Coins & Collectors

GOLDEN ANNIVERSARY EDITION

SECOND EDITION

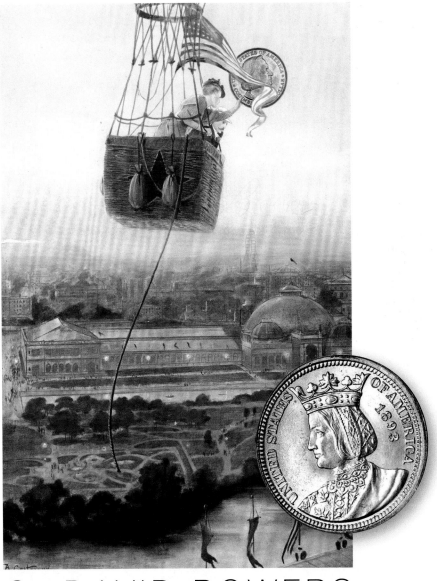

Q. DAVID BOWERS

FOREWORD BY JOEL J. OROSZ

Coins and Collectors
Golden Anniversary Edition
(Second Edition)

Whitman
Publishing, LLC
PUBLISHING SINCE 1934
www.whitman.com
© 2014 Whitman Publishing, LLC
3101 Clairmont Road • Suite G • Atlanta, GA 30329

ISBN: 0794842720
Printed in China

Correspondence regarding this book may be mailed to Whitman Publishing, Attn: Coins and Collectors, 3101 Clairmont Road, Suite G, Atlanta GA 30329; or emailed to info@Whitman.com (subject line: Coins and Collectors).

Disclaimer: No warranty or representation of any kind is made concerning the accuracy or completeness of the information presented, its use in purchases or sales, or any other use. Much information in this book has never been published in a single volume before, and in the future corrections, amplifications, and additions may be made.

If you enjoy *Coins and Collectors,* you will also enjoy *America's Money, America's Story* (Doty), *History of the United States Mint and Its Coinage* (Lange), *Numismatic Art in America* (Vermeule), *100 Greatest American Medals and Tokens* (Bowers and Sundman), *Pictures From a Distant Country: Seeing America Through Old Paper Money* (Doty), *Abraham Lincoln: The Image of His Greatness* (Reed), *Milestone Coins: A Pageant of the World's Most Significant and Popular Money* (Bressett), and other books by Whitman Publishing. Whitman is a leading publisher in the antiques and collectibles and American history fields. For a catalog of related books, hobby supplies, and storage and display products, please visit Whitman Publishing online at www. Whitman.com.

A SPECIAL PRESENTATION BY

Stack's Bowers Galleries

America's Oldest and Most Accomplished Rare Coin Auctioneer

East Coast Office 800.566.2580 • West Coast Office: 800.458.4646
Info@StacksBowers.com • StacksBowers.com
New York • Hong Kong • Irvine • Paris • Wolfeboro

Coins &Collectors

GOLDEN ANNIVERSARY EDITION

Richard A. Beck

Jan. 29, 2017

Sunset From the Roof of the Manufacture Building, by André Castainge, from *World's Columbian Exposition: Art and Architecture* (Walton, 1893), a limited-edition multi-volume study of the World's Fair and its exhibits and buildings. Learn more about the fair and its famous coins and medals in chapter 10.

Contents

The book you are holding in your hands—*Coins and Collectors, Golden Anniversary Edition*—is both a piece of numismatic history and a glimpse into the hobby's future. This volume comes from a very distinguished family. Its father was *More Adventures With Rare Coins* (2002); its grandfather was *Adventures with Rare Coins* (1979); and its great-granddaddy was the original *Coins and Collectors,* from way back in 1964. Each of these "illustrious predecessors" (to borrow a term from a Hard Times token mentioned in chapter 33) was published just as numismatics was down in the dumps, and each helped stimulate the hobby toward better days.

Many of today's collectors owe their enthusiasm for coins to cracking open one of these volumes, and getting "hooked" on their fascinating stories. I know whereof I speak, for I was there in 1964 when this series of books began, and I was one of those transformed by their tales into a lifelong enthusiast: what an earlier generation would call a genuine "coin crank."

When I first dipped my toe into numismatics, back in 1962, coin collecting—all across the United States—was not just growing, it was *metastasizing.* You could hardly heave an egg down the main street of any Cold War–era town without splattering a newly opened coin shop. Numismatic clubs sprouted like mushrooms after a rain, and newsstands sagged under the weight of coin newspapers, magazines, catalogs, and books. Powering this "numis-tsunami" were the ubiquitous Whitman coin folders. Royal blue in color, unfolding into three panels, with row upon row of die-cut openings for every date and mintmark of a given coin series, their "holes" virtually cried out to be filled to completion.

Whitman made folders for every denomination, but by far the most common was that for the humble Lincoln cent. In the early 1960s, even a nickel still had purchasing power, so the farther you went up the denomination chain, the more collectors got priced out of the market. Cents were cheap, and most collectible Lincolns could still be found in everyday circula-

tion if you were persistent and lucky. You could plug those nasty holes in your Whitman folder with circulation finds worth $5, $10, even $20, and all each of them would cost you was one red cent. Who could resist the allure of building a valuable coin collection on the cheap?

Certainly not my father, Joseph F. Orosz, who since the 1950s had been among the ranks of the roll searchers. Starting in 1962, the year I entered kindergarten, he allowed me to accompany him to the local branch of the Industrial State Bank, where he would buy rolls of "pennies." They came in sturdy coral-hued rectangular pasteboard boxes, each stamped in bold black letters: "$20 Cents." They were stacked on our kitchen table, temporarily bedecked with a protective newsprint spread of back issues of the *Kalamazoo Gazette,* for a session of searching and sorting.

The first roll was opened and dumped, and then the hunt was on! Any "wheatie" went into the "keep" pile, as did all "S" mintmarks. Anything minted before 1934 was of definite interest; anything dated 1925 or earlier got our immediate attention. We were always hoping against hope to snag one of fabled "four keys": 1931-S, 1914-D, 1909-S, and the major-domo of them all, the 1909-S V.D.B. It took us thousands of rolls, but we actually found three circulated 1931-S cents; one 1914-D, which my Dad graded as "V.T." (short for "Very Tired"); and one magical afternoon, I spied a 1909-S. Euphoria mixed with foreboding as we turned it over, and spent the better part of the next 10 minutes vainly searching for any trace of the devoutly-to-be-wished-for letters V, D, or B. Disappointing as that was, of course, we still had a very fine 1909-S, with a retail value—according to the *Guide Book of United States Coins*—of $29, which seemed a small fortune to a young boy in 1963. We never did find a 1909-S V.D.B., but it didn't prevent us from fantasizing about experiencing such outrageous good fortune.

All of this happened during the long-ago "Camelot" of the Kennedy Administration, but interestingly, we roll-searchers had a high-tech gadget at our disposal back then that no one has today: the Scan-O-Matic. A camel-colored rectangular plastic box perched on four stubby legs, it had a brown tube on the top-right side, and a lighted magnifier window on the left. Drop half a roll of cents down the tube, then use the slide sticking out of the right-hand side to maneuver the obverse of the first cent leftward into the magnified viewing area. Then push the slide all the way in until it hits a stop, a hidden spring flips the coin, and then you slide it backwards to view the reverse. Finally, with both sides examined, you pull the slide farther to the right, a spring pushes up a door to allow the coin to fall out of the bottom of the contraption. Once you got the hang of it, you could really get on a roll (so to speak), examining magnified images of the obverse and reverse of coin after coin, the process punctuated by the satisfying "clink" of examined "pennies" dropping into the growing pile beneath the machine. (Obviously, we weren't quite as fanatical about the condition of our coins back in the early 1960s!)

Today, 50 years on, these memories are suffused with the amber glow of a gooseneck lamp on a penny-covered kitchen table, the brilliant coins twinkling like starlight. But all things must pass, and the fact was that we roll searchers were literally destroying our own hobby. Every treasure we triumphantly plucked from circulation reduced the store of available rarities, and made success the next time a bit less likely. It took only a few years for legions of roll searchers to scour from circulation the collectible coins it had taken generations to amass. And worse, these "desirables" were not being replaced; mintages in the hundreds of millions assured that the coinage of the early 1960s would never be rare.

The time of reckoning finally occurred during the memorable year of 1964. The rising price of silver meant that the value of this precious metal in all dimes, quarters, halves, and dollars was approaching—and would soon exceed—the face value of the coins themselves. Millions of non-collectors suddenly started searching through their change to pull 90%

silver coins from circulation. In a matter of months, coin shortages became a coast-to-coast scourge. Officials at the Treasury Department blamed collectors for the shortfalls, but in fact it was the entire citizenry who saw an honest opportunity to profit, and seized it.

By the end of 1965, for my Dad and me, and all our fellow roll searchers, hard times had descended like a ton of the new copper-nickel-clad coinage. Cents and nickels were increasingly picked over. There was no point in even attempting to fill a Whitman folder for dimes, quarters, or halves, for 90% silver coins had been effectively removed from circulation. The roll-searching hobby was approaching a wall at high speed, so close that we could count the individual bricks.

A numismatic lifeline arrived for me, strangely enough, courtesy of the bargain book cart at the Portage Public Library. Portage, where we lived, was and is the most populous suburb of Kalamazoo. Its public library, as of the mid-1960s, was located in a strip-mall storefront, and the cramped space necessitated the discarding of earlier editions of a book when a newer edition was purchased. The discards, priced at 10 cents per volume, landed on a cart strategically parked by the circulation desk.

In the autumn of 1966, I was checking out my usual rhyming fare of age-appropriate histories and mysteries, and glanced at the sale cart. One of the discards was *Coins and Collectors*, by a David . . . no, wait, there was an intriguing "Q" in front of his name . . . Q. David Bowers. I had never heard of the book or its author, but there was no time to leaf through it, for other library patrons were waiting behind me in the checkout line. So I dug a clad dime from my pocket, and—unbeknownst to me at the time—my numismatic future was transformed.

Not that it happened instantly. In fact, once back home, the first few pages of the book left me completely flummoxed. My Dad owned current copies of Whitman's flagship publications, the *Guide Book of United States Coins* (Red Book) and *Handbook of*

United States Coins (Blue Book). These helped us identify our coins, and told us what they were worth. I knew that coin dealers published lists of stock for sale at fixed prices, and catalogs of public-auction sales. That was numismatic literature to me—publications that answered the questions: What is my coin? What is it worth? How rare is my coin?

That's what gobsmacked me about *Coins and Collectors*. It offered not a single coin for sale, nor did it provide a solitary coin valuation. Instead, it was packed with *stories* about coins and the characters (and I mean *characters*) who collected them.

Chapter 1 was titled "The Romance of Coins," and before I was five pages into it, I had learned about the Randall Hoard of 1816 to 1820 large cents, and the romantically named "Economite Treasure," a vast cache of early American coins unearthed in Pennsylvania. By chapter 2, "The Beginnings of Numismatics in America," I was hooked, devouring story after story about colorful pioneering collectors such as Joseph Mickley and Matthew Stickney, immersing myself in the stranger-than-life saga of the 1804 dollar, and chuckling over the description of a fistfight between two 19th-century coin dealers at a public auction: "The two numismatic sages were soon mixed up on a dusty floor in a manner that would have made football adversaries envious of their combative qualities, until, in a badly circulated condition, they were dragged apart by dismayed spectators."

New delights jumped off page after page: the rapid inflation—and spectacular implosion—of the 1930s commemorative coin bubble, and the shocking (to a nine-year-old) picture on page 142 of a *topless* depiction of Britannia on a British coin!

For me, *Coins and Collectors* unfolded a world of possibilities. It revealed that numismatics is a perpetual banquet of delights, some of the dishes big and flashy, others small and subtle, but all of them mouthwatering. Collectible coins had disappeared from circulation? Said Q. David Bowers, "So what?" Have you considered the realm of old copper coins? What about

pattern emissions of the Mint? Maybe coins of the world? U.S. colonial coinage? Perhaps numismatic literature? The buffet was crammed with every imaginable delicacy, and it was clearly open for business.

There had never before been a numismatic book quite like *Coins and Collectors*. Instead of answering "What is this coin?" it asked "What is fascinating about this coin?" Instead of answering "What is this coin worth?" it asked "Why is this coin worth collecting?" Why did a man who had been a coin dealer since 1953 write such a revolutionary book? Dave realized that the roll-searching craze could not last forever, and that when the last hole had been plugged in the last album, roll searchers would need something to do, and somewhere to go, or they would leave numismatics in droves.

Coins and Collectors was Dave's solution to this problem. With superb timing, he published this book in 1964, the year the storm clouds were gathering. By late 1965, as the exodus of silver from circulation was beginning, and with coin shortages developing, the numismatic hobby slumped into the doldrums. *Coins and Collectors* offered disillusioned roll searchers a viable alternative to leaving the hobby. Most importantly, Dave understood that *enthusiasm* was the key to staying power; those who had it kept on collecting, while those who lacked it fell away. This was why the stories in *Coins and Collectors* focused on the romantic, delightful, and even comic aspects of numismatics: these stirred excitement and enthusiasm in a way that prices alone never could.

Coins and Collectors was a consequential book, and it turned out to be the opening act of a long-running show. In 1979, just as he was about to conduct the first auction of the Garrett Collection, one of the greatest cabinets of rare coins ever formed, Dave authored a worthy successor, *Adventures with Rare Coins*. The title had changed, but the content was very much in the tradition of *Coins and Collectors*. The chapter titles of this book tell us that Dave had lost none of his passion for the hobby: "The Secret of the Sierra," "Pike's Peak Gold," and "A Numismatic

Adventure." These concepts alone bestir within the reader a sense of romance and excitement, even before the tales begin!

The stories Dave tells in *Adventures with Rare Coins* have a "you are there" feeling to them: Witness the underhanded dealings at the 19th-century Philadelphia Mint! Watch as long-squirreled-away Morgan dollars disgorge from the Treasury vaults in the early 1960s! Delight in the very distinctive (and sometimes quirky) personal tokens created during the national bicentennial by the Patrick Mint! Wit and wisdom is dispensed in equal measure, as in this quote from 19th-century dealer Ed. Frossard (taken from an 1876 magazine), on the ideal method for treating "rusted" coins: "The best way of cleaning rusted or worn coins in our opinion is to clean them out of your collection and replace them by such specimens as will not need cleaning."

Just as in 1964, Dave's timing in 1979 was impeccable. Fed by the booming market in silver and gold, rare coins were skyrocketing in value. When, in 1980, the Hunt brothers failed in their attempt to corner the silver market, the bubble burst, and the coin market fell like a soufflé. But once again, just as when the bottom had dropped out in 1965, there was a book by Dave Bowers to guide collectors into new, more sophisticated, realms of numismatics.

Not content to rest on his laurels, Dave continued to sell great coin collections (Brand, Norweb, Eliasberg, Bass, Childs), and to write more books about coins. Shortly after the turn of the new millennium, however, he sensed the need for another book of "Adventures." Third-party grading was by then 15 years old, and "slab" collectors were often no more connected to the broader hobby than had been the roll searchers of the 1960s, or the "silver bugs" of the 1980s.

So it was time, in 2002, for the third book in what by then had become a series: *More Adventures with Rare Coins.* The title may have been familiar, but the format was experimental. Instead of broad thematic chapters like "The Gold Rush," *More Adventures*

was organized around 50 different specific "Adventures" focused on individual coins and personalities. These ranged from the familiar (the story of my old nemesis, the 1909-S V.D.B.) to the unusual (the 1868—yes, *1868*—large copper cent), to the downright obscure (the 1787 Washington and Columbia medals). Unlike generic "slabs," every individual numismatic item has a story to tell, and Dave delighted in giving them voice.

Just as history and romance had provided an antidote to the "filled-folder blues" and the "broken-silver fever," so too did they prove efficacious against "slab fatigue." Once again, a generous dose of enthusiasm helped to transform jaded collectors into passionate numismatists who wanted to learn what was so *fantastic* about the 1804 dollar; what was so *shocking* about President Theodore Roosevelt's "pet crime" with the MCMVII double eagles; and what was so *thrilling* about recovering 1857-S double eagles from the briny deep. Could there be a more effective antidote to the "same old same old" in slabs than pure numismatic fascination?

Now, in 2014, *Coins and Collectors* is celebrating its 50th anniversary; *Adventures with Rare Coins* its 35th; and *More Adventures with Rare Coins* its 12th. Each book did superb service in its own time to recast casual collectors into dedicated numismatists, transforming the disappointed and the disillusioned into the excited and the enthusiastic. What better way to celebrate this legacy than to add to it?

Hence the fourth volume in the series reaches back to its beginnings by reviving the title of the book that started it all: *Coins and Collectors.* Happily, the hobby in 2014 is not facing the looming crises that were on the horizon in 1964, 1979, and 2002 when the earlier books were published. We will soon discover, however, that dramatic and romantic numismatic stories will serve the coin hobby just as well in good times as in bad.

And *Coins and Collectors, Golden Anniversary Edition* is a book chock-full of drama and romance.

"Dr. Bowers" diagnoses the epidemic causing "The Unc. Roll Fever," which swept the hobby in the early 1960s. One modern coin—the 1950-D Jefferson nickel—soared to an astounding $1,500 per roll in 1964, only to crash-land shortly thereafter. Forty-seven years later, such rolls were selling for barely more than a fifth of their 1964 high ($340 including shipping). Dr. Bowers notes that not all numismatic fevers break so badly, as he demonstrates in the case history of the 1856 Flying Eagle cent. A coin that sparked feverish interest from the moment it fell from the dies, this little gem keeps rising in value even though it has been the favorite target of coin hoarders over the past 150 years. Dave relates that Pittsburgh collector John A. Beck pack-ratted an impressive 531 examples of 1856 Flying Eagle cents, but—incredibly—this was only the second-largest hoard, and not even close to the largest, which clocked in at an astronomical 756 pieces!

If, like me, you can't resist a good mystery, then the enigmatic 1783 Georgius Triumpho token, known to numismatists since the first publication about it in 1798, but never adequately explained, will fascinate you. On the obverse, is that George III of Great Britain or George Washington of America? On the reverse, is Britannia in a balloon, ascending triumphantly to freedom, or is she behind bars, languishing in helpless captivity?

If scandal is your cup of joe, take a peek at the naughty "Parisian Varieties" counterstamp. It seems that the Parisian Varieties troupe's "Frenchy, Spicy, and Sparkling" brand of entertainment was just too "Spicy and Sparkling" for New York's finest in 1876, so their "Frenchy" show was raided by the police. (One witness testified that he could not positively identify one of the arrested actresses, because in court she had her clothes on!)

And so it goes through dozens of stories. You'll learn which famous collector once received a letter addressed only to "King of Coins, U.S.A." You'll dis-

cover the identity of the very first dealer in numismatic items in the United States, who started his business long before the Civil War broke out. You'll find that the classical (and today much-beloved) Educational Notes of 1896 were so unpopular when introduced that they were swiftly replaced by other designs.

I fearlessly predict that you will find in this *Golden Anniversary Edition* stories just as fresh, surprising, and compelling as I found in my second-hand copy of the first *Coins and Collectors* nearly half a century ago. Yes, five decades have come and gone, but the books of Dave's *Coins and Collectors* and *Adventures* numismatic storytelling series march on, as vital as ever. If you want to measure the impact these volumes have had upon the coin hobby, all you need do is to compare its flourishing state—the packed bourses, the record prices, the new discoveries, the growing specialty clubs, the vibrant activity on the Internet—with the declining state of similar pastimes. Philately has retreated, both in number of collectors and value of stamps. In fact, name your collectible—autographs, toys, books, porcelain, dolls—and you will find the hobby associated with it in a diminished and contracting state. None of these avocations has had a Q. David Bowers to be its troubadour, or a series of books packed with fascinating stories to stoke enthusiasm.

How fortunate we in numismatics have been, therefore, to have had Dave Bowers as our bard for the past 50 years, and his stories as our guides to the sheer *joy* of collecting coins. So savor this latest in a long line of tales that both connect to a glorious past and point the way to a future bright with promise. If you do, I can easily imagine you as a veteran numismatist, 50 years from now, telling young collectors, "I trace my enthusiasm for the great hobby of coin collecting back to 2014, when I first read *Coins and Collectors, Golden Anniversary Edition*."

Joel J. Orosz
Kalamazoo, Michigan

I have enjoyed numismatics ever since I was a young teenager. A common or rare coin on its own has certain characteristics—design, weight, grade, and price among them. Beyond these considerations, more than just a few coins, tokens, medals, and currency notes have interesting stories. Ownership of a coin can be worth 1 point, a story about it can be worth 1 more point, but if you own a coin with a story 1 + 1 can equal 3, not just 2.

It was back in 1964 that I wrote *Coins and Collectors.* The book attracted wide attention and sales. Now in the *Golden Anniversary Edition* nearly all of the stories are new, spiced with a few reprises of favorite from various articles and books I've written since then. Some are short, others are essays. Some of the items are rare and expensive, but most are affordable. Enjoy!

To this introduction I append a commentary written by Robert W. Benroth and published in *The Numismatist* in 1942. I never met him, but we think alike!

Q. David Bowers
Wolfeboro, New Hampshire

Robert W. Benroth on Collecting

JANUARY 1942

It is the firm belief of many coin collectors that the main requisite of a true coin collector is a good imagination. Some coin collectors collect for the purpose of appreciation in the value of their coins, having a complete turnover in their collection every few years. Others collect for the beauty involved in the minting of well-designed, finely-struck coins, while still others are just plain collectors, collecting only because of a hereditary individual frugality. In all probability this later type of collector comprises over 50% of the coin collectors of today. They are "here today, gone tomorrow"

to some other field of collecting that at the moment takes their fancy.

The collector who collects for profit will collect coins as long as they appreciate in value, but will leave in a "bear" coin market for other fields of greater profit. The collector who collects for the beauty involved in individual coins will be with us always, for coins of beauty are many, and beautiful coin designing and minting are some of the boons of modern civilization.

This article deals with the coin collector who collects coins because of his imagination. He lives with each individual coin of his collection, reminiscing through the facilities of his mind and historical knowledge of that individual coin, the period in history when that coin was a medium of exchange, or that period, personage, or event that it commemorates. . . .

He will look at his Pine Tree shilling and go back in his imagination to the days when the Pilgrim fathers were settled in New England, where in 1652 the Court of Massachusetts appointed John Hull, strictly against the laws of England, as mint master, to strike some silver coins for use in the New England territory. He will imagine this as the first act of revolt against England. He will see, in his mind's eye, John Hull, mint master, keeping one coin in every 10 as his wages for operating the mint, and will think of his coin as one of the 10 that John Hull claimed. He will reconstruct the life of the Hull family until that great event of their lives, the marriage of their daughter and the granting of her dowry of her weight in Pine Tree shillings, when again his mind's eye will picture his individual shilling as going into the balancing scale as a part of her dowry. . . .

He will pick up his Fugio cent and live back in the days of George Washington and the problems that confronted our ancestors at the beginning of our nation. He will even imagine George Washington as having this individual coin in his possession some time or other during his term as first president of the United States.

He will examine his Jackson cent and relive the great political fight and hard times during the presidency of Andrew Jackson, and his Civil War tokens will reconstruct, in his mind's eye, the great struggle between the states in which his father or grandfather may have played an important part.

The silver trade dollar will make him visualize the continual fight by the so-called "silver bloc" in Congress, bringing him up to the present day when silver is still a very important issue for almost any congressional consideration.

He will pick up his "Gypsy Rose Lee" quarter of 1916 or 1917 and imagine back to the First World War days when women were "coming into their own" and public opinion demanded that more clothes be put on Liberty.

His commemoratives will make his imagination run riot, for every commemorative has some historical background of great interest or is dedicated to the life of some great personage of the past or present.

He will pick up his Bridgeport commemorative half dollar and live back in the days of the Cardiff Giant and Jenny Lind, made famous by P.T. Barnum, whose likeness appears on this coin. His Cincinnati commemorative will have him humming the beloved Southern ballads of that famous composer, Stephen Foster, and his Columbian half dollar will bring about the rediscovering of America while traveling with Christopher Columbus on the *Santa Maria* in 1492.

In fact, a collector who has an imagination can pick up almost any coin and, by perusing his history books, reconstruct in his mind, many an enjoyable evening of reminiscing. Yes, the coin collector with an imagination is, in all probability, the basis of the science of numismatics, for he lives, breathes, and talks his coins until the end.

Coins
&Collectors

GOLDEN ANNIVERSARY EDITION

As the first coin struck by the federal government under the Mint Act of April 2, 1792, the 1792 half disme has long held a special position in American numismatics. Several hundred examples survive today, and each is highly prized.

The 1792 Silver Half Disme

The story of the 1792 half disme is well known. Some of the tale is legend and tradition, other elements are fact. The two seem to overlap.

James Ross Snowden in his *Description of Ancient and Modern Coins in the Cabinet Collection in the Mint of the United States,* 1860, gave this description:

> Obverse: A female head, emblematic of Liberty, facing to the left. This is popularly supposed to represent the features of Martha Washington, who is said to have sat for the artist while he was designing it; the hair is short and unconfined; immediately beneath, the date; the whole being encompassed by the Lib(erty) Par(ent) of Science and Industry. On the reverse is a small eagle volant, beneath which is described the value half-disme; legend, Uni States of America. This piece is said to have been struck from the private plate of Washington; it is not unlikely, considering the great interest which he took in the operations of the infant mint, visiting it frequently and personally superintending many of its affairs. This coin made its appearance in the month of October, 1792.

Unfortunately, no letters, newspaper accounts, or anything else has been located to verify that Washington visited the Mint "frequently," although Philadelphia was the capital of the United States then, and the president did not live far away. As to the "private plate," or silverware, of Washington, although old pieces were sometimes melted down to make new, there is no record o f this either. As to Martha posing, the likeness on the coin does not even slightly resemble any surviving portrait of her. So, we see that "legend" was off to a good start!

Writing in *Coins and Coinage: The United States Mint, Philadelphia,* 1881, Andrew Madsen Smith picked up and expanded upon Snowden's commentary:

> In the beginning of October, 1792, three presses were put in operation and were first used for striking the half-dismes, of which Washington makes mention in his annual message to Congress on the 6th of November, 1792, as follows:
>
> "There has also been a small beginning in the coinage of half-dismes; the want of small coins in circulation calling the first attention to them."
>
> This half-disme has upon its obverse a female bust,

Tradition and Romance

The 1792 silver half disme. This example is one of four pedigreed to the family of Mint Director David Rittenhouse.

emblematic of Liberty, facing to the left. This is popularly supposed to represent the features of Martha Washington, who is said to have sat to the artist while he was designing it. The hair is short and flowing. Immediately beneath the bust is the date 1792, surrounded by the legend "LIB(erty), PAR(ent) OF SCIENCE AND INDUSTRY." Reverse: Eagle on the wing, beneath the same is inscribed: "HALF DISME." Legend: UNI(ted) STATES OF AMERICA." This coin is said to have been struck from the private plate of Washington, which is not unlikely, considering the great interest he took in the operations of the infant mint, visiting it frequently, and personally superintending many of its affairs. This half-disme made its first appearance in October, 1792; but was not generally circulated and has now become one of the rare coins of our national coinage.

Dye's Coin Encyclopedia, John S. Dye, 1883, included this:

> The half dime was the first coin struck by the United States Mint, located in Seventh Street between Market and Arch streets, Philadelphia, Pa. The coin presses, three in number, were imported from abroad and arrived at the Philadelphia Mint on Friday, the 21st of September, 1792, were put into operation on the 9th of October, and first used for striking the half dimes of 1792.[1]

In contrast to the above, an earlier account as part of *New Varieties of Gold and Silver Coins,* by Jacob

R. Eckfeldt and William E. Dubois, curators of the Mint Cabinet, 1851, which included the mention of the 1792 half disme, stated this early issue was "not actually coined in the Mint."

Thus, there is the question of when and where they were struck, or were there two striking events?[2]

The first Philadelphia Mint began business in 1792 and was continued in operation until replaced by a new facility in 1832. Shown is the main building where coinage took place.

The July 1792 Coinage

Over the years the 1792 half disme has attracted the attention of several leading scholars who have pieced together information that was not generally known until the early 21st century.[3]

Tradition has it that in mid-July President George Washington personally arranged for a supply of silver to be delivered to the Philadelphia shop of John Harper, located close to where the foundation stone for the United States Mint would be laid on the 31st of the same month. (This scenario seems to have been unknown to Messrs. Snowden, Smith, and Dye as cited above.) Using equipment destined for the Mint, workers struck about 1,500 silver half dismes one by one using a hand press. No presses from abroad or anywhere else were yet in service.

Nearly all of these coins were placed into circulation, where they found immediate use, as verified by most of the several hundred survivors today showing significant wear and by the president's annual message.

Historical research regarding the July outside-of-the-Mint coinage has come from two main sources. The first is the 1792 *Memorandum Book* by Thomas Jefferson, with two entries of particular interest regarding this issue. This is a personal journal of Jefferson's, but no mention of these comments has been preserved in any official Mint documents known.

Jefferson noted on July 11, 1792, "Delivd. 75 D. at the Mint to be coined."

Since structures on the site of the new Mint had just been purchased a few days before and some were being razed and others rehabilitated, it is likely Jefferson refers to another location where the coinage would take place. The first foundation stone for one of the new buildings would not be laid until July 31.

Then following this entry is another two days later, dated July 13, 1792: "Recd. from the mint 1500. half dismes of the new coinage."

This confirms an actual coinage in July 1792.

Jefferson then left Philadelphia for Monticello, his home in Virginia. His record makes no statement as to what he did with these half dismes. Did he spend them? Give them to the Mint officers for distribution? Did he hold onto them until he met with George Washington on October 1, 1792, at Mount Vernon? The written record is frustratingly silent. However, it would seem likely that "want of small coins in circulation" would have compelled Jefferson to get them into the channels of commerce, rather than wait a few months to return the silver coins to Washington after such great lengths were accomplished to get them coined in July.

Prior to mintage of the half disme, there was no coin circulating in the United States with a precise value of five cents. The Mexican half-bit or medio and the Spanish half pistareen both traded extensively, especially in the American South, for the equivalent of 6-1/4 cents. Half pistareens were made of debased silver, so their value fluctuated with the perceived fineness of the coin. It was the closest thing to a five-cent piece in American commerce until the half disme came along.[4]

The McAllister Memorandum

The second document of importance is a memorandum created in 1844 by John McAllister Jr., a Philadelphia numismatist who summarized the reminiscences of Adam Eckfeldt, the retired second chief coiner of the Mint. Eckfeldt was in 1792 a part-time contractor for the facility. Although some portions of this memorandum have been discounted as fanciful, other parts are likely accurate.

Eckfeldt recalled that the half dismes were struck before the North Seventh Street mint was opened, in the cellar of John Harper, a saw maker and also part-time contractor at the Mint. This memorandum went on to say that silver bullion or coin in the amount of $100 was provided by President Washington, and the half dismes were not struck for circulation but rather for Washington's use as "presents" for friends in Europe or in his home state of Virginia. This would suggest a mintage of 2,000 pieces.

While Eckfeldt was right about the timing of the striking, and probably accurate about using John

Harper's cellar, no one has ever found any hard evidence that Washington provided the silver or ever presented any of these half dismes to his friends. One would think some would have survived with notations inscribed such as "Gift from President Washington, keep." As noted, nearly all of these half dismes were spent around the time of issue, with many eventually showing evidence of years in circulation. A few were obviously saved and treasured, such as four retained by Director of the Mint David Rittenhouse and consigned to auction by his heirs to Henry Chapman's auction held with the American Numismatic Association convention in Philadelphia in August 1919.

Frank H. Stewart in his *History of the First United States Mint,* 1924, quotes the following letter he received on June 12, 1915 from Dr. George S. Gerhard, a Philadelphia physician:

> The David Rittenhouse silver "Half disme" (never in circulation) came into my possession many years ago having been given to me by my half uncle, David Rittenhouse Sergeant, a son of Jonathan Dickinson Sergeant (my great grandfather) by his second wife, Elizabeth Rittenhouse. David Rittenhouse Sergeant, when I was a young boy, had a number, perhaps eight or nine, of these coins which he had inherited from his mother and what has become of them I do not know.

Although the McAllister memorandum was not published until 1943, the gist of its contents was recounted in an article appearing in the February 6, 1853, issue of the *Philadelphia Dispatch.* The story quoted current Mint personnel Franklin Peale and William E. Dubois, respectively the successor and the son-in-law of the late Adam Eckfeldt. It was through this newspaper story that Eckfeldt's reminiscences first entered the consciousness of numismatists.

Coinage at the Mint in November

As to the coinage of 1792 half dismes within the Mint on October 9, 1792, facts are scarce, and no contemporary documentation has been found. Forensic evidence—examination of surviving coins—may provide confirmation. Joel Orosz, Leonard Augsburger, and Pete Smith have studied the situation carefully. Orosz writes:

> On the coinage front, Pete has taken the lead in a thorough variety study. He has examined, either through photos or the actual coins, more than 100 specimens of the approximately 250 surviving half dismes. He has determined that there are four die states, with two substates each for state 1–3, and a single state 4. States 1-A, 1-B, and 2-A form the great majority of the examined specimens, and are distinguished among each other by the die cracks forming on the reverse in states 1-B and 2-A. However, between states 2-A and 2-B, significant areas of roughness develop in the reverse field. In our view this was caused by die rust. Such extensive die rust cannot have developed overnight during the three-day July striking period.

> Our hypothesis is, therefore, that after the first striking was completed July 13, the reverse die was improperly stored and developed rust, which shows on the coins from the second striking on October 9. This provides solid proof that both Eckfeldt/Jefferson and Snowden were correct as to the when and where of half disme striking.[5]

Orosz further suggests that as most high-grade pieces in existence today are from later die states, likely the October striking was to test the presses and more were saved as souvenirs.[6]

How Many Were Minted

If it is agreed that about 250 of the 1792 half dismes exist today, and that all but a handful show signs of circulation, can the mintage be estimated from that figure? In the absence of facts I suggest that the 1794 silver dollar may provide at least part of the answer. Dollars were first produced that year, and 1,758 were released. All but a handful show evidence of circulation. These have been the object of close study by several numismatists, most importantly Jack Collins and Martin Logies. About 140 different examples have been accounted for today. This suggests that about 8 percent of the original mintage of 1794 dollars survives.

If the same conservation ratio holds true for the 1792 half disme, with 250 known, this by mathematical calculation indicates an original mintage of about 3,200 coins. Deduct 1,500 coins of the July mintage and this suggests about 1,700 made in October. I suggest that the figure is probably slightly larger, as it was more likely for a small-face-value half disme to be saved than it was for a silver dollar, equal to more than a day's wages in the early 19th century.

On November 6, President Washington, as noted, stated "There has also been a small beginning in the coinage of half-dismes; the want of small coins in circulation calling the first attention to them." Although some were undoubtedly made to test the presses, the quantity was such that most went into circulation for use in commerce. It seems likely that he remembered the October mintage rather than the off-site production months earlier in July.

Additional Commentary

The half disme's designer and die cutter is thought to have been Robert Birch, who produced the motifs on

contract. The appearance is quite similar to that used on the famous Birch pattern cents of the same year.

Just as the 1652 Pine Tree shilling variety Noe-1 is a candidate for being the "poster example" of an American colonial coin, perhaps the 1792 half disme would be ideal as such for a Philadelphia Mint coin. There is so much history in this piece that an hour-long presentation could be made concerning it, and still not all information would be given.

An Early Auction Appearance

From the earliest days of numismatic interest in America down to the present time, the appearance of a high-grade 1792 half disme at auction has attracted attention. This account in the *Philadelphia Bulletin,* February 21, 1851, describes an early auction offering and is of further interest as a report on the first major auction of rare coins in America:

Great Sale of Coins.

Messrs. M. Thomas & Sons commenced last evening the sale of the collection of coins, medals, and autographs of the late Dr. Lewis Roper, deceased, of this city. It is probably unequalled by any private collection in the United States, and the announcement of its sale created quite a stir among our virtuoso.

The sales last evening were confined to American coins and medals; the bidding was very spirited, and some of the prices paid were extremely high. A half dollar, with the head of Washington, dated 1792, brought the enormous price of $18. Two Washington cents, date 1791, brought respectively $1.62½ and $1.75, and one of 1792 brought $2.12½. Four other Washington cents were sold for $2.20. An American silver dollar of 1838, with the flying eagle, brought the extravagant price of $5, and a half dollar of the same coinage, $7.25! Two dollar pieces of 1836 brought $3.25; one 1839, $1.75, and a dollar and half dollar of 1794, $1.75; while another half dollar of '39 sold for $2.10.

Four old Massachusetts shillings brought $3.60, and a three penny Massachusetts piece sold for $2. A "half disme" of 1792 brought $2; two old Annapolis shillings, $1.75; a half cent of 1792, $2.40; a gold dollar of 1836, $2.37; two old cents and eight half cents, $1.50; and a three-cent silver piece, 90 cents. The actual value in metal, of the lot of American coins, scarcely exceeded $10, and yet they brought about $66.

Among the medals sold was a gold one issued on the storming of Stony Point, valued at $30. It sold for $38. Two silver medals of Washington, $3.24; a silver medal of George II., $1; a copper medal, (Kittanning destroyed by Colonel Armstrong, September 8, 1756) $1; Libertas Americana, $2.12; copper medals of Jefferson, Madison, and Monroe; $1.75 each; do. of J.Q. Adams, $2.50; gilt medals of J.Q.

Adams, $1, and 62½ cents, respectively; 62½ cents and $1.12 were paid for copper medals of Martin Van Buren, and 50 cents and $1 for similar medals of John Tyler. Sic transit gloria mundi!

A copper medal of Com. John Paul Jones sold for $2.12; one of Commodore Decatur, $2.12; one of Commodore Hull, $2, and a number of other naval medals at prices ranging from 50 cents to $1.50. A gold locket, with the head of Washington ruled on glass, was struck off at $2; a fragment of old Independence bell at 50 cents.

The great mass of the collection remains unsold, and the sale will be continued this evening. Among them are several hundred ancient Roman and Greek coins of gold, silver, and copper; Italian, Papal, and Episcopal coins; English coins, from the time of Canute to Victoria; French coins, from Charlemagne to Napoleon, and other coins of all the European nations, besides numerous medals of great historical interest. There is also a collection of numismatic works, and numerous rare and valuable autographs.

CHAPTER 2

The favorite design created by Frank Gasparro during his long career at the U.S. Mint, including as chief engraver from 1965 to 1991, was the Eisenhower dollar.

Frank Gasparro and the Eisenhower Dollar

Chief Engraver Gasparro

A 1971 Eisenhower dollar, Denver Mint issue.

Over the years I have enjoyed visiting the Philadelphia Mint on various research trips, often accompanied by a photographer. It was and still is pleasant to call upon the Engraving Department and visit with the artists there. On several occasions in the 1960s and 1970s I had long talks with Chief Engraver Frank Gasparro, who served at the Mint for nearly 40 years, until his retirement in 1981.

Born in Philadelphia on August 26, 1909, Frank became interested in art at a young age. While in grade school he enrolled in classes at the Samuel Fleisher Art Memorial School, with which he maintained connections for the rest of his life, until his passing on September 29, 2001. In 1928 he enrolled in the Pennsylvania Academy of Fine Arts, a stint followed by the award of two scholarships that made it possible for him to study in France, Italy, Germany, England, and Sweden. He returned to America in 1932 and began his professional career as a sculptor working on various commissions. In the depth of the Great Depression, patrons were scarce. In 1937 he signed with the Federal Art Project division of Franklin D. Roosevelt's Works Progress Administration, which gave artists a steady salary while they worked on Post Office murals, civic sculptures, and other projects. Frank was assigned to making sculptures for local parks, including children's wading pools.

In April 1942 he was appointed as an assistant engraver at the U.S. Mint, working under Chief Engraver John R. Sinnock and then for a brief time under Sinnock's successor, Gilroy Roberts. When Roberts left to join the private Franklin Mint, President Lyndon B. Johnson appointed Frank to the chief engraver position, starting on February 11, 1965. By that time he had designed many medals and some coins, the last including the reverses for the Lincoln Memorial cent (1959) and the Kennedy half dollar (1964). In later years he would design many other medals and coins.

The Eisenhower Dollar

In 1991 when I was doing research for the two-volume *Silver Dollars and Trade Dollars of the United States: A Complete Encyclopedia* (published in 1993) I interviewed Frank Gasparro at length. His favorite commission was the 1971 Eisenhower dollar. He later sent me this letter describing the experience:

> The happiest and most rewarding experience in my Mint career was the day I was commissioned to design the Eisenhower dollar. It was like training daily for an athletic event. I was ready. Only I had to wait twenty-five years. This is my story.

I remember that happy day in 1945, when I made every effort to take off from my Mint work to go to New York City from Philadelphia. I was to see the "D" Day–World War II victory parade down Broadway to honor our hero, General Eisenhower. I admired him greatly. I stood with the rest of the bystanders to celebrate Eisenhower's welcome home. Everyone shouted and waved.

Amidst all the rousing enthusiasm, I stepped back from the crowd and made a quick pencil profile sketch of our hero. I was pleased with my efforts. Then I took the train home to Philadelphia, and back to work the next day.

In my off hours, I modeled in wax and then cast in plaster a life size portrait of Eisenhower from memory and sketches, in the round. Meanwhile, I also started to chisel and engrave in soft steel, three inches in diameter a profile portrait of him. It took a long time; as you know steel is hard to move. Meanwhile, time moved on.

Late in 1970 (after twenty-five years), the director of the Mint, Mary Brooks, phoned me in Philadelphia from Washington (I was then chief engraver). She informed me that the Eisenhower dollar bill passed in Congress.

In my capacity, I was requested to design and produce working dies, for the Eisenhower dollar, fast. I knew in my bones, I could make it. Time was tight and there was no time for a national competition. So, I had to work hard and long hours. This was the Thanksgiving weekend, I started. The new dollar had to be struck January 2nd, 1971 (6 weeks in planning).

I was ready, I had my Eisenhower early profile, in hand. The dollar reverse had to portray the Apollo XI eagle insignia, as requested by the congressional bill. In this area, I was fortunate, having pursued many years in research of the American eagle. Luckily my sketches were approved, with no changes. The rest is history.

(Signed) **Frank Gasparro**
November 21, 1991.

Later Years

Frank and I kept in close touch in later years. His favorite traditional design was the Liberty Cap as on the Libertas Americana medal and the cents and half cents beginning in 1793. In 1976 he used this motif for a medal struck for the American Numismatic Association's annual convention.

In 1977 he was commissioned to design a mini-dollar, a small-size dollar coin to replace the Eisenhower dollar scheduled to be discontinued. He thought his Liberty Cap motif to be ideal, and working with Ed Rochette, executive director of the American Numismatic Association, he gained permission for the government to use the portrait he created in 1976. All seemed to be set for a 1979 Liberty Cap dollar. Then politics intervened, and he was directed to use the portrait of Susan B. Anthony, women's rights advocate, instead—much to his dismay. More is told in my *Expert's Guide to Collecting and Investing in Rare Coins*.

Starting in 1983 he produced for my company, Bowers and Merena Galleries, a series of one-ounce silver Proof medals. I suggested that one of these be a self-portrait, which he did and which is illustrated here. The mintage was 320 pieces.

Gasparro by Gasparro—a 40.4 mm silver medal designed by Frank Gasparro, a self-portrait showing the engraver at work.

Gilt plaster model by Frank Gasparro prepared in 1977 for the anticipated mini-dollar. (Smithsonian Institution)

A Gasparro design for the dollar's reverse.

CHAPTER 3

One coin led the investment market from 1951 to 1964, and all eyes were upon it.

The 1950-D Jefferson Nickel Excitement

Summer Seminars

The 1950-D nickel.

In the late 1970s into the 1980s I conducted a class, "All About Coins," for the American Numismatic Association's annual Summer Seminar at Headquarters on the campus of Colorado College in Colorado Springs. Each year I spent a week discussing American coins from the colonial era to the latest Proof sets. My typical class attracted several dozen students. The text was *A Guide Book of United States Coins* with copies furnished with the compliments of Whitman Publishing.

Among the brightest and best attendees were members of the group known as Young Numismatists. Teenagers interested in coins have a large appetite for information and the ability to retain it. Over the years, going way back in history to the 19th century, many of the most successful professionals started in the hobby before they were of voting age. In the late 1850s teenaged Augustus B. Sage founded the American Numismatic Society. In the 1870s S. Hudson Chapman (born 1857) and his brother Henry (1859) went to work in the Philadelphia shop of J.W. Haseltine, and in 1878 hung out their own shingle. From that point into the 20th century the Chapman brothers conducted the most accomplished rare-coin auction firm. B. Max Mehl, the most prominent dealer in the early 20th century, started as a teenager.

My Summer Seminar class inspired a number of young students to go on to become important collectors and several—Dwight N. Manley, Dan Ratner, and Kerry Wetterstrom among them—to become successful professional numismatists.

Of the five days in each seminar, three were spent in a classroom. I hasten to say that most attendees were older than teenagers, and I had a nice share of retirees. "Bert" Bressett, wife of Ken Bressett, attended one year, liked it, and came back the next year.

The House that Nickels Built
Of the other two Summer Seminar days, we spent one touring and going behind the scenes at the Denver Mint and the other going to Cripple Creek, a former gold-mining camp high in the Rockies on the west side of Pikes Peak. After gold was discovered there in the early 1890s, a great "rush" ensued, and within a few years the Cripple Creek Gold District had tens of thousands of residents and was called the richest gold camp on earth. Into the 20th century the production slowed, and by the 1980s there was just one mine, the El Paso, that was in operation. The community, while not a ghost town, had fewer than a thousand residents, most of whom were engaged in the tourist trade. At the Hotel Imperial melodramas, such as

Stock certificate for the Hannibal
Gold Mining Co., Cripple Creek,
1896, one of several hundred such
companies in the gold district.

Old-time buildings on Bennett
Avenue, the main street of Cripple Creek (1979).

The Gold Mining Stock Exchange
built in Cripple Creek in 1896 was
long since converted to other uses
when I photographed the top front
of this structure in July 1979.

Lady Audley's Secret and *East Lynne,* were staged each
summer. In later years the town evolved into a gambling mecca and its character was changed. Today it is
quite unlike it was when my classes went there.

For the Cripple Creek ride I was joined by Adna
Wilde, who at one time was executive director of the
ANA and another time its president, and Bill Henderson, ANA treasurer and a highly successful local
banker. On the ride up through Ute Pass heading out
of Colorado Springs to the gold country we would
each take a turn at the microphone in the front of our
chartered tour bus. During the next hour we would tell
stories of the areas we passed through, adding comments about numismatics and gold as appropriate.

Not far along the way and set back from the road
was a nice vacation home constructed to the order of
A.J. Mitula, a rare-coin dealer who had been a prominent advertiser in the 1950s. "That is the house that
nickels built," I would point out as we passed by.

The story goes back to 1950. At that year at the
Denver Mint only 2,630,000 nickels were minted—
fewer than in any year since the 1931-S. In comparison, in the year before, 36,498,000 1949-D nickels

were minted. When the mintage figure was published in early 1951, there were fireworks! Everyone wanted to get some, preferably a $2-face-value roll of 40 coins. From February to early summer, prices jumped all over the place. Dan Brown, a well-respected Denver dealer, was a wholesale source for new Denver Mint coins as they were released. He took advance orders for 1950-D nickels, but was unable to fill them.

Thousands of collectors went on a campaign to get some, but few dealers had any to offer. The demand was incredible. In the meantime, dealers and others scoured banks to see what they could find. Some were lucky and struck pay dirt. Others had to do without.

1950 DENVER NICKELS
(BR. UNC. MINT)
$20.00 Roll

WILL TRADE FOR:
Uncirculated Lincoln Cents
Gold Coins
Commemorative Halves
Uncirculated Rolls
(Very Good Supply)
Anxious to do business

WEIDENHEIMER'S
KINSLEY, KANSAS

Weidenheimer's asked $20 per roll. (*Numismatic Scrapbook Magazine*, April 1951)

In Houston, Texas, aforementioned A.J. Mitula, who conducted the Mitula Stamp & Coin Co., was in the right place at the right time. Although facts are scarce, it seems that a large proportion of the 1950-D mintage was distributed in the Houston area. Reportedly, he was able to buy more than a million of them somewhere! The usual trade method at the time was to tip bank tellers and ask them to look out for desired rolls. Seemingly, most of these were wholesaled to other dealers. Profits were sufficient to build his Colorado vacation home.

By the summer of 1951 the excitement diminished, and about $5 per roll was the retail asking price, seemingly with no shortage. After a year or two of quiet, the 1950-D nickel was again in demand. Many coin buyers were investors, not collectors, and modern rolls and Proof sets were what they desired. With its glaringly low mintage the 1950-D remained enticing.

Soon, the 1950-D nickel became the poster example of a modern coin turning into a fantastic investment. As the price for a roll passed $8, then $10, the demand increased. By the late 1950s such rolls were selling for $15 or so each. At that time Harry J. Forman in Philadelphia was one of the most active dealers in bank-wrapped rolls. He agreed to sell me a bunch for $15, stating that he was out of stock and would be replacing them soon. He was "caught short," as the price went past this point. As Harry and I did a lot of other business, I suggested that we forget the deal.

A non-collecting friend of Ken Bressett's heard about all of the investment action, wanted to buy some, and had Ken locate a couple of rolls, which he then tossed into a desk drawer and forgot. In 1960 the launching of *Coin World* and the excitement over the "rare" 1960 Small Date Lincoln cent ($50-face-value bags sold for $12,000 or more), the greatest boom in coin investment took place. While prices rose all over the map, front-row center was the 1950-D nickel. The price of a roll went to $200, then $500, then up some more. In 1964, when the price of a roll crossed the $1,200 mark and challenged $1,400, Ken called his friend, reminded him of the two rolls, and encouraged him to sell—which he did, for $1,200 each! Other smart sellers did the same, not all at $1,200, some for a bit less and others for a bit more, but over the $1,000 mark. Later the price crashed to about $325 per roll.

On November 12, 2011, a seller on eBay advertised rolls of 1950-D from the estate of A.J. Mitula for $340 each, including shipping, and sold five rolls. In the case of this nickel, fame was indeed fleeting.

Postscript: The 1950-D nickel excitement was built nearly entirely on speculation, not on basic numismatic demand by collectors. Today as you read these words, probably more than 99.9 percent of the *other* Mint State coins listed in the *Guide Book* are worth much more than they were in 1964.

Dan Brown's apologetic advertisement in the *Numismatic Scrapbook Magazine*, February 1951.

It seems that H. Feinberg, America's largest dealer in bank-wrapped rolls of coins, was out of 1950-D nickels. (*Numismatic Scrapbook Magazine*, March 1951)

R. Green, the business of Charles Green conducted under his wife Ruth's name, stated that 1950-D nickels were "the most over-rated U.S. coin," but was eager to buy some to fill customers' demands. (*Numismatic Scrapbook Magazine*, February 1951)

By spring several dealers were offering the elusive nickels, including Gerald Kimmell, who claimed to have unlimited quantities. (*Numismatic Scrapbook Magazine*, April 1951)

Lester M. Cox pitched $12 rolls as a great investment. (*Numismatic Scrapbook Magazine*, April 1951)

By May the price had settled down. (*Numismatic Scrapbook Magazine*, May 1951)

CHAPTER 4

Voted No. 1 by panelists for the 100 GREATEST AMERICAN MEDALS AND TOKENS book, this medal has been highly sought ever since the art and science of numismatics took root in our country.

Revisiting the Libertas Americana Medal

The Iconic Portrait of Liberty

An illustration of the Libertas Americana engraved by John E. Gavit in 1850, at which time he was a partner in the firm of Gavit & Duthie, Albany, New York. The obverse inscription omits the 4 day date that was on the medal.

The 1776-dated Libertas Americana medal, struck in France under the direction of Benjamin Franklin, is *the* medal to have if you only want one in your collection. Its fame is ever enduring. In 2002 this was an entry in my *More Adventures With Rare Coins* book. Since that time Whitman Publishing issued *100 Greatest American Medals and Tokens.* This book was written by Katie Jaeger and me and presented the results of votes submitted by leading collectors, dealers, and researchers. The Libertas Americana landed in the No. 1 spot. To me this was not a surprise.

It is estimated that today about 100 to 125 are known in copper and 45 to 55 in silver. The typical grade of an example ranges from about Proof-55 to 62. Although all were struck with a Proof finish at the Paris Mint, sometimes these are given Mint State grades today. Two original gold examples were made, but they are untraced today. In 1976 the Paris Mint restruck 500 examples in .920 fine gold (slightly over two ounces each) and sold them in fitted cases with a serial number assigned to each. I have one of these in my collection and prize it highly. Perhaps someday I'll have an original copper or silver impression.

A Libertas Americana medal in silver, an original impression.

Creating the Medal

The obverse of this 47.6 mm medal depicts the goddess of America, a portrait that numismatists call Miss Liberty, facing to the left, with LIBERTAS AMERICANA above and the historical date, 4 JUIL 1776, below. Behind the rich tresses of her hair is a liberty cap on a pole, the cap being the ancient symbol of freedom.

The dies for this beautiful work of medallic art were engraved in Paris in 1782 at the behest of Benjamin Franklin, who conceived the medal and suggested the mottoes. A French artist, Esprit-Antoine Gibelin, sketched the design, and the die work was done by Augustin Dupré.

Franklin, who was in France at the time, described the medal in a letter to Robert R. Livingston (secretary of foreign affairs under the Confederation) on March 4, 1782:

> This puts me in mind of a medal I have had a mind to strike, since the late great event you gave me an account of, representing the United States by the figure of an infant Hercules in his cradle, strangling the two serpents; and France by that of Minerva, sitting by as his nurse, with her spear and helmet, and her robe specked with a few *fleurs de lis.*
>
> The extinguishing of two entire armies in one war is what has rarely happened, and it gives a presage of the future force of our growing empire.[1]

On April 15, 1783, Franklin advised Livingston:

> I have caused to be struck here the medal which I formerly mentioned to you, the design of which you seemed to approve. I enclose one of them in silver, for the President of Congress, and one in copper for yourself; the impression in copper is thought to appear best, and you will soon receive a number for the members.
>
> I have presented one to the King, and another to the Queen, both in gold, and one in silver to each of the ministers, as a monumental acknowledgment, which may go down to

future ages, of the obligations we are under to this nation. It is mighty well received, and gives general pleasure. If the Congress approve it, as I hope they will, I may add something on the die (for those to be struck hereafter) to show that it was done by their order, which I could not venture to do until I had authority for it.

One of 500 Libertas Americana medals restruck in gold at the Paris Mint in 1976

This was an age of allegories and allusions, and many coins, tokens, and medals revealed stories to those who studied them. In other instances, the stories are still hidden, as with the 1783 Georgivs Triumpho token described in chapter 13. Franklin's description of the reverse, "representing the United States by the figure of an infant Hercules in his cradle, strangling the two serpents; and France by that of Minerva, sitting by as his nurse, with her spear and helmet, and her robe specked with a few *fleurs de lis*," is subjected to an expanded explanation:

Minerva (France with a shield ornamented with fleurs de lis) is fending off a ferocious lioness (England), with its tail between its legs, an heraldic symbol of defeat, NON SINE DIIS ANIMOSUS INFANS (the brave infant was aided by the gods) is around the border above. Below are the dates of American victories over the British at Saratoga in October 1777 and the climactic Yorktown in October 1781.

In the annals of American numismatics Louis E. Eliasberg is a unique figure. Beginning in the mid-1920s, by 1950 he accomplished what no one had ever done before or will ever do again: he completed his collection with each and every date and mintmark of federal coin from the 1793 half cent to the 1933 double eagle. Beyond that, he shared his collection widely through many exhibits.

Louis E. Eliasberg, "King of Coins"

"King of Coins"

Louis E. Eliasberg and selections from his collection. (Baltimore *Sun*, March 25, 1962)

Today, the aura of Louis E. Eliasberg Sr., (1896–1976) looms larger than life. He was a collector of legendary proportions whose likes will never be seen again.[1] Although he was well known in his time, today the details of his life are even more appreciated and better understood through his collection and the bringing of it to market. I admit some involvement in this, actually quite a bit, not only in the sale of his marvelous collection but also in the writing of a book-length biography, *Louis E. Eliasberg, Sr., King of Coins.* The "king" title came from an article in *Life* magazine, which was a color spread featuring gem coins from his collection as well as an overview of his accomplishments, and was selected by his son Richard for use with the book. Beyond numismatics, Louis was well known for his creation and operation of the Finance Company of America.

His son Richard recalled:

> *Life* magazine expressed an interest in writing an article on the collection and sent a photographer to Baltimore to photograph the coins. At the time, these pictures of the coins were the finest that had ever been taken and published. The article appeared in print in April 1953.
>
> Thousands of inquiries were sent to *Life* magazine regarding this article, and my father received about 7,000 letters directly. Unbelievably, he reviewed every letter personally and furnished an answer. *Life* magazine indicated they received more letters on that particular article than on any other except the 1937 article regarding President Franklin D. Roosevelt's efforts to pack the Supreme Court! My father's accomplishment became so well known that the U.S. Post Office delivered a letter to him that was simply addressed "King of Coins, U.S.A."

Double-spread feature on the Eliasberg Collection in *Life* magazine.

GEMS FROM THE GREATEST COLLECTION OF U.S. COINS

In brief, starting with a numismatic interest about 1925, Eliasberg, a Baltimore banker, built his holdings slowly—gathering commemoratives, half cents, silver coins, and other pieces of interest as they became available. Then in 1933, when the holding of gold coins by the American public was no longer permitted but numismatists were allowed to retain prized specimens, his attention focused on that area. Eliasberg was an avid student of American monetary history, and he felt that inflation would soon become rampant, never mind that 1933 was still in the depths of the Great Depression. In this focus, and in numismatics, he had great foresight and, indeed, was ahead of his time. The tempo of coin acquisitions accelerated, especially in the field of American gold.

The Clapp Collection

In 1942 Eliasberg took advantage of a truly marvelous opportunity: the estate collection of John H. Clapp became available through Joseph and Morton Stack, New York City dealers. This comprised an extensive collection of United States coins from half cents to double eagles, missing many rarities but well filled in with basic dates and mintmarks. Also, many important world coins were included.

The price was a staggering $100,000, a remarkable amount that can be appreciated by comparing it to the total realization for the William F. Dunham Collection sold the year before, in June 1941, by B. Max Mehl, for $83,364. Much of the Dunham figure involved rarities ($11,575 for the 1822 $5 and $4,250 for an 1804 dollar, as examples) that the Clapp Collection did not have. Instead, the Clapp cabinet contained basic date-and-mint issues in incredible condition—including many obtained directly from the mints at the time of issue, beginning in 1893. John M. Clapp, a Pennsylvania oil man, may have been the only numismatist to order a full set of coins directly from the Carson City Mint, this in the year that it ended production.

Page 80 of the notebook inventory of the Clapp Collection that was formed beginning in the late-19th century.

It may be correct to say that across the board the Clapp estate had the highest quality of any comprehensive collection of United States coins ever formed!

After the Clapp coup, Eliasberg was in the home stretch. With a copy of *Green's Check List* on hand, and with most of the United States coins crossed off, he needed just a few rarities to complete the seemingly impossible—to get one of each date and mint of United States coin from the very first, the 1793 half cent, to the very latest.

Completion!

Coin by coin, sometimes privately, other times in auction competition, Eliasberg added the needed pieces—a 1913 Liberty Head nickel here, an 1822 $5 there, from another source an 1804 silver dollar, then the unique 1870-S $3 gold, and others. Finally, it was down to the finish line, with just one piece needed— the 1873-CC Liberty Seated dime without arrows at the date. On November 7, 1950, he secured this, a coin recently sold in the Numismatic Gallery offering of the Adolphe Menjou Collection. Now the impossible had been achieved!

As time went on, the scope of the Eliasberg holdings became known. Generously, the owner made the collection available for viewing at selected banks, where the complete collection was mounted in special holders, in glass frames pivoted to vertical metal posts. Under the watchful eye of a guard and also an assistant to answer questions, the public could see all of the treasures. Often it was Louis Eliasberg himself who was there to meet and greet the public. At one time the collection was displayed in the Smithsonian Institution, where it attracted an amazing 1,500,000 visitors! At a later time it was set up at the Philadelphia Mint, where it was also a magnet for the public.

My Reminiscences

After finishing his American coins in 1950, Eliasberg added selected world pieces to his holdings, and also kept his United States cabinet current by adding modern issues, Proof sets, and the like, as they were made.

In the summer of 1975 he gave me a call and invited me to come to Baltimore to spend a week. The purpose, he said, was to become immersed in his collection, go through it with him coin by coin, and give my opinion as to the current significance, value, and anything else that came to mind regarding the various pieces, especially the rarities.

In the years since completion in 1950 the numismatic scenario had changed, and he had not kept pace. Additional examples had been discovered of certain varieties, others had been the subject of research, and

still others had captured market fancy and had sold for strong prices. Although Eliasberg had meticulously kept a card index with catalog prices and auction records, he wanted my inside view or take on the collection, its marketability, and other aspects, including the current psychology of the coin hobby.

Louis Eliasberg in his office.

He offered to pay my way to Baltimore and have me stay in a suite at the Lord Baltimore Hotel, which was owned by a friend. I said I could do this easily enough on my own, no charge, as this was truly a privilege—something I might *pay* to do, not the other way around! However, he demurred, stating that if I paid my way he might feel an obligation to me, which he did not desire. Instead, he wanted my opinions, after which he may or may not do anything with them. Accordingly, I was to be his guest.

This worked out well, and in August 1975 I found myself in Baltimore, taking my meals with Louis Eliasberg each noon at the Center Club, in the evening also with his wife, and during the day spending time in the lower-level vault at the Maryland National Bank, punctuated by occasional visits to his office in the venerable Munsey Building, a marvelous old office structure complete with marble floors in the hallways.

From the vault each day we would take a group of coins and wheel them on a metal cart to a private room. There we would go over them in detail, and I would tell what I observed, pointing out any that to me seemed to be very special. Of course, the basic rarity of the issues was known, but in recent times there developed a great market price differential between an "average" Uncirculated coin and one that was a superb gem. The inventory cards did not note such differences. And there were gems galore! Indeed, coin after coin was the finest I had ever seen—and by that time I had viewed quite a few collections.

After a very pleasant visit I departed, but we kept in touch. That autumn he prepared a manuscript for a talk, "Why, When, and How I Assembled the Most Complete Collection of United States Coins," which he sent to me for editing and comments. This was presented on November 9, 1975, at the Evergreen House, owned by The Johns Hopkins University, and important numismatically as the former home of notable collector T. Harrison Garrett and his son, John Work Garrett. Eliasberg asked if I could share his thoughts by publishing his talk in our company magazine, *The Rare Coin Review,* which we did. I had no inkling that four years later I would be at Evergreen House on another mission—to work with the University in the marketing of the Garrett Collection, in cooperation with Susan Tripp, curator at the Evergreen House, and her husband, coin expert David E. Tripp, whose professional link was later with Sotheby's, the art auction house.

Unfortunately, Mr. Eliasberg was in declining health, and on February 20, 1976, he passed away, leaving a legacy of accomplishment that had never been achieved before and will never be done again. Today, regardless of one's financial means, it is com-

pletely and utterly impossible to get one of each date and mintmark. Certain key rarities are widely scattered, and unlike the situation when Mr. Eliasberg acquired his 1933 $20, the Treasury Department now holds that such pieces cannot be legally owned except for a single example reputedly once held by King Farouk of Egypt. The unique 1870-S $3 is now out of reach, being owned by the Harry W. Bass, Jr., Foundation and on loan exhibit at the American Numismatic Association headquarters in Colorado Springs. The only 1822 $5 in private hands is a treasured possession of a Texas connoisseur and fine friend.

Louis E. Eliasberg's heirs included his two sons, Louis Jr. and Richard. In 1982, then a principal of Bowers and Ruddy Galleries (with Jim Ruddy), I was contacted by Louis Jr., who had inherited the U.S. gold coins section of the numismatic estate. Arrangements were made to showcase these for auction and, separately, to write a book. The auction was held in New York City the following October, 1982, and brought record prices, including for the aforementioned 1870-S $3 and 1822 $5, each at $687,500. This was a big media event, with an appearance on the NBC *Today* show, an interview on another network with Jane Bryant Quinn (of *Newsweek*), and more. It seemed that the whole world became excited about this extraordinary event! The book, *United States Gold Coins: An Illustrated History,* proved popular, has since gone through multiple editions, and in 1986 was quoted by Secretary of the Treasury James A. Baker III in his introductory remarks when he inaugurated the gold bullion-coin program.

Some years later, his other son, Richard, contacted me, and arrangements were made to consign the balance of the U.S. coins from the Eliasberg Collection—consisting of copper, nickel, and silver coins, ranging from half cents to silver dollars and trade dollars, plus patterns, territorial gold, and other specialties. This proved to be a garden of numismatic delights, and with the staff I jumped into the project with great enthusiasm.

In front of us were many rarities that had not crossed the auction block for years, some of them not since the 1890s when they first went into the Clapp Collection! In connection with that, the second offering, which crossed the block in 1986 and 1987, I wrote the earlier-mentioned book, *Louis E. Eliasberg, Sr., King of Coins.* This sale had its highlights, including the first public auction of any American coin over the $1 million mark, the 1913 Liberty Head nickel at $1,485,000, with the buyer being Jay Parrino. Later, it went to my fine friend Dwight Manley, with whom I worked in the California Gold Marketing Group, dispersing the fabulous golden treasure from the SS *Central America.* As I contemplate the Eliasberg Collection I can still see in my mind's eye the splendid 1796 half cents, the incredible Mint State 1793 Liberty Cap cent and the "Abbey" 1799 cent, the 1873-CC No Arrows and 1894-S dimes, the 1876-CC twenty-cent piece, the 1838-O and 1853-O No Arrows halves, the fantastic 1804 dollar, the 1884 and 1885 trade dollars, and other rarities. Wow!

The 1982 auction of the Eliasberg gold coins and two sales, 1986 and 1987, of the copper, nickel, and silver collection, still echo in the halls of numismatics today. Many coins have changed hands again, with the Eliasberg pedigree being second to none in terms of desirability when attached to a particular specimen. In the years since that time, every once in a while we get one or a few coins consigned to a sale—always providing an opportunity for some pleasant reminiscing!

Another chapter in the Eliasberg epic took place in April 2005, when Richard Eliasberg consigned the world and ancient coins to American Numismatic Rarities, of which Christine Karstedt was president. (Later, ANR merged into what became Stack's Bowers Galleries.) The sale, held in New York City, was a star-spangled event—with participants from 37 different world countries! Many pieces sold for double, triple, or even five to ten times their estimated values. When all was said and done, the realization crossed the $10 million mark. The total Eliasberg Collection checked in at more than $55,000,000, far and away the most valuable numismatic property ever to be sold, with no close competition up to that time. Since that time the John J. Ford, Jr. Collection sold by us edged it out by a few million dollars.

In my life in numismatics—as a collector beginning as a young teenager in 1952, followed in 1953 with my entry as a dealer while I was going to school, later as a professional numismatist full time—I have had many wonderful experiences. Knowing Louis E. Eliasberg Sr. and his family is high on the list, and I will be forever grateful for the opportunity.

CHAPTER 6

In late 1856 and early 1857 the Mint struck pattern one-cent pieces of small diameter with the Flying Eagle design, intended to replace the large copper cents in use since 1793. The new cents were recognized as being scarce from the outset. Even since then the ownership of an 1856 Flying Eagle cent has been a source of pride and a badge of distinction.

The Famous 1856 Flying Eagle Cent

An Ideal Rarity

The 1856 Flying Eagle Cent.

If there is an *ideal* American rarity the 1856 Flying Eagle cent is a candidate. These pieces, actually patterns, were struck from several 1856-dated die combinations in that year and in early 1857. The original quantity minted was perhaps 800 or more pieces, followed by perhaps a couple thousand restrikes later made at the Mint for collectors. When numismatics became a widespread national activity in 1858, the 1856 Flying Eagle cent, by then considered to be rare, was an object of desire. To accommodate the demand the Mint coined restrikes beginning in the spring of 1859. Accounting for attrition, disappearance, and other negative effects, there are probably about 1,500 or so 1856 Flying Eagle cents in existence now.

Today the fame of the 1856 Flying Eagle cent endures. Whenever one turns up at auction it is a candidate for a picture and a glowing description. The late Abe Kosoff once stated that to start an auction with an 1856 Flying Eagle cent was a symbol of good luck, and he did this on some occasions. Today there are enough of these around that anyone with the necessary funds can buy an example, although all are expensive. The comforting factor is that if history repeats itself, such coins will increase in value over a period of years. I am not aware that during any generation the market price of an 1856 Flying Eagle cent failed to increase substantially over the price of a generation before.

Original Mintage Details

No records are known concerning the production of pattern 1856 Flying Eagle cents. It was the practice of the Mint at that time to produce whatever pattern coins of various types were needed, but not to include them in regular production figures. For some patterns the *distribution* numbers are known from surviving correspondence. This is only partially true here.

According to documents in the National Archives, distribution included the following:[1]

> 264 pieces or more to congressmen.
>
> 200 to Representative S.D. Campbell.
>
> 102 to Secretary of the Treasury James Guthrie.
>
> 62 to senators.
>
> 4 to President Franklin Pierce.
>
> 2 to the Mint Cabinet.

In addition to the above 634 coins, additional pieces were given to newspaper and magazine editors across the country, dignitaries, the Mint staff, interested numismatists, and others. These figures suggest a total approaching 1,000 coins, if not more.

The late numismatic researcher Walter Breen, who was a master at guesswork, posited that an additional "several hundred were held in stock in the Mint for later distribution to coin collectors, or to trade them for Washington medals for the Mint Cabinet."[2] If this was so, these can be added to the total suggested above.

Reviewing the New Cents

In its issue of February 7, 1857, *Harper's Weekly* inserted an illustration of an 1856 Flying Eagle cent and furnished this commentary, in part:

> You see for yourselves the patriotic design—the wreath entwined with the vine and Indian corn on the one side, and that everlasting American eagle, 'spreading its wings and soaring aloft,' on the other. The bird, by-the-by, has rather an anserine than an aquiline look, and is said to be the same as once was set loose upon golden wings in a previous issue of half eagles, but having been again caged, in consequence of its barn-yard fowl appearance, is now to be turned adrift for a humbler flight. . . .

The account went on to suggest that the old phrase, "Not worth a red cent," would be of no use now that copper cents were to be replaced, "for the new cent is not red, being of a gray, silvery aspect."

The *Buffalo Commercial Advertiser,* January 8, 1857, printed this:

The New Cent

The editor of the Providence, R.I. *Journal* has been permitted to see one of the new cents just struck off at the Mint. He describes it as a little larger than a dime, and nearly twice as thick.

NOT A RED CENT.
We give you, out of the abundance of the liberal resources of our establishment, a " counterfeit presentment" of the new cent.

You see for yourselves the patriotic design—the wreath entwined with the vine and Indian corn on the one side, and that everlasting American eagle, "spreading its wings and soaring aloft," on the other. The bird, by-the-by, has rather an anserine than an aquiline look, and is said to be the same as once was set loose upon golden wings in a previous issue of half-eagles, but having been again caged, in consequence of its barn-yard fowl appearance, is now to be turned adrift for a humbler flight.

The cut gives an exact representation of the size, with the exception of the thickness, which is about equal to that of two half-eagles put together. The composition is of copper and nickel. As the former metal has become dearer, from the fact of its supply not having kept up with the manufacturing demand for it, the Government gains by the alloy, as, although the nickel is comparatively dear, the quantity used of the mixed metal is smaller. The intrinsic value at one time of the single copper cent was only 1-50th part of the dollar; now, with the heightened value of copper, it has risen to nearly 1-86th. The new cent only costs 1-65th part of the dollar.

Provided the act of Congress, which establishes the new cent, becomes a law, which it has not as yet, we think the public will be a gainer by the new coin. Its smaller size makes it much more convenient for handling, and less burdensome for transportation, while the neater look and the freedom from the *brassy* odor, renders it much more acceptable to fastidious delicacy. Ladies may now venture to touch with their ungloved fingers small change without being, like Lady Macbeth, unable to wash out with Cologne, or any other toilet detersive, the "damned spot" of a base contamination.

There is a great deal that is interesting in the history of the old American cent, which we would like to have eliminated. Will our "Notes and Queries" tell us something about the old Washington Penny, for which eager collectors are willing, it is said, to pay for in weight of gold? Let us know something, also, about the whereabouts of these rarities. Franklin, as well as Washington, we believe, has honored the penny with his name. What was his design? Is it a fact, that at one time, our cents—eagle, stars, and all—were manufactured in Great Britain, at the celebrated Soho Works of Birmingham, belonging to Bolton and the great Watt, and imported in the gross by our hardware merchants, and sold at large profits to small dealers for their own purposes?

We will lose an American proverb, now widely circulated, by the issue of the new coin. "He's not worth a *red* cent" will be of such general application that it will not have any specific meaning, and will be of course dropped, for the new cent is not red, being of a gray, silvery aspect.

The *Harper's Weekly* article.

On one side is a flying eagle, with the inscription "United States of America, 1856," around the circle: On the other is 'One Cent' within a wreath. It is altogether the handsomest coin of so low a denomination that we have ever seen.

Restrikes Add to the Supply

In late 1856 and early 1857 the numismatic hobby comprised hundreds of enthusiasts, but likely no more than a thousand nationwide. This changed dramatically when in early 1857 it was announced that the large copper cents familiar since childhood would be discontinued. Excitement knew no bounds as thousands of citizens looked through their change, visited banks, and otherwise set about collecting as many different dates of cents as possible.

Newspapers in New York City, Boston, and elsewhere ran features on coins, and the monthly *Historical Magazine* was founded. This situation acted as a catalyst for coin collecting throughout 1857, which increased in interest and activity that year and then went into high gear in 1858, when the American Numismatic Society was formed and other developments occurred.

Collectors realized that Flying Eagle cents dated 1856 were quite scarce, as although many had been distributed, very few had gone to numismatists. The market value of a nice example advanced to as much as $2, which at the time was more than equal to a day's pay for many American workers. Even at this price they were hard to find, as most had been scattered, with many being spent by the recipients.

Beginning in spring of 1859, Mint Director James Ross Snowden decided to restrike these in quantity along with many other coins from earlier dies, ranging from Gobrecht silver dollars of 1836 to 1839 to illogical combinations that made little sense, strikings in off metals, and the like. Thus was initiated an era of privately produced restrikes and numismatic

novelties that continued unabated until the summer of 1885. No records were kept, and the profits went secretly into the pockets of Mint officials.

Whereas the original 1856-dated Flying Eagle cents had lustrous or Mint State surfaces, the restrikes were all Proofs, this being considered a *better grade*. Today, circulation strikes are recognized as varieties collectible separately from Proofs, and neither is "better" than the other. Each represents a different method of manufacture. Throughout numismatics there are many varieties which are common in Mint State but rare in Proof finish, and for some the opposite is true.

It is not known how many Proof 1856 Flying Eagle cents were restruck. A reasonable estimate might be 2,000 to 2,500. Restriking is thought to have continued through the 1870s and from several pairs of dies that differ very slightly in their characteristics. Rick Snow, a longtime professional numismatist, has studied and published these in his books on the Flying Eagle and Indian Head cent series.

All of a sudden 1856 Flying Eagle cents became available in 1859 and the price dropped from $2 to about $1 each. From that time to the present era the price has advanced more or less steadily. By the turn of the 20th century a nice Mint State or Proof coin sold for $10 to $15. By the end of the 1990s, by which time hundreds of thousands of people collected coins seriously, the price was more likely $30,000 or more.

Famous Hoards

In the late 19th and early 20th centuries several numismatists thought it desirable to hoard as many 1856 Flying Eagle cents as possible. A great sport, this!

The first extensive study of such hoards was published by John F. Jones in *The Numismatist*, April 1944. Since then others have taken up the topic.

R.B. Leeds, of Atlantic City, New Jersey, began scooping the coins up in the 19th century. Henry Chapman auctioned the Leeds Collection on November 17 and 28, 1906, and included the following in his commentary:

BROTHER JONATHAN'S NEW BABY.

Harper's Weekly cartoon, February 21, 1857, showing the
new cent. Brother Jonathan was a popular allegorical
term for the United States, much like Uncle Sam is today.
The illustrated eagle is flying in the wrong direction!

For many years he was an ardent collector, turning his attention to accumulating all the examples he could of certain dates, his especial hobby being 1856 Eagle cents of which he had 109 specimens, the greatest collection ever offered of this very rare cent. Mr. Leeds was a firm believer in the rarity and value of this coin, and bought all that he could for many years past. The advance of the past 10 years has proved his judgment to have been correct.

In the auction Proofs sold from $8 to $10.50; Uncirculated, from $6 to $10; Very Fine to nearly Uncirculated $5.50 to $6.50; Good and Very Good, $4 to $5.50.

George W. Rice, a wealthy building contractor in Detroit, began collecting coins in 1864. At an early time he took a fancy to 1856 Flying Eagle cents. By the early 20th century he had obtained 756 examples—far and away the largest hoard ever! This was not at all pleasing to Commodore W.C. Eaton, who penned a letter to *The Numismatist,* July 1916, stating that Rice's numismatic gluttony made the current price of $5 for a specimen "absolutely absurd . . . for anything under a brilliant Proof," and that such activity was "quite contrary to proper ethics." Rice's cents seem to have been sold privately, as no catalog of them has ever been found.

The best-known hoard of 1856 Flying Eagle cents was that formed by John Andrew Beck of Pittsburgh. Born in Chestnut Ridge, Pennsylvania, on January 5, 1859, Beck spent part of his youth with his parents in Texas, but the family was forced to return to Pennsylvania in face of Indian depredations in the West. His father developed brine wells near Pittsburgh, from which liquid salt was taken, building a large wholesale trade in that commodity. He also drilled for oil. Upon his father's death, John eventually acquired the business. He collected his first scarce and rare coins at the age of 10. The passion continued, and into the late-19th century he bought territorial gold coins (including dozens of octagonal $50 pieces), large quantities of Mint State $3 coins, and many other coins, including 1856-dated Flying Eagle cents, mostly from the Chapman brothers and, after 1906, from Henry Chapman. It seems that along the way he acquired many coins from the Leeds hoard. At one time he posted a standing offer of $10 for any 1856 Flying Eagle cent regardless of grade.

Beck died on January 27, 1924. His estate was handled by the Pittsburgh National Bank & Trust Company, of which he had been a director. An inventory revealed 531 Flying Eagle cents. Although many coin dealers knocked on the bank's door, Beck's vast coin collection remained intact. Finally, in the early 1970s the estate administrators turned over the coins to Abner Kreisberg and Jerry Cohen, of Beverly Hills, to sell in the best manner they saw fit. Most of the gold coins and other rarities were sold at auction but it was decided by Jerry and Abner that most of the Flying Eagle cents would be best sold by private sale.

When the cents arrived at their office I was among the first to see them. All of the coins had a rather dull appearance, "vault grime" so to speak, from inattention for decades. However, some basic dipping in acetone, a solvent that simply removes dirt and grease, did wonders, and the coins regained their original appearance. It was thought that the availability of hundreds of pieces would dampen the market, but the opposite proved to be true. The coin hobby was in a period of great strength at the time, all of the 1856 Flying Eagle cents found ready buyers, and the price increased!

Among classic silver rarities in the American series the 1876-CC twenty-cent piece both is famous and has a rich historical background. Fewer than 20 are believed to exist today.

A New Denomination Proposed

The Carson City Mint. (Stereograph panel by John Scripture, 1870s)

The Rare 1876-CC Twenty-Cent Piece

Produced only from 1875 to 1878, and for circulation only in one truly significant year, 1875, the twenty-cent piece is the most short-lived of all regular American coinages. This denomination has a unique connection to the state of Nevada.

Although a twenty-cent piece had been suggested in the United States as early as 1791, and in neighboring Canada the twenty-cent piece had been distributed in quantity in 1858, it was not until February 1874 that the notion of this denomination was translated into reality this side of the border. The scenario in 1874 was centered on the West Coast. Small-denomination minor coins including Indian Head cents, two-cent pieces, nickel three-cent pieces, and Shield nickel five-cent pieces had never circulated there to any extent, nor was the silver three-cent piece used in commerce. For this reason, the San Francisco Mint produced none of these denominations. Half dimes were made in San Francisco through 1873, when these silver coins were abolished, and most pieces quickly disappeared from circulation. Thus, in 1874 the smallest denomination currently being made for circulation was the dime or ten-cent piece.

One theory for the creation of the twenty-cent piece involves the complexity, under these circumstances, of making change in commerce. If someone wanted to buy an item priced at 10¢ and did not have a dime, and offered 25¢ in payment, he might receive a Spanish-American silver one-real "bit" worth 12-1/2¢, although most had disappeared from circulation (their legal-tender status had expired in 1859), as there was no way of giving 15¢ back, absent a circulating 5¢ coin. If an item was priced at 5¢ retail, a buyer would have to pick up two of them as there were no coins to conduct a solo 5¢ purchase. By rather complicated reasoning, if the twenty-cent piece became a reality, someone could make a 5¢ purchase, tender a 25¢ piece in payment, and receive a twenty-cent piece as change. Or, for a ten-cent purchase a twenty-cent piece could be offered, and change of 10¢ would be given.

Perhaps a simpler explanation is that which appeared in the *American Journal of Numismatics,* July 1875, to the effect that the twenty-cent piece was made to replace Spanish silver coins that still circulated in the West and Southwest. These two-real coins, often dating back to the 18th century and usually very well worn, were said by many to be worth 20 cents or so, but they usually traded in commerce for 25 cents. Such "two-bit" coins, as they were called, were legal tender in America until the summer of 1860, but by 1874 most had disappeared from circulation in the East and Midwest.

In February 1874 Senator John P. Jones of Nevada introduced a bill for the twenty-cent piece. At the time Nevada was America's leading silver-producing state. While fortunes for the Comstock Lode in Virginia City, Nevada, had been at a high crest in the 1860s and had prompted the establishment of the Carson City Mint a few miles away from Virginia City, by the 1870s the demand for and price of silver had fallen sharply, and times were difficult. New markets were needed. Certainly, a new silver denomination such as the twenty-cent piece would help. Jones in his proposal suggested that the twenty-cent piece would facilitate change-making and help eliminate the use of the few Spanish-American coins still in circulation in the West.

An 1875 pattern twenty-cent piece, the variety classified as Judd-1392.

An 1875 pattern twenty-cent piece, Judd-1398.

In 1875 a number of different patterns were made, most of them quite different from the quarter dollar, including having the head (rather than the full figure) of Miss Liberty on the obverse and having a shield on the reverse. However, it seems that diversity was not wanted.

The Twenty-Cent Piece Becomes a Reality

The adopted obverse design features Christian Gobrecht's motif of Miss Liberty in a seated position, stars surrounding, and the date below. The reverse was a new motif by William Barber and depicts a perched eagle, somewhat similar in configuration to that used on the trade dollar, surrounded by UNITED STATES OF AMERICA and the denomination expressed as TWENTY CENTS. The edge is plain, unlike other silver denominations of the era, which had reeded edges.

In 1875 the Nevada-born (so to speak) twenty-cent piece made its debut.

On March 3, 1875, the coin became legal. It was soon realized that just because a coin of this denomination was available, merchants did not necessarily change their habits, and the piece was a failure virtually from its inception. Most were coined at the San Francisco Mint, where they could be obtained in exchange for gold coins (current Legal Tender Notes did not circulate in the West). The *San Francisco Bulletin* told this on June 4, 1875:

> Samples of the new 20-cent coin were received in this city this morning from the Carson [City] Mint. The officers of that Mint were anxious to make the first coin of this description on the Pacific Coast and, accordingly, had everything in readiness upon the arrival of the dies from Washington [*sic;* dies were sent from Philadelphia].
>
> The first coins were struck off on the 1st of June. . . . It is of course a little smaller than the quarter dollar

and has the words "Twenty Cents" in place of the words "Quar. Dol"; otherwise there is but little difference in the general appearance of the two coins. Some care will be necessary in receiving changes not to take them for more than their face value. The new coin has a clean look and was probably made from Consolidated Virginia bullion.

Twenty-cent pieces were immediately confused with quarter dollars of somewhat similar size and design, as predicted by some. For example, a ticket taker on the ferry connecting San Francisco and Oakland took in a twenty-cent piece, thought it to be a quarter dollar, gave change for a quarter, and alerted others to the danger of such coins.

At the time there were no silver coins of any kind in circulation in the Midwest and East as specie (gold and silver coin) payments had been suspended by the Treasury Department in 1862, during the Civil War when citizens were hoarding coins, and payments had not yet resumed. Thus, mintage of the new silver twenty-cent pieces was concentrated in the Western states in anticipation of demand there, as per these circulation-strike mintage figures:

1875 (Philadelphia Mint): 36,910 coins.

1875-CC (Carson City Mint): 133,290.

1875-S (San Francisco Mint): 1,155,000.

Things did not go as expected. The *San Francisco Bulletin* reported on November 22, 1875, that $231,000 face value in such coins had been struck, but only $5,000 to $6,000 worth had been paid out. All of the others had been shipped to the East to be held by the Treasury Department until silver coins, which had been trading at a premium in terms of Legal Tender Notes, were exchangeable at par. This did not happen until April 20, 1876. It is presumed that at that time large quantities of 1875-CC and 1875-S twenty-cent pieces were paid out in the East, far from where they were coined.

By early 1876 the denomination was an object of confusion and derision, and circulation-strike coinage declined precipitously. The next year the production figures were as follows:

1876 Philadelphia Mint: 14,640 coins.

1876-CC: 10,000. Nearly all of which were melted. Therein lies a story!

After that time, coinage of the twenty-cent piece was limited to several hundred Proofs each year for collectors, in 1877 and 1878, after which the denomination was no more.

In 1878, Senator John Sherman testified before a House committee about the twenty-cent piece and said that it had been created "only because Senator Jones asked for it." Dr. Henry R. Linderman in his book, *Money and Legal Tender,* said it was a mistake to introduce the piece, but that it was a proper denomination between a dime and a half dollar and should have been used instead of a quarter dollar. It will be recalled that there is no $25 bill.

1876-CC twenty-cent piece.

Front Row Center:
The 1876-CC Twenty-Cent Piece

For decades the 1876-CC has been recognized as one of the most famous and most desired of all American coins. Fewer than 20 examples are known to exist, most of which are in Mint State. The appearance of a specimen at auction is always a cause for excitement!

Records as cited above reveal that 10,000 1876-CC twenty-cent pieces were struck. However, by the time they were produced the denomination was rendered effectively obsolete, so apparently nearly all were melted. The destruction of these coins is probably the subject of the following order written by Mint Director Henry Richard Linderman on May 19, 1877, addressed to James Crawford, superintendent of the Carson City Mint: "You are hereby authorized and directed to melt all 20-cent pieces you have on hand, and you will debit 'Silver Profit Fund' with any loss thereon."

In 1876 at the Carson City Mint selected samples of all coins were set aside for examination by the Assay Commission (which met annually in Philadelphia) on Wednesday, February 14, 1877. Presumably, a number of 1876-CC twenty-cent pieces were shipped east for the Commission. This group of coins later probably constituted most of the supply available to numismatists. It seems likely that a few were paid out in Nevada in 1876 and 1877, accounting for a handful of worn and impaired pieces known today.

Perhaps the first specimen of the 1876-CC twenty-cent piece to attract notice in a catalog was that sold in the R. Coulton Davis Collection sale by New York Coin & Stamp Company, January 20 through 24, 1890. At that time only a few numismatists collected coins by mintmark varieties, and virtually nothing was known of the 1876-CC. I will say more about Davis later.

The rarity and desirability of the 1876-CC twenty-cent piece was first showcased to a wide audience in a landmark monograph, *Mint Marks, A Treatise on the Coinage of United States Branch Mints,* by Augustus G. Heaton, published in 1893. Heaton was a professional artist, a poet, and an early president of the American Numismatic Association. His painting, *The Recall of Columbus,* hangs in the Capitol and was used as the design for the 50-cent commemorative stamp for the World's Columbian Exposition. Prior to that time, numismatists had been concerned primarily

with dates, and whether a coin had a mintmark or not made little difference. Heaton, a facile writer, listed 17 "causes of attractiveness" for collecting mintmarks, as delineated below.

Causes of Attractiveness

1st. Mint Marks in their progressive issue at New Orleans, Dahlonega, Charlotte, San Francisco, and Carson City show the direction of our country's growth and its development of mineral wealth.

2d. Mint Marks in their amount of issue in varied years at different points offer the monetary pulse of our country to the student of finance.

3rd. The denominations of any one Branch Mint, in their irregular coinage and their relation to each other at certain periods, indicate curiously the particular needs of the given section of the land.

4th. A knowledge of the Branch Mint coinage is indispensable to an understanding of the greater or less coinage of the Philadelphia Mint and its consequent numismatic value.

5th. A knowledge of the coinage of the different Branch Mints gives to many usually considered common dates great rarity if certain Mint Marks are upon them.

6th. Mint-Mark study gives nicety of taste and makes a mixed set of pieces unendurable.

7th. Several dies were used at Branch Mints which never served in the Philadelphia coinage, and their impressions should no longer be collected as mere varieties.

8th. The very irregularity of dates in some denominations of Branch Mint issues is a pleasant exercise of memory and numismatic knowledge.

9th. This irregularity in date, and in the distribution of coinage, gives a collection in most cases but two or three, and rarely three or more contemporaneous pieces, and thus occasions no great expense.

10th. As the Branch Mints are so far apart their issues have the character of those of different nations, and tend to promote correspondence and exchange, both to secure common dates in fine condition and the rarities of each.

11th. The United States coinage has a unique interest in this production at places far apart of pieces of the same value and design with distinguishing letters upon them.

12th. As Mint Marks only occur in silver and gold coins they can be found oftener than coins of the baser metals in fine condition, and neither augment or involve a collection of the minor pieces.

13th. As Mint Marks have not heretofore been sought, or studied as they deserve, many varieties yet await in circulation the good fortune of collectors who cannot buy freely of coins more in demand, and who, in having access to large sums of money, may draw therefrom prizes impossible to seekers after older dates.

14th. The various sizes of the mint marks O, S, D, C, and CC, ranging from the capital letters of average book type to infinitesimal spots on the coin,

as well as the varied location of these letters, defy any accusation of monotony, and are far more distinguishable than the characteristics of many classified varieties of old cents and 'colonials.'

15th. Mint Marks include noble enough game for the most advanced coin hunter, as their rarities are among the highest in value of United States coinage, and their varieties permit the gathering in some issues of as many as six different modern pieces of the same date.

16th. The face value of all the silver Mint Marks to 1893, being less than one hundred and fifty dollars, they are within the means of any collector, as aside from the economy of those found in circulation, the premiums for rarities are yet below those on may coins of far inferior intrinsic worth.

17th. As the new Mint at Philadelphia will have a capacity equal to all existing United States Mints, it is probable that others will be greatly restricted or even abolished in no long time, and that Mint Marks will not only cease as an annual expense, but be a treasure in time to those who have the foresight to collect them now.

In his text Heaton further mentioned the 1876-CC twenty-cent piece in two places, noting in the preface that it was "excessively rare in any condition," and in the main text the following: "The pieces of 1876-CC have become very rare, as we have mentioned in our preface, from the negligence of western collectors, or the indifference involved in mintmark rarities."

845 — STATE CAPITOL, CARSON CITY, NEVADA.

The Story Continues

The June 1894 issue of *The Numismatist* included this filler:

> Three of the rare 20-cent pieces of 1876 from the Carson City Mint have lately turned up in Uncirculated condition. It was not two days before they were incorporated into three of our leading collections where their presence is highly appreciated.

In due course other examples of the rare 1876-CC twenty-cent piece appeared, including in the Dr. S.L. Lee Collection auctioned by J.W. Scott & Co. on June 12, 1899. The Lee cabinet was a particularly fine one, and many other delicacies were included. The buyer of the 1876-CC twenty-cent piece was well-known numismatist John M. Clapp. This coin passed to his son John H. Clapp in 1906 and into the Louis E. Eliasberg Sr. Collection in 1942 as noted in chapter 5. Mention of this specimen was made by Edgar H. Adams in *The Numismatist,* March 1911, in his column, "Live American Numismatic Items":

> Mr. Elmer S. Sears is exhibiting one of the greatest prizes of the mint mark field—an Uncirculated specimen of the extremely rare 20-cent piece of 1876, of the Carson City Mint. This piece is remarkable for the fact that although ten thousand are said to have been struck at the Nevada mint in that year, still not more than four pieces can now be located. One of these is owned

by Mr. John H. Clapp of Washington, another by Mr. Virgil M. Brand of Chicago, and the third by Mr. H.O. Granberg of Oshkosh, Wis.

The Adams account brings together several of the most famous names in numismatics at the time. Elmer S. Sears was for several years a partner with Wayte Raymond in the U.S. Coin Co. Virgil M. Brand (1861–1926), a wealthy Chicago brewer, devoted most of his life to coins and assembled a magnificent holding. In the 1980s, in connection with presenting Brand estate coins at auction on behalf of certain heirs and the Morgan Guaranty Trust Co., I wrote a book-length biography of this remarkable man. Granberg had one of the finest cabinets of his era within which were the 1804 dollar and the 1884 and 1885 trade dollars, among other delicacies.

Another 1876-CC was offered by Édouard Frossard in the J.G. Hubbard Collection sale on December 10, 1900, and was purchased by S. Benton Emery (whose collection was sold by Bowers and Merena, November 1984, this coin appearing as lot 492). From such beginnings in the late-19th century the 1876-CC became highly prized, and it has been a mark of distinction if a major cabinet includes an example. In 2013 Stack's Bowers Galleries offered the Battle Born Collection of Carson City coinage consigned through Nevada dealer Rusty Goe. One of the showpieces was a beautiful 1876-CC twenty-cent piece.

Certain of these are pedigreed to the Maryland estate hoard, one of the more remarkable finds in the American series. In the late 1950s, Baltimore dealer Tom Warfield found a group of seven, eight, or possibly nine splendid Mint State coins in his home town. Each piece was a lustrous gem, delicately toned, and

virtual perfection. It is my opinion that these may have come from someone who once served on the earlier-mentioned Assay Commission which in 1877 reviewed the prior year's coinage. The genesis of this cache was never revealed, but was variously thought by others to have been T. Harrison Garrett (who died in 1888, had a fabulous collection, but did not seem to have acquired many mintmarked issues; in my opinion, he can be eliminated as a possibility, especially as his estate did not contain even a single specimen of the 1876-CC twenty-cent piece), Waldo C. Newcomer, or Frank G. Duffield. Even the name of Louis E. Eliasberg Sr. was mentioned. I suggest that R. Coulton Davis, Philadelphia pharmacist with close ties to Mint officials, could be in the running, if held-over coins from the Assay Commission were indeed the source.

Four of these coins were sold to me. I subsequently distributed them into as many different collections. Several more were sold to John J. Ford Jr., of New Netherlands Coin Co., who recalled showing one to Morton Stack, who expressed great surprise and admiration, then quickly showing him a second coin, and selling him these and others.

An amplification of the preceding is provided by this recollection by Harvey Stack:

> In 1970 we sold the B. Frank Collection which had an 1876-CC twenty-cent piece in it. The coin showed some wear. After this was sold, John Ford came to the sale with five more coins, one a superb gem, the others attractive Uncirculated as well, that he got from a Maryland dealer. These were all sold to various people who attended the Frank Collection sale.[1]

There are treasures and there are more treasures, but few are as curious as this one.

A Treasure Hidden in the Woods

An Unlisted Token Is Exciting to Russ Rulau

Selections from the hoard.

One of the 47 Miss M.J. Drury 18.9 mm aluminum tokens.

In 1996 I received a call from my longtime friend Dave Sundman, president of Littleton Coin Company. They had just purchased a trove of old coins, tokens, and other numismatic things found on an old New England farm once owned by a Mr. Miller, an odd duck it seems. Included were 47 GOOD FOR tokens in aluminum, bearing the name of MISS M.J. DRURY, of Williamstown, Vermont. After some checking, Dave was not able to find any record of such tokens—not particularly surprising, as there was no reference book on 20th-century tokens of that state and as the field of Good For tokens comprises countless thousands of varieties.

I did know, however, that Good For tokens are rare in general for the northern New England states of Vermont, New Hampshire, and Maine. Why this is, I can only guess. In their day they were paid out by trade-stimulating devices, slot machines, and other novelties and were redeemable in cash at the counter or in merchandise. Such tokens were produced in large numbers by Meyer & Wenthe (Chicago), S.H. Quint & Sons (Philadelphia), and other private minters. It seems that if one saloon in, say, Cincinnati, ordered some Good For tokens and they became popular, other businesses in the same city would do likewise. From a numismatic viewpoint this resulted in many towns and cities for which Good Fors are common and others for which they are rare or none are known at all. My town of Wolfeboro, New Hampshire, is in the last category. I suggested to Dave Sundman that as it was in aluminum it might date from the first or second decade of the 20th century.

The tokens and the pill box in which they were found.

As to value, I suggested to Dave that he drop a note to Russell Rulau, who was in the midst of updating the third edition of his *Standard Catalog of United States Tokens 1700–1900* book. He might have some information.

The result was unexpected: Of the thousands of Good Fors known to Russ, this was the only one in which an issuer was identified by the word MISS. He knew of MR. tokens and MRS. tokens, but not a single one with MISS. He was as excited as all get-out! Therewith, because of this unusual feature he listed it in the next edition of his *Standard Catalog,* never mind that the token was issued after 1900!

Dave Sundman sent me a token for my collection, and offered the other 40-odd pieces for $95 each in an offer sent to Littleton customers. I took a picture of mine (shown on page 35), and then tucked it in a safe-deposit box. Using the Internet and otherwise poking around I endeavored to learn more about Miss Drury and the hoard.

Alexander Kennedy Miller

I don't know if Alexander Kennedy Miller of East Orange, Vermont, ever met Miss M.J. Drury of Williamstown in the same state. I do know that, somehow, Miller acquired a little pasteboard box filled with her tokens.

Born on July 14, 1906, the only child of Edward S. and Jane Kennedy Miller, Alexander spent much of his early life in Montclair, New Jersey, the heir to a family fortune based on the flour business and, later, securities. He became a collector of license plates by age 16, a portent of the future. Miller attended Rutgers University on a scholarship to study mechanical engineering. In the 1930s he engaged in "expert automobile repairing" and offered Miller's Flying Service for "aeroplanes rebuilt and overhauled," according to one of his old business cards. He also conducted the Miller Flying Service, which specialized in fast delivery of packages and mail.

He married Imogene Raymond (born in 1917) in 1941. The couple had no children. In World War II he endeavored to be a pilot in the U.S. Army Air Force, but was declined due to his age, after which he served in the Royal Canadian Air Force. He loved Stutz automobiles, drove several, and collected others that he put in storage.

Miller retired, and with his fortune still substantial sought respite in rural Vermont in 1946. He and his wife Imogene purchased a rustic old farm in the small village of East Orange—a time-capsule sort of place without central heating, with only limited electrical service, and with hardly any amenities or modern conveniences. The roof was patched with pieces of tin. Imogene's raincoat was made of plastic bags. Both

Edward L. Huber, Alexander's grandfather, was at one time the largest wholesale flour dealer in America. Alexander's father, Edward S., was a prominent Wall Street securities and investment dealer.

A Treasure Hidden in the Woods

Gyrocopter operated by the Miller Flying Service of Montclair, New Jersey, to deliver mail and other items.

Alexander Miller in one of his favorite Stutz automobiles.

way leading to their house. Callers were often greeted with religious messages and quotations from the Bible. The neighbors felt sorry for them and offered charity, which was politely refused. One way or another, the Millers got along and lived happily.

W. Murray Clark, owner with his family of Clark's Trading Post in Lincoln, New Hampshire, recalled communicating with Miller over the years and visiting him upon occasion in East Orange. At one time Miller had some Indian Head cents, and Clark had some brass lamps and other auto parts. A trade was to be arranged. The two met on the first floor of the Miller home, but after some give-and-take discussions, Clark came to the conclusion that the Vermonter wanted high retail prices for his coins, but wanted to acquire the auto parts below wholesale. End of transaction. Murray Clark also had the impression that Miller had brought many of his various coins with him from New Jersey, and had acquired relatively few after his move.

Alexander Miller relished his surroundings and remained there until his death from a fall from a ladder while installing storm windows, in autumn 1993 at age 87. His wife Imogene, age 78, died in Montclair, New Jersey, in February 1996. The will provided that the estate was to go to religious groups. The Internal Revenue Service stepped in with a claim for many years of unpaid taxes. The house and outbuildings were checked—to reveal a wonderland of antique treasures!

For starters, there were more than 30 classic cars, most of them of the highly desired Stutz marque. In fact, this was the largest Stutz collection ever! Poking

were what we could easily call eccentric, for they did not elect to modernize the place at all. Instead of driving upscale cars they went around town in dilapidated Volkswagen "Beetles." When one stopped working, they left it as an eyesore to rust near the wooded drive-through a woodpile revealed about a million dollars in gold bullion (worth much more today) buried in various spots, and further looking around unearthed $900,000 in stock certificates and promissory notes, a bundle of $1,000 bills, bags of silver dollars (with many of the 1878-S issue) found under the floorboards of an abandoned schoolhouse on the Miller property, negotiable bearer bonds taped to the back of a mirror, and 47 little Miss M.J. Drury tokens struck in aluminum.

Various experts were called in. The automobiles were auctioned on the premises by Christie's on September 7, 1996. There were 47 of them, all of which were sold, commanding a total price of $1,863,064. Including other items the realization was $2,185,220. Stars of the sale included a Stutz Model 4C Bearcat (1916) at $173,000, 6D Bearcat (1913) at $118,000, DV32 Roadster (1933) at $167,500, and Eight Supercharged (1930) at $151,000. Among non-Stutz vehicles was a Rolls-Royce Springfield Silver Ghost (1926) crossing the block at $129,000. At the low end was a junky Volkswagen Karmann Ghia for $81.

Real Audet, of Green Mountain Coin Co., was a consultant for the bank handling the estate and collected bids on numismatic items from interested parties. Dave Sundman related that Jim Carr, of Pelham, New Hampshire, was on the Littleton staff at the time and assisted staffer Jim Reardon in making an offer for the coins and other items. Once acquired, they sold readily. Other items went elsewhere—making a lot of collectors happy.

The Millers had no Social Security numbers nor had they ever bothered to file tax returns. Uncle Sam stepped in with a demand for $7 million or so, and the state of Vermont claimed about $1 million, and 50 others tried to put their fingers in the treasure pie.

Dave Schenkman's Story

Learning of my interest in this curious scenario David Schenkman, known as an expert numismatist specializing in tokens, wrote with this account:

My family has owned a house in Vermont since the 1950s, and my parents spent their summers there for many years. The water system consists of a primitive hydraulic ram which pumps water, at a very slow rate, up to holding tanks in the attic.

In the late 1960s my dad noticed a small classified ad in the *Yankee Trader* magazine offering to swap a hydraulic ram for Stutz Bearcat parts "or $5 cash." My father sent him $5 with a note saying that he didn't have any Stutz parts but would like the ram and would pick it up eventually.

My wife and I, who lived in the Boston area at the time, used to go to the house frequently, and from there drive around the state stopping at flea markets, antique shops, etc. looking for tokens and medals. One day, as we were leaving, my dad told me the ram story and asked me to pick it up if we got to that part of Vermont. We decided to do so, and since we only had the man's name, and the town, we had to ask around to find out where he lived. Eventually we found a group of men who were hanging around outside a house drinking beer. In reply to my question, one of them said, "Oh, you mean Nutsy Stutzy," and told me how to get there.

We followed his directions and found the place, which was outside the town. There was what I remembered to be a large airplane hangar–like building, and a door at one end was open so I went in. There, a distinguished-looking man in coveralls was working on an antique car. He stopped, and in a rather irritated tone asked what I wanted. I told him why I was there, and he remembered about the ram. While he was looking for it I asked him some questions about the car he was working on, and he realized that I knew something about old cars (my first car, which I bought when I was 15, was a Model A Ford and since I couldn't afford to pay anyone to do repairs, I learned to do them myself). So, he asked if we would like to see the rest of his cars, and he spent the rest of the afternoon showing us his collection, which took up the entire building. I had never seen so many classic cars in one place!

The man was obviously very eccentric. When I asked if he ever drove the cars he said that although he had rebuilt the engines in some of them, he had never started them to see if they would run.

In addition to the cars, the walls were lined with rows of old porcelain license plates. There was a large group of mechanical banks on one wall, and there were old high-wheel bicycles hanging from the rafters. He showed us an old bicycle that he said had been custom built for Diamond Jim Brady. Everywhere we turned there was more neat stuff!

At some point of our visit he asked what I collected. When I told him I was a coin collector he said if we ever got back this way to stop by and he'd show us his collection. Unfortunately, shortly thereafter we moved to Maryland and I never saw him again.

Miss Millie J. Drury

Pursuing another tangent, I learned that Miss M.J. Drury's first name was Millie. In the early years of the present century, continuing into the 1920s, Miss Drury operated a retail business and, later, a lunch room in the lower level of the Grange Hall in Williamstown, Vermont. The building later burned, and today no trace of it remains, although the local historical society has an old-time photograph showing part of her sign there.

In 1909 her business consisted of selling "fancy goods," toys, and novelties. At the time, fancy goods were generally defined as including small items that added to the enjoyment of life—such as clocks, vanity mirrors, binoculars, china plates, etc. Her business was not particularly well financed, and in 1909 it was said that her assets were less than $500. Of course, in that era, such an amount went much further than it would today. Moreover, she may have elected to keep her net worth private, and her credit rating may have been a guess. It seems that she loved the town, told many people of the quality of life there, and was a one-lady Chamber of Commerce!

Millie was also interested in local history, and at the dedication of the Williamstown Public Library on December 6, 1911, was a speaker. She was very active in her town, but does not seem to have had a husband or children. In 1924 *Walton's Vermont Register* lists her as selling drugs, newspapers, etc. Her brother, Hiram S. Drury, owned a bakery and lunchroom.

Millie Drury died at age 79 in the Waterbury State Hospital for the mentally ill, a sad ending.[1] Today her elusive Good For tokens remain, a testament to her Yankee ingenuity and a slice of old-time New England history.

CHAPTER 9

Coins counterstamped with advertising messages were little billboards that could be carried in one's pocket. The Model Artistes (or Artists) exhibition in New York City used silver coins to publicize the attraction and at the same time serve as a 25-cent admission pass.

Don't Miss the Model Artistes

George Lea

ADMIT / TO THE / MODEL ARTIST'S / 127 GRAND ST. / NEAR B.WAY advertising counterstamp on a 1797 Spanish-American two-real silver coin. Worn nearly smooth, it was ideal to show the message clearly. Counterstampers often chose well-worn coins for this reason. The two-real pieces were legal tender in America in the early to mid-1850s and were worth 25 cents in commerce.

Model Artistes, part of the Franklin Museum, showed nude women posing to imitate statues and classic painting scenes, and was located up one flight of stairs at 127 Grand Street near Broadway in New York City beginning in 1856. The proprietor, George Lea, had Spanish-American two-real silver coins, worth 25 cents, counterstamped to advertise his business. These were marked ADMIT / TO THE / MODEL ARTIST'S / 127 GRAND ST. / NEAR B.WAY, not following the *artistes* spelling.

Cleverly, these could be turned in at the entrance as the price of admission, as was done by several other attractions including Parisian Varieties in the same city two decades later.[1] Under different names such as living pictures, tableaux vivants, and the like, similar shows were held by many entrepreneurs in various cities during the last half of the 19th century. Often these were advertised, but other times a "model artist" might hold forth without publicity, except for word of mouth, in a saloon or gambling parlor or at a party attended by men. As an example, the *Boston Courier*, October 5, 1855, carried this:

> There was a private exhibition of "model artists" at No. 66 Margin Street on Saturday evening. The police entered the house, arrested two unfortunate creatures called Elizabeth Watson and Sophia Cannon, and locked them up for trial.

Sometimes such displays were closed down by the authorities, but most often they were ignored. Obscenity was hard to define, and the proprietors often took the stand that they were educating their customers in classic art, or, in the case of "living pictures" of scriptural scenes, furnishing instruction in the Bible!

George Lea, an Englishman but born in Paris in 1819, came to the United States 19 years later and became a leading factor in such shows. Trained as a pharmacist, he worked in that trade in New York City, eventually operating several drug stores there. Lea shifted careers and operated several variety theaters in New York City. He purchased the remaining term of the June 1852 five-year lease on White's Melodeon at 49 Bowery for $600. This had been opened by Charley White on November 24, 1846, and "was the first cheap theatre in New York City." Minstrelsy was the main attraction. White closed on April 22, 1854, and Lea opened two days later, having closed his Franklin Museum at 175 Chatham Street.[2] This was not far from Lea's Minstrels, which he conducted at 165 Chatham Street.

By the spring of 1856 Lea was deeply involved in theater activities. For a while he operated a pharmacy at 186 Grand Street, then offered it for sale, as "the proprietor, being engaged in other business, cannot attend to it."[3] He also offered a saloon (restaurant) for sale at 36 Howard Street. He had his fingers in multiple business pies.

Nudity at the Franklin Museum

For a time Lea conducted in the city a model artists' show called the Temple of the Muses. In the late spring of 1856 he transferred that entertainment to a new venue. The *Neu Work Herald,* May 6, 1856, ran this classified notice:

Temple of the Muses

316 Broadway, will close on Saturday May 10—Grand closing scenes—Two performances each day, commencing at 3 and 8 o'clock, by Madame Warton's troupe of Model Artists (27 in number).

Notice—On Monday Madame Warton will open at 127 Grand Street, one door from Broadway.

On May 12, 1856, the same newspaper included this:

Franklin Museum

127 Grand Street, one door from Broadway. Open every afternoon at 3 and evening at 8 for the purpose of given a series of Magnificent Living Statuary by Madame Warton's troupe of Model Artistes, twenty-seven in number, comprising a company of the finest-formed women in the world.

Other advertising stated that this was the only place in the city where the original troupe of Model Artistes could be seen. Business must have been good. On August 20 the *Herald* posted four advertisements for the attraction, one of them noting that the tableaux included Sappho, Fortune Teller, the Three Graces, and Innocence. In the meantime George Lea continued to manage the Melodeon.

The Mayor and the Models

The *New York Tribune* was not at all fond of New York City mayor Fernando Wood and took many opportunities to criticise him, such as in this article published on October 20, 1856:

Our Model Mayor Among the Model Artists

On Friday night the police, by order of the mayor, arrested certain women who are part and parcel of an exhibition popularly known as "model artists."

It seems that certain policemen were made to disguise their office and go as spectators. After feasting their eyes upon the fancies of the spot for several nights, on Friday night, in the third act of the Venus Rising from the Sea, when the women were grouped around a revolving platform, six valiant policemen sprang upon the stage, and, seizing as many females, drew their clubs, showed their stars, and, in the midst of the wildest confusion, dragged them into the hall, refusing to allow them to put on their clothes or divest themselves of their stage attire.

Dressed in nothing but their silk tights and transparent skirts, with no bonnets on, and but ball-room sandals upon their feet, these women were dragged into the street and carried off to the Eighth Ward Station House where they were kept all night, without a change of clothes, although friends had carried garments for them thither.

"The Three Graces. As exhibited by the Model Artists of New York." Lithograph print showing a typical Model Artistes show of the era.

The same model-artist exhibition flourished in Broadway, at Gothic Hall, during the entire administration of our model mayor; yet he never interfered with it in any manner, although many complaints were made, and even the governors of the New-York Hospital tried in vain to put a stop to the horrid music discoursed daily and nightly from the balcony.

Their gross signs were displayed, and men and boys stood at the door distributing prints of naked women to the immense throng of people in Broadway, without the slightest reproof from city authorities. Grand juries presented in vain, and the suffering sick people in the hospital appealed in vain. But at length Gothic Hall was taken down and the model artists removed to Grand Street, some distance out of Broadway, into a place where, instead of flaunting them in the public's face, it costs some little trouble to find them.

And now, all of a sudden, our virtuous mayor is shocked at the indecencies which, under a toleration which was equal to direct patronage, he protected for a year and a half in Broadway in defiance of constant protest by the people.

The excuse for the present action is that the exhibition "injures property in that neighborhood," the property being the new unoccupied marble building on the Broadway corner, owned by Benjamin Wood, brother of the model mayor, and displaying from its roof, "For Mayor, Fernando Wood."

On Saturday morning, in further glorification of our model mayor, these women were paraded through Broadway, in the same state of semi-nudity, to the mayor's office. The policemen say they acted in strict obedience to orders. The women were kept at the mayor's office and duly exposed to a crowd of foul-tongued spectators, and then dismissed on their own recognizance, with a virtuous admonition from—Fernando Wood.

Answering to the alleged offense, on January 20, 1857, George Lea appeared before Judge A.D. Russell in the Court of General Sessions. He was charged with "keeping a disorderly house," a term for prostitution, in his "model artist establishment." Charles Bird, an associate, was charged as well. His bail of $1,000 was posted by a surety, John Dearborn of 93 Third Avenue. Soon afterward, Mr. Phillips, Lea's counsel, had the charge quashed on the grounds that no arrest warrant had been issued for the ladies and that no examinations had been conducted with the people charged.

Raids on exhibitions or businesses considered to be obscene were common in the larger cities. They were often a secret source of revenue for certain city-hall officials who could elect not to interfere with alleged risqué shows. In nearly all instances, as here, the shows continued selling tickets.

The Model Artists Continue

Perhaps aspiring to compete with P.T. Barnum, proprietor George Lea advertised in 1857 that he desired to purchase or rent "Living curiosities of every description suitable for exhibition." Another notice sought living curiosities "together with all kinds of birds, monkeys, &c." Offers could be presented in person at the Franklin Museum at 157 Grand Street or sent by mail to 186 Grand Street, the latter being Lea's pharmacy address. In July 1857, Arnold Mockeritz, the three-year-old "Bearded Boy," who had been exhibited by Lea, died while in the care of Lea's wife, Catharine, at their home. An autopsy found a cancerous growth as the cause.[4]

On January 16, 1858, the Benefit of George Lea was held at the Franklin Museum, featuring 70 performers. The show was then closed briefly for a transition following the final appearance of Madame Warton's troupe per an announcement in the *New York Herald* four days later:

Remember, the Franklin Museum, 127 Grand Street, is reopened for the winter season. Performances every

afternoon and evening by the new troupe of Model Artistes consisting of Thirty Young Ladies, who will appear in a collection of living pictures, with other beautiful entertainments. . . .

Another notice in the same issue advised that the tableaux included the Greek Slave, Venus Rising from the Sea, Bathers Surprised, Adam and Eve, Venus Attired by the Graces, the Three Graces, and "others equally interesting," 16 in all. Orchestra seats were 50 cents, a seat in a box was 25 cents, and a private box $1.

Elsewhere on the same page was this:

Wanted: Several Young Ladies to Appear on the stage at the Franklin Museum, 127 Grand Street, one door from Broadway; also a young lady to attend bar. Apply after 1 P.M. at the box office.

For whatever reason Madame Warton's troupe of ladies was back on the bill by March.

The Franklin Museum was not without competition in the city. In January 1858 the police raided the Francisco Hotel on Howard Street, kept by August Meyer and his wife, and arrested them "and half a dozen young girls who were at the time exhibiting themselves in a nude state as 'model artists'." The place had been in business for some time and catered to "lewd citizens and country bumpkins." The girls were convicted as vagrants and sent to a penitentiary for six months.[5] Apparently, Meyer did not have the right connections with City Hall.

In the evening of February 18 in New York City the "Model Artist exhibition" on Broome Street, which featured nude women who "were always willing to favor the 'gentlemen' visitors with an exhibition whenever a sufficient amount could be subscribed to pay them for their trouble," was raided by the police.

Among the patrons were three police captains. An effort was made to keep the situation quiet, but word leaked out.[6] No prosecution was made.

On Monday, December 16, 1858, a "Benefit for the Manager, George Lea," featured 100 young ladies in the Model Artiste exhibition. Occasional advertisements continued to appear in 1859.

The 1860s

On February 23, 1860, the *New York Herald* printed this:

Franklin Museum

127 Grand Street, one door from Broadway, will reopen on Saturday, February 23. Having during the recess been thoroughly renovated and remodelled and an entire new company engaged, it will open on Saturday afternoon and night, in a magnificent style, a troupe of Model Artistes comprising some of the most beautiful young ladies in the world will appear in a new series of Tableaux Vivants introduced under the direction of Madame Warton.

Admission: Orchestra 50c, boxes 25c, private boxes $1, seats on the stage $3. Strangers will observe that the Franklin Museum is the only place where Model Artistes are exhibited in the United States. Established over 20 years.

On May 17, 1860, an unsigned advertisement in the *New York Herald* sought performers:

The proprietor wishes to engage talent of every description, and having four places of amusement open every night in the city, viz: the new Gaieties, 616 Broadway; the Broadway Pavilion, 600 Broadway (the old Gaieties); the Broadway Varieties; and the Franklin Museum, he thinks he can complete with any other person in the world—and can engage all kinds of performers at all kind of salaries and give them long or short engagements. Apply at 616 Broadway.

Later Years

By the summer of 1861 a number of ladies and others once associated with the now-closed Franklin Museum were with the Melodon at 539 Broadway, which offered a varied program. Lea continued his involvement and became a factor in the management of various stage shows, of legitimate drama as well as suggestive nudity, in several cities.

Then the tide turned. Through unwise speculation in securities he lost most of his net worth during the Civil War. In 1867 he went to Port Jervis, New York, opened a pharmacy, and in time was back on his feet. Ever the showman, he managed a number of entertainment and tourist operations. In that city in the 1880s and 1890s he was listed as the proprietor of Lea's Opera House, also known as the Grand Opera House, which seated 1,500. George Lea died in Port Jervis on August 20, 1902.

CHAPTER 10

The World's Columbian Exposition held in Chicago in 1893 was the greatest of American world's fairs. A wonderful numismatic legacy resulted.

Numismatics and the Columbian Exposition

Planning the Exposition

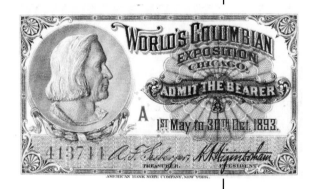

Columbian Exposition admission ticket.

The first world's fair held in the United States was the 1876 Centennial Exhibition in Philadelphia. It was a grand event set up on a 236-acre site in Philadelphia.[1] Nearly 200 buildings were filled with displays and attractions. The Main Exhibition Building was 1,832 feet wide, 120 feet deep, and 75 feet high, occupying 21.5 acres. It and most other buildings were temporary structures of wood with a steel frame. On opening day, May 10, President U.S. Grant addressed a large audience with Emperor Dom Pedro of Brazil at his side, the first major foreign head of state to visit the United States. By the time the gates closed on November 10, attendance had reached 10,164,489. By all accounts it was a grand success.

By 1890 it was time for another world's fair. The subject was ideal: to celebrate in 1892 the 400th anniversary of Christopher Columbus's discovery of America (not that it had been lost in the first place). It was intended to create the greatest such event ever—to outdo the 1876 Centennial Exhibition, the 1889 Paris Universal Exposition, and all others. Where to hold it? St. Louis, New York City, Washington, D.C., and Chicago all competed for the honor. The decision was made by Congress, which passed an act on April 25, 1890, naming Chicago, in view that more money to construct the fair had been pledged by backers of that location.

Bird's-eye view of the Exposition.

The mostly undeveloped Jackson Park and some surrounding land, a 686-acre site on the shore of Lake Michigan, was selected for the Exposition grounds. In January 1891 a group of architects met in Chicago to plan the buildings, which were subsequently constructed mainly in the classical style reflecting Greek and Roman influences, and with exteriors made of an artificial composition called "staff," resembling marble, giving rise to the name "White City" for the structures. In November of the same year Dr. George F. Heath of Monroe, Michigan, since 1888 publisher of *The Numismatist,* organized a meeting of interested collectors in Chicago in November 1891, who formed the American Numismatic Association. The attendees went to the fair site to see the work in progress.

The Exposition was intended to showcase American progress in art, architecture, technology, science, agriculture, and other endeavors. No expense was spared to create a virtual city, complete with 160 buildings (many of which were connected by canals plied by gondolas and small steam-powered craft) and 65,000 exhibits devoted to commercial, national, artistic, and other subjects. Separate structures showcased the attractions and products of different states and 45 foreign countries. Sculptures and other works of art decorated many of the open spaces as well as building interiors.

The Exposition

Unpacking exhibits in the Fine Art Building. (*Harper's Weekly,* April 15, 1893)

The best-laid plans went astray, and construction fell behind schedule. Until the buildings were ready, exhibits could not be set up. A dedication ceremony was held on October 21, 1892, but work was far from complete, and many displays and exhibits had not arrived. Frederick Law Olmsted, the designer of New York City's Central Park, and Daniel Burnham laid out the grounds. The theme of Beaux Arts, neoclassical French architecture, was decided upon. In the twilight of the Victorian era it epitomized ornate design.

The Fine Art Building as shown on an official souvenir postcard.

Opening day, May 1, 1893. (*Harper's Weekly,* June 10, 1893)

President Grover Cleveland at the opening ceremony. (B.W. Kilburn stereograph)

The gigantic Ferris Wheel, center point of the Exposition. (*Columbian Exposition Album*, 1893)

Finally, on May 1, 1893, after an estimated $30 million had been spent on the facilities and nearly everything was in place, President Grover Cleveland officiated at a noon ceremony and pushed an electric switch that unfurled flags and set machinery in motion. The gates were opened to the public. An estimated 300,000 visitors thronged the grounds. This was, of course, the 401st anniversary, not the 400th, of Columbus's landfall.

The prime attraction was the gigantic Ferris Wheel, which loomed over the Exposition grounds and was visible from a long distance beyond. The wheel, which was not ready until June, measured 250 feet in diameter, was powered by two 1,000-horse-power engines, and held 36 wooden cars with a capacity of up to 60 riders each. Tickets were sold for 50 cents each, bringing in receipts of $726,805.50. Alternating electric current provided by Westinghouse illuminated the "White City" at night in a spectacular display. Among the visitors were teacher Katherine Lee Bates and friends on the way to Colorado College. Later, after viewing the vista from Pikes Peak, she composed *America the Beautiful,* with "Thine alabaster cities gleam, undimmed by human tears" inspired by her experience in Chicago.

Midway Plaisance featured many concessions and amusements. "Little Egypt," a scantily clad hootchy-kootchy dancer said to be immoral in her gyrations (all the better to attract customers), was publicized nationwide. The *John Bull*, a locomotive built in 1831 and owned by the Smithsonian Institution, rode the rails from Washington to Chicago and back under its own steam power. Krupp, the German manufacturer of ordnance, displayed a gun weighing more than 100 tons, suitable for firing a projectile weighing over a ton for a distance of 15 miles.

M. Welte & Sons of Freiburg, Germany, set up a large orchestrion (automatic orchestra) that was later sold to the Atlantic Garden in New York City, where it entertained patrons into the 20th century. Quaker Oaks, Pabst Blue Ribbon Beer, Juicy Fruit Gum, and Cream of Wheat cereal were among the new products

Machinery Hall, Administration buildings, and fountain viewed from the Liberal Arts Building. (B.W. Kilburn stereograph panel)

The Welte orchestrion played concerts to visitors. After the exposition closed it was sold to the Atlantic Garden, a large beer hall in The Bowery in New York City.

Exhibit of music boxes set up by Mermod Frères of Ste. Croix, Switzerland, and managed by Jacot & Son, Mermod's American distributor. (*Shepp's World's Fair Photographed*)

introduced at the fair. Many electrical devices were demonstrated, including an all-electric kitchen.

The nation was in the midst of a depression, the Panic of 1893, which reduced revenues. Another negative was that Buffalo Bill's Wild West Show had hoped to set up at the fair, but was rejected and did business outside of the grounds, taking in many dollars that might have otherwise gone to the exposition. The record attendance was on Chicago Day, October 9, when 716,881 visitors were on hand. By the time the fair closed on October 30 nearly 25 million admissions were registered.

Columbian Souvenir Half Dollars

1892 Columbian souvenir half dollar.

To raise funds and promote the Exposition, five million souvenir (as they were called) half dollars were authorized by Congress. These were to be sold to the Exposition management for face value, after which it was planned to offer them to the public for $1 each.

In 1892, hundreds of newspaper articles were published about the new half dollars, and interest was intense. Chief Engraver Charles E. Barber of the U.S. Mint was tapped to create the obverse design of the souvenir coin. It was soon learned that no authentic portrait could be found of the Great Discoverer. Barber copied his visage from a medal dated that year and issued in Spain, this having been taken from a statue in Madrid by Jeronimo Suñel, in turn based on a fanciful portrait by Charles Legrand.

George T. Morgan, an assistant engraver who joined the Mint in 1876, designed the reverse. Depicted was Columbus's flagship *Santa Maria,* taken from a recent model made in Spain. Below, two globes represented the Old World and New World and were reminiscent of Spanish Pillar dollars.

In a special ceremony the first coins came off a press at the Philadelphia Mint on November 18, 1892. Wyckoff, Seamans & Benedict, makers of the Remington typewriter, offered $10,000 for the very first coin and soon donated it to the Columbian Museum (later

known as the Field Museum of Natural History). More than 2,000 were struck on the first day, with the 1st, 400th, 1,492nd, and 1,892nd coins being given to Colonel James W. Ellsworth of the Exposition commission. Ellsworth was one of the leading numismatists of his day and had a magnificent collection that included many rarities. He avoided publicity, however, and scarcely a word about it appeared in journals of the day.

The coins sailed off to a good start. From the five million authorized, 950,000 were struck in 1892, plus an unknown small extra quantity for testing by the Assay Commission. In time all found buyers.

Newspaper Reports

Many commentaries concerning the Columbian half dollars appeared in various papers throughout the autumn of 1892 and early 1893. It seems as though everyone had an opinion, many of them centering on the seemingly unconscionable profit to be made by selling a fifty-cent piece for one dollar. Samples:

> From the *Philadelphia Call:*
>
> The average man won't stick about the World's Fair souvenir half dollar. Any other will do as well. Perhaps the proposition to sell the 50¢ souvenirs at the World's Fair for $1 is an evidence of what visitors to Chicago may expect in the general increase in prices.

> *Pittsburgh Chronicle:*
>
> The coinage of the souvenir half dollars has begun at the Philadelphia Mint, and the superintendent expects to have 30,000 of them ready by the end of the month. Talking about money making, did you ever see anything like the profit Chicago will get out of the remelting of old half dollars and making "souvenir" coins of them?

San Francisco Examiner:

The newest thing out. Buy your half-dollar for a dollar and sell it for two dollars. We don't hear much about the two-dollar victims yet, but suppose they will be forthcoming. The picture of Columbus upon the souvenir coins will be ideal, so it is stated. It is not altogether clear how it could be anything else, since the roving gentleman neglected to leave any authentic portrait. Those available range from figures of a pallid student to a bewhiskered brigand, each probably as wrong as the other.

Galveston Daily News:

The front side of the coin has an elegant likeness of the late Sitting Bull. This, however, is said to be meant for Columbus. The patriotic American can take his choice, and the know-nothings certainly will claim the head to be intended for Sitting Bull because of that gentleman being an American. On the right shoulder appears the letter B. This certainly indicates the location of either a boil or a barnacle. There is also a likeness of Columbus' ship under full sail.

At first blush the ship seems to be on wheels, but closer examination shows that the two wheels are the eastern and western hemispheres. The ship seems to be surrounded by a herd of porpoises, but probably this is meant for waves. There is also a fishing pole rigged out of an after port in the cabin of the ship, and one gathers an idea that the venturesome mariner is either baiting his hook and lying about a bite he has just had, or has hauled in a fish,

for the line is taken aboard ship. The figures 1492 appear beneath the vessel. The coin is of the same size and weight as the old run of half dollars, and for all they are sold at a heavy premium, the purchasing power is but ten beers.

Minneapolis Times:

A dollar will go no further in Chicago than in some other places, but Chicago is the only town that can sell 50¢ for $1.

Colorado Sun:

The World's Fair people count upon making a good thing by selling their five million souvenir half dollars at premium. The Chicago propensity for speculating in futures cannot be restrained.

Philadelphia Ledger:

If it were not known in advance whose vignette adorns the Columbian souvenir half dollar, the average observer would be undecided as to whether it is intended to represent Daniel Webster or Henry Ward Beecher.

More Half Dollars in 1893

1893 Columbian souvenir half dollar.

The public had not yet arrived, and the year 1893 beckoned. Anticipating a sellout, the Philadelphia Mint set about coining more half dollars, but with the new year's date added. To use up the authorization, 4,052,105 of the new 1893 coins were minted, including 2,105 destined for the Assay Commission.

Displays of Columbian half dollars helped promote sales of the souvenir and were set up in many places. In the rotunda of the Administration Building was a model of the Treasury Building in Washington, constructed of Columbian half dollars, measuring 20 feet long, 11 feet wide, and four feet high. In the Liberal Arts building an obelisk 20 feet high was made of such half dollars, billed as the only official souvenirs of the Exposition.

The 1893 Isabella commemorative quarter.

Isabella Quarters

In January 1893, although the fair had not yet opened to the public, half dollars were selling like hotcakes. Mrs. Potter Palmer, well-known Chicago socialite, patron of the arts, and *grande dame* of the Exposition, suggested to the Appropriations Committee of the House of Representatives that $10,000 of the money earmarked for the Board of Lady Managers of the World's Columbian Exposition be given in the form of a special issue of souvenir quarter dollars. This was translated into a law approved March 3, 1893, which stated that the production of these quarters would not exceed 40,000 and that the pieces would be of standard weight and fineness.

In light of the 5,000,000 authorization for the half dollars, this certainly was a modest request. The Isabella quarter, as it was called, caused no excitement at all, newspaper notices were almost non-existent, and at the exposition itself the only place they could

SOPHIA HAYDEN, ARCHITECT.   DRAWN BY ALBERT RANDOLPH ROSS.   PUBLISHED BY PERMISSION OF THE NEW YORK PHOTOGRAVURE COMPANY.

WOMEN'S BUILDING.

The Woman's Building, where the Isabella commemorative quarter dollars were sold for $1 each. (*Century Magazine*, September 1892)

be purchased was in the Woman's Building. To make marketing matters worse, the quarters were priced at a dollar each—obviously a poor value in light of half dollars being available for the same amount.

Requiem for the Souvenir Half Dollars

Although excitement for the Columbian half dollars had been intense in late 1892 and early 1893, interest faded, buyers became scarce, and most of the coins remained stored in the cloth bags in which they were put up at the Mint. After the gates to the fair closed about 3,600,000 remained unsold, of which about 1,400,000 were held by the Treasury in Washington, 960,000 in Chicago, and 147,700 at the Philadelphia Mint, although reported figures varied. This posed a dilemma, for the managers of the Exposition felt that the million-plus people who had paid a dollar each for them should be protected. They suggested that the government melt them down.

The Treasury Department disagreed. A compromise of sorts was made. James W. Ellsworth agreed to pay the Treasury $40,300 to transport the coins back to Philadelphia and melt most of the remainder. The bargain seems not to have been kept, at least in part. In 1894 the Treasury announced that remaining coins were available for face value to anyone who desired them. Not many people were interested. In time it was reported that 2,501,700 were melted and the rest placed into general circulation. Soon they were familiar in pocket change.

The May 1896 issue of *The Numismatist* gave an update on the Columbian half dollars, reporting that in a typical bank holding of $20,000 face value in coins, fewer than $10 would be in such half dollars. It was noted that at the Sub-Treasury "they are sorted out and kept by themselves, and are not paid out unless asked for. The demand is slight, but it is expected that by Christmas time the business firms will want them to give out in change as a sort of an advertisement, for that is the way they did last Christmas."

Report on the Isabella Quarters

As to the Isabella commemorative quarters probably no more than about 15,000 found buyers, including several thousand purchased by the Scott Stamp & Coin Company, which had two sales exhibitions at the fair. When the event ended the Board of Lady Managers still had about 25,000 on hand. What to do with them? Mrs. Potter Palmer and several of her friends bought 10,000 for face value. Returned to the Mint were 15,809 unwanted coins.

The Mint melted those that came back. There is no record of them being available for face value from that source. Mrs. Potter and her friends parceled out their holdings at a profit, but discounted from the dollar retail price, over a period of years, including thousands sold to S.C. Stevens of Stevens & Co., Chicago's leading rare-coin dealer.

The Columbian Exposition Award Medal

Exhibitors whose exhibits were evaluated by official committees were given an award medal designed by the combination of sculptor Augustus Saint-Gaudens, who did the obverse, and Chief Engraver Charles E. Barber, who did the reverse. This was an unlikely combination, as Saint-Gaudens was quite contemptuous of Barber's abilities, later calling his various work "wretched."

Augustus Saint-Gaudens's proposed designs for the Columbian Exposition award medal. These motifs were rejected, and a new arrangement was made for Saint-Gaudens to create the obverse and for Charles E. Barber, chief engraver of the Mint, to do a new reverse. (*Century Magazine*, June 1897)

The accepted award medal obverse
by Augustus Saint-Gaudens.

The accepted award medal reverse
by Charles E. Barber. This was presented to Paul Lochmann, a leading
Leipzig, Germany, maker of music
boxes under the Symphonion name.

Award-winning Symphonion Model
38B hall clock with music box exhibited by Paul Lochmann at the 1893
Exposition. This descended in the
Lochmann family and was sold at
auction in 2001. (Sotheby's, London)

The original Saint-Gaudens motif for the reverse showed a nude boy, but this was viewed as risqué and was rejected by the Mint, which had him prepare another design. There was certainly a double standard in effect, for on display at the exposition itself were many statues of nude males and females from classic history. The award medals were in bronze, 77 mm in diameter, and on the reverse had a plug inset into the die with the recipient's name. These are very collectible today, and hundreds exist.

I have one presented to Paul Lochmann, a Leipzig manufacturer of disc-type Symphonion music boxes, who exhibited at the Exposition. This descended in his family and along with a related Symphonion Model 38B hall clock containing a music box was sold by Sotheby's in London some years ago, then to an American collector, then to me.

Tokens, Medals, and Elongated Coins

Some other medals of large size depicted the figure of Miss Liberty as found on the contemporary Morgan silver dollar, while others showed attractions of the fair itself, such as the Ferris Wheel, the prime drawing card. Some years ago Nathan Eglit compiled *Columbiana, The Medallic History of Christopher Columbus and the Columbian Exposition of 1893*. This launched a new generation of enthusiasts who sought such pieces. Today, all medals of the event are in strong demand.

Also of interest were the very first elongated or rolled-out coins, which were issued by several different vendors. These were made by putting a coin, usually a cent or nickel, into a hand-cranked press with two rollers, with a curved die on one side, which was impressed into the coin while at the same time stretching it out. These are very collectible today and beyond cents and nickels can be found on dimes, quarters, tokens, and other coins, including at least one on a Morgan silver dollar.

The three Series of 1896 "Educational Notes" are the epitome of classical design for American paper money. So highly prized and desired by numismatists today, they were of short-lived production and somewhat controversial in their time.

The Ornate "Educational Notes" of 1896

Turn-of-the-Century Beauties

The $1 Educational Note with the ornate vignette, *History Instructing Youth.* A vista of Washington, D.C., is in the distance and the names of famous Americans are around the border. (Friedberg-224, Whitman 59)

Of the many interesting and beautiful notes issued by the Treasury Department from the first Demand Notes of 1861 down to the present day the three 1896 Silver Certificates known as Educational Notes are particularly outstanding. The designs, made in the late Victorian era, were inspired in part by the art at the World's Columbian Exposition. In *100 Greatest American Currency Notes* voters placed each high on the list. Educational Notes were made in three denominations: $1, $2, and $5.

Creating and Issuing the Notes

On November 1, 1893, Thomas F. Morris signed on as chief of the engraving division at the Bureau of Engraving and Printing. By that time plans had been discussed to create a new series of Silver Certificates, enlisting the talents of artists in the private sector who were known for their murals, specifically E.H. Blashfield, Will H. Low, and Walter Shirlaw. The idea was to create "scenic" motifs on various denominations. Their motifs were then to be engraved by artists at the Bureau of Engraving and Printing.

In time, serious work was done on values of $1, $2, $5, and $10, with motifs and sketches made for the $20, $50, $100, $500, and $1,000 as well. Only the three lower denominations were ever produced, creating the beautiful Educational Notes that are so highly prized today.

The Series of 1896 $2 and $5 notes were released in 1897, a year after the series date. The $1 bills were first paid out in the summer of 1896. There was widespread complaint about these denominations. The *Washington Times,* May 1, 1897, reported:

The Bureau of Engraving and Printing is engaged in making plates for the five and two dollar bills of the latest series. These bills when printed were too dark and the number denominations too indistinct for rapid use at the banks, and the Treasury received many complaints concerning them. To remedy this evil, new plates are being made which will make the bills much lighter in color, the figures in the corner of the bill will be plain and distinct.

On August 15, 1897, the *New York Times* reported that the three designs of the Educational Notes were "doomed to be retired before fully completed. The whole series has proved unsuccessful from the point of view of the handlers of money. . . ." Bankers further complained that the bills became smudged soon after they were placed in circulation and were difficult to count quickly.

Detail of the vignette, *History Instructing Youth.*

As incredible as it may seem today, the Educational Notes were not honored in their own time, not even by numismatists. Each of the three designs was replaced within a few years, in contrast to certain other motifs of the denominations that were continued in use for a decade or more. However, collectors love them dearly now!

$1 Educational Note, Series of 1896: *History Instructing Youth*

Among the three Educational Notes the $1 is the most plentiful, most readily available, and most affordable in the marketplace today. As is true of the two other denominations, market values have advanced steadily over a period of time.

The face motif is *History Instructing Youth,* with the goddess and her pupil positioned approximately where the Lee mansion is, across the Potomac River from Washington, D.C. The panorama of America's capital city spreads before them, with the Capitol, the Washington Monument, and more. Around the border at the left, top, and right within wreaths are the names of famous people in American history: Longfellow, Sherman (presumably William Tecumseh, not John), Lincoln, Irving, Cooper, Fulton, Calhoun, Clay, Jackson, Adams (either John or John Quincy, probably the former), Jefferson, Washington (within a wreath larger than the others), Franklin, Hamilton, Perry, Marshall, Webster, Morse, Hawthorne, Bancroft, Grant, Farragut, and Emerson. Today, in the early 21st century, it might challenge the owner of such a note to be able to relate a few words concerning each of these prominent figures selected for the honor. The face design was by Will H. Low, a talented artist in the private sector, with engraving by Charles Schlecht, and with some changes by Thomas F. Morris. All of the notes of this issue have a small red Treasury seal with spiked border. On the back of the note George and Martha Washington appear in separate portraits, designed by Morris and engraved by Alfred Sealey and Charles Burt.

Detail showing the Constitution text and several names of famous Americans.

The printing of the new $1 notes began on April 18, 1896, and distribution took place in the summer. The word *tranquility* was spelled this way, with a single *l*, in the Constitution, illustrated on the right side of the face of the note. Correct preferred spelling in the 1890s was *tranquillity*, and the Bureau of Engraving and Printing was criticized for making an error. However, a reading of the original Constitution revealed the *tranquility* style, and it was preserved. There was a little flurry and for a time a premium of 10 to 25 cents was paid by those seeking such bills for investment and who thought the "error" would be corrected.[1]

During the tenure of Thomas F. Morris (from November 1, 1893, until his untimely passing in 1898), he helped design several other motifs featured in *100 Greatest American Currency Notes*. Morris had an interest in numismatics, as did his son, Thomas Jr., who contributed articles years later to the *Essay-Proof Journal* and *The Numismatist* and collected obsolete bills with interesting vignettes. A commentary published in *The Numismatist* in June 1934 included this:

Certain changes were made of the original design as submitted by the artist and after weeks of toil by the

engraver, Charles Schlecht, who had just previously finished the government's beautiful Columbian Diploma (also designed by Will Low) and who did the figures and the balance of the featured design, the lettering and scroll work was entrusted to Mr. Kennedy. Certain changes in the style of lettering were, however, made and one or two minor changes were also done.[2]

Following complaints by bankers and others this beautiful Educational Note was replaced by the Series of 1899 issue featuring an eagle at the center of the face.

Varieties of the $1 Notes
These signature varieties were made. Attributions are to Arthur and Ira Friedberg, *Paper Money of the United States*, and to my *Whitman Encyclopedia of U.S. Paper Money*.

Friedberg-224 • Whitman-59 • Tillman-Morgan (1893–1897) • Small red Treasury seal with scalloped border • 33,952,000 estimated printage

F-225 • W-60 • Tillman-Roberts (1897) • Small red Treasury seal with scalloped border • 23,392,000 estimated printage

$2 Educational Note, Series of 1896: *Science Presenting Steam and Electricity to Industry and Commerce*

The $2 Educational Note features a group of five allegorical figures on the face, titled *Science Presenting Steam and Electricity to Industry and Commerce*, the artistry of Edwin H. Blashfield. Illustrated are the goddess *Science*, two other goddesses, and two youth, representative of ornate art, architecture, and design in the fading years of the Victorian era. This motif was originally made for the proposed $50 denomination, but that value was never issued. Instead, it was adopted for the $2, as here showcased, replacing a design by Will H. Low showing two figures, *Peace,* a woman, and *War,* a man (also called *Peace* and *Defense*).

Electricity was very much in the limelight; in fact it *created* the limelight with an arc of current. The World's Columbian Exposition of 1893 had been illuminated by electricity, and there were many exhibits featuring this increasingly popular source of power. In the 1890s America was being wired for household and industrial power, the telephone was gaining in popularity, and citizens looked forward to the benefits electricity would bestow.

Blashfield, born in New York City on December 15, 1848, was educated at the Boston Latin School, and in 1865 was among the first 16 students to inaugurate the Massachusetts Institute of Technology, which in time became one of America's leading universities. He then studied art in Paris. His talents were recognized, and in the early 1890s he was tapped as a member of the artistic team that decorated the World's Columbian Exposition, creating the murals on the Liberal Arts and Manufacturing buildings. Blashfield was roundly criticized by engravers within the Bureau of Engraving and Printing, especially by Thomas Morris, as part of an overall dislike for the policies that created Series of 1896 notes, in which three outside artists encroached on what they believed was in-house prerogative to create new paper-money designs. The rest of the face of the $2 note and all of the back was designed by Morris. The face engraving of Blashfield's and Morris's artistry was the work of Charles Schlecht and G.F.C. Smillie.

Roso Marston, a young girl about 13 years of age, modeled three of the figures for Blashfield, all except *Steam* and *Electricity* (those positioned closest to *Science*), which were modeled by young boys. By that that time she had spent much of her life on the legitimate stage, including in the title role of the popular play, *Editha's Burglar.* When Blashfield had her pose she was currently appearing as Eunice in *Quo Vadis* at the New

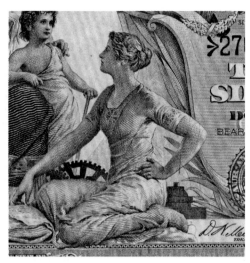

Detail showing Commerce, one of two figures modeled by young Roso Marston.

York Academy of Music. Among other commissions, she had posed for Augustus Saint-Gaudens.[3]

On the back two prominent Americans are depicted: Robert Fulton of steamboat *Clermont* fame, and Samuel F.B. Morse, highly accomplished as an artist but better known as inventor of the telegraph. Thomas F. Morris engraved the back.

Varieties of the $2 Notes

F-247 • W-367 • Tillman-Morgan (1893–1897) • Small red Treasury seal with spiked border • 9,400,000 estimated printage

F-248 • W-368 • Bruce-Roberts (1897–1898) • Small red Treasury seal with spiked border • 11,252,000 estimated printage

$5 Educational Note, Series of 1896: *Electricity Presenting Light to the World*

The $5 Educational Note features the ornate and elegant motif *Electricity Presenting Light to the World,* also called *Electricity as the Dominant Force in the World.* Walter Shirlaw created the grand allegory for the face of this issue, one of the most dynamic action groups ever seen on American currency.[4] At the center, Liberty (or perhaps Electricity) holds aloft an Edison bulb

The $2 Educational Note with the vignette of *Science Presenting Steam and Electricity to Industry and Commerce*. (F-247, W-367)

are scarce, and this may be more folklore than anything else.

The back was conceived by Thomas F. Morris and mostly engraved by G.F.C. Smillie, with portraits of generals U.S. Grant and Philip H. Sheridan engraved by Lorenzo Hatch. This was part of the Treasury Department policy of featuring Civil War military heroes (Union side only) on paper money. It is interesting to contemplate that Grant, a great general but considered to be a poor president, is perhaps overly represented on United States currency. It hurt when Morris's concept of a naval design for this denomination was discarded and replaced by outside artist Shirlaw's motif. At the congressional inquiry of 1897, Bureau of Engraving and Printing chief Claude Johnson testified concerning the $5 note (excerpted):

which casts rays on the scene below. To the left, a god in the clouds uses bolts of lightning to urge fiery steeds onward. At the right a flying goddess attracts a dove, with the U.S. Capitol in the distance. Thomas F. Morris engraved certain of the details, while the main allegory was engraved by G.F.C. Smillie.

This is Neoclassicism at its height—an elegant scene that stands as one of the most popular currency motifs in the view of collectors today, with more than just a few considering it to be the ultimate in federal paper-money artistry. The uncovered bosoms of certain of the figures in the scene caused several Boston society ladies to rally against the design, and some banks to resist taking them—the origin of the term "banned in Boston," according to some. Facts

Mr. Morris, since his own design was rejected, was indignant, had a disagreement with all the artists, and there was pulling between the artists and Mr. Morris all the time, to such an extent that in several cases I started to recommend Mr. Morris's dismissal. He aggravated me so. That was the especial policy of that administration; the Secretary of the Treasury had ordered this Bureau to do certain work, and it was Mr. Morris's duty to carry into effect whatever policy was adopted by the Treasury's Office and being executed through this office.

The $5 Educational Note with the vignette of *Electricity Presenting Light to the World.* (F-269, W-800)

Detail of the central vignette.

I went to New York and met Mr. Shirlaw, who had been in his early life a bank-note engraver. He was also an artist of some note; had studied in Europe ten years. I suggested to him to make a design, which he did. . . . Of course, that character of work took better engraving than ever had been done in this Bureau before. Naturally, we would employ the best talent. Mr. Smillie was employed, and Mr. Schlecht for the purpose of executing that work, and adding to the stock of the Bureau generally. Mr. Schlecht had engraved the Columbian Exposition diploma. Mr. Smillie was considered one of the five first-class engravers in the country and had done work for the American and the Hamilton, the Western, and the Canadian bank-note companies.

I will say that, in my opinion, if both designs had been properly transferred, and Mr. Morris had made the counter numbers distinct, as he should have done, that they would have been very successful. [The Shirlaw counter or denomination designs were rejected by Morris.] Now, this is a photograph of Mr. Shirlaw's border. Mr. Morris would not use that border, and put this other border in. You see that the 5 is very distinct. I do not mean to say that that border is altogether satisfactory. The 5 shows that it was intended to have a very plain 5, and Mr. Morris changed it. . . .[5]

Varieties of the $5 Notes

F-268 • W-799 • Tillman-Morgan (1893–1897) • Small red Treasury seal with spiked border • 17,300,000 estimated printage

F-269 • W-800 • Bruce-Roberts (1897–1898) • Small red Treasury seal with spiked border • 10,700,000 estimated printage

F-270 • W-801 • Lyons-Roberts (1898–1905) • Small red Treasury seal with spiked border • 6,932,000 estimated printage[6]

CHAPTER 12

John Allan, America's First Rare-Coin Dealer

John Allan.

The Erie Canal, begun in 1817 and completed in 1826, was the greatest public-works project in the United States up to that time. To commemorate its opening and success, Charles Cushing Wright was commissioned to engrave dies for a special medal. At the time there were few numismatists in America. One of them, John Allan, was especially appreciative of Wright's work.

The Erie Canal Medal

In chapter 4 I discussed the famous 1783 Libertas Americana medal. The 1826 Erie Canal medal is another classic and is the subject of this chapter. And the list could be expanded. Almost completely forgotten is the 1838 New Haven medal, one of the most important productions of its time (see chapter 20). Both the Erie Canal and New Haven medals are among the greatest of early American issues. Both were engraved by Charles Cushing Wright. Beautiful medals have always been appreciated by numismatists—a passion predating interest in collecting federal coins by dates and mintmarks. Most historic medals are relatively inexpensive in comparison to coins of equal rarity. Today the Token and Medal Society and the Medal Collectors of America are two groups that study the field and publish magazines.

In 1839 the editors of the *American Journal of Science* tapped John Allan to contribute an article, "On Coins and Medals, with a notice of the Medal which has been recently struck to commemorate the settlement of New Haven, Connecticut."[1] At the time the art and science of American numismatics was in its infancy and no more than a few dozen collectors and scholars were active in the field. The inauguration of the Mint Cabinet display at the Philadelphia Mint in June 1838 had accelerated interest recently as had scattered articles in magazines distributed to highly educated readers, as here.

Born in Kilbernie, Ayrshire, Scotland, in 1777, John Allan emigrated to the United States and secured a position in New York City as a bookkeeper. In his adopted country Allan became an active numismatist in the early years of the 19th century and continued his interest for decades thereafter. In 1820 he was one of only three American subscribers to Mudie's set of National Medals issued in England.[2] By 1827 the active numismatists in New York City in addition to Allan were Philip Hone (who served a term as mayor), Pierre Flandin, James Thornton, A.D. Moore, and Michael Moore.

As was true of most early collectors of coins and medals, John Allan's interests were far-ranging and also included books, antiques, artifacts, and curiosities. His collection of snuff boxes was memorable and was widely admired. In his house on Pearl Street, opposite Centre Street, and, beginning in 1827, in his home on Vandewater Street he greeted many visitors who shared his enthusiasm. Allan also sold coins to others and is remembered as America's first rare-coin dealer. He had artistic talent and created many sketches and illustrations for books including *Washington's Life* and Robert Burns's *Poems*.

On December 10, 1855, he and G.A. Leavitt and R.L. Delisser formed a partnership to conduct an auction business under the name of Leavitt, Delisser & Co. In premises at 377 and 379 Broadway the firm sold

John Allan medal published by
John K. Curtis in 1859. Dies by
George H. Lovett.

books, art, antiques, and some coins and medals. In 1859 John K. Curtis, a prominent New York City rare-coin dealer, issued a medal from dies by George H. Lovett featuring Allan on the obverse and the Latin inscription: JOHANNES ALLAN. ANTIQUARIUS SCOTUS. NATUS FEB. 26, 1777 ("John Allan, Scottish antiquarian, born Feb. 26, 1777").

In 1862 in *The Old Merchants of New York City,* volume I, Walter Barrett included this about Allan: "He is famed for an antiquarian collection of everything relating to our city." Allan died in New York City on November 19, 1863, having been inactive in the hobby for the last several years of his life. His properties were later sold in a series of auctions.

Allan on Medals

The 1839 *American Journal of Science* article began with an overview of medals in history and their importance:

As to the question, at what period of the world the study of coins and medals commenced, or at what precise time they were first fabricated, we are ignorant, although several writers have endeavored to trace their origin to a very remote antiquity. The states of Italy were the first, after the revival of literature and the fine arts, to com-

mence the study and striking of coins and medals; and the modern governments of Europe have all, more or less, followed their example.

Medals have been admired by many of the wisest and best of ancient and modern times; by Pliny, Alfred, Petrarch, Cambden, Selden, and others; for they have beauties inherently their own, which being founded on the immutable principles of human nature, must ever afford delight to the human mind. Novelty, beauty and sublimity are the three great sources of moral and intellectual pleasure, and the incitements to these are well supplied by medals. They display the usages of society, and the habits and forms of persons, with whom history having made us acquainted, we long to see the faces on which their minds and characters were impressed.

From a similar feeling we are delighted with the exhibition of the battles, edifices, religious rites, costumes, and innumerable other interesting circumstances belonging to the age, or illustrating the characters and actions of eminent individuals. Hence Greece and Rome, the noblest states in ancient times were most distinguished for their attachment to, and production of coins and medals. A vast number of these have been spared by the destroyer *time,* to attest the pains and success with which they were executed, thus evincing the high importance attached to them in those ages, not only as commemorating passing events, but as gratifying the ardent wish of posterity, to look back into remote times, and thus to obtain the most important aids to history.

FRONTISPIECE

History protecting Medals from the Ravages of Time

Published by the Proprietor T Prattent Coth Fear W Smithfield London 1796

Frontispiece of *The Virtuoso's Companion*, 1798, showing Time, the destroyer of medals. Numismatic passion was high in Great Britain at the time.

No adequate conception can be formed by persons who have paid no attention to the subject, how highly subservient medals may be made to the gratification of private taste, to the perpetuation of the memory of objects of personal history, of domestic endearment, and individual honor; to the illustration of the success of well laid plans of public enterprise, to the commemoration of marriages and births, to perpetuating the knowledge of new inventions, and of the memory of men eminent for learning and talent, and for public as well as private virtues.

As medals are the least perishable of all the materials upon which the artist displays his powers, they continue current on the tide of time when the productions of all other arts have sunk into oblivion. A desire to possess modern as well as ancient medals exists, at present, in the most distinguished academies, and among individuals of all enlightened countries: medals are eagerly sought for public libraries, and museums, and governments employ the mint in striking medals and coins to heighten the splendor of the existing administration and to extend and perpetuate their civil and military renown.

Another source of pleasure and amusement which attends the study of medals, is the finish and beauty displayed in their workmanship, by the designers and engravers. We have already remarked that the states of Italy were the first after the revival of literature to commence the study and striking of medals. The papal medals form a magnificent series. Germany possesses many cabinets of coins and medals and many books which have been written on the subject in that country. Russia and Sweden have each a series of medals in honor of national victories. Holland has a similar series, commemorating her struggles for liberty, and her final emancipation from the Spanish yoke. France has an immense national collection. England, till lately, was behind the continent in her medallic history. Several fine medals were struck by the celebrated Simon, in Cromwell's time; and a very excellent series by Croker to celebrate the victories of Marlborough in the reign of Queen Anne.

A series of English sovereigns was engraved and struck by Dassin, a native of Geneva, in the reign of George the first—and recently, an additional series consisting of forty, has been struck to commemorate the national achievements during the late war with France, and the powers on the continent. But many elegant private medals of individuals in Britain have been executed; of men who have been eminent in various walks of life, or who by their talents have added to the discoveries in the sciences, in agriculture, or the mechanical and other arts. For the improvement on the steam engine by Watt, a medal was struck, but where is the medal in honor of Fulton?—where is that in honor of Whitney?

The most distinguished collection of medals of the present day is the Napoleon series of one hundred and sixty, commemorating the civil and military actions of that extraordinary man; they were done chiefly from the designs, and under the direction of the celebrated Denon. Most of them are beautiful in design and execution, and unequalled by any of modern times. Several medals were struck at Paris to commemorate the American Revolution. Congress, some years since, made an appropriation to have the whole

series placed in the national library at Washington; the vessel that had them in charge (if I recollect right) was lost, and whether any further action has been had, or any progress since made, I am ignorant.

A medal was struck on Commodore Truxton's victory,—and another on the war with Tripoli under Commodore Preble. Medals also were struck by order of Congress, to carry down to posterity the naval victories of the United States, in the late war with Great Britain.

John Allan continued his discourse by stating that a medal had been struck "to commemorate the union of Lake Erie with the Atlantic, by the great canal." The dies were engraved by Charles Cushing Wright, who was on his way to fame.

Charles Cushing Wright

Charles Cushing Wright is widely considered to have been the most accomplished of American die engravers from the mid-1820s until his passing in 1854. The Erie Canal medal and the New Haven medal are among his triumphs.

He was born in Damariscotta, Maine, on May 1, 1796. Details of his early life are sketchy. He worked for a silversmith in Utica, New York, about 1817, later in Albany and in New York City, and after that in Savannah, Georgia, and Charleston, South Carolina. In Charleston he met and fell in love with Lavinia Dorothy Simons. Her mother did not like him, and would not give her daughter permission to marry. No matter, they wed on September 18, 1820, and her mother did not attend the service.

An advertisement in the *Charleston Courier* of April 22, 1823, gave his shop address as 161 King Street. Later that year Wright moved to New York City, where he engaged in diecutting. In October 1823 he joined the bank-note-engraving firm of Maverick &

Durand, conducted by Peter Maverick and Asher Brown Durand, the latter who became one of the most famous early-19th-century American artists. A proof of a copper plate is signed "Durand & Wright 1823." Another trade style was C.C. Wright & Durand, and others included C.C. Wright & Co, Wright & Smith (with Daniel D. Smith), and Wright & Prentiss.

The full extent of Wright's work on dies for medals and tokens is not known and would furnish an excellent subject for a book-length study. His Erie Canal medal is recognized as one of the most outstanding examples of medallic art of the era.

The Erie Canal Medal

Construction of the first convenient cargo route through the Appalachians from the Atlantic to the West was slow and difficult. Work on the 363-mile-long "Great Canal," as it was sometimes referred to, began at Rome, New York, in 1817, and after two years, only 15 miles had been completed. Strident opponents to the massive state expenditures for the project began calling it "DeWitt Clinton's Big Ditch," a reference to the governor of the state, and demanded that the work be abandoned. Supporters persevered, immigrant laborers toiled, and when the waterway was completed, the City of New York hosted the biggest celebration the nation had ever seen.

On October 26, 1825, the first canal boat, the *Seneca Chief,* left Buffalo. A flotilla of sailing ships and steam barges joined it on the Hudson River at Albany, and escorted it to a landing at New York's Battery on November 4. The Grand Canal Celebration began. "The wharves and shores and the roofs of many buildings were crowded with onlookers. . . . Castle Garden, the Battery and every avenue to the water were thronged to a degree altogether beyond precedent. The ships and vessels in the harbor were filled even to their riggings and tops."[3] Loud cheers resounded from every direction when a jubilant Governor DeWitt Clinton ceremoniously poured a jar of Lake Erie's water into New York Bay.

The Erie Canal medal struck from dies engraved by Charles Cushing Wright in 1825, and distributed on November 4 of that year. The medal is dated 1826.

Detail of Wright's signature on the reverse of the medal.

Richard Riker was chairman of the Committee of Arrangements for the Grand Canal Celebration, which included the issuance of a commemorative medal, per this contemporary account:

> The Corporation of the City having voted that a MEDAL should be struck, in commemoration of the great event of opening the navigable communication between Lake Erie and the ocean, the arrival in our harbor of a loaded flotilla, charged with the productions of the immense regions, surrounding the wide Western Lakes, and the measureless water-courses of our Northern Continent the same general idea of a device, was adopted, as on that of the badge worn by the Corporation guests on the celebration day.
>
> On the face of the medal is represented Neptune, who, with brotherly cordiality, returns Pan's visit to the ocean; the motto – "UNION OF ERIE WITH THE ATLANTIC." Under this emblem are the initials of the artists, R. DEL., W. Sc. On the reverse is the armorial bearings of the state, the sole agent in the great work; on the right of which are appropriately represented canal aqueducts and locks; and on the left is a view of the harbor and city of New York; the motto "ERIE CANAL COMM. 4 JULY 1817, COMP. 26 OCTR. 1825:"
>
> The contracted words in this motto in full are "COMMENCED," and "COMPLETED." Underneath the above is the sculptor's name "C.C. WRIGHT"; and below are the words in small Roman capitals "PRESENTED BY THE CITY OF N. YORK."
>
> *Artists:* The medal was engraved by Mr. Charles C. Wright, (of the firm of A. B. and C. Durand, Wright and Co., corner of Broadway and Canal Street.). The lettering by Mr. Richard Trested, engraver and die sinker, 68, William Street, upon dies made by Mr. William Williams, worker in iron and steel, corner of Liberty and Green streets. The medals, themselves, were most elegantly *impressed* by Mr. Maltby Pelletreau, (of the firm of Pelletreau, Bennett, and Cooke, 170 Broadway) at their Gold and Silver Manufactory, No. 12 Rose Street, by means of his very powerful and exquisitely adjusted screw press.
>
> The superlative beauty of the medal (to everyone who has seen it) renders it perfectly unnecessary for us to say more, than that all pronounce it to be a *chef d'oeuvre* of the fine arts; each artist, in his respective department, having manifested himself to be an accomplished master of his art; which, by this combination of talent has aided in producing a work of such superior excellence as to rival the best masters of the old world. We must, however, in justice to the sculptor decide, that although each has crowned himself with a never fading wreath of fame that a ray of superior lustre reflects upon the brow of the artist who engraved the dies.
>
> *The Box.* When it had been determined by the city authorities that a medal should be struck, the Committee of the Corporation (aldermen King and Davis) were charged, amongst

Wooden box made by Duncan Phyfe for the Erie Canal medal and the printed labels on the underside of the lid and under the medal at the bottom.

their other commissions to Buffalo, with procuring a sufficient quantity of the most curious woods, such as birds-eye and curled maple, red cedar, &c. the produce of the western forests, for making boxes to inclose the medal. This was procured, and deposited in a canoe, now in the City Hall, made by the aboriginal red men, on the shores of Lake Superior; and embarked on board the "Seneca Chief," the first canal boat from the lakes, which navigated the length of waters from Erie to the ocean.

We may here take notice, that the logs of cedar were procured by Mr. Miles, son of Capt. Thaddeus Joy, of Buffalo, from an island in Lake Erie. The boxes are made of these woods which inclose the medals presented to the invited guests. The boxes for the semi-metal [white metal] and silver medals are likewise made of these very curious woods. On the inside of the lid is the crest of the City Arms; with the inscription "Presented by the City of New York;" and on the inner side of the bottom "This Box was made from a piece of Wood, brought from Erie in the first Canal-boat, the Seneca Chief." The gold medals are enclosed in elegant square red morocco cases.

The makers of the curious wood boxes were Mr. Daniel Karr, turner, 222 William Street; and Mr. Duncan Phyfe, Murray Street. The maker of the morocco cases for the gold medals was Mr. Robert Tanner, morocco case maker, 67, Liberty Street.

The route of the Erie Canal (the black line extending from Buffalo to Albany) as shown on an 1825 map by R.T. Welch & Co.

Excavating the Erie Canal. (Cadwallader D. Colden, *Memoir Prepared*, 1825)

Entrance of the Erie Canal at Albany. (Cadwallader D. Colden, *Memoir. . .*)

Erie Canal aqueduct crossing a river at Little Falls, New York. (John H. Hinton, *History of the United States*, 1850)

"Three of these in gold were ordered in 1826 to be sent to the three surviving signers of the Declaration of Independence."[4] The date 1826 is on each medal, including those struck and issued in 1825.

Much more could be said about Wright. Suffice it to say here that the Erie Canal medal brought him great fame and was a worthy predecessor to the 1848 New Haven medal discussed in chapter 20. He died on July 7, 1854, leaving a unique numismatic legacy that includes some of the most beautiful art medals and many tokens and store cards from the 1820s onward.[5]

The Erie Canal Medal in Numismatics

Harold E. Hibler and Charles V. Kappen, authors of *So-Called Dollars* published by the Coin & Currency Institute in 1963, listed the Erie Canal medal as HK-1 in white metal and HK-1000 in silver. This book has been widely circulated over the intervening half century and has served to focus attention on the issue. In *100 Greatest American Medals and Tokens*, 2007, the medal was voted as No. 8.

An estimated several hundred survive today, of which perhaps a couple dozen or so are accompanied by their original boxes. Strikings are in white metal (pewter) and silver, the rarity of each being about equal. In England die sinker Edward Thomason issued

Life on the Erie Canal. (E.L. Henry painting)

Edward Thomason's 91.3 mm copy of C.C. Wright's Erie Canal medal.

a larger-diameter medal incorporating much of the same design and dated 1825. It was Thomason who struck the Mudie's National Medals referred to earlier.

In his 1845 biography, *Sir Edward Thomason's Memoirs During Half a Century,* the author told this:

> His Royal Highness the Duke of Saxe Weimar, in 1825 and 1826, travelled through the United States, and I understood he was present at the completion of the Grand Canal, uniting the Erie with the Atlantic. The American government employed their best artist in medal engraving to engrave a pair of medal dies (of small size, about one inch and a quarter in diameter) to commemorate this important undertaking, which was accomplished towards the end of the year 1825.
>
> The Duke, on his return, landed at Liverpool, and called upon me as he passed through Birmingham, and was so obliging as to present me with one of the American medals. His Royal Highness was well aware of the inferiority of the workmanship, both as to the execution of the dies and the making of the medal, but it was the best their artist could do.
>
> As so important an event was worth recording upon a medal, 1 had a pair of dies engraved, about four times the size, by one of my first artists, the *allegory* of the medal being exactly a *facsimile* of theirs. On the *Obverse* was a River God encouraging Neptune for a time, whilst he conducted him to the River Erie—the *Legend,* "Union of Erie with the Atlantic." On the *Reverse* was the Eagle standing upon, and in the attitude of protecting one-half of the Globe. A ship at a distance—an escutcheon with the sun rising out of the water, and in a garter the word Excelsior. The Legend—"Erie Canal, commenced 4th July, 1817, completed 26th October, 1825."
>
> The Americans were delighted with this production, and seemed to acknowledge, without jealousy, the vast distinction between English and American artists.

CHAPTER 13

Of all tokens associated with 18th-century America—or was it associated at all?—more has been written and theorized about the 1783 Georgivs Triumpho than about any other.

The Enigmatic 1783 Georgivs Triumpho Token

A Mystery in Copper

The 1783 Georgivs Triumpho token.

I love a mystery! And, if it is a numismatic mystery, so much the better! A first-class puzzle is the 1783-dated copper token depicting the portrait of somebody-or-other on the obverse and the inscription GEORGIVS TRIUMPHO. Although this has been described in print for more than 200 years, since at least 1798, facts concerning it are still elusive!

Georgius Triumpho tokens come on the market with some frequency, with the result that they are not expensive in the context of 19th-century pieces. Curiously, I have never seen one that I would call choice Mint State, although some, such as the illustrated example, come close.

This chapter shares some of the information I have found about it.

Description of the Token

Obverse: Portrait of King George III facing right, similar to the image found on the 1782 Irish halfpenny.[1] Left: GEORGIVS. Right: TRIUMPHO. The first word clearly has a V, the second word a U. In numismatic literature the token is nearly always referred to as Georgius Triumpho. Louis Jordan adds this:

> On the obverse there are small die cracks in both G's in GEORGIVS; the cracks run from the final cross stroke in the center up to the serif at the start of the letter. In the same word there is also a small die crack in the E from the top horizontal to the serif on the center horizontal. On the S punch the bottom of the S was not as deeply cut as the top portion, this has slightly raised the surface of the bottom section of the letter, thus the bottom bow shows a slight ridge from the top of the final serif to the center of the letter. In TRIUMPHO note that the verticals of the H are not even.[2]

Reverse: At the center is a seated figure of Britannia, waist up, adapted from the full figure used on contemporary British halfpence, inspired by the seated figure on ancient Roman coins. The figure was later used on Connecticut state copper coins of 1785 to 1788. In her right hand (the observer's left) is a branch and her right hand holds a pole. She is seated in a box or behind a railing with 13 vertical bars. At each corner is a fleur-de-lis, the symbol of France. Left: VOCE. Right: POPOLI (instead of the usual POPULI, but POPOLI was used elsewhere such as on certain Voce Popoli tokens of Ireland dated 1760). The date 1783 is below. Again I quote Louis Jordan:

On the reverse there is a major die crack in front of Liberty running through her right shoulder and continuing down into the gate. This crack is absent from the first examples struck. It seems to have been due to a die clash and first appears in a state similar to the example shown above. In its final stages the crack becomes much more pronounced moving to the top of the head and further down into the gate area. Also note that the bottom of the spear, seen above the 7 in the date, is not properly aligned with the upper portion of the shaft. In the legend the top of the second O in POPOLI is very weak. Also in the date, the top portion of the 8 is broken on the right side near the center.[3]

The typical example is about 25.8 mm diameter.

James Conder, 1798

An Arrangement of Provincial Coins, Tokens and Medalets, issued in Great Britain, Ireland, and the Colonies, within the last 20 years, from the farthing to the penny size, by James Conder, was published in London in 1798. This gave rise to the term *Conder tokens* still used today to describe copper pieces dated in the 1780s and 1790s. His was not the first listing, but happened to be the one that posterity smiled upon. Conder lived in Ipswich, Suffolk. On the title page is this notable quotation:

"It is certain that medals give a very great light to history," *Addison*

Among his listings was this token:

No. 45
O. A laureled bust in profile, "Georgius Triumpho"

R. A Figure standing behind Railing, "Voce Popoli." Ex "1783"

The American Antiquarian Society, 1855

The American Antiquarian Society in Worcester, Massachusetts, is the largest repository of printed material—books, newspapers, broadsides, pamphlets, you name it—in the United States today. Its collections range from the earliest of colonial times down to the cut-off date of 1876, the year of the American centennial. Some years ago I was elected a fellow of the AAS, an honor I cherish. On a number of occasions I have visited the Society and have immersed myself in various archival items.

The *American Antiquarian Society Proceedings,* October 22, 1855, published in 1857, include this as part of the "Report upon the American Coins and Tokens in the Cabinet of the American Antiquarian Society," by Nathaniel Paine:

The rare "Tory copper," or, as it is most generally termed, "Georgius Triumpho," comes next in order, and may be described as follows: —
Device. — A bust, with face to right.

Legend. — "Georgius Triumpho."

Reverse. — The Goddess of Liberty erect, with a branch of laurel in her right hand, and a liberty-pole in her left. In front, a frame, with fleur-de-lis at each corner.

Legend. — "Voce Popoli."

Exergue. — 1783.

This piece was issued in England

in the year 1783. It is said to have made its first appearance in Georgia, but was probably not designed for exclusive circulation in that state. Good specimens of this coin sell for from one to three dollars each.

The "most generally termed" comment suggests that by 1855 the token was widely known to numismatists, a small community that probably did not exceed a couple hundred serious collectors, most of whom specialized in Greek, Roman, and European coins, medals, or early American colonial coins, among other pursuits. By that time there were a number of cabinets of such pieces, including in the New-York Historical Society and P.T. Barnum's American Museum. There were no reference books on American coins except for Joseph Barlow Felt's *An Historical Account of Massachusetts Currency,* 1839, the contents of which were limited by the title. In 1842 the Assay Department of the U.S. Mint published a book by Eckfeldt and Dubois, *A Manual of Gold and Silver Coins of All Nations, Struck Within the Past Century,* which primarily treated the bullion content of coins and had no numismatic text.[4] Early American numismatics is a fascinating field of study, and I tell more in chapter 20.

Who said it "made its first appearance in Georgia" is not known, and I have found no confirmation of such an initial distribution.

Montroville W. Dickeson, 1859

In early 1859, Dr. Montroville W. Dickeson's master work, *American Numismatical Manual,* was published. Dickeson was primarily known as an archaeologist who excavated many Indian burial mounds, especially in the Midwest. He was also a numismatist, a seller of a metal safe for storing valuables, and a landlord in Philadelphia to coin dealer E.B. Mason Jr. This large and impressive quarto volume included 256 numbered pages, numerous color lithograph plates, and other material. Slightly revised and retitled *An Ameri-*

can Numismatic Manual, the book was also issued in 1860 and 1865 editions. The publisher was J.B. Lippincott & Co., Philadelphia. Apparently, at least several thousand copies were issued totally, for the work became widely circulated and even today is readily available.

This was the first large book with significant content on the entire spectrum of American coinage. Much of it was a distillation of information that had appeared earlier in various articles and books. Other information was obtained in consultation with Mint Director James Ross Snowden, other Mint officers, prominent numismatist Joseph J. Mickley, and "numerous private individuals." What Dickeson didn't know he often guessed at, without noting that this was the case. As an initial work it contained many errors, but the majority of the information was correct, and without doubt it had a strong influence on the growth of the hobby in America.

Today, one cannot help but wistfully contemplate the vast numbers of coins available to Dickeson for study. As an example, in a discussion of 1787 New Jersey coppers, he noted that he was able to describe die varieties of this year "from the examination of several thousand specimens." When discussing 1793 cents, Dickeson described pieces he "found in cabinet collections and *circulation*" (italics added).

For the token under discussion he gave this:

Georgius Triumpho

Device.—A bust, the head laureated, and facing to the right. 1783.

Legend.—GEORGIVS TRIUMPHO.[5]

Reverse.—The Goddess of Liberty erect, facing to the left—holding a laurel branch in the right hand, and supporting the liberty pole with the left. In front of the figure, a frame, with fleur-de-lis

The Enigmatic 1783 Georgivs Triumpho Token

President George Washington.

King George III.

at each corner, and on the field of the same, thirteen stripes, emblematic of the thirteen United States.

Legend.—VOCE POPOLI

Exergue.—1783.

Of this copper, known as the "Tory penny," we have found only one type and three varieties.

It has a history. From the head of the bust, being an effigy of George III, and the legend, GEORGIVS TRIUM-PHO, much hostility was manifested toward it at the time of its appearance; the lingering evidences of which still prevail among those who possess or see it, the legend being supposed to refer to the triumph of George the king instead of George the patriot.

There being, at the time of its issue, no victory for his British majesty, but, on the contrary, the greatest triumph that has ever been achieved by man for his race, the acknowledge-

ment of our national independence, no basis exists for prejudice against this harmless copper, not purely constructive.

Gotten up in England, it is said to have made its first appearance in this country in Georgia, though we have found no evidence to show that it was designed for exclusive circulation in that state; which we are informed, unfortunately contained an undue proportion of the partisans of the British monarchy and its king—a circumstance calculated to excite and strengthen the impression that it was designed at least to reflect upon the triumph of the Revolutionary cause.

We are informed the feeling ran so high in Virginia and elsewhere against it, that many of them were mutilated and destroyed. We must, however, relieve the Tories of Georgia, of that day, of any connection or complicity with either its origin or circulation.

It is related of this unhappy class, that, about this time it emigrated in a body to the Island of Jamaica, since which, those composing it have incurred by their sins—moral and physical—a condition of degeneracy which must ultimately result in their total extinction. A portion, perhaps the entire remnant of them, finally found a home at Key West, where they are known by the name of "conchs"— mere wreckers [men who salvaged wrecked ships, common in the area] and fishermen, picking up a precarious living, and who, by isolation and close intermarriage, are as distinguished for very moderate physical power and mental ability, as the lowest of the human species anywhere.

In regard to the effigy upon this coin, it is not the only instance in the colonial currency, as this work discloses, where either carelessness, ignorance, or the want of something more appropriate has given us a fac-simile of the head of George III., as represented upon British coins; but, in our opinion, not designed to have any intended connection with the then living original, the numerals being left out, and thereby rendering the head as applicable in intention to George Washington as George De Este or Guelph.

Further, the Goddess of Liberty with the pole, and the thirteen stripes—emblematic, clearly, at that date, of the States of the Union—were too distinctive of a fact that could not be ignored, to suppose that royalty or Toryism would adopt as emblems such distasteful evidences of their own humiliation. We trust then we have established the claim of the GEORGIUS TRIUMPHO to equal favor with its associate colonial coins.

The *Universal Review*

This *Universal Review* of October 1859 included a lengthy article, "American Numismatics," which discussed the Dickeson book and quoted much text from it. The unnamed author took issue with a number of statements, including this regarding the Georgivs Triumpho token:

Another is more remarkable, and has given rise to a good deal of discussion,—it bears the date 1783; but it presents a fair portrait of the king, with the singular motto, GEORGIUS TRIUMPHO; reverse exhibits the old figure of Britannia, the lower portion covered by a kind of gridiron having thirteen bars, and the equivocal legend, VOCE POPOLI [sic].[6] That the portrait of the king is not a caricature, that the reverse legend may mean either loyalty or independence, that the stripes look more like a gridiron than anything else, seem to show that the piece was designed by one who bore no enmity to monarchical government. Dr. Dickeson, however, seems to think that to admit this would be a disgrace to the American people, and we must, therefore, let him get them out of the difficulty in the best way he can. He says:— [Dickeson's text is given here]

On this we beg to remark; first, that the goddess Liberty is the figure of Britannia, as accurately as could be copied from an English halfpenny, and that the pole or spear has *no cap*. Secondly, that the portrait is unmistakably George III, and must have been meant for him, as the workmanship is good. So skillful an engraver as he who designed this coin would have represented George Washington a little better than by making him a *facsimile* of his royal rival. The way in which the token was received proves what the popular feeling was about it, and the name Tory halfpenny may still be used with strict propriety.

The Historical Magazine

The token and commentaries about it moved Fisk Parsons Brewer, curator of the coin cabinet at Yale, to submit the following inquiry to *The Historical Magazine,* published in the issue of July 1860. (Launched in 1857, the periodical contained many items of numismatic interest in an era before there was any journal specifically dedicated to the field.)

Georgius Triumpho Copper

What evidence is there that the Georgius-Triumpho copper was struck in this country, or has any reference to Washington? Specimens of the coin are not rare, but those who are without one can see it engraved in Dickeson's *Num. Manual,* or *Harper's Magazine* for March, in both of which it is classed with American tokens. It, however, does not bear Washington's name, or his portrait, or any allusion to America; except perhaps that there is a figure of Liberty on the reverse, standing behind a railing which contains 13 bars.

The date is 1783, in which year the principal events, commemorated by tokens, were the treaty with England and Washington's resignation as commander-in-chief. The legend on the obverse,— *Georgius Triumpho—I, George, triumph,*—taken by itself, might refer to the close of the Revolution; but the legend of the reverse, *Voce*

Popoli, seems to be a continuation of the sentence, and the whole sentiment, "I, George, triumph by the popular voice," has no special application to this year of Washington's life.

On the other hand, the portrait is evidently that of King George of England, being almost a *facsimile* of his laureated head as it appears on an Irish half-penny of 1782, now lying before us. The female on the reverse, with her left hand raised and holding a long staff which rests upon the ground, and with a branch in her right, although she might be used to represent Liberty, is certainly the usual figure of Britannia. Why the die-sinker made her standing and placed her behind the singular railing, which reminds one of the front of a witness-box, is not clear, unless he considered it their proper position in uttering the popular voice.

The words *Voce Populi* are found on an Irish token of the year 1760, the first of George Third's reign, as legend around a laureated head, behind which is the letter P—the reverse the figure and name of Hibernia. If the Georgius-Triumpho token refers to King George, the legend would be quite appropriate. Twice in the year 1783 did the sovereign change his ministers. The second or coalition ministry, lost their place through their efforts to carry Mr. Fox's India Bill—the bold innovations of which had excited violent opposition among the people, and finally on the part of the king himself. In one day the bill was defeated in the House of Lords, and the two Secretaries of State were peremptorily dismissed from office, the king declining

1783 Nova Constellatio copper, Crosby 1-A. The date numerals are identical to those on the 1783 Georgivs Triumpho copper and the letters are a close match as well. Likely, both dies were from the same hand. Heavy clash marks on the obverse at the 11 o'clock and 2 o'clock positions are from another die coming into contact with it on two occasions. The clash marks show the dentils from the other die(s).

Detail of the date numerals in the 1783 Nova Constellatio copper, Crosby 1-A.

Detail of the Georgivs Triumpho date.

a personal interview. Says Prof. Goodrich, in his "British Eloquence": "The course taken was regarded by all concerned as an extreme measure on the part of the crown to repel an extreme measure of Mr. Fox, which endangered the rights of the king and the balance of the Constitution. The great body of the people gave it their sanction, and rejoiced in a step which they would have resisted in almost any other case, as an invasion of their rights." Well might the king say, *"Georgius triumpho voce popoli."*

In view of these facts, it would be interesting to know what direct evidence there is that the token in question had a reference to Washington? F.P.B.

Modern Commentary

Today the 1783 Georgivs Triumpho token remains mysterious in several respects. Certain of the 19th-century questions have never been resolved. Does the token relate to King George III or to George Washington? What is the significance of the reverse motifs?

Quite a few modern scholars have addressed the question, including (alphabetically) Walter Breen, George Fuld, Ron Guth, Michael Hodder, Louis Jordan, John Kleeberg, John Kraljevich, Eric P. Newman, John Pack, Andrew W. Pollock III, Mike Ringo, Robert A. Vlack, Byron Weston, and Dennis Wierzba. Other names could be added. More has been said about this token and more has been speculated in the pages of the *Colonial Newsletter* and the *C4 Newsletter,* and in various auction catalogs and Internet postings, than for any other token of its era.

As to the obverse portrait it does not resemble the George Washington we know but, instead, is a fairly close copy of the image of King George III used on certain contemporary Irish halfpence as noted above by early writers. Offhand, this would seem to settle the

matter in favor of the British monarch. However, in more than just a few instances engravers of the 18th and early-19th centuries used a portrait on one coin or token to illustrate an entirely different person on another. In 1783 in England there were no easily obtainable images of Washington. The Voltaire medal of Washington, made in France several years later in 1789, had a fictitious portrait for the same reason. Although the 1783 date was used on certain other Washington tokens such as the Draped Bust, Military Bust, and UNITY STATES issues with true Washington portraits, these were struck years later into the

19th century, presumably using the 1783 date of the treaty that officially ended the Revolution (which had concluded with the Battle of Yorktown in 1781). Still, it can be argued that if a British diesinker needed to use a fictitious portrait of Washington he would not have selected that of the current monarch.

It is agreed that the obverse depicts "George Triumphant." While the 1860 commentary by F.P.B. (Fisk Parsons Brewer) in *The Historical Magazine* made a case for George III being triumphant in domestic politics in 1783, this has not been shared by present-day researchers. While the image is of George III, it is considered generic in this use by many writers.

The Georgivs Triumpho token was probably struck in Birmingham, England. The numeral punches in the 1783 date are identical to those used on Nova Constellatio coppers of this year, Crosby variety 1-A (Whitman-1860), the "Large US," which is anomalous among the issues of that series.[7] The die work indicates a hand not as experienced as that which made the rest of the coinage (genuine issues). As to whether it is a contemporary counterfeit, or an authorized issue by a different diesinker, is not known. Both the Georgivs Triumpho token and Nova Constellatio Crosby 1-A are likely from the same hand. Another mystery!

In a letter published in the October 10, 2011, issue of *Coin World*, Andrew W. Pollock III opined that the reverse motif of the Georgivs Triumpho token might actually show a balloon gondola, with the seated figure standing in a basket with corners having fleur-de-lis ornaments. "John Pack suggested to me that the reverse motif may represent America's aspirations for independence being buoyed aloft by means of assistance received from French military allies," Pollock continued.[8]

The Pollock idea about the hot-air balloon may have merit. America was indeed grateful to Marquis de Lafayette and other Frenchmen who helped the Continental Army to victory. Paris was the center of aerial activity, at first with tethered hot-air balloons, and then on December 14, 1783, the first free flight was made in a craft constructed in 1782 by the Montgolfier brothers.[9]

The obverse die of the Georgivs Triumpho tokens was later muled with two irrelevant reverse dies.

Eric P. Newman suggests that the 1783-dated *Nova Constellatio* pieces may not have been struck until 1785, for no contemporary accounts concerning them have been located before that year.[10] The design seems to have been copied from the 1783 5 units decimal pattern piece made in America in the year dated. It seems certain that the Georgivs Triumpho tokens were actually made and circulated in the mid-1780s and thus, if George Washington were intended, are the first tokens to bear his image, in this case fictitious.

While many of the British tokens of this era were made as numismatic or cabinet pieces, this was not true of the Georgivs Triumpho. Nearly all known examples show extensive circulation. While most were used in the British Isles, some circulated in the United States, seemingly including in Georgia and Virginia per the above accounts. One served as an undertype planchet for a 1787 New Jersey copper (Maris 73-aa, W-5430), struck by Matthias Ogden at his mint in Elizabethtown. Other New Jersey coppers have been reported with the same undertype.[11] Another was found in South Carolina by a metal detectorist.

What is my opinion?

I have no conclusive answer. To add my commentary to certain others given in recent times, I consider the obverse to relate to King George III of Britain, not to George Washington. The diesinker obviously used the image of the current monarch. I consider the reverse to relate to America with the 13 bars signifying the 13 colonies and the fleur-de-lis a nod to French assistance during the Revolution. The seated figure of Britannia may be in a cage or behind bars, if so signifying she had been bested by the United States. Or, perhaps she is ascending in a balloon to freedom. I consider this to be a *satirical* token intended to poke fun at George III. In the same era the Conder token series comprises dozens of various satirical issues. What do *you* think?

Wyman in his day was one of America's best-known ventriloquists and magicians, even performing in the White House for the Lincoln family on several occasions. His counterstamped coins served as admission tickets to his public shows.

Wyman the Wizard

John Wyman, Ventriloquist

WYMAN / WIZARD / & / VENTRILO-QUIST counterstamp on a well-worn 1782 Mexican silver two-real coin. These coins were legal tender in the United States and traded for 25 cents. This counterstamped example served as an advertisement for Wyman and also an admission pass to his show.

John Wyman Jr., known as Jack to his friends, performed on stage as Wyman the Wizard. I first learned of him through his counterstamps—WYMAN THE WIZARD countermarked on well-worn Spanish-American two-real silver coins, the matrix of choice for so many who advertised on these "little billboards" during the mid-19th century. Worth "two bits" or a quarter, no doubt such pieces also served as admission tickets to his stage show. I first discovered the joy of various counterstamps in 1955 and have delved into their history ever since.

Wyman was born on January 19, 1816, in Albany, New York. After attending the Albany Academy he went to Baltimore at the suggestion of his father and went to work for an auction house. This did not suit him, and he practiced ventriloquism—the art of voice projection. He was on stage by the time he was in his early twenties. The Baltimore *Sun* of November 27, 1837, carried this advertisement:

> Baltimore Museum and Gallery of Fine Arts, corner of Baltimore and Calvert streets.
>
> The proprietor very respectfully announces to the public that he has made a short engagement with Mr. J. Wyman, the Western Ventriloquist, who will display his peculiar and astonishing powers, commencing this evening, November 27, 1837, and continue for a few evenings during the week in the Saloon of the Museum.

Sharing the bill was Mr. T.S. Hyatt, who delivered a lecture on phrenology, and the Roman Twins, "nearly similar in formation to the well-known Siamese Twins." Admission was 25 cents. Among those who enjoyed Wyman's presentations was President Martin Van Buren.

The *New York Commercial Advertiser*, August 22, 1840, included this listing for Peale's New York Museum of Natural History and Science, Broadway, opposite the City Hall and Park—also known as Peale's Museum:

> Miss J.E. Wyman, the accomplished lady magician, will introduce with astonishing rapidity and brilliancy, a variety of the most inexplicable, mysterious, and wonder-working and marvelous magical Deceptions, Illusions, Necromantic and Physical Experiments ever yet attempted, consisting of Metamorphosis and Illusions, &c., embracing all the principal beauties of Manual Dexterity, with Rings, Birds, Money, Sorcerer's Banquet, &c.
>
> Mr. Wyman, the much admired Ventriloquist, will hold

a colloquy between two supposed persons, the Ne Plus Ultra, or Automaton Speaking Figures. He will also give various Acoustic Illusions in imitation of Birds, Bees, Saw, Pig, &c., &c. objects animate and inanimate, to show the difference between the art of imitating sounds and the powers of Ventriloquism. After which he will introduce the much admired Conversing Spectator.

In May 1841 he and a Miss Wyman (possibly a daughter or sister), "the celebrated magician 15 years of age," were on the stage again at what was now called the Baltimore Museum. Admission was 50 cents. The show was popular and continued until early autumn, after which the duo went to Harrington's New Museum at 76 Court Street in Boston, in the building that earlier housed the New England Museum. New experiments and "costly apparatus" were featured. Admission was 25 cents. The two Wymans returned to Baltimore where they finished out the year and continued into 1842. They were very popular there and consistently played to a full house, according to the Baltimore *Sun*.

Wyman enjoyed playing jokes. In a Baltimore hotel he saw a man raise a glass to his lips to sip a julep. All of a sudden a dog barked and growled at his heels. The patron turned but saw nothing, but then heard a voice coming from the julep glass, "I am rum, and rum is the devil." The man dropped the glass. Score one for the temperance movement![1]

In 1843 he appeared in various venues without mention of Miss Wyman, including an extended stay in Charleston, South Carolina, which continued to be a favorite stop in later years. Talking automaton figures were part of the program which also included magic tricks and illusions. In Baltimore in May of that year he engaged in discussions with as many as four different voices coming from various points in the theater.

In the mid-1840s and continuing for years afterward Wyman was a regular at P.T. Barnum's American Museum in New York City. Other popular venues included Newark, Baltimore, Washington, and other cities in the area. Mr. Sutton, Mr. Haskell, and other ventriloquists toured in the same era, but none were as popular as Wyman.

Wyman the Wizard.

The magician's tricks off the stage made news now and again, as when Wyman saw a man about to cut into a watermelon on a cart in front of a hotel in Philadelphia. As he was about to take his first poke the melon shrieked, "Oh, murder! You kill me!" With that the owner dropped the melon and ran from the cart as Wyman walked quietly away.[2]

In another instance Wyman was walking down the street when a jockey approached him, trying to sell a pony. Wyman asked how old the horse was. "Seven last spring," was the reply, whereupon the horse spoke up: "Oh, what a lie! I am thirteen and you know it as well as I do."[3]

In spring 1851 he was on stage in Bleecker Hall in Albany, where his stand was continued into early May, with "positively the last" appearance advertised for Saturday the 3rd. As was true for other itinerant performances he was "held over" if admissions continued to be satisfactory. During the next several years his show continued to attract excellent audiences.

Counterstamped Coins

In autumn 1854 Wyman added "the Wizard" to his name, and continued it for years afterward. During this decade he counterstamped a number of Spanish-American silver two-real coins with WYMAN THE WIZARD, which could be spent at the door to gain admission. At the time the Spanish coins were more plentiful in circulation than were Liberty Seated quarters of equivalent value.

At the Hibernian Hall in Charleston in December 1855 "For Nine Nights Only" Wyman's "Soirees Fantastiques" promised many novel and humorous acts in exchange for 25 cents, the usual admission, On August 7, 1856, P.T. Barnum advertised in the *New York Tribune* that at his American Museum in New York City it was the:

Fourth and last week of that remarkably popular and successful artist, Wyman the Wizard, who will present his amazing feats and experiments every afternoon and evening at 3 and 7½ o'clock, besides his exquisite Ventriloquial Scenes in 8 voices, his life-moving figures, &c.

On August 30 in the same paper Barnum advertised that it was "Positively and unequivocally the last week of that great artist, Wyman the Wizard." This time it seems that the artist moved on, for a few days later in the *Newark Daily Advertiser* this notice appeared:

Wyman
The Wizard and Ventriloquist

With his life moving and speaking automatons at Library Hall, Fair Week, Wyman has lots of new and wonderful tricks—the disappearance of a man—suspension of a boy in the air—the spirit rapping drum—electric chair—inexhaustible bottle, and many others.

From there he went to Baltimore where he appeared at Peale's Museum, then to Richmond on October 13 to start a three-week stand. He then went back to Washington, where he remained until March. His show provoked "uncontrollable laughter," advertisements promised.

P.T. Barnum's American Museum (in the distance, left of center), New York City's most popular tourist attraction, was a frequent venue for Wyman the Wizard. (Currier & Ives)

In the summers of 1857 and 1858 he was back at Barnum's American Museum, and in the same years he was a regular at Peale's Museum in Baltimore and other venues in that area. The Illuminated Mystic Temple was among his new attractions. In 1857 he assisted in an investigation of the Fox sisters, Leah, Margaret, and Kate, who had attracted attention nationwide in an era in which spiritualism had many advocates. By "spirit rapping," in which an unseen presence made rapping noises on a table, they could receive messages from long-departed souls, answer questions, and do other superhuman things. In connection with the *Boston Courier* and several Harvard professors, he posed questions to the Fox girls for which they could not give answers. However, the popularity of the spiritualists continued unabated.

In 1858 it was reported that Wyman had made an arrangement with Barnum to travel through Europe for the next five years.[4] However, in ensuing summers he was back in New York City at the American Museum and with engagements in Washington vicinity. On October 20, 1860, the *Richmond Whig* announced that his 20th annual visit to the city was about to take place.

A Typical Entertainment

An advertisement in the *Hartford Courant,* October 16, 1862, described his current show:

Allyn Hall

Four Nights

Commencing Monday,
October 27th

WYMAN The Unequalled Magician and Ventriloquist. New and Wonderful Experiments.

Everybody is astonished at the amusing and wonderful performances of Wyman the Wizard and Ventriloquist, Professor of Physical and Mechanical Sciences, who will appear every afternoon at 3 o'clock and every evening at 8 o'clock, in his brilliantly Illuminated Magic Temple of Witchcraft, Fascination, and Delusion.

He will be assisted by his splendid apparatus and other implements of Equivocation and Deceit clothed in inscrutable mystery, and yet so beautifully executed as to defy the closest investigation.

The Programme will be varied each evening, selected from the following extraordinary feats:

The Famous Crystal Casket. Mysterious Cabinet. Mystic Scrap Book. The Cauldron Fantastique. The Electric Watches. Mechanical Amalgam. Le Chapeau Prolifique. Mysterious Laundry. Dove Sprite. Filtration. Celebrated Gun Feat. Great Bank Note Feat. Miraculous Restoration. Le Casquet Du Diable. Inexhaustible Bottle.

These feats will appear incredible to the sense, impossible to the eye, and improbable to the imagination. They will bewilder the one, elude the other, and defy the whole. Including Changes, Transformations, Secret Manipulations, Ocular Deceptions, Passes, and *Necromantic Illusions!*

Consisting of Dissolution! Reproduction! Separation! And Re-Union! Of an infinity of objects belonging to the Company combining the rapidity of motion and its imperceptible effects on the observer, illustrating the Arts and Mysteries of the Ancient Magicians, Hindoo and Brahmin Astrologers, Egyptian Sorcerers, Indian Jugglers, and the marvels of the Eastern Magiis of old.

During the evening Mr. Wyman will perform his Ventroquilism which will embrace Novel Scenes, Humorous Dialogues, Laughable Incidents, Imitations, &c. Illustrating the Wonderful Power of the Human Voice. The Exhibition closing with

*Wyman's Laughable
Life-Moving Figures!*

Which are exhibited in the following order: The Polander, The Ball Tosser, Harry Helm, Polka Party, Somebody or Nobody, Old Dan Tucker, Madam Metamorphoses, Comical Joe in his Great Act of Horsemanship.

Mr. Wyman will be assisted at each Entertainment by the wonderful blind pianist Mr. Michael McCarty, who has been blind from infancy. The brilliancy of his performances upon the Piano Forte has been highly commended by the press and applauded by the public whenever he has appeared.

In addition to the unparalleled excellence of the Entertainment, the Manager will give to his patrons a magnificent Hallett & Davis full Grand Piano Forte (to be seen at Messrs. L. Barker & Co.'s Music Store) worth $750! One rich Red Black Silk Dress Pattern worth $30; one Double-Face Green Brocade Dress Pattern worth $25; one Purple Moiré Antique $35; one pattern Blue Irish Poplin $23; one pattern brown Irish Poplin $28. These splendid gifts are to be seen in the windows of Messrs C.S. Weatherby & Cp. Also, Twelve New Style Hats (Monitors) at Mr. L. Daniels' new store.

Notwithstanding the great expense attending the exhibition and the large sum expended in the purchase of the Presents enumerated above, the manager is confident that by placing the price of admission within the reach of all his success will justify the confidence he has in an appreciative public.

Prices of Admission

Single admission, 25 cts.; Four Tickets admitting four persons or one person four times with a numbered ticket—giving the holder a share in the presents, $1. Children under 12 years, 15 cents.

The Gifts will be distributed on the evening of the Fourth Day, Thursday.

A committee will be selected by the audience at each entertainment who take charge of the distribution. Not more than 2,000 numbered tickets will be given out. It will not be necessary for persons who attend the first of the entertainments to be present at the distribution of gifts.

Single tickets do not share in the gifts.

The Grand Piano to be given away will be played at each performance.

Tickets for sale at Messrs Barker & Co.'s and Brown & Gross. Seats can be secured without extra charge.

Doors open at 7. Commence at 8 o'clock.

This advertisement was coded "oct 16 tfd," reflecting that it was run daily beginning on October 16 "till forbid" or canceled. Thus Wyman's stint in Hartford was open-ended, until audiences diminished.

Continuing Performances

In early autumn 1863 the entertainer was on stage at the Odd Fellows' Hall in Washington, a familiar venue he had played many times before. Wyman had great staying power, and patrons returned year after year to re-experience their favorite scenes and to enjoy new ones. On at least four different occasions he gave private performances at the White House for President Abraham Lincoln and his family.[5]

During the Civil War he traveled to various Northern cities with stands in Boston, Milwaukee, New York, and other venues, mostly on the East Coast. In the late 1860s and early 1870s he traveled extensively in Dixie, including New Orleans, where he played to packed houses, according to press notices.

The distribution of gifts was expanded to include at least something for everyone in the audience. These ranged from lithographed scenes to combs and other small articles of nominal value. In addition some watches, table sets, and other larger gifts were distributed in limited numbers to certain lucky ticket holders. Performances continued until at least 1874. An article on illusions published in 1876 referred to Wyman the Wizard in the past tense, stating that in one of his acts he used to draw from a small carrying case a series of trunks ever increasing in size, up to a large Saratoga trunk of the type used to carry a season's clothing and supplies by rail.

Wyman never claimed mysterious or occult powers and thus was never "exposed," although his tricks were analyzed. His specialty as advertised comprised magic and illusions—great fun for all!

He lived in Baltimore, Washington, and, for a long time in Philadelphia. In his final years he resided in Burlington, New Jersey.

His books told of his trade, including *Wyman's Hand-Book of Magic* (1850) and *Jokes and Anecdotes of Wyman, the Magician & Ventriloquist* (1866). In 1860 he published and distributed *Ventriloquism Made Easy, Also, an Exposure of Magic, and the Second Sight Mystery,* author being Ebenezer Locke Mason Jr., who at the time was on the cusp of becoming one of Philadelphia's leading rare-coin dealers (I discuss him in chapter 27).

Wyman passed to his eternal reward on July 31, 1881, in Burlington, New Jersey, and was buried in the Oak Grove Cemetery in Fall River, Massachusetts.

CHAPTER 15

In 1997 my American Coin Hoards and Treasures *book was published. It sold widely and was reprinted. Ever since then I have been keeping a "Treasures Book 2" file, which I may use someday. Meanwhile, I revisit one of my favorite scenarios. Of the various topics in my first book, the Randall Hoard is one of the most often referenced.*

Revisiting the Randall Hoard

Information Not Widely Known

When I was a young coin dealer in the 1950s, Mint State large copper cents of the 1816 to 1820 years were easy to find, especially those dated 1818 and 1820, the most plentiful of all. The reason for their availability was not widely known at the time, although Walter Breen had written about them in "Survey of American Coin Hoards," in the January 1952 number of *The Numismatist*. Monthly magazines being what they were and are, this and articles on other subjects were forgotten soon after publication. Most collectors I knew in the early 1950s had either not read the article or didn't remember it. Accordingly, availability of all of those bright-red (with some spots) cents of a few particular years was a mystery to many, including those who had them for sale.

Reference books on American coins were few and far between, with hardly any published in recent years. The annual red-covered *Guide Book of United States Coins,* a new edition of which came out each summer, was the one-volume "library" of most collectors. The *Standard Catalogue of United States Coins,* published by Wayte Raymond, was issued sporadically and had certain information not in the *Guide Book,* so I had both and read each from cover to cover. I was an exception.

I was fond of large copper cents and maintained a nice inventory of them. Among my sources was Charles "Suitcase" Foster, who lived in Rushville, New York, wherever that is, and came to Empire State Numismatic Association and other shows in the East. He carried his inventory in one or more suitcases and always had a nice supply of 1818 and 1820 cents. I would buy a half dozen or more of each for several dollars each, then restock the next time I saw him.

One day I was visiting Honesdale, Pennsylvania, the town of my birth, when I was contacted by an elderly lady who invited me to come to her home to see her family's coin collection. On her dining-room table she laid out many coins, including piles of 1816 to 1820 cents stacked like poker chips! There were perhaps a hundred or more all told. Some invoices revealed that these and most others had been purchased from Philadelphia dealer Henry Chapman in the 1910s. They hadn't been examined since. I asked if I could buy at least some them and was told that the time would come, but not yet. The time never did come, and I don't know where they are now.

Today there are no such groups remaining, so far as I know. Individual coins appear with frequency, especially those of 1818 and 1820, less often for 1816 and not frequently for 1817 either. The 1819 cents are less scarce. Now a Mint State 1818 or 1820 is a candidate for a color illustration in an auction catalog! I could never have imagined such a thing when I first started in business.

Discovery of the Randall Hoard

While notices about the Randall Hoard differ in some details, it seems to be the consensus that a *small* wooden keg (or perhaps more than one keg) filled with Uncirculated copper cents was found beneath a railroad station platform in Georgia after the Civil War, but before autumn 1869. Or were they buried in the ground?

The cents may have been hidden during the 1861 to 1865 Civil War to prevent discovery, per some stories. Even then, Mint State coins would have been unusual as most had been redeemed by the Treasury Department. If they had been stored beneath a railroad platform, that would date the deposit no earlier than the 1830s, as there were no railroads in the South before then. Alternatively, the hoard may have had nothing to do with any railroad platform. And were the coins really found in the South?

As usual with coin hoards, facts are scarce. One reason is that hoards are often found on property belonging to someone else. Another is that the discoverer avoids publicity because mentioning large quantities of previously rare coins might depress the market. However, that was not the case here.

Before the Hoard

In 1859 in his *American Numismatical Manual,* Dr. Montroville W. Dickeson wrote of cents of various years, but at this time the Randall Hoard was not known, nor would it be until after the Civil War. Thus, in 1859 the 1820 cent was viewed as being rare. The Dickeson work has many errors and a lot of guesswork, but some of the information may be relevant. Extracts from Dickeson:

> 1816 cent: They are quite plenty, and can be procured looking as fresh as when they first came from the Mint.

> 1817: The metal of which they were composed is well milled and very hard, which protects the face of the coin. They are hence in a good state of preservation.

> 1818: Plenty and well preserved.

> 1819: Equally plenty, and in good order with the preceding emission out.

> 1820: The slight milling of the edges of these coins renders good specimens difficult to be obtained.[1]

What the Hoard Contained

The knowledge we have today of the Randall Hoard is due in large part to the publication in 1869 of an answer to a correspondent. Ebenezer Locke Mason Jr., Philadelphia coin and stamp dealer (of whom more is told in chapter 27), published this in his magazine, supposedly advice to a reader, L.M., who had sent an inquiry:

L.M. Troy. Beware of bright pennies of old dates. Buy them as restrikes, but not as originals. We can send 1816, 1817, 1818, 1819 (large and small dates) and 1820 U.S. cents for 25 cents each, or fair ones for 2 cents each.

If there is one characteristic Mason seems to have had in short supply it is truthfulness.

This evoked a response from veteran dealer Edward D. Cogan, who wrote this to Dr. Charles E. Anthon, for publication in the *American Journal of Numismatics*. The date was January 11, 1870:

My Dear Sir:—

When I presented to our Society, through my friend Mr. Betts, at the last meeting, the cents of 1817, '18, '19, and '20, I did so upon the full conviction that they were from the issues of the U.S. Mint, struck in the years of which they bear the date. Judge, then, of my surprise to find in Mason & Co.'s magazine, of this month, a caution against buying these pieces as being re-strikes.

I believe all these pieces were purchased of Mr. J. Swan Randall, of Norwich, in the state of New York, and I immediately wrote to this gentleman, asking him whether he had any idea of their having been re-struck from the original die, and herewith I send his reply, which exculpates him from having reason to believe that he was offering anything but original pieces; and from his statement I must say I believe them—as I have from the time I purchased them—to have been

struck at the Mint in the years of their respective dates.

Yours faithfully,

Edward Cogan.

Randall's letter, datelined Norwich, January 7, 1870:

Edward Cogan, Esq.
Dear Sir:—

I should not sell coins that I knew or believed to be re-strikes without letting it be known. The bright, Uncirculated cents I have sold of 1817, 1818, 1819, 1820, and 1825, I am very sure *are not re-strikes*. I bought them of Wm. H. Chapman & Co., dry goods merchants of this village, and the head of the firm, W.H.C., informed me that he got them of a wholesale merchant in New York, who informed him that he got them from a merchant in Georgia; that he took them as a payment on a debt, and that the Georgia merchant wrote him that they were found since the war in Georgia buried in the earth.

Mr. Chapman said to me that he was in New York about the time the cents were received there, and that the merchant who had (ditto) thought they were too large to use, and did not know what to do with them; and that he (Chapman) thinking that his customers here would be pleased with bright cents, offered ninety cents a hundred for them, which was immediately taken.

Chapman & Co. commenced paying them out here, and their bright appearance and old dates made many think they were counterfeits, and they were called "Chapman's counterfeits," and the firm stopped paying them out.

I then went to the store and asked W.H. Chapman if he had disposed of many of his bright cents. He replied, "No. I made a bad bargain," and laughed about their being regarded as his counterfeits.

I then offered to take them at the price he paid—ninety cents a hundred—and he was very willing to let me have them. They were loose together in a small keg,[2] and the great mass of them were of 1818; and a great many, though apparently Uncirculated, were more or less corroded or discolored. I enclose herewith one of the 1817 and 1818, discolored on one side and bright on the other, From this statement, you will see that there can be very little doubt about their being the genuine issues of the United States Mint of their respective dates.

Very respectfully,

John Swan Randall

So much for the "railroad platform" story! Randall's memory seems to have been faulty, for the date distribution differs from the years Mason wrote about

and that are generally attributed to the hoard today.

Randall passed to his final reward on January 1, 1878, without passing any information that would allow the Georgia finder to be interviewed. Shortly thereafter, on May 6 through 9, 1878, Edward D. Cogan offered the remaining coins at auction, comprising 85 pieces dated 1817, 1,464 of 1818, 67 of 1819, and 500 "various dates," presumably including many dated 1820. This shows that cents of 1816 were either sold by that time or were not possessed by Cogan.

Hoard Cents in Later Years

The typical specimen seen today with a Randall Hoard pedigree is a mixture of bright original red with flecks and stains of deep brown or black. Few if any are pristine (uncleaned, undipped) full mint red.

According to Walter Breen's research sponsored by Wayte Raymond in the 1950s, the most readily available variety attributable to the Randall Hoard is 1818 Newcomb 10, followed by 1820 N-13.[3] Curiously, both of these varieties are usually seen with die breaks linking the stars and date. Then, follow in descending order of rarity, the 1817 N-14, the 1816 N-2, and the 1819 N-9 and N-8 are encountered.

However, by 1988 Breen revised his thoughts and stated that 1816 N-2 and 1819 N-9, although traditionally ascribed to this hoard, were from other groups, and that the Randall hoard included specimens of 1825 N-9.[4] Inasmuch as a few 19th-century commentaries did not mention 1816, but did include 1825, perhaps this is nearer the truth, but who knows?

Perhaps if Agatha Christie were alive she could sort the clues and figure it out!

Alden Scott Boyer, who began collecting coins at the age of six, is a poster example of an enthusiast for whom coins and numismatics enhanced his long life.

The Many Interests of Alden Scott Boyer

Boyer on the Numismatic Scene

Alden Scott Boyer in 1921.

Among the numismatic personalities from the past one of my favorites is Alden Scott Boyer. It is unusual for me to begin a tribute with an obituary, but in this instance the memorial to him printed in *The Numismatist* in September 1953 covers a lot of interesting things I might not have otherwise mentioned:

In Memoriam

Alden Scott Boyer
(1887–1953)

The sudden passing of Alden Scott Boyer, at his office, on June 16, 1953, was a shock to his family, friends, and associates. He was a well-known manufacturing chemist and an ardent lifelong collector. To me, a friendship that was mutual, understanding, and enjoyable, is now stilled.

His devoted service to collecting and collectors was an inherent and profound characteristic. He lived in an aura of collecting, beginning in childhood with baby ribbons, advertising picture postcards and tobacco tags. Alden regularly advanced into numismatics by studying and collecting Revolutionary period currency, encased postage, and fractional and large specie currencies. And, lastly, his final numismatic collecting was concentrated on classical Greek ancients.

Along with being a consummate collector, Alden Boyer was one of the Chicago Coin Club founding members and served as its president 1919–1927. He was elected to the American Numismatic Association general secretary office 1921–1922, first vice president 1925–1930, and to the presidency for 1932–1933.

Alden Scott Boyer was born in Cresco, Iowa on January 29, 1887, of an American mother, Cora Fobes Boyer, and a French father, M. Albert Boyer, who migrated from Valley Field, Quebec, Canada, to Hiawatha, Iowa in 1860. He graduated from Northwestern School of Pharmacy in 1908. He married Marie Gunderson of St. Ansgar, Iowa, in 1909, and lived in Reeder, North Dakota until 1912. His enthusiasm for analytic chemistry led the Boyers to move to Chicago in 1912 where he established the Boyer Chemical Company and in 1923 set up a French cosmetic division,

The Society Perfumeur in Paris.

Together the Boyers, Marie and Alden, became universally known as collectors, Marie, with her lectures on romance of perfumes, daguerreotypes and laces, and Alden, on the romance of photography, mechanical music, bicycles, wooden Indians, books, old silver, and coins. The more than forty years of this matchless collecting team ceased with Marie's passing on May 1, 1950. The A.N.A. was saddened by that event. On July 8, 1950, he married Elizabeth Marie Johnson of Hamilton, Ohio.

Alden Scott Boyer can no longer take an active part in future collecting activities, but what he accomplished in his active years will be felt and appreciated by those who may strive to fill the tremendous void that his passing has made obvious.

He is survived by his widow, Elizabeth Marie Johnson Boyer, and a sister, Helen Boyer Horton of Pittsburgh, Pennsylvania. Interment was at Hamilton, Ohio.

Boyer the Numismatist

By the late 1910s he and his wife Marie were well known on the collecting scene in Chicago. Alden could write and talk about numismatics from ancient times down to the latest Mint issues. He was a close friend of Virgil M. Brand's, whose numismatic interest and knowledge were parallel to his—except that Brand, a bachelor, ate, slept, and dreamed coins, far and away the most important part of his life. On the other hand, Boyer, whose business became increasingly profitable, enjoyed many aspects of life and traveled widely, often to France in connection with his business and where at one time he and his wife resided. He was known to lapse into speaking French while attending coin-club meetings—probably reflective of his sense of humor.

Marie was an avid collector in her own right, as noted above. During the American Numismatic Association convention in Chicago in August 1920, attended by about 75 members, Marie hosted 14 ladies at the Boyer home at 201 East Chestnut Street, providing a program of music and entertainment. At the time Alden was president of the Chicago Coin Club. At the 1920 convention Samuel W. Brown, of North Tonawanda, New York, displayed five Liberty Head nickels dated 1913, the year that the Buffalo nickel was introduced to replace the older design. Brown was interested in numismatics and in 1908 attended the ANA convention in Philadelphia, where he worked at the Mint. As there is no official record that any 1913 Liberty Head nickels were ever struck, it is presumed that he made them for his own account. In 1920 he was endeavoring to find buyers, but without success. He gave one to Boyer to contemplate, but no interest was shown. Not long afterward Brown wrote this:

> Dear Mr. Boyer
> I would appreciate it very much if you would return the 1913 Liberty Head nickel you have with your coins in the Masonic Temple vault in your city. I have a deal pending for the sale of this coin, and it is necessary that I have it within the next 10 days. If you will, kindly send it by express, charges collect, and estimate the value at $750. Thanking you for your courtesy in this matter.

Soon afterward, five 1913 Liberty Head nickels were in the hands of Stephen K. Nagy, of Philadelphia, one of the more mysterious figures in numismatics at the time. I interviewed Nagy several times in the 1950s, and he regaled me with stories about his handling of rarities, restrikes, and more. At one time he

COLOR PLATE XIII

Lot 807
The Fabulous 1913
Liberty Head Nickel
Finest Known

The Eliasberg Collection 1913 Liberty Head nickel was auctioned by the author in 1996. It was the first rare coin ever to cross the million-dollar mark. Shown is the catalog plate.

his effort to sell copies of the *Star Rare Coin Encyclopedia,* a premiums-paid guide, for a dollar.

After Green's death his holdings were widely dispersed. Many of the coins went to Stack's in New York City, who sold to many clients, including King Farouk of Egypt. The five nickels went to Eric P. Newman in St. Louis in the early 1940s. Newman in time became recognized as one of America's leading numismatic scholars, earning more Heath Literary Award medals from the ANA than anyone else in history. He sold the nickels one by one.

The finest of them, and the only one with a deep Proof surface, went into the Louis E. Eliasberg Collection. In 1996 I was auctioneer at the podium when that coin sold for $1,585,000 the first coin in history to break the million-dollar mark.

Back to our main subject: Mr. Boyer. For much of the 1920s to *The Numismatist* he contributed a monthly column, "A Little News from Alden Scott Boyer," which always contained interesting items.

Boyer formed several different collections. When the challenge of finding new things faded, he passed the items on to others and began a new specialty. His first major endeavor was colonial paper money. This went to the Ludger Gravel Museum in Montreal, Canada. Then followed obsolete bank notes issued from the 1790s to the early 1860s, continuing into federal paper money from 1861 onward. This large and important collection was consigned to B. Max Mehl, the Fort Worth, Texas, dealer who sold it to James M. Wade of New York City. Years later the Wade Collection was bought by Aubrey and Adeline Bebee, leading dealers in Omaha, who in time donated it to the American Numismatic Association Museum in Colorado Springs, where it remains an attraction today.

had a 1926-S $10 gold piece, he said, acquired from the Philadelphia Mint, where the dies for San Francisco coinage were made. Today such a variety is unknown.

Regarding the 1913 nickels, they later found a buyer in Colonel Edward H.R. Green, son of the famous millionaire miser Hetty Green, memorialized as the "Witch of Wall Street." Edward lived profligately on the family fortune, collected everything from pornography to antique wooden whaling ships, and owned the 100-stamp sheet of 1918 inverted 24¢ "Jenny" airmail stamps and one of the finest cabinets of rare coins ever assembled. He died in 1936. By the late 1930s the 1913 Liberty Head nickel had become one of the most famous American rarities, due in large part in its use in a nationwide advertising campaign by B. Max Mehl in

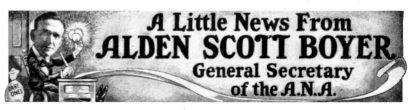

A Little News From
ALDEN SCOTT BOYER,
General Secretary
of the A.N.A.

Masthead of Boyer's popular column in *The Numismatist.*

Coin-Operated Devices

In the 1930s Boyer became an avid collector of antique mechanical musical instruments, particularly those with a coin slot, but extending to others as well. In 1938 he announced the opening of the Chicago Coin Device Museum of Old Coin Controlled Machines and Automatic Musical Instruments in Boyer Building No. 1 at 2700 Wabash Avenue and with additional displays at Building No. 6 at 2701 Wabash Avenue.[1]

To visitors he gave a souvenir card, "Music Box: A Short Story about 'The Regina,' 'Queen of Music,' Music Box of 1886, by Alden Scott Boyer." The text began:

> The Regina was the most popular musical instrument in America in its day, and its makers made a fortune. The Regina preceded phonographs and was invented in 1886.
>
> In around 1896 every home in America that could afford one had a Regina music box in the parlor. The more modest homes had the square table models that cost $100 to $150, while the homes of the rich had large models costing from $465 to $1,000, a tremendous price in that day. The Regina with its changeable tune discs killed the Swiss cylinder music box business overnight, because with a Regina there was no end to the music library that one could buy and play. . . .[2]

In 1939 he sent a letter to potential owners of machines, such as makers of coin-operated devices and route operators, noting in part:

> Offer us any of these you have— broken or complete—in any condition:

A Style H orchestrion made in Chicago in the teen years by the J.P. Seeburg Piano Co. Alden Scott Boyer was the first large-scale collector of music boxes, coin-operated pianos, orchestrions, and related devices. Today the pursuit involves thousands of enthusiasts in America.

> Any old nickel-in-the-slot pianos—Pianos with drums—Music boxes—Automatic violins—Automatic banjos—Slot machine pianos—Race horse pianos—Profit sharing pianos (or their rolls)—Made by Regina, Wurlitzer, Resotone, Mills, Seeburg, Nelson-Wiggen, etc.

By 1941 he had two full-time technicians at work restoring and maintaining his treasures.[3] The museum grew to include many other items ranging from cigar-store Indians to gold ingots from the American West. After Boyer's passing at the age of 66 on June 16, 1953, his collection was dispersed by private sales to interested buyers. For many years I have searched for a description of the ingots in particular, for very few numismatists had such things. Their nature remains a mystery today.

A rarity among early American tokens, this is a ticket to ride on the first horse-drawn railroad in New York State and one of the earliest in America. Fewer than 100 such pieces are believed to exist today.

Take a Ride on the New York & Harlem Railroad

An Early Rail Line

The earliest type of New York & Harlem Railroad car.

Among the earliest of American transportation tokens are the little octagonal pieces bearing on one side a coach on wheels and on the other an inscription. These trace their origin to the New York & Harlem Railroad, or *Harlaem* as it is spelled on the token. More properly it could be called a street railway. The motive energy was not by a steam engine, at least not at first, but by horsepower in the literal sense of the word. Each coach was drawn by two trusty steeds hitched to the front. Running on steel rails, it was certainly the first such line in New York State and one of the earliest in America.

The enterprise was incorporated as the New-York & Harlem Railroad on April 25, 1831, to link Harlem, a fine farming and residential district, with the lower reaches of Manhattan. Among the incorporators was John Mason, the president of the Chemical Bank and a well-to-do land owner whose name was lettered on the side of the first car put into service. Mordecai Noah, a journalist, playwright, and diplomat, was another principal. Others were engaged in such pursuits as law and sales, and some owned land in Harlem and stood to benefit from the connection.

A route was chosen along the eastern side of Manhattan as it was thought that the rise of steamship commerce on the Hudson River on the western side might present unfavorable competition. It was planned that in Harlem passengers could connect with the New York & Albany Railroad to go farther north, but this arrangement never materialized.

The coaches were designed by John Stephenson. Ground breaking took place on February 23, 1832, in the Murray Hill district near 4th Avenue. Progress was made in stages. The first section was opened on November 26, 1832, and carried passengers along the Bowery—the main area in the city for entertainment—from Prince Street north to 14th Street. Construction proceeded apace, and on June 10, 1833, it was open to the north along Fourth Avenue up to 32nd Street. On May 9, 1834, the line was

opened north to Yorkville, including through the Murray Hill Tunnel. Next came development continuing on Fourth Avenue to Harlem, including via the Yorkville Tunnel, opened to passengers on October 27, 1837. In that year steam locomotives burning wood were introduced but were limited to operating only on the northern section of the tracks above 23rd Street, as they were forbidden in the Manhattan commercial district. Then followed the opening on May 4, 1839, of tracks farther south through the Bowery, Broome Street, to City Hall and Park Row.

Tokens for a Ride

The finest of the 14 tokens in the John J. Ford, Jr. Collection. The B & S initials represent Bale & Smith, New York engravers and minters. (enlarged)

Tokens good for a ride were ordered from Bale & Smith, who signed them B & S on the obverse. This firm was composed of James Bale and Frederick Smith at 16 Maiden Lane, by 1834 successors to Wright & Bale at the same address. From 1835 to 1838 the firm was at 68 Nassau Street, then at 96 Fulton Street until well into the 1840s. In numismatics the tokens are part of the Hard Times series, loosely defined as from 1832

to 1844. Perhaps as many as a hundred of the New York & Harlem tokens are known today, in nickel alloy and usually weakly struck on the obverse due to the hardness of the metal. These must have been well used

Another famous and highly desired token is the Carry Me to Atwood's Hotel three-cent pass, also made by Bale & Smith. The hotel was located at the terminus of the line as of November 1832, when the first stretch of rail was opened. Information regarding the operation of the hotel remains elusive.

in their time, as most examples show significant wear. The John J. Ford, Jr. Collection auctioned in 2013 had a remarkable, indeed unprecedented, group of 14 pieces, only two of which could claim to be well struck, one of which is illustrated here.[1]

The expansion of the railroad was not without difficulty, including lawsuits. Not everyone agreed that coaches on rails were a good idea running along routes traveled by pedestrians and other horse-drawn vehicles. This was overcome in part by recessing the rails slightly below the level of the street, so as not to interfere with other traffic. In later years the line was blended into others. In one form or another the Harlem name was used for decades afterward.

CHAPTER 18

Minstrel Shows

A minstrel-show poster of the 1840s.

There are numismatic connections to virtually all elements of American entertainment including, as here, minstrelsy.

Show This Coin,
See the Minstrel Show

Minstrel shows, closely related to vaudeville shows, were a popular form of entertainment in America during the 19th century. In the early days, from the 1830s to the Civil War, most troupes consisted of several white performers in blackface, imitating Negroes (as African-Americans were usually referred to) in comic routines, skits, jokes, songs, and other entertainment. The performers were often referred to as "Ethiopian delineators." Black people were parodied as being carefree, superstitious, and gullible—as easily fooled. Music was played on the banjo, fiddle (violin), and other instruments, with the tambourine and clacking bones often added.

Jump Jim Crow was a song-and-dance routine performed by Thomas Dartmouth Rice in the late 1820s and 1830s. The melody became famous nationally, and, years later, "Jim Crow" became a synonym for a black person who behaved differently and was subjected to different rules than were whites. As little was needed in the way of props or equipment, and as a typical performing company had fewer than a half dozen people, shows could be given on short notices in many different venues. The typical program appealed to young and old alike.

As time went on, shows became more sophisticated, and troupes included props and backdrops and a half dozen or more performers who often satirized popular plays, gave fake political speeches, imitated famous people, and devised other scenarios. Music ranged from popular favorites such as Stephen Foster melodies, to *Dixie* (first performed in the North in the late 1850s), to show songs and spirituals. In the era before the popularity of Harriet Beecher Stowe's 1852 book, *Uncle Tom's Cabin*, minstrelsy gave white theater audiences a humorous view of life on Southern plantations and the comic fun and games of life there.

Gradually, minstrelsy became mainstream and some troupes were booked into large theaters and opera houses. Later shows in the North were criticized by abolitionists as falsely representing Blacks as a happy-go-lucky lot and ignoring the reality of the trials and tribulations of slavery. Although minstrel shows continued into the 20th century, the genre was largely replaced by vaudeville, which might include a blackface act or two but did not center on plantation life.

Several minstrel troupes advertised by counterstamping coins—usually Spanish-American silver two-real coins which were legal tender in America until 1859 and traded for 25 cents. These were stamped in large numbers and could be used as admission tickets. Several such troupes are discussed here.

Geo. Christy and Wood's Minstrels

In 1851 Henry Wood (whose brother, Fernando, would later be elected mayor of New York City) leased a 1,600-seat theater at 444 Broadway, a venue earlier known as Fellows' Opera House. Jerome B. Fellows was his partner. Performances of Wood and Fellows' Minstrels attracted large audiences. Fellows departed in February 1852, after which time the show was known as Wood's Minstrels.

George Christy and Wood's Minstrels advertisement counterstamped on a 1787 two-reales coin.

On October 31, 1853, Wood took as a partner George Christy, who had been in Ethiopian minstrelsy since the early 1840s, and formed the Original George Christy and Wood's Minstrels. The former was stage manager and the latter business manager. The show was given at 8 o'clock every evening. Admission was 25 cents. "This company has no connection with any other" was added to notices, as the Christy name was used elsewhere, such as by E.P. Christy in Christy's Original Minstrels at 472 Broadway, which was well known in the entertainment industry and viewed George Christy and Woods as upstarts not worthy of patronage. There was much enmity between the two Christys played out in print.

Early in the morning of December 20, 1854, fire broke out in the City Assembly Rooms upstairs in Christy and Wood's Minstrel Hall, which also housed J.W. Gray M.D.'s drugs-and-medicines business. The building was heavily damaged but remained standing. The flames spread rapidly and several other buildings were set afire, including the McKinstry carriage manufactory, Lyon's Magnetic Powder depot,[1] Duncomb's Saddlery, and Mix's coach factory.

Henry Wood, owner of the minstrel business, reported a loss of $10,000 to $15,000 with no insurance. Christy lost a wardrobe he had gathered over a period of 20 years. Ironically, Wood had agreed to sell the business for $30,000 on the next Monday, December 25.[2]

Christy and Wood's Minstrels survived, at least for a while, and went on to play in Boston and other venues as well as in a hall at 472 Broadway. Matters worsened, and in March 1856 the troupe's assets were scheduled to be sold at auction.[3]

In any event, Henry Wood remained in control and George Christy continued to direct and participate in the shows. In August 1856 he announced that his Temple of Negro Minstrelsy still known as Christy and Wood's Minstrels would reopen on the 25th of the month at 444 Broadway in restored and enlarged premises, now seating 1,800, an increase of 200 over earlier times. "It is needless to say that we have taken every precaution to guard against fire." A hydrant had been placed "in the centre of the hall, so arranged as to be perceptible to all, with hose attached, so that a full head of water could at any time be turned on by anyone in the vicinity."

In early September 1857 the company performed for 12 nights in Philadelphia to more than 26,000 people. On October 1, 1857, the troupe moved to Wood's Buildings, 561 and 563 Broadway near Prince Street, an edifice known as the Marble Palace. A token was issued showing the building and lettered, "Admit to Wood's Minstrels, 561 & 563 Bd Way, N.Y."[4] In spring 1859 a diorama of a sleigh ride in the city was an added attraction. Each Thursday evening was The Old Night in which old-time melodies were featured. This venue was discontinued on September 3, 1859. Then it was back to 444 Broadway. Not long afterward the program was known simply as Wood's Minstrels. On July 7, 1862, the company moved to 514 Broadway. The business was discontinued about 1866.

Broadway Varieties

Also involving Henry Wood in this era was another show, Broadway Varieties, that had been fitted out in January 1856 in Mechanics Hall at 472 Broadway. Wood was the lessee and owner, and R.G. Marsh was the manager. The venue was called a "miniature theatre." The Marsh Children (as the act was titled) and other youngsters were featured in juvenile skits. To advertise the theater a number of Spanish-American silver two-real coins were counterstamped ADMIT TO / BROADWAY / VARIETIES. Worth 25 cents, these could be used as admission tickets.

Broadway Varieties advertised on a two-reales coin.

Throughout the year the theater earned favorable comments. Business must have been less than desired despite this, for in January 1857 Broadway Varieties was available to rent by the week or the month by applying to Henry Wood. By July the March Children act was playing at Laura Keene's Theatre under the direction of R.G. Marsh.

In 1859 an unrelated Broadway Varieties was set up on the ground floor at 127 Grand Street, the Franklin Museum address but now advertised as two doors from Broadway (instead of one, as before), and billed as "the cheapest amusement in the world," *cheapest* presumably referring to the admission charge of a dime. "Thirty talented performers appear in a miscellaneous variety of entertainment. Novelty and entertainment. Remember the price: ten cents."

Sprague & Blodgett's Georgia Minstrels

Sprague & Blodgett's Georgia Minstrels counterstamp on an 1873 Liberty Seated half dollar.

Sprague & Blodgett's Georgia Minstrels, a later counter-stamper of coins that served as admission tickets, was owned by whites but featured black performers, as did several other "Georgia Minstrels" troupes of the second half of the 19th century. The troupe gave their first known performance in Missouri in 1876. Famous members of the troupe included James Bland, Billy Kersands, and Sam Lucas—meaningless names today, but well-known and deeply appreciated stars in their time.

Sprague's Georgia Minstrels

Sprague's Georgia Minstrels, formerly known as Sprague & Blodgett's Georgia Minstrels, was operated by Z.W. Sprague alone from 1878 to 1880. Sprague was involved with Sprague's Olympic Theatre in Chicago. The troupe toured the West and Midwest and played in Havana in 1878. The company disbanded in 1880.

The *Columbus* (Georgia) *Daily Enquirer* published this on October 12, 1877:

> Atlanta, Ga., October 11.
> Sprague & Blodgett's Georgia Minstrels are no humbug, but a fine company, and are playing here to immense audiences. The most culti-

Show This Coin, See the Minstrel Show

vated and refined ladies of Atlanta attend as there is nothing to offend good taste. They go to Columbus for tomorrow night.

Sidney Herbert

The Canton, Ohio, *Repository* published this on January 21, 1879:

Amusements

Sprague's Georgia Minstrels made their second appearance in Canton at the Opera House last evening to a crowded gallery and comfortably filled circles on the floor below. Since their appearance last season Manager Sprague has reorganized the company, having retained a few of the most meritorious members of the old organization, and added several new and excellent faces and features.

About six weeks ago he returned with the present company from Havana, Cuba, where he played a month's successful engagement at the Lersandi Theatre, under the Orrin Brothers, and while fulfilling this engagement he secured Jose De Sallis, whose violin solo was one of the most prominent features of the show last evening.

Sam Lucas and James Bland, on the ends, were original and funny, the latter reminding us of Dick Goldrick in his quaint way of saying funny things. The orchestra music was very fine, more so, in fact, than the various efforts of the quartette, three of whom are laboring under the effects of severe colds. The performance taken as a whole was very creditable. The company left this morning for Alliance where they play tonight.

This notice was in the Harrisburg, Pennsylvania, *Patriot* on February 27, 1879:

Sprague's Georgia Minstrels

The above named famous minstrel troupe will perform at the Grand Opera House, this city, tonight. The troupe comes here with the endorsement of the press everywhere, that it is a large, first-class combination, which can without hesitation be placed at the head of the minstrel profession. The Buffalo, N.Y. *Courier* gives them a send-off in this style:

"If a solid, hard-working merit an intense desire to please, coupled with sterling talent, is any introduction to public favor, then the Georgias are entitled to a full meed of praise, which they certainly received from the large and delighted audience which gathered at the Academy last evening.

"The entertainment from beginning to end was void of any reprehensible feature and gave every satisfaction. Where all was so fresh and sparkling it would be invidious to specify, but certainly the quartette singing of the troupe was excellent. The laughing song of Warburton and Layton was immense and brought down the house all save a 'hilarious cuss' in the gallery who kept on laughing all through the show until it became somewhat monotonous.

"The orchestral music, especially the cornet playing of Harris, must not be forgotten. The 'Home, Sweet Home' of Layton was the finest trick banjo work we ever saw or heard. On the whole the troupe gave every satisfaction."

After he discovered numismatics in 1966 Harry Bass jumped into the hobby with both feet, aided at the outset by noticing a small star.

Harry W. Bass Jr., Numismatist and Scholar

Connoisseur
Par Excellence

Harry W. Bass Jr.

During my career in numismatics I have had the good fortune to know personally many of the great figures in our hobby. Many still live, but others have passed to their eternal reward.

In our field there are *buyers* who have built collections solely for intended profit, and there are others, a smaller class, who have bought coins, tokens, medals, and paper money and who have made numismatics a central part of their lives. For these the profit has always come naturally—no effort required. In contrast, investors who do not immerse themselves in learning are apt to follow miscellaneous and often bad advice, with mixed results.

In the class of connoisseurs I need but mention Louis E. Eliasberg, Amon Carter Jr., Emery May Holden Norweb, John J. Ford Jr., Oscar G. Schilke, John J. Pittman, and others from the past with whom I have spent time and shared their interests.

Looming large among such great figures is Harry W. Bass Jr., an American numismatic legend.

Harry was a director of the Texas Bank and Trust Company in Dallas. In 1955 a friend of his was seeking some "new" Washington quarters with a D mintmark, struck that year in Denver. He had heard that the mintage was fairly low in the context of the series, and he wanted a few to set aside for the future. Through the bank Harry was able to find a $10-face-value roll containing 40 coins. About 10 years later the same friend encountered Harry and casually remarked that the roll of quarter dollars had performed quite well investment-wise, and that a local coin dealer had offered him $100 for it!

"That captured my attention," Harry later reminisced. "I looked at numismatics being first, perhaps, an investment vehicle."

This was not unusual. The investment potential of coins has always attracted people to the hobby, as has the desire to acquire silver or gold. Many buy coins for such purposes but go no further. Not Harry Bass. He had to learn more.

He subscribed to *Coin World* and *Numismatic News,* joined the American Numismatic Association and the American Numismatic Society, and contacted dealers to get on their mailing lists. In the meantime he bought all of the books, old catalogs, and other printed material he could find.

In May 1966, by which time he already had a fine library, he gave bids to a friend who attended a Paramount International Coin Co. sale held in New Orleans. His very first purchase at auction was an 1876 gold dollar, lot 511. It showed evidence of circulation and was in Extremely Fine grade, one of the lesser-quality pieces known of this scarce date, which when found is likely to be in Mint State. From this inauspicious beginning he went "onward and upward."[1]

A Special 1803 $10 Gold Coin

Among Bass's other acquisitions at the same auction was a $10 gold piece dated 1803. Upon inspecting the coin he was surprised to see what appeared to be a tiny extra star, perhaps from a punch intended to place a star on a half-dime die, embedded in the rightmost cloud above the eagle on the reverse. Seeking more information, he turned to the standard references on hand, including *A Guide Book of United States Coins* and then to a monograph on early $10 coins written by America's leading scholar at the time, Walter Breen. Unbelievably, although this particular die was described, the curious 14th star had not been noticed! Harry had made his first major numismatic discovery, a eureka! moment, the precursor to many that would follow.

The coin business was in a slump at the time. The bull market that began in 1960 with the influx of hundreds of thousands of new buyers ran out of energy in 1964 and was licking its wounds by the year that Harry stepped in as a buyer.

The 1966 ANA Convention in Chicago began on Monday, August 15, with Professional Numismatists Guild Day, a dealer bourse to which collectors, including Harry W. Bass Jr., were sent private invitations, reflecting a rapidly expanding recognition of him as a coin buyer. At the show the auction was conducted by veteran dealer Abe Kosoff. A later report told this:

> Half cents and large cents went above estimates in most instances and patterns were very active with prices frequently higher than Judd's listing. Paper money was spotty, sometimes active, sometimes dull.
>
> U.S. gold went below expectations although good prices were realized for

a number of the highlights. A new record of $6,100 was set for the 1907 eagle with periods and rolled edge. Choice type coins went very well, the 1795 half dime fetching $850; a 1796 dime, $2,325; 1805 dime, $675; a 1796 quarter, AU, at $4,100; 1807 quarter, gem, at $1,500; and an 1831 Small Letters variety quarter at $410 must be a new world's record by far.

An 1848 "CAL" quarter eagle fetched $3,850 and the 1862 over 1 quarter eagle went for $2,600. An 1879 Stella at $5,100 was reasonable. The 1873 Proof $3 gold fetched $3,300, the $20 gold of 1929 went for $1,600, and the 1931 for $1,750.[2]

The 1803 eagle that caused a lot of excitement when Harry Bass found a tiny stray 14th star on the rightmost cloud on the reverse.

It continued to be a buyer's market, which was very pleasing to Harry. A consummate businessman, investor, and planner, he would rather buy in a "down" market than in a rising one, a contrarian philosophy that is so rare among coin buyers but so effective. After all, the coins remained as rare and numismatically desirable as ever.

Harry was at the convention, with his *special* 1803 eagle with the stray 14th star on the reverse. He went from dealer to dealer, collector to collector, but could find no one who had ever heard of the variety before! Walter Breen, who was in attendance as well, congratulated him on this significant discovery.

Building a Collection

With sufficient financial resources to acquire just about any coin that captured his fancy, Bass set about building a fine collection. At first he collected here and there, this and that, acquiring such diverse pieces as tokens issued as advertisements and whimsies by early-20th-century dealer Thomas L. Elder, obsolete currency of the 1830s issued by the Republic of Texas, a silver tankard inlaid with European silver coins, a selection of private gold coins, Civil War store cards issued in Cincinnati by rascally coin dealer Robert Downing, a handful of silver coins (highlighted by an important and rare 1794 dollar), and other desiderata.

In the January 1977 issue of *The Numismatist*, Harry Bass, now with more than a decade of experience, advertised his personal interests, including United States gold coins by die varieties, pattern issues, Proof coins struck before 1858, silver coins struck before 1837 in MS-65 or better grade, numismatic books, Mexican 8-escudos pieces, and Western Americana. "Please contact me if you have any of the above items for sale. I'm willing if necessary to buy whole collections to obtain the pieces I need." He had other specialties as well. On April 10, 1980, after attending one of the sessions of our auction of the Garrett Collection for The Johns Hopkins University, he wrote a two-page letter that included this (at the time I was deeply involved in research on Hard Times tokens, a long-term project):

Doris and I enjoyed seeing you at the sale, and I was pleased to be able to introduce your wife to Doris. Congratulations on another great sale. In fact, I want to congratulate you on the way you and your firm have handled this whole undertaking. . . .

I am most pleased by the manner in which you have been able to document the history of these coins individually together with the manner in which you have been able to utilize them in your milestone work, "The History of United States Coins as Illustrated by the Garrett Collection."

Regarding the Hard Times tokens and my literature on the subject, I am sending under separate cover, insured for $5,000, all of the material that I have. In all probability, little of it will be of any real value to you, but since they all are original items I feel that it would be best that you have all of it at one time to peruse (and to caress!). . . .

I hope that some of this material will be of benefit to you in your forthcoming work on Hard Times tokens. I am one of your great admirers as a numismatist and author and am most happy that I may have some material that will be of some benefit to you in your endeavor.

Most cordially

[Harry]

In time he settled upon early gold coins of the 1795 to 1834 era as the prime focus of his interest, perhaps from the emotions ignited by his discovery of the stray 14th star. During the next 30 years he bought and bid aggressively whenever a choice specimen came up for sale or for auction competition.

Harry W. Bass Jr., Numismatist and Scholar

Harry and I corresponded frequently over the years and also had many visits and conversations. He was a regular attendee at our auction sales. In time I learned a lot from him.

Acquisition Strategy

Harry realized at an early time that a listed price for a *rarity* represented either what such a piece had sold for in the past, or was a ballpark estimate put down by a catalog compiler who had to come up with *some* figure, but could find no market data. Thus, equipped with the knowledge found deep in his library, he knew that if a particular gold coin, a rare medal, a Hard Times token, or an elusive piece of currency was listed at, say, $1,000, but that during the past 100 years only three or four had come on the market, and none recently, he could bid $2,000, or $5,000, or even $10,000 to acquire an example at auction, and then *own it,* while everyone else was waiting to buy one at the catalog or old auction price! Of course, after Harry bid and bought the item for $10,000 and had it in his possession, the next round of published price guides would list it at $10,000 and a similar piece might cost a later buyer $15,000 to $20,000 or more. It was a win-win strategy.

On the other hand, if an item was listed at $1,000, but Harry found that each year a half dozen of them were sold at auction and even more were held in the private stocks of dealers, he could bide his time and wait for a piece that was just right in terms of *quality.* These were the days before we had MS-61, MS-62, etc., or certification services, and one person's "superb gem" might be another's "*almost* Uncirculated."

In time, this undefined grading caused Harry to do several things: First, he learned on his own everything that he needed to know. As well as any *dealer* I ever met, Harry the collector had a keen eye and knew the gem from the so-so, the pristine from the cleaned. Further, he chose to buy from dealers and others in whom he placed trust, based upon his experience with them.

In summary, Harry was a very sophisticated buyer.

At the Eliasberg Sale

I recall that during our auction presentation of the Eliasberg Collection of U.S. Gold Coins in 1982, the first in a long string of Eliasberg auctions, Harry Bass came to lot-viewing in New York City. He brought his magnifying glass, loupe, and stereo microscope, and also many coins from his collection, and from morning to night in an area we set up for him he made notes of die varieties and compared them with his own, particularly for issues of the early era in American coinage, 1795 to 1834.

Harry planned a full-court press with multiple agents giving him advice and representing him on specific pieces. Although he discussed with me his general plans, no single person or agent knew what the others were doing. Harvey G. Stack later told of Harry's bidding technique in the Eliasberg event:

> Harry was sure that if he bid himself, others not as knowledgeable as he would use his bidding as a "crutch" to bid against him. He didn't want to create his own competition.
>
> Harry asked me to represent him at the sale and gave me a list of special lot numbers he wanted me to bid on. I asked him for his limits, and he said, "Just watch me." We made up a special signal. He wore his jacket and had a handkerchief in his breast pocket. Whenever we came to a lot he wanted, he would signal by touching the handkerchief in his pocket. When he removed his hand, I was to stop bidding. I could only bid when he was touching the handkerchief.
>
> I was not sitting near him. He sat in the first row, and I positioned myself five rows behind him with a good view of the handkerchief in his pocket. The plan worked perfectly the first part of the sale, and I acquired for him a goodly number of coins.

The tense moment arrived when the unique 1870-S three-dollar gold piece was offered for sale, and I knew from my list he wanted to bid on it. When the bidding opened at about $120,000 and started to advance towards $200,000, Harry did not move. He waited. As the bidding approached $300,000, he moved his hand to the handkerchief and held on to it.

I began bidding and continued in $25,000 increments till it reached $425,000, and suddenly his hand dropped, and the bidding continued to $500,000. Once again Harry's hand returned to the handkerchief and dropped after I bid $575,000 for him. Suddenly a bid came at $600,000 and the room gasped.

Harry didn't move. The auctioneer was calling for "any more" and just as the gavel was about to drop, Harry's hand returned to the handkerchief and I immediately bid $625,000 and won the coin [$687,500 with the buyer's fee added]. The applause that followed showed the excitement we all felt in the room. Stack's was given the credit of acquisition, and it was only later that year Harry revealed he was the buyer.[3]

I could expand upon Harvey's comment and tell of a dozen or more strategies Harry Bass used at other sales. A common technique was to have Mike Brownlee, a Texas dealer who was very close to Harry and acted as an advisor and agent, bid on rarities in our sale. Mike would sit somewhere near the front and would raise his bidder paddle in an obvious manner. Everyone knew he was bidding for Harry. Then, if the price went beyond his authorization he would frown, give an expression of disappointment, then look around the room to see who else was bidding. Mike was the main advisor in the conducting of the Goliad Corporation set up to buy, sell, and hold coins—giving Harry the opportunity to use corporate credentials in certain matters.

In the meantime Harry had laid plans with me or the auctioneer. These varied from sale to sale, so that no one in the audience would be the wiser. For one sale it might be, "If I am sitting in the audience and then stand to observe the action, I am bidding, unless I sit down again." Or, "If I have a pen in my hand I am bidding."

I hasten to say that such arrangements were not unique. Other leading buyers who were well-known specialists often did the same thing—so that less informed bidders would not ride on their coattails.

John J. Ford Jr. was a master at this and sometimes had several agents taking part. Sometimes strategies didn't work quite right. At one of the Garrett sales John had his eye on buying most of the 1783 Nova Constellatio silver pattern coins and gave secret instructions to Herb Melnick. On a particular lot, John bid for a while, then dropped out. Melnick, ostensibly a dealer competitor, raised his paddle while keeping an eye on John for signals. Then he stopped bidding. John had no choice but to break silence and call out, "Herb, keep bidding!"

At another of the Garrett sales Art Kagin and his son Don attended, but did not sit near each other. For one rarity, both had their paddles in the air. Our auctioneer asked, "Are you sure, Art, that you want to bid against your son?" The lot was reopened, this time with just one Kagin bidding.

Over the years a number of amateurs have ridden the coattails of knowledgeable dealers and collectors, by following their actions and topping them in the final bid. Raymond N. Merena has told the story of a lady who collected coins over a period of years, by bidding at auction. He remarked at the beautiful quality of the pieces she showed him, and asked her if she had studied numismatics extensively. She had not, and revealed that her secret was to quietly watch one of America's leading quality-oriented dealers as he bid to acquire coins for his inventory, topping him by a bid on items she found appealing.

In another instance a rare double eagle in one of our sales, a coin that I estimated would bring about $4,000, was bid up to $20,000. The underbidder came up to me and asked, "Should I have bid more? I don't know much about the coin, but I was intrigued by the catalog description. I was following what another bidder was doing."

The winning bidder later told me, "I didn't know much about the coin, but I felt safe as there was a strong underbidder."

Many other stories could be related.

Onward

As Harry continued to build his collection and library he communicated with me at an increased pace. He enjoyed discussing the technicalities of minting procedures, early die varieties, numismatic tradition, and more. Although there were many fine dealers in America, not many were interested in such esoterica, so perhaps I was unique as a professional numismatist who was also consulted frequently on obscure matters not related to rarity and price.

On one fine day in the late 1980s he called me to say that no longer would I be receiving any letters from him. He had been immersed in the new world of computers for several years, and henceforth we would be communicating only in this medium. I was an amateur in this field and was learning how to use my Mac Plus with its floppy discs. Microsoft Word 1.0 was a challenge to learn as well. There were helpful hints, such as while users were waiting to save a file they could use the time go get a cup of coffee! All of this seems so strange to relate now—when the Internet is part of everyday life! Now, a million (or however many) email messages later, I remember Harry as my very first Internet correspondent.

Harry didn't stop there. For several years beginning in 1972 he served as a councillor for the American Numismatic Society and from 1978 through 1984

Harry relaxing with a handful of modern foreign currency.

he was the Society's president.[4] I remember thinking at the time, how *lucky* the Society is to have his talents. During his administration many notable accomplishments were made, effectively laying the groundwork to lead the Society, founded in 1858, into the new millennium. At the ANS, director Leslie Elam and librarian Frank Campbell were his closest friends and contacts. On December 2, 2003, a dedication ceremony was held at the Society for the Harry W. Bass, Jr. Library.

David Calhoun, Doris Bass, ANS president Don Partrick, and Michael Calhoun at the Bass Library dedication.

Doris Bass and Don Partrick at the dinner hosted by the ANS with the ceremony.

The Society for many years has served as a bastion for numismatic research and study, and today it has the largest numismatic library in the world. Harry

established a leading-edge data base for their library and collection, the first in the numismatic field worldwide. Outside of the hobby, he created or advised concerning computer systems for his various business interests.

Harry continued his research, collecting, and other numismatic activities with enthusiasm, into the late 1990s. He then became ill with throat cancer. Although his pace necessarily diminished, his enthusiasm continued. By the time of his death on April 4, 1998, he had formed the largest collection of die varieties of early gold ever gathered by a single individual, with no equal in museum collections either. His passing engendered tributes from far and wide. To say he was fondly remembered would be an understatement.

The Bass Collection

Many of the coins, tokens, medals, and paper money in Bass's estate, items nearly all outside of his 1795 to 1834 gold collection, were consigned by his foundation to my company, Bowers and Merena Galleries, in Wolfeboro, New Hampshire. Working with his widow, Doris, the Harry W. Bass Jr. Foundation, and his stepsons David (in particular) and Michael Calhoun, we presented a series of sales in the "Grand Format" catalog style to showcase items that sold for a total of well over $40,000,000, breaking countless auction records. In 2012 we had a reprise sale with paper-money rarities. Doris sent to me a treasured memento, the large walnut coin cabinet Harry had used to hold his collection. Today I use its wide flat drawers to store old prints and paper items. If I correctly recall Harry's story about it years ago, it came from the estate of Henry Chapman. Who knows what it has held over the years!

Kept by the Foundation was the Core Collection, a rich legacy for observation and study, including through the medium of electronic copying—making information available easily and at a distance, a concept pioneered in numismatics by Harry and his associate in the Harry W. Bass Jr. Foundation, Ed Deane.

American Numismatic Association Headquarters on the campus of Colorado College in Colorado Springs. The Harry W. Bass Jr. Gallery within is one of its prime attractions.

Mint Director Jay Johnson, Doris Bass, and ANA president Bob Campbell at the outdoor ceremony dedicating and opening the Gallery on July 14, 2001.

Entrance to the Bass Collection exhibit.

Many of the interior exhibits.

Visitors viewing a selection of rare United States pattern coins.

Another section of the Gallery.

This rare 1815 half eagle on display was purchased by Harry Bass in the sale of the collection of Ambassador and Mrs. R. Henry Norweb.

Many other significant coins beyond early gold were preserved in the Core Collection, including a selection of beautiful patterns (other than those we auctioned), a complete set of $3 gold, a splendid Ultra High Relief MCMVII (1907) $20, and other items. Christine Karstedt and I arranged for the Foundation to work with the American Numismatic Association in Colorado Springs to build the Harry W. Bass Jr. Gallery to display the treasures on loan, where they may be seen today.[5] A special ceremony was held at ANA Headquarters, with the Bass family present, to dedicate the exhibit.

Possessed of a firm but gentle turn of mind, Harry Bass tapped the good parts of the hobby, while ignoring non-productive controversies of the day. Further, he was an advocate of the saying, "If you can't say something nice, don't say anything at all." Quick to praise and reluctant to criticize, he appreciated the good in everyone, and became one of the most widely liked personalities in numismatics.

After his passing I was invited to contribute a tribute to *Harry W. Bass, Jr.: Memories of His Life,* edited by Margo Russell and Leslie A. Elam and published by the American Numismatic Society, and to other memorials. To establish a permanent record I wrote an award-winning book, *The Harry W. Bass, Jr. Collection: A Museum Catalogue and Sylloge,* for the Foundation.

Harry W. Bass Jr.: A Sketch of His Life

Harry Wesley Bass Jr., was born to Wilma Schuessler Bass and Harry Wesley Bass on January 6, 1927, in Oklahoma City. By that time his father was well established in the oil business, especially in explorations and "wildcatting." At age five he moved with his family to Dallas, where he attended the Bradfield Elementary School and, later, the Texas Country Day School (today known as St. Mark's School of Texas). The carefree days of summer were often enjoyed at the family's Delmar Ranch on the Bosque River near Waco, an expanse which in time grew to be the largest working spread in the central part of Texas.

From an early time Harry was active in outdoor activities, including hiking, team sports, and skiing—although the latter involved traveling to distant mountain areas such as in Colorado.

"If Harry W. Bass, Jr. had a coat-of-arms, it would more than likely consist of an oil derrick, the GOP elephant and a pair of skis," a 1962 biographical sketch noted.[6] If the story had been written a few years later, "coins" could have been added, and a few years later, "computers." As befitted a multi-talented person, Harry had multiple interests and specialties and usually delved into them very deeply.

His family recalls that his motto was "Integrity, Integrity, Integrity," and wherever he went, in each activity he conducted, he was widely admired by his peers. Indeed, Harry would always "tell it like it is," adding perception, knowledge, and reason to his statements.

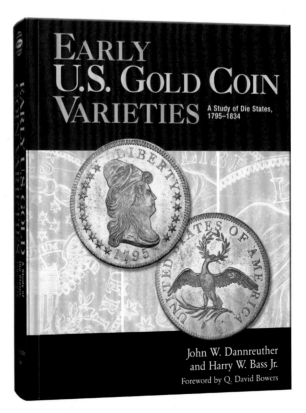

Harry's notes on early gold coins formed the basis for this book.

He had one sibling, his brother Richard D. Bass, who later became prominent in many activities including the operation of the Snowbird ski resort in Utah and in outdoor adventure. At an event held by the Appalachian Mountain Club a few years ago Dick, a prominent figure in that organization, told me that he had climbed the highest peak in each of the continents.

After attending the University of Texas and Southern Methodist University, Harry signed with the U.S. Navy for a two-year hitch, during which he spent most of his time in the Pacific region of operations. After leaving the service he returned to SMU. He then went to Canada, where for three years he was involved in oil drilling and exploration. Returning to Dallas, he immersed himself in the family oil business.

In the 1950s, influenced by Senator Robert Taft, Harry took a great interest in Republican politics. In 1952 he cast his first vote in a presidential election, for Dwight Eisenhower (during the 1948 election he was in Canada and did not vote). In January 1957 he entered the contest for Dallas County chairman for the Republican Party and won in a landslide. After that he was prominent in GOP politics for many years. In time he was a prime factor in what proved to be a successful effort to elect George Herbert Walker Bush to the United States Senate. It might be said that if it were not for Harry, the roster of past residents in the White House would be different from the names we know today.

Harry loved people, and over the years he was associated with many groups and organizations. Locally, he was a member of the Dallas Country Club, the Brook Hollow Golf Club, and the Idlewild and Calyx groups. Beginning in 1954 he served as president of the Sertoma Club, a well-known service organization, in Dallas. He was also active in alumni activities of the Phi Delta Theta fraternity.

For a long time photography was one of Harry's strong interests, and in pursuit of this activity he acquired much equipment and ranged far in quest of challenging subjects.

In 1953 he spent a week in Aspen, Colorado, and was introduced in a significant way to skiing, which he did not like at first. However, that soon changed, and he became an avid fan, as did his brother Dick. High in the Rocky Mountains to the west of Denver the resort town of Vail was established, and flourished in the 1960s—literally a community built on the attractions and pleasures of skiing in combination with the rental or ownership of condominiums and homes nestled in some of the most scenic slopes of the Rockies. By the mid-1970s Harry and his family became very prominent in the management of the fortunes of Vail and the development from scratch of a new community, Beaver Creek. Today in downtown Beaver Creek there is a special memorial site dedicated to him.

In the mid-1970s Harry, then divorced, met Doris Calhoun. The couple fell in love and kept each other company while attending different sporting, civic, and society events. Harry married Doris in 1979 and gained two great stepsons, David and Michael Calhoun, to add to his family of several children from his first marriage.

The union was a happy one, and Harry tended to Doris, with great care and affection. I recall an instance in which she fell from a horse and was injured, at which time Harry immediately canceled his scheduled attendance at several important numismatic events.

In March 1967 *The Numismatist* noted that Bass, by that time an established rare-coin collector, had made a significant donation to the American Numismatic Association, and was pursuing the hobby at a rapid pace, even though he had been involved for less than a year.

You know the rest of the story!

This chapter is a companion to chapter 12 and discusses another medal engraved by Charles Cushing Wright, today remembered as the greatest American medalist of the era from the 1820s to the early 1850s.

The 1838 Celebration in New Haven

Yale University, a New Haven landmark. (Library of Congress)

The 1838 New Haven Medal, a Numismatic Icon

On December 27, 1836, members of the Connecticut Academy of Arts and Sciences resolved to appoint a member to provide a discourse on the coming 1838 bicentennial observation of the town's founding. Professor James L. Kingsley was selected at the next meeting. It was subsequently decided to select April 25, 1838, as the anniversary day, allowing for a 10-day difference in the current calendar in comparison to that in use in 1638. Producing the commemorative medal was an essential part of the year-long festivities.

Kingsley prepared a discourse and delivered it on the appointed day, after which it was published in an octavo volume of 116 pages. During the year Reverend Leonard Bacon, a member of the committee charged with the celebration, delivered a series of speeches on various aspects of his church in relation to New Haven history. These together with notes and documents were published in a 408-page octavo book in 1839. By that time the Academy had close to 170 members, of whom about half resided in New Haven.[1]

The New Haven Medal

John Allan in his 1839 narrative praised the Erie Canal medal (see chapter 12) and then continued:

> Since that time, no medals worthy of commemoration have been executed either by individuals, or any of the states or cities of the United States, till lately, New Haven in the state of Connecticut, has taken the lead, and on the return of the second centennial anniversary of the founding of the colony by Eaton and Davenport, has had a medal engraved and struck to commemorate the first settlement of the City. The medal does honor to both the designer and engraver, as well as to those patriotic citizens of New Haven, at whose instance it was done. The writer has one.
>
> On the obverse is a view of the place where New Haven now stands, as it was in April 1638, with the band of pilgrim settlers under a tree, listening to a sermon on the first Sabbath in the wilderness, from the Rev. John Davenport, their spiritual leader, while the aborigines on the opposite bank of the river are looking on; the reverse has a view of New Haven as it is at the present day, or rather a bird's eye view of the public square or green, now in the centre of the

town, with the different churches, the state house, colleges, &c.

Legend on the top of the obverse, ("Quinnipiack, 1638") the Indian name,—underneath, "The desert shall rejoice."—On the reverse, "and blossom as the rose." "New Haven, 1838." On the exergue, a ship in full sail, a steamboat, railroad cars.

May this patriotic effort of New Haven be imitated by every town and state in the union, and may every college and literary institution possess a cabinet of coins and medals!

Remarks.—An eminent artist has pronounced that this medal is the best hitherto executed in this country. It has been struck both in bronze and in silver. The medal is 2 1/8 inches in diameter; the silver 1/8 inch thick; the bronze 3/16 inch thick. The silver medal weighs 1 oz. and seventeen and a half pennyweights and sells for six dollars.

The bronze 3 oz. and two pennyweights sells for three dollars. The impression of the medal is in high relief, and its most minute lines are exceedingly sharp and well defined. The costume and manner and even the features of the pilgrims are highly characteristic and illustrate the humble beginning of this now large and beautiful town. The numerous objects grouped together to indicate its present prosperity, although on a crowded field, are perfectly distinct; the architecture of the public buildings is so exactly copied that they are instantly recognized by an eye that is familiar with them, and the exuberant foliage of this city of groves, is gracefully dis-

played among its squares and temples.

This medal was designed by Mr. Hezekiah Augur, the well-known sculptor, with the advice of Mr. Ithiel Town, and it was executed in New York, by Mr. John [sic] Wright. For sale at the bookstore of Young & Ulhorn. For a very interesting account of the rise and progress of the colony, see Prof. Kingsley's excellent historical discourse, and the volume of historical sermons—of deep interest—by the Rev. Leonard Bacon.

A $1 note of the New Haven Bank with a vignette at the lower left showing the 1838 Sabbath discourse.

Detail showing the "First Sabbath, Quinnipiack 1638."

Yale College and the Connecticut State House (the Greek Revival building to the right of center). (John H. Hinton, *History of the United States*, 1850)

The above account led readers to credit Ithiel Town, a highly regarded local architect, with advising on the design. As Town had died on June 13, 1844, he could not have been involved. His misplaced fame was repeated in later accounts. The vast repertoire of Town's architectural work included wooden bridges, imposing mansions, two churches on the village green, the Tontine Hotel, the Alumni Hall for Yale College, and the Connecticut State House.[2] He traveled in Europe with artist and inventor Samuel F.B. Morse in 1829 and 1830 and was one of two architects involved in the founding of the Academy of Design in New York City. He also designed state capitols for Indiana and North Carolina. For larger buildings he specialized in the Greek Revival style.

Hezekiah Augur and the New Haven Medal

The New Haven medal was created under the supervision of the joint committee formed by the Connecticut Academy of Arts and Sciences to conduct the bicentennial observance. As noted above, the design

was by Hezekiah Augur. Born in New Haven in 1791, he was instructed by his father to follow his trade, that of a carpenter. This did not suit, and at the age of nine he was apprenticed to a grocer who also mended shoes, where he enjoyed being a cobbler. This did not satisfy his father either, and he gave the young man the then-remarkable sum of two thousand dollars to set him up as a partner in a dry-goods business. Within three years that not only failed, but resulted in debt. Hezekiah's next venture was running a fruit stand.

In the meantime he enjoyed carving in wood, as he had since childhood, to his parent's dismay. His father died, after which Hezekiah was freed from bondage, so to speak, and determined to devote his life to art. He also had a mechanical turn of mind and made and sold an invention for making worsted lace that brought him a large sum of money. From this point onward he was in comfortable but not wealthy circumstances. He also invented a wood-carving machine used in making legs and other ornate piano parts, and made the first bracket saw.

Professor Samuel F.B. Morse was impressed with Augur's wood carvings and encouraged him to sculpt in marble. He did this and made a head of Apollo, followed by a head of Washington and a statue of Sappho. For a commission for Congress he made a bust of Chief Justice Oliver Ellsworth that today is on view in the Supreme Court Building in Washington. Art historians credit a pair of marble statuettes, *Jephthah and his Daughter,* as his finest work. In 1835 Yale College raised funds to acquire these. By 1848 his work in sculpture was well known. Augur was a logical choice to create the designs for the New Haven medal, both sides of which were in relief. Although he had no formal education, in 1833 Yale made him an honorary alumnus. Augur died in January 1858 and left a small estate.[3]

Jephthah and his Daughter. (Yale University)

Obverse 1 of the 1838 New Haven medal.

Two Varieties of the New Haven Medal

There are two varieties of the 1838 New Haven medal, which share a common reverse die:

Obverse 1: This obverse is distinguished by having the signature C.C. WRIGHT above DES (ERT) and having a round-top 3 in 1838. Both dies show John Davenport standing, his head tilted to the side, with his right arm raised and his index finger pointing and his left hand at the front of his coat. He is preaching to a group of settlers as two seated natives look on from the left. Obverse 1 has the rays of the sun in the field to the left. A heavy tree branch overhead shows clusters, perhaps of pine. At the top border is QUINNIPIACK 1638. At the bottom border is THE DESERT SHALL BLOOM. The inscription on both sides is adapted from Isaiah xxxv, 1 and 2. This was widely

Detail of Obverse 1 showing the signature of C.C. Wright.

Obverse 2 of the 1838 New Haven medal.

Reverse A of the 1838 New Haven medal, the common die used with obverses 1 and 2.

Detail of reverse A, showing the die crack at the right side of the last rail car, as used with obverse 1.

Detail of reverse A, showing the advanced die crack at the right side of the last rail car, as used with obverse 2.

quoted in the early 19th century and referred to the coming of the Lord and appeared in many variations. This die was used first, as evidenced by the state of die cracks on the common reverse.

Obverse 2: This obverse, also attributed to Wright, is not signed and has a flat-top 3 in 1838. On obverse 2 there are no rays to the sun and the tree is of a deciduous type and has large leaves with prominently engraved veins. Details of the onlookers vary slightly as do those of other features. This die was the second used. On the reverse a die crack at the right side of the last rail car is significantly more advanced than on the preceding.

Reverse A: The reverse shows a cityscape as viewed from the water, a montage of buildings. At the shoreline a puffing locomotive heads to the right, towing a tender and three passenger cars. In the foreground are a sidewheel steamboat, a sailboat, and a rowboat on the water. Above is NEW HAVEN 1838. At the bottom border is AND BLOSSOM AS THE ROSE. After a run of medals in combination with obverse 1 the die, now with the crack on the last rail car, was slightly retouched and was mated with obverse 2.

The New Haven Medal in Numismatics

When in 1840 a notice of the New-York Historical Society stated it was a repository of selected coins and medals, only two of which were specifically cited: an Elizabeth silver shilling of England and an 1838 New Haven medal.

Over a long period of years occasional examples, nearly always in copper, were mentioned in print. In 1861 in *A Description of the Medals of Washington,* James Ross Snowden, erstwhile director of the Philadelphia Mint, included this in his "Supplemental List of Medals in the Cabinet":

> No. 16. New Haven, Connecticut.—The *obverse* represents New Haven (or Quinnipiack) as it was in 1638; and the *reverse* as it was in 1838. *Obverse.* The Desert Shall Rejoice.

Reverse. And Blossom As The Rose. This was probably struck on the occasion of a centennial *[sic]* celebration in 1838. *Size 33.*

In 1864 in New York City, in an auction cataloged by Joseph Sabin (who signed the preface and dated it April 4, 1864), Bangs, Merwin & Co. offered more than 5,000 lots of books, engravings, prints, relics, and other items from the John Allan estate, including:

> Lot 4299. New Haven medal in silver. Original. Fine Proof. Nearly or quite unique in this medal. Size 38.

From June 20 to 24, 1882, Philadelphia dealers S.H. and Henry Chapman offered at auction the celebrated collection of Charles I. Bushnell, including this:

> Lot 368. New Haven Medal. Roger Williams preaching to the Colonists and Indians. QUINNIPIACK 1638, THE DESERT SHALL REJOICE. Rev. View of Harvard College, etc.; NEW HAVEN 1838, and BLOSSOM AS THE ROSE. Silver. Very rare. Size 38.

Not unusual for the Chapman brothers at the time, they mixed up their facts, sometimes ludicrously, as here. Roger Williams, who founded the Providence Plantations (Rhode Island), was not the preacher shown. Harvard College was of course in Cambridge, Massachusetts, and not in New Haven, Connecticut!

The 1907 collection catalog of the New Haven Colony Historical Society included this:

> No. 55 Two Duplicate Copper Medals commemorative of the two hundredth anniversary of the settlement of New

Haven. Vignette, John Davenport preaching under oak tree, Quinnipiac, 1638, "the desert shall rejoice." On reverse side, representation of New Haven, 1838, "and blossom as the rose." Designed by Hezekiah Augur, 1791–1858, sculptor of New Haven— struck by the Connecticut Academy of Arts and Sciences.

The 1907 collection catalog of the Mint Collection in Philadelphia listed this:

No. 239. Quinnipiack–New Haven, 1838. *Obv.* QUINNIPIACK 1838. A religious meeting under a tree; below, The Desert Shall Rejoice. *Rev.* NEW HAVEN 1838. View of the campus of Yale University; below, And Blossom As The Rose. Electrotypes. 56 mm.

Again, facts were scarce. Depicted was a composite cityscape of New Haven including a small boat, a sailing ship, a locomotive and rail cars, and more— hardly the Yale campus.

In 1977 the Token and Medal Society published R.W. Julian's magnum opus, *Medals of the United States Mint, The First Century 1792–1892*. An original New Haven medal was illustrated and given the catalog number of CM-37. Julian noted that in 1888 it was hoped that a new version would be made:

The listing of this medal is based on a letter written to Superintendent Daniel Fox on March 5, 1888, by New Haven officials. They wished to have a certain medal struck at the Mint honoring the 250th anniversary of New Haven and mentioned in passing that they believed the earlier one had been struck at the Mint in 1838. There was no 1888 medal struck at the Mint due to a lack of time.

CHAPTER 21

With a counterstamped Liberty Seated half dollar in hand the owner could gain admission to a hall where "the highest order of artistic talent and the most beautiful and accomplished ladies will provide entertainment attractive to the most fastidious lovers of the refined and charming in art." This is another favorite from my collection.

Take a Peek at the Parisian Varieties

A Popular New York Theater

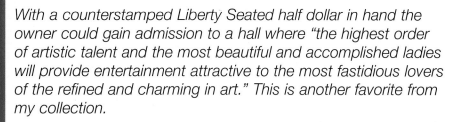

Parisian Varieties advertisement in the *New York Dramatic News*, June 10, 1876 (see the third column).

Parisian Varieties, located at 16th Street and (actually *near*) Broadway, New York City, presented diverse stage acts. An advertisement in the *New York Daily Tribune* on September 14, 1875, included this:

Parisian Varieties

This elegant temple of amusement, late Robinson Hall, will reopen Wednesday evening, September 15, 1875, as a first-class variety theater presenting a constantly changing succession of brilliant novelties, choice specialties, humorous bagatelles, new and original sketches.

The highest order of artistic talent and the most beautiful and accomplished ladies will provide entertainment attractive to the most fastidious lovers of the refined and charming in art.

Twenty star artists, elegant ballet arranged by M. Blandowski, entitled "La Coquette." The irresistible funny farce entitled "The Nocturnal Muddle." Emotional poem vivant entitled "The Brooklyn Seminary for Finishing Young Ladies."

A pleasant combination of terpsichorean eccentricity, modern morality, and female beauty with a jolly termination entitled "The Parisian La Chateaux Quadrille."

Evenings at 8. Matinees Tuesdays, Thursdays, and Saturdays at 2.

Business was excellent in ensuing weeks, according to reports, and the venue was ideal for family entertainment. Despite any allusions gained from the title, the Parisian Varieties program was not risqué—at least not yet.

Regular advertisements in the New York papers reflect changes in the features. On February 14, 1876, a listing in the *Commercial Advertiser* invited patrons to a "Temple of Sensational Art" with "all former efforts surpassed." Sixty artists were on stage. Acts included Fattie Stewart's tricks, Delmonio, New Tableau, Aubrey & Monites, James Messenger, "Don't Go Tommy," French dances, and Annie Morton.

A Company Goes on the Road

Advertisements announced that on March 25 and 26 in Providence, Rhode Island, "The New York Parisian Varieties! From Broadway and 16th Street, New York" would hold forth for two days at the venerable Academy of Music, a well-respected venue that hosted quality performances. G.A. Henderson was listed as business manager, J.F. Swords as treasurer. This was a traveling road show. In the meantime performances continued in New York City.

> The liveliest, funniest, and most artistic entertainment ever given in America. Pronounced by the public and press the largest and most brilliant array of talent ever selected for presentation to public notice. Playing with astonishing success for the past six months to crowded houses. . . .
>
> The entire entertainment is chaste, elegant, humorous, and artistic. Prices 25c, 50c, and 75 cents. . . . Monday, March 27, at Pawtucket.

On Thursday, March 30, 1876, the troupe was on stage in a one-night stand at the Music Hall in Lowell, Massachusetts. On April 6 the company was back at the Academy of Music in Providence, starting a run of several days. The next stop was Hartford, Connecticut.

Advertising on Coins

Silver coins of all kinds had disappeared from circulation in the late spring of 1862, when the outcome of the Civil War was uncertain and citizens hoarded "hard money." It was thought that they would reappear after hostilities ended in 1865, but that was not the case. Silver coins were held by speculators, banks, and exchange houses and were available only at a premium in terms of Legal Tender Notes—paper bills with no backing in silver or gold coins.

Finally, on and after April 20, 1876, currency and silver coins were at par with each other. Vast quantities of long-hidden silver coins flooded the marketplace. Thousands of Liberty Seated half dollars were counterstamped PARISIAN VARIETIES / 16TH ST & B'WAY. N.Y. in the left and right obverse fields.

Parisian Varieties counterstamp on an 1875 Liberty Seated half dollar.

These were, in essence, a ticket to gain entrance when the half dollar was surrendered—a situation imitating the "free ticket" half dollars distributed by Yankee Robinson for his circus in the mid-1850s and the Spanish-American two-reales silver coins stamped by Model Artists, Broadway Varieties, and others in that decade.

Silver trade dollars had been introduced in 1873 for use in commerce with China, but they were legal tender in the United States as well. On July 22, 1876, Congress repealed this status, after which trade dollars in circulation were often refused by banks and shopkeepers, or received only at a discount, such as for 75 or 85 cents. Some of these were counterstamped with Parisian Varieties advertisements as well.

Today, somewhat more than 50 Liberty Seated half dollars are known with this imprint, mostly dated in the mid-1870s, and a handful of trade dollars exist as well.

Take a Peek at the Parisian Varieties

On Stage in New York

The road show played other stops in New England, after which many of the troupers returned to 16th and Broadway.

In the meantime in New York City the entertainment included the Scotch Bell Players (198 bells), The Elephant (presumably a live animal, but who knows?), Sculptor's Dream, Peerless Zitella, and other acts. As with other stage shows, the management booked a continuing stream of itinerant showpeople and acts.

W.H. Woodley, manager of the New York show, announced that beginning on Monday evening, May 22, 1876, and continuing for a week a lightweight wrestling match would be given on stage with William J. Austin, American champion, challenging M. Lucien Marc, champion from Paris.

In other news:

> Mrs. Leonna LeClare, a trapeze performer in the Parisian Varieties, in New York, had a severe accident on the 6th. One of the tricks was to throw herself backward, slide downward, catch by the insteps, and swing. As she was trying to do this in the upper trapeze her foot slipped and she fell on her husband, who was in the lower trapeze, and then she fell on the cushioned orchestra railing, and from there bounded to the main aisle, a total distance of about twenty feet. She is confined to her bed but not in any danger.[1]

In New York City many theaters closed during the warmer summer months. Parisian Varieties remained open, the "most comfortable, coolest, and best ventilated theatre in New York, having immense windows opening into gardens." The entertainment was "Frenchy, Spicy, and Sparkling" in July.[2] Beer, wine, and tobacco were available to patrons. In August, advertisements mentioned "100 Brilliant Star Artists."

The *Morning Telegraph* printed this on August 20, 1876:

> A "Lovely Ladies Levee" has proved a very attractive card at the Parisian Varieties during the week and was supplemented by a series of spicy songs and sketches. On the 21st a new and lively program is announced.

Soon advertised was a "complete change—entire new bill and company," features including "The Forged Will," "Light and Shades of Everyday Life," "Oneida Community," "Tableaux Vivants," and "Ireland & America."[3] Among those on stage was Minnie Hall, who seems to have been a regular at the theater. In September, "Sitting Bull," "Legs on the Brain," and "Handsome Harry" were among the headlined attractions. Management claimed that its audience comprised "the elite of the world."

Surprise!

This newspaper account appeared: the *Herald* printed this revelation on Monday, October 16, 1876:

The Robinson Hall Raid

> At the Washington Place Police Court yesterday, before Justice Bixby, Captain Williams of the 29th Precinct arraigned the 56 prisoners, men and women, whom he had arrested in the theatre known as "The Parisian Varieties" at Robinson Hall in East Sixteenth Street on Saturday evening.
>
> For giving indecent exhibitions, the proprietor and manager, were held for trial at the Court of Special Sessions in default of $1,000 bail each. The dancers, principal among whom were Minnie Hall and Bertha Neokirk, were required to furnish $50 each.
>
> A similar disposition was made in

the case of the men arrested in the theatre, Mr. Christrup, the leader of the orchestra, being required to furnish $300 bail to appear as a witness against Robinson. . . . The neighborhood of the courtroom was crowded with sightseers desirous of witnessing the spectacle of the unfortunate women being taken to court.

Many if not most of the girls were young, some of "tender age." Many were crying and distraught as their parents and others watched, some of them handing bail money to the clerks. Those who could not pay were sent to the House of Detention for the time being.

Business As Usual

The theater remained open, and performances continued. Raids on various New York City places of public accommodation were not unusual in this era. Typically, after a flurry of newspaper publicity the alleged miscreants resumed their regular activities, often by making private arrangements with city officials. An advertisement in the *Daily Graphic*, October 30, 1876, announced:

Parisian Varieties

16th St. and Broadway. Evening at 8; matinees Tuesday, Thursday, and Saturday at 2.

Gigantic array of talent. Grand olio. 100 artists. Eighteen new acts. Three hours' lively times. Everything new. My Wife's Garter. Two Lone Widows. Sailing Under False Colors. Les Neapolitaines. The Eaton Boy. The Area Bells. Hungary Musicians. A company of great artists. Benefit of Harry Spriggs November 8. Tremendous bill. Sixty volunteers.

On the evening of Tuesday, November 7, 1876, the various theaters in the city announced from the stage the telegraphed results of the national presidential election and local contests.

As part of a routine fire-safety inspection of theater buildings, on Friday, December 15, a visit was made to the Parisian Varieties. It was reported that the gallery or balcony accommodated 180 people and had a satisfactory exit. The main floor or parquet had 500 loose seats. On each side six large windows looked out upon gardens. It was recommended that one window on each side be removed and a door put in its place. The dressing rooms were under the stage and connected to a large room beneath the parquet, with a passage opening into Sixteenth Street.[4]

The Final Curtain (Almost)

The Morning Telegraph reported this on Sunday, December 17, 1876:

Attractions of a very spicy local character occupied the Parisian Varieties stage during the past week. These consisted of illustrations of academic studies in two sketches entitled "Scenes at Solaros" and "Vassar Outdone" which provoked considerable merriment.

Miss Jessie Fox, Signor Emi, Francis Melrose, the Sanyeahs, Breyame and Sawtelle, Minnie Hall, Emily Prior, Charley Fox, and a large company assisted in a very amusing program.

After the 18th the house will be called the Criterion Theatre and will be under the management of Mr. J.F. Swords, and an entire change will be made in the style of entertainment. Several original burlesque novelties will be presented, including "Ernani, or, the Horn of a Dilemma."

J.F. Swords had been with the Parisian Varieties including with its road show. The Sanyeahs act, husband and wife, included Mlle. Sanyeah, an acrobat who had been with Yankee Robinson and other entertainers earlier. Her surname was really Haynes, which spelled backward and with an added "a" was Sanyeah.

In January 1877 it was reported that the hall had been closed for some time, but that before any reopening took place the alternations recommended by the fire inspectors would be made.

"Good Old Times Resumed"
On January 22, 1877, the *Daily Graphic* published this:

Parisian Varieties

Sixteenth Street and Broadway. Good old times resumed with a company sure to startle the natives. Every evening at 8. Matinees Tuesday, Thursday, and Saturday at 9. Admission 20c and 30c. Reserved seats 50c.

Within a week the show advertised "Greatest combination of talent in America." Now, boxes were available for $5 and $10 in addition to regular seats.

In March, "Petty Sins and Pretty Sinners" with "les poses plastiques" was on the bill along with Mr. Burton Stanley in "Foiled," other acts, and "30 beautiful young ladies." In the same month "A Husband's Ghost," "Dancing Quakers," "The Royal Japs," "Around New York in Three Minutes," "Living Statues," and other features were on the bill. "Living Statues" meant a display of nude women posing to imitate well-known classic marble statues—a performance

considered artistic rather than suggestive. The earlier-mentioned Model Artists specialized in this theme.

An advertisement in the *New York Herald*, May 2, 1877, seems to indicate that the program had drifted even further toward attractive women and suggestive displays:

Keep Your Eye On Us: Grand display of beauty, art, and nature by the largest combination known. Every artist new. Every act new. Grand ballet. 50 lovely women. Captivating songs. Exciting dances. Perfect female models. Artistic sketches and naughty hits.

On May 7, George Francis Train, a well-known local eccentric man of wealth and former presidential candidate, was headlined in "Paris in Sight: War, Pestilence, Deluge," seemingly a departure from the "girly" acts. Admission was only 25 cents.

After about this time the advertisements stopped. In the autumn, E. Fellows Jenkins, secretary and general superintendent of the Society for the Prevention of Cruelty to Children, testified in court that he had visited Parisian Varieties often, in his official capacity.

"What is the reputation of the Parisian Varieties?" the judge asked him.

"Very bad," was the reply.

In a situation involving a Mrs. Rogers, mother of two children, Jenkins said when queried if he could identify her: "I think so, but it is rather difficult to identify a woman in an ordinary lady's dress as one you have seen in a 'model artist's' exhibition."

Jenkins also said that the theater had been raided "once or twice" in recent years.[5]

CHAPTER 22

On July 4, 1829, dignitaries and others gathered to watch the laying of the cornerstone for the second United States Mint. For this occasion silver half dimes of the hitherto-used Capped Bust design were made.

July 4, 1829

Obverse and reverse of the 1829 Capped Bust half dime (enlarged).

Half Dimes for a Mint Cornerstone Ceremony

Hazard's Register of Pennsylvania, July 1829, included this account:

Mint of the United States

The foundation stone of the Edifice about to be erected at the S-W corner of Chestnut and Juniper sts., under the provisions of the law for extending the Mint establishment, according to a plan thereof approved by the president, was laid, on the morning of the 4th of July, at 6 o'clock, in presence of the officers of the Mint, and a number of distinguished citizens.

Within the stone was deposited a package, securely enveloped, containing the newspapers of the day, a copy of the Declaration of Independence, of the Constitution of the United States, and of the Farewell Address of General Washington; also, specimens of the national coins, including one of the very few executed in the year 1792, and a half dime coined on the morning of the 4th, being the first of a new emission of that coin, of which denomination none have been issued since the year 1805.

Within the package was also enclosed a scroll with following inscription.

"Mint of the United States."

"This Institution was originally established by Act of Congress April 2d, A.D. 1792, Gen. George Washington being President of the United States, and the following fifteen States members of the Union, viz;—New Hampshire, Massachusetts, Rhode Island, Connecticut, Vermont, New York, New Jersey, Pennsylvania, Delaware, Maryland, Virginia, North Carolina, South Carolina, Georgia, Kentucky.

"The operations of coinage commenced in the year 1792. The coinage effected from that period to the 1st of January, 1829, was as follows;

"Gold coins; 132,592 eagles: 1,344,359 half eagles: 39,239 quarter eagles—making 1,566,190 pieces of gold coin, amounting to $8,395,812 50.

"Silver coins: 1,439,517 dollars: 41.604,347 half dollars: 1, 855,639 quarter dollars: 5,526,250 dimes: 265,543 half dimes—making 50,691,286 pieces of silver coin, amounting to $23,271,499 90.

"Copper coins: 50,882,042 cents: 6,138,513 half cents—making 57,029,555 pieces of copper coin, amounting to $539,512 984.

"Total amount—109,278,031 pieces of coin making $32,206,825 38½."

An extension of the Mint establishment was authorized by Act of Congress, March 2d, 1827, John Quincy Adams being president of the United States, and the following twenty four states members of the Union, via: Maine, New Hampshire, Massachusetts, Rhode Island, Connecticut, Vermont, New York, New Jersey, Pennsylvania, Delaware, Maryland, Virginia, North Carolina, South Carolina, Georgia, Tennessee, Kentucky, Ohio, Indiana, Illinois, Missouri, Louisiana, Mississippi, Alabama.

In fulfillment of the law for extending the Mint establishment, this foundation stone of the Edifice designed for that purpose, was laid on the 4th day of July, A.D. 1829.

Gen. Andrew Jackson, being President, J.C Calhoun, Vice President, Martin Van Buren, Secretary of State, S.D. Ingham, Secretary of the Treasury, John H. Eaton, Secretary of War, John Branch, Secretary of the Navy.

Officers of the Mint. Samuel Moore, Director. James Rush, Treasurer. Adam Eckfeldt, Chief Coiner. Joseph Richardson, Assayer. Joseph Cloud, Melter and Refiner. William Kneass, Engraver. George Ehrenzeller, Clerk.

Architect of the Edifice. William Strickland.

Builders. Robert O'Neile, Carpenter. Jacob Souder, Mason.

The 1829 Half Dime

Whether those on hand at the ceremony each received specimens of the new half dime is not known. As noted concerning the piece placed in the box, this denomination had last been struck in 1805, following an intermittent coinage that had begun with the half disme in 1792. Were half dimes struck in quantity in the wee hours of the morning of July 4, preceding the 6 a.m. ceremony, or was there just one? It seems that enough would have been made to use them as souvenirs. On the other hand the first recorded delivery from the coiner to the treasurer of the Mint consisted of 10,000 pieces on July 25. The next delivery was 40,000 coins on August 5. By year's end there had been 17 deliveries totaling 1,230,000 pieces. Such coins are common and inexpensive today in circulated grades.

An estimated 20 or more Proof 1829 half dimes are known, this figure being higher than for any other in the 1829 to 1838 Capped Bust series. The quantities of Proofs struck were not recorded in the early days. The availability of Proof 1829 half dimes today suggested that quite a few were made, taking into account that most of them given out to non-collectors at the ceremony would not have been carefully preserved.

The motif is the Capped Bust type by John Reich, an assistant engraver at the Mint who introduced it on the half dollar of 1807, after which it was used on the dime beginning in 1809 and the quarter in 1815. It seems likely that the half dime was chosen for the ceremony because the Capped Bust was a novel design for that coin, for those who were aware of such things, and also as an inexpensive silver coin for distribution. As the first quantity delivery was not made until a few weeks later, if half dimes were distributed to the public on July 4 they were probably paid for by giving equal face value in silver coins to the Mint, so as not to affect the records. It strains credulity to suggest that as the new half dime was publicized at the time, none were available for anyone. But, who knows?

The National Numismatic Collection at the Smithsonian Institution includes more than 1.6 million specimens of coins, tokens, medals, and paper money, including many unique items. It is a treasure owned by the American public. Selections from the collection are on public display.

The Coin Collection at the Smithsonian

The Mint Cabinet Organized

Adam Eckfeldt.

Beginning about 1821, Adam Eckfeldt and possibly others at the Philadelphia Mint started saving specimens of current coinage.[1] It is likely that sometime during the 1830s, Baltimore collector Robert Gilmor Jr. suggested the idea of the Mint forming its own collection.[2] In June 1838 the Mint Cabinet was formally organized, and on March 3, 1839, Congress recognized the growing collection and voted an annual appropriation of $300 for its maintenance, the initial amount being $1,000 to launch the display. "The cabinet began with a small collection of Proof pieces and some of the more interesting foreign coins that had been sent in as bullion, which the coiner, Adam Eckfeldt, had preserved," a later curator commented in 1906.[3] Interestingly, in 1838 the term *Proof* had not been used yet to describe mirror-finish pieces, the designation not coming into popular application until the 1850s.

In 1838 William Ewing Dubois became curator, a position he maintained (in addition to other Mint duties) for years thereafter. By the early 1840s Jacob Reese Eckfeldt and Dubois had greeted many visitors. They created *A Manual of Gold and Silver Coins of All Nations, Struck Within the Past Century,* which was published by the Assay Department of the Mint in 1842 and became known as the *Assay Manual.* Although it was not a numismatically oriented volume, but was intended mostly for bullion and exchange dealers, it contained the first illustration of an 1804-dated silver dollar, from a plate pantographically engraved by running a stylus in a medal-ruling machine over the surface of the Mint Cabinet coin.

Alexandre Vattemare

Among the early visitors to the Mint Cabinet was Nicholas Marie Alexandre Vattemare, known as Alexandre Vattemare. As he is an important figure in American numismatics in the cradle days of the hobby he is deserving of notice here. Born in Paris on November 8, 1796, by age seven he was an expert ventriloquist, able to project—seemingly—his voice in different directions, making it appear that inanimate objects could speak, far antedating the earlier-mentioned Wyman the Wizard. From 1815 to 1835 he was on stage in more than 550 cities, mostly in Europe. His repertoire included ventriloquism as well as putting on acts in which in costume he played all of the different characters ranging from chimney sweeps to royalty and even fights between dogs and cats.

From 1839 to 1841 he toured America and Canada, with an early performance billed as Monsieur Alexandre at the Park Theatre in New York City on October 28, 1839, earning "incessant applause," per a newspaper account.

Alexandre Vattemare at age 26.

In the meantime he pursued interests in literature, monetary systems, and numismatics. During his American visit he met with congressmen and sold them on the idea of an international exchange system between libraries and museums, to spread knowledge.

In Philadelphia he was gifted with a signed copy of the Constitution. Traveling through 13 states and the eastern reaches of Canada he endeared himself to civic as well as academic leaders. More than 36,000 exchanges of books and related materials had taken place by the time he sailed back to Europe in June 1841. He returned to France with hundreds of coins, more than a thousand books, hundreds of engravings and prints, and many mineral specimens.

In a return visit in 1847 that lasted into 1850 Vattemare brought 50 cases of material from France. In 1848 Congress awarded him a stipend of $5,940 to further his exchange program. Among other accomplishments he was instrumental in the founding of the Boston Public Library.

On various visits to the Mint he was presented with Proof sets which he later donated to the Bibliothèque Nationale in Paris. Upon visiting Matthew A. Stickney, the well-known Salem, Massachusetts, collector, Vattemare was watched very closely by his host, who was somewhat fearful that by sleight-of-hand he might purloin his prized 1804 silver dollar![4] On a trip to Albany in 1850 he had come upon a room "knee-deep" in old historical documents of New York State, reminiscences of colonists, etc., these papers being considered waste to be used for cushioning for shipping newly published four-volume sets of *The Documentary History of New York*. He recognized the immense value of these papers and was instrumental in having them preserved by the archives of the state and cataloged by Dr. E.B. O'Callaghan, who had prepared the *Documentary History*.[5] The exchange program worked well for a time in the 1850s, after which interest waned.

In 1861 Vattemare was the author of *Collection die Monnaies et*

Proof sheet engraved by Rawdon, Wright & Hatch for Alexandre Vattemare's *American Album*. (Christie, Manson & Woods)

Médailles de l'Amerique du Nord de 1652 à 1858 (short title), a wonderfully detailed account of United States coins and, especially, medals, including those of the colonial period. This described nearly 400 examples of North American coinage; Vattemare suggested that the second silver dollar design of 1795 featured "the head of Liberty with the traits of Mme. [Martha] Washington." Probably this was his own observation, and was not based upon any specific information he obtained from Mint officials.

Meanwhile, Vattemare held a vast collection of coins, medals, bank notes, and other items, including many of American numismatic interest sent to him in later years, up to the time of his death in Paris in 1864. He had represented that they had been acquired for public use, but he never implemented this with the majority of his acquisitions.[6]

Mint Cabinet Catalogue Issued

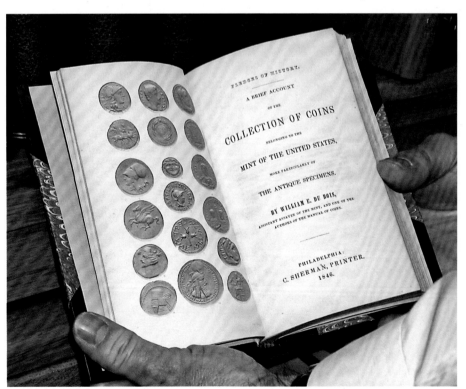

Pledges of History, by William E. DuBois.

In 1846 the Mint Cabinet was first cataloged, by William E. Dubois, assistant assayer at the Mint, in *Pledges of History: A Brief Account of the Collection of Coins Belonging to the Mint of the United States, More Particularly of the Antique Specimens.* The preparation of this text was simplified by printed labels for the ancient coins in the display cases being placed in a form that would also suit a pamphlet. It was noted at the beginning of this volume that "most of the letter-press is the same as that posted in the margin of the glass cases."

Through a private contribution, 140 copies of the cabinet's catalog were provided to such societies and individuals as would appreciate the subject. A vignette designed by Chief Engraver James B. Longacre decorated the volume. Besides a general history of money and the specimens in the collection, a table was included to classify the contents of the collection by each nation, empire, kingdom, or duchy, covering both ancient and modern times—and noting 385 examples from the United States out of a total of 3,802 specimens. The coins from all periods consisted of 605 in gold, 2,047 in silver, 324 in the alloy called billon (an alloy of copper with silver added, popular in the mid-19th century, scarcely heard of since), 822 in brass or copper, and 4 in platinum. By that time platinum, not considered to be a precious metal, had been used in certain Russian circulating coinage.

The 1850 Book

In 1850 Messrs. Jacob Reese Eckfeldt and William E. Dubois published a small book of 62 pages, *New Varieties of Gold and Silver Coins, Counterfeit Coins, Bullion with Mint Values.* This was intended for use by bullion and exchange brokers and gave exchange rates for various silver and gold coins. Further, it furnished a useful supplement to the 1842 *Assay Manual* by the same authors. Included was information on gold coins privately minted in California. This work was also issued in modified form in 1851 and 1852, these two later versions also including a reprint of the text of Dubois's 1846 *Pledges of History* work, the latter being out of print at the time. As is true of the 1842 book by the same authors, the 1850 volume and its two later editions were distributed in fairly large quantities. Some had tiny samples of California gold flakes mounted under mica on an inside page, an interesting promotional idea.

While the 1850 book was not focused upon the Mint Cabinet, it did contain much valuable information about certain coins on display there, particularly private and territorial gold issues.

A Visit to the Mint Cabinet (1851)

In the second edition of this work, 1851, the Mint display was described in part:

> The suite of apartments in the Mint appropriated to the exhibition of coins, ores, and national medals occupies the front of the building in the second story and measures 16 feet wide by 54 feet long. Originally there were three rooms, connecting with each other by folding-doors; the removal of these has made one large saloon, with recesses, very commodious and suitable for the use to which it is applied. The eastern and western rooms are of uniform size and construction; the central one has a dome and skylight, supported by four columns; with a corresponding window in its floor (protected by a railing) to light the hall of the entrance below.
>
> The ancient coins are displayed in eight cases, mounted in pairs, and placed erect against the walls in the wide doorways and the middle room. The modern coins are variously arranged; part (including all those of the United States) being in a nearly level case which surrounds the railing above mentioned; and part being in upright cases, disposed along the walls of the middle and west rooms.
>
> The ores, minerals, and metallic alloys are placed in the west room;[7] in the eastern are shown the national and other medals, and the fine beams used for the adjustment of weights. The middle room also contains portraits of the directors of the Mint, beginning with Rittenhouse, the first director. All the cases are fronted with glass, and, besides allowing an inspection of every specimen, present an agreeable *coup d'oeil* on entering the room, especially by the middle door.
>
> Visitors are admitted at prescribed hours, if attended by an officer or conductor of the institution. The collection was commenced in June 1838. Long before that date, however, Adam Eckfeldt, formerly chief coiner, led as well by his own taste as by the expectation that a conservatory would someday be established, took pains to preserve master-coins[8] of the different annual issues of the Mint, and to retain some of the finest foreign specimens, as they appeared in deposit for recoinage.

The Mint Cabinet also served as a gathering place for numismatists, who were warmly welcomed. Proof coins and sets were provided on request as were medals. (In the same city the piano and musical-instrument repair shop of Joseph J. Mickley was a coin club of sorts.)

Joseph N.T. Levick, a Philadelphia numismatist who later moved to New York City and who began his interest in rare coins sometime prior to 1855, described a visit to the Mint early in that decade:[9]

Cents in those days were easily found in circulation in such condition as to satisfy a collector; always excepting, of course, those rare dates of 1799 and 1804, which were considered scarcer than the 1793s, and even those dates were to be had of collectors by exchanging.

I quite well remember what an advantage the Mint was to us who lived in Philadelphia, for we had the privilege of going to the institution and selecting from trays or drawers subdivided for each date. From these I procured some excellent specimens of cents for their face value; and many of us collectors, knowing this channel, thus secured cheap cents. We also took the precaution to lay aside quantities of fine pieces to trade with, and for some years afterwards, the market was well stocked with cents. The employees of the Mint, however, soon learned to know the increasing value of these coins, and also commenced laying aside the finer pieces and more unusual dates. Our game was blocked by this discovery, for we saw thenceforward that the desirable cents were missing.[10]

James Ross Snowden

The first Mint director to take a serious interest in the Mint Cabinet was James Ross Snowden, who entered the post in 1853. By a few years later he became particularly fascinated with the tokens and medals of George Washington, of which the Mint Cabinet had but a handful. Offering to trade patterns and restrikes as well as duplicates, Snowden and the staff significantly added to the display. On February 22, 1860, the Washington Cabinet was dedicated as a part of the Mint Cabinet. A special medal was struck for the occasion, from dies engraved by Anthony C. Paquet.

The Washington Cabinet medal by Anthony C. Paquet.

In the same year, a book was published under Snowden's name, *A Description of Ancient and Modern Coins in the Cabinet of the Mint of the United States.* The volume was primarily researched and written by William Ewing Dubois and George Bull (curator of the Mint Cabinet). This 412-page volume was and still is highly regarded and contains much useful information, including the first notable listing of pattern coins ever to reach print. Certain commentary must have been derived from conversations rather than old Mint records, as there are scattered inaccuracies as might be expected from any first effort.

In the following year another Snowden book was published, the lavishly illustrated, printed, and bound 204-page work, *A Description of the Medals of Washington.* Illustrated were items relating to the title subject as well as certain other pieces, all from the Mint Cabinet.

Trading Coins

By October 25, 1873, the Mint Cabinet contained 6,484 specimens of coins and medals; the cost of these, including gems, minerals, etc., was $12,443, according to curator Dubois. On July 14, 1881, Dubois died. He was succeeded as Mint Cabinet curator by his son Patterson, who capitalized his surname as *DuBois.* Patterson, who had been at the Mint since about 1866, resigned in late summer 1886 to become managing editor of the *Sunday School Times.* He is best remembered today for a small article he contributed to the *American Journal of Numismatics,* January 1883, "The Pattern Piece," which told of the utility of patterns, the story of what might have been.

Apparently, Patterson DuBois had been engaging in some coin swapping. In October 1886 the editor of the *American Journal of Numismatics* remarked that the curator of the Mint Cabinet had been exchanging duplicates of rare colonials for some gold coins it lacked, such trades being rumored as "far more profitable to the dealer than the government."

R.A. McClure's Effort

After Patterson DuBois's departure, others became involved with the Mint Cabinet, with R.A. McClure named as curator, moving up from the assistanceship he had held for a number of years. So far as is known, McClure's numismatic credentials were modest at best. A native of Pennsylvania, he had been hired at the Mint in 1868 and was soon associated with the Mint Cabinet. In 1877 his wages were $4.25 per day. In 1887, E.L. Royal was assistant curator to McClure.[11]

Yet another edition of the descriptive catalog of the Mint Cabinet was prepared in 1891 by McClure, titled *An Index to the Coins and Medals of the Cabinet of the Mint of the United States at Philadelphia.* In the transmittal letter of May 12, 1891, from O.C. Bosbyshell, superintendent of the Philadelphia Mint, to E.O. Leech, director of the Mint, Washing-

ton, D.C, this new edition of the descriptive catalog was described as being "very complete."

It was intended that the book be funded by the federal government in the interest of education, that 20,000 copies be printed, and that it showcase "such a valuable, historical collection, in some enduring form, so that it can be more understandingly studied and comprehended." However, the scarcity of copies today suggests that far fewer were made, unless thousands of these books remain in some long-forgotten room or warehouse.

Moreover, good intentions notwithstanding, McClure furnished little information not known to numismatists of the era, with the result that the book is of little use to scholars today.

At the Columbian Exposition

In 1892 much of the Mint Cabinet, amounting to about 7,000 coins and 2,000 medals, was moved to Chicago, Illinois, and set up by the Treasury Department as part of a large exhibit at the World's Colum-

The United States Mint exhibit with cases and displays from the Mint Cabinet. (*Shepp's World's Fair Photographed*)

bian Exposition, which opened to the public a year late, in 1893, as discussed in chapter 10.

Perhaps a reflection of McClure's expertise—or, more appropriately, lack of it—is the review by Dr. George F. Heath, in *The Numismatist,* February 1894. Heath noted that there were a number of coin exhibits at the Exposition, the primary one being that of the Philadelphia Mint, displayed in the Government Building, and "arranged in so jumbled and amateurish a manner that but little benefit could be derived from it." However, for uneducated viewers the display seemed to have worked out well: "If, however, the exhibit was designed to interest the novice, as we must believe it was, it was a decided success. All day long the space around the cases was crowded by an anxious and expectant mass of humanity, and the comments on the coins, one could hear from the tyro, were decidedly refreshing and interesting, and the explanation often given to the gaping looker-on by someone more or less 'up' on the matter proved that a little learning may be an amusing as well as a dangerous thing."

The main attraction in the Mint Cabinet was the "Widow's Mite," it was stated, with the 1804 dollar and 1849 double eagle coming in for their share of attention as well. Further from Heath:

> The coining press, used in our mints, in operation also attracted considerable attention and souvenir medals struck in brass found ready sale at 25 cents each. In this connection it is worthy to note that while medals of the cheaper class struck in brass, copper, bronze, aluminum or white metal, were offered for sale and hawked all about over the grounds of the city, the better class representative of a higher art so much sought after and obtained in our Centennial Exhibition in 1876 were conspicuous for their absence.[12]

The wooden and glass cabinets used in the Mint Cabinet display at the Exposition were subsequently brought back to Philadelphia and employed there in the front room on the second floor. In 1894, McClure estimated the Mint Cabinet to be worth "upwards of $58,000." Apparently, this represented the *intrinsic value,* not the market value, of the pieces.[13] As such, the figure had no numismatic relevance.

Zerbe Visits the Mint Cabinet

In the early years of the present century, Farran Zerbe (see Thomas L. Elder's comments about him in chapter 24) was in the midst of extensive travels around America. He roved widely, often filing reports with *Numismatist* editor Heath. In August 1903 he told of a visit to the Philadelphia Mint, which since 1901 had been in a new facility. He lamented that in the Mint Cabinet display not a single coin from the Confederate States of America was to be seen, but, on the other hand, a fascinating collection of 140 New Jersey coppers was on view. The condition of certain United States coins was less than ideal, as Zerbe related:

> I found many of the silver Proof coins of late years partially covered

The Mint Cabinet circa 1900.

with a white coating. On inquiry I learned that an overzealous attendant during the last vacation months when the numismatic room was closed took it on himself to clean the tarnished coins, purchased some metal polish at a department store, and proceeded with his cleaning operation. Later a coating of white appeared on the coins, which was now slowly disappearing.

I expressed my displeasure at this improper treatment of Proof coins, and the custodian explained, "that is nothing. I have been here eight years and they have been cleaned three or four times in my time."

Zerbe speculated that should this cleaning continue, in the future one would have nothing left except plain planchets and badly worn coins! More from Zerbe was printed in November 1904, when he suggested that as the Mint Cabinet had been subject to damage and abuse, the American Numismatic Association might offer its services to enlarge, improve, and contribute to the preservation of the coins:

"That the National Collection should be in charge of someone with a knowledge of coins and their care, has repeatedly been made manifest," he commented, then repeating what he had said earlier and giving additional details, including the disappearance of a certain $50 pattern:

A few years ago during the summer vacation when the Mint Cabinet was closed, one of the custodians thereof in his desire to improve the appearance of tarnished Proofs, subjected them to a scouring process, using an ordinary kitchen compound for this purpose; thus producing cleaned coins of the Proofs, some of

them unique, as they were the only evidences of patterns that existed.

Another instance was in the destruction of what, to my mind, was the most interesting specimen among the patterns of the proposed coinage for this country. From dies that had been prepared for a $50 gold piece, but one piece had been struck, this in gold. Not only was it in this sense unique, but the only metallic evidence that existed, indicating the entertainment by the government of issuing a coin of so large a denomination. In recent years the one in authority to so act, decided that $50 was too much to be tied up in a specimen of this kind and elected that a base metal copy would answer the purpose. He had the $50 gold piece melted, and from the amount received therefrom, he endeavored to improve the collection, but how did he do it? He purchased a number of ordinary Spanish and Mexican silver pieces. . . . Evidences of the $50 pattern were restored by producing a bronze copy, but this copy is not unique, several pieces being struck. The original piece in gold was as much a part of the record of the Treasury as any document, and such should have been preserved.

What Zerbe didn't know is that at least two impressions had been struck in gold, not only one, and that both pieces were preserved, filtering out of the Mint into private hands, namely Philadelphia dealer J.W. Haseltine, through whom they surfaced a few years later, to much fanfare, in a transaction involving Haseltine and Stephen K. Nagy and their customer William H. Woodin.

T. Louis Comparette

In 1905, T. Louis Comparette, Ph.D., was appointed as curator. From the time of W.E. Dubois's death in 1881 until the naming of Comparette in 1905, the Mint Cabinet suffered much under the incompetent McClure. As Zerbe observed, former glittering gem Proofs were now reduced to cleaned, hairlined coins. The treatment was irreversible. Otherwise the National Numismatic Collection would have countless superb gems today.

Under Comparette's watch at least the Mint Cabinet rebounded in its reputation. In March 1906 he contributed an article to *The Numismatist,* "On the Utility of a Cabinet of Historic Coins," which gave the history of the Mint Collection and noted that by 1906 it comprised "about 15,000 pieces, and includes many rare and scientifically important specimens." A comparison was given to numismatic museums elsewhere, including 350,000 coins in the Bibliothèque National in Paris, 270,000 of the Royal Cabinet of Coins, Berlin, and 250,000 in the British Museum, followed by 180,000 in the Numismatic Cabinet in Munich, 120,000 in the National Archaeological Museum in Madrid, and 95,000 in the National Numismatic Museum in Athens.

On May 28, 1910, Comparette became an associate member of the American Numismatic Society. In 1912 the first edition was printed of his large book, *Catalogue of Coins, Tokens, and Medals in the Numismatic Collection of the Mint of the United States at Philadelphia, Pa.* Subsequent editions were published in 1913 and 1914. Regarding the United States series, the catalog was nothing more than a bare listing of dates and, occasionally, a mintmarked variety. Little effort was made to give numismatically interesting and important information (such as the time of acquisition and source of specimens, their grades, and their historical or numismatic significance). Accordingly, similar to in this respect to McClure's catalog, it contains little of use to present-day scholars.

In the meantime, Comparette was quite active on the numismatic scene. During the excitement surrounding the 1907 release of the new $10 and $20 coins, featuring designs by Augustus Saint-Gaudens, Comparette was the Mint's spokesperson. In January and February 1914 he brought rarities from the Mint Cabinet to the American Numismatic Society, 155th Street and Broadway, New York City, for a memorable display that, among other things, featured four 1804 silver dollars (but none from the Mint Collection).

During most of the year 1922 the Denver, Philadelphia, and San Francisco mints were closed to visitors, due to concern raised after a robbery at the Denver facility. During this time the Mint Cabinet was not on view. Reflective of this, Secretary of the Treasury Andrew W. Mellon wrote to Charles D. Walcott, secretary of the Smithsonian Institution, on February 8, 1923:

> It has recently been deemed advisable in the interest of safety to close the United States Mints to visitors. As you are aware, there is a large numismatic collection in the Mint at Philadelphia. Since the Mint is to be permanently closed [!] to visitors, the inspection of the collection by the public is no longer possible.
>
> There is an important and very beautiful selection of coins, tokens, and medals, perhaps the largest and most complete numismatic collection owned by the government. The logical place for this collection would seem to be in the National Museum in Washington, and I am writing to see if you would consider it feasible to have the collection transferred there. . . .[14]

The Smithsonian Institution

Prior to 1923, the Smithsonian Institution had its own numismatic collections, although in the United States series they mounted no challenge to the Mint Cabinet in Philadelphia.

The Institution's founding dated back to the early 1800s. James Smithson, an Englishman who died in Genoa, Italy, on June 27, 1829, and who had never visited America, bequeathed the bulk of his estate to the United States "for the increase and diffusion of knowledge." Smithson was interested in numismatics (although this does not seem to have influenced his bequest decision), as evidenced by the inclusion in his estate of "two pasteboards containing medals, coins . . . etc."[15]

In 1838, Richard Rush was appointed by the U.S. government to arrange shipment of gold coins representing the value of the estate and the transportation of the coins to America. This amounted to 104,960 gold sovereigns, 8 shillings, and 6 pence.[16] The gold sovereigns were placed into 105 bags of 1,000 coins, except for one bag which had 960 sovereigns, 8 silver shillings, and 6 copper pence. Shipment was made to America aboard the *Mediator*. Although no effort was made to save any of the sovereigns as mementos, apparently two may have been retained.

On August 10, 1846, the Smithsonian Institution was founded by an act of Congress. On May 1, 1847, the cornerstone was laid to its first building.

In 1858 the National Institution for the Promotion of Science, organized on May 15, 1840, began to transfer its extensive collections—including coins and medals—to the Smithsonian, an effort that was not completed until 1883. In the early 1840s the National Institute, as it was called, had mounted displays in rooms in the Patent Office Building and was "very prosperous."[17] Its collections included coins from local museum operator John Varden and also the Columbian Institute for the Promotion of Arts and Sciences, the charter of which had expired in 1838.

By 1886 the Smithsonian had 1,055 coins, medals, and related numismatic items in its collection. About this time a number of pieces were placed on display. In 1891, Dr. R.E.C. Stearns, an associate curator, prepared an exhibit of Indian shell money, medals of historical events, and tokens. The filled cases remained in place until 1893, when they were taken down to make room for an expanded exhibit related to natural history.

In 1909 Theodore T. Belote was named assistant curator of the Division of History at the Smithsonian.[18] In time, Belote developed and refined an interest in numismatics and wrote several papers. By 1914 he had supervised the arrangement of more than 6,000 coins, tokens, medals, and notes in 27 flat cases plus vertical cabinets, the latter including some that had been at the Columbian Exposition. In the process "Belote . . . saw to the cleaning of every coin and medal to be displayed, but no details are [known] of the methods he employed."[19]

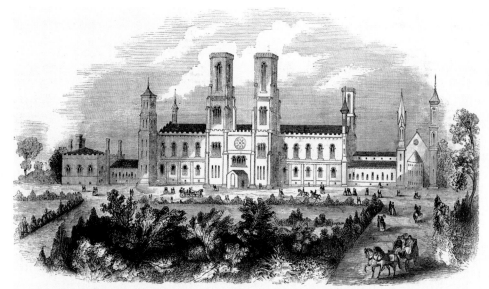

The Smithsonian Institution in its early days. This building, known as "the Castle," stands today and is used for special events. (*Gleason's Pictorial Drawing-Room Companion*, April 24, 1852)

The Move to Washington

On April 3, 1923, Andrew Mellon, secretary of the Treasury, approved Director of the Mint Robert W. Wooley's recommendation for the transfer of the Mint Cabinet from Philadelphia to the Smithsonian Institution. Among the dissenters was S. Hudson Chapman, Philadelphia coin dealer, who felt it would be a great loss to his city. On the other hand, the American Numismatic Association voiced its approval (in *The Numismatist,* May 1923).

On May 28, 1923, the Mint Cabinet specimens arrived at the Smithsonian. Involved in the move were 18,291 pieces from Philadelphia. These were added to 21,523 already on hand in the History Department under the supervision of Theodore T. Belote. Henceforth it was generally called the Mint Collection, although nomenclature was hardly standardized. It is remembered that in 1912 the catalog title of the holding was, in part, Numismatic Collection of the Mint. The term "cabinet" was becoming increasingly obsolete.

By spring 1924, exhibits combining the old Smithsonian collection with the newly arrived Mint Cabinet specimens had been nearly completed. Modifications and rearrangements were made in 1925 and 1926.

In 1925, seeking to help with the exhibit, the American Numismatic Association set up the "A.N.A. Smithsonian Committee," for which ANA President Moritz Wormser did much work. In 1927, through the benefactions of Robert P. King, the ANA began to organize its own collection, and in 1928 part of the ANA's holdings were loaned to the Smithsonian.

The October 1926 issue of *The Numismatist* included an article, "The Numismatic Group of the National Historical Collections," by Belote, which told of the function of the Mint Collection housed at the Smithsonian.

In 1931 the numismatic exhibit was moved from a dingy, dark area to a well-lighted section of the Arts and Industries Building, in which location it remained for the next several decades. In 1933 there were 45,802 specimens in the collection.[20] In 1932 and 1933 a special exhibit of Hard Times, Civil War, and other tokens was prepared, and in 1934 a case of pattern coins was added to the display.

However, "over the next two decades the lack of a numismatist and a trained staff, an ever-increasing workload, and general neglect of the hall led to the continuing deterioration of the coins and medals on display as well as in the reference collections. There is a report that mentions the cleaning of the silver coins in 1937."[21]

Visiting the Collection

On August 23, 1937, a coterie of collectors attending the ANA Convention in Washington visited the Mint Collection, as later reported:

> On Tuesday afternoon buses conveyed the party to the Smithsonian Institution to view the government collection of coins and other historical exhibits installed in this wonderful building. The coins are located in a large room close to the entrance, and there we were greeted by Dr. A. Wetmore, of the Department of History, and Theo. T. Belote, curator of the collection. The collection of coins lent to the Smithsonian by the ANA occupies four large cases in this room, each fairly well filled, but with room for additions, which the ANA will probably make from time to time.[22]
>
> It was soon discovered by someone in the party that the 1804 dollar in the collection was not in its accustomed place. It was explained by Mr. Belote that it had been temporarily transferred to a case containing many of the other rarities in the collection. One of the cases is devoted to commemorative half dollars, and it was noted that a few

of these issues are not represented. Most of the commemoratives are shown in duplicate, with both sides visible. It might be explained that no specific appropriation is made for the purchase of coins, and the only money available for this purpose is what the division can save from other appropriations.[23]

In March 1947, *The Numismatist* included a letter from William Guild, a Massachusetts reader, who reported the following:

Having just returned from a trip to Washington and a visit to the Smithsonian Institution to study the collection of coins on display, I am shocked. I first talked with (of all things) the curator of history who has charge of this exhibit and he told me the following: He has no list of the coins for distribution and apparently has not even a list for his own use. This irreplaceable collection is rapidly deteriorating from tarnish and filth which sifts into the cases and literally, on one case, the dirt was so thick that you could have scooped it up in your fingers. There are certain cards on which apparently coins were placed at one time which are now blank—for what reason I do not know.

The coins are displayed in such a way that it is practically impossible to see the details on any except those at the very front edge, and there is literally no illumination except what comes in through the windows at the opposite side of the large hall. In referring to the Adams-Woodin pattern book,[24] there are several coins mentioned as being in the Mint Collection which are not even in the display which, in the face of the curator's statement that 'All the coins are in the display' makes his statement a little difficult to understand.

The curator told me that he has no funds available for proper cataloguing or protection of the coins nor for any further extension of the collection and by and large, the whole situation looks like pretty much of a mess to me. I am sending this letter to you as I feel that this is something that should be taken up on a national and official basis as it seems just too bad that these irreplaceable specimens should be thus neglected. Hoping that you may be able to find space to publish this letter so that this situation may come to the attention of the ANA membership and hoping that the ANA will take cognizance of the situation and make definite recommendations to cure the condition, I am, Cordially yours. . . .

In 1947 I was living in Baltimore and in the third grade. Our family took a train to Washington and visited the Smithsonian and looked at the coin exhibits, which were in a dingy room as described above. There was no curator, guard, or other person on hand to answer questions, and no one else was in the room for the half hour or so I spent looking in the glass-fronted cases.

Stuart Mosher Arrives in 1948
In 1948, the Mint Collection consisted of 54,175 specimens. Stuart Mosher was named curator in August of that year. Mosher, an accomplished numismatist, had worked since the 1930s with Wayte Raymond and Moritz Wormser (founder of New Netherlands Coin Co.), among other commercial activities,

and had edited *The Numismatist* since 1945 (a position he would continue to hold until 1954). When Richard S. Yeoman was compiling information for a new work to be titled *A Guide Book of United States Coins* (released in November 1946 with a 1947 cover date), he relied heavily upon Mosher for guidance and expertise, and gave him the very first numbered copy of the book when it was released.[25]

In 1946 Mosher moved to McAllen, Texas, where he became the personal curator for O.K. Rumbel, a numismatist who later sold certain of his coins through New Netherlands Coin Co., including at the 1952 American Numismatic Association convention auction. In the 1940s and early 1950s, his brother-in-law, Alan W. Faxon, worked with Wayte Raymond and distributed certain of Raymond's books and albums.

Writing in *The Numismatist,* December 1948, Mosher informed collectors that:

> The National Coin Collection in the Smithsonian Institution is being given a general overhauling. It is being cleaned, labeled and rearranged. The cases are being repainted inside with a much lighter tone of paint and arrangements are being made to provide additional lighting. So far, six cases out of the 110 in the coin room have been completed and the results seem highly satisfactory.
>
> Our own opinion is frequently substantiated by visitors who remark, "Why don't they fix the rest of the cases up like those?" Quite a few members of the ANA have visited us here, since we became acting curator of numismatics about the first of September, and without exception they approve of the work that is being done on the collection. Their attitude has been very encouraging.
>
> About the time this issue of *The Numismatist* is in your hands, the entire section of United States coins will have been finished and a good start made on the foreign sections. It will be perhaps many, many months before the work is completed but, when it is, the indications are that the time and work will be well spent.

According to a later curator, Mosher did indeed clean many of the "tarnished coins" "by methods recommended by the Bureau of Standards. Unfortunately, some of those methods would hardly pass any tests today."[26] On the same subject, Dr. George J. Fuld (whose family owned a chemical company in Baltimore) recalled this:[27]

> We had a lot of direct contact with Stuart Mosher in 1948 and 1949, having bought his collection on the condition that we wrote the first "Token Collectors" pages in *The Numismatist.* Since dad and I were both chemists, he consulted us at least once before cleaning the Smithsonian silver coins.
>
> The procedure he wanted to do (and did!) was dipping the coins in potassium cyanide. This same lethal procedure killed Sanford Saltus, the American Numismatic Society member, as you know from your study of numismatic history.[28] We tried to discourage him—we told him that any residual cyanide would horribly tone the coins—they would have to have been cleaned with lots of distilled water, preferably sonically, but I am sure this was never done—there was no abrasive cleaning, only the cyanide. They looked pretty for a year or so, and then started to turn, as you know.

Mosher died on February 20, 1956, having been ill for about two years. Mendel Peterson, who was especially well known in the field of undersea exploration for treasure, was named as acting curator, a position he occupied for the next several months.

The Stefanelli Team

In October 1956, Dr. Vladimir Clain-Stefanelli (the "Clain" part of his surname was rarely used, conversationally or in correspondence, by his friends) was named acting curator (soon to become curator) of the Mint Collection, which in 1959 Congress set apart as the Division of Numismatics within the Smithsonian Institution. Previously, Dr. Stefanelli had managed Coin Galleries for the Stack family in New York City, and before that he had been associated with Robert Hecht in the business of Hesperia Art, a New York City firm specializing in classical numismatics. In 1953, when Hecht dissolved the New York office and moved to Europe, he noted: "I have known Dr. Clain-Stefanelli for six years and only as a friendly and cultivated person, a proficient and profound scholar, and a judicious numismatist." Vladimir later wrote, "An electrolytic apparatus was installed in 1957 for cleaning tarnished and corroded coins. . . ."[29]

In May 1960, *The Numismatist* noted that under the direction of Dr. Vladimir Clain-Stefanelli the Numismatic Department of the Smithsonian Institution was making great strides forward, after having been more or less moribund for many years. Further:

A survey of the gold coins struck in the United States was completed by Acting Curator Vladimir Clain-Stefanelli and published in abridged form in various issues of the *Washington Star.* Some progress was made in the *Dictionary of American Engravers and Medallists,* and also in the arrangement of collation of source material for a corpus of Greek coinage from Kallatis, Dionysopolis, Istros, Markianopolis, Nikopolis, Odessus, and Tomis.

Dr. Clain-Stefanelli's research on 'Re-attribution of Some Alexander Coins' continued, and a 'Chronology of the Lysimachus series of Kallatis' was worked out, based on a comparative study of the dies as well as on stylistic, historical, and intrinsic elements. The results of this study formed the subject of a lecture presented at the annual meeting of the Board of Regents of the Smithsonian Institution. . . . In connection with their research projects, Dr. and Mrs. Clain-Stefanelli traveled extensively, visiting mints in the United States and Canada. Paper currencies and other source material of the colonial period formed the subject of research at the American Antiquarian Society in Worcester, Massachusetts.

Dr. Stefanelli's wife, Elvira Eliza Clain-Stefanelli, was a talented scholar and writer. In 1957 she was named as first assistant curator (elevated to associate curator in 1959). Together the team brought a new level of sophisticated curatorship and expertise to the Mint Collection, the first truly enlightened and scholarly oriented management since the Eckfeldt-Dubois era of the 1850s! They were both fine friends of mine and helped me with many research inquiries. In reciprocation I went to Washington on several occasions to examine and discuss certain American coins, including a 1787 Brasher doubloon, and I facilitated the donation of the Norweb family's 1913 Liberty Head nickel to the collection.

In 1960 Louis E. Eliasberg Sr. lent his complete collection of United States coins by date and mint-mark sequence, and during the several months it was on display it attracted an unprecedented 1.5 million viewers, as mentioned in chapter 5. Clearly, coins, if attractively presented, could draw large crowds.

New Exhibit Opened

The March 1961 issue of *The Numismatist* included this:

> The Smithsonian Institution's new exhibit of Monetary History will open on Saturday afternoon, March 18, 1961, at 3 o'clock in the Arts and Industries Building, Jefferson Drive, and Ninth Street, on the Mall, Washington, D.C. Numismatists are invited to attend, according to Dr. V. Clain-Stefanelli, Curator of Numismatics, Smithsonian Institution.
>
> The Hall of Monetary History and Medallic Art illustrates the major lines of the development of money economy from the beginning of primitive barter to the establishment of our modern monetary systems. This is an entirely new approach in numismatic exhibition in that the exhibits have been arranged to show the evolution of money within the sequence of the most significant historical events and as an integral part of the cultural development of human society.
>
> Special emphasis has been given to the development of the various forms of currencies in North America and their role in the economic and political growth of the United States. The Hall also features the world's largest collection of gold coins on public display, that of the late Paul A. Straub, as well as the renowned United States Mint Collection, and selections from the Willis H. du Pont Collection [Mikhailovich Collection] of Russian coins and medals.

In 1961 and 1962, the Union Carbide Corporation advised on "a new and promising method of protecting silver coins against corrosion. The product tested was a low-viscosity solution containing 7.5% silicone solids in a solvent system formulated primarily for spray application."[30] However, I recall that the Stefanellis were not satisfied with such a chemical process, and when Richard Picker, a New York coin dealer, located a supplier of clear Lucite plastic holders with protective faces, the Smithsonian curators ordered many of these and were delighted with the results. Unlike certain previous caretakers, curators, and well-intentioned chemists, outside consultants, et al., the Stefanellis *knew* coins. No doubt under their watch the careless cleaning of coins on multiple occasions ended forever, or at least to the time I write these words (I hope that future caretakers will be numismatically inclined).

During the ensuing decades the husband-and-wife team did much for the hobby, including the presentation of forums and special discussions, the publication of articles, and a generous welcome given to numismatic scholars who desired to utilize the collection. In time, a fine research staff was hired.

Upon Dr. Stefanelli's death in 1982, his wife Elvira, known as Liza to her friends, became curator.

New Premises, New Exhibits

In 1963 the Numismatic Division and entire Hall of Numismatics was moved to the new Museum of History and Technology at the Smithsonian, and the exhibits were arranged in January 1964. Coins that had been on loan from the American Numismatic Association were returned, later to be shown at the ANA's headquarters building. At the time the staff, in addition to Dr. and Mrs. Stefanelli, included Charles D. Wilkinson, Carl J. Jaeschke, and R. LeGette Burris.

Keeping in step with changing coin technology, a special "Our New Coinage" display was opened in September 1965, illustrating the clad-metal coinage that had replaced the 90% silver alloy in use in prior years.

In 1967 Josiah K. Lilly, a pharmaceutical executive with the firm bearing his surname, passed away,

The Coin Collection at the Smithsonian

leaving in his estate a collection of about 6,500 gold coins valued at $5,534,808. The holding included a nearly complete set of United States gold date-and-mintmark varieties, except for the 1870-S $3 (that unique coin was in the Eliasberg Collection). For many years Lilly had worked exclusively through Stack's to build this marvelous holding, and not a single coin was acquired elsewhere!

A bill was filed in Congress to authorize the government to acquire the collection on behalf of the Smithsonian Institution by granting tax relief to the Lilly estate. Such an acquisition would make the Smithsonian Collection "the foremost in the world." Appointed by the administrators of the Lilly estate were professional numismatists Abe Kosoff and Hans M.F. Schulman, who performed the appraisal. Paul A. Rawley, vice president of the Merchants National Bank & Trust Co., Indianapolis, Indiana, supervised the liquidation of the Lilly estate. Kosoff's appraisal report was submitted on September 5, 1967.

Congress was very slow in its action toward the donation, and in the meantime plans were made with Peregrine Pollen, president of Parke-Bernet Galleries, New York City, to auction the coins if the gift proposal was not passed by Congress. News releases were prepared to the effect that Kosoff would be the cataloger of the collection.[31] To the delight of the numismatic community and as a treasure for posterity, the Lilly Collection finally went to the Smithsonian, after which highlights from the fabulous cabinet were put on display. Lilly's fine collection of stamps was sent to Robert Siegel, New York City, for auction.[32]

In the 1970s the Chase Manhattan Bank Money Museum was shuttered, as the bank felt that it was not contributing to the "bottom line" of profits, this in an era in which profits were just about the most important consideration for any business. Public relations and altruism often suffered. The prized 1804 dollar displayed by the museum for many years was given to the American Numismatic Society, while the rest of the collection went to the Smithsonian Institution. The transfer was completed in 1980, thus providing

the latest chapter in the history of a collection the Chase National Bank had purchased from Farran Zerbe in 1928. In earlier times parts of the collection had been set up by Zerbe at the 1904 Louisiana Purchase Exposition, the 1914 Panama-Pacific International Exposition, and other venues.

In the 1980s Elvira Clain-Stefanelli continued as curator, while Cora ("Cory") Gillilland, who joined the staff in 1965, served as associate curator. Mrs. Gillilland had her own set of memorable accomplishments, including the writing of articles, the presentation of forums, and, especially, the creation of a fine

While president of the American Numismatic Association, I visit with Elvira Clain-Stefanelli, in 1983.

book published in 1992, *Sylloge of the United States Holdings in the National Numismatic Collection of the Smithsonian Institution. Volume 1: Gold Coins, 1785–1834.*

Elvira Eliza Clain-Stefanelli wrote many articles and monographs over a long period of time, participated in several Coinage of the Americas conferences held by the American Numismatic Society, and more. Her *Numismatic Bibliography,* published in 1985, became a standard reference on the title subject. To the *American Numismatic Association Centennial Anthol-*

ogy, which accompanied the history that I wrote, she contributed two research articles, "From the Drawing-board of a Coin Engraver," and "Old Friends—Common Goals: The Evolution of Numismatics in the United States."

The curatorial staff was very appreciative of the historical artifacts the museum possessed, and during the period under the Stefanelli management, many sketches, documents, and other items were showcased in publications and exhibits, bringing new insights to the engraving and artwork of Christian Gobrecht, James B. Longacre, William and Charles Barber, George T. Morgan, and other coin and medal designers.

In the 1990s she was honored by a special *festschrift,* or collection of research papers contributed by her friends to be published in a book in her honor. Invited participants were from all over the world. I was honored to be included.

Dr. Doty Named Curator

In May 1986, *The Numismatist* carried this account:

> Richard G. Doty has been appointed curator of Western Hemisphere numismatics for the National Numismatic Collections at the Smithsonian's National Museum of American History, effective April 21, 1986. Doty will have charge of the massive collections of United States paper money, as well as equally large holdings of currencies and financial documents from other countries. He also will administer the collections of Roman, medieval and Latin American holdings, including the Josiah K. Lilly Collection of Spanish-American gold coins, one of the world's most comprehensive collections outside South America.

> Doty, who has served as curator of the American Numismatic Society since 1974, will contribute substantially to the ongoing reorganization of the approximately 900,000 items in the National Numismatic Collections. As a staff member of the National Museum of American History, he also will serve on committees involved in steering general museum policies.

> Doty holds a Ph.D. in Latin American Studies from the University of Southern California and most recently was assistant professor of United States and Latin American History at the University of Guam before joining the ANS. His recent publications include *The MacMillan Encyclopedic Dictionary of Numismatics* (1982), *Money of the World* (1978), *Paper Money of the World* (1977), and *Coins of the World* (1976).

Doty's writing and research continued, and he created many articles, gave public presentations, and wrote additional books, the latter including a study on American coinage from the earliest days onward, and the definitive history of the Soho Mint (in Birmingham, England; a maker of many tokens and medals associated with the American series).

In 1996 the U.S. Mint produced commemorative silver dollars and $5 gold coins honoring the Smithsonian.

A footnote was added to the history of the National Numismatic Collection when it was announced in the numismatic press in March 1999 that budgetary constraints might force the closing of the exhibits and facilities as they were presently known, the collection might have to be put in vaults, and in the future only occasional exhibits would be mounted. I talked with the Smithsonian people at the time and was told that an animatronic display, a la

Commemorative silver dollar honoring the 150th anniversary of the Smithsonian Institution.

Disney, might be mounted in that space to show baseball heroes in action. At the time a craze for collecting baseball trading cards was sweeping the nation, and just about every town and city had shops devoted to selling them. As might be expected, the fad faded and most shops later closed.

This news spurred a rallying cry from the numismatic community, which, it was hoped, would result in this priceless treasure receiving the budget and recognition millions of coin collectors believe that it deserves. However, it seemed that the news articles were more form than actual substance, as Dr. Richard Doty advised that while the direction of the exhibits might be changed (the current one having been in place for a long time), there was every expectation that the integrity of the collection would be maintained.[33]

In the meantime, Elvira Eliza Clain-Stefanelli declined official retirement, and while the day-to-day overall curatorship and work was left to others, she maintained a keen interest in the National Numismatic Collection and activities concerning it. I conversed with her at length at the American Numismatic Association convention in August 1999.

Transition

Transition took place, budgetary constraints intervened, and it was all that Dick Doty could to do keep pace with suggestions and fend off ideas that seemed to be negative. There were many positive situations, however, such as when the Bureau of Engraving and Printing moved its massive collection of proof sheets of federal currency, including for more than 10,000 National Banks, to the Smithsonian.

In the meantime, Doty expanded his outreach to researchers and allowed numismatists such as Peter Huntoon, Jeff Garrett, and me to spend time with the collection and make detailed studies.

Dr. Brent Glass, director of the Museum of American History, held a special reception for numismatic leaders in 2005 at the "Castle" building. On view were treasures from the National Numismatic

The author with Dr. Brent Glass at the 2005 reception.

Collection. The program consisted of commentary on the importance of coins and related subjects and plans for the future.

In 2008 "Stories on Money," a gallery exhibit of rare coins, was opened on the main floor of the Smithsonian's National Museum of American History. Dr. Glass welcomed collectors, the press, and others to a ceremony. The gallery, still in place as a prime attraction, includes many of the "rarest of the rare" items from the collection.

Entrance to the "Stories on Money" exhibit with grandson John Bowers, numismatic researcher and coin dealer Jeff Garrett, and Whitman publisher Dennis Tucker to the right.

Associate curator Jim Hughes, Mary Counts Burleson (president of Whitman Publishing), curator Dick Doty, and me at the Smithsonian.

In the meantime Dick Doty and his staff welcomed visitors and also mounted displays including each year at the annual World's Fair of Money convention held by the American Numismatic Association. In recent years Karen M. Lee has helped with much of the outreach for the National Numismatic Collection, including working with researchers and scholars, exhibitions, and more. In 2012 her book on U.S. Mint chief engraver George T. Morgan (*The Private Sketchbook of George T. Morgan, America's Silver Dollar Artist*) utilized the Smithsonian archives and earned high praise, including an "Extraordinary Merit" award from the Numismatic Literary Guild.

In 2013 Whitman Publishing released the latest in a string of books by Dick Doty, *Pictures from a Distant Country: Seeing America Through Old Paper Money*. The "distant country" was the United States of long ago, distant in time.

A book-length study of the National Numismatic Collection has been under discussion in recent years. Then, tragically, Dick Doty succumbed to lymphoma and died in April 2013, leaving behind many saddened friends and admirers. At the American Numismatic Association convention in Chicago in August 2013 I sponsored a special memorial service to celebrate his life and accomplishments and Dennis Tucker of Whitman Publishing took care of arrangements. Speakers included Tucker; family members including Dick's widow, Cindi Roden Doty, and his brother-in-law; Karen Lee (associate curator of the National Numismatic Collection); coin dealer, researcher, and NNC advocate Jeff Garrett; and me.

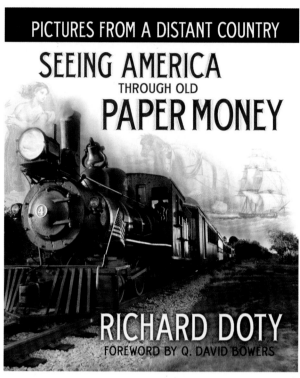

Dick Doty's book released in 2013.

Dick Doty at the World's Fair of Money, August 7, 2009.

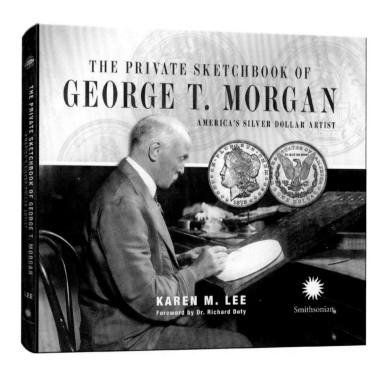

Treasures from The Smithsonian's Numismatic Collection have been featured in numerous books.

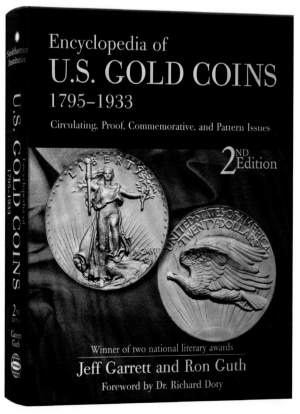

CHAPTER 24

The Early Years

Thomas L. Elder in 1908.

During the early 20th century Tom Elder was the most prominent figure in New York City coin sales and auctions. He was quite a colorful character.

Thomas L. Elder, Outspoken and Dynamic

Thomas Lindsay Elder was born in Dayton, Pennsylvania, on November 22, 1874. At the age of 13 Tom, then living in the "small railroad town" of New Bethlehem in the same state, collected Indian arrowheads, tobacco tags, and other curiosities. In 1887 his father presented him with a small coin collection, which Tom found to be fascinating, thus igniting his interest in numismatics. These were times of national prosperity, engendering unprecedented intense interest in collecting things, and more than a dozen periodicals, most of which would prove to be short-lived, sprang up to cater to the needs of those pursuing coins, stamps, relics, birds' eggs, fossils, and other items worthy of study and acquisition.

His dad, who frequently traveled to New York City, would stop at the store of J.W. Scott and buy coins and arrowheads. Meanwhile, teenager Tom looked forward to reading a little periodical (a copy of which I have never seen) titled *Golden Days for Boys and Girls.* Published by Philadelphia newspaperman James Elverson, it included puzzles, stories, pictures, and other features including an exchange column with advertisements. Tom Elder placed his own notice, and soon thereafter was corresponding and swapping with the likes of Robert P. King (who was later to become prominent in the study of numismatic items relating to Abraham Lincoln; King also formed a large cabinet of Washington tokens and medals, which my company bought in private treaty in the 1950s), R.L. Read (of Attleboro, Massachusetts), and others not well remembered today, including W.A. Bodendoerfer and A.W. Reeves.

Becoming a Part-Time Dealer

In 1896 Elder started in a small way to buy and sell coins on a commercial basis, realizing that this was a good way to add to his ever-growing cabinet while, hopefully, turning a profit at the same time. In 1897 he was vice president of the American Society of Curio Collectors, a position he held past the turn of the century. In its 1902 *Yearbook* Elder was credited with helping build the group, alerting members about fake military relics, and more.

In September 1899, now located at 343 Princeton Place, East Pittsburgh, Elder advertised in *The Numismatist* that he would trade medals and foreign coins for a good camera, this being in the decade that saw the rise of popular photography, pushed along by George Eastman (of Kodak fame) and the Anthony manufacturing and distribution interests. Obviously, Tom Elder was tuned into the events of his day and rode with them. Educated at Park Institute and also at Beaver College, both near Pittsburgh, he sampled the intellectual joys of music, art, and reading.

In 1900 he became a full-time coin dealer. Well, *almost*. He still had a "day job" to help pay expenses. Also, he was known in other circles as an expert telegrapher; he could "hear" the words as they were clicked in dots and dashes. Later he was to write: "I spent the entire summer of 1901 in Buffalo [where the American Numismatic Association convention was held that year] and collected coins there also." At the Pan-American Exposition held in Buffalo that summer, President James McKinley was shot by an assassin. Elder was tapped to be the official telegrapher for the government and relay the news of McKinley's lingering agony, and finally his death, to the world.

Elder's 1902 token, 31 mm.

By 1902 Elder issued his first token. It advertised his business and, for good measure, included the Latin motto MOVEO ET PROFICO ("I move and I am proficient"), but he was embarrassed as the last word should have been spelled as PROFICIO. He later stated that 1,000 were made in aluminum and 100 in copper.

RARE COINS!
This May Mean Dollars to You!!
Do you know that certain U. S. CENTS, NICK-LES, DIMES, QUARTERS, HALF DOLLARS, DOL-LARS, COLONIAL PIECES and PAPER MONEY, are worth from $5.00 to $500 each? Many coins in actual circulation today are worth many dollars over face. **Get Posted on Coins!** My New 1904 Coin Book contains over 100 pages, 300 pictures of rare coins, and treats not only of Ancient, Mediæval, and Modern Foreign Coins, American Coins and Scrip, but also illustrates British Coins from the Roman Conquest down to modern times. Invaluable book to you if you have money or **use** money. Send for it today; prepaid only 25 Cents.

☞ I Buy Coin Collections, And Have Over 35000 Coins, Bills And Gems For Sale. Retail lists free.

☞ Circular giving prices I pay for Rare Coins, 06 cents.

THOMAS L. ELDER,
Box 11, Station A.,
PITTSBURGH, - PA., U. S. A.

Feb. 22-04

Mr. Beck.

I have a Very good 1799 (over 1798) cent, will sell for only $16.50. Cost me $16.00 Can you use this rare variety?

Yours truly,

Thomas L. Elder

Postcard notice by Elder in April 1904, shortly before his move to New York City. The recipient was numismatist John A. Beck of Allegheny, Pennsylvania.

Dealing Full-Time

In the summer of 1902, Elder was employed by the Pittsburgh Provision & Packing Company. He was offered the position of private secretary to the Honorable Alfred S. Moore, of Beaver, Pennsylvania. The post paid $2,500 per year, but necessitated moving to Nome, Alaska, to which location Moore had been named by President Theodore Roosevelt as a district court judge. Around this time he really did become a full-time coin dealer. In April 1903 *The Numismatist* took note of this:

> At present his whole time is given to his coin business which in a few years has developed to a considerable proportion. This is mainly due to persistent and judicious advertising, honorable dealings with his patrons, and promptness, three elements so necessary to success in any business.

New York City

In May 1904 Elder moved to New York City, where

he remained for most of his business career, which continued into the 1940s. Along the way he wrote 294 auction catalogs, claiming at one time that he could describe 1,000 lots in a *single day.* Although this seems amazing at first blush, a reading of the terse descriptions in certain of his catalogs suggests that he was speaking the truth! Notwithstanding the conducting of many auctions simply intended to move merchandise out the door, his repertoire also included the presentation of many fine cabinets described with detailed information that is still of great interest and utility to scholars today.

Elder was active in the American Numismatic and Archaeological Society, based in New York City, founded in 1864 and succeeding to the interests of the early American Numismatic Society (which was active in 1858 and 1859 before expiring). For the Society in 1906 he served on a committee seeking to improve art in coinage and met with President Theodore Roosevelt on the matter. Roosevelt was deeply immersed in the project, which in 1907 led to Augustus Saint-Gaudens creating the Indian Head gold eagle and the MCMVII High Relief double eagle. In the same year Farran Zerbe, *at the time* having a friendly disposition toward Elder, or at least not a negative one, visited New York City and subsequently wrote of seeing Elder:

> The large artistically arranged and modern equipment of the suite of rooms which Thomas L. Elder devotes to his coin trade are a delight for anyone to visit. Mr. Elder reports good business, in fact too good to give his publication *The Elder Monthly* the attention it should have. This paper is not as old as its name implies. Like a bunch more of us, Tom says he is sometimes misunderstood. To know him is to appreciate him for his personal qualities, and to quote him: "My bite is not near as severe as my bark."

In time, Zerbe would be bitten. Following the death of Dr. George F. Heath (ANA founder and editor and publisher of *The Numismatist*), Zerbe, then president of the ANA, journeyed to Monroe, Michigan, to visit with widow Lucy Heath. Everyone thought he was going to negotiate for her to turn the magazine over to the Association. Surprise! Zerbe bought it for himself, anticipating making a profit. As if this were not enough, he rigged the next ANA presidential election to put his pet candidate, Dr. R.M. Henderson, into the office. Moreover, Zerbe was viewed as a promoter without a conscience. In *The Numismatist,* July 1909, Elder excoriated Zerbe in a lengthy commentary that included this relating to Zerbe and his election-rigging cronies:

> All shiftiness, evasiveness, hypocrisy, will be bared by me, and there has been a lot of it indulged in by the bunch. This time you have not simply a lot of "poor and holed" to address, but some of them do their own thinking. How it must pain you to talk to anybody who does his own thinking. Your oily, oozy, slimy phrases will make about as much impression as a pea shooter against a belt of armor plate. Never again will the American collectors be deceived.[1]

On October 5, 1908, at the popular Café Martin, New York City, Elder hosted a banquet in connection with his auction of the James Wilson Collection, one of the most important sales of the era. *The Numismatist* later reported.

> In addition to ANA members, many collectors who had come to view and participate in the Wilson Collection were on hand, resulting in what was many times referred to as "the largest and most notable numismatic gathering ever held."

Even super-collector Virgil M. Brand was on hand, and Brand rarely traveled far from his Chicago home.

At the time of his banquet, Elder was engaged to Miss Sophie Faskett Howley, whom he married the following month, after which they went to Atlantic City and, presumably, enjoyed the interior of one of the commodious hotels lining the Boardwalk, for it must have been cold on the beach.

The New York Numismatic Club

On December 11, 1908, Elder was back in New York City, attending an informal get-together at Keen's Old English Chop House at 36th Street and Sixth Avenue.[2] The New York Numismatic Club was formed on that occasion. It went on to years of brilliant successes and was to include in its membership over a period of time many of the most prominent numismatists in the greater New York area. At the first regular meeting of the organized club, at the same venue a month later, among those in attendance in addition to Elder were Joseph Mitchelson, Elliot Smith, Albert R. Frey, Frank Higgins, Edgar H. Adams, D. Macon Webster, William H. Woodin, George H. Blake, Wayte Raymond, Victor D. Brenner, and Bauman L. Belden.[3] Nearly all of these would become "greats" in the hobby, and some already were.

In 1909 Elder was coauthor with Ebenezer Gilbert of *The Varieties of the United States Cents of 1796,* followed by a solo work the next year, *United States Cents of 1794.* The latter was a revision of the Frossard-Hays work on 1794 large cents using the collection of Ebenezer Gilbert for illustrations.[4] Then as now, there was something *special* about cents of this particular year, as at once they consisted of a wide selection of varieties and many interesting diecutting idiosyncrasies within the group.

During this time Elder continued war against the wily Farran Zerbe, which Elder fought with paper notices and specially produced medals.[5] Elder took dead aim at Zerbe and the American Numismatic Association, calling the latter the A.N.ASSo., and personifying it on a medal as a jackass.

Additional venom was later directed via medal inscriptions at "pacifists" Henry Ford and William Jennings Bryan, who resisted America's entry into the World War. And woe to any Elder customer who showed up at one of his auction sales but had not paid an earlier bill. From the podium, Elder was apt to say something like, "Here comes a deadbeat," as the victim entered the room and all heads turned.

On December 11, 1914, Elder read a letter to the New York Numismatic Club telling of his extreme displeasure with the current Barber silver coinage, which he deemed to be quite inartistic. Over the next two years, he would say more on the subject. Finally, in 1916 the dime, quarter, and half dollar were redesigned to create some of the most beautiful motifs in American coinage, an action due at least in part to Elder's prompting.

Thomas L. Elder was a key factor in persuading the Mint and the Treasury Department to redesign all of the silver denominations currently in use. The result consisted of the 1916 "Mercury" dime by sculptor A.A. Weinman, the Standing Liberty quarter dollar by Hermon A. MacNeil, and the Liberty Walking half dollar by Weinman.

Elder on Collecting

Elder was a missionary for the hobby, and he was always ready to speak or write on the subject. In December 1916 the lead article in *The Numismatist* was by him and was titled "Collecting—With Special References to Coins, Medals and Paper Money." Elder noted, in part:

Collectors as a class are, I believe, somewhat misunderstood, and occasionally maligned. The best type of collector is a most valuable member of society. By the best collector I mean one whose pursuit, study and research in connection with his hobby have magnified his imaginative, aesthetic, romantic and intellectual qualities. His wide and varied experiences with various odd and interesting objects, and his painstaking care of them, have given him a remarkable fund of out-of-the-way information, as well as patience, a sense of order and practicality.

Contrary to current opinion, the best collector is far from eccentric. He is the finest sort of an example of the cultured and refined man. Collecting keeps people busy at odd moments, and hence keeps them out of mischief. It emphasizes in no uncertain way that keeping young is largely the result of the mental attitude, for collecting, above all other panaceas, meatless diets, and physical exercise even, keeps people young. I have for a correspondent a man who is 94 years of age. At last report he was still riding a bicycle. . . .

The instinct to collect is not only in many cases deep-rooted, but I venture the assertion that it is universal. It is expressed in some form by every child or adult. Even the poor, misguided miser, who enjoys the sight of his glistening gold falling through his fingers, has a few collecting instincts, such as Russell Sage and Hetty Green have expressed it after a fashion.[6]

In most people it lies dormant in the sense that we collectors know it. Does not every child have at some time an attack of the "postage stamp fever," which, like the measles, is often soon over and forgotten?

How to develop this collecting instinct, which is universal, is a matter of prime importance. It is a matter for we collectors to ponder over and put into practical working form. In collecting small metal objects like coins or medals we have an immense advantage over the collectors of china, furniture and other cumbersome or fragile material. Our coins are indestructible, and they may be neatly laid down in small spaces in our compact cabinets. Other objects, like weapons and manuscripts, will rust or discolor unless the greatest care is used. Owning a collection which is one's own is far better than seeing another in a museum. A good picture in our own home is of more value than a public gallery full which we may only look at. In coins remarkable finds have been made by individual collectors and are still being made. . . .

Coins and medals are always worthy of collectors' attention, and, contrary to the crude ideas of the public, our science is in no way an inconsequential study—and it has attracted many of the world's best scholars and thinkers. Its close relation, since the beginning of the seventh century BC, with the best in art and sculpture, and its intimate relation to history, give it first rank among the collecting hobbies. Most Americans do not begin to realize that coin collecting is the hobby of aristocratic Europe. Kings, princes, princesses, dukes, and earls belong to the numismatic societies. And we know that the royalty have always associated with the most brilliant men and women of their time. Besides these, generals, scientists, educators, lawyers and artists of highest standing are members.

Elder continued the article with comments concerning various coins, medals, paper-money issues, and other collecting aspects.

In the early 20th century Elder issued many medals on subjects that ranged from the 1909 Hudson-Fulton Celebration to pacifists who did not want America to enter the World War.

On Washington's birthday, February 22, 1922, Elder hosted a banquet for numismatic notables at Engel's Chop House, West 35th Street, New York City. Speakers included T.L. Comparette, Carl Würtz-

Elder medal of 1917 aimed at members of Congress who did not want to declare war on Germany.

bach, Russell Drowne, Albert R. Frey, and Frank C. Higgins, all prominent figures in the hobby. Comparette was curator of the Mint Collection.

In the summer of 1924 he gave a talk, "Our Numismatic Successors," which was printed in *The Numismatist* the following November. Economic times were tough in the rare-coin business, perhaps with Mehl's sale of the James Ten Eyck Collection the turning point for recovery. The nation had undergone an economic depression in 1921 and 1922, and although recovery was underway, by 1924 there were not many free-spending collectors in the old style. Elder's comments included these (here excerpted):

Our Numismatic Successors

The present-day numismatists have to prepare and pave the way for those numismatists who are yet to come, for those who shall take our places in collecting. We can do this by improving our grade of numismatic work and by making it easier for future numismatists to work and study. How can we best contribute to this end?

There are a number of ways. Badly we need books on American numismatics and paper money, especially books on our political medals and tokens and a convenient work on

Elder medal of 1908 satirizing William Jennings Bryan in his third and final run on the Democratic ticket for president of the United States.

American colonial and Continental coins. There are plenty of neglected subjects in American numismatics. American numismatics can be greatly enriched by the addition of a considerable number of numismatic works.

If we are able to improve the American taste for the history of our own America, naturally our collectors will turn toward the collecting of more purely historical coins, medals, tokens and paper money.

Our numismatic successors are to inherit nothing better than we leave them. They will inherit our tastes or culture or lack of them. It is clearly up to us to determine the quality of this new collector's technique and availability. As present-day custodians of numismatics we are obliged to prepare a place and way for the future curators of the science.

Coin collecting has curious beginnings and has strange comrades as to stations in life. It is the hobby of the small boy or girl, or the young clerk, the street-car conductor, the college professor, the student, the banker and the head of big business. It is well its adherents have such a diversity of callings. The field of collecting has many branches. People collect things from needles to anchors. I won't say that one person in 100 is a collector, but the chances are one in 100 is not too high an estimate. Let us say one in every 200. This would give us over 500,000 people who collect something. Everybody knows there are at least 100,000 stamp collectors here. Let us eliminate, say, half of these and estimate 50,000 active stamp collectors. Then compare the figures with our estimated 2,500 coin collectors, a number who have some interest in collecting coins, even if not over half are active numismatists. This estimate of about 1,250 actives would indicate a rather meager body of serious coin collectors and students of numismatics and paper money.

It is to youth, then, that we have to look for our numismatic legatees. Nearly all boys or girls, at some time or other, show an inclination to collect something, such as postage stamps, coins, minerals, or curiosities. The pursuit of these has given untold pleasure and benefit. The great question is, "How can we turn their attention to coins, medals and paper money? How can we make them permanent collectors and not spasmodic accumulators who give up the pursuit after a brief interest?" In order to have our ranks largely added to, this is a subject of the first importance and about which we must strive for a solution.

The numismatic market continued to be on "hold" throughout the rest of the decade. There was improvement after 1924, but it was only slight. This was very strange, for at the same time the auction prices for art, manuscripts, books, Currier & Ives prints, and nearly all other collectibles hit all-time highs in the era later memorialized by F. Scott Fitzgerald's *Great Gatsby*.

A Seeming Contradiction

In the 1920s Elder was America's foremost exponent for the collecting of tokens and medals and the interrelationship of history and numismatics, not to mention the publication of reference books, as noted above. He could have used much of his knowledge to

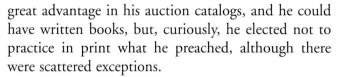

great advantage in his auction catalogs, and he could have written books, but, curiously, he elected not to practice in print what he preached, although there were scattered exceptions.

Elder was probably the dealer with the largest reference library, who used it the least when preparing his catalogs. Perhaps with the stress of turning out a continuous stream of auctions, attending club meetings, and running an over-the-counter coin shop in America's busiest city he had little time left over to devote to a cozy acquaintance combining his typewriter, his by now almost innate knowledge, and his reference books.

Later Years

Meanwhile, Elder was making money. Economic conditions perked up after 1924. In his best business year, 1929, he grossed $125,000, even though the coin market did not share the runaway excitement evident with other collectibles. This had a benefit in a way, for during the Depression of the 1930s the prices of art, antiques, prints, books, and other highflyers crashed, but rare coins, although there was a slump, did quite well. Starting with President Franklin Roosevelt's calling in of gold coins in 1933 and the popularization of "penny boards" and the launching of the *Standard Catalogue of United States Coins* in 1934, the numismatic market became more active than ever!

In the 1930s Elder became the numismatic columnist for *Hobbies,* a national magazine with sections on different aspects of collecting, one of them being rare coins. The publication "paid" its contributors by giving them "free" advertising space.

In 1934 he decided to emulate B. Max Mehl and printed thousands of copies of his latest effort, the *New Premium Coin Book*. Sales fell far short of expectations, and for years afterward he had boxes of copies on hand. In the same era he made mass mailings to banks and others who were receiving gold coins turned in by the general public. More than anyone else in numismatics, Elder thus rescued countless thousands of Charlotte and Dahlonega coins, pre-1834 rarities,

and other pieces, probably comprising at least 50 percent of what survives today in those categories. Mint and Treasury employees who substituted common gold coins for rare ones (in vault holdings and in deposits) were also major sellers to him.

In February 1937 Elder offered his business for sale, using multiple exclamation points (perhaps he had been following Mehl too closely):

> After having held successful coin sales since 1903 (over 33 years), we, the oldest living cataloguers, will sell our business in New York City, for a stipulated price. With this consideration will go the mailing list, lease and location, where we are the best-known buyers and cataloguers of coins, medals and paper money. We are offered more material for auction on good commissions than we can handle!
>
> Our successor is assured a sale business. Ours is the leading sale business in the country today! The buyer would jump promptly into the numismatic limelight as the country's leading coin sale proprietor! With our goodwill would go our personal assistance in conducting the buyer's initial sales, ensuring his immediate success and leadership! An exceptional opportunity for a young man of ambition who has a sum to invest in such a business. We lead. One sale brought almost $50,000—4 coins brought $22,600. Nobody can equal this record. If seriously interested, and with some cash to invest, write for liberal terms. We did a $125,000 business one year (1929).

By 1937 the New York City auction mantle had fallen on the shoulders of brothers Joseph and Morton

Stack, who were up and coming in the field and pursued it with great energy.

In 1940, by which time Elder had moved to Pleasantville (a little town north of New York City, and perhaps best known at the time as the home of *Reader's Digest*), he conducted his final auction, a mail-bid sale. No buyer had stepped up to take over his business, and it simply lapsed. In most winters he went south to North Carolina, as he had usually done for many years.

Thomas Elder died on May 11, 1948. *The Numismatist* included this in his obituary:

> For over half a century he had been one of the country's leading coin dealers and his death, while not entirely unexpected, comes as a great shock to all who knew him. A native of Pennsylvania, he established himself as a full time dealer in New York City about the turn of the century.

His love for coins, his keen mind, and his dynamic personality soon won for him a coveted place in the coin dealing profession. He never relinquished it. He was a prolific writer and many of his articles will be found in past volumes of *The Numismatist*. He could, and often did, prepare a thousand-lot catalogue in 24 hours. His memory was so good, even to dates, that it was rarely necessary for him to consult a reference book.

Later, his inventory and what remained of his business interests were transferred to his son-in-law, Paul S. Seitz of Glen Rock, Pennsylvania, who conducted his own coin business, advertised widely in the *Numismatic Scrapbook Magazine* and *The Numismatist,* was early in the game of selling plastic holders, and was highly admired.

CHAPTER 25

I have learned that people either like to collect things or they don't. Few non-collectors ever change. Likewise, once a collector, always a collector. In this chapter I share some ideas on the subject.

The Mentality of Collecting

"Collected Wisdom"

"We all have our hobbies."

Some years ago Ron Thompson read one of my columns in *Coin World* and sent me a related article, "Collected Wisdom," published in *The Chronicle of Higher Education,* June 28, 2002. The thesis: "a new wave of scholarship examines the centuries-old 'mental landscape' of collectors." Peter Monaghan, the author, is one of the many who have endeavored to determine what makes a collector "tick." The introduction to the article is fascinating:

> Captain James Cook, as he sailed about the Pacific in the late 1700s, was so eager a collector that mocking Tongans offered him rocks and twigs. One local wit even tried to sell him a turd on a stick. As many as one in three modern-day Americans and Britons, too, collect anything and everything, from works of the Old Masters to varieties of dirt.

Monaghan went on to quote Susan M. Pearce, a professor at the University of Leicester, England, who suggested that "collecting is a way of creating self-identity."

Few would argue with this, and in numismatics this has been proven time and again. Having handled as many important coins as anyone I know, I can state that of the countless collections I have purchased intact or sold at auction over the years, no two have ever been alike.

From the very word "go," collecting coins is an individual pursuit. If I were to give two collectors each $500 today, chances would be good that not even a single coin in a given grade would be duplicated between the two buyers. Even if I gave $50,000, the same would be true. Every collection is very personal, reflecting the tastes of its owner.

Specialize in Something and Live Longer!
Again quoting Dr. Pearce, although some not in the loop think that a collector can be "a bit of an oddball," the fact is that:

> The statistics show quite clearly that they're just as likely to be married or to have children or to have a stable home as anyone else. They're not people who find it difficult to make relationships with humans and use objects as a substitute, but they just make their relationships at least in part through objects, which is interesting. I don't sense any pathology.

That's nice, for we collectors like to think we are "normal"! Moreover, hobby relationships, at least in numismatics, last for a long time, even decades. In 1957 a group of young and enthusiastic coin collectors formed the Rittenhouse Society. These included Ken Bressett, Walter Breen, Grover Criswell, George J. Fuld, and Dick Johnson. As I write this, Breen, Criswell, and Fuld have passed to their final reward, but none of us during our lifetimes ever stopped being a collector and a friend to others sharing his interest. Remarkable!

In addition, and departing from Pearce's thesis, collecting can increase your lifespan as can specializing in some other pursuit that is intellectually challenging and emotionally satisfying. Or, at least I believe that it can. A number of years back I learned that of the niche professions in America, those who bought and sold antiquarian and out-of-print books had, on average, lived longer than the rest of the population. I have read that those who do challenging crossword puzzles or engage in research not only live longer, but are less apt to get Alzheimer's disease. Mental activity seems to go hand in hand with good health.

I also learned that librarians and violinists have longer life spans. The common thread between book lovers and violin lovers is that each has broadened his/her life to include a field that presents challenges, is never ending, and cannot be conquered completely—always leaving something still to be strived for. Also, one can retreat into a library, or with a violin into a quiet room, and become lost in another world—one in which the latest stock-market news or accounting scandal, or terrorist act, or political coup is not at all important. Becoming involved in a discipline such as collecting, playing music, or studying a specialty brings with it a special tranquility.

For a numismatist this tranquility comes automatically. No collector has ever had *everything*—not even Virgil M. Brand, who, upon his passing in 1926, had more than 350,000 coins. Alden Scott Boyer, discussed in chapter 16, started collecting at age six and was still going at it when he died in retirement. Along the way he continued investigating different numismatic specialties.

People to People

Among other perspectives I could mention, collecting can bridge international borders, or as Simon and Garfunkel put it, troubled waters—possibly a very good thing in today's world of xenophobia, terrorism, and fear.

I recall that in 1971 I was traveling with my family in the Schwarzwald or Black Forest district of southern Germany, not far from the border with Switzerland. I was interested in tracking down some information regarding the company of Imhof & Mukle, manufacturers of orchestrions made generations earlier in Vöhrenbach, a town in the area. As luck would have it, it was in the middle of the summer, and as we did not plan ahead and had no reservations for a place to stay, we were in a bit of a quandary as where to spend the night.

In poking around Vöhrenbach we learned about a local businessman, Willy Rombach, who, it turned out, was related to the Imhof family. A few minutes after talking with him—we had never met or corresponded and I had never heard of him before—he offered my family use of his beautifully furnished guesthouse!

How often in travels have I seen similar situations. In the days before the fall of the Berlin Wall I had a "guest" pass from the Deutsche Demokratische Republik (East Germany) to do research on automatic musical instruments during several trips to Leipzig and elsewhere. In the late-19th and early-20th centuries that city was the world's leading center for the manufacture of disc-type music boxes and automatic pianos and orchestrions. I had written extensively on the subject, including in the *Encyclopedia of Automatic Musical Instruments,* 1,008 pages in size, published in 1972 and one of the best 16 books of that year, according to the American Library Association (this recognition brought in more than 4,000 orders to the publisher!).[1] The book had been circulated worldwide by the time I applied and was known in East Germany. At the time I was co-owner of the Mekanisk Musik Museum in Copenhagen, a popular tourist attraction housed in a brick mansion at Vesterbrogade 150.

I was apprehensive at first, for the United States, unlike Denmark, had no diplomatic relations with East Germany. My concern was short-lived. Everyone I met welcomed me as an authority on the history of this field. I and my traveling companions, Claes O. Friberg and Bonnie Tekstra, met with many enthusiasts and historians. All of us were warmly greeted at every stop and felt right at home.

In the early 1960s I used to spend a lot of time in London in search of rare coins and collections. This was not like going behind the Iron Curtain, but I was a stranger in the city, at least at first. My off hours and weekends were often pleasurably spent with coin dealers and collectors—sampling clubs and restaurants, walking through the pastureland at Stonehenge (before there was even a sign identifying the place), tramping up the stone stairs of the Tower of London, or visiting some old ruin in the provinces, or wandering through the Sunday morning flea market in Portobello Road. With one or another of my British numismatic friends on hand as a guide, I always felt comfortable.

If there is a point to the preceding, it is that a shared hobby, collecting, or research interest has no boundaries, and politics are not important. I rather imagine that if I were to visit Baghdad, Kabul, Moscow, Teheran, Beijing, Tel Aviv, or any other world city tomorrow, and were to have dinner with a numismatist, we both would have a good time—the world around us notwithstanding.

Moreover, the race, religion, creed, or color of a person is absolutely irrelevant and unimportant when two people of the same mind—librarians, numismatists, violinists, you name it—meet to share their interests. I imagine that the worldwide clients of my company include just about every known variation of human classification.

In 1956 President Dwight D. Eisenhower invited the American Numismatic Association to become involved in his People to People Program, promoting international understanding. Two years later in 1958, Admiral Oscar H. Dodson, ANA president at the time

and a world traveler, thought this was a great idea. An invitation was extended to Dr. Rastislav Maric—formerly professor of Classical Philology at Belgrade University and at the time the curator of the National Collection of Coins in the Yugoslav National Museum—to come to this convention as a guest of the ANA. Yugoslavia was a Communist country with sealed borders. Dr. Maric responded with enthusiasm, but red tape between his country and our State Department resulted his being denied permission.

Today many of the former Communist countries are capitalistic, hold elections, and permit unlimited travel. Focus in the early 21st century has shifted to lack of understanding between America and certain Islamic countries. In today's troubled world the People to People concept could be revived with benefits to all.

Trophies

Not only do people collect different things, they have different reasons for doing so. Some people like "trophies" that can be admired by their friends and visitors. No doubt the late William Randolph Hearst was in this category as was the late Norton Simon. Hearst showed his treasures to his friends who visited his San Simeon mansion high above a desolate stretch of California coastline. Simon gained control of the Pasadena Art Museum, renamed it the Norton Simon Museum of Art in 1975, and filled it with important paintings and sculptures, amidst great controversy which is now mostly forgotten. The Breakers and Biltmore family mansions of the Vanderbilts, once trophies of conspicuous consumption, are now enjoyed by the public. The Henry Ford Museum in Dearborn, Michigan, filled with the late mogul's "toys," is wonderful to visit.

In numismatics Art Lovi comes to mind—among more than just a few collectors who had lots of money and who mainly bought for "show," to impress their friends. Art, who didn't know much about numismatics, had a well-fortified bank account. He bought a set of four 1879 and 1880 $4 Stellas, other Proof gold coins, various rarities, and the like, and mounted them in revolving, spotlighted glass cases at coin conventions. Attached telephones permitted listeners to hear about the display. It was gaudy to be sure, but Art enjoyed it immensely, including standing near to greet anyone who seemed interested.

Aubrey and Adeline Bebee, coin dealers and longtime friends of mine from Omaha, bought a 1913 Liberty Head nickel and an 1804 silver dollar as trophies—they did not collect either series—and later donated them to the American Numismatic Association.

Buyers spend tens of thousands of dollars to buy Rolex, Patek Philippe, and other Swiss watches as they enjoy their tradition, their trophy value, and, sometimes the complexity of their mechanisms. A Timex watch for $20 keeps better time. Similarly in a way, I collect antique mechanical musical instruments. My Yale Wonder Clock, a contraption that plays a steel music disc while displaying a series of changing advertisements and dispenses tokens, is fascinating to own and is valued into the tens of thousands of dollars, but better music can be found for free on YouTube!

A Midwestern friend who collects coins, automatic musical instruments, and automobiles told me he went to Italy on two occasions to take delivery and test-drive new bright-red Ferraris made to his specifications. He doesn't drive them at all, but enjoys seeing them in his private museum in the Midwest.

On this subject, I cannot see the point of a connoisseur paying thousands of dollars for a bottle of champagne owned by royalty a century ago, if it is not opened and poured into glasses. But, come to think of it, I would not consider spending my "pet" 1857-S double eagle from the SS *Central America* treasure!

I am not sure that collecting "trophy" items brings the camaraderie and peace of mind mentioned earlier in my commentary, but I mention that sport here as it is part of the equation. While some who buy for "show" miss much of what collecting has to offer, others get deeply involved in a nice way. Collectors of Duesenbergs, Thomas Flyers, and even Edsels often share them at car meets. Owners of paintings loan

them for museum and gallery displays. Often in later years the public benefits when many such things are gifted to foundations or societies.

In numismatics there is a solid place for trophy collectors who do not explore the history and tradition of their prizes. They liven up things and make interesting headlines. They also buoy the market and in some seasons propel prices to new highs. In coins I have seen many instances in which someone who does not collect early silver dollars buys a famous and rare 1804, or another person buys an MCMVII (1907) Ultra High Relief double eagle but owns no other coins in the same series. Such things make the news. In contrast, some numismatic fields such as colonial and early American coins, tokens, obsolete bank notes, historic auction catalogs, Betts medals, and the like are nearly if not completely owned by dedicated specialists who enjoy possessing and studying them and, unless strongly prompted, are not interested in discussing their values.

I also say that many buyers of trophy coins purchase them in order to fill in gaps in their collections. Most buyers of 1856 Flying Eagle cents acquire one to add to their display of Flying Eagle and Indian Head cents. Over the years I have had many customers buy a Mint State 1909-S V.D.B. cent because in their childhood this was the Holy Grail of coins that could be found in pocket change—but few people were so lucky.

Quintessential Aspects

For many buyers there are two aspects that are most important: grade and price. A coin is found, paid for, and put into a safe-deposit box.

In contrast many enthusiasts who have been at the game for a long time derive a great deal of pleasure from the study of the objects themselves, the more obscure the better. The late Byron Johnson was such a person, as was Bob Lindesmith, to mention just two people whose disciplines ran across many different numismatic specialties. In his time, Byron would walk a mile to see a curious feature on a pattern half dollar that had not been noticed before, and Bob would do the same if you suggested that he might want to view a piece of obsolete currency of unusual rarity or characteristics. Steve Tanenbaum, who neither exhibited nor wrote articles, spent several decades of his life dealing in and studying American tokens, primarily of the 19th century. He made many new discoveries and shared his knowledge with anyone who had similar interests. More in the mainstream of numismatics was Harry W. Bass Jr. As I have mentioned, he would spend countless hours studying his coins and reading about them.

Personally, the things I collect—numismatic and American history books, music boxes, Civil War tokens, Hard Times tokens, counterstamps, "Good For One Tune" tokens (many of which cost me $5 to $10 each), paper money of New Hampshire—I enjoy as tangible links to a bygone era. I often gaze at the specimens in detail to study their die or engraving work and other aspects, and often delight in learning their history as I do in owning the items themselves. To me, a token worth $20 can be every bit as fascinating as an item worth a hundred times that amount. I scan or photograph my numismatic items, put them in safe-deposit boxes, and enjoy them by projecting their images in large size on a screen—making them easier than ever to study and appreciate.

I also collect *information.* I love curious and obscure facts, interesting accounts I have never read before, and the like. A lot of this sort of stuff has found its way into this book, as you can tell by now! Most information costs nothing but yields great pleasure in the thrill of the hunt. I suppose bird watching, which I do not do, would be analogous. Most of us delight in learning new information that NASA reveals about the mysterious moons of Jupiter and Saturn.

Collecting can be a lot of fun. Once a collector, always a collector. The careful study and pursuit of any hobby can be rewarding in many ways—new friendships locally and around the world, new challenges, always something interesting to discover.

CHAPTER 26

The greatest American gold treasure of all time. I enjoyed being part of the excitement.

The SS *Central America* Treasure

Gold in California!

Gold Mining in California.
(Currier & Ives)

The Gold Rush started on January 24, 1848, when James Marshall discovered a gleaming flake in the tail race of a sawmill on the American River in an area controlled by John Sutter, whose rectangular fort was near Sacramento. The structure housed stores, workshops, and various facilities to accommodate the ranch hands and others who worked in the area for Sutter doing farming, animal husbandry, lumbering, and other activities. Soon, other flakes were found. Marshall, hoping that he found gold, but not at all certain, went back to the fort where he and Sutter, following instructions in an encyclopedia, confirmed that it was indeed precious metal. Eureka! This, meaning "I found it!" became the rallying cry, according to legend.

As Sutter did not want to disturb the operations and commerce of his fort he urged secrecy. The news could not be contained, it soon reached San Francisco, and by late spring the Gold Rush was on! Farmers abandoned their fields, merchants left their shops, sailors on shore did not return to their ships. All headed to the new Golconda, with instant riches beckoning.

In the days before telegraph and other modern connections, the news did not reach the East until late summer, and even then it was viewed by many as a hoax or fantasy. Finally, in December 1848 an emissary sent from California reached Washington, D.C., with a small container of gold. This was shown to President James Knox Polk and others, and then sent to the U.S. Mint. The excitement knew no limits!

Most of the gold that arrived in Washington in December 1848 was sent to the Mint and coined into an estimated 1,389 $2.50 pieces, each stamped on the reverse with CAL. to indicate their significance.

In 1849 tens of thousands of people headed west to tap this golden bonanza. Some went overland and others went by sea, crossing by land in Panama. Still others took the long way by sailing around Cape Horn at the tip of South America. By late spring and early summer 1849 the banks of the American River were crowded with prospectors, as were many tributaries. Tales of fortune abounded and still more people came. San Francisco, earlier called Yerba Buena, changed from a sleepy village to a dynamic city.

As the years passed, assayers, bankers, and other commercial interests were established in San Francisco, Sacramento and other towns, with gold remaining a focal point of interest. Important to the present account, miners, banks and others would receive gold, then take it to an assayer who would melt it, cast it into bars or ingots, and then test it for its purity. At regular intervals ingots and coins made from California gold, including at the San Francisco Mint (which opened for business in late March 1854 in a renovated building that earlier had housed the private minting and assaying business of Moffat & Co.), were packed in wooden cases and shipped to the East.

The SS *Central America*

One day in late August 1857, well over $1.6 million (at the $20.67 per ounce value of the time) in golden ingots and coins was packed aboard the steamer SS *Sonora,* which headed south from San Francisco along the Pacific coast, docking offshore at Panama City, Panama. At that point the passengers and treasure transferred by small boats to land and were put aboard the 48-mile-long Panama Railroad and carried to the port of Aspinwall on the Atlantic side. Soon, the SS *Central America,* earlier known as the SS *George Law* and recently renamed, arrived in port, and the

passengers and gold went aboard, to head north to New York City.

All was serene with sunny skies and pleasant temperatures. A stop was made in Havana, but a cholera epidemic was raging, and only a few passengers went ashore. One man who intended to board in Havana stayed too late in his hotel and missed the connection. Out of Havana the ship steamed forward under continuing sunny skies and pleasant weather. Not long afterward, storm clouds arose, and the wind increased. No doubt this was a squall and would soon pass. Such

The loss of the SS *Central America.*

was common in September. However, the wind intensified, the waves rose, and by Thursday, September 10, the seas were very high and the SS *Central America* was almost helpless. Water was taken aboard through cracked and twisted planks, flooding the hold and extinguishing the fires for the steam boiler, placing the vessel at the mercy of the elements.

On Saturday morning, September 12, two sailing ships, the bark *Ellen* and the brig *Marine,* were nearby, and with heroic effort all of the women and children of the *Central America* were placed on lifeboats and rowed to safety. In the early evening, Captain William Herndon fired rockets of distress and flew the Stars

The *Central America* in mountainous seas.

Finally, in September 1986, what looked like the remains of a steamer sidewheel cover with some scattered coal nearby was seen on the ocean floor at a depth of 7,200 feet 200 miles off of the coast of North Carolina. In order to lay claim to the treasure and protect their rights, the discoverers retrieved a lump of coal, took it to a court in Virginia, and registered a claim. The area was later explored by the remote-controlled vehicle *Nemo* and, in time, the ship's bell was recovered, making identification of the *Central America* positive.

After multiple dives *Nemo,* with mechanical arms and baskets to store the golden treasure, recovered the coins and ingots. This led to what for me was a great adventure.

A Great Adventure

A selection from the hundreds of gold ingots recovered from the wreck of the *Central America,* with an 1857-S double eagle added to indicate the size.

and Stripes upside down, a sign of impending disaster. At about 8 o'clock, with Herndon standing on the cover of one of the sidewheels, the ship slipped below the waves, taking with it hundreds of passengers. Many perished, but some clung to bits of driftwood and debris, to be rescued later by passing ships. The *Central America* and its gold went to a watery grave 7,200 feet below the surface.

The news was sensational at the time, an unprecedented marine disaster of an American mail steamer.

Discovery of the Treasure

In the 1980s Tommy Thompson, Bob Evans, and Barry Schatz, scientists in Columbus, Ohio, discussed the long lost SS *Central America*, and immersed themselves in study, trying to determine where the ship may have been during the hurricane. Forming the Columbus-America Discovery Group, they plotted a tract of ocean involving hundreds of square miles off the coast of southern Virginia. With sophisticated equipment aboard their ship, the *Arctic Discoverer*, the treasure seekers began a determined search, using underwater cameras and other equipment to scan the bottom.

Of all of the wonderful experiences in my life, being involved with the gold treasure from the SS *Central America* will forever be one of the greatest. As I write these words I reflect on scenes from the past—signing with Dwight N. Manley and the California Gold Marketing Group to present the coins and ingots to the public, researching and writing a book describing the California Gold Rush and the fabulous treasure that was lost and then found, and the people I met and worked with.

As no greater American gold treasure was ever lost, no greater one will ever be found. The *Central America* find will forever remain unique. Writing in *Coin World* in 2000, editor Beth Deisher called it the story of the year.

One of the 5,402 1857-S double eagles, nearly all mint-fresh, recovered from the SS *Central America*.

Presenting the Long-Lost Treasure

After the discovery of the ship there was a lot of excitement and publicity—far too much, in fact. Claimants with alleged ties to old insurance companies no longer in existence, people who felt they contributed to the research, and others descended and filed suits. It was not "finders keepers," it turned out. After resolution of legal issues in the courtroom, the coins and ingots were finally made available in 1999, with the finders being awarded 92.4 percent of the treasure.

The owners decided to sell their holdings. On behalf of a group of investors, Dwight Manley (who as a teenager was a student in my American Numismatic Association Summer Seminar, mentioned in chapter 3) formed the California Gold Marketing Group (CGMG) to distribute the fabulous treasure, which

comprised more than 7,500 sparkling gold coins and more than 500 gold ingots from Gold Rush assayers, over 8,000 items in all.

To draw attention to the collecting community and to begin the distribution, Christie's, the art auction house, was tapped to hold a sale of selected coins and ingots, due in part to negotiating an arrangement the company had made earlier with the treasure finders. I was "guest cataloger" for Christie's, which, I suppose, is a rather rare distinction, as the internationally known firm has its own large staff. I was invited in view of my special knowledge of the Gold Rush and its coinage.

The "Ship of Gold"

The sale was a great success and paved the way for a general distribution that began in the next year. Front-row-center in the program was the "Ship of Gold" exhibit—a modern representation of the side of the SS *Central America* that stretched across the front of the dealers' bourse area of the American Numismatic Association's annual summer convention, held in 2000 in Philadelphia.

Visitors alongside the "Ship of Gold" display at the ANA convention in Philadelphia in August 2000.

Dwight Manley, Bob Evans, and Dave Bowers with an ingot from the treasure.

Andrew Bowers views the "Eureka!" ingot in a gallery in the "Ship of Gold" exhibit. Weighing 933.94 ounces, .903 fine, and with a stamped value of $17,433.57 (when gold was $20.67 per ounce), this was the largest of more than 500 gold ingots recovered.

Along the side of the ship were "portholes" through which visitors could see some of the recovered items. A gallery featured contemporary newspaper accounts of the 1857 loss of the ship, prints and tintypes from the Gold Rush, and more. To the right was a mini-theater with a continually running film showing elements from the deep-sea recovery of the treasure. To the left was a reproduction of the Kellogg & Humbert Assay Office.

Treasure discoverers Tommy Thompson and Bob Evans were on hand to greet visitors, sign autographs, and discuss the items on display. On one afternoon Bob Evans with me as a helper presented a program about the treasure in a Numismatic Theatre presentation (part of the ANA's educational programs). About 400 people packed a large room from wall to wall—far and away the largest attendance at any Numismatic Theatre before or since!

Later, the "Ship of Gold" display went on a road show. One stop was at the California State Fair held in Sacramento, where Dwight Manley estimated more than 500,000 admissions! The California Historical

Society headquarters in San Francisco was another stop, where festivities included a special reception for members and invited guests.

The Tucson Gem & Mineral Show, the world's largest annual gathering dedicated to the title subjects, was a memorable stop as well. I, Chris Karstedt, Dwight Manley, Bob Evans, and others were on hand. There were so many people lined up to see the display that for the first time in show history crowd control, with stanchions and belts organizing visitors in line, was necessary. I was told that earlier the Hope Diamond was an attraction one year, and that the world's finest collection of Fabergé eggs was the drawing card at another time—but crowd control was not needed!

In the meantime the thousands of Mint State 1857-S double eagles, the hundreds of ingots, and the other coins and items were offered for sale, mostly by private treaty as opposed to public auction. Within a relatively short time all were gone!

There were some concerns that the aftermarket might not hold. In actuality, the value of most items increased as years went by.

Crowd control was needed at the "Ship of Gold" exhibit at the Tucson Gem & Mineral Show.

Of all the characters on the 19th-century numismatic stage Ebenezer Locke Mason Jr. is one of the most difficult to understand. He was the embodiment of the saying, "Do as I say, not as I do."

A "Character" *Par Excellence*

Ebenezer Locke Mason Jr.

Trying to Understand "Ned" Mason

There are coin dealers and there are coin dealers.[1] From the first of the line, John Allan in New York City, who started in the early 1820s, to the latest advertiser in *Coin World* or *Numismatic News* there have been tens of thousands of people in the coin trade. One of the most curious was Ebenezer Locke Mason Jr.—"Ned" to some friends, "Eben" to others—who would make an interesting study in psychology. As evidenced by his writings, he was the most aware, most knowledgeable person in numismatics in the 1860s and 1870s. Only he could discern the motives, sometimes suspicious, of other dealers, and only he had the ability to review the catalogs and works of others so as to advise readers of the errors found.

Mason was born in North Yarmouth, Maine, near Portsmouth, on March 21, 1826. His father followed various trades including sales of ready-made and custom clothing at No. 1 Jones' Row, Fore Street, Portland, and, later, harness making. He and his family moved to Philadelphia in the late 1830s.

Ned and Jo

By 1855 Mason was employed in the counting room of Mr. Newell, a commission merchant, on Front Street below Chestnut Street in Philadelphia.[2] He would reside there into the early 1870s. In the same building Joseph N.T. Levick worked as the chief bookkeeper for Freeman & Simpson. Ned and Jo, as they called each other, became close friends. Both were to become prominent in numismatics. Writing in the third person, Mason recalled:

> When those two youths first met neither had any special predilection for old coins, but were rather inclined to social enjoyments, in which the fair sex was an important factor. About a year subsequent to this acquaintance Ned "was on the road," as a showman says, with a public exhibition, and Jo remained at his post posting away at his accounts, and when the two met again both had become interested in coins; Jo as a collector, Ned as a speculator. The first interview after a year's separation occurred in 1856 in front of the general post-office, then in Dock Street, this city. Jo had the nucleus of a prospective large coin cabinet, in a few choice pieces, and Ned had gathered some old coppers and silver coins during his peregrination as a showman. . . .

Dealing in Coins

Although Mason did not chose to reveal the nature of his life as a showman in the late 1850s, it may have involved ventriloquism, as in 1860 he wrote

a book on how to practice this deception and illusion, *Ventriloquism Made Easy, Also, an Exposure of Magic, and the Second Sight Mystery.* He was a close friend of the publisher, Wyman the Wizard, whose numismatic connection is described in chapter 14 of this book.

One of the illustrations.

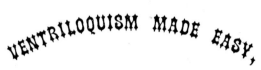

ALSO, AN EXPOSURE OF

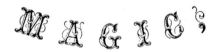

AND THE

SECOND SIGHT MYSTERY,

By E. MASON, Jr.
(OUR NED.)

452197759

All things being are in mystery: we expound mysteries by mysteries;
And yet the secret of them all is one in simple grandeur :
All intricate, yet each path plain, to those who know the way ;
All unapproachable, yet easy of access, to them that hold the key.

PHILADELPHIA:
WYMAN THE WIZARD, PUBLISHER.
C. E. P. BRINCKLŒ & CO., PRINTERS, No. 23 NORTH SIXTH STREET.
1 8 6 0.

The title page of Mason's 1860 book.

Concerning his travels, Mason recalled:

The writer was connected with a popular exhibition, traveling from North to South, and visiting all the important cities and towns en route. While thus engaged, we made it a daily practice to visit all the old junk shops, confectioners, bakers, grocers, &c., and collect all the old and curious coins we could find—at the same time leaving a card, with address, to establish future trade; and this practice led to a very general hunt, in the places aforesaid, for coins, and in many instances we were surrounded at the opening of the Exhibition with men and boys eager to dispose of large quantities of old cents, &c. In one instance while passing through North Carolina, we purchased 10,000 copper pieces; in another, at Norfolk, Virginia, 64 brass Washington tokens of 1783, and 46 Connecticut coins, besides a large quantity and variety both foreign and American.

Time passed on—Jo went on with his collection and Ned with his traveling exhibition until 1860, when the two friends met again at Mason's Coin Shop, 451 N. 2nd Street, this city. Jo continued to accumulate fine coins and Ned alternated coins with shows, picking up in the winter many rare and valuable pieces which were sold in the summer at his coin store.

These coins, or the best of them, were disposed of to Mr. Cogan and Mr. Dickeson of this city. The gathering of coins afforded us an agreeable pastime, as well as a profitable occupation; and the constant accumulation of coins led us to enter the field as a dealer in this city, in 1860. While thus occupied we advertised very extensively in the large cities offering what appeared to be fabulous prices for rare U.S. cents. Many of our friends will remember the advertisements, headed with glaring capitals, "$25 PAID FOR U.S. CENTS OF 1799." The public manner in which we made known our wants induced many persons to send us packages of coins by express. . . .[3]

The campaign for cents involved emblazoning the message on the side of a horse-drawn wagon and driving through the streets of Philadelphia and nearby towns. Another account tells of a similar search in and around Boston. At the time such a rare cent would have been worth this amount only if in a very high grade. Average circulated examples were worth only a few dollars.

Another reminiscence told this:

While making a coin speculating tour of the chief cities and towns of North Carolina, during the year 1859, we visited the promising little village of Charlotte, and its neighboring gold mines. After satisfying our curiosity by a personal examination of the different methods of extracting the precious metal, and witnessing the slow and laborious process of mining, as conducted by Negro slaves, with the aid of mule power, we accepted an invitation from the landlord of the prominent hotel in Charlotte, to visit the U.S. Branch Mint, then in operation at this town.[4]

At the time there was hardly any numismatic interest in mintmarked coins and little knowledge thereof. In his *American Numismatical Manual* Dickeson stated that a "C" mintmark meant the coin was struck in California!

Ned Mason, Aeronaut

Continuing his narrative:

Time passed on—Fort Sumter had been fired upon, the North rushed to arms, the South followed suit, and ordinary business and pleasure were alike discarded by the people of each portion of the country to take a hand in the more serious business of engaging in "grim visaged war." The coin store was closed and the coin dealer was with the men at the front; so also was his companion Jo, though each ignorant of the other's occupation. Time passed on—McClellan with his vast army was working his way on the Peninsular by slow sieges toward Richmond.

[In December 1861] Ned had become an aeronaut of the Army of the Potomac, and was engaged reconnoitering the Confederates in the vicinity of Yorktown. While thus employed, Ned was ordered to take a balloon in a certain direction where the operations of the Confederates could be observed on the opposite side of the river, near Gloucester. While up in the balloon about 150 feet high, and while being thus towed by a detail of soldiers who marched in three angular lines drawing the balloon along by ropes, through the long rows of soldiers attracted by the unusual spectacle, his attention was attracted to an officer in a bright blue uniform and silk sash, waving his sword and crying at the top of his voice:

"Hello! Is that Ned Mason up there?"

By the use of a field glass we discovered our coin collecting friend, whose appearance had changed considerably, and whose title was Lieut. Levick, of Sickle's Brigade, New York. The next salutation was,

"Have you got any coins?"

We replied:

"Come up to our balloon camp, front of Yorktown, and see."

The next morning, bright and early, the orderly announced "Lieut. Levick wishes to see Capt. Mason," and our curiosity tent was honored by a visit from our old chum, who

remained far beyond his limit of absence, so enthusiastic was he in the discussion of coins and the examination of the objects of art and war the aeronaut had collected and heaped up near the outer pole of his wall tent. Time passed on—the aeronaut returned to his coin store, and the Lieut. to his book-keeping; but both now frequently exchange notes on the exciting times of the past and continue their love for numismatology.

Back in the Coin Business

So far, so good. A young man with wide-ranging interests is established in rare coins. Nothing eccentric or unusual. According to his own account Mason, back in business in Philadelphia as Mason & Co., was busy publishing priced catalogs of rare coins, with the 14th edition appearing in 1866.[5] Little is known of these today, and I don't recall ever having seen one. The "& Co." included a brief partnership with J.W. Haseltine, who was later to become prominent in Philadelphia coin sales and auctions. In 1867 at his store at 434 Chestnut Street he launched *Mason's Coin and Stamp Collectors' Magazine,* which, with some variation in the title, was published into 1871 to the extent of six volumes and 66 issues. The March 1869 issue included the memorable *Mason's Photographic Gallery of the Coin Collectors of the United States, #1,* depicting 48 individuals. There never was a #2.

The magazine gave Mason a forum to dispense much useful knowledge about numismatics, to share his experiences, and from this bully pulpit to criticize his competition and much else.

Among his experiences he related that in the summer of 1867 he, coin dealer and token issuer Charles K. Warner, and collector William Fewsmith hired a light wagon and drove about 100 miles to see the collection of a Mr. Bodey, which was valued at $2,000 by the visitors, but was not purchased. At the time this represented a very valuable cabinet. Early the next year he moved to 50 North 10th Street below Arch, a "now thriving and fashionable" district. The new office was described as commodious and on the ground floor. Visitors were welcome.

In 1868 he was also a partner in Mason & Wells at 50 North Tenth Street, which advertised to buy and sell coins. On July 1 and 2, 1868, the collection of Philadelphia lawyer John C. Nippes was sold by Thomas Birch & Son, one of the city's most prominent auctioneers, in sweltering summer heat into the nineties. The catalog "is the production of a novice," Mason wrote. Further:

> There sat our good, big, fat friend Cogan, in front of the auctioneer, sweating, sweltering and suffering for the benefit of his bidders and that little 10 percent. Friend Cogan was not the only sufferer and wet-shirted philosopher. The writer, who turns 215 pounds, was wringing wet with the huge drops of perspiration, which rolled down cheeks, neck, arms, and legs, until we felt like a man overboard in his best clothes. We noticed among the overheated crowd of attendants at the sale, Messrs. Cogan, Kline, Martin, Agnew, Adams, Smith, 'Moneta,' Vaux, Wells, Randall, and Jester.[6]

The City of Brotherly Love must have had its shortcomings, or else Broadway beckoned, for in November 1868 Mason wrote:

> Wishing to remove our business to New York, we are prepared to arrange with a good, active and industrious man, to take the entire control of the Coin and Stamp business in this city. A good stock of Coins and Stamps; good fixtures, iron safe, etc., and a good location at a good rent. Whoever takes

this chance, will have the advantage of connecting with the New York Office, and will be supplied with, coins, stamps, and publications, necessary for the successful prosecution of the enterprise. A few hundred dollars required.

No qualified buyers appeared, and it was business as usual.

Mason's First Auction

In the 1860s J. Colvin Randall was an active dealer in Philadelphia and also a scholar, one of the first to study federal coins by die varieties. Rather than conduct his own sales, typically he consigned to others, such as Mason, who put Randall's name as consignor on the front of his first auction catalog, which was dated October 28–29, 1868. The venue was the sale room of none other than Thomas Birch & Son, with the elder Birch wielding the gavel. Bidders each held a copy of Mason's text, and many if not most had viewed the coins beforehand, as they were spread out on tables in the auction room.

Mason, who was doing his best to be a really *important* dealer, his status now increased as a magazine publisher, wrote this account of his Randall sale:

> Many strange faces were scattered through the rows of well-known numismatists. There, at the counter, spectacled, pencil in hand, set our inevitable friend and brother coin dealer. Cogan . . . whose jovial, good nature always keeps the audience in a pleasant and enjoyable manner. Among those present were the well-known collectors, R.C. Davis, William Fewsmith, A.M., Dr. Dickeson, Kline, Wells, Campbell, Ralston (recently returned from Europe), Martin (he of the Post Office), Mahoney, Jenks,

Jackson, Petrie (of hotel renown), Roberts, Jones (the numismatic author), Porter, Alexander, 'Moneta,' Moore, Leutze, Snyder (he of the Reading Railroad), and the welcome and inevitable 'Cash' (he of the Treasury Department).

Of those represented by Messrs. Cogan, Mason, and Kline, we caught the names Harris, Sanford, Elliott, Ufford, Bailey, Bohea, Staeblein, Duncan, Clark, Phillips, Rust, Abbott, Emerson, Payfer, Wilder, Mott, Hennessy, Gschwend, Cook, Barnhard, Marshall, Bates, Oram, Keeney, Dawley, Porter, Converse, Steel, Bollar, Sellers, Winsor, Birch, and some half dozen others.

From this account the auction was a smash success. And how nice it was the good-natured Edward D. Cogan lent a pleasant and enjoyable ambience that, by implication, might otherwise have been missing.

About the same time Cogan was writing his own commentary of the catalog and sale, which was published soon in the November issue of the *American Journal of Numismatics*, stating in part that certain dimes in Mason's auction "were ridiculously overdescribed." Several other similar remarks were made. In the December issue of the same magazine there were heated remarks by both Mason and Cogan. The latter suggested that Mason may have "written the most contemptible, and in some respects, unintelligible and withal untruthful twaddle, that ever was written, and he ought to have been ashamed to insert it in his magazine."

In his own magazine, Mason could always have the last word, and he soon published the rebuttal he had mailed off to the *American Journal of Numismatics* stating that Cogan's recent criticism of the cataloging and conduct of the Randall sale was unfair. The affair escalated, and Cogan printed a three-page leaflet

attacking Mason. Thus precipitated one of the bitterest of the internecine dealer feuds of the era. Randall must have sided with Mason, for on October 18–19, 1869, Mason issued another catalog bearing Randall's name.

In time Mason conducted at least 34 auction sales. The first set the record for controversy.

Expanding Operations

Mason's second auction was held in Philadelphia on April 13 and 14, 1869. He told of its success, not missing the opportunity to take a swipe at the Mint Cabinet collection:

> E.J. Farmer's collection of coins was disposed of at public sale and gave universal satisfaction to all concerned. There has seldom, if ever, been a sale that attracted as much attention as this. Not that the coins were superior to those offered in previous sales, but simply from the fact that several pieces were eyed with selfish longings by more than one collector.
>
> The excitement was created principally by the exhibition of the finest 1796, 16 star, U.S. half dollar that had been seen in the country. Day after day came the lovers of numismatics to feast their eyes upon this beautiful coin. It was vaguely hinted that Uncle Sam might purchase the piece to improve his disreputable collection, at the marble Mint in Chestnut St. Philadelphians said that the coin should not leave the city. If the Mint did not purchase it, some bold, patriotic and sensible collector, would buy it himself, if he had to sell his new velocipede to raise the needful.
>
> There were other attractions in the sale. A magnificent series of Roman and Greek silver coins, many of them

of the highest rarity; also a *unique* "Virginia shilling," or as Brother Cogan terms this peculiar little brass piece "store card." Let it be what it may. . . . Here, too, we had a 1794 U.S. dollar, 1796 half cent, two pieces that create a lively bidding and competition at any sale when offered. There were other pieces, and other reasons, which caused that large collection of gentlemen and scholars assembled in Birch & Son's spacious rooms, on Tuesday, April 13.

Lorin G. Parmelee, the Boston collector, captured the 1796 half dollar. "Happily for the present owner, Mr. Cogan, who had an unlimited bid, withdrew, thinking the piece had reached its fictitious value. There were 950 lots sold, realizing not far short of $1500."

In the late summer of 1869 Mason announced that he had opened a branch Coin Depot at 54 Wall Street in the heart of New York City's financial district. He observed that the numismatic hobby was growing rapidly. In 1868 there were about a thousand serious collectors in the United States and Canada, a number that doubled by late 1869. About 200 of these had important collections, he estimated.

In *Mason's Coin & Stamp Collector's Magazine,* November, 1869, Mason took aim at Alfred S. Robinson, an otherwise respected banker, bullion dealer, token issuer, and coin dealer of Hartford, Connecticut, while stating that his own sale was a great success:

> Since our last issue we have two coin sales to chronicle—one made under the auspices and *mis*-management of a Mr. Robinson, of Connecticut, which took place October 15, at the sales rooms of Bangs, Merwin & Co. The catalogue of this sale was an outrageous infringement on good numismatic taste, and reflects great *dis*-credit upon the author, Mr. R. The coins were as a whole as poor a congregation of trash as we remember to have seen offered at public sale. We pity the buyers of the pieces in the Robinson sale, and we trust they will control their feelings, when comparing the coins purchased with the catalogued description of the same.

> The other coin sale was under the auspices of the publishers of this journal, and was a success, realizing nearly $2,000. The following are some of the principal pieces, with the prices at which they were knocked down: Woodgate & Co.'s liquor dealers card brought $5.50, Isle of Man penny, $2.50, Barbados penny, $2.25; U.S. half eagle of 1821, $12.50.

Woodgate & Co. was operated by none other than Joseph N.T. Levick, Mason's longtime friend.

By his extensive criticisms, briefly sampled above, Mason aroused the ire of others in the stamp and coin business. The January 1870 issue of the *American Stamp Mercury and Numismatist* was an attack on Mason probably by an anonymous contributor to publisher Ferdinand Trifet (who is further noticed in chapter 35 of this book):

> We shall now proceed to expose the ignorance of this Mason (no, he is not a Mason, but a numismatic hod-carrier, if we may be allowed to coin an expression), and show that while he presumes to sit in judgment on things numismatic he is himself ignorant of the simplest rules and usages of the science. We shall call only himself to witness against himself—"out of thine own mouth will I judge thee."

Trying to Understand "Ned" Mason

While convicting him of ignorance in the science of numismatology, we shall also take occasion to show up some of his amusingly—stupid blunders in orthography and syntax. On page 1 of the first number of vol. 1 of his magazine, in the second paragraph, Mr. Mason calls the Sommer Islands shilling the 'Summer Island shilling.' In the fifth paragraph of the same article he says of New England coins, "although very rare, [they] are frequently found in good condition." Here, in one simple sentence, are to be found as many absurdities as the celebrated Roche was guilty of when he said "I am writing this with a pistol in each hand, and my sword between my teeth."

In the same article, in the sixth paragraph, he further says "The Pine Tree money bears in appearance a slight resemblance to the ancient Roman silver coins." This is certainly "rare" information, when we remember that the only resemblance between the coins in question is in the color of the metal of which they are made. Truly, a most profound person, this Mason—a worthy guide—a great man!....

We will not tire the reader by taking *seratim,* the numbers of Mason's magazine and laying bare the blunders in them. We, therefore, pass to the third volume, No. 11. On page 123, in an article on "The New Jersey Cent, 1787," he says "we now believe it genuine, with a doubt." What does this mean? Can a belief be coupled with a doubt and be a belief? We think not.

One has positive properties, the other negative. Both cannot, therefore, prevail in the mind at the same time. But it seems this fellow does not know when he contradicts himself in terms. The best of the joke, however, is that on the next page 124), in an article about the same coin, he says "we now have the pleasure of stating that the New Jersey coin is pronounced a genuine and original piece.".....

But, great a man as Mason evidently considers himself to be, his peacock pride is sometimes hurt by the criticism of unfeeling men upon his ungainly tracks in the (to him) muddled mazes of orthography. A correspondent of the New York *American Journal of Numismatics,* over the signature of C, has taken him to task for bad spelling. Mason whines that the 'proof-reader' is 'the proper person to blame for errors of any kind occurring in printed matter.' Alas! Poor proof-reader, if you have to shoulder all errors made by Mason, we pity you.

In vol. 3, No. 4, page 37, Mason makes his melancholy lament. But the richest part of the affair is that in this very article we find several typographical blunders. The word infallible is spelled 'infallable'; heinous is spelled 'henious'; and both these errors occur in one short sentence.

Undeterred, Mason continued his glaring errors, diatribes, and other actions, seemingly thinking that for some reason he was right and all others were wrong.

In the spring of 1870 Mason moved his office to 139 North Ninth Street. He described the new premises:

The interior of a coin store: the furniture of which consists of a counter, showcase, coin cabinets, a few armchairs, desk, pigeon holes for letters, and a glass partition separating a small portion of store which is used for private bargains, such as buying and exchanging coins, conversation room, etc.[7]

The federal census of 1870 lists Mason, age 44; his wife Levinia, 37; and children Mena W., 1, Camille, 10, Clarance (*sic*), 7, and Genevieve, 8.

The Fewsmith Sale

Beginning on October 4 at the auction sale rooms of Leavitt, Strebeigh & Co., Clinton Hall, Astor Place, New York, Mason held a four-day sale of the collection of William Fewsmith, an event that probably marked the high point of his career. By this time he and Cogan had settled their differences.

Catalogues of the collection can be had on application to the auctioneers, or Edward Cogan, 95 William Street, New York; Henry Cook, 74 Friend St, Boston; A.C. Kline, 212 South Eighth St., and Mason & Co., 139 North Ninth St, Philadelphia. The collection embraces several thousand choice and rare American and foreign coins and medals. Catalogues, extra size, printed on tinted paper, wide margin, will be mailed on receipt of ten cents to prepay postage.

Mason would have more to say about Henry Cook. In the meantime he announced that excepting W.E. Woodward's 1867 sale of the Joseph J. Mickley Collection, this was the greatest auction in American numismatic history. Not everyone agreed. Moreover there seems to have been some trouble in Mason's

paradise, as in December 1870 he wrote this in his magazine:

A handsome reward will be paid to any party informing us from whence and whom came the report that the Fewsmith Cabinet of coins had been tampered with before the sale of October 4, and that all the choice cents in that collection had been reserved for private parties.

This vile report lessened the pecuniary results of said sale, and we wish to publish the name of the miscreant who would see to undervalue and injure another's private property for selfish motives. The report was circulated extensively in Boston, and was mentioned to Elliot of Lowell, Colburn, Crosby, Trifet, and others of Boston. Mr. Trifet denies giving publicity to the report, but heard it frequently mentioned before the sale. All communications upon this subject confidentially considered.

The Cook matter was next. Mason had sent Boston rare-coin dealer Henry Cook an unsolicited package of 25 auction catalogs to distribute to his customers. Cook sent them back forthwith and requested reimbursement from Mason for the 50 cents he had to pay in return express charges. Mason then printed a criticism of Cook, stating that he was mainly a shoe cobbler, was on an old street in Boston, and had premises

in which decayed boots with initial-chalked soles occupies the greater portion of the shelves and floor. This eccentric Crispin [ancient Roman shoemaker who was beatified] rejoices in the name of coin dealer, finding time between his half soling and cement patching to buy and sell old coins and medals; also catalogues and conducts coin sales.

Within his little four by sixteen feet coin and shoe shanty he has created a two and half feet counter upon which rests a case of coins. An upright case stands in the southeast corner of the front part of the store, in which medals, old silver spoons, and broken jewelry are prominent.

Thus, our eccentric knight of the awl represents a coin dealer of standing at the Hub. At various times, we have had occasion to send this Mr. Cook catalogues of sales for his especial and pecuniary benefits. We consequently sent him 25 catalogues for the sale of December 21.

Mason continued:

Is Henry Cook a coin dealer or a cobbler? If he claims to be the former of these respectable callings, is he dealing justly with his numismatic patrons by refusing to distribute the catalogues of a coin sale?

Although Mason criticized Cook for being in two businesses at the same time (shoes and coins), Mason himself also dealt at one time or another in stamps and real estate in addition to coins.

Off to Europe

On April 11, 1871, Mason filled out a passport application that was signed and witnessed by J.W. Haseltine. The document described the traveler as:

5 feet, 9½ inches tall, broad and high forehead, light hazel eyes, slightly aquiline and prominent nose, full mouth, round chin, dark brown hair, florid and slightly parchment complexion, and square face.

Mason advised his customers that he was off on a "coin hunting" tour and could be reached c/o W.S. Lincoln & Son, 464 New Oxford Street, London. Previous to going he purchased 125 "large and small Proof sets" of current coinage from the Mint. These would have been minor sets (with the cent, two-cents, nickel three-cents, and nickel five–cents) and larger sets (with those coins plus the silver issues through the Liberty Seated dollar). On the way over on the *City of London* he endeavored to sell some to his fellow passengers, but was only able to find one or two buyers.

Mason returned that summer, and in September announced that he was thinking of opening a branch office in London. This never happened. Meanwhile, his Wall Street branch must have been short-lived, for nothing more was said about it.

In the autumn he went on two domestic coin-hunting trips, the first through New Jersey, New York, Connecticut, and Massachusetts, and the second through much of the same territory. On December 21 he was the overnight guest of Alfred S. Robinson, the man previously described as an incompetent cataloger. The two must have smoked a peace pipe! Despite the seeming success of the Fewsmith sale and, perhaps, advantageous buying while in Europe, Mason's business operated at a loss in 1871.

In January 1872 his publication was renamed *Mason's Monthly Coin Collectors' Magazine,* published by Mason & Co. Coin & Medal Depot, Assembly Building, 10th and Chestnut Streets, Philadelphia, a new location for his business. Challenges continued, and he had difficulty publishing his magazine.

The Clay Sale

In December 1871 the collection of Charles Clay, M.D., of Manchester, England, crossed the block in the auction rooms of George A. Leavitt & Co., New

York City. The catalog was prepared by William H. Strobridge, one of the more highly regarded professionals of the day. Trouble was that during an earlier visit with Clay in England, Mason had endeavored to buy the Clay collection. Seeking to curry favor in this regard, he mentioned it glowingly in his magazine. Now it was out of reach. Mason could not "let go" and fired this in the January 1872 issue of his journal:

> The catalogue of Dr. Clay's collection of coins, medals, etc., prepared by Clay and revised by W.H. Strobridge, Brooklyn, N.Y., with a view of making a sale . . . is one of the most peculiar books ever presented to the numismatic public. This we believe to be the only catalogue of coins in which the uniform and simple system of arranging the pieces according to denomination has been ignored, and the confusing, inconvenient style of 'mixing things' adopted.

Mason said that half cents and cents were mixed together in a manner "that bidders at the sale were frequently led into the error of bidding upon a half cent when the cent was the object of their thoughts and competition." Mason complained that three different silver dollars—1801, 1802, and 1803—were all put into one lot. Some errors were characterized by "overdescription, while others consist of typographical blunders. . . ."

Many coins were overgraded, Mason advised his readers. Further, there were many counterfeits among the colonials. He criticized many descriptions lot by lot. In a separate article he reviewed the sale, stating that Strobridge and Woodward were in the front row, and that the room had a first-class audience throughout. Mason gratuitously declared that Clay would realize about $5,000 in currency, as opposed to the $6,500 in gold Mason had offered for the collection earlier in the year. He commented, generously, that if Woodward had held the sale, it would have brought $8,000 to $10,000.

In July 1872 the frequency of publication of the magazine was changed and it was renamed and continued as *Mason's Quarterly Coin Collectors' Magazine.* The magazine gave up the ghost in October.

In the meantime in July Mason went on another trip through the Eastern states. In New Haven, Connecticut, he was the guest of Mr. and Mrs. Parsons. He became ill, blamed it on bad water served by Mrs. Parsons, and wrote in his magazine that he was considering suing her.

Later Years

Matters worsened—due in part to the Panic of 1873, Mason stated. In the absence of publishing a magazine he kept most of his comments to himself, probably to the gratitude of the collecting community. In 1879 he was in possession of one of four original 1861 Confederate States of America half dollars and the reverse die used to strike them. These were offered here and there and were finally bought by J.W. Scott & Co., who made restrikes by stamping the die on the reverse of 1861 Liberty Seated half dollars for which the reverse inscriptions and motif were removed on a lathe.

In June 1879 Mason published *Mason's Coin Collectors' Herald* from 143 North 10th Street, Philadelphia. The first issue took up the subject of the 1861 Confederate *cent,* stating that neither engraver Robert Lovett Jr. nor anyone else had been able to substantiate the tale that these were made for the Confederate States of America. This was a true statement, and today the matter remains controversial.

Mason's financial matters were in better order, and on June 29, 1879, he sailed to Europe aboard the SS *Pennsylvania.* He visited Glasgow and Edinburgh in Scotland, then went to Liverpool, England, and other cities before returning home.

Back in America he kept busy buying and selling coins, publishing his magazine, and taking trips to visit collectors and dealers. In June 1880 Mason took to task Lancaster, Pennsylvania, dealer Charles Steigerwalt for having his *Coin Journal* "pretty well filled with numismatic articles taken, without credit, from *Mason's Coin Collectors' Herald.*" Mason claimed that a number of other publishers were stealing his information as well.

Mason moved to Boston and set up as Mason & Co. at 235 Washington Street. In 1883 during the Without CENTS Liberty Head nickel excitement he offered circulated pieces for 8¢ each with a "discount by the 100," Uncirculated specimens for 10¢ apiece, and Proofs also for 10¢. He advertised as an antiquarian.

On February 13, 1885, Mason married Emilie E. Atkins, age 59, one year his senior. The two headed off to Europe, where he intended to buy coins, only to learn that in London two American dealers had recently preceded him.

From 1886 to 1890 he conducted 15 auction sales in Boston, none of them of memorable content.[8] Numismatically, he seems to have faded away.

Mason died in 1902. His passing was little noted by the numismatic community and his numismatic greatness, such as he had espoused it, unrecognized. In the 1990s Charles E. Davis, numismatic bookseller, reprinted in three volumes the series of Mason's magazines, thus making their interesting contents easily available to a new generation of collectors and researchers.

Unrecognized until recent times, this interesting Jefferson nickel seems to be quite rare.

A Curiously Misplaced Mintmark

A Nickel Catches My Eye

Some time ago I noticed in *Coin World* a feature by Mike Diamond ("Case of the Moving Mintmark") pointing out that the 1975-D Jefferson nickel, total mintage 410,875,300, was normally found with the D mintmark downward from the right side of the 5 of the date, but one die had the D high and between the 5 and the Jefferson portrait. The regular 1975-D is, indeed, a common nickel—with more around than the total of all men, women, and children in the United States! While mintmarks vary considerably on many United States coins, including those of the 20th century, the position of the D near the portrait was extreme.

What to call such a variety? I contacted Ken Bressett, senior editor of the *Guide Book of United States Coins,* who suggested "Misplaced Mintmark," abbreviated as Misplaced MM. Ken has done his share of naming varieties, with many designations to his credit—including Doubled Die (for many varieties), Matron Head (for cents of 1816 and following years), and more.

The term has been used elsewhere, as by Bill Fivaz and J.T. Stanton (of the *Cherrypickers' Guide to Rare Die Varieties of United States Coins*). He has abbreviated it as MPMM (a convention that does not necessarily follow the words exactly any more than UVM does for the University of Vermont). MPMMs are found on various cents (in particular) but also on other coins, often varying slightly up or down or to the left or right of the "normal" position. To my mind these are not really *misplaced,* but are in the correct usual position with some variance up or down and to the left or right. Perhaps "Wandering Mintmark" might be more appropriate for these? In any event, studying such varieties has a long tradition. In the early 20th century

1975-D Jefferson nickel with the D mintmark in the regular position used on other nickels of the era.

1975-D Jefferson nickel with the D mintmark misplaced in a unique and different position.

Commodore W.C. Eaton submitted a number of articles on the subject to *The Numismatist*. His movable mintmarks, such as for Lincoln cents described in the March 1912 issue, were not dramatic—a little bit up, a little bit down, or slightly to the left or right. At least, on Lincoln cents of the early years the mintmark was always below the date. I would not call these *misplaced*. If one had been placed above the date, that would indeed be misplaced. If the 1975-D nickel with Misplaced MM catches on, perhaps the nomenclature will be revised. Who knows?

I contacted the author of the *Coin World* article, Mike Diamond, and it turned out he had an example for sale, which I purchased for $25. It arrived in due course, is illustrated here, and is what I would call Extremely Fine to About Uncirculated grade. Then began a further search. I contacted David Sundman, owner of Littleton Coin Company, who maintains in-depth stocks of certain modern issues. (If you need 50,000 examples of a particular Statehood or America the Beautiful quarter, Littleton Coin can probably help! Although few people want even close to this many, for me Littleton has been a handy place to order each year or so one of each example of current coinage.) Dave checked hundreds of 1975-D nickels in his inventory, but not a single one had the wandering mintmark!

Will History Repeat Itself?

I was reminded of a situation back in 1962. In that year two Jamestown, New York, dealers, C.G. Langworthy and Robert Kerr, found a 1938-D Buffalo nickel with not one but two mintmarks! They contacted *Coin World* about it, and editor Margo Russell passed the inquiry to me to give an opinion, as I often did (and still do) for unusual things. Under magnification I verified that there were indeed two mintmarks—a D punched over a clearly visible earlier S! This was incredible

Similar to the 1975-D now under discussion, when I saw my first 1938-D/S (D Over S) nickel I considered it to be a rarity, perhaps a fantastic rarity.

I had never seen such a thing. Were there just a few specimens known? Or would dozens or hundreds turn up? Perhaps it was as rare as the 1913 Liberty Head nickel. I didn't know.

No one had ever heard of or seen coins with two different mintmarks, or even suspected that they existed. Or at least that is what I thought at the time. There were plenty of *overdates,* one date numeral punched over another, but no varieties of what were later designated as overmintmarks, an obvious term I made up and which has endured.

This sensational news was published on the front page of the September 14, 1962, issue of *Coin World*. It was one of the most spectacular discoveries of modern times. I received letters and telephone calls from all parts of the United States. In following weeks and months more 1938-D/S nickels turned up, a few at first, then several dozen, and within a year or two, several hundred. Investors and hoarders with rolls of 1938-D Buffalo nickels looked through them in the hopes of finding the coveted D/S variety. Today as you read these words, the 1938-D/S is easily available in Mint State and thousands have been found, but is several times more elusive than the very common regular 1938-D.

It can be theorized that in late 1937 and/or early 1938, when dies were being prepared for the coinage of the 1938 calendar year, Mint workers realized that no production of Buffalo nickels would take place in San Francisco, but Denver would be making 1938-D coins. Moreover, it was known that the Buffalo design would be discontinued soon. On hand were at least a half dozen reverses with S mintmarks. Rather than waste them, the S mintmark on each was overpunched with a D, after which the dies were sent to Denver and used. While a number of overmintmarks in various series have been discovered since then, in 1962 this was shocking news.

Years later I was reading the November 1928 issue of *The Numismatist* and was startled to find this comment submitted by Will W. Neil, a Baldwin, Kansas, pharmacist (excerpt):

Mint Marks, Or What Have You?

Regarding the specimen in question, it is at first glance an ordinary Morgan-type silver dollar of 1900 from the New Orleans Mint, but upon closer examination of the mint mark it has the appearance of the O having been punched in over the letters CC.

If this is so, then, undoubtedly, in this instance a reverse die was taken from the Carson City Mint to the mint at New Orleans [*sic;* actually the punching was done in Philadelphia], where the usual O was punched in the die over the CC and used in conjunction with an obverse die of 1900.

Thus, the laurels for reporting the first "over-mintmark" in American numismatics goes to Neil (whose collection was auctioned years later by B. Max Mehl).

Back to the 1975-D Misplaced MM Nickel

Regarding the curious 1975-D nickel, my excitement increased. I published my own query in *Coin World*, in my "Joys of Collecting" column, to see if anyone might tell me more about the variety. Did someone have a roll of them? I did not know what to expect. If a nickel die had a useful life of 1,000,000 impressions at the time, this meant that the 1975-D Misplaced MM, if made from a single die, is 400 times rarer than a regular 1975-D. On the other hand, if the errant die was spotted by a pressman and removed, or if it broke, the mintage could have been far less. How rare is it?

Just one other turned up. Randolph Grimes sent me an image of a worn example he had set aside years earlier when he spotted it and found the mintmark position to be highly unusual.

As I write these words the 1975-D Misplaced MM nickel seems to be very rare. On the other hand, probably only a tiny fraction of people owning 1975-D nickels know of the variety. I expect there are others waiting to be identified. If this were to be listed in *A Guide Book of United States Coins,* it would become well known and, in time, its relative rarity could be confirmed. Certainly there are more around. However, it seems that it will remain relatively scarce.

Other Coins with Two Mintmark Positions

Going a bit further, I contemplated mintmarks in American numismatic history that were *intentionally* placed in two different positions. Hence they are not Misplaced MMs or the result of a mistake. Here are some that are very dramatic and, for the most part, quite affordable, at least in circulated grades.

The 1872-S silver half dime exists with two mintmark positions of the S on the reverse, one being high above the wreath bow and the other below it. Each is quite collectible.

In 1875, dimes of the Carson City and San Francisco mints were made in the same variations, with the mintmark above the bow and the mintmark below. Both are easily enough found.

Early in 1917 Liberty Walking half dollars, of the new design introduced in 1916, were produced at three mints—Philadelphia, Denver, and San Francisco.

1872-S half dime with its S mintmark high above the wreath bow.

A Curiously Misplaced Mintmark

1872-S half dime with the S mintmark below the wreath bow.

1875-CC dime with CC mintmark above the wreath bow.

1875-CC dime with CC mintmark below the wreath bow.

1875-S dime with S mintmark above the wreath bow.

1875-S dime with S mintmark below the wreath bow.

1917-S half dollar with S mintmark on obverse.

1917-D half dollar with D mintmark on obverse.

1917-S half dollar with S mintmark on reverse.

1917-D half dollar with D mintmark on reverse.

On the branch-mint issues the D and S mintmarks were on the obverse, below the date. Partway through the year the standard was changed and the mintmarks were removed to the reverse. Each variety is quite collectible today, with the 1917-S on the obverse being viewed as a key issue.

When I cataloged the Louis E. Eliasberg Collection (with staff assistance of course), it fell upon me to

do the Liberty Walking half dollars. Assignments were split among experts, myself included, and while I usually worked with colonial coins, territorials, patterns, and early American issues, I did some modern pieces as well.

When examining the 1917-S half dollar with the mintmark on the reverse, I noticed on the obverse, below the date, where the mintmark had been on earlier issues, an area that showed marks of a grinding tool. It seemed to me that this particular obverse die once had a mintmark, but when reverse dies with mintmarks arrived at the San Francisco Mint from the

The reverse of a 1908-D No Motto $10 with its mintmark in a position found on no other variety in the series. Also shown is the reverse of a 1908-S with its mintmark in the place found on nearly all other Indian Head eagles.

main mint in Philadelphia, this particular obverse die was kept fit for use by removing the S. Interesting!

Another case that comes to mind, which Ken Bressett reminded me of, is the 1908-D $10. These were made in two reverse varieties, without the motto IN GOD WE TRUST and, beginning in August of that year, with the motto. The typical position for a D mintmark as evidenced by the 1908-D With Motto and also later Denver Mint coins is at the left border opposite the end of the eagle's perch. However, the 1908-D Without Motto, all by itself, has the D in a completely different location, at the border above the branch tip. As there are two different types here, this is not a case of having two mintmark positions of the same basic date and mint.

Until the modern era, mintmarks were punched into working dies by hand, using a letter punch. In several visits to the Philadelphia Mint in the 1970s and 1980s I would always stop by the Engraving Depart-

ment and chat with Chief Engraver Frank Gasparro, who became a friend, and later I visited his successor, Elizabeth Jones, also a friend. I would also talk with the other engravers who were busy hand-sculpting, modeling, sketching designs, and the like. Mike Iacocca (cousin of Lee Iacocca of Chrysler automobile fame) was in charge of punching mintmarks on coins. He had guide charts that someone made up with lines showing in what position the mintmark should be placed on a coin. Mike asked me if I would like to put a D mintmark on a Roosevelt dime die he was preparing, and I said yes. In retrospect I should have put it on the left side of the torch! However, I minded my business as a guest, and entered it properly. (My apologies to numismatists for not creating a rare variety!)

Mike and I became friends as well. He proposed making for me a portrait medal, and during a visit (accompanied by Mint staff) to the American Numismatic Association convention in August 1985 he asked me to sit so he could finesse a model of my portrait which he had made earlier from a photograph. However, the medal never came to be and I don't know where the model is today. I suppose if it is at the Mint I should see if it could be found! This was to have been a private medal—not unusual, as most Mint sculptors and engravers have done private work many times.

There you have it. A quick glance at a *Coin World* article about an unusual 1975-D led to an interesting adventure, still continuing, as described here.

Engraver Mike Iacocca modeling the author for a portrait medal that never came to be.

The years of the late 1850s saw a flurry of tokens issued by and for numismatists. William Bramhall issued a very curious token depicting Abraham Lincoln.

The Tokens of William L. Bramhall

Among the tokens in my collection several particularly interesting ones were made for and distributed by William L. Bramhall, born in 1839. By 1858 Bramhall was deeply involved in numismatics. He then went off to the Civil War and left the hobby behind. Early in 1866, by which time he was living in Washington, D.C., he came into contact with an old friend from New York, Augustus B. Sage, per Sage's recollection (written on March 26, 1867, and published in the *American Journal of Numismatics*), which mentions a recent encounter:[1]

> A few weeks since, in Washington, I met our mutual friend, and one well known to your readers, William Leggett Bramhall. Mr. Bramhall served with distinction during the war as captain of volunteers, was severely wounded in the head, and was breveted major, lieutenant-colonel and colonel, for gallant and meritorious services.
>
> He was looking very well, although he told me he suffered occasionally from his wounds. He still collects, though not to the same extent as formerly. I believe Bramhall's [1859 auction] was the first extensive sale of business cards or tokens in this country.

Reading a copy of this letter prompted Bramhall to sign up with the American Numismatic and Genealogical Society. He became a corresponding member on October 10, 1867.

Suitably inspired, Bramhall contributed this informative letter to the *American Journal of Numismatics* for the August 1867 issue (modern images and notes added):

> Washington, D.C., July 3d, 1867
> To the Editor of the American Journal of Numismatics.
>
> Dear Sir: Through the great kindness of some one of my former numismatic friends and associates, of your city I have for a year past been in receipt of your able and interesting Journal, which, as I have long since discontinued collecting numismatic treasures, has been read with an interest which I had supposed I had ceased to possess in the subject of which it so ably treats.
>
> Through the several articles in your Journal, I have discovered that most of my numismatic companions of the days before the war—who still live—continue to pursue the

William L. Bramhall

study of the cultivating and refining science of numismatics; and I have often thought that, were my time less occupied and my facilities here for collecting even moderately good, I should be strongly tempted to resume my former position in the "numismatic world."

I have thought too, that it was, perhaps, my duty to contribute, for collectors, the little numismatic light I still retain, instead of hiding it under a pint measure; and, animated by this feeling—whether from an egotistic or a generous disposition I cannot myself determine—I have concluded to send you the following statement in regard to the issue of certain medalets in 1859 and 1860, placing them at your service, if they shall be deemed of any value or interest to collectors of the "private American coinage":—

Having for a time made the collection of American political and advertising medalets a specialty, I designed and issued, in October 1859, through the works of the Scovill Manufacturing Co., of Waterbury, Ct., a "Republican token" intended both as a political toy and as material for exchange with other collectors.

The following description may serve to identify it:

Obverse: An American eagle (similar to that on the recent issue of the quarter dollar); Legend: "Success to Republican Principles."

Reverse: inscription: "Not One Cent for Slavery;" Legend: "Millions for Freedom." Edge milled. Size of the American quarter dollar.

The number struck was: in silver, 6; copper, 15; brass, 1,000; and lead, 1.

A little less than a year afterward, on the opening of the presidential campaign of 1860, I had the reverse die altered by the addition of two palm leaves crossed over the inscription; a six-pointed star under the word "Cent"; and, in the exergue, "1860." Of this new type of the medalet, I had struck only 7 in silver; 75 in copper; and 15,000 in brass,—all of them having plain edges.

I am satisfied that no more pieces than I have above stated were ever struck, as the dies have always been in my possession, except when used for the striking of the before-mentioned pieces; and as I received a certificate from the company as to the number actually struck. The reverse die I destroyed before the war.

In May 1860, immediately after the nomination of Abraham Lincoln for president, I obtained—through the kind assistance of my friend, George B. Lincoln, of Brooklyn—a profile photograph of his honest face, which was taken at Springfield for my special purpose.[2] I engaged the services of Mr. George H. Lovett, of New York, who immediately commenced engraving the dies for a small medalet, which soon after appeared, and it was the first—and bore the best likeness of Mr. L.—among the very many issued during that long and exciting political contest.

Reverse: inscription: "the Hannibal of America—•—1860", within a wreath; Legend: "Abra—ham Lin—coln Honest Abe of the West." Edge plain.

Of these, only 7 pieces were struck in silver, 35 each in copper, brass, and tin; and 250 in nickel,—inclusive of specimens retained by Mr. Lovett.

The appropriateness of the inscription used for the reverse, was, at the time of its issue, severely criticized by some. Although there was nothing then foreshadowed in the character of Mr. Lincoln to warrant his comparison to the Carthaginian warrior, it was intended to illustrate his reputed boldness, and his success in political warfare; and at the same time to inscribe, in conjunction with the two syllables between the hyphens in the legend, the full name of his associate upon the ticket. The hyphens referred to in the legend were designed to exhibit the singular fact that the last syllable of the Christian name and the first of the

One of the most fascinating tokens of Bramhall's era was the one he issued with Abraham Lincoln on the obverse and by means of a punning inscription, cleverly mentioning his running mate, Hannibal Hamlin, on the reverse. The subtle humor seems to have been lost on many observers, who felt that designating Lincoln as "the Hannibal of America" was an insult.

I will describe it, though perhaps imperfectly, as follows:

Obverse: A profile bust of Abraham Lincoln, in citizen's dress, facing to the right, and surrounded by a dotted circle; Legend: "* Abraham Lincoln * Natus Feb. 12. 1809."

The punning reverse die was altered by deeply punching the word WIDEAWAKES at the center, with a background of ruled lines and with leaves above and below. All of this was great fun for Bramhall, who enjoyed the excitement such pieces provided to the numismatic community.

surname of Mr. Lincoln comprised the surname of his political Lieutenant: Mr. Hamlin. This was the first political medalet struck in nickel of uniform size with the nickel cent.

Before the close of the political contest referred to, there being a demand for a quantity of these medalets, and the reverse die having been injured, that die was altered by substituting for the legend an oval shield bearing on a scroll "Wideawakes"— above and below it, a rose and leaves. Of this new type there were struck but 21 pieces in silver; 35 each in copper, brass, and nickel; and about 1,500 in block tin. The reverse die of this medalet has since been destroyed by myself.

In the winter of 1858–9, I had issued a business card, the first token of any description, I believe, of the size of the nickel cent, struck in that metal. It was executed by Mr. George H. Lovett, and the nickel planchets were procured by him at the U.S. Mint at Philadelphia. It is as follows:

Robbins, Royce & Hard token with "Wholesale Dealers" obverse and George Washington reverse. The obverse and reverse designations are per Bramhall, but many collectors would call the Washington side the obverse.

Obverse: Inscription: "Robbins, Royce & Hard, Wholesale Dealers in Dry Goods, 70 Reade St., New York."

Reverse: A nude bust of Washington, profile, facing to the left; Legend: "Represented by Wm. Leggett Bramhall." Edge Plain.

There were struck, of these only 7 silver; 52 each copper and brass; 250 nickel; and 15 block tin. The card not answering my purpose, I had a new obverse die cut for it, as follows:

Robbins, Royce & Hard token with new obverse.

Inscription: "Robbins, Royce & Hard, Jobbers of Staple Fancy and Dry Goods, 70 Reade & 112 Duane Sts., New York.

Of this type Mr. Lovett struck only 20 silver; 35 each copper and brass; 15 block tin; and several hundred in nickel.

During the autumn of 1860, the "raging fever" for "store cards" and political tokens having nearly reached its height, I was importuned by many of my numismatic friends to issue a limited number of "mules" in the different metals.

Muling of the two Robbins, Royce & Hard obverses.

Muling of a Robbins, Royce & Hard die
with the altered "Wideawakes" die.

other four metals used. Of the three sets of silver, seven each, I retain one in my little case of reserved numismatic treasures; another is now, I believe, in the cabinet of Robert Hewitt, Jr., Esq., of New York; and the third is possessed by my old friend and late comrade in arms, Captain Joseph N.T. Levick, of New York.

In contributing this statement I am well aware that I am imparting information of but slight importance to the numismatic world; but it is all that I have to give you, and I freely furnish it for the use of your Journal, or the Society of which I am proud to have been an active member soon after its original organization. Wishing your Journal the great success which it fully deserves, I have the honor to be,

Very Respectfully,

Your Servant,

W.L.B.

I must say that I had always looked with detestation upon this illegitimate system of coinage, and had already been quite disgusted with the profuse muling, re-issuing from old dies, and issuing from imitation dies, which had lately been practiced to a great extent in this country; but I have to confess that I was finally so far persuaded by the entreaties of some of my friends as, half reluctantly, to give the order to Mr. Lovett to combine the five parts of dies and thus issue seven sets or "mules" in five metals each. The number of these mules was limited to 3 of each in silver, and to 15 each in each of the

Bramhall's Early Life

Some biographical notes may be of interest: William Leggett Bramhall was born on July 26, 1839, in Buffalo, New York. His father, Charles H. Bramhall, was well known in his time. In 1845 he was appointed by Governor Silas Wright to be judge of the Common Pleas Court in Albany. Later he served for a decade as warden of the Port of New York. In the Reconstruction era after the Civil War he was appointed judge of the Circuit Court in Richmond. William's mother, née Eliza Hogeboom, was a daughter of Judge Tobias Hogeboom of Columbia County, New York, who in 1844 was a presidential elector.

Young William enrolled at the Albany Academy for his elementary education, and then went to the Kinderhook Academy, from which he graduated in

1855. He moved to New York City in that year and secured a position as a clerk with Tracy, Irwin & Co., importers of dry goods.[3]

IMPORTANT
TO CASH BUYERS
WE WOULD CALL THE ESPECIAL ATTENTION OF
ALL CASH BUYERS
TO OUR
Very Large and Full Assorted Stock
OF
Staple and Fancy
DRY GOODS,
Yankee Notions,
WHITE GOODS & HOSIERY,
WHICH WE OFFER
CHEAP FOR CASH.
Robbins, Royce & Hard,
70 Reade and 112 Duane Streets,
NEAR BROADWAY.

Advertisement by Robbins, Royce & Hard, where William L. Bramhall worked beginning in 1858.

By 1858 he was clerking at Robbins, Royce & Hard, dry-goods and novelty merchants.[4] In this year or in early 1859 he met with local engraver and die sinker George H. Lovett and commissioned him to make some tokens to advertise his employer. These were the size of the contemporary copper-nickel cent. The intent was to make them for numismatic trading and sale. One side depicted George Washington and the other side, made in two versions, had information about Bramhall's employer. The striking was done by the Scovill Manufacturing Co. in Waterbury, Connecticut, as mentioned above.[5]

Bramhall joined the American Numismatic Society in November 3, 1858, and was welcomed at the group's "first semi-annual meeting" held at the Omacatl Club, an organization of boat-rowing enthusiasts, at 811 Broadway. At the time the Society met in various places where a room could be secured. That evening Sage, who had founded the Society at a meeting in his home in March 1858, was appointed curator of its cabinet, which by that time had a small selection of coins and artifacts, some donated by Sage himself. On January 6, 1859, Sage resigned so he could devote all of his time to his rapidly growing coin dealership, including the publishing of medalets made to his order by George H. Lovett. Bramhall was appointed curator to fill the vacancy.

At the American Numismatic Society specially called meeting on Thursday, March 24, 1859, Bramhall moved the following resolution:

> Whereas—The question as to the coinage of the American cent in the year 1815, remains a matter of doubt and dispute, therefore—Resolved that the Committee on American coins, be and is hereby instructed to investigate and report regarding the same.

The resolution passed. At the time there were many questions regarding the rarity of American coins. Dr. Montroville W. Dickeson's book, the *American Numismatical Manual*, had just been published by Doubleday, at $7.50, and was in the process of being distributed. The text stated that the author doubted that any cents were made in 1815, but many fakes altered from 1813 had been seen.

Bramhall also proposed amending the by-laws at the meeting and donated an 1819 large cent to the cabinet. At the same Society meeting Dickeson was elected as an honorary member.

At the next regular meeting, Thursday, April 7, Bramhall resigned as curator in view of the pending incorporation of the Society; under law, all of the officers had to be at least 21 years of age.

Torchlight parade reception given to the Wide-Awake Club of Newark, New Jersey, by the Hartford club during a visit to that Connecticut city in July 1860. (*Frank Leslie's Illustrated Newspaper*, August 11, 1860)

The premises of Bangs, Merwin, & Company (earlier known as Bangs, Brother & Co.) at 13 Park Row, New York City, 1859. In front is a horse-drawn omnibus.

In the meantime he pursued the study of law, a career objective, and delved into Republican Party politics. The presidential election of 1860 was of particular interest, as noted above, prompting him to take the exceptional step of having a friend acquire from Abraham Lincoln a special portrait to use on the tokens George H. Lovett created.[6] The Wide-Awakes, an enthusiastic group of Republicans active in the late 1850s and in the Lincoln campaign, were likewise memorialized.

With his family connections he seems to have lived comfortably while in New York City, enjoying the advantages offered by the metropolis.

The Bramhall Collection at Auction

As referred to in the *American Journal of Numismatics* letters quoted above, in spring 1859 Messrs. Bangs, Merwin & Co. presented an auction described on the title page as *Catalogue of the Valuable and Extensive Cabinet of American and Foreign Coins, Tokens, Medals &c. herein minutely described, the property of William Leggett Bramhall, Esq., late curator of the American Numismatic Society.*

The title page also noted:

This is undoubtedly the most complete collection of American coins and tokens ever offered at public sale in this city, and, together with a general assortment of English coins and medals will be sold at public auction by Messrs. Bangs, Merwin & Co. at their sales room, No. 13 Park Row, N.Y., on May 4th and 5th, 1859, commencing at precisely 7 o'clock, P.M.

Among 595 numbered lots were these listings:

Lot 116. Full set of cents, including all the dates, and

many types and varieties. Some very fine. 100 [pieces]

Lot 211. [under "American Advertising Tokens"] Chesbrough, Stearns & Co. 37 Nassaw-street. [Nassau wrongly spelled.] Extremely rare. Brass. [1]

Lot 220. Smith's Clock Est. "Time is money." Four types; Phalon, 35 Bowery. All fine and scarce. [5]

Lot 225. D. Sweeny & Son. Hotel Check; Miller's Hair Invigorator, Bowery; Strasburger & Nuhn. Two types. All very fine and rare. [5]

Lot 434. Connecticut cent, 1786. "AUCTORI CONNEC:" Woman's head facing the right, date in small figures, not mentioned by Dickeson.[7] Fine [1]

Lot 437. Connecticut cent, 1787. The "Laughing Effigy Piece." Very fine, and very rare. [1]

Lot 464. Dollar, 1794. Stamped B.L. FOWLER. Otherwise exceedingly fine. Very rare. [1]

Lot 478. Dollar, 1854. Very fine and rare. [1]

Lot 479. Dollar, 1856. Very fine and scarce. [1]

The "minute descriptions," such as they were, may have been done by Bramhall himself. A separate listing of 111 addenda, sold on May 6, seems to be in the style of another cataloger.

I have not been able to learn anything about how the young numismatist formed his collection or why he elected to sell it. Perhaps they were duplicates or otherwise unwanted pieces. At the time—and the tradition continues today—it was common practice to put the name of a consignor on a catalog cover of an offering that included items from multiple sources. The main part of the sale totaled $352.65, a respectable sum in those days.

The Bramhall catalog does not seem to have attracted much notice, and even in a later era few numismatic bibliophiles considered it to be important.

Bramhall, Civil War Hero

In 1860 William L. Bramhall joined the 7th Regiment of the National Guard of the New York State Militia. On April 19, 1861, on President Lincoln's first call to arms for three-month enlistments, he went with the militia to Washington. In July he fought in the Battle of Bull Run. Union troops were routed by the Confederates, signaling that the Civil War (as it later was called) was not going to end quickly.

For the second presidential call to arms Bramhall was authorized to recruit a company for the Columbia County Regiment headquartered at Chatham, New York. His men were sent to the 91st New York Volunteers while Bramhall was in Albany serving as a military instructor and drill officer. On January 1, 1862, in New York City he enlisted in Company B of the 93rd Regiment, New York Volunteers, and was appointed as sergeant-major of the regiment by Colonel John S. Crocker. On May 1 he transferred to Company G, where he served as first sergeant. On May 9, 1863, he was commissioned as first lieutenant

The Battle of Bull Run.

of Company G. On this occasion he hosted a reception to the officers of the regiment and to General Joseph Hooker's staff. That autumn he served for several months as judge advocate of the General Court Martial at the headquarters of the Army of the Potomac.

On May 5, 1864, at the Battle of the Wilderness he was struck by a musket ball and sustained a severe scalp wound. With 11 other wounded officers of the regiment he was taken to a house in Fredericksburg, Maryland, and placed on the bare floor. Later he was sent to the Seminary Hospital in Georgetown, D.C., then to the Officers Hospital at the Naval Academy in Annapolis. He seemed to have recovered and was back in action at Deep Bottom when he suffered a severe sunstroke on July 29. By that time Bramhall had seen action in the battles of Yorktown, Williamsburg, Antietam, Fredericksburg, Chancellorsville, Gettysburg, and Petersburg in addition to those already mentioned. On November 5, 1864, he was discharged on a surgeon's certificate of disability.

In Civilian Life

After the war Leggett moved to Washington, where he became a partner in the law firm of Crocker, Robert-

son & Bramhall. On September 27, 1865, he was commissioned major by brevet in honor of his meritorious service and on September 8, 1866, he was commissioned as colonel by brevet. In that month he was a delegate to the Pittsburg Soldiers' and Sailors' convention and while there was mustered into the recently organized Grand Army of the Republic group.[8] Colonel Bramhall was active in Company "I" (9th) of the Army reserves.

In 1868 he married Anna Tabor Holland in a ceremony held in Buffalo. The couple had no children.

After leaving his law practice he engaged in many other activities. He was a painting contractor, deputy collector of taxes for the District of Columbia (for five years), and an agent for the Niagara Fire Insurance Co., and he conducted a real-estate brokerage. He returned to law in 1880, and in the late 1890s he was a campaigner for William McKinley. He died in Washington of heart disease on February 17, 1902, and was buried in Arlington National Cemetery.

Apart from the tokens issued by William Bramhall there were many other interesting pieces made by muling irrelevant dies to create numismatic delicacies. High on the list of combinations without logic is this 22 mm issue combining the obverse of an 1860 Lincoln presidential campaign token with a reverse die made for tokens sold to Southerners who opposed the North! The dies were by Benjamin C. True and the minting was done by John Stanton in Cincinnati. (Listed as a Civil War token in the Fuld reference, 506/514a)

CHAPTER 30

Among the most curious and interesting National Bank Notes are the very rare $5 "Black Charter" notes of the First National Bank of Central City, Colorado Territory, in a gold-mining camp high in the Rocky Mountains.

Rare Territorial Notes from Central City

Arcadia in the Rockies, Perhaps

Bird's-eye view of Central City circa 1876.

The Arcadians, saith the writer of old, regarded themselves as the most ancient people in Greece. Their habits were simple; and the quiet and happiness of their life among the mountains; their passionate fondness for music, in which they excelled; their delight in dancing; which they practiced assiduously; and their generous hospitality, for which they were noted, made them pass among the ancients for favorites of the gods; and although they were a brave and martial people, the name of their land became the synonym for a land of peace, simple pleasures, and untroubled quiet.

So began *Echoes from Arcadia*, a book of reminiscences published by Frank D. Young, the founding cashier of the First National Bank of Central City in Colorado Territory and prominent in the political and intellectual circles of the community.[1]

Billing the gold camp of Central City as Arcadia raised some eyebrows among later historians, who approached the settlement's history from a different perspective. Caroline Bancroft in *The Gulch of Gold, A History of Central City, Colorado*, emphasized some of the more rough-and-tumble aspects, successes but also failures, and more—a story of the people, some of whom endured great challenges and difficulties. The third notable historian of the district, H. William Axford, in *Gilpin County Gold*, featured the business angle, following the career of Peter McFarlane, and along the way telling of the trials and tribulations of life in the gold camp. Reflecting upon Young's comments, Axford was quick to point out that designating the city as an equivalent of Arcadia was a myth. It was anything but, in his view.

Actually, to cashier Young, Central City was indeed Arcadia. He and his attractive wife were active in social affairs, music, and theater. He accentuated the positive, as the old song goes. The negative was there as well, but he chose to look on the brighter side, even when accused, seemingly wrongly, of misdeeds as a town leader in politics and banking.

In a way, the same is true of other stories of Eldorado. Take for example San Francisco, epicenter of the Gold Rush in California, which had its low life, but also its high life, tents as well as mansions. A half dozen different people describing the city by the Golden Gate could give as many different perspectives. Cripple Creek, in Colorado, which was developed in the 1890s, similarly was adventure and romance for some and just plain hard work for others.

For many historians, Colorado mining towns are incredibly interesting to contemplate in terms of adventure, discovery, and good times. At least a dozen books on this vein have been written about Cripple Creek alone. Nolie Mumie, M.D., who enjoyed numismatics, was possessed of endless intellectual curiosity and visited many gold camps and wrote extensively about them. Muriel Sibell Wolle, in *Stampede to Timberline*, told of mining cities then and now, and added her own sketches as to what they looked like in later years when she visited.

The stories of Central City tell of a small district, three communities linked together in the mountains above Denver. Barely two miles long from one extreme to the other, the interlocked settlements consisted of Nevadaville, Central City, and Black Hawk. Where one began and the other ended was difficult for anyone to tell.

As to whether Central City was Arcadia during the era of the First National Bank, or was a rough-and-tumble mining camp, the reader can decide. In its glory days it was a magnet for distinguished visitors who came to see for themselves what they had been reading about in newspapers and magazines. They had missed out on the California rush, but here was a chance to observe first-hand the one in Colorado.

Horace Greeley, editor of the *New York Tribune*, came, as did Schuyler Colfax (speaker of the House of Representatives when he visited on May 27, 1865, later to become vice president under Ulysses S. Grant), P.T. Barnum, U.S. Grant (two times, once as a general and once as president), and even a Rothschild from the French banking family. In 1873 Grant, in his second visit to the city, dined at the Teller House as part of a trip through the mountains. After alighting from his coach, he walked on a path of solid-silver ingots laid from there to the door.

One visitor, Bayard Taylor, a raconteur, novelist, international traveler, and *New York Tribune* correspondent, visited on June 26, 1866, and wrote this account:

Commencing at Black Hawk, where the sole pleasant object is the Presbyterian Church, white, tasteful, and charmingly placed on the last step of Bates Hill, above the chimneys and mills in the uniting ravines, we mount Gregory Gulch by a rough, winding, dusty road, lined with crowded wooden buildings: hotels, with pompous names and limited accommodations; drinking saloons, "lager beer" being a frequent sign; bakeries, log and frame dwelling-houses, idle mills, piles of rusty and useless machinery tumbled by the wayside, and now and then a cottage in the calico style, with all sorts of brackets and carved drop-cornices.

In the centre of the gulch rushes a stream of muddy water, sometimes dammed up to broaden the bed and obtain a little more foothold for houses. Beyond the large mill built by ex-General Fitz-John Porter for an unfortunate New York company, who paid a large sum to repeat the experience of the national government, Black Hawk terminates; but the houses, mills, drinking saloons, and shops continue just the same, and in another half-mile you find yourself in Central City.

This place consists mainly of one street, on the right-hand side of the gulch; the houses on your left, as you ascend, resting on high posts or scaffolding, over the deep bed of the stream. Half-way up there is a single cross-street some three hundred feet in length, where the principal stores are jammed together in an incredibly small space. With one exception, the buildings are frame, dry as tinder at this season; and a fire, starting at the top of the town, with a wind blowing down the ravine, would wipe out the place in half an hour.

The whole string of cities has a curious, rickety, temporary air, with their buildings standing as if on one leg, their big signs and little accommodations, the irregular, wandering, uneven street, and the bald, scarred, and pitted mountains on either side. Everything is odd, grotesque, unusual; but no feature can be called attractive. I took quarters at the St. Nicholas Hotel, of which I will only say that the board is five dollars per day. . . . .

In this population of from six to eight thousand souls, one finds representatives of all parts of the United States and Europe. Men of culture and education are plenty, yet not always to be distinguished by their dress or appearance. Society is still agreeably free and unconventional. People are so crowded together, live in so primitive a fashion for the most part, and are, perhaps (many of them), so glad to escape from restraint, that they are more natural, and hence more interesting than in the older states. Owing to the latter cause, no doubt, it is sometimes difficult to recognize the staid New Englander in the sunburnt individual in sombrero and riding-boots, who smokes his pipe, carries his pocket-flask, and tells any amount of rollicking stories. He has simply cast off his assumed shell and is himself; and I must confess I like him all the better…

Some friends took me over the hill to Quartz Gulch the other day, in order to try some mountain-brewed ale. After the intense still heat of the air the beverage was very refreshing and greatly superior in its quality to the lager beer of the mountains. The owner of the brewery lives in a neat log-cabin, the steps whereto are ores of gold and silver, and inside the rough walls an accomplished lady sat down to her piano and played for us some choice compositions.

There is also a theatre here, with performances every night. Mr. Waldron, of California, takes the leading tragic and melodramatic parts, while Mr. Langrishe, the manager, is himself a very admirable comedian. A good deal of swearing is introduced into the farces, to please the miners. I went in one evening and found the house crowded. There is a daily paper here and one in Black Hawk, both well supported, I believe—certainly very well printed. The editorial dialect, to meet the tastes of the people, is of an exceedingly free-and-easy character. A collection of very curious specimens, both of approbation and attack, might easily be made; but I am too fatigued by the thin air to make the attempt to-night. . . .

There is an immense number of fools in the world, and many of them either found their way to Colorado, or invested in mythical mines of fabulous productiveness. More than the usual amount of folly and swindling was located here for a time—hence the reaction, the effects of which are still felt.

Before leaving Central City, I must say that it is the most outrageously expensive place in Colorado. You pay more and get less for the money than in any other part of the world. I am already tired of these bald, clumsy shaped, pock-marked mountains; this one long, windy, dusty street, with its perpetual menace of fire; and this never-ending production of "specimens" and offer of "feet," and shall joyfully say good-by to-morrow morning.

My friends in Central City will not take offence when I say that I left—not them, but the place—with a cheerful sense of relief. I had been for four days jammed down among the torn and barren hills, and yearned mightily for a freer outlook and more attractive scenery.[2]

To Taylor this was not Arcadia.[3]

Grace Greenwood visited Central City and recorded her impressions in a letter sent on September 4, 1871, to be published as part of a continuing series she was doing for the *New York Times*:

Central is a wonderfully busy and interesting place. Through its steep, rugged, and narrow streets pour swift, ceaseless currents of travel and traffic,—carriages stages, loaded carts and wagons, trains of packed mules, miners in their rough, but picturesque garb; mounted drovers, eager-eyed speculators, sleepy-eyed Mexicans, sullen Indians, curious squaws, sunburned, lounging tourists. But the picture were somewhat somber, but for the pleasant lights given it by groups of merry children and bright-faced, handsomely dressed ladies.

It is evident that there are happy homes in Central, and churches and school-houses, and that people think of something besides mines, though the town is built on Pactolean gulches, seven times washed; though the hills above it look like the walls of gigantic fortresses, thickly pierced as they are with tunnels, like monstrous portholes; though hundreds of men in it lie down to prospect in dreams, and rise up to pay or dig; though for many the gold fever dries up the very juices of youth, tinges all life with a fearful moral jaundice. People here, they say, mine in their cellars and wells and back yards, and a careful housekeeper examines her teakettle for gold deposits once a week. Gold is "in the air" in dusty weather; and if you live long enough here, you may "eat your peck" of gold, instead of dirt of the common sort.

Colonel Frank Hall, the secretary of the Territory, to whom I fortunately had letters, did the honors of the town for us,—took us to the Miners and Mechanics' Institute where we saw rare and beautiful mineral specimens; to shops, where elegant jewelry and silver-ware of native ore and home manufacture are sold; to the banks, where we saw both silver and gold, in bewildering quantities and in all forms,—nuggets and bars and dust, and in the ponderous shape in which it comes from the crucible. All this kindness, and much beside, was done with a charm of finished courtesy which, though it did not "gild refined gold," made us realize that there was something in Central better than gold.[4]

To Greenwood, a well-traveled writer for magazines and newspapers from the 1840s onward, Central City fitted Frank C. Young's description nicely!

"The Richest Square Mile on Earth"

Gold was discovered at the confluence of North Clear Creek and a mountain stream in the mountains west of Denver by John H. Gregory on May 6, 1859. The region was part of Kansas Territory. Almost overnight the population of the area, soon called Gregory Diggings or Gregory Gulch, swelled from zero to 5,000, then 10,000, then as many as 15,000 by July, as fortune seekers came from all directions.[5] The California Gold Rush was in the decline, having had its best year in 1853. Kansas Territory was the new Eldorado, with no competition. Gilpin County, the home of Nevadaville, Central City, and Black Hawk, was called the richest square mile on earth. And, indeed, gold was everywhere.

By the summer of 1859, there had already been a year of excitement in nearby Denver. This had begun in 1858 in the prairie to the east of the Rockies with the discovery of gold in stream beds in and around Cherry Creek. One settlement of log cabins was aptly named Auraria, from a town in Georgia of the same name, derived from *aureus*, Latin for gold. The other was Denver City, on the east side of the waterway. The two towns merged in April 1860.

Mining was done by panning and sluicing. Most adventurers were successful and filled little bags and bottles with gold dust and nuggets at the rate of about $5 to $10 value per day. Enthusiasm spread, and soon the rallying cry, PIKES PEAK OR BUST, became famous, as lettered on the sides of Conestoga wagons headed for the latest promised land. Never mind that Pikes Peak the mountain was not in the district at all, but was about 75 miles to the south. In 1859 and 1860 newcomers arrived every day, often after having read exciting accounts in the Eastern newspapers.

While panning for gold in streams in the Denver flatlands continued to be worthwhile, it was the 1859 strike in Gregory Gulch high in the Rockies that promised a fortune. The rush was on! In the first year, most mining was still done by sluicing and panning, the traditional style. From October 24, 1859, until February 28, 1861, Central City was in a district called Jefferson Territory by its proponents. This encompassed parts of Kansas and other territories. Although Jefferson Territory elected officials in a democratic process and legislation was enacted, it was never officially recognized by the United States government.

In the spring and summer of 1860 expansion continued, and Central City took form, centered slightly west of the original gold find. The Consolidated Ditch was completed, bringing a greater supply of water into the area. Deep-rock mining yielded ore from several veins. Mills with 5, 10, or 15 stamps were set up, with more than 100 in place within the first few years. A single stamp could crush three-quarters of a ton of ore if operated around the clock, as many were. The life of such machinery was short, and when their usefulness ended they were sold as scrap iron or left derelict on hillsides. Average daily pay for a miner was $4 to $5.

During the first several years there was much lawlessness and rowdyism in Gilpin County, after which things settled down to an orderly nature, except for the occasional Saturday night scuffle. It was common practice to run out of town anyone who stole mining tools or jumped a claim, with the threat of death if they returned. This seemed to work. Serious crime became rare in the district, and sensational cases were the exception, hardly a "Wild West" scenario.

In the early days the post office at Gregory Diggings was known as Mountain City. The facility was established on January 17, 1860. (Miners lived in the region, but there was no permanent settlement; in other words, there was no city of *Mountain City*—just the post office!) In time the mining area expanded up the hill, and became known as Central City. On February 28, 1861, Colorado Territory was established. However, the post-office name was not changed to Central City until years later, on October 8, 1869. The

Central Overland and Pikes Peak Express completed a railroad connection in the spring of 1860.[6]

News traveled very slowly in the early days. It was not until November 7, 1863, that a Pacific Telegraph Company line was strung into Central City. In 1872 the Colorado Central Railroad line connected Black Hawk with Denver and other stations, and it was announced that within a year a link would be made to Central City. That did not happen. The grade from that point up to Central City was nearly 500 feet in slightly more than a mile, through very rough terrain, and it was not until 1878 that the line was completed.

Central City Flourishes

In the 1860s and 1870s Central City was second only to Denver in terms of population in the territory. In 1869 Frank C. Young described the greater population of the district as being American-born but with a fair sprinkling of Germans, several hundred Celts, and some few Scandinavians. In the last several years there had been an influx of robust people from the tin mines of Cornwall, and these promised to outnumber the native element. The people from Cornwall did not like the Celts in Nevadaville, he stated, and much rowdyism ensued.[7] Beginning in the summer of 1870, several hundred Chinese workers streamed into town, having completed their work on the transcontinental railroad. Some worked the streambeds for gold (although the ravines were mostly depleted by this time), as they were not allowed in underground mines. They kept to themselves and led quiet, peaceful lives.

Central City was long and narrow, squeezed between two mountains. Lawrence Street, paralleling Eureka Gulch just west of Gregory Gulch, was the busiest thoroughfare and ran east to west. At the western end, Eureka Street was an extension and was also a thriving place. On the combined streets were located the Teller House, opened in 1872 to become the largest hotel in the district (named for Henry M. Teller, lawyer and prominent Colorado politician) and the Rocky Mountain National Bank, the First National Bank, and various mercantile houses.

The Teller House was the scene of a lot of legitimate fun, including dances held in the evening when dining chairs and tables would be cleared away in the second-floor restaurant, and patrons would dance to the accompaniment of fiddlers. The facility became a favorite, taking the place of the run-down Connor House, the main hotel up to that time, and of the St. Nicholas Hotel, also rather seedy.

Branching off to the south, just before the Teller House, were Pine Street next to the hotel and, separated by a row of business blocks, Main Street. These two thoroughfares were home to saloons, theaters (such as they were), and gambling parlors, among dry-goods stores and other enterprises. Several bordellos were in operation—how many was never recorded. Stores and shops, laundries, equipment purveyors, and other businesses flourished, as did several churches and schools. At one time the district had eight church congregations with more than 2,000 seats for worshipers.

Miners who worked hard played hard, like as not spending most of their pay on gambling and drinking in the local saloons. Games of faro, roulette, and poker went on through the night, usually in small rooms with a stove for warmth and a side bar providing alcoholic comfort. Relatively few miners banked their wages.

Young women eligible for marriage were in short supply in Central City, prompting the *Daily Register* to include this in an issue of March 1871:

> Girls are plenty, and men scarce in Maine. At a recent Leap Year sleigh ride in a village in that state, it was found that there were not enough men to go around, so they allotted two girls to each young man, and then had to take in several old widowers to make up the necessary number.
>
> This is all wrong, and if a few hundred of those girls would only come to Colorado, we will promise them at least two beaux each, in young, true,

and sturdy fellows for their next Leap Year ride. Wake up girls, and come to where you are needed and appreciated.[8]

Some local young women may have been eligible and willing to marry, but many were busy courting miners and others in saloons, dance halls, and other places where sporting men frequented, such as in Jane Gordon's bordello on Pine Street. Historian Fred Holabird has estimated that half the saloons in mining camps were actually bordellos.[9] Such saloons usually offered assignations in rooms on the second floor above.

At the corner of Main Street where Lawrence Street evolved to become Eureka Street, on a site later occupied by the First National Bank building, was one of the most popular spots in town in the 1860s and early 1870s. This was an unpretentious one-room log building, 32 by 16 feet on the interior, that housed the office of Hinckley's Express, later the Pikes Peak Express, and served as the popular distribution point for mail and packages when they arrived, typically in a Concord coach drawn by a span of six horses. In the same space was Waill's jewelry store, the law office of Purkins and Weld, the office of Dr. Smith, and that of district recorder D. Tom Smith. Frank Fossett described the scene, or at least part of it:

The Express office occupied a space nine feet by six, enclosed by a picket fence. Here was packed and piled the large amount of express matter, and the immense quantity of letters and the distributing boxes they required. The office was open from 7 o'clock a. m. to 9 p.m., and had two delivery windows and a man at each. For a long time it was the only mail distributing office in the mountains. During the summer months and often in winter, two long lines of men, num-

bering from 100 to 300, were always awaiting the opening of the windows in the morning, and there was seldom much diminution of the crowd (except from 2 to 6 p.m.) until closing time at night.

Men who had trudged many a weary mile over mountain and ravine to hear from the dear ones in some far eastern home, after keeping their places in the lines for an hour, were doomed to the disappointment of seeing the windows close just before they reached them. Delivering letters was then a slow business, owing to the charge of twenty-five cents per letter by the express company, and as gold dust was the currency of the country, time was required to weigh out the payment in gold dust from the pouch of each man receiving a letter. For this purpose scales were used inside of the office window as at all points of trade in those days. Men experienced much difficulty in hearing from home, as letters were usually directed simply to Pike's Peak, with no town or other locality written upon them. The thousands on thousands of missives from wives, sweethearts, parents or friends, first came to Denver and were then sent to whatever part of the mountains a man was thought to be, and for a long time to Central only.[10]

Similar to the situation in other mining towns, Central City aspired to culture—the Arcadia factor, perhaps. In the winter of 1866, into 1867, the Miners and Mechanics Institute was organized, with banker Frank C. Young as secretary. By 1870 the shelves were "laden with nearly 1,000 volumes of carefully selected and well bound works on art, science and literature (besides numerous monthly journals, and weekly and daily periodicals)," while in the same building "rare and costly cabinets of ores, minerals, fossils, petrifactions and specimens of the precious metals, will give even the casual observer abundant evidence of the earnest and effective manner in which the live members of this association have conducted their arduous labors."[11] In time, 200 people paid $10 each to become full members of the Institute.

The First National Bank of Central City

The First National Bank of Central City was organized on September 15, 1873, with a capital of $50,000, and was chartered on October 31 as No. 2129. It succeeded Thatcher, Standley & Co., a private banking firm, in the same office location on Lawrence Street. Joseph A. Thatcher was the founding president, Joseph Standley and Otto Sauer were vice presidents, and Young was cashier. These men were also incorporators of the bank, as were Samuel Mishler, William Marten, and Hugh C. McCandron. Sauer, a prominent merchant and developer in town, later became the bank's president.

The doors were opened for business on January 4, 1874.[12] A few months later on the morning of May 21, cashier Young heard shouts as fire broke out a few blocks away on Spring Street. Thatcher was on a trip to the East at the time. Realizing it was only a matter of time until the flames reached Lawrence Street, Young and the bank janitor, a black man named Henry Poynter, resolved to save what they could. Into a large metal lard can they stuffed $100,000 in paper money, $300,000 in securities, and other valuable papers. Poynter and Young took the large gold-weighing scales and apparatus, ledgers and records, and other items and put them into the vault. Poynter then headed off with the can and secretly buried it under the porch of his home. Young stayed to watch as the flames licked the roof, then consumed the building. Much of the downtown district was laid to waste.

Several days later the rubble had cooled to the point at which the safe could be opened. Although some papers were scorched, everything else was found to be intact. Poynter unearthed the paper money and securities, which were intact as well.[13] The First National Bank quickly went back into business in temporary facilities on the same side of Lawrence Street, between Church and Spring streets, in what became known as J.O. Raynolds' Beehive, an appropriate name as multiple businesses set up shop there after the disaster. The fire stopped at the Raynolds building, where fireproofing precautions had been taken—a good thing, as the owner was the Colorado agent for the Hazard Powder Company, provider of explosives for blasting.

Early in 1875 a contract was let for a new building, described by the *Register* as "a large, fine, two-story, seventy feet on Eureka, forty-five feet on Pine, and twenty-four feet on Main Street. The first floor is occupied by the bank and is lighted by three large windows of French plate glass. The circular counter is of the finest walnut, the center panels of veneered French walnut. For workmanship there is nothing like it in Colorado Territory."

The interior had a wooden-fronted division separating the lobby from the work area behind. At the right was a window marked GOLD, and to the left was one marked CHECKS. Near the GOLD window on the right, behind glass, was an assay scale where customers could watch their gold being weighed.

In the new building a large vault was built in the right-hand corner to house a 6,000-pound Herring safe. The rest of the Eureka Street front was occupied by Chase & Sears, tobacconists, and the United States Post Office. The upstairs "accommodated one-half dozen lawyers, one physician, the clerk of the District Court, and the law offices of Judge James B. Belford, Colorado's first congressman." The flume carrying Eureka Creek was channeled under the bank building and the street and caused flooding problems over the years.[14]

"Black Charter" Notes

In the 1860s and 1870s, National Bank Notes were printed in New York City under contract with the American, National, and Continental bank-note companies. At the Treasury Department in Washington, D.C., accounts were kept of each denomination issued by each bank. In time the bills sustained wear and damage and were returned to the Treasury to be redeemed. Clerks had to carefully read the face of each note to determine the name of the bank and its location. The name was usually prominent, such as First National Bank, but the town and state were in much smaller type and were sometimes difficult to read. From 1863 until December 31, 1872, the total number of banks chartered rose to 2,073.

In 1873 the typical National Bank note of any denomination had overprints on the face, including the Treasury seal in red and two serial numbers, also in red, one being sequential for the given bank and the other being part of an overall Treasury Department system without regard to the issuing bank. In that year a plan was implemented to print the bank charter number as well. This brilliant move made it possible to instantly identify at a glance the particular bank that issued a bill presented for redemption. The Act of June 20, 1874, made this official. Charter numbers were used on notes from that time forward.

As to my own interest in this particular bank it came about some years ago when doing general research on state-chartered banks and National Banks (usually capitalized even when discussed generically). I learned of so-called "black charter numbers," these in contrast to the red charter numbers imprinted on the notes of thousands of banks beginning with Series of 1875 notes.

As an early experiment in adding charter numbers to the Series of 1875 notes the Treasury Department directed the Continental Bank Note Company, contractor for the popular $5 denomination, to enter numbers directly on certain printing plates. Numismatic researcher Peter Huntoon found that this procedure was used from November 15, 1873, to May 15,

1874.[15] This was prior to the Act of June 20, 1874, which required the addition of such numbers that resulted in the Series of 1875 (this information being imprinted on the face of each note in addition to the charter number). As these $5 notes had the charter number printed at the same time as the face design, it was in black.

The experiment with black charter numbers was abandoned after at least 10, possibly as many as 14, banks had plates made with this feature. Later charter numbers were overprinted in color as a separate process, the style employed for *thousands* of different banks. As chance would have it, one of the recipients of "Black Charter" notes was the First National Bank of Central City.

First National Bank of Central City, Colorado, $5 "Black Charter" Note. The black charter number is vertically at the upper left and also horizontally at the upper right. Plate F, federal serial Z516561, bank serial 8578. Colorado Territory address. Signed by F.H. Messinger as cashier and A.N. Rogers as vice president. Messinger succeeded Young as cashier in 1880.

The Original Series four-subject $5 plate made by the Continental Bank Note Company for the First National Bank of Central City in 1873 bore plate letters A-B-C-D. The notes carried Allison-Spinner Treasury signatures and a plate date of November 15, 1873, and the location was shown as Colorado Territory. A total of 2,475 Original Series sheets of the $5s were printed from the plate and sent to the bank between 1873 and 1876. These probably were signed in ink by cashier Frank C. Young and president Joseph A. Thatcher. Because Thatcher often traveled, a vice president could have signed some for him. Amazingly,

The unique discovery note—the only known $1 First National Bank of Central City, a bill with an imprint of Colorado Territory. The grade is such that only a dedicated specialist in territorial-note rarities could love it.

not a single Original Series $5 note from this bank is known today!

Original Series $1 and $2 notes were printed in a sheet as $1-$1-$1-$2 with plate letters A-B-C-A. Only 2,475 sheets were printed, yielding 7,425 $1 notes and 2,475 $2 notes. Until November 2013 only a single $2 note was known to exist, and no one had heard of a $1 note. On Thursday, November 7, at the Whitman Coin & Collectibles Expo in Baltimore, Tom Denly said he had just purchased a note of a variety not hitherto known to exist. He handed me a well-circulated $1 of the Original Series! Wow! I thought about it and thought some more. That evening at dinner at Morton's steakhouse I asked Tom what he wanted for it. He replied that $5,500 was the price. I bought it on the spot!

Now my "Central City collection" includes two notes: the unique Original Series $1 and one of about 18 known Series of 1875 Black Charter notes. From a value standpoint the Black Charter is famous as a rare "type." Some numismatists with no particular interest in Colorado desire such notes as relatively few exist in comparison to thousands with regular red charter numbers. As to the demand for my unique Original Series $1 in, perhaps, Good-4 grade, as the only note of this denomination known for this Colorado bank (no Series of 1875 $1s were made), it probably would attract a specialist, as it did attract me. However, numismatists who would rather have a common note in high Uncirculated grade and who do not notice bills that have been in circulation would wonder why the heck I bought it!

CHAPTER 31

A curious token dated 1846 was distributed by an unknown person or persons for reasons that have eluded modern researchers. In some ways the inscriptions seem to relate to the Mormons—but do they?

Let the "Egle" Fly

A Mysterious Token

The curious "Let the Egle Fly" token dated 1846. 26 mm.

Among the mysteries in numismatics is the curious 1846-dated copper token with the inscription "Let the Egle Fly." Actually, there are two mysterious tokens, the other also discussed below.

The obverse of mysterious token no. 1 features a face surrounded by rays of glory. Around the border is lettered LET THE EGLE FLY / J.S.G.S.L.C.O. Dentils are around the edge. Punches were used for the letters as evidenced, for example, by the E's all being similar. Dentils around were added individually by hand and are of irregular length and spacing. A little dot seen on the nose of the face is a centering point for a compass that was used to draw a circle around the die so that the letters would be arranged at the same distance from the center.

The reverse has an eagle with a shield on its breast, evocative of federal silver and gold coin designs of the time, except that on the token the eagle has no legs. A prominent centering dot is within the shield. Eleven stars are around the border, added by a punch. The date 1846 is below, from number punches, arranged so the digits slant slightly to the right. Irregular dentils are inside the rim. On the two specimens studied, each shows extensive die cracks at the bottom and lower right. The die has buckled slightly in that area.

The overall appearance of the token is somewhat crude and rustic. The engraver seems to have cut the obverse and reverse motifs directly into the die, while individual punches were used for the letters, numerals, and stars. It can be surmised that this is not the work of one of the leading shops in the token trade.

As to the number known I suggest perhaps half a dozen. Other estimates have ranged from only two to about a dozen. All or nearly all show signs of wear, indicating that they must have passed from hand to hand in commerce, perhaps at the value of a cent. In the early 19th century all sorts of copper tokens were commonly used in commerce for the value of a cent. Or they could have been lucky pocket tokens for the Mormons in that pivotal year, as discussed below.

What does the obverse motif represent in combination with the inscription? What do the initials stand for? Does the 1846 date represent the year the die was made, or does it observe some event or philosophy of that year, but was made later?

Does this token have a connection with Mormon history?

I give two modern citations below.

A Mormon Collectible

The Early Mormon Collectibles web site, an Internet forum for the title subject, includes this:[1]

Rare Mormon Coin

Let the Egle Fly

Rare Mormon Coin/Token

Coin/Token. Great Salt Lake City, 1846 (?). Copper, 26 mm, scarce. Radiant surface in 8-lobed cartouche. Around LET THE E[A]GLE FLY. J.S.G.S.L.C.O. Rv: Eagle displayed. U.S. shield on its breast, 11 stars above. The eagle is of unusual design. Reeded edge (Bangs & Co. January 27, 1888, Lot # 321, Dr. Jay M. Galst collector).

Cataloger David Proskey in 1888 called this a pattern Mormon eagle ($10) coin and the initials for "Joseph Smith, Great Salt Lake City." The "O" not explained. This is the only known specimen and in Very Good condition. It fetched $3.60 in 1888. "We doubt this is a pattern eagle; more likely a very old, clumsy token produced in Utah after the Mexican War" (David Proskey). $4500.00

John J. Ford Jr. Token Description

The sale of tokens and medals from the John J. Ford, Jr. Collection, conducted by Stack's Bowers Galleries in August 2013, included this:

Lot 22121.

Non-local. "1846" Let the Egle [sic] Fly. Rulau Ut-SL 7. Copper. 26 mm. MS-61 BN (NGC).

Golden brown toning with faint violet highlights. Struck on a planchet made from crudely refined copper showing pitting which we assume was due to the presence of impurities in the metal. Rulau notes that David Proskey considered this to be a pattern Mormon $10, and in 1888 Proskey expressed the view that J.S.G.S.L.C. signified "Joseph Smith, Great Salt Lake City."

Rulau noted that the letters in the inscription are J.S.G.S.L.C.O., and that Proskey never conjectured about the meaning of the final "O." Perhaps if Proskey were cataloging the same piece today he would conjecture instead "Joseph Smith—Great Salt Lake Coinage Office." Rulau thought the piece was actually a token dated to the era between 1846 and 1848…

The attribution of this token has been a matter of considerable discussion. The Mormons did not establish Great Salt Lake City until 1847, the year after the date of the token. And yet, the letters J.S.G.S.L.C. are sufficiently distinctive that it would be difficult to assign any other attribution. As to the initials J.S., these letters could relate to the founder of the religion, Joseph Smith, who was killed in 1844. At least a dozen or so examples are known today, and nearly all show signs of circulation. These are not numismatic issues made for collectors but in their time were used in circulation.

What do the inscriptions mean? The token, though dated 1846, could have been made later when Great Salt Lake City was a reality. In any event, Joseph Smith was a memory. "Let the E[a]gle Fly" could relate to some hope that Smith's aspirations or indeed the Mormon faith would take wing. Again, there is room for conjecture and little in the way of fact.

Dave Bowers, in an Internet discussion with Bob Leonard earlier this year, felt that it does have a Mormon

connection, but the circumstances of issue have yet to be determined. Proskey and Rulau felt the same way.

On the other hand, Bob Leonard suggests that it may not be from Utah at all and could have a genesis in Pennsylvania or New Jersey, based on the first known appearance at auction. One thing remains clear, that this is an interesting early American token of considerable rarity and charm and one that holds a secret, perhaps very important, that remains to be discovered.

Salt Lake City.

Perhaps a Related Token?

In *The Numismatist* in July 1911 Edgar H. Adams, under "Live American Numismatic Items," included what seems to be a token closely related in spirit and precisely related in date:

A little token in brass which is illustrated here and dated 1846 has attracted the interest of a number of collectors, and there is considerable conjecture as to its exact attribution. The date, taken in connection with the emblems on the obverse and reverse, would seem to indicate association with the Mormons.

The date was one of the most important in the history of that sect, for it was during 1846 that the great exodus took place from Nauvoo, Ill., which had the final result of the Mormons founding the City of Great Salt Lake in 1847 and of causing the desert-like valley of Salt Lake to bloom like a garden and become the center of one of the most prosperous communities in the United States.

The use of the emblems of the beehive and the clasped hands by the Mormons are well known to numismatists. The beehive was a favorite device of the followers of Joseph Smith and Brigham Young. It is the principal emblem on the state seal, and the first name of the Mormon territory was the "State of Deseret," the significance of the latter word being "honey bee." The emblem of the clasped hands was used on the first Mormon coinage of 1849, and the beehive was afterward used on the five-dollar gold piece of 1850 issued by the Deseret Assay Office.

The two inscriptions of UNION IS STRENGTH and DO YOUR DUTY were particularly appropriate to the year 1846, for at no time during the eventful career of the Mormons as an organized body were they subjected to greater trials than at the beginning of their vast relay expedition from the Mississippi River to California.

Items from Mormon History

Joseph Smith Jr., born in Sharon, Vermont, on December 23, 1805, moved with his family to New York about 1817. Beginning in the early 1820s he claimed to have experienced certain visions from on high that directed him to find engraved tablets with ancient writings describing a Judeo-Christian congregation in America. He published what he designated as the English translation of the plates as the *Book of Mormon* in 1830. In the same year he established the Church of Christ, with followers who were inspired by the ancient people and activities described in the book. In time they became known as Latter Day Saints. The Mormon religion caught hold quickly, and during the decade it attracted thousands of followers.

In 1831 Smith and many of his followers moved west, hoping to establish their Zion, a city of hope and glory. Independence, Missouri, was intended as the location of what was to be called New Jerusalem and was an outpost to the Mormon community that had been set up in Kirtland, Ohio (where they issued their own paper money). Smith drew up detailed plans for the settlement, including buildings and streets. Due to financial difficulties and conflicts with anti-Mormon elements in Missouri, the Zion plan was dropped.

Smith and his followers left Kirtland and established Nauvoo, Illinois. Critics of the Mormon practice of polygamy and of the honesty and integrity of Smith resulted in various actions, including a printed exposé of the religion. Smith ordered that the printing press used for this be destroyed. Matters went from bad to worse, and Smith was thrown in jail in Carthage, Illinois. A mob stormed the facility and killed him. The Church of Jesus Christ of Latter-Day Saints

The Mormon mint in Salt Lake City (center right). (Howard Stansbury, Exploration and Survey of the Great Salt Lake of Utah, 1852)

lived on. He was succeeded as leader by Brigham Young.

Great Salt Lake City, as it was first called, was well-envisioned in 1846, the date on the two tokens, and was established in 1847 by Brigham Young and his followers, who had come there, arriving on July 24, to establish a modern Zion, a center for their religion. In 1868 "Great" was dropped from the name. It became the headquarters for the Mormon religion, as it remains today.

During the War with Mexico, 1846 and 1847, many Mormon men served with the United States Army. In early 1848 they headed home, many of them having come from San Francisco. They were in the right place at the right time. Gold was discovered on the American River by James Marshall in January. Word spread and thousands went to the area. The Mormons set up at Mormon Bar in the river, which proved to be incredibly rich. Later in the year most continued to the east.

In Great Salt Lake City a mint was established to coin the metal the men brought. Coins bore the inscription G.S.L.C.P.G., for Great Salt Lake City Pure Gold.

CHAPTER 32

The 1955 Doubled Die cent was featured in my first book, Coins and Collectors, *published in 1964. I revisit it here.*

Memories of the 1955 Doubled Die Cent

One Day in 1955

On one particular day several presses were coining cents, with workers dumping the coins into a box where they were then collected and mixed with the cents from other coining presses. Late in the afternoon a Mint inspector noticed the bizarre doubled cents and removed the offending die. By that time somewhat over 40,000 cents had been produced, about 24,000 of which had been mixed with normal cents from other presses.[1]

Coins are where you find them—and that's sometimes in circulation.

One day in 1955 at the Philadelphia Mint a coinage die was being prepared for a cent. In the course of impressing the working die with the hub die several times, a slight misalignment occurred. The result was a 1955 die with the letters and numbers on the face of the coin all being doubled. Instead of reading IN GOD WE TRUST, the famous 1955 Doubled Die (as they came to be known) reads IINN GGOODD WWEE TTRRU-USSTT.

The decision was made to destroy the cents still in the box behind the press and to release into circulation the other 24,000 or so pieces mixed with others. This was to have an untold effect on numismatics. The coins, which were nonchalantly released into circulation, subsequently attracted the interest of collectors all over the country.

Jim Ruddy

These 1955 Doubled Die cents were first noticed by collectors later in the same year when they began appearing in the hands of the public. Shortly after that time Jim Ruddy, who had left his employment as a technician at the General Aniline & Film Co. (makers of Ansco film products), went into business as a rare-coin dealer, renting a second-floor space at 258 Main Street in Johnson City, New York. The Triple Cities Coin Exchange (from the trio of Johnson City, Endicott, and Binghamton communities) was an instant success, nicely launched when Jim was given the estate coins of Claude R. Collier, an old-time numismatist who had recently passed away. At the 1954 American Numismatic Association convention in Cleveland Collier had received an award for being a member for 50 years. The coins and accompanying rare stamps included many rarities and sold quickly when Jim offered them.

One day a man walked into his office and showed him two curious 1955 cents with the doubled features. As of that time nothing had appeared about them in the three monthly hobby publications—*The Numismatist*, *Numismatic News*, and *Numismatic Scrapbook Magazine*. There was hardly any interest in modern varieties at the time, apart from basic dates and mintmarks, quite unlike today when the *Cherrypickers' Guide to Rare Die Varieties*, by Bill Fivaz and J.T. Stanton, lists hundreds of oddities from the late 20th century onward.

Jim paid 25 cents each for the two cents. Word spread that he was doing this, and others came calling with coins. Fearful that he would accumulate too many, he stopped buying! These were modern cents with no known market for them.

Distribution and Increased Popularity

Jim asked questions and learned that in each instance the bright-as-new 1955 cents had been found in packs of cigarettes. The vending machine price was 23 cents at the time. To make change for a quarter, each pack had two cents inserted on one side beneath the cellophane wrapper.

In time the story was picked up by the papers. *Numismatic News* called them 1955 "Shift cents." A market developed, and Jim went back to buying them—now from people who found them in pocket change. On April 15, 1958, Jim and I formed Empire Coin Co., which soon moved into its own three-story building at 252 Main Street. We became a focal point for those seeking these oddities.

The price climbed to $1 per coin and then to $2, and it seemed that everyone wanted one. Our buying price increased in step, reaching about $5, at which point we advertised brilliant Uncirculated coins for $7.50. We were overwhelmed with orders and sold out!

The demand was on! The price kept climbing. We corresponded extensively with collectors who had coins for sale. We learned that there were just three key distribution areas: in and around Johnson City, in the area of Pittsfield in western Massachusetts, and, in particular, in Boston and nearby towns. We had an artist make an engraving of a cent showing the doubling and published it in newspapers in those areas, offering to pay $10 each. In a visit to Boston I noticed that several coin shops had clipped our advertisement, removed our name, and posted it in their front windows. At the time there were a half dozen or so active coin dealers in that city, plus Arthur Conn in the suburb of Melrose. We raised our buying price to $20 and our selling price accordingly.

Thousands of people in the New York–Massachusetts area looked through their pocket change and hundreds suddenly found themselves many dollars richer. One man in Greene, New York, found 17 specimens! A nun in a convent near Boston found one coin, sold it for $20, and then found another. In this way several thousand 1955 doubled-die cents have turned up over the years.

We bought many of them, typically now in grades of Extremely Fine to About Uncirculated, with occasional Uncirculated pieces mixed in. At one time we had 800 on hand—meanwhile offering them for sale. We probably handled several thousand all told. Eventually, Ken Bressett gave the variety the "Doubled Die" name when it was first listed in *A Guide Book of United States Coins* (13th edition, published in 1959 with a 1960 cover date).

Along the way there were lots of stories. Harry Lessin, a Connecticut attorney, liked the Doubled Die cents and bought many over the years, certainly more than a hundred. Bob Bashlow, the eccentric New York City dealer, bought many from us when they were under $20 each Uncirculated, then sold them back, and later in a rising market bought more.

A dealer who was well known for his braggadocio told New Jersey dealer Edmund A. Rice that he had some original rolls of 1955 Doubled Die cents. Ed called me to see if he should inquire on my behalf. I told him that there were no such things, for when the doubled-die cents were distributed they were mixed with other cents of the same date, seemingly in a ratio of about one doubled die to five or six regular ones. Ed went to the dealer and said he had a customer, but was told that they were not for sale. "I'll give you $500 just to *see* a roll," he countered. Considering inflation, this was probably like offering $5,000 or more today. The dealer said he was too busy to do that! Ed called him a liar.

Today a gem 1955 Doubled Die cent, once risky to buy for 25 cents, sells for many thousands of dollars.

President Andrew Jackson's presidency of 1829 to 1837 was among the most controversial in American history. Certain aspects of his activities were memorialized on cent-sized and related tokens, most of which were satirical in nature. Today they are widely collected.

Jackson: "I Take the Responsibility"

A Controversial Figure

Portrait of Andrew Jackson engraved by James B. Longacre for The National Portrait Gallery, 1834, volume I, 1837.

Over a long period of years I have enjoyed reading through 19th-century newspapers, magazines, and other accounts to observe history as it was happening. Andrew Jackson figured in many accounts for a long period of time. His heroism during the January 8, 1815, Battle of New Orleans was never questioned. However, when he entered politics in the 1820s, continuing through his presidency from 1829 to 1837, his actions were praised by many and condemned by others. There was little in the way of middle ground. Similarly, modern historians often view him from different angles. Did he lead the country through a great period of prosperity, or did his actions destroying the Second Bank of the United States launch the Panic of 1837?

Lyman H. Low, New York City rare-coin dealer and writer, and a man of excellent numismatic knowledge, in 1886 published the first standalone study of tokens of this era, 18 pages in length, titled *Descriptive Catalogue of Hard Times Tokens Issued for and against the United States Bank, and with Reference to the Financial Troubles of 1834–1841*. The bank went out of business in 1836, but the controversy continued, the opposition to Jackson and his successor, Martin Van Buren, being led by Daniel Webster. The Constitution was a focal point. Was it being wrecked? A pro-Webster token of 1840 shows the allegory of the Constitution ship being wrecked on rocks in during the Van Buren administration, with the Panic reminder date of 1837 on one side and on the other side, a "Webster ship" of 1841 under full sail, the date suggesting that if Webster's advice would be followed in 1841, when the Sub-Treasury Bill would take effect, all would be well.

In July 1898 in the *American Journal of Numismatics*, of which he was an editor, Lyman H. Low began his second and much more extensive study of the series, complete with many fascinating historical notes. Then in 1899 his book, *Hard Times Tokens: An Arrangement of Jackson Cents Issued for and Against the United States Bank*, was published. This consisted of 65 numbered pages plus plates. In this book and in the supplement published soon thereafter, Low described 164 different die varieties of Hard Times tokens, using a single number for a die combination, with additional notation as to the metal of striking.

The author defined the Hard Times period as dating from 1832 to 1844, which is quite out of step with the facts. The panic did not start until 1837, although there were shivers in the economy by 1834, and it ended in spring 1843. However, Low wanted to include many political tokens relating to the presidential election of 1832 and the mid-term elections of 1834, so he used artistic license. Similarly, there is a single cent-sized token dated 1844, by J. Cochran, a bell founder in Batavia, New York. To include this rarity he extended his Hard Times era to include this year.

Lyman H. Low, pioneering scholar of the Hard Times token series.

51. *Obv.* Same as *rev.* of No. 44. *Rev.* THE CONSTITUTION above, · AS I UNDER-STAND IT · below. Donkey standing *l.*, on the side of which, LL. D; above, ROMAN | FIRMNESS and below, VETO On the obverse, H beneath chest is omitted on cut. Borders 4. Edge 1. Metal Æ. Size 28, 29.

The spaces on the safe appear to be in at least three conditions, differing as follows :— 1st, the vertical lines in front are but lightly defined in four of the spaces ; the horizontal lines on the end are totally wanting in six of the twelve spaces ; in the upper three they show lightly at the top ; in the lower three, strong and full : 2d, all spaces appear to have been retouched, only four remain unfilled and these on the end : 3d, every space is filled, and all I have seen of 52 are from this finish ; in fact, the whole die seems to be brought out stronger.

The date of this token and others muled from the obverse die (Nos. 44, 52, 53) is somewhat uncertain ; they evidently refer to Jackson, who was shown with sword and purse in No. 12. The feeling which led to the adoption of the device however manifested itself for some time after the Whigs had taken the reins of government, for the *Albany Argus*, 1 October, 1842, said :— " The liberties of the Country were alarmingly threatened under Mr. Van Buren's administration by a union of the purse with the sword in the same hands."

Low's entry for a popular Jackson token.

In the late-20th century Russell Rulau developed an intense interest in the Hard Times series and published a series of monographs, then the large reference book, *Standard Catalog of U.S. Tokens 1700–1900*, which included much information. Rulau discarded the Low numbering system and created a new one with HT numbers, grouping all of the political varieties—Jackson, Van Buren, Webster, suspension of specie payments, etc.—in the first part of his listing, then the store cards (merchant's advertising tokens) alphabetically by state and town in the last part.

From a numismatic viewpoint the Hard Times token series is one of the most interesting and fascinating. Over a long period of time it has attracted many sophisticated students and buyers. This chapter sets the scene and explores the field.

161. *Obv.* J. COCHRAN BELLFOUNDER above, and below, completing the circle, ✸✸✸ BATAVIA ✸✸✸ surrounding a female head, laureated, in profile to left. *Rev.* AN ARMY FOR DEFENCE outside of an unfinished wreath of olive leaves and berries formed by a single branch tied at the base with a bow of ribbon, between the end of which and the stem is the date 1844 ; within the wreath the inscription NOT | ONE | CENT | — | FOR · TRIBUTE the last line curving upward. Borders 4. Edge 1. Metal Æ. Size 28.

I believe that the first knowledge of this piece by collectors, certainly the first mention of it which has been found on record, so far as I have been able to discover, dates from its appearance in a public sale held in New York, on December 1, 1896. The motto " Millions for Defence " had ceased to be a popular cry ; the era of peace and good feeling, save for the growing opposition to slavery, was regnant ; the war with Mexico had not begun, and the special signification of the reverse legend is therefore difficult to discover ; it is doubtful if it be anything more than a modification of the earlier motto. I attribute it to Batavia, now a wealthy city in Genesee County, N. Y., then a prosperous town. No other specimen is known to me.

Low's description and illustration of the 1844 Cochran token.

Jackson's Early Life

Andrew Jackson was born in Waxhaw, North Carolina, on March 15, 1767, the son of Andrew and Elizabeth Hutchinson Jackson. His education was intermittent, causing many later critics to call him illiterate. No matter; he read law for about two years, and then entered practice in Tennessee, where he was viewed as very competent. He became well-to-do and built a mansion, The Hermitage, near Nashville, and was a slave owner. He was a ready debater and quickly rose to challenges. In a

Jackson: "I Take the Responsibility"

duel with a man who had insulted his wife, Jackson was the winner. In 1796 and 1797 Jackson served as a congressman, then as a senator for the next two years, followed by a judicial position on the Tennessee Supreme Court until 1804.

As a major general in the War of 1812 he became known as the "Hero of New Orleans." On January 8, 1815, his forces devastated a large corps of British soldiers—even though, unbeknownst to the combatants, the war had ended by a peace settlement perfected in Europe in December 1814. Jackson was appointed governor of the newly acquired Florida Territory in 1821, where his actions against the Seminole Indians were often harsh and unfair, and he served as a United States senator from 1823 to 1825. In 1824 he ran for president, but lost to John Quincy Adams.

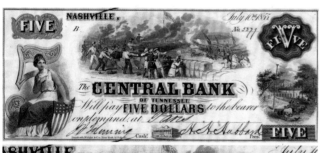

The Battle of New Orleans, January 8, 1815, and the victory of Andrew Jackson as depicted on a $5 note of the Central Bank of Tennessee in Nashville. Engraved and printed by Danforth, Wright & Co.

The First Jackson Presidency

In 1828 Jackson and incumbent John Quincy Adams squared off again in a particularly vitriolic contest for the presidency. John C. Calhoun, who had served as vice president under Adams, joined Jackson on the

1828 ticket. Jackson won, was inaugurated on March 4, 1829, and went to the White House. Contrary to the policy of his predecessors, the doors of the Executive Mansion (as it was called in those days) were opened to everyday citizens for his inaugural ceremonies—many coming in everyday clothes and some

Chief Justice John Marshall administering the oath of office to Andrew Jackson on Inauguration Day, March 4, 1829.

standing with dirty shoes on chairs in order to get a better view. There had been no advance planning for this, nor was there any security or police protection. Thousands thronged in, breaking cut glass and china, and creating a huge mess. Jackson slipped out to Gadsby's boarding house, where he had been staying prior to the inauguration. This was much to the dismay of certain elements of Washington society, who considered the new president to be without finesse or manners.

Matters worsened. Jackson's Cabinet became dysfunctional when certain men appointed through John C. Calhoun's recommendations became disloyal to the president's interests. Central to the matter were the actions of Margaret O'Neale Eaton, known as

Peggy Eaton, wife of U.S. senator John Henry Eaton. Peggy's parents owned the Franklin House, a popular Washington hotel that was frequented by many important officials. Bright, slender, and red-headed, she flirted with and enjoyed the company of many men—sometimes intimate, it was alleged. At age 17 in 1816 she married John B. Timberlake, age 39, a purser in the Navy. The couple had three children.

In 1818 Peggy met John Henry Eaton, a widower, age 28, newly elected as a senator from Tennessee. Seemingly the two embarked on what became a lengthy affair. Earlier, when Jackson was a senator, he boarded at the Franklin House from 1823 to 1825 and became a close friend of the O'Neale family. Timberlake died in 1828 in the Mediterranean Sea while on a four-year voyage. The circumstances of his passing were controversial. Did he commit suicide because of his wife's disloyalty? Peggy married Eaton in early 1829, at the onset of the Jackson administration.

Late-19th-century portrait of Peggy Eaton, probably fanciful, as no image is known of her when she was a young lady.

Eaton was appointed as secretary of war in Jackson's Cabinet. The new Mrs. Eaton, whose reputation had been questionable for a long time, was ostracized by the wives of other Cabinet members and officials, who shunned her at functions. Floride Calhoun, wife of the vice president, was particularly vehement in her condemnation.

Subsequently Jackson, who sided with Peggy, broke with his vice president and relied on unofficial advisors (his "Kitchen Cabinet," so called because they were said to meet in the White House kitchen). Secre-

On April 13, 1830, at the Democratic Party's annual Jefferson Day party, Jackson stood and proposed a toast, "Our federal union—it must and shall be preserved." This was a counter to his rebellious vice president, John C. Calhoun of South Carolina, who strongly defended states' rights against actions of the federal government, such as the enactment of tariffs that restricted the shipment of cotton, the main export product of the South.

Jackson: "I Take the Responsibility"

tary of State Martin Van Buren, who staunchly defended Peggy through all of this, was rewarded with an ambassadorship to England, after which he became vice president. Some historians have suggested that if it hadn't been for Peggy Eaten, John C. Calhoun would have ridden on Jackson's coattails to become president.

The country became very polarized, with Democrats following Jackson's every step, while the National Republicans or Whigs opposed just about everything he did. A major clash arose with Calhoun and the state of South Carolina, which threatened to nullify federal import tariffs and was considering seceding from the Union. A compromise was negotiated by Henry Clay, otherwise a Jackson opponent.

The Second Bank of the United States

The First Bank of the United States was authorized by Congress in 1791 and discontinued business in 1811 when its charter expired. It was controversial from the beginning. The federal government held only a minority interest, much stock was purchased overseas, and yet it had the cachet of a national bank. This was felt to be unfair competition in an era when state-chartered banks owned by private American stockholders were in a rapid period of growth.

Some years later in 1816, a time of financial distress, enough votes in Congress were gained to launch the Second Bank of the United States, also with a 20-year charter. It was felt that this would prop up the banking system, which in many states was in turmoil. The capital was set at $35,000,000, with the federal

Headquarters of the Second Bank of the United States in Philadelphia. Built in the Greek Revival style, it was one of the most imposing structures in Philadelphia. (William H. Bartlett, *American Scenery*, 1839)

government taking only $7,000,000. Again, it was in effect a privately owned bank, but with a federal cachet. It became just as controversial as its predecessor, perhaps even more so. The main problem was the same: unfair competition. Bank of the United States bills could be spent anywhere, while those of state-chartered banks had a limited trading area. By the end of that year more than $150,000,000 in bills had been printed for the main office as well as its branches. All were of common designs and differed only in the imprints designating the branch cities.

State-chartered banking began in 1782, and by the late 1820s hundreds of institutions were in business, mainly along the Eastern Seaboard. These were operated by private investors who had obtained state

Henry Clay as depicted later on an 1844 medal when he was running for the presidency. Issued by his proponents in Rhode Island, the reverse die with the state motto, Hope, and shield and anchor was used in late 1864 or early 1865 by an officer of the Rhode Island Numismatic Association to strike a series of tokens with various obverses, today cataloged as rare Civil War tokens with Fuld numbers from 481/482 to 481/493C.

charters to engage in banking with set capital and certain requirements. Although there were many exceptions, most were sold stock in the range of $50,000 to $100,000. Such banks could issue paper money, often up to the amount of their stated capital. Various bills were ordered from engraving firms, mainly centered in Philadelphia at the time. Among those who engraved bank plate were Robert Scot, William Kneass, and Christian Gobrecht, each of whom would later serve as chief engraver at the U.S. Mint. In the 1830s James B. Longacre, also destined for the Mint chief engravership, was a prominent bank-note engraver as well.

The paper money of these state banks tended to circulate regionally. A $10 note issued in Pittsburgh would be received in that area, but would likely be rejected or received only at a discount if spent in Charleston or Boston. Further, while most of the state banks were solvent, some were of questionable liquidity and would not redeem their paper in gold or silver coins even for those who lived locally. In contrast, notes of the Bank of the United States were viewed as worth their face value in coins no matter where they were spent.

The branch bank in Portsmouth, New Hampshire, entered the scene and through circumstances became important in the controversy. It had been in operation since 1817. With a capital of $200,000 the branch was larger than its state-bank competitors. Isaac Hill, well-known New Hampshire banker and political figure, was until recently the president of the Merrimack County Bank in Concord, the best politically connected bank in the capital city. He was a close friend of Andrew Jackson's and in the election of 1828 led the Jacksonians in the presidential election victory in the Granite State. Hill was appointed as second comptroller of the Treasury Department. As a long-time banker in the private sector he resented the Bank of the United States, an institution commonly referred to as "The Monster" by those who were against it.

Not long afterward the Jackson administration took on an anti-Bank stance. In his first annual message to the House and Senate, December 7, 1829, this was included toward the end:

> The charter of the Bank of the United States expires in 1836, and its stockholders will most probably apply for a renewal of their privileges.
>
> In order to avoid the evils resulting from the precipitancy in a measure involving such important principles, and such deep pecuniary interests, I feel that I cannot, in justice to the parties interested, too soon present it to the deliberate consideration of the legislature and the people.
>
> Both the constitutionality and the expediency of the law are well questioned by a large portion of our fellow citizens, and it must be admitted by all, that it has failed in the great end of establishing a uniform and sound currency.
>
> Under these circumstances, if such an institution is deemed essential to the fiscal operations of the government, I submit to the wisdom of the legislature, whether a national one, founded upon the credit of the government and its revenues, might not be devised, which would avoid all constitutional difficulties; and, at the same, time, secure all the advantages to the government and country that were expected to result from the present bank.[1]

Charter Renewal Proposed

The renewal of the Bank of the United States charter came up before Congress in the summer of 1832. Battle lines were drawn, with Jackson and his supporters on one side and his opponents, including Webster and Clay, on the other.

The bill was determined in the Senate on June 11, 1832, and was passed by 28 votes to 20. It was voted upon in the House of Representatives on July 3 and was passed 109 to 76. It was then sent to President

Jackson for his signature, and was returned to Congress on July 4, marked "Vetoed."

Jackson went on to declare that as much stock was held by foreigners the benefits of rechartering would not benefit America, that the bank was an unfair monopoly, that of the 25 directors 20 were elected by stockholders and thus the arrangement was similar to a state bank, and more. It was right to abolish it. It was, indeed, a "monster."

Jackson's statement went on to discuss his view of the constitutionality of the Bank of the United States, which had been questioned: "Each public officer who takes an oath to support the Constitution, swears that he will support it *as he understands it*, and not as it is understood by others." This phrase would find its way onto anti-Jackson tokens.

In the meantime the economy was robust. Recently imposed tariffs had restricted imports, with the result that factories and mills prospered as never before. As the state of the nation often affected presidential elections then as now, when Jackson announced he was going to seek reelection he had many supporters.

Jackson's Second Administration

The sides were thus polarized for the presidential election of 1832. On one side was Jackson and on the other side Clay, the latter backed by advocates of the Bank of the United States. Each enlisted friendly legislators to make tedious speeches, complete with personal attacks and accusations of dishonest and dishonorable actions, before the adjournment of Congress, which took place at 6 a.m. on July 16. At the polls in November, Jackson overwhelmed Clay with 56 percent of the popular vote and nearly five times as many Electoral College votes.

In an effort to cripple the Bank, whose charter was still in effect and would remain so until 1836, Jackson ordered that future federal deposits, instead of being sent to the Bank of the United States, be given to various state-chartered institutions, this to take place on October 1, 1833, "or sooner, provided the necessary arrangements with the state banks can be

made."[2] "The president thinks that the state banks ought immediately to be employed in the collection and disbursement of public revenue, and the funds now in the Bank of the United States drawn out with all convenient dispatch."

The state institutions were officially called "deposite banks," but popularly referred to as "pet banks." The amount to be deposited in the banks of each state was based upon the number of Electoral College votes of that particular state.[3]

On March 4, 1833, Jackson was inaugurated for his second presidential term. In the meantime, the economy continued to experience great prosperity from development of the West and the sale of public lands, as well as expansion of railroads, canals, and domestic works. The president's many detractors kept harassing his every move, and on March 28, 1834, Jackson was censured by Congress for having removed funds from the Bank of the United States. Some years later in 1837, when Jacksonians were in control of

Token celebrating Jackson's reelection in 1832. (HT-5 in the *Standard Catalog of U.S. Store Cards 1700–1900*, by Russell Rulau)

Congress, this censure was expunged from the record, causing an uproar.

On January 8, 1835, the United States public debt was officially registered as $0, for the first and only time in the history of our country. The Treasury had a surplus that year and returned money to each state. These were indeed good times, but not for everyone. In New York City, for example, commerce had slowed and petitions were made to continue the Bank of the United States, which was in the process of winding down.

Tokens of 1832 and 1834

This set the scene for several varieties of copper and brass tokens, some picturing Jackson, others with different messages, reflecting hopes, policies, and contentions of the 1832 presidential election, the veto of the bank charter, the 1834 mid-term elections, and more.

In April 1834 the Whig Party made gains in the states of Connecticut and New York. The city papers proclaimed the event, such as this in the *New York Courier & Enquirer*, April 11: "We subjoin the result of the election, as far as ascertained, and it will be

This token related to Jackson's reelection of 1832 declares his anti-Bank stance and reiterates his 1830 Jefferson Day toast that challenged Calhoun. It must have been popular in its time, as three slightly different obverse die varieties are known. (HT-1)

perceived that we have indeed achieved a GLORIOUS VICTORY." This set off vigorous Whig efforts during the next two years.

The various state elections in 1834 furnished subjects for several varieties of Hard Times tokens.

Token celebrating the Whig victories in New York State in April 1834, a brief triumph for the anti-Jackson forces. (HT-14)

Another celebratory token for the Whig victories. (HT-15)

None are more curious than those depicting William H. Seward and Gulian C. Verplanck. The Whig Party, which opposed Jackson and other Democrats, scored wide victories this year. In New York the Whig con-

Campaign token for William H. Seward. (HT-26)

Jackson: "I Take the Responsibility"

vention to nominate candidates for state governor and lieutenant governor opened in Utica on September 10. In the several preceding months there was speculation as to who would be chosen. During this time brass

Campaign token for Gulian C. Verplanck. (HT-30)

tokens were issued depicting Seward and Verplanck. It seems that the engraver had no likeness of Verplanck, so he used Seward's portrait on both! In an era before prints were widely used in newspapers, many recipients of the tokens probably didn't know the difference. When final balloting took place in Utica, Seward was the landslide winner with 119 delegate votes, trailed at a long distance by 1 for James Kent, 1 for Peter R. Livingston, and 1 for Verplanck. In November Seward lost to the incumbent, Governor William L. Marcy, a Democrat and staunch supporter of Jackson.

This satirical token reflects the president's victory over those who wanted to recharter the Bank of the United States. (HT-9)

The obverse of HT-70 shows Jackson in a strongbox holding a purse (representing the United States Treasury). The reverse dated 1834 satirizes him as a jackass with LL.D. on its flank (reflecting the derision of his foes when Harvard awarded him an honorary doctorate in June 1833), noting that he interpreted the Constitution "as I understand it." Some called Jackson stubborn and obstinate, but an admirer said he had "Roman firmness." (HT-7)

The obverse of HT-25 shows Jackson with a purse (the Treasury) in one hand and a sword in the other. The inscription is taken from a message from the president to Congress, April 15, 1836, when he stated that in contrast to a government supported by monopolies and aristocratical establishment, ours is "a plain system, void of pomp." The reverse is as the preceding. (HT-25)

The year 1836 saw the record purchase of $24.8 million worth of public lands, up sharply from $14.7 million in 1835 and only $4.8 million as recently as 1834. To slow the rampant speculation, on July 11, 1836, Jackson issued his Specie Circular, stating that henceforth public lands could be purchased only by paying in gold and silver coins, no longer in bank bills or promissory notes.

Jackson decided not to run for a third term as president, but to retire to his Hermitage home in Tennessee. Vice President Martin Van Buren was the logical choice as his successor and was placed on the ticket as the Democratic candidate. Opposing him was William Henry Harrison, a military hero with regard to his victory at the Battle of Tippecanoe. The Whigs ran four different candidates in the hope that they would win over Democratic candidate Van Buren, and the

The Hermitage, in Nashville, Tennessee.

winner among the four Whigs would be settled by the House of Representatives. This unprecedented strategy did not work, and Van Buren won easily.

In many areas in the East the economy remained strong through the end of the year, punctuated by a few business hiccups. That changed in early 1837 when the "Flour Riot" erupted in New York City's Chatham Square.[4] A crowd had gathered to protest the high prices of bread, meat, and fuel. Angry citizens drove off the mayor and the police and stormed a warehouse holding flour.

In March, stock prices on Wall Street fell across a wide front of issues. Anxiety gripped the financial community. Banks and trading-company failures made news headlines, and there was concern about the future. On March 4, 1837, Martin Van Buren took the oath of office and Andrew Jackson departed, leav-

Martin Van Buren.

ing behind a very successful administration, in the minds of his advocates. (His detractors differed.)

Van Buren promised to follow "in the footsteps of my illustrious predecessor." Jackson looked forward to spending time at his Hermitage in Nashville.

The favored "pet banks" held federal deposits until in 1837 under a Van Buren proposal they began to be moved to Sub Treasury offices operated by the government. The transfers were too slow, some said, leading to the issuance of tokens with a tortoise (a diamondback terrapin such as are indigenous to Chesapeake Bay) carrying a safe marked SUB-TREASURY.

The "illustrious predecessor" had left Van Buren with a somewhat confused scenario and what seemed to be a new wave of economic problems. At a March 1837 meeting in New York City, Daniel Webster told a crowd that the growing financial difficulties were due to government interference with private banks and, in particular, Jackson's Specie Circular that abruptly ended Western speculation. An appeal was made to newly inaugurated Van Buren to help strengthen the

Jackson: "I Take the Responsibility"

economy, citing examples, including that real-estate values in the country had dropped by $40 million within the past six months.

At the time there were 788 banks in the United States (as of one reporting period in 1837; the number

An anti–Van Buren token with his quotation, "I follow in the steps of my illustrious predecessor," referring to Jackson, who is represented by a jackass. The obverse with a tortoise carrying a strongbox refers to the slow movement of federal funds to the newly established Sub-Treasury offices. (HT-34)

was constantly changing), with capital of $291 million. These institutions had $149 million worth of paper money in circulation, backed by $38 million worth of specie. Deposits totaled $127 million. Outstanding loans amounted to $525 million.

Matters worsened and there were more bank and business failures. A brave face was maintained by many, including the influential *New York Journal of Commerce.*

May 10, 1837

Despite optimism in certain quarters the credit and cash crunch became deeper. On May 10, 1837, New York City banks suspended specie payments under a state law which permitted them to do this for a one-year period.[5] By this time there were about 100 bank failures in that city and surrounding areas, causing a loss of about $15 million. This had a domino effect, and within the next few days, most of the larger banks

elsewhere in the East stopped paying out gold and silver coins. In an era before the telegraph, news spread by dispatches sent by rail and, in the interior, by coach or horseback.

In time, virtually every bank in the United States suspended paying out coins. By the end of the year, additional hundreds of banks had closed their doors forever. Many of these had assets of dubious value, and some had no assets at all except a printing press or, more likely, some bank-note ordering forms from one or another of the engraving and printing firms that were all too eager to deliver as many notes as were

Hard Times token HT-66 memorizes the date that specie payments were suspended. The reverse shows a phoenix (commerce) rising from the ashes; by November 1837 many banks had resumed specie payments.

Although Andrew Jackson left office on March 4, 1837, satirical currency (as here) and tokens continued to be produced. This one was copyrighted on August 21, 1837.

requested. The country was awash in "broken bank" notes worth only the paper they were printed on.

Coins of all kinds disappeared from circulation, eventually including copper cents—those for just a short time. In order to maintain commerce, paper "shinplasters" were issued by merchants, banks, towns, and others. Denominated in cents, most of these scrip bills were as worthless as the broken-bank notes they supplemented. Cent-size copper tokens, known to a later generation of numismatists as the aforementioned Hard Times tokens, were made by the millions and helped fill the need for small change. The pivotal date of May 10, 1837, is included in the inscription on certain of these and is generally cited as the beginning of the Hard Times era, although for numismatists the era began in 1832, as noted.

Daniel Webster railed against Van Buren during his presidency and, similar to the arguments against Jackson, he stated that the Constitution was being wrecked. This inspired several Hard Times tokens with an 1837-dated obverse and an 1841-dated reverse, the latter suggesting that if, in 1841, Van Buren would no longer be president and the pro-Constitution stance of Webster would be adopted under a Whig administration, all would be well.

One can "read history" by the devices and inscriptions on these tokens. No wonder that they are so popular with collectors and have been for a long time.

A Hard Times store card. In 1833, the date on this token, clothing merchant Francis L. Brigham operated two sales facilities. The main depot was at No. 1 Cheapside, New Bedford, premises in a long building that housed multiple shops. The other was in the Union Lodge Building at 94 Main Street on the island of Nantucket off the coast of Massachusetts (HT-175). A few years later Brigham became a dentist in New Bedford.

Anti–Van Buren token issued in 1840 with allegorical motifs. One side is dated 1837 as a reminder of the Panic with the president's Experiment ship wrecked on a rocky shore, in contrast with smooth sailing anticipated in 1841 with the hope that the Constitution, which had been challenged many times by Jackson, would sail forward. (HT-19)

By early 1857 counterfeit gold and silver coins were said to be endemic in commerce. Dr. James T. Barclay had a proposal to eliminate or at least vastly reduced them. Pattern coins were prepared.

A Report on Counterfeiting

Counterfeit gold coins.

Chormann's Special Pattern Coins of 1860

In the mid-1850s there was great excitement concerning false coins and paper money in circulation. Dr. James T. Barclay, a concerned citizen, stepped to the fore and convinced Congress to investigate the methods of counterfeiting coins and to see if changes could be made to restrict the practice. Further, he suggested that new methods could be devised to prevent coins from wearing as quickly as they did. He saw three problems:

1. That the coins of the United States sustain a very serious loss from the ordinary wear and tear of circulation, and that much of this amount can be as easily saved as lost.

2. That our coins are extensively, profitably, and speciously counterfeited and impaired in value, and government thereby subjected to great expense, and society to serious inconvenience and loss on account of this great and growing evil.

3. That every method of counterfeiting at all specious and dangerous can be entirely prevented, and that all the other attempts upon the integrity of coin that have hitherto been devised can either be altogether frustrated, or so materially obviated as to be rendered virtually impossible.

Newspaper clippings, comments from bankers, and other insights were presented to indicate that of the $250,000,000 estimated value of silver and gold coins in circulation, perhaps one-half of one percent, or more, were counterfeits.

Barclay was like the Pied Piper—his song was irresistible to legislators, who agreed to form a committee to implement his suggestions per the Act of February 26, 1857. A committee of two professors—K.E. Rogers and Henry Vethake—was appointed on July 18 and given apartments within the Mint to set up machinery and experiment. The two men filed an extensive report on April 17 (the original titles of these classes are given below in italics followed by comments I have added, as false coins have always been of interest to numismatists):

1. Imitation by casting. This process involved pouring metal into molds and had been practiced since ancient times. False pieces of base metal such as lead then could be silver plated. The committee said that casting was exclusively limited to silver coins and "though not very specious, is dangerous."

2. The gilding fraud. Dies could be made by casting and creating molds from genuine coins. Inferior metal would then be used to strike coins which could be gilded to imitate gold or could be silver plated. "This fraud, it must therefore be clearly seen, is a most specious and dangerous one. Our inquiries lead us to believe that it is carried on, at the present time, to a formidable extent."

3. Coining alloys resembling gold and silver, but containing neither. This is self-explanatory. Cheaper metals or alloys were used and coins were struck from false dies.

4. Counterfeits with alloy above the standard amount. "This fraud consists in coining a compound containing a liberal proportion of precious metal, but still much poorer than the genuine coin. It is attended with so little profit, compared with other modes of counterfeiting, on account of the skill and machinery required that it is not extensively practiced." A century later in the mid-1900s this became a popular way to counterfeit bullion coins, especially double eagles, an operation mostly done in foreign countries.

5. The encasing process. "This mode of counterfeiting consists in enveloping a cheap metal within thin soldered disks of precious metal, and then striking the planchet in a coining press." In 1857 Dr. Barclay said this was the "most dangerous which has attracted his notice." Other than a stir about this method at the time I am not aware it was a widespread problem later, if it ever was.

6. Altering and gilding certain silver coins, in imitation of gold coins. This also seems to have been much ado about nothing, or very little. Barclay claimed that older half dollars could be gold plated to pass as eagles. Such a coin would still have the design of a half dollar, quite unlike that of an eagle!

7. The facing fraud. "This species of deception is accomplished by removing one of the faces of a silver coin, and soldering the thin face of a gold coin of similar dimensions upon the silver coin suitably gilded. Thus the half dollar of 1801 harmonizes sufficiently well with the eagle

of our earlier coinage to deceive the unpracticed." Again, this seems naive. The 1857 committee, perhaps to justify its existence, seems to have used a lot of words to say relatively little. The comments quoted here are but a tiny fraction of the original text.

8. The sawing and inserting fraud. "This fraud is practiced by sawing apart the two faces of a gold coin, and inserting between them a planchet of base metal, by solder, in place of the precious metal thus removed, the circumference being gilded to conceal the interposed metal." Several notices of fakes of this type were published in the era; they were viewed as a great threat by Mint officials. However, the practice does not seem to have been widespread.

9. The drilling and plugging fraud. "This method of impairing coin is performed by drilling the coin edgewise and plugging the perforation with base metal, the outer extremity being closed with precious metal." Several contemporary notices of this have been found as well.

10. The eviscerating fraud. This consisted of using a lathe to remove metal from the back and interior, leaving the face and reeded edge, and then fitting a thin sheet from the back of another coin to it. This is used by modern watchmakers today. As a fraud in 1857 this would have yielded most of the gold from two $20 coins plus a new $20 made as a shell filled with platinum (not a precious metal at the time). These were also a real threat in the 1850s.

11. The peripheral fraud. "This fraud consists in removing from the circumference of coin more or less of the metal by means of the turning-lathe and chisel or the file. Several dimes' worth of precious metal may be thus removed from the larger coins, and yet the reeding be so perfectly restored by the simplest mechanical device that the loss cannot be discovered except by means of measurement or weighing. It is a process easily executed, and one which we have reason to believe is practiced to very considerable extent." This may have been so, but to me it seems complicated, and I am not aware it was ever a problem.

12. The galvano-plastic fraud. This consisted to making electrotype shells of the obverse and reverse of a coin and "the hollow portion being filled with a platinum alloy of proper weight, the two are adjusted and soldered together."

13. The sweating fraud. "This method of reducing the value of coin consists in abstracting a portion of precious metals by means of mercury."

14. Chemical reduction. "This fraud, sometimes also called 'sweating,' is performed by exposing coin to the action of dissolving liquids; for silver, nitric acid is usually employed, and for gold, the mixture of nitric and hydro chloric acids. This process is greatly more lucrative than the one with mercury, and is, indeed, in our opinion, by far the most dangerous of all the methods by which our coinage is tampered with." This was widely done, resulting in a gold coin with a somewhat pebbly surface. Such are not uncommon today and are usually referred to as "jewelry pieces."

Seeking a Solution

Regarding the wearing away of precious-metal coins in circulation, Barclay figured that the larger the amount of surface area on a coin in proportion to its weight, the more attrition would occur. Hence, the loss was greatest on lower denominations. He proposed that if coins were made thicker and of smaller diameter, this loss would be reduced. The committee gave this logical comment:

That this obviously important principle of contracting the surface in order to diminish the abrasion should not have been carried further than has been done in our coinage, is ascribable doubtless to the fear of the drill and saw—a fraud to which the increased thickness would invite.

The committee further thought that while the 14 methods of counterfeiting could be practiced, in reality they were all labor intensive and were not likely to ever be large scale. There was, however, a suggestion for the modification of the coinage, so secret that it could not be given in the report.

John C. Breckinridge, vice president of the United States and president of the Senate, was very impressed with the prospect. James F. Heiskell, Barclay's attorney, set about making arrangements. Ernst G. Chormann, an engraver in the private sector, was contacted to make pattern coins, and David Gilbert, a skilled mechanic at the Mint, was selected to make suitable coining machinery, as that already at the Mint was not satisfactory. Chormann wrote to Heiskell on May 19, 1860:

Dear Sir,

Being conversant with the plans proposed by Dr. J.T. Barclay for the improvement of the coinage, (having been engaged in the recent experiments connected therewith,) I will agree to engrave all the dies (for the facial and peripheral devices) that may be required for the production of a specimen coin, for the sum of twenty-five hundred dollars ($2,500.) I will guaranty the same to be in accordance with recent experiment, embracing Dr. J.T. Barclay's method of improving the coinage of the United States.

Respectfully, your obedient servant,

E.G. Chormann

41 N. Chestnut Street

Gilbert wrote to Heiskell on the same day:

> Dear Sir,
>
> Having had several interviews with Dr. James T. Barclay, and by him been made acquainted with certain plans for improving the coinage of the United States, and my having been for about fifteen years in the employ of the mint of the United States as a practical machinist, and having knowledge of the machinery and coining operations of the mint, and at the request of Mr. James F. Heiskell, said Dr. James T. Barclay's agent, I herewith engage to construct the machinery, and to produce the mechanical results as proposed by said Dr. James T. Barclay, or his agent, Mr. James F. Heiskell.
>
> My estimate for machinery and services is for the sum of eighteen hundred dollars; payment to be made at such times and ways as may be agreed upon at the time of contracting.
>
> Very respectfully submitted by
>
> David Gilbert

The arrangement met with favor, and the Senate passed an appropriation to further it.

However, the Barclay ideas were rejected by those in charge at the Philadelphia Mint. On September 8, 1860, Heiskell sent a letter to Secretary of the Treasury Howell Cobb that included this:

> We would undertake, after proper legislation, so as to be placed independent of the Mint officers, (for whose co-operation we can never hope, bitterly arrayed as they have ever been against the improvement,) to remodel, prepare, and introduce the new coinage, calling to our aid skillful designers and artificers to make the whole worthy of this great coin manufacturing government, and would condition that our compensation should be a percentage for a certain number of years on the amount that might be conclusively shown to be saved over a like number of years under the old coinage. . . .

Secretary Cobb wrote this to professors Rogers and Vethake on September 12, 1860:

> Gentlemen,
>
> Your letter of the 31st of May enclosed a letter from Dr. Heiskell containing the estimates of Messrs. Chormann & Gilbert of the expense of producing a specimen for the purpose of showing Dr. Barclay's processes and discoveries. They offered to make the necessary dies and machinery for $4,300, being $2,500 for the former, and $1,800 for the latter.
>
> Near the close of the last session of Congress an appropriation of $5,000 was made applicable to this purpose. The amount beyond the estimates, $700, will probably be required to furnish the necessary bullion for a sufficient number of the specimens to illustrate Dr. Barclay's improvements, which I desire may be fully and fairly done.
>
> Soon after this appropriation was made I addressed Dr. Heiskell, as agent and attorney of Dr. Barclay, as to the best and most satisfactory mode of applying the appropriation. I have now received his answer of the 8th instant, in which he suggests that you

be requested to cause a coin to be made in accordance with the estimates before referred to. Allow me, therefore, to request you to take the necessary and proper steps to have a coin of the denomination of eagle or half eagle, as you may deem most suitable to exhibit Dr. Barclay's views, struck off, at an expense not to exceed the $4,300 estimated by Messrs. Chormann & Gilbert.

I have to-day sent a copy of your report to the director of the mint, and requested him to furnish you with all proper facilities in regard to such specimens.

Very respectfully,

Howell Cobb

Secretary of Treasury[1]

Pattern Coinage

Although no instructions from Barclay have been found, it seems that the main element of his proposal was to have a smaller distance between the obverse and reverse fields than that on regular coins. The motifs would be in high relief and raised decorations such as ridges would use metal that might ordinarily been employed to make the coin thicker. A thin coin would eliminate the possibility of removing gold or silver from the interior of a genuine struck coin.

Whether the Chormann pattern coins were produced within the Mint, per the space reserved for the experiment, or outside of the Mint in view of the staff opposition to Barclay, is unknown. It seems that within the Mint is the more logical possibility as Mint equipment and coinage metal were involved.

Not only did Chormann make patterns, but Chief Engraver James B. Longacre made some as well. Correspondence from attorney Heiskell to Secretary Cobb (quoted above) reveals that should the Barclay ideas have been adopted for regular coinage, a royalty

was expected. Likely this proved to be a fatal flaw in any implementation. Further, not long afterward the secessionist movement commenced with the withdrawal of South Carolina from the Union on December 20, 1860. Secretary Cobb packed up his belongings and decamped to the South to become an official of the Confederate States of America.

Auction Listings

In August 2006 at the World's Fair of Money (summer American Numismatic Association convention) in Denver, Heritage Auctions offered the following:

Lot 4064: 1861 Copper and Lead Die Trials by Ernest G. Chormann. A fascinating lot of die trials. . . . Chormann was a Philadelphia engraver and die cutter and he was listed in Boyd's Directory 1860–1, with an address of 41 North 6th Street. These are high quality trials, suggestive of Mint quality. Three are in lead, and two of those have an Indian head central motif inside a scalloped rim, the reverses are also scalloped with different finishes. The third lead piece is larger (half dollar sized) with a central motif that imitates Gobrecht's Seated Liberty design, again inside scallops with punches below for digits, the reverse has a copy of the eagle seen on contemporary Seated Liberty coinage, a scallop around, and CHORMANN F. below the eagle. Four copper pieces are also included, each with 1861 in the center and the initials EGC in a triangular position around the date, scalloped outer design and in relief; the reverses have a rosette within the same scalloped relief. An interesting group of die trials that deserves more extensive investigation.

In August 2013 at the World's Fair of Money in Chicago, Stack's Bowers Galleries offered these items from the John J. Ford, Jr. Collection, as cataloged by John Pack of the firm:

The pieces offered below are at once exciting and fascinating. As far as we are aware, these are the first such pieces to come to light and be presented in their proper historical context. These were unknown to Judd and Pollock, and are thus not included in the standard references on United States experimental and pattern coins; however, it seems that they very much belong in the appendices of any further editions. We are aware of a small group of related pieces that surfaced in a Philadelphia estate some years ago, but those were not understood at the time and were never published.

The whereabouts of those pieces is unknown to us today. However it is worth noting that they were associated with several trial strikes of Clark, Gruber & Company coins, and were punch-linked to those pieces, identifying Mr. Chormann as most likely the die-cutter for that well-known Colorado firm.

22001 (ca. 1860) Private Experimental Coin. J-Unlisted, P-Unlisted. Rarity-8. Silver. Plain edge. MS-60. 11.1 grams. 24 mm. Obv: Indian head styled after Longacre's small cent design in sunken cartouche of ribbon with 12 curves, faint C in field below bust. Rev: raised federal-style shield at center surrounded by fine engine-turned scrolling, within a broad scalloped ring, in relief. Beyond the outer curves, a circle with dot at each inward curve of the outer ribbon. Deep steel gray with bold design elements and plenty of retained luster and eye appeal. Highly attractive and extremely rare.

22002 (ca. 1860) Private Experimental Coin. Judd Unlisted, Pollock-Unlisted. Rarity-8. White metal. Plain edge. AU-55. 7.4 grams. 24 mm. Obv: Indian head styled after Longacre's small cent design in sunken cartouche of ribbon with 12 curves, faint C in field below bust. Rev: sunken federal shield with five concentric 12-curved ribbons, CHORMANN / F / PHILa. on three lines in shield depression. Light pewter gray. Lustrous and very pleasing. Extremely rare, and possibly Unique.

22003 (ca. 1860) Private Experimental Coin. J-Unlisted, P-Unlisted. Rarity-8. Silver. Plain edge. MS-60. 7.8 grams, 24 mm. Obv: sunken federal shield with five concentric 12-curved ribbons. CHORMANN / F/ PHILa. on three lines in shield depression. Rev. raised federal-style shield at center surrounded by fine engine-turned scrolling, within a broad scalloped ring, in relief. Beyond the outer curves, a circle with dot at each inward curve of the outer ribbon. Olive and chestnut over deep gray surfaces, accents of bright silver in the recesses. Visually striking and extremely rare, if not unique.

22004 (ca. 1860) Private Experimental Coin. J-Unlisted, P-Unlisted. Rarity-8. White metal. Plain edge. AU-55. 12.3 grams, 31 mm. Obv: accurate copy of the obverse circulating Liberty Seated coinage motif in

recessed cartouche with ribbon-like border with 12 curves, C flanked by tiny rectangles below Liberty. Rev: accurate copy of an eagle from the reverse of a Liberty Seated coin in an oval cartouche, CHORMANN beneath in tiny letters. Sharply struck and largely brilliant with just a hint of rub on the design high points. A thick (3+ mm) planchet adds to the overall heft and appearance. Visually striking and extremely rare.

22005 (ca. 1860) Private Experimental Coin. J-Unlisted, P-Unlisted. Rarity-8. White metal. Plain edge. AU-50. 11.7 grams, 30.5 mm. Obv: accurate copy of the obverse circulating Liberty Seated coinage motif in recessed cartouche with ribbon-like border with 12 curves, C flanked by tiny rectangles below Liberty. Rev: accurate copy of an eagle from the reverse of a Liberty Seated coin in an oval cartouche, CHORMANN beneath in tiny letters. Light pewter gray. An internal bend is noted, likely as made, creating a high point the central eagle. A duplicate of the preceding, but still extremely rare.

22006 (ca. 1860) Private Experimental Coin. J-Unlisted, P-Unlisted. Rarity-8. White metal. Plain edge.

Chormann's Special Pattern Coins of 1860

MS-60. 12.3 grams, 31 mm. Obv: accurate copy of the obverse circulating Liberty Seated coinage motif in recessed cartouche with ribbon-like border with 12 curves, C flanked by tiny rectangles below Liberty. Rev: accurate copy of an eagle from the reverse of a Liberty Seated coin, with a 12-curve ribbon around. CHORMANN. F. beneath in tiny letters. Light pewter gray. A small area of oxidation to the right of the seated Liberty, but lustrous and attractive. Extremely rare, and possibly unique.

Thin-planchet, large-diameter pattern $5 gold coin made by Chief Engraver James B. Longacre in 1860 following Ernst Chormann's ideas. Judd-271 as listed in *United States Patterns* by J. Hewitt Judd.

In 1860 Chief Engraver James B. Longacre made some pattern gold half eagles with larger diameter than standard and with very thin planchets. After this time little more was heard about the Chormann ideas.

Ernst G. Chormann

Ernst G. Chormann, whose first name was also spelled as Ernest, was born in France about 1821. His wife, Mary, was a native Pennsylvanian and was a year younger. By 1853 he known as an engraver, a profession he followed for many years, although he was sometimes listed as an artist as well. He did work on dies as well as on copper and steel printing plates. In 1855 he engraved an award medal for the Pennsylvania Institute of Philadelphia, a standard die that was used for years afterward. Examples are in the cabinet of the American Numismatic Society. In 1856 he engraved the dies for the St. Louis Agricultural and Mechanical Association medal.

In the late 1850s Chormann did some work for Chief Engraver James B. Longacre. He was well known at the Mint by the time that he was selected to make dies to illustrate Dr. James T. Barclay's coinage ideas. In the Scott & Co., 50th Sale, May 28 and 19, 1883, lot 469 was described as: "1861 Indian head surrounded by stars, same as on $3 gold piece, beautiful head by *Chormann*, pewter; rev. blank, size 65, probably a pattern for a $50 gold piece."

In August 1861 in Philadelphia he raised a volunteer group of soldiers known as Col. E.G. Chormann's Independent Rangers of the 8th Pennsylvania Cavalry. Thomas Furniss was captain. Their exploits were memorialized in the *Pennsylvania Rangers War Song*, lyrics by James V. Murray, played to the tune of *I'm Afloat.*

Chormann was interested in mechanical things, especially relating to optics, but in other fields as well. Beginning in the late 1850s many patents were awarded to him. After the Civil War he was usually listed as an artist. He and his wife were members of local society and were listed in *Boyd's Philadelphia Blue Book*. Their son, Ernest Jr., was born in the early 1850s and practiced law in Philadelphia.

CHAPTER 35

A collector with a nose for popular Civil War tokens will hunt down an example of this amusing piece.

"Good For a Scent"

A Token Attracts Attention

Civil War token issued by Joseph H. Merriam, with a dog's head on the obverse and an advertisement for Merriam's Toad Seal Press on the reverse. (Fuld MA-115-D-2b variety)

For many years Joseph H. Merriam, die sinker and token maker, held forth with his business in downtown Boston, advertising that he had entered the profession in 1850.[1] His first directory listing was in 1854 at the rear of 147-1/2 Washington Street, offering "Seal press, brands, and seals." He also manufactured door and window fasteners. In 1856 the Merriam brothers, Joseph H. and John C., did business at 37 Faneuil Hall Square. Within a year Joseph moved to the address he would occupy for the token-issuing period under discussion, a location variously listed as 19 or 20 Brattle Square at the corner of Elm Street. In 1861 he advertised:

> Jos. H. Merriam. Letter-Cutter, Die-Sinker, and Medalist. 18 Brattle Square, corner of Elm Street, Boston. (Established 1850). Name-Punches, Stencil Plates, Medals, Branding Irons, Seals, Embossing Presses, Steel Letters and Figures, Metallic Labels, and Fancy Dies of all kinds, executed with dispatch, and in a style not to be equaled.

By 1864 he was a partner with William N. Weeden in Merriam & Co. at the same address and advertised as seal and letter engravers. Products of the era included the Eagle, Toad, and Omega seal-embossing presses. The Toad was pictured on a token. At the time Joseph Merriam boarded at 285 Washington Street. By 1865 he owned a small farm in South Hadley, Massachusetts, which was taken care of by others.

Circa 1870 the business was succeeded by W.C. Brigham & Co., which advertised:

> Established 1850; Successors to Jos. H. Merriam. 18 Brattle Square. Seal Engravers and Stencil Cutters, Embossing Presses, Hand and Ribbon Stamps, Steel Dies, Letters and Figures, Medals, Checks, Metallic Labels, &c. Proprietors of Merriam's Pat. Lion Press, Merriam's marking Can and Inks. Business stencils a specialty.

A Memorable Civil War Token

Among the tokens issued by engravers of the era before and after the Civil War, Merriam's products were distinguished for having deeply cut dies and being boldly struck. His best-known tokens were Civil War store cards with a dog's head on the obverse and the inscription GOOD FOR A SCENT. Although as a class they are not particularly rare, they are so popular with collectors today that any auction offering draws a wide circle of bidders.

It was not always so. They did not please everyone. A commentary on

The "Scent" die combined with Joseph H. Merriam's advertisement. (Fuld MA-115-E-1a)

the die was provided by "Nemo" (possibly numismatist Charles Chaplin) in the *American Stamp Mercury and Numismatist*, published by Ferdinand Trifet in Boston in 1869:

> We have a "Copperhead," issued by our friend Merriam of Brattle Square. This medal bears a dog's head with the inscription, "Good for a scent," and is the "head scenter," both in design and execution, of all the mushroom crop of tokens that sprang up during the latter part of the war, nine-tenths of which are a disgrace to the die-sinking profession and should be scouted by every coin and medal collector in the land.[2]

Chaplin and Trifet

Forgive me if I divert momentarily from Merriam. The names of Chaplin and Trifet prompt me to say that in recent decades members of the Numismatic Bibliomania Society in particular have been researching the stories of numismatists of the 19th century, a fascinating pursuit. As to Chaplin, he was a printer in Boston, a dedicated member of the Boston Numismatic Society, and a contributor to Trifet and others. As to whether "Nemo" was one of his pen names, I don't know. He seems to have several, usually attached to

pieces that combine the critical with the humorous. "Gointoem Strong" is perhaps the best known, including for a farcical article on the descriptions used by auction catalogers which appeared in the May 1869 issue of the *American Numismatic Journal*.

Ferdinand Trifet, who nearly always signed as F. Trifet, conducted a stamp business at 57 Court Street, later 20 State Street, in downtown Boston. The first issue of his periodical *American Stamp Mercury* bore the date of October 25, 1867. Trifet soon caught on to the fact that the rare-coin market was expanding rapidly, and this specialty was added to his trade. The July 1869 issue added *and Numismatist* to the title.

Not many criminals use their own publications to confess their misdeeds. Trifet was an exception. In the same issue of his magazine he stated that he began collecting stamps in 1861, and in 1866 became acquainted with S. Allan Taylor of Boston. Then:

> A short time after this I sold my collection to Mr. Lemuel Pope of Cambridge and established myself in the stamp business on a small scale. In buying of persons in this city I very frequently got badly swindled with counterfeits, but at that time I had no scruples in selling them over again without warranting them.
>
> At that time I had set up and printed 200 each of the figure issues of the Sandwich Islands. I also in conjunction with Messrs. Taylor, Seltz, and Frost, all of Boston had engraved a fine wood-cut copy of the 3-1/8 Luzon stamp, paying one quarter of the expenses and receiving one quarter of the stamps. I carried on this nefarious business until June 1867 when at the urgent solicitation of personal friends and prominent collectors of Boston, who promised to give me all the help and encouragement in busi-

ness, provided that I should have nothing to do with counterfeit or fictitious stamps, issued a circular in which I stated that on and after date (June 20, 1867) all stamps sold by me would be warranted genuine. Of course, this made certain parties of this city threaten vengeance and destruction, which, I am happy to state, I am still waiting for. . . .

After the July 1870 issue, *and Numismatist* was dropped from the masthead. Apparently his foray into coins did not pan out as expected.

"Once a crook, always a crook" seems to define Trifet, if E.L. Mason Jr., a leading Philadelphia rare-coin dealer (and the subject of chapter 27), is in this instance to be believed (his statements varied widely). In 1869 Trifet was back at the game of selling fake postage stamps, according to Mason.[3] In 1870 Mason wrote that Trifet was busy selling fake Proof half cents of the 1840s.[4] He may have been hoist on his own petard, for by March 1871 he was bankrupt.[5]

Merriam's Civil War and Sutlers' Tokens
The 1863-dated SCENT obverse die was combined with several different reverses advertising Merriam's own business. Further varieties were made for a number of other New England businesses.

Store card of Dunn & Co.'s Oyster House of Charlestown, Massachusetts. The reverse shows the Bunker Hill Monument. (Fuld MA-200-A-3a)

Store card of A.W. Gale, who operated a restaurant in the railroad depot in Concord, New Hampshire. This is the state's only Civil War store-card variety. (Fuld NH-120-A-1a)

Numismatists attribute these and other issues by various die sinkers to Fuld numbers, as used in *U.S. Civil War Store Cards*, giving the state abbreviation first, then a number indicating a town or city within that state, then a letter from A onward, one for each merchant, then a lowercase letter such as *a* (for a copper striking), *b* (brass), *d* (copper-nickel), *e* (white metal), etc. Accordingly, MA-115-G-1a, a token made by Merriam for Tuttle's Restaurant in Boston, has MA for the state, 115 (the number for the city of Boston), G for the tokens of Tuttle, 1 for the first of several Tuttle die combinations, and *a* for copper.

Another Joseph H. Merriam Civil War store card. (Fuld MA-115-E-2b)

Somewhat oxidized white-metal store card of F. Pfeiffer of Norwalk, Virginia. Although it is dated 1863 it was struck after the Civil War. (Fuld VA-580-A-1e)

Other varieties with the dog's-head obverse include one for F. Pfeiffer of Norfolk, Virginia. David E. Schenkman, who has studied Merriam's tokens in detail, found that Pfeiffer did not enter business until after 1870, suggesting that this die was used by Merriam's successors in business.[6] The Pfeiffer tokens typically show wear and oxidation, suggesting they actually circulated and were not made as collectibles for the numismatic trade.

Inside a sutler's tent. (*Frank Leslie's Illustrated News*, November 29, 1862)

Merriam made Civil War store cards from other obverse dies as well. Compared to the output of token makers elsewhere, such as in Cincinnati, New York City, and Waterbury, his output was relatively small.

In 1861 the War Department set up a system of sutlers, as they were called, these being appointed individuals or partnerships that sold goods to soldiers. In permanent posts and in some occupied towns the sutler operated a store, the shelves of which were lined with stationery, pens, ink, cards and games, clothing, cooking and eating utensils, tobacco in various forms, patent medicine, knives, books, newspapers, toiletry items, knick knacks, and more. In traveling companies and on the battlefield sutlers set up in tents or operated from the rear of wagons.

Sutlers' tokens are related to Civil War store cards and probably should be included in that category, as they were issued by merchants. However, numismatists have always considered them to be a separate series. *Civil War Sutler Tokens and Cardboard Scrip*, by David E. Schenkman, 1983, is the standard reference on these. Joseph H. Merriam made such tokens for Harvey Lewis, sutler to the 23rd Massachusetts Regiment.

Modular Dies

Some years ago I was studying the dies made by Merriam, looking for variations in punches and arrangements. In viewing a series of four store cards issued by C.F. Tuttle's Restaurant in Boston I noticed that the letters around the reverse die were identical on each of the four denominations, 5, 10, 25, and 50 cents. I also noticed that there was a tiny raised circle around the center number visible on some examples. It was but a short leap to conclude that these were *modular* dies. The reverse die with the denomination was placed on the bottom in the coining press and became the anvil die, so called. The obverse die with the steer's head was the hammer or top die. To go from one denomination to another a small circular mini-die with 5, 10, 25, or 50 was placed in the recess in the reverse die. The sutler's tokens of Harvey Lewis were also modular.

Four different denominations made by Joseph Merriam for Tuttle's Restaurant. These used a common obverse die combined with a modular reverse die into which a small insert bearing the denomination could change the value. (MA-115-G-1a to 4a)

Four different denominations made by Joseph Merriam for Harvey Lewis, sutler for the 23rd Massachusetts Regiment. These were also modular dies permitting the denomination to be changed. (Schenkman MA-B-010C to MA-B-050C)

Apart from an interesting and rare Wass, Molitor & Co. $10 gold coin of 1855, for which a 5 digit was inserted in a hole drilled in the space after 185, I was not aware of any earlier modular dies in the American series. It could have been that the Wass, Molitor & Co. die was made with an earlier date but not used, and then had a new final digit inserted.

In time, modular dies came into common use, such as for adding the names of recipients of World's Columbian Exposition award medals. As far as I am aware, Merriam's modular dies are unique in the Civil War series.

Other Merriam Tokens

Beyond the Civil War and sutlers' tokens discussed above, Joseph H. Merriam issued dozens of commemorative medalets, large-diameter store cards of plain appearance (with lettering and digits but without motifs), and other pieces. Production of these commenced in a large way in 1860 when he issued medalets for presidential contenders Republican Abraham Lincoln, Democrat Stephen A. Douglas, and Constitutional Union Party candidate John Bell. Edward Everett, famous Massachusetts orator, politician, and educator, who was Bell's running mate, was also a

token subject. The market for these seems to have been numismatists, not potential voters in the general population.

The great boxing match between American John C. Heenan and British Tom Sayers was in the headlines, and tokens featuring each of them were made in quantity.[7] The visit of Albert Edward the Prince of Wales to the United States was another Merriam topic. He continued the production of these commemorative or souvenir tokens through the Civil War and for a short time afterward. As numismatic buyers were scarce after 1859, most of Merriam's tokens are elusive in the marketplace today.

Henry Clay, Benjamin Franklin, Abraham Lincoln, George B. McClellan, George Washington, and Daniel Webster were among the historical and political figures showcased on Merriam tokens. Civil War generals Joseph Hooker and Philip Kearney, actor Edwin Forrest, the SS *Great Eastern*, the Boston Masonic Temple, Washington's Tomb, and the United States Army were among other subjects. Certain of Merriam's commemorative token dies (but not Civil War dies) were acquired later by James A. Bolen, a Springfield, Massachusetts, engraver and numismatist who combined them with some of his own dies.

One of the most intricately engraved medalets from the mid-19th century depicts William J. Mullen. It was an interesting project to try to learn more about it.

An Ornate Medalet

The 33 mm medalet honoring William J. Mullen and depicting his manufactory of watch dials and cases.

Meet William J. Mullen and His Medal

When the Stack's Bowers Galleries catalog of the John J. Ford, Jr. Sale No. XXIII arrived in the summer of 2013 I stopped everything and spent a few days poring through it—on and off. These tokens and medals had been collected by the late John J. Ford Jr., from the late 1940s to the end of his life in the early 2000s. The basic listing had been cataloged by George Fuld years earlier, and then was later finessed by a company staffer. I had my eyes on quite a few things and may have been the single largest buyer at the auction.

If there is a message to this chapter it is that it is not at all unusual for collectors of tokens and medals to be able to buy great American classics for very modest sums. In this instance I mention lot 22504 in the sale, a 33 mm copper token of William J. Mullen, of New York, graded MS-63 BN by NGC. I was the winner for $176.25, including the buyer's fee. This would be pocket change for a specialist in Morgan silver dollars and is not enough money to buy even the commonest American gold coin.

Mullen in Philadelphia

On February 22, 1832, the centennial of George Washington's birth, marble masons marched in a parade in Philadelphia with a wagon on which was placed a recently made cornerstone intended for the Washington Monument. In 1833 William J. Mullen was on the committee to erect this, perhaps inspired by one completed in Baltimore in 1829. Proponents hoped to raise funds by subscription, but there was not sufficient interest. They turned to the city provide the money.

On February 19, 1833, the councilmen passed an ordinance authorizing the erection of such a monument in Washington Square. Arrangements

The Washington Monument, in Baltimore, completed in 1829.

were quickly made to have a large parade, but the time was so short that only about 12,000 to 15,000 people participated, a fraction of those who had thronged the procession of the birthday parade in 1832. After the procession ended, participants gathered in the square to hear a prayer, an introductory address, and an oration. Completing the ceremony, the cornerstone was laid in a small excavated area—evidently disturbing some graves, as the square had been used as a potters' field for indigent burials. In time the cornerstone was covered up, and the monument was never built. The cornerstone contents included "an emblematical sketch of the centennial celebration by William J. Mullen, Esq.," "a silver medal struck off during the centennial procession and presented by the gold and silver artificers for the cornerstone, several specimens of copper coin, by several citizens, of the years 1771, 1772, 1791, 1797, etc.," newspapers of the day, and other items.[1]

On August 26, 1834, Mullen was one of five delegates from Philadelphia who attended the Reform Convention in Harrisburg to discuss amending the Constitution of the state of Pennsylvania. He became known as a reformer, a do-gooder in the best sense of that term. Mullen was an abolitionist, he spent years in the temperance movement, and he led other programs to improve human dignity and quality of life.

Mullen in New York City

In early 1834 he moved to New York City and formed a partnership, Mullen & Ackerman, with Abraham Ackerman. Located at 101 Warren Street, the firm specialized in gold watch dials and jewelry. Mullen resided at 85 Mercer Street. In 1834 they exhibited watch cases at the 7th Annual American Institute Fair, held in Niblo's Gardens, and received a diploma. This facility seems to have been short-lived, as by 1835 his business address was variously given as 173, 174, and 175 Broadway.

A report of the first Annual Fair of the Mechanics Institute, held in New York City in 1835, included this:

No. 43. *A Case of Watch Dials.* William J. Mullen, New-York City. The Committee considers these specimens of American workmanship worthy of special notice, both for originality of design and elegance of workmanship. They have never been equaled by any articles of the kind, foreign or domestic; and when it is considered that heretofore a large sum of money has been sent abroad annually for these articles, the Committee feels at liberty to express unqualified praise in favor of the articles here exhibited; they therefore award to Mr. Mullen the Silver Medal of the Institute.

Mullen also exhibited a map and three engravings at the same event.

In 1835 he was president of the Gold and Silver Smith's Temperance Society in New York City, a division of a larger organization that had 18,643 members totally according to a report, with some divisions not yet reporting. Among their activities were giving lectures, distributing tens of thousands of copies of the *Temperance Almanac*, and otherwise spreading the word about the evils of alcohol. Among the group's successes was gaining a 5 percent reduction in marine insurance premiums for vessels operated by those who did not drink ardent spirits.

In 1836 at the 8th Annual Fair of the American Institute he was given a gold medal and this citation:

William J. Mullen, 173 Broadway, New-York, manufactures gold and silver watch dials. Dials are made in great variety, elegance, and perfection. Mr. M. deserves much credit in having, by his skill, contributed to render us, in relation to this article, independent of foreign importations.

A report of a visit to that event in the *Commercial Advertiser*, October 18, 1836, included this description of an oil painting on view:

> William J. Mullen, manufacturer of gold watch dials, has been painted by Otis in his own shop with the implements of his craft about him. Mr. M. looks very pleasantly in his picture—and has reason to be satisfied with the increased variety and beauty of the gold watch dials contained in a large case below.
>
> From the indication of all these dials, we judged that it was high time the center figure was out of the office. The dials are very perfect and are made up of many new patterns. Mr. Mullen has a new machine (represented in the picture) by the aid of which he transfers the likenesses of men or animals, or any given figure, flower, or other ornament, to the dial in a very few minutes.
>
> Among the likenesses we obtained was that of Napoleon crossing the Alps, from the picture of Sully. It is in gold, on a ground-work of silver— exquisitely wrought. Mr. Mullen's factory, judging from this picture, must be a very interesting place for the lover of mechanic arts to visit.

An Ornate Factory Scene

The *New York Gazette* also reported on the event and gave more details:

A Painting by Otis

> Among the specimens of art now exhibiting at the fair is a painting, 10½ by 6½ feet, by Otis, of the interior of the factory of Mr. William J. Mullen.
>
> It is a firelight scene, emanating from the forge, the reflection of which on Mrs. Mullen, who occupies a central position on the canvas, produces a beautiful effect. Mr. M. is represented in the act of performing a chemical operation in the manufacture and color of his beautiful watch dials.
>
> The ease, elegance, and beauty of the main figure are spoken of by amateurs of the art in the highest praise. The piece also represents the workmen in their different occupations, at lathes, presses, &c., and the little son of Mr. M. sitting at his father's feet engaged in the mischievous work of destroying dials.
>
> Another figure prominent in the painting is Mr. M.'s rose engine, a machine containing upwards of 22,000 parts, and one of the most complicated of its kind ever manufactured. This machine is used for producing every species of elegant devices in the manufacture of watch dials and backs, a great variety of patterns of which may be seen in Mr. M's case in the saloon. It is but recently that these neat and delicate articles have been manufactured in this country, and as Mr. M. is the original inventor, he deserves the patronage of the public and will doubtless find remuneration for is skill and enterprise as a mechanic.
>
> The painting is, on the whole, one of the first class, got up with great accuracy in all its parts, and the artist has shown in its execution many brilliant flashes of genius. For this work we understand Mr. Otis was awarded a premium by the Institute.[2]

The above description may relate in a tangential way to Mullen's 33 mm copper token, although the token has cherubs or putti rather than humans, and the scenario differs. The artist was Bass Otis (1784 to 1861), active and well known in the East.

Afterward Mullen served on the committee that conducted the yearly American Institute events. These gave artists, manufacturers, and others the opportunity to showcase their products. A gold medal, the highest award, could be won on multiple occasions, but later wins were honored by a printed certificate, not another medal. Mullen continued to be active in the temperance movement and also followed the progress of phrenology, which was rapidly becoming a pseudo-medical sensation.

Niles' National Register, May 18, 1839, included this mention of an unnamed firm in the same business, with a nod to Mullen:

> Watch dials. According to the New York Transcript, there is in that city one of the most extensive watch dial manufactories in the world. The style and quality of the work are described as infinitely superior to those of any foreign manufacture—not excepting even the French, Swiss, or English. The business done by this concern is immense—the annual consumption of gold and silver, for material, amounting to three or four hundred thousand dollars.
>
> Mr. William Mullen, formerly of Philadelphia, has also a very extensive establishment in New York.

Back in Philadelphia

By 1842 Mullen, seemingly having a fortune, was back in Philadelphia. Continuing in the business, at least for a while, in October of that year he exhibited watch cases at the Fair of the Franklin Institute. He then turned his emphasis to public causes, reform, and wel-

fare, and remained a staunch advocate of temperance. On November 28, 1844, he helped organize a discussion on capital punishment, held in the lecture hall of the Franklin Institute. In April 1846 he helped organize and was elected the first president of the Philanthropic Association. In the same year he helped found and was the first president of the House of Industry, which helped indigent and unfortunate women in the Philadelphia area.

In April 1848 he addressed a meeting of citizens at the Philadelphia Museum on the "best means for the preservation, civilization, &c., of the Indian tribes west of the Mississippi and on this side of the Rocky Mountains."

In 1849 Mullen was instrumental in founding the Female Medical College of Pennsylvania, the world's first institution of higher learning for women who wanted to enter the medical profession. There were six branches of study at the facility: Anatomy and Physiology, Principles and Practice of Medicine, Obstetrics and Diseases of Women and Children, Surgery and the Institutes of Medicine, Materia Medica, Pharmacy, and Chemistry. By 1852 it had 40 students from across the country.

In 1854 he was appointed prison agent to investigate people who had been unfairly incarcerated. He served for many years in this position. He worked with about 1,200 to 1,500 cases each year. At the time it was common practice to jail tenants who were behind in their rent, after which time landlords took what they wanted from the premises. Other petty debts were offenses that led to incarceration as well. Mullen worked with unfortunate men, securing the release of many, and helped them to find employment and get settled. On one instance a citizen angrily protested his work—stating that as the city spent a lot of time capturing criminals and jailing them, why should it pay for Mullen to try to release some of them.

The 1860 federal census lists his occupation as prison agent, age 55 (born in Pennsylvania). Living in the household were Caroline, age 45 (North Carolina), Wesley, age 20 (New York), Alfred, age 16

(Pennsylvania), Julia, age 14 (Pennsylvania), and William Jr., age 11 (Pennsylvania). George D. Sergent, clerk, also lived there, as did Mary Drouin, servant, age 18, born in Ireland.

Mullen became highly honored as a humanitarian, and in Philadelphia few knew about his earlier stint in New York City as a manufacturer. In honor of his work with the Female Medical College of Pennsylvania, Albert E. Harnisch (born in 1843) sculpted a bust and also a statue of Mullen that were displayed at

Mezzotint illustration of the Mullen statue by artist John Sartain. (Pennsylvania Academy of the Fine Arts)

the 1876 Centennial Exhibition in Philadelphia. Listed as No. 1226 under art at that event, the smaller piece was described as "Bust of William Mullen, first president of a college for women." Mullen died in Philadelphia on July 21, 1882.

Two Mullen Tokens

Numismatists recognize two tokens relating to Mullen. The first relates to his manufactory of watch dials and faces. A notice was taken of it in the *Coin Collector's Journal*, August 1885:

> This token is in every way the most artistic of the series, and while it does not approach some of the finer specimens of the English tokens of 1789–1798, it is by far superior to very many of that series. The head upon the obverse is bold and finely drawn; the legends upon the reverse are in such minute letters that they cannot be read without the aid of a strong glass, when each comes out in a perfection of form which is highly creditable to the die-sinker, to say the least. The allegorical scene upon the reverse, although somewhat crowded, is also of fine execution and no mean design. . . .

That is high praise considering that the writer compared it to the entire corpus of English-language tokens from the 1780s to 1885! How curious it is that the token almost became forgotten in later years, including through the 20th century.

Charles I. Bushnell in *An Arrangement of Tradesmen's Cards, Political Tokens, etc.*, issued in 1858, a work dedicated to C.C. Wright, listed this as No. 96 under New York tradesmen's tokens. The description included "Dies cut by Lander, N.Y. 1837." Russell Rulau in the *Standard Catalog of United States Tokens 1700–1900* attributes the dies to Louisa Lander, 1847, age 21, and the striking by C.C. Wright.

Maria Louisa Lander, born in Salem, Massachusetts, on September 1, 1826, known to her friends as Miriam and professionally as Louisa, grew up in a family of artists and began sculpture at a young age. In 1847, the year stated by Rulau, she would have been

21 as he said, but the subject of the clock dial and case manufactory would have been anachronistic as by then Mullen had left the business behind. On the other hand, Mullen may have wanted in 1847 to sponsor a medal honoring his commercial past.

Lander produced such works as *To-Day* and *Galatea*. In 1855 she went to Rome to study art and sculpture with Thomas Crawford (best remembered today for his *Freedom* statue placed on the dome of the U.S. Capitol in 1863). In early 1858 she sculpted a bust of Nathaniel Hawthorne, who was in Rome at the time, and developed a friendship with him and his family. Not long afterward Hawthorne penned this to his publisher William Tichnor in America:

> Miss Lander, a lady from my native town, has made an excellent bust of me, of which I will enclose a photograph, if I can get one. Even Mrs. Hawthorne is delighted with it, and, as a work of art, it has received the highest praise from all the sculptors here, including Gibson, the English sculptor, who stands at the head of the profession. Miss Bremer declares it to be the finest modelled bust she ever saw. I tell you this in the hope that you and Fields may do what may be in your power to bring Miss Lander's name favorably before the public; for she is coming back to America (for the summer only) and might be greatly benefitted by receiving commissions for busts, etc. She is a very nice person, and I like her exceedingly. If you happen to see her, she will give you the latest and most authentic news of me and mine.[3]

This pleasant situation ended when Hawthorne renounced her friendship for posing in the nude for artist Raphael Vittorio. Also, while he admired the bust when sculpted in clay, he did not like the finished product in marble.[4] In 1862 her sculpture *Virginia Dare* was publicly exhibited in Washington and seems to have drawn many visitors. For much of her life Louisa resided in Salem, city of her birth, punctuated by extended stays in the nation's capital. The 1880 census lists her as a sculptor, age 51, living with her sister Elizabeth, keeper of the house, age 65, with a servant, Hannah Driscoll, age 26, born in Ireland. Louisa Lander died in 1923.

The 36 mm token honoring William J. Mullen as an advocate of prisoners' rights, using an adaption of the portrait on the earlier 33 mm token of the watch-dial factory. The 36 mm token probably dates from 1862, the last date on the inscription.

The second token uses an adaptation of the portrait bust as the first, but altered to show a toga rather than the point of Mullen's neck. Although Lander may have sculpted the portrait, she was not a medalist and probably had nothing to do with the dies of either token. Charles Cushing Wright died in 1854, so he had no connection with the second token, which was likely produced in 1862, the date of the bottom of the medal. The inscription refers to Mullen's prison work. The token, perhaps considered a small *medal* at the time, seems to have been a tribute to his efforts.

Per the above, each token has yet to reveal mysteries such as the engraver of the dies, the occasions for which they were struck, the method of distribution, and how many were made.

CHAPTER 37

Morgan dollars are the most popular of "classic" American coins. Within this eagerly collected series is a subset with special romance and historical connections: the silver dollars of Carson City, Nevada.

Those Carson City Morgan Dollars!

Searching for Coins

The Carson City Mint in 1878. (*Frank Leslie's Illustrated Newspaper*, February 23, 1878)

Generations ago when there were no reference books on coin mintages and values (the first was Wayte Raymond's *Standard Catalogue of United States Coins* in 1934), no *Guide Book of United States Coins* (the first edition was published in 1946), and no grading standards, assembling a coin collection was a great challenge.[1] Of course, that was part of the fun. In that long-ago era dealers were a source of supply, and auctions were held regularly.

One numismatist, E.S. Thresher, of Kansas City, took on an even greater challenge—finding coins locally and regionally from miscellaneous sources. In July 1925 this letter from him was published in *The Numismatist*:

On June 1, 1919, I started an experiment to see how long it would take to find every date and mintmark of the coins of type now in circulation, that is, silver dollars since 1878, half dollars, quarter dollars and dimes since 1892, nickels since 1883 and cents since 1864. I put every date and mintmark on a card which I carried in my pocket, and whenever I found one I checked it off.

Not being in a business where cash is handled, I had to depend on such coins as I would get for pocket money, except cents. For these I had access to the collections of about 200 "penny-in-the-slot" machines.

Several interesting points have developed in these six years. Practically all that time I have spent in Kansas City. Similar experiments in different parts of the country probably would show different results. Following are the dates and mintmarks I have not yet found. Of course, I hardly expected to find the 1894-S dime or the 1913 Liberty Head nickel in circulation:

Silver dollars—1878-S, 8 feathers[2]; 1884-CC, 1885-CC, 1889-S, 1892; 1893-S, 1894, 1897, 1899, 1923-D.

Half dollars—1893-S, 1895-S, 1897-O, 1904-S, 1905, 1908-S, 1919-S, 1921.

Quarter dollars—1893-S, 1896-S, 1899-S, 1901-S, 1909-O, 1909-S, 1911-D, 1913-S, 1914-S, 1915-S, 1923-S.

Dimes—1893-O, 1894-S, 1896-S, 1901-S, 1915-S, 1924-S.

Nickels—1913 Liberty Head; 1924-S.

Cents—1924-S.

It will be seen that coins of the San Francisco Mint are by far the scarcest in this part of the country. It is hard to explain the finding of such scarcities as the 1895 dollar, 1916 new type quarter and 1877 cent, and yet not come across so many others of far larger coinage.

I have also kept a record of other oddities found in circulation. I have received no Liberty Seated dollars, but have found 16 half dollars, 12 quarters and 21 dimes of the Liberty Seated type, many with the dates illegible; 67 nickels of the old 5 [Shield] type, of which I could read the date on only eight.

Among the silver dollars he was seeking were the 1884-CC and 1885-CC, great rarities at the time.

As you probably know, the order of rarity among Morgan silver dollars changed dramatically in November 1962. Around the country it was customary for a lot of people to go to their banks in the holiday season to get some silver dollars for gifts. Silver dollars of the 1878 to 1921 Morgan design and the 1921 to 1935 Peace design were held at face value by many such institutions, but not in quantity as they were no longer in general circulation. There were a few scattered exceptions. In Nevada they were in wide use on the roulette and other gaming tables, and occasionally in the Rocky Mountain states they would be given out in change.

In 1962 to fill the demand for "new" dollars, a vault at the Philadelphia Mint, sealed since 1929, was opened. (In 1929 millions of Morgan dollars packed in cloth bags of 1,000 coins each had been shipped there from New Orleans, where the Mint had struck such coins continuously from 1879 to 1904.)

In the meantime, collecting Morgan dollars had become very popular with numismatists who sought to get one each of the nearly 100 dates and mintmark varieties struck at Philadelphia, Carson City, New Orleans, and San Francisco from 1878 to 1904 plus the tag-along coinage at the Denver, Philadelphia, and San Francisco mints in 1921. Among New Orleans coins in Uncirculated grade there were several notable rarities: 1898-O, 1903-O, and 1904-O. By 1962 I had been a coin dealer for nine years and I had never *seen* a Mint State 1903-O! The *Guide Book* listed it for $1,500, or multiples of the price of an 1856 Flying Eagle cent! No other Morgan dollar was listed higher. In 1941, when B. Max Mehl offered the William Forrester Dunham Collection at auction (mail-bid sale), the Mint State 1903-O was called out for its rarity. It was thought, logically enough, that most of the 1903-O dollars had been destroyed under terms of the Pittman Act of 1918, when 270,272,722 silver dollars of earlier dates were melted.

Lo! and behold. When the sealed vault was opened in 1962, millions of mint-fresh New Orleans silver dollars were found, including hundreds of thousands of the 1903-O.[3] This precipitated a nationwide treasure hunt. Banks were besieged with requests, and the vaults of the Federal Reserve Banks and other banks were emptied of the coins. It was realized that in 1910 millions of Carson City Morgan dollars had been shipped from storage in that city to the Treasury Building in Washington, D.C. For a number of years the occasional bag of CC dollars was opened, much to the delight of numismatists. With the great silver rush, the Treasury Building holdings were mostly paid out, until the Treasury decided to hold back three million Carson City dollars and sell them in a series of public auctions to be held by the General Services Administration (GSA). This was done, and eventually all were gone.

With these Treasury sales, certain of the low-mintage issues, including the 1884-CC and 1885-CC that E.M. Thresher was not able to find, now were common—along with the previously rare 1903-O and some others.

Carson City Update

The order of rarity changed, and dramatically. As you read these words the most difficult Carson Morgan dollar to find in Mint State is the 1889-CC. Only a single coin was in the GSA sales program. Second rarest, and by a distance, is the 1879-CC. After than the 1893-CC is the most elusive. The most common are the 1882-CC, 1883-CC, and 1884-CC.

Assembling a full set of CC dollars is a reality for many collectors. There are 11 different. If you want to be super specialized, you can expand the set by two coins. The 1879-CC exists in two varieties: the standard Large CC mintmark and the curious Large CC Over Small CC. The mint letters were small on the 1878-CC dollar dies. In 1879 it was decided to make them larger, and a die with a small mintmark had the letters partially effaced and large letters punched over them. Most collectors are happy with just a single 1879-CC, however. More interesting are the two varieties of 1880-CC dollars. The earlier has the feathers in the arrows with parallel tops, as in 1878. The later coins have the top feather slanted—immediately obvious upon inspection. If I were assembling a set of Morgan dollars I would want one of each of the 1880-CC.

I am often asked as to my opinion on how to start someone collecting coins—a son or daughter, a friend, or a business acquaintance. One of my popular recommendations is to have them buy an 1882-CC, 1883-CC, or 1884-CC dollar, study it carefully, and also read something about the history of the Carson City Mint. I also recommend buying a copy of *A Guide Book of United States Coins*. An hour or so spent leafing through the pages may or may not open the door to what I consider to be the world's greatest hobby. If it does, further steps include subscribing to one or more of the numismatic newspapers and magazines and building a small library (the Whitman Publishing web site or your favorite bookstore are places to start).

The Story of the Carson City Mint

In the late 1850s the western section of Nevada had few inhabitants and consisted of little except sparsely vegetated high prairie and mountain landscapes. Abraham Curry, who came from New York State, went to Nevada and purchased a tract of land on which he established Carson City in 1858. In local parlance, and also in numerous entries in the *Annual Report of the Director of the Mint*, the town was known simply as Carson.

In 1859 a band of travelers located gold- and silver-bearing black sand about 15 miles away from Carson City. Henry Comstock aggressively sought and gained control of the beginning operation, and soon exploited a very valuable property which eventually became known as the Comstock Lode. Although the district was primarily known for its silver, vast amounts of gold were also found there. Word of the bonanza spread westward to California, where many gold-seekers had found the yellow metal elusive during the "rush" and had been reduced to employment on farms, in stores, and in other less adventurous pursuits. The Comstock Lode beckoned, and by the early 1860s the district, centered in Virginia City, was teeming with miners, nearly all of whom worked as laborers in large mining operations. Unlike in the early days of the Gold Rush in California, in Nevada there was little opportunity for the one-man mine. Largest of all Virginia City operations was the sprawling Gould & Curry facility.

Prosperity was the theme of the day, and fortunes were made not only in mining but in railroading, gambling, and other related ventures. On March 2, 1861, Nevada was granted territorial status, and on October 31, 1864, it became a state.

From 1859 through the early 1860s, most gold and silver from Virginia City was shipped by rail to San Francisco, the leading financial center of the West Coast. The San Francisco Mint converted much of the

Those Carson City Morgan Dollars!

metal to coins. The bonanza of riches from the earth spawned a number of very powerful political figures in Nevada, and repeated calls were made to establish a mint in the state. This would give Nevada a status of its own and was envisioned as a giant step in the establishment of the state as an important financial center in its own right, as opposed to being a feeder to San Francisco.

In Washington, Treasury Secretary Salmon P. Chase favored a mint in Nevada, while Mint Director James Pollock felt that with existing mints at Philadelphia, New Orleans (inactive since 1861, when Civil War exigencies forced its closing), and San Francisco, a new mint would be redundant. It would make much more sense, he felt, to enlarge the San Francisco facilities, which at the time were cramped and poorly ventilated (this was eventually done, and a new building opened there in 1874).

A Nevada mint was to be, and the Act of March 3, 1863, set forth the necessary details for a beginning, including salaries for those employed there. One of the most powerful figures in Nevada was Abram (also spelled Abraham) Curry, an owner of the Gould & Curry mine and the man who founded Carson City. He sold the government a tract of land there in 1865. Following an authorization on July 18, 1866, construction began on a cut-stone building 60 by 90 feet in floor plan, two-and-one-half stories high, estimated to cost $150,000. When the project was finished in autumn 1868, costs had mounted to $426,000.

Thompson and West's *History of Nevada*, 1881, described the facility:

> Granite from the prison stone quarry. Pict style of architecture. Portico, Ionic. Hall, 12 feet in width; main hall 12x40; on the right of the entrance. Paying teller's office, 13x16 feet. Coining room, 19x19. Spiral staircase conducts above. Whitening room 10x14.5, with a vault in solid masonry 5x6. Annealing furnace and rolling room, 17x24. Gold and silver melting room 10x24. Melters' and refiners' office, 12x19 feet. Deposit melting room 14.5x19. Deposit weighing room, 19x19, with a strong vault 6.5x10.5 feet. Treasurer's office, 13x16, with a vault five feet square. Engine room, 16.5x53 feet. Beside which there is a cabinet, adjusting room, ladies' dressing room, humid assay room, assayer's office, assayer's room, watchman's room, two store-rooms, attic, basement. As a preventive against fire the floors are double, with an inch of mortar between. The foundations are seven feet below the basement floor and laid in concrete. Building two and a half stories high.

On November 1, 1869, a large Morgan & Orr press shipped from Philadelphia did a test run minting coins or tokens, the nature of which is not known today. There were delays, the dies for coinage did not arrive until early in 1870, and the first mintage for circulation was on February 10, when Liberty Seated silver dollars were made. In 1870 the silver quarter dollar and half dollar denominations were also made, as were gold coins of $5, $10, and $20 values. Dimes were minted in Carson City for the first time in 1871, trade dollars in 1873, and twenty-cent pieces in 1875.

In 1878, when Morgan silver dollars were first struck, other CC silver coins from the dime to the trade dollar were made for the last time. Later coinage consisted of silver dollars and the three same gold denominations.

From the outset the Carson City Mint was unpopular with many of the important figures in the silver mining and refining business. Curry was a competitor, and the thought of having him benefit from their ore was not pleasing. Apparently, the railroads cooperated in this situation against Curry, for tariffs were set up which made it cheaper to haul bullion hundreds of miles to San Francisco than 15 miles to Carson City! Actually, the equation is not as simple as that, for once minted, the coins would mostly have to be shipped to San Francisco or some other commercial center anyway, for the inhabitants of Nevada were not numerous enough to use much of the production in everyday commerce. As it turned out, Curry was superintendent for only a brief time. He left in September 1870 to make what turned out to be an unsuccessful bid for election as lieutenant governor on the Republican ticket. He was followed in the Mint office by H.F. Rice, erstwhile Wells-Fargo express agent.

Throughout the history of the Carson City Mint, many efforts were directed toward closing it down, including by the Treasury Department. Many allegations were made concerning the inefficiency of operations there, the poor security, poor refining practices, etc., few of which had any foundation in fact. Coinage of all denominations was suspended in 1886, and it was thought by some that the Mint would never

$20 Silver Certificate, Series of 1888. Newly minted silver dollars were segregated in Treasury Department vaults as backing for the currency. First called Silver Certificates of Deposit, these were authorized under the Bland-Allison Act of September 28, 1878, the same legislation that spawned the Morgan silver dollar.

reopen. But it did in 1889 and continued in operation into 1893. In 1900 it was realized that it would remain closed forever, and much of its equipment was sent to the Philadelphia Mint. In 1910 quantities of stored silver dollars were dispatched by rail to the Treasury Building in Washington, as stated above. Since October 31, 1941, the building has housed the Nevada State Museum, where various coin exhibits can be seen today.

Carson City in 1878

On February 28, 1878, President Rutherford B. Hayes signed the Bland-Allison Act. This was a nod to Western silver mining interests who were experiencing difficult times. Throughout the decade the price of the metal had been falling in the marketplace. This was caused by two primary factors: 1. In Europe the striking of high-silver-content coins was discontinued by some countries, and large quantities of earlier coins were melted, releasing quantities of bullion; and 2. In America the production of silver expanded with new discoveries in Utah and, in particular, Colorado. The new legislation provided for Uncle Sam to buy tens of millions of ounces of silver each year and convert it into silver dollars to facilitate storage and inventorying. As there was relatively little need for such coins in circulation, hundreds of millions piled up in vaults. In 1918, many were melted, as noted. Still, hundreds of millions remained. The act also provided for Silver Certificates of Deposit, initiating the currency series that became known simply as Silver Certificates.

In 1878 the new dollars were struck at Philadelphia, Carson City, and San Francisco. In 1879 New Orleans joined the group.

In that year *Frank Leslie's Illustrated Newspaper* was one of the most popular periodicals in the country. Each issue was filled with engravings depicting people, places, things, and events. To pique interest the publication started a serial story, "Across the Continent: The Frank Leslie Excursion to the Pacific." The February 23, 1878, instalment included this:

Those Carson City Morgan Dollars!

The commercial district of Carson City. The Mint is on the right. (*Frank Leslie's Illustrated Newspaper,* February 23, 1878)

A Visit to Carson City

Via the Virginia and Truckee Railroad we reach Carson City at seven o'clock of a Sunday morning. It is a sort of "halfway house" between Reno and Virginia City, and considers itself a fine thriving, full-grown town—quite an old-established one, having had twenty years' time wherein to improve and beautify and to run up its population to three thousand five hundred souls.

It is not a fair city to look upon—few of these Western centers of young civilization are such; it is only a straggling place set on a flat plain, with the glorious snowy "sierras" stretching away to north and south, a shining rampart behind which the sun goes down in glory. There are the usual broad streets with stone paved channels of clear running water on either side, in lieu of our muddy gutters of the East; sparse rows of cottonwood trees with their smooth, pale yellow

bark; square two-storied houses, in the most severely simple style of domestic architecture; planked sidewalks, stores, saloons; the long low railroad buildings and platform, and a little square enclosure of fresh, thick green grass, in the midst of which a fountain is playing, and scatters a wide cool shower as the breezes toss it.

Indians lounging along the line of the cars, of course—calico rags, red paint, blankets and papooses are their distinctive features; a few American citizens, clothed as with a garment in that careless self-sustained, half-barbaric freedom which influences the very cut of hair and beard, and the putting-on of the clothes, in a Far-Westerner; men and boys of all sizes, but as always, no women.

Being stationary for an hour at Carson City, we leave our car, and wander off on a stroll through the streets. They don't invite the pedestrian to a very extended ramble; in ten minutes one could make a brisk circuit of them all. There is the main street, running north and south, with its goodly stone buildings, the Mint and the State Capitol, and the straggling show of shops (most of them with open windows and doors, and a view inside of the proprietors making ready to open business for the day); the cross-streets, with their few neat and many shabby private dwellings, all of the peculiarly bare and utilitarian type prevailing in streets aforesaid—terminating in dreary no-thoroughfares of waste lots, strewn with ashes and old timber and barrel-hoops, and given over apparently to the Indian population, whose shanties are scattered about this Sahara; the solemn figure of a man, in a red blanket, stalking away from us, and disappearing in a low hovel in the lee of a great lumber-yard, and the shapes of two or three squaws, barefooted and with generously molded figures compressed with difficulty in their ragged calico gowns, remain among the pictures in our memories of Carson City. . . .

Besides the churches, the Capitol and Mint, Carson has a large and very excellent schoolhouse, and three good

The Nevada State Capitol. (*Frank Leslie's Illustrated Newspaper*, February 23, 1878)

hotels on the main street; two daily newspapers express the vox populi, and the society is said to be unusually good. This last statement we must needs take on faith, our social observations being confined to Indians and those specimens of the male population who tuck their pantaloons in their boots, cultivate many beards, and eschew "biled shirts"—a picturesque and essential element, if not a "high-toned" one.

Local Reception of the New Dollars

The Carson City *Morning Appeal* printed this article on April 17:

Dies at Last

Yesterday morning the new dies for the U.S. Mint arrived from Philadelphia. There were ten obverse, ten reverse, and six collars. The dies were hardened yesterday and the big Ajax press will start up today. There are 632,325 blanks ready for the press and when they get to work will turn out the dollars at the rate of 30,000 per day. We have had our little say about the dollars coined in Philadelphia, and how the Coiner here is driven to follow in his footsteps, or rather the press whacks, of the concern on the Delaware.

Great disgust was expressed at the general appearance of the dies. All that has been said as to the wretched workmanship of the Philadelphia dollar will be equally true of the Carson dollar, and it can't be helped. The die represents the same wide, flat, pelican-bat of the wilderness, and will show up all the defects of the coin. The C.C. in the

Those Carson City Morgan Dollars!

die is very indistinct, and looks as if it would turn out two periods. We wish it may, and that the inartistic appearance of the coin will lead the government to employ a new designer and give us a new die, dollar and deal. The United States ought to be ashamed to issue such a piece of workmanship, and at least should allow a small discount on the face of the thing.

The same edition noted this under the heading "Pencil Scratchings":

A few new dollars were struck off yesterday as samples.

Grumbling about new coin designs was typical. The *Argus*, published in Boston on March 26, 1793, quoting an account from New Jersey, gave this review of young America's first coin from the new Philadelphia Mint:

The American cents (says a letter from Newark) do not answer our expectations. The chain on the reverse is but a bad omen for liberty, and liberty herself appears to be in a fright. May she not justly cry out in the words of the apostle, "Alexander the coppersmith has done me much harm; the Lord reward him according to his works!"[4]

In fact, the *only* American coin ever to get consistent rave reviews was the MCMVII (1907) High Relief double eagle designed by sculptor Augustus Saint-Gaudens. Today, numismatists dearly love 1793 copper cents and George T. Morgan's silver dollars!

Carson City Morgan Dollars

I now give an overview of the 11 different dates of Carson City silver dollars, their mintages, and my estimates of surviving examples today.

1878-CC

1878-CC.

Mintage: 2,212,000

The Carson City Mint produced a large number of dollars of the new design, starting in April. (The production of dollar-size silver trade dollars had stopped shortly before.) Nearly all were very sharply struck—as continued to be the case for the majority of Morgan dollars made in this mint in ensuing years.

Dies prepared: obverse, 30; reverse, 30

Estimated quantity melted: 1,000,000 or more, mostly under the provisions of the 1918 Pittman Act

Approximate population MS-65 or better: 3,000 to 6,000

Approximate population MS-64: 10,000 to 20,000

Approximate population MS-63: 30,000 to 60,000

Approximate population MS-60 to 62: 120,000 to 160,000

Approximate population G-4 to AU-58: 75,000 to 125,000

Availability of prooflike coins: Fairly common semi-prooflike; DMPL coins are scarce, cameo DMPL more so.

Characteristics of striking: Usually very well struck.

Known hoards of Mint State coins: 60,993 were held back from the 1962 to 1964 Treasury release and subsequently sold by the General Services Administration. An estimated 100,000 to 125,000 or more additional coins were released by the Treasury during the 1940s, 1950s, and early 1960s.

1879-CC

Mintage: 756,000 (both varieties)

1879-CC, Large CC mintmark.

1879-CC, Large CC Over Small CC detail.

1879-CC, Large CC detail.

Tariffs posted by railroads made it cheaper to send silver bullion hundreds of miles distant to San Francisco for coinage than to send it 15 miles to the Carson City Mint, as noted above. As a result, silver bullion was scarce at Carson City, and the mint stopped production of dollars after only a relatively few had been coined. All coinage operations were suspended from March 1 to June 30, 1879, and again from November 1, 1879, to May 1, 1880.[5]

Apparently, 1879-CC dollars were rare in their own time. In a pioneering article he wrote on die varieties for *The Numismatist* in 1898, silver-dollar specialist George W. Rice had never seen an 1879-CC. On the other hand, Augustus G. Heaton, in his 1893 treatise, *Mint Marks*, noted that on the 1879-CC the mintmark is more over the D of DOLLAR than the space between the D and the O, and further: "It is not very common." Apparently, by 1893 Heaton saw or knew of at least several specimens.

LARGE CC OVER SMALL CC:

> *Approximate population MS-65 or better:* 20 to 40
>
> *Approximate population MS-64:* 300 to 500
>
> *Approximate population MS-63:* 800 to 1,200
>
> *Approximate population MS-60 to 62:* 1,750 to 2,500
>
> *Approximate population G-4 to AU-58:* 1,500 to 3,000
>
> *Availability of prooflike coins:* Prooflike coins are rare, and DMPL pieces are extremely rare
>
> *Characteristics of striking:* Average to below-average sharpness

PERFECT CC:

> *Approximate population MS-65 or better:* 125 to 150
>
> *Approximate population MS-64:* 900 to 1,300

Approximate population MS-63: 1,600 to 2,400

Approximate population MS-60 to 62: 3,250 to 4,500

Approximate population G-4 to AU-58: 3,500 to 5,000

Availability of prooflike coins: Prooflike coins are available, more so than for the Large CC Over Small CC. DMPL pieces are rare, but are more available than for Large CC Over Small CC.

Characteristics of striking: Ranges from average to fairly sharp.

Known hoards of Mint State coins (both varieties as a class): Harry J. Forman had a bag of 1,000 (ex J. Grove Loser). Loser had at least two bags, and C.J. Dochkus and Aubrey E. Bebee had one each. The Treasury had earlier unintentionally paid out another to someone in "Montana or Seattle." 4,123 were held back from the 1962 to 1964 Treasury release and subsequently sold by the General Services Administration. About 600 of these were the Large over Small CC variety, with the balance being the Small CC issue. Most were in grades MS-60 to MS-62 and extensively bagmarked. Probably about 10,000 or so Mint State coins remain today.

1880-CC

Mintage: 591,000 (both varieties; net 495,000 after melting)

The mint at Carson City suffered from sporadic shortages of silver, due to the local preference for shipping bullion to distant San Francisco. However, in 1880 enough metal was on hand that 591,000 dollars were made. Relatively few of these were passed into circulation at the time; most were stored at the mint. Coinage was suspended from November 1, 1879, to May 1, 1880. Some dies were made by overdating those of

1880-CC, Parallel Arrow Feather (PAF).

1880-CC, Parallel Arrow Feather (PAF) detail.

1880-CC, Slanted Arrow Feather (SAF) detail.

1879; see *A Guide Book of United States Coins* and other references.

In February 1881, the Assay Commission determined that a number of 1880-CC dollars were of insufficient silver fineness.[6] Because of this, 96,000 of them were subsequently melted at the mint, leaving a net production figure of 495,000 coins.

In the early days of the 1900s, the 1880-CC was virtually unknown in Uncirculated grade in collections. Typical grades offered in auctions ranged from Very Good to Very Fine. Apparently, 1880-CC dollars were released only in limited numbers at or near the time of coining, and after that no quantities were paid out by the Treasury. No one knew that vast numbers of mint-sealed bags still existed!

The 1880-CC dollars with Parallel Arrow Feather (PAF) are several times scarcer than those with the Slanting Arrow Feather (SAF). Probably, only 10 to 20 percent of the known Mint State coins of this date are of the second reverse. The market price of the PAF does not reflect this, as many numismatists opt to collect only one of this date and mint.

Dies prepared: obverse, unknown quantity; reverse, unknown quantity

Estimated quantity melted at later times: Possibly 300,000 or more, probably mostly in the form of mint-sealed bags, melted under terms of the 1918 Pittman Act; plus 96,000 melted at the mint in 1881.

Approximate population MS-65 or better: 15,000 to 25,000

Approximate population MS-64: 30,000 to 50,000

Approximate population MS-63: 70,000 to 100,000

Approximate population MS-60 to 62: 100,000 to 150,000

Approximate population G-4 to AU-58: 10,000 to 20,000

Availability of prooflike coins: Third Reverse coins are available but somewhat scarce. Second Reverse coins are very rare

Characteristics of striking: Striking quality varies widely. Many average and lightly struck pieces exist, as do sharply struck coins. Some have distracting planchet striations.

Known hoards of Mint State coins: 131,529 were held back from the 1962 to 1964 Treasury release and subsequently sold by the General Services Administration. Prior to that as many as 100 bags (100,000 coins) were paid out in the Cash Room of the Treasury Building, including at least several thousand coins that caused a market sensation in 1938.

1881-CC

Mintage: 296,000

1881-CC.

Coinage at Carson City was suspended from April 1 to October 1, 1881. Accordingly, only 296,000 silver dollars were struck in 1881, the second-lowest mintage of the early 1878 to 1885 series. By most standards, 1881-CC should be a rarity today. But it is not. Unlike the higher-mintage 1879-CC and 1889-CC dollars, large quantities of 1881-CC were stored by the Treasury, to be released 80 years later to delight a generation of numismatists unborn when the coins were made. Many dies were made, but few were chosen. Of 25 pairs of dies shipped from Philadelphia (where all dies are made) to Carson City, only a few were used.

Dies prepared: obverse, 25; reverse, 25

Estimated quantity melted: Relatively few

Approximate population MS-65 or better: 15,000 to 30,000

Approximate population MS-64: 40,000 to 55,000

Approximate population MS-63: 60,000 to 80,000

Approximate population MS-60 to 62: 70,000 to 90,000

Approximate population VF-20 to AU-58: 1,000 to 2,000

Approximate population VG-8 to F-15: 2,500 to 4,000

Availability of prooflike coins: Semi-prooflike coins are often seen. Full prooflike coins and DMPL pieces are readily available but are much scarcer than regular (frosty surface) Mint State coins.

Characteristics of striking: Nearly always seen sharply struck.

Known hoards of Mint State coins: Bags were released by the Treasury in 1954 and 1955—about 50, per the estimate of Steve Ruddel, who was active in the market at the time. Harry J. Forman had several bags from C.J. Dochkus in 1957 and 1958. Others came from storage at the San Francisco Mint in the late 1950s, and from the Treasury in 1962 to 1964. 147,485 coins were held back from the 1962 to 1964 Treasury release and subsequently sold by the General Services Administration; this latter figure amounted to more than half of the original mintage!

1882-CC

Mintage: 1,133,000

1882-CC.

In the silver-dollar department the Carson City Mint was busy in 1882 and 1,133,000 spewed forth from the presses by year's end, the highest production since 1878. But larger mintages were to come in 1883 and 1884.

Dies prepared: obverse, 15; reverse, 15

Estimated quantity melted: Possibly 200,000 to 300,000, nearly all under the 1918 Pittman Act and/or the 1942 Silver Act

Approximate population MS-65 or better: 25,000 to 35,000

Approximate population MS-64: 75,000 to 100,000

Approximate population MS-63: 150,000 to 200,000

Approximate population MS-60 to 62: 350,000 to 450,000

Approximate population G-4 to AU-58: 8,000 to 16,000

Availability of prooflike coins: Prooflike coins, including DMPL specimens, are plentiful on the market

Characteristics of striking: Most are very well struck, but a few are weak on the eagle's breast feathers and on the hair above Miss Liberty's ear.

Known hoards of Mint State coins: The Cash Room in the Treasury Building in Washington had a huge quantity of 1882-CC dollars. These were released sparingly over a period of time. Steve Ruddel stated that about 50 bags (50,000 coins) were released from the Treasury Building in 1955, and that many more came out before 1962. 605,029 coins were held back from the 1962 to 1964 Treasury release and subsequently sold by the General Services Administration. Others were released by the Treasury in the 1950s and early 1960s.

1883-CC

Mintage: 1,204,000

1883-CC.

The Carson City Mint was busy this year, and before the calendar turned over to 1884, some 1,204,000 silver dollars had been struck, virtually all from metal obtained nearby in the Comstock Lode.

Dies prepared: obverse, 10; reverse, 10

Estimated quantity melted: Very few; probably 100,000 or so at most

Approximate population MS-65 or better: 35,000 to 45,000

Approximate population MS-64: 110,000 to 125,000

Approximate population MS-63: 250,000 to 300,000

Approximate population MS-60 to 62: 500,000 to 550,000

Approximate population G-4 to AU-58: 12,500 to 25,000

Availability of prooflike coins: Prooflike coins are readily available, and even DMPL coins are seen with some frequency. The most common Carson City dollar with these finishes.

Characteristics of striking: Most are well struck,

although some other specimens have the eagle's breast feathers lightly defined.

Known hoards of Mint State coins: For much of the present century, a vast reserve of 1883-CC dollars was stored in the Treasury Building in Washington, D.C. From this source, examples trickled out over a period of years, with a significant release occurring in 1938 and 1939. Many bags were given out at face value in the 1950s, when dealers such as Charles J. Dochkus sought to buy them, but demand was such that the market could only absorb limited quantities. At the time, the wholesale price for a $1,000 face value bag was apt to be about $1,200—not a source of windfall profits. Steve Ruddel stated that about 50 bags (50,000 coins) were released from the Treasury Building in 1955, and that at least that many were released of all other CC-Mint Morgan dollars except 1879-CC, 1889-CC, and 1893-CC.[7] By the late 1950s, the Treasury stopped paying them out. 755,518 were held back from the 1962 to 1964 Treasury release and subsequently sold by the General Services Administration.

1884-CC

Mintage: 1,136,000

1884-CC.

1884 represented the last full year of operation of the Carson City Mint during the early period. In 1885 it would be open for coinage for only part of the year.

Dies prepared: obverse, 10; reverse, 10

Estimated quantity melted: Very few

Approximate population MS-65 or better: 30,000 to 35,000

Approximate population MS-64: 110,000 to 120,000

Approximate population MS-63: 350,000 to 375,000

Approximate population MS-60 to 62: 550,000 to 575,000

Approximate population G-4 to AU-58: 5,000 to 10,000

Availability of prooflike coins: Common in prooflike as well as DMPL. Most have cameo contrast and are in lower grade levels, although many high-grade coins exist as well. Tens of thousands survive totally. This is the second-most common (after 1883-CC) Carson City dollar with PL or DMPL finish.

Characteristics of striking: Usually seen well struck.

Known hoards of Mint State coins: The 1884-CC Morgan dollar is one of the most remarkable coins in the annals of silver-dollar history. The original production amounted to 1,136,000 pieces. Of that number, 962,638, amounting to 84.7% of the original mintage, were still in the hands of the Treasury Department after March 1964, when a halt was called to the great Treasury release that began in October 1962. Earlier, in 1938, bags of this date were also released, and during the 1950s the Cash Room at the Treasury Department paid out a further steady stream of 1,000-coin

bags. Steve Ruddel stated that about 50 bags (50,000 coins) were released from the Treasury Building in 1955.[8]

1885-CC

Mintage: 228,000

1885-CC.

The Carson City Mint was closed to coinage in November 1885, by which time 228,000 1885-CC dollars had been struck. 200,000 of these were made in January and February, and were thus listed as having been produced in fiscal year 1885 (July 1, 1884, to June 30, 1885). Additional coins to the amount of 28,000 pieces were struck in August 1885 (which was in fiscal year 1886), giving rise to the old-time theory that there were "1886-CC" dollars, which was not the case. All the mintage figures cited here are for calendar years, as is the case for listings elsewhere in numismatics today.

Although 228,000 1885-CC dollars were minted, it is apparent that very few were actually placed into circulation at the time. To suggest that as many as 28,000 were used in the channels of commerce might be an exaggeration, for today worn coins are few and far between and, in fact, are the rarest of all Morgan dollars in circulated grades (not including the Proof-only 1895, of which worn pieces are occasionally seen).

Dies prepared: obverse, 10; reverse, 10

Estimated quantity melted: Very few; perhaps 25,000 under the Pittman Act

Approximate population MS-65 or better: 15,000 to 20,000

Approximate population MS-64: 25,000 to 35,000

Approximate population MS-63: 50,000 to 60,000

Approximate population MS-60 to 62: 80,000 to 90,000

Approximate population G-4 to AU-58: 2,000 to 4,000

Availability of prooflike coins: Common. Many DMPLs have cameo contrast.

Characteristics of striking: Usually very sharply struck.

Known hoards of Mint State coins: Bags were released in the 1950s; 148,285 coins were held back from the 1962 to 1964 Treasury release and subsequently sold by the General Services Administration.

1889-CC

Mintage: 350,000

1889-CC.

The Carson City Mint, which had produced its last gold and silver coins in 1885, reopened on July 1, 1889. Coinage resumed in October.

Dies prepared: obverse, 10; reverse, 7 (at least 3 pairs were used from this quantity)

Estimated quantity melted: Unknown, but probably at least 250,000

Approximate population MS-65 or better: 80 to 150

Approximate population MS-64: 400 to 800

Approximate population MS-63: 1,500 to 3,000

Approximate population MS-60 to 62: 5,000 to 8,000 (including several thousand coins still undistributed in bags)

Approximate population G-4 to AU-58: 3,500 to 7,000

Availability of prooflike coins: Nearly 50 percent of all known Mint State coins have prooflike surfaces. Numerous DMPL coins exist, mostly at the MS-63 level or below. Population included in the above Mint State figures.

Characteristics of striking: Usually seen well struck.

Known hoards of Mint State coins: At least 1,000 coins and possibly as many as 3,000 were in the 1962 to 1964 Treasury release[9] and possibly as many as seven other bags (7,000 coins) came to light in the 1950s and 1960s. This coin is somewhat of an enigma in Mint State, for the actual market availability of coins and the number of pieces certified is much less than the number of reported mint-sealed bags would indicate.

The 1889-CC in Mint State is far and away the rarest Carson City Morgan dollar and handily outdistances its closest rivals, the elusive 1879-CC and 1893-CC. As such, it has acquired an aura of fame in recent years. Offerings of coins in higher grades are apt to be one at a time (instead of by the roll or bag). A Mint State coin is a candidate for a picture and effusive description in an auction catalog.

Further on hoard coins: When Carson City silver dollars were being paid out from the Cash Room at the Treasury Department in Washington, many thousands of all issues, 1878 to 1893, were distributed, except 1889-CC. Apparently only a few single coins and rolls were given out, some of them as early as 1933 and 1934. By the 1950s, possibly only a few hundred coins remained on hand at the Cash Room. I have found no record of bags being distributed from Washington during that decade or any time later.

It is probably the case that more 1889-CC dollars were stored at the San Francisco Mint and/or in bank stocks in the West than at the Treasury Building. In 1925 and 1926, quantities of 1889-CCs were paid out at face value from storage at the San Francisco Mint. Bags that came to light in the 1950s are all from the San Francisco Mint vaults, so far as I know. In the 1950s a bag of 1,000 pieces was released in Montana, followed by another in the early 1960s. Apparently the first bag contained many heavily marked coins, "sliders" if you will, of a quality that today would be called AU-55 or 58. In addition, at least two intact bags were in existence in 1976 (one of these is from the Ben Stack group mentioned below). Probably, these have not been distributed.

Harry Warner of Mill Valley, California, told Walter Breen that he once owned a bag of 1,000 coins. Ben Stack told Harry J. Forman that he bought two bags in 1954 by advertising in the Las Vegas Sun, and another was acquired in this way or by buying it separately. One of these bags went to Irving Davidoff, owner of the Klondyke Coin Exchange in New York City; another was dispersed at $140 per roll of 20 coins ($7 apiece); the third was still owned by Ben Stack as of February 1976, for he offered it to me at that time.

Only one solitary coin was left in the Treasury when the government decided to hold back CC dollars after payouts were halted in March 1964!

1890-CC

Mintage: 2,309,041

1890-CC.

Record mintage: The 1890-CC was minted in larger quantities than any other Carson City silver dollar. Many were released into circulation in the 19th century.

Dies prepared: obverse, 15 or more (?); reverse, 16

Estimated quantity melted: Probably more than 1,000,000 under the 1918 Pittman Act

Approximate population MS-65 or better: 1,000 to 2,000

Approximate population MS-64: 3,000 to 5,000

Approximate population MS-63: 10,000 to 20,000

Approximate population MS-60 to 62: 20,000 to 50,000

Approximate population G-4 to AU-58: 80,000 to 160,000

Availability of prooflike coins: A high percentage of Mint State coins are prooflike, usually DMPL, but nearly all are in lower grades, with bagmarks. Only 2 to 3 percent of DMPL specimens are MS-65 or finer.

Characteristics of striking: Usually seen well struck.

Known hoards of Mint State coins: Many bags were released from storage in the Treasury Building in Washington from the 1930s through the 1950s, and some were paid out in the 1950s from storage in the San Francisco Mint. In addition, 3,949 were held back from the 1962 to 1964 Treasury release and subsequently sold by the General Services Administration. Despite its record mintage the 1890-CC is somewhat scarce in Mint State in comparison to the typical Carson City dollar of the early 1880s.

1891-CC

Mintage: 1,618,000

1891-CC.

Hundreds of thousands of 1891-CC dollars were put into circulation in the late-19th century. Historically, the 1891-CC is one of just a few Carson City dollars that has been readily available ever since day one. During the century or so since the pieces were minted, Mint State coins have been among the most easily obtainable Carson City Morgan issues. However, after 1962 to 1964, when it was found that few remained

in Treasury hands in comparison to the large quantities of CC dollars in the early 1880s, the 1891-CC became scarce in a relative sense.

Dies prepared: obverse, 24; reverse, 23

Estimated quantity melted: Hundreds of thousands, probably mostly under the 1918 Pittman Act

Approximate population MS-65 or better: 1,400 to 2,200

Approximate population MS-64: 6,000 to 10,000

Approximate population MS-63: 20,000 to 40,000

Approximate population MS-60 to 62: 40,000 to 70,000

Approximate population G-4 to AU-58: 90,000 to 170,000

Availability of prooflike coins: Prooflike and DMPL coins are readily available. Nearly all are in grades below MS-65, and nearly all lack eye appeal.

Characteristics of striking: Usually seen well struck and with good luster, but there are exceptions.

Known hoards of Mint State coins: Many were held at the San Francisco Mint for storage. In 1925 and 1926, in the early 1940s, and particularly in 1942, many bags of these were paid out at face value—so many in the 1940s that silver-dollar dealer specialists such as Norman Shultz stopped buying them. By late 1942 the 1891-CC dollar was by far the commonest Carson City issue in collectors' and dealers' hands in Mint State. These continued to be paid out at face value to dealers and others in the 1950s, and also shipped as part of Nevada casino coins. Harry J. Forman bought at least

10 bags from John Skubis and Arnold Rosing; these originally came from San Francisco Mint storage. Numerous bags were released by the Treasury from the 1940s through the late 1950s. 5,687 leftover Treasury hoard coins were sold by the GSA in the 1970s (plus 19 later sold in a "mixed lot" offering).

1892-CC

Mintage: 1,352,000

1892-CC.

Hundreds of thousands of 1892-CC dollars were put into circulation in the late 19th century. Historically the 1892-CC, like the 1890-CC and 1891-CC before it, was never considered to be a rare date. Enough were dispersed at or near the time of mintage that examples have been readily available on the market. However, in comparison to some of the 1878 to 1885 Carson City dollars sold by the GSA in the 1970s, the 1892-CC is relatively elusive today.

Dies prepared: obverse, 10; reverse, 10

Estimated quantity melted: Probably hundreds of thousands under the 1918 Pittman Act

Approximate population MS-65 or better: 1,000 to 1,800

Approximate population MS-64: 3,000 to 5,000

Approximate population MS-63: 8,000 to 15,000

Approximate population MS-60 to 62: 20,000 to 35,000

Approximate population G-4 to AU-58: 75,000 to 140,000

Availability of prooflike coins: 1892-CC dollars with prooflike surfaces are scarce, and DMPL coins are scarcer. Exceedingly rare in MS-65 DMPL or finer. Most have deep mirror surfaces and if not extensively bagmarked are very attractive.

Characteristics of striking: Most are well struck, but some are flat at the centers.

Known hoards of Mint State coins: Scattered bags were released from storage in the San Francisco Mint in the late 1940s and early 1950s. The Redfield hoard (1976) is said to have had a bag or more of 1892-CC, but most coins were damaged by a counting machine. None were left in the Treasury Building to be sold by the GSA.

1893-CC

Mintage: 677,000

1893-CC.

After 1893 the Carson City Mint was closed to further coinage, although it remained in business as an assay office and refinery. Thus ended an era in American coinage and numismatic history. The Carson City Mint had produced coins from 1870 to 1885 and again from 1889 to 1893.

Dies prepared: obverse, 10; reverse, 5

Estimated quantity melted: Probably several hundred thousand under the 1918 Pittman Act

Approximate population MS-65 or better: 50 to 100

Approximate population MS-64: 1,000 to 2,000

Approximate population MS-63: 2,000 to 4,000

Approximate population MS-60 to 62: 15,000 to 30,000

Approximate population G-4 to AU-58: 4,500 to 9,000

Availability of prooflike coins: Prooflike specimens are elusive, and are usually flatly struck at the centers. DMPL coins are exceedingly rare.

Characteristics of striking: Usually weakly struck at the center, but exceptions exist.

Known hoards of Mint State coins: Mint bags of 1893-CC dollars came on the market as early as 1920 at face value through the Cash Room at the Treasury in Washington and, in particular, from storage at the San Francisco Mint. However, the quantity was small in comparison to certain other Carson City dates, particularly those of the early and mid-1880s. The supply seems to have been exhausted by the late 1950s, and there are no records of any quantities being paid out after that time. However, during the 1950s the 1893-CC was sufficiently plentiful that Harry J. Forman handled at least 10 bags (10,000 coins), and other quantities were bought and sold by other dollar specialists. One solitary coin turned up in the General Services Administration's holding held back in March 1964.

The Redfield estate contained several thousand coins, most of which were severely damaged. Regarding this, in 1982 in his *Morgan and Peace Dollar Textbook* Wayne Miller related the following: "One of the most amazing acts of incompetence in the history of numismatics occurred during the dispersal of the Redfield hoard. Apparently the company which was engaged to inventory and appraise the hoard ran several thousand Mint State dollars through a coin counter! The damage was most evident with the 1893-CC dollars, many of which evidenced a large, very noticeable scrape on Liberty's cheek or the eagle's breast. Although most of these dollars are well struck, with good lustre, they are virtually unsaleable." Today they do find a market but at deeply discounted prices.

The Oregon Trail Memorial commemorative half dollars were marketed in fits and starts and not at all consistently or successfully. Today, the 14 different date-and-mintmark varieties are highly prized by collectors.

Following the Oregon Trail

By 1926 quite a few commemorative half dollars had been issued to memorialize various people, places, and things—starting with the World's Columbian Exposition coins in 1892 and 1893.

There was little logic to certain of the issues. Alabama celebrated the centennial of its statehood in 1819, but after the fact persuaded Congress to issue appropriate half dollars in *1921*, some "plain" and others with 2X2 in the field, signifying its status as the 22nd state. Pilgrim Tercentenary half dollars were made in 1920, but with many remaining unsold, additional coins were minted with the irrelevant date of 1921. The 1924 Huguenot-Walloon half dollar honored the 300th anniversary of the settling of Huguenots and Walloons in North America, and the founding of New Netherland (today's New York City) in 1624. The obverse depicts Admiral Gaspard de Coligny and William the Silent, who had nothing to do at all with the celebration in question. Moreover, this was primarily a religious tercentenary and was sponsored by church officials, causing some justifiable dissent at the time.

Commissions or other groups, sometimes even single entrepreneurs, enlisted political connections to influence Congress to pass laws authorizing such coins. The cost to the issuers was only face value plus die preparation and shipping. They could charge whatever they wished when selling them.

The Oregon Trail

An omen of more illogical things to come occurred in 1926 when a group of entrepreneurs from New York City sought to memorialize by means of commemorative coins the travails endured by pioneers who migrated westward on the Oregon Trail in the early 19th century. The Oregon Trail never did pass anywhere near New York City, and 1926 was not the centennial or other significant anniversary of anything connected with the westward travels of people to the Pacific Northwest in the 1840s, but that didn't make any difference.

The Oregon Trail Memorial Association, Inc., a corporation organized under the laws of the State of New York, secured the approval on May 17, 1926, of a Congressional resolution authorizing:

> The coinage of 50-cent pieces in commemoration of the heroism of the fathers and mothers who traversed the Oregon Trail to the far West with great hardship, daring, and loss of life, which not only resulted in adding new states to the Union but earned a well-deserved and imperishable fame for the pioneers; to honor the twenty thousand dead that lie buried in unknown graves along two thousand miles of that great highway of history; to rescue the various

Commemorative Capers

Obverse of the Oregon Trail commemorative half dollar.

important points along the old trail from oblivion; and to commemorate by suitable monuments, memorial or otherwise, the tragic events associated with that emigration—erecting them either along the trail itself or elsewhere, in localities appropriate for the purpose, including the city of Washington.

Reverse of the Oregon Trail half dollar.

Further, the hitherto unprecedented quantity of "not more than six million" coins was authorized, a number eclipsing the overly generous five million authorization for the 1925 Stone Mountain issue—far more than needed.

On the surface the motivation seemed to be good enough, even if numismatically or historically illogical, for by 1926 the Oregon Trail was well known in history and legend, and doubtless many American citizens had family ties to the famous migration along that route.

Laura Gardin Fraser, by then the grand lady of commemorative half-dollar art, designed the obverse, and her sculptor husband James Earle Fraser, who had created the 1913 Indian Head / Buffalo nickel, designed the reverse. Mrs. Fraser did the models for both sides. The die hubs were the work of the Medallic Art Company of New York, which by this time had been an important player on the commemorative scene for years.

The obverse depicted a relief map of the United States behind the figure of an Indian facing to the viewer's right, a bow (spanning the continent) in his right hand and his left hand outstretched.

The reverse depicted a Conestoga wagon drawn by two oxen, heading to the left toward a setting sun of monumental proportions, with resplendent rays.

Minting and Distribution

Proponents of the issue were quick to realize that if varieties were created the market could be expanded. In 1926 the Philadelphia Mint struck 48,030 pieces, followed soon thereafter by San Francisco Mint pro-

duction of 100,055 coins, the first time that a single commemorative issue had been struck at more than one mint, setting a precedent which would be expanded and abused in the years to come.

The Oregon Trail Memorial Association offered the Philadelphia coins for $1 each, and sales got off to a good start. Eventually all were sold (except for 75 returned for remelting, probably consisting of mis-struck or damaged coins). The Association then requested an additional 100,000 pieces, these from the San Francisco Mint, which produced the coins in October and November of the same year. While thousands of pieces from the additional coinage were disposed of quickly, it was soon evident that the market had been saturated, and most of the mintage remained unsold. Still, the Association sought to have 1927-dated varieties made—but the Treasury Department declined until all of the 1926-S coins were delivered and paid for.

In 1928 at the Philadelphia Mint an additional 50,028 were made and put in a vault there. For the next five years collectors wondered what would happen to them, and several inquiries in this regard were printed in the pages of *The Numismatist*.

In 1933 the problem was solved, after a fashion, by the Mint's melting 17,000 unsold specimens of the 1926-S coinage, enabling the 1928 coins to be released by the Treasury Department. Are you following this? Certainly it was confusing to numismatists at the time.

Early in 1933 sales of 1928 coins (and also unsold 1926 and 1926-S coins) were handled by the Oregon Trail Memorial Association, which found an indifferent reception to its offerings. Coming to the rescue was the Scott Stamp & Coin Company of New York City, which agreed to market the issues under what it stated was an exclusive contract. Well-known numismatist Wayte Raymond, representing the Scott interests, suggested that the 1928 half dollars be made "rare" by melting all but 6,000 of them.

Raymond, who had saved the day somewhat by selling at least some of the 1928 issues, now desired to capitalize on the gullibility of collectors and their need to complete sets by having more varieties coined. He figured that if additional Oregon Trail half dollars could be minted with the date 1933, they could be sold effectively at the Century of Progress Exposition held that year in Chicago.

The Scott firm, billing itself as "sole distributor of Oregon Trail half dollars," advertised in *The Numismatist*, September 1933:

> The Oregon Trail Memorial Association issues a new half dollar dated 1933 to commemorate the Century of Progress. 5,000 1933 half dollars were struck at the Denver Mint; 2,000 have been reserved for patriotic societies; 3,000 are offered to the public.
>
> 1928 Oregon Trail half dollars. None ever sold until this year. All of these coins, except 6,000 pieces, have been remelted by the U.S. Mint. We offer the 1928 and 1933 half dollars at $2.00 each. Postage and registration extra.

As it turned out, 242 of the 1933-D half dollars, probably defective, were later returned to be melted, resulting in a net distribution of 5,008 pieces. This represented the first time the Denver Mint produced commemoratives. The various mints experienced difficulty in striking the Oregon Trail halves, and numerous pieces were rejected because of weakly struck rims.

And Still They Come

Wayte Raymond contemplated what the Scott organization should do and decided to proceed full speed ahead by promoting additional varieties from different mints and in relatively small quantities and selling them into three markets: the general public, coin collectors, and speculators. It turned out that speculators, while they may have been interested in other things, did not take a fancy to the Oregon half dollars, perhaps because the series had a bad reputation by that time. Besides, America was deep in the economic Depression. Individual collectors and dealers absorbed a few thousand of each of the succeeding issues, and relatively few others were sold to the general public.

In 1934 at the Denver Mint 7,006 Oregon Trail half dollars were minted, followed by a 1936 Philadelphia coinage of 10,006, and by 1936 San Francisco coins in the amount of 5,006. In 1937 Oregon Trail halves were struck only at Denver, and to the extent of 12,008, a large figure for the time. Up to this point, issue prices had been quite erratic. The 1926 and 1926-S pieces had been offered for $1 each. Then when Scott got into the act the price was doubled; and the 1928 issue, released in 1933, went on the market at $2 per coin. Seeking to increase sales, in view of the tremendous unsold quantity of 1928 issues, the 1933-D was pegged at a slightly lower $1.50. That didn't stimulate activity to the extent desired, so for the 1934-D the price was raised back to the $2 level. In due course the issues of 1936 and 1937 were listed at $1.60 each. All of this was confusing at the time.

Raymond promoted and sold the Oregon Trail issues dated from 1928 through 1936, save for some quantities set aside by the original Association for direct sale in bulk to historical societies. Apparently 1936 coins were sold by both the Scott Stamp & Coin Co. and the Oregon Trail Memorial Association, the latter doing business from a mail drop at 1775 Broadway, New York City.

Over a period of time the promoters assigned special names to certain issues. Thus the 1926 was known as the Ezra Meeker coin (Meeker, still living, had traveled the route in 1851), the 1928 as the Jedediah Smith issue (Smith was an explorer of the American West and led a group of pioneers to *California* in 1826), the 1933-D as the Century of Progress Exposition half dollar, the 1934-D as the Fort Hall, Fort Laramie, and Jason Lee coin (a confusing, catch-all name; Lee was a missionary), and, finally, the 1936-S was designated as the Whitman Centennial coin, also referred to as the Whitman Mission coin (the mission of Marcus Whitman was to convert Indians to Christianity; Whitman, his wife, and 12 others were killed by Cayuse warriors in 1847). The names attached to these half dollars were not widely publicized and were little heeded by collectors and are almost completely forgotten today.

Twilight on the Trail

Oregon Trail issues of 1937, 1938, and 1939 were marketed by the Association, by which time the arrangement with Raymond and Scott had been discontinued. In 1937, Oregon Trail half dollars were minted only at Denver, to the extent of 12,008 coins. These were offered for sale at $1.60 each.

In 1938 Oregon half dollars were issued for the first time as a set from all three mints, with a coinage of 6,006 for Philadelphia, 6,005 for Denver, and 6,006 for San Francisco, the odd specimens being reserved for the U.S. Assay Commission. Sets of three were advertised for $6.25 each. The final and lowest mintage in the series consisted of 1939 sets of three pieces made to the extent of 3,004, 3,004, and 3,005 respectively at the various mints. The price was raised to $7.50 per set.

By the end of 1939, well over a decade after the original coinage of 1926, only 264,419 Oregon Trail half dollars had been minted, a far cry from the six million authorized, and, deducting 61,317 returned for melting, just 202,928 had achieved distribution or were still on hand in the stocks of the Scott Stamp &

Coin Company and the Oregon Trail Memorial Association. As late as 1943 an outfit named the American Pioneer Trails Association was attempting to sell quantities of 1936 and 1937-D halves. Several observers later suggested that, if Congress on August 5, 1939, had not forbidden further issues of commemorative coins authorized prior to March 1939, Oregon Trail coins would probably still be minted today! Wayte Raymond kept some for himself. Years later I bought some of these through John J. Ford Jr. and Olga Raymond, Wayte's widow.

Collecting Oregon Trail Half Dollars

In his 1937 monograph, *The Commemorative Coins of the United States*, well-known coin dealer B. Max Mehl stated: "This is one of the most beautiful, artistically designed, and well struck coins of the entire series." To list other accolades would take many pages. Suffice it to mention that some years ago when the Society for U.S. Commemorative Coins (SUSCC) surveyed its members to determine their favorites from hundreds of motifs created from 1892 to date, the Oregon Trail half dollar was the hands-down winner.

As most of the coins were sold to dealers and collectors rather than the general public, today nearly all are well preserved—in choice Mint State or finer. One in Very Fine grade would be a rarity.

The quality of the surface finish on the various Oregon Trail issues is different, with earlier examples tending to be frosty and lustrous and later issues, particularly those dated 1938 and 1939, having somewhat grainy or satiny fields.

Arranged in a collection by date sequence, a set of the 14 different varieties associated with this long-lived series makes an attractive exhibit. However, relatively few individuals have attempted to form such except as part of a complete overall commemorative collection. I am an exception, and about 10 years ago I asked Melissa Karstedt, an auctioneer and associate at my company who has a sharp eye for quality, to hand-pick for me a complete set, which she did over a period of time by cherrypicking for quality. (I also had her do this for a set of Peace silver dollars from 1921 to 1935.) With careful examination she found "high-end" certified MS-64 coins, most of which are very inexpensive considering their rarity, that are as nice as many certified as MS-65.

You might want to give it a try.

Here is a summary of the 14 varieties:

Oregon Trail Half Dollars, 1926–1939

Figures are for the total number minted plus the net number actually distributed (many of the earlier issues were melted)

1926 • Mintage: 48,030 • Distributed: 47,955

1926-S • Mintage: 100,055 • Distributed: 83,055

1928 • Mintage: 50,028 • Distributed: 6,028

1933-D • Mintage: 5,250 • Distributed: 5,008

1934-D • Mintage and distribution: 7,006

1936 • Mintage and distribution: 10,006

1936-S • Mintage and distribution: 5,006

1937-D • Mintage and distribution: 12,008

1938 • Mintage and distribution: 6,006

1938-D • Mintage and distribution: 6,005

1938-S • Mintage and distribution: 6,006

1939 • Mintage and distribution: 3,004

1939-D • Mintage and distribution: 3,004

1939-S • Mintage and distribution: 3,005

THE SOCIETY OF MEDALISTS FIRST ISSUE

LAURA GARDIN FRASER, *Sculptor*

THERE are many persons who desire to collect medals but are unable to do so because the medal is used in most instances as a specific award. The scope of subject matter which bears no relation to a particular person or occasion embraces many forms of expression and the sculptor has a large field of choice. In this case, I felt that a sporting subject would be a departure from what one has been accustomed to seeing in medallic art. Therefore, I chose the hunter with his dog because it presented the opportunity of telling a story embodying a human and animal element. It has been studied as to correctness of detail so that it should have an appeal to those who are interested in out-of-door life. The ruffed grouse forms the reverse. It may be considered as a national game bird and is distinct in character and very decorative.

It is to be hoped that there is sufficient merit in the rendering of this work to appease the collector whose interest is in the art of the medal.

Laura Gardin Fraser

THE SCULPTOR

In recognition of her achievements in sculpture, Laura Gardin Fraser has been awarded the Watrous gold medal, the Shaw Memorial prize, the Helen Foster Burnett prize of the National Academy of Design. She personally deems the most distinguished honor that of the American Numismatic Society Saltus gold medal given on the art of the medal.

In competition with several sculptors, her designs were chosen for the Congressional medal presented to Colonel Charles A. Lindbergh, the official George Washington medal of the Bi-Centennial Commission, the National Geographic Society medal to Admiral Richard Evelyn Byrd, the American Bar Association medal, the National Sculpture Society award, the Horse Association of America Polo and Irish Setter Club medals.

Among horse lovers, she is best known for her life-size portrait statue of Fair Play, sire of Man o' War, now to be seen on the estate of Joseph E. Widener in Kentucky.

Society of Medalists issue No. 1 by Laura Gardin Fraser, The Hunter.

Two Medals by the Frasers

Under the auspices of the American Federation of Arts, the Society of Medalists was formed by railroad man and philanthropist George Dupont Pratt and others in 1928, with the purpose of encouraging interest in medallic art. Subscribing members were to receive two medals each year, designed by artists and sculptors of high rank and reputation. It was announced that if 1,000 members would join, the annual dues would be $8. By January 1929 nearly 200 had signed up. The first medals were issued in 1930 to great acclaim. The 129-medal series endured until 1995, when orders received by the Society became insufficient to sustain the costs of operation. By a decade later interest was gaining momentum and several of the varieties are now quite difficult to obtain.

The Medallic Art Company, with its Janvier pantographic equipment, was the ideal choice for a mint, because it allowed artists to model their designs in a 9- to 12-inch format, to be mechanically reduced onto medal dies. Almost every important sculptor in the country submitted potential designs to the Society's review committees, who extended the invitation to create a medal to just two artists per year.

The first five participants, Laura Gardin Fraser, Paul Manship, Hermon MacNeil, Frederic MacMonnies, and Lee Lawrie, were thrilled to have total control over the subject matter, design, shape, metallic content, and finish—something not available to them as commissioned makers of commemorative and award medals. They were joined by a stellar lineup of successors: John Flanagan, Herbert Adams, Carl Jennewein, Chester Beach, Walker Hancock, Adam Belskie, James Earle Fraser, Marcel Jovine, Karen Worth, Alex Shagin, and many more. The result of all that unleashed talent and imagination was a 65-year-long emission, representing 129 different artistic approaches and as many creative visions.

Laura Gardin Fraser created No. 1 in 1930 and James Earle Fraser created No. 45 in 1952. The medals and their descriptive leaflets are shown here.

THE SOCIETY OF MEDALISTS
ARCHITECTURAL LEAGUE, 115 EAST 40TH STREET, NEW YORK
FORTY-FIFTH ISSUE   June 1952

JAMES EARLE FRASER
Sculptor

FROM THE ARTIST

My belief is that in art wherever possible we should use the lore of our people. With this thought in mind I selected two of the most romantic, hazardous and important subjects of our pioneer days, the Prairie Schooner and the Pony Express.

These were not fairy tales, but very real events so I have treated them realistically.

As a small boy in Dakota, I saw prairie schooners crossing the plains. They went the full distance to their objective. With the pony express, however, only one object went all the way and that was the medalla which was changed from pony to pony and rider to rider. In ten days the mail was carried the distance from Westport, Missouri, to San Francisco.

These were great and thrilling adventures in American history.

James Earle Fraser

ABOUT THE ARTIST

FRASER, JAMES EARLE: Sculptor: b. Winona, Minn. Nov. 4, 1876: s. Thomas Alexander and Caroline E. (West) F: ed; pub. schs. Mitchell, S. D. Chicago, Minneapolis: Chicago Art Inst., Ecole des Beaux Arts and Colorossi and Academy Julian, Paris: Nov. 27, 1913 m. Laura Gardin. Instr. Art Students League, New York, 1906 to 1912.

At the age of seventeen modeled portrait bust of John Riley and made a model for the equestrian statue "The End of the Trail."

Several other works of this period were lost in a fire; in particular a bust of his father.

Went to Paris at twenty years of age. Through winning a competition for best work of art in the American Art Association, attracted the attention of Augustus Saint-Gaudens. Assisted him for two years, principally on the Sherman statue.

In 1902 made a marble portrait relief of Baby Hathaway Brewster.

In 1902-3 made a model for an equestrian statue of Cherokee Indian, eighteen feet high, for St. Louis World's Fair, and a seated statue of Thomas Jefferson.

Among the portrait busts are: Sonny Whitney, Jock Whitney, A Basque, Sage Goodwin, June Evans, Henrietta and John Deming, Sherman and George Pratt, Roland Harriman, Theodore Roosevelt for the Capitol, Washington, D. C., Theodore Roosevelt for San Juan Hill, Cuba, Robert Bacon, Eastman Chase, Pat Ford, Warren Delano, Senator Elihu Root, John Nance Garner, Harvey Firestone, a mask; Young Artist, Metropolitan Museum; Dr. William-Polk; Augustus Saint-Gaudens.

Among the heroic statues and memorials: John Hay, Cleveland; Bishop Potter, St. John the Divine; Alexander Hamilton, south portico of the Treasury Bldg., Washington, D. C.; Albert Gallatin, north portico of the Treasury Bldg., Washington, D. C.; Thomas Jefferson, Merriwether Lewis, William Clark in Jefferson City, Mo., Capitol; John Ericsson monument in the Mall, Washington, D. C.; Canadian Officer in Winnipeg, Canada and Figure of Victory, Montreal, Canada, for the Bank of Montreal, both won in international competition; the Mayo Memorial Statues, Rochester, Minn.; Heroic Statue of Lincoln at beginning of Lincoln Highway, New Jersey; General Patton Statue at West Point; Benjamin Franklin, Springfield, Ill; Marble statue of Franklin for Franklin Institute, Philadelphia.

Among the symbolic sculptures are: Two heroic figures at the front of the Supreme Court Bldg., Washington, D. C.; Pediment with twelve figures, all double life size on the south facade of the Archives Bldg., Washington, D. C., one of the two largest pediments ever made; Four pediments, fifty feet long, twelve figures in each pediment, one and one-half life size, carved in stone; New York State Memorial to Theodore Roosevelt, an equestrian statue with four granite portrait statues of Audubon, Daniel Boone, William Clark and Merriwether Lewis on the columns over the portico, figures thirteen feet high, carved in granite; Two Bridge Groups in Chicago on Michigan Avenue, north end of the bridge; Four figures, seven feet high in the Elks Memorial, Chicago; Primitive Inventor, Water Power, figure in front of City Hall, Niagara Falls; Pioneer Women; Two Equestrian Groups each nineteen feet high for Lincoln Memorial Plaza, Washington, D. C. Collections of his medals have been bought by the Governments of Italy and Belgium.

Honors: Awarded two Gold Medals, one for the art of the medal and the other for sculpture in the round, Panama, P. I. Exposition 1915; Saltus medal for Art of the Medal; Awarded Medal of Honor, National Sculpture Society; The Century Association's Medal of Honor; The Gold Medal of the American Academy of Arts and Letters and National Institute of Arts and Letters.

Decorated Knight Order of Vasa (Sweden). Elected National Academy 1917; member National Institute of Arts and Letters, (V.P.); Academy of Arts and Letters; Member National Sculpture Society (President 1925-26); Century Association, Architectural League, National Arts Club.

Home: Eleven O'Clock Roads, Westport, Connecticut.

Society of Medalists issue No. 45 by James Earle Fraser, New Frontiers.

CHAPTER 39

Over a long period of years many hobby leaders have shared their passion for numismatics. Here is a selection from The Numismatist, *official journal of the American Numismatic Association. Today in the world of automation and instant gratification it is interesting to revisit the spirit of yesteryear as reflected in these commentaries.*

"What They Say" About the World's Greatest Hobby

Dr. George F. Heath

May 1900

"The secret of success in coin study is to go slowly over each specimen, examine it with reference to size, weight and material, view the portrait from different positions, study the armor and decorations, decipher, letter by letter, the inscriptions, supplying the abbreviations—in short, follow the order in which our descriptions are given.[1] Attend to only one thing at a time. To dwell on each topic until a perfect mastery of that is secured is a sure way to make acquisitions profitable and subsequent progress easy, rapid and delightful."

A.B. Coover

September 1908

"A well-conducted hobby is a necessary auxiliary to every man's business or profession. To the businessman, the professional man, the man who does the hardest kind of labor, the possession of a hobby is a safety valve by which he eases the strain and pressure brought to bear upon the various parts of the body. To the man who spends a stated number of hours each day in the pursuit of his profession or trade, a few minutes, or hours, spent in a different line of thought, will rest, as nothing else will, the various nerve centers which are soon run down by long continued use.

Hobbyists are of different types. Some collect simply to gather objects or to satisfy personal whims, but the true hobbyist is one who was not content to acquire, but also had to know the details connected with his collection.

Knowledge of the origin, use, and material is of more value to the man with the hobby than the object itself. The collector who gathers about him a large collection of coins, stamps, or other objects, and who does not make an effort to learn all of the available history of the same, loses a greater part of the pleasure that is to be had in the ownership of a collection. However, as much as he is to be pitied, he must not be condemned, for at some future time his collection may fall into the hands of one who will appreciate it in the proper manner."

John W. Scott

December 1910

"Fine coins have proved to be about the best investment of modern times. U.S. cents which were bought for a few dollars 20 years ago now sell readily at 10 times their cost, while gold has got beyond the reach of all but the very rich. A $2½ gold piece which sold at auction for $39 lately changed hands at $3,000, and the demand is greater than the supply.

To derive either pleasure or profit from coin collecting the cabinet must be formed on some definite plan. A desultory accumulation of the coins of various nations will never increase in value while a complete collection in any line is always valuable. Take for instance the proclamation coins of the Spanish kings in South America. They can be bought cheap when found and are veritable numismatic historic documents, proving the sovereignty of the king in all the towns and territories for which they were struck. Or one can find another line cheaper still, equally interesting and referring to our own country.

The quaint series of 'store cards' bear business advertisements of our early merchants. Family histories may be traced, business locations defined and trade combinations studied on these interesting tokens. They were apparently used by all for we find pieces issued by conjurers and undertakers, shoemakers and blacksmiths, jewelers and grocers, in fact every calling is represented and nearly every city of consequence in the country commemorated. They commence with the birth of our country, remain plentiful up to the middle of the Civil War, and reach from Canada to New Orleans. Many can be purchased at five and 10 cents each, which in future years will realize as many dollars, when got together in a representative collection showing the extent and commerce of our country."

Frank C. Higgins

January 1911

"The difference between the collector and numismatist may be almost precisely likened to that between what is commonly called a builder and an architect. Both represent appreciation, capacity, activity, interest and zeal, both are mutually helpful, but the latter represents just so much more profundity of research, technical ability, scientific attainment and professional training than the former.

The main appeals of a coin are its history and artistry."

"What They Say" About the World's Greatest Hobby

Waldo C. Moore

December 1918

"It is difficult to give any general advice about collecting; it is a matter of taste. If one means to become a collector, and not merely a possessor, it is wisest to choose perhaps a somewhat limited field. To collect everything numismatic means to acquire much that does not interest, and therefore one often becomes discouraged. The more acquired the more one finds there is to be gotten, and the farther one seems to be from a constantly receding goal. Decide what interests most and then make the tackle. In this way the collector may in time be able to assemble a collection that will be worthwhile.

Now and again the collector may hear of a certain specimen of numismatic art fetching a very large price indeed, and so be led to believe that that represents its market value; the consequence being that should another piece of the same design be placed within reach, he may think it a very good stroke of business to buy it for something less than was paid for the first. The fact is, that until one is made fully aware of all the circumstances, and perhaps sentiments, associated with the sale of any numismatic item for what seems to be a high price, one cannot pronounce any opinion as to whether the price was excessive or the reverse; and it is most unsafe to take it for granted that because a thing sells for a certain price to a certain collector today it will sell for the same price to a different collector tomorrow.

It is in the possession of some special line, after all, that the real joy lies. Numismatics is a broad term. The average dealer in numismatics has a hotchpotch of unrelated specimens on tap. The collector does not want his collection to be like that unless he be the proprietor of a town museum. The average collector should choose some special line in numismatics and follow the same consistently, seeking for the finest examples in season and out.

A collection is desirable when it means something. The collection should be made a means, not an end. There is a charm and beauty in it when it is chosen with good judgment, which the devotee can never adequately express nor the Philistine ever understand."

Theodore J. Venn

February 1920

"My observation has been that the majority of collectors either have been so from early manhood or else have taken it up as a diversion after the more active portion of their life had been spent. In other words, few numismatists are made between the ages of 25 and 50.

Consequently, our main efforts must be directed toward the younger generation and those who have passed the meridian. The intervening years appear to be a period of hibernation so far as creating much enthusiasm in numismatics is concerned. There are exceptions, of course, but these merely prove the rule."

Thomas L. Elder

February 1923

"Not nearly all the best collectors are made by starting out when young men. DeWitt Smith did not commence to collect until late in life. Mr. Clarence Bement started to collect when around 60 years of age. The start in many cases was made very quickly and without previous sober thoughts of coin collecting. The taste to collect coins seems to come as a sort of flash or inspiration suddenly acquired. But I do say the collecting instinct, the instinct to collect something, was already present. That instinct was not so suddenly born. All of these noted collectors had already made collections of other objects.

One of the fortunate things to remember is that nearly every young boy at some period of his youth wants to collect something. Nearly all boys have the stamp fever. That fever may be only a rash which comes up brightly and then entirely disappears, but it is a favorable sign. It shows the youthful mind is impressionable. One of the things I most regret about present-day American college education is that less stress than ever is put on historical and classical studies. The average college student today takes a scientific course, or at least he is perhaps less apt to take a course in history than in any other study offered. College statistics prove it.

A lack of taste for history usually means a lack of imagination. If a young man takes a good serious course in history while at college, he will, if he ever collects coins, make the most desirable sort of a collector. If he doesn't, he is more apt to make a date collector. Now, date collectors are all right, and we need them, but the point I want to emphasize is that far more knowledge is gained from historical coins than from a series of dates on the same kind of coins. More knowledge of art is also gained through a study of art and historical coins than the others."

Winston S. Churchill

August 1926

"Many remedies are suggested for the avoidance of worry and mental overstrain in persons who over prolonged periods have to bear exceptional responsibilities and discharge duties upon a very large scale. Some advise exercise, and others, repose. Some counsel travel, and others, retreat. Some praise solitude, and others, gayety. No doubt all these may play their part according to the individual temperament. But the element which is constant and common in all of them is change.

Change is the master-key. It is not enough merely to switch off the lights which play upon the main and ordinary field of interest; a new field of interest must be illuminated. The cultivation of a hobby and new forms of interest is therefore a policy of first importance to a public man. To be really happy and really safe, one ought to have at least two or three, and they must all be real."

"What They Say" About the World's Greatest Hobby

Thomas Mayr

January 1928

"The hobby from which I have derived the greatest pleasure and which has been the most valuable to me is collecting old coins. Why I started to collect I do not know. I had several old coins, but did not take any interest in them. Then one day came to me the inspiration to collect coins. Why, whence and how I received the inspiration, I know not. Probably from some exaggerated advertisement or article which told of the fabulous fortunes to be made by knowing coins. Although I soon found out the very valuable coins would hardly ever come into my possession. I still persevered in collecting, for I had discovered how worthwhile and valuable the hobby was.

The best thing about the hobby is its creation of a desire for further knowledge of the countries which issue money. I say best, because an inspiration to strive for learning is here gained that could not be received elsewhere. When once received, this desire cannot be resisted. When a coin from a little known land is procured, one is sure to look up the history and geographic conditions of that country. Thus, knowledge is gained for which one would not have thought of looking before."[2]

Spink & Son, Ltd.

December 1928

"Lucullan Luxury: You do not know what a denarius is? Lucullus once spent 50,000 of them on a single supper in ancient Rome, so it was an $8,000 affair!

What did the parrot say? 'Pieces of eight. Pieces of eight!' Long John Silver taught him the byword of the Spanish Main; and you don't know what it meant!

Coins, all kinds, are the very essence of history. We can show you both denarii and pieces of eight if you are intrigued."

Harvey L. Hansen

February 1929

"A great many collectors simply collect for the pleasure of collecting and possessing. They are not to be criticized so much as they are to be sympathized with. They are losing the best part of collecting, that which comes from connecting their finds and possessions with the knowledge of the world in history, art, heraldry, geography, economics, and so forth. So many of us in our daily rush find time pressing and do not take the trouble to study seriously the pieces that come into our hands.

Let me plead for a relatively small collection, every piece of which the collector is familiar with in a thorough manner. The question then arises, where shall we find out about the coins in our possession? The books you will need are not always available in local libraries. These will, from time to time, be quoted in our American numismatic publications, in auction catalogues, and especially in European catalogues. Spink's *Numismatic Circular* lists many every month, so do German and French publications.

In order to avail yourself of these offers I would suggest that some of the money you plan to spend for coins be spent for reference books. In other words, budget your spendable resources and follow a definite program. Not so romantic, perhaps, but productive of results. Books are necessary in order to make you a numismatist instead of a collector. *Research* is the word every collector should become familiar with and practice."

Charles N. Schmall

June 1932

"The majority of sincere coin collectors are individuals in moderate circumstances, who make up for their lack of wealth by their honest enthusiasm for their chosen hobby, their fidelity, their love of the beautiful, their taste for art, and their fondness for the numismatic memorials that have descended to us from the dim and distant past to delight us with their mute messages from our revered forefathers.

The true collector buys without counting the cost or contemplating the possible future losses or profits; he is free from the cold, calculating

designs of the mere hoarder or speculator. To him, an old coin is not to be scorned nor despised merely because of its poor presentation due to the ravages of time, or its cheapness of price. Every antique coin is entitled to its share of respect, be it cheap or costly; intact or impaired; Fine or Poor. The dealer who refuses to handle the cheaper grade of coins misses a large and lucrative clientele.

I have, in my collection, coins ranging in price from two cents to $250. Strange to say, I have derived the most pleasure from the coins costing less than 50 cents each.

When I meet a collector who boasts that he admits into his cabinet only the highest rarities in the finest condition I know immediately that he can never make the acquaintance of about 98% of the available pieces, and that he is totally devoid of the instincts and attributes of the true collector. From such a deluded and misguided dilettante I flee as quickly as from a contagious disease lest I be infected with the germ of sordid commercialism and robbed of the genuine pleasure to be found in real collecting."

Robert K. Botsford

July 1933

"It is absolutely necessary for a well-balanced individual to have both a vocation and an avocation.[3] The vocation feeds the body. The avocation feeds the soul. There is a distinct place for both of these activities, and it is not wise to go to extremes with either one.

"What They Say" About the World's Greatest Hobby

The border line of each blends into the other with a nicety. Yet each individual must maintain a physical and a mental poise in order that he may escape the ravages that beset the fanatic.

Mr. Average Citizen is a coin collector and is generally interested in odd or unusual dates, designs or figures. He wants to know the whys and wherefores. But, as a general rule, there is no individual to whom he can turn for immediate information that is of a comprehensive nature. This situation is similar to the child who wants to know the great facts of life, and knows not where to inquire concerning them. It is really surprising to find that the bankers of our country are but slightly versed in numismatics. In fact, it is quite rare to find a banker who is even a coin collector to any marked extent. True, he has accumulated a number of odds and ends that he values but little. So, if one is desirous of traveling on the numismatic path he must depend on what he can pick up from dealers' catalogues and other odds and ends of numismatic literature that he is able to secure.

Coins—gold, silver, nickel, copper—of this age and of the ages long since gone by are a medium of exchange recognized for their bullion value at any period and any time. They speak the universal language of values known and recognized by mankind. History is written upon their faces. Great events are recorded on the coins used by man. The likenesses and images of the world's famous personages are handed down to posterity on the coins of the various nations. . . .

The great numismatists of the United States are the kindliest of men, ever ready and ever willing to be of service. They take great pride in their collections and are always ready to show their choice specimens to those who will appreciate the rarity and handle properly.

Just go to visit some well-versed numismatist and find out what a real man he is. Call on him and let him see and know how much you are interested. Why, my friend, you have a treat in store for you that will live for years as one of the happiest, most pleasant memories of a lifetime. Words cannot give you the revelation that you will receive of what a brother really is until you spend some hours with such a man. That is, providing you are a numismatist at heart and long to learn the vast facts of the world's coins and how this kindred spirit has acquired and taken care of the specimens that have come into his possession. . . ."

And for good measure, this:

Dr. Dean Miltmore

November 1945

"As a coin collector in a modest way, my observations, while attending those who are seriously ill mentally, may be of some interest to your readers. In the course of years I have seen a thousand cases, (not all in institutions) and I have yet to see or hear of a single one who was even an indifferent collector of coins or of other objects of collectors' interest.

As for the practical application of this fact, collecting can hardly be used as a means of treatment for those actually in a mental institution; there the emphasis for the convalescents is principally on manual training. But for the average person, with the cares and worries of everyday life, a collector's hobby (coins, stamps, or something of the sort) should have a definite place in mental hygiene. This of course does not exclude other recreations, such as nature study, out-of-door sports, and scouting for instance. When evening comes, I know of nothing better to get one's thoughts off his troubles, real or imaginary, and to compose his mind for sleep, than an hour or so with his coins.

This need not be an expensive hobby; it may be much less so than the theatre. A coin need not be rare—the eagle cent of 1857 is as interesting as that of 1856. A coin need not be in fine condition. For the purpose under discussion, an ancient bronze that requires an hour or so to remove the corrosion and bring out the inscription may be better than one that needs no such treatment. If successful, it gives a splendid thrill. It is good mental hygiene. The cares that infest the day shall fold their tents like the Arabs, and as silently steal away.

Essay on Snakes in Ireland: There are no snakes in Ireland.

Essay on Numismatics and Insanity: Coin collectors do not become insane."

CHAPTER 40

It was not until the 1840s that there were at least several dozen collectors of coins in America. Here I discuss the hobby prior to the opening of the Mint Cabinet in 1838. A nod to Joel Orosz for certain information in this chapter, most particularly about Pierre Eugène Du Simitière and Gilmor. See also my book American Numismatics Before the Civil War, *1998.*

The Beginning of Numismatics in America

In 18th-Century England

Halfpenny-size copper token satirizing the collectors of such pieces.

In America the art and science of numismatics received a large boost in June 1838 when the Mint Cabinet was opened. In the next decade at least a couple of hundred, probably more, collectors were active. In 1857 when the small-diameter Flying Eagle cent replaced the traditional large copper cent, interest multiplied tenfold or greater. Other surges in the hobby took place when in 1883 the new Liberty Head nickel created a nationwide sensation, another in the 1930s when "penny boards" and albums became popular, and another in 1960 when the Small Date Lincoln cent and the launch of *Coin World* combined to change the primary emphasis of the hobby from collecting to investing. Today in the age of computers and instant gratification, many call numismatics an *industry*. To me it remains an art and science, as it was in the beginning.

In sharp contrast, in Europe the collecting of coins had longtime traditions by the time of the American Revolution, and by the late 1780s the typical collector in London could consult a shelf full of reference books, bid in auction sales, and visit museum exhibits of coins. In England the discipline had been particularly popular since the late 1780s, when a flood of halfpenny-size copper coins bearing political motifs, advertisements, slogans, illustrations of buildings, and other subjects reached circulation. The collecting of these became a pleasant pursuit in the British Isles, and in time a number of firms in Birmingham (in particular) and other cities produced many issues especially for numismatic sale. One of these was self-deprecating and bore the legend ASSES RUNNING FOR HALF PENCE.

Many British numismatists desired to add a few coins to their cabinets from that former British possession, America. Thus in the 1790s, when

Wondrous animals could be seen at Bayley's Museum at 212 Piccadilly in London, per this token. Depicted on the obverse is a rattlesnake, a reptile found only in North America. (29.7 mm)

collectors in the United States were not saving their own country's specimens, such pieces were avidly collected on the other side of the Atlantic.

Meanwhile, in the United States there is not a single record of a collector who was interested in, for example, the copper coins of Vermont when they were struck from 1785 to 1788, or, a few years later, the copper cents and half cents of the 1790s. Today it is difficult to envision tens of thousands of citizens contemplating mint-fresh 1793-dated cents and then simply spending them!

Pierre Eugène Du Simitière

The earliest numismatically inclined person in America for whom we have a fairly detailed biographical record was Swiss-born Pierre Eugène Du Simitière (1737 to 1784), who settled in Philadelphia by 1774.[1] Among his sources for specimens was John Smith, of Burlington, New Jersey, who furnished him with desired pieces by 1766, and possibly as early as 1763. Du Simitière later remembered that Smith's holdings were "considerable." In the same decade, a Major James, of Philadelphia, is also said to have had a cabinet of ancient coins as well as modern European pieces and was in touch with Du Simitière on matters numismatic.

Not only did Du Simitière collect specimens, but he was also involved in the production of medals for the Continental Congress. Accordingly, he prepared a sketch depicting General Washington standing with a figure of the goddess Liberty or Columbia, overlooking Boston Harbor.[2] This commission is reflected by a payment made by Congress on November 29, 1776: "Paid P.E. Du Simitière for designing, making and drawing a medal for General Washington, $32." However, this medal was never produced. Next was a medal that Du Simitière seems to have designed, struck, or caused to be struck, and was actually used in the Revolutionary War. A newspaper account related on August 12, 1776:

The Congress have struck a number of silver and copper medals, which are distributed among the officers of the army, who wear them constantly. On one side are two vases swimming on the water, with the motto 'Frangimur si collidimur';[3] on the other is an emblematical device; four hands clinched together and a dove over them, beneath them is a serpent cut in pieces. These medals were designed or executed by P.E. Du Simitière.[4]

A 1737 Higley copper threepence. (Eric P. Newman Collection)

On April 26, 1779, Du Simitière wrote about numismatics to Governor George Clinton of New York, noting in part, "Coins and medals ancient and modern I have collection of, but now a days these are become scarce, notwithstanding I meet with some now and then."[5] By this time his cabinet included seven (!) rare Higley copper coins of the 1737 to 1739 era and nine Massachusetts silver pieces as part of an inventory of 135 specimens. In 1783 he wrote to Clinton to see if he had any old paper money issued by the State of New York.[6]

Later Du Simitière prepared an outline titled "Sketch of a Plan of a Work intended to illustrate the Revolution in North America by Medals, Seals, Coins,

Devices, Statues, Monuments, Badges &c," which was never expanded into monograph or book form.[7]

By this time his American Museum, founded in April 1782 at his home on Arch Street, above Fourth Street, Philadelphia, had attracted wide attention and even some gifts. A small coin was given by a Lutheran minister, Reverend John C. Kunze, whose "very fine collection of coins and medals" was donated to the New-York Historical Society by his heirs on July 14, 1818, but was later stolen in its entirety from that institution.[8]

Du Simitière died in October 1784. A half year later, on March 19, 1785, the contents of his American Museum were dispersed under the auctioneer's hammer. The listing included lot 19, "A mahogany Cabinet containing ancient and modern Gold, Silver, and Copper Coins and Medals; among which there are some very curious bronzes," and lot 36, "A collection of Parchment and Paper Money." The buyer of lot 19 seems to have been Matthew Clarkson, whose own estate was later auctioned on October 29, 1800, and which included "a valuable cabinet, containing silver and copper coin, medals &c. some of which are very ancient."[9]

Eliot and Andrews

Among other pioneer numismatists was Reverend Andrew Eliot (1718 to 1778), pastor of the famous Old North Church in Boston, who by 1767 had an extensive cabinet which included many New England silver coins.[10]

Silver issues of New England, produced from 1652 until the early 1680s, were widely circulated in the Northeast. Most famous were the Pine Tree shillings. Most early American cabinets of coins included a few specimens of such pieces.

Another early Boston numismatist of note was John Andrews, a hardware merchant at No. 4 Union Street, per the first Boston directory (published in 1789). By that time he had been a selectman since 1785, a position he continued in until 1790. It was related decades later that his residence was "a beautiful

A 1652-dated Pine Tree shilling. The various Massachusetts Bay Colony silver coins circulated widely in the Northeast for many years. (Die variety Noe-1) (Richard August Collection)

estate at the northerly corner of Winter and Tremont [then Common] streets—an antique wooden house in the midst of a delightful garden, extending down Winter Street, in the rear of what is now Hamilton Place." The home had been occupied earlier by Sir Francis Bernard, British governor of Massachusetts, perhaps until he was recalled to England in 1769.

A letter from Andrews to William Barrell, of Philadelphia, December 25, 1772, asked him to procure on his behalf any genuine ancient coins he might find. In later years Andrews moved to Jamaica Plain, near Boston. Eventually, his estate coins were purchased by the secretary of the Massachusetts Historical Society on behalf of that institution.[11]

William Bentley

In 1787, William Bentley, D.D., of Salem, Massachusetts, entered in his diary some interesting observations of coins then in circulation, creating one of the earliest records of the types known to exist.[12] His notes for September 2, 1787 included:

> About this time there was a great difficulty respecting the circulation of small copper coin. Those of George III, being well executed, were of uncommon thinness, and those

stamped from the face of other coppers in sand, commonly called "Birmingham," were very badly executed.[13] Beside these were the coppers bearing the authority of the states of Vermont, Connecticut and New York, etc., but no accounts how issued, regularly transmitted.

The Connecticut copper has a face of general form resembling the Georges, but with this inscription, AUCTORI: CONNEC: The edge plain, but the face fretted on one side near the edge. On the reverse is a woman resembling the Britannia of the English coppers with the staff & cap of liberty in one hand & the branch of peach in the other & shield behind, the inscription INDE: ET: LIB: underneath, 1787, & late dates.

among the thirteen. A rising sun over the mountains to denote the Green Mountain boys, a name assumed in the war, & a plow below. Inscriptions forgotten. Of all the executions the Vermont is the most perfect. A mint is said preparing for the Commonwealth of Massachusetts. It may be noted that the New York and Connecticut coin face opposite ways.

The New York copper is like the other excepting that it has no fret on the face near the edges & has the following inscriptions. On the face, NOVA EBORAC: separated by roses. On the reverse, VIRT. ET. LIB: underneath 1787.

On the *Vermont coppers*, a specimen of which I have not before me, are new emblems adapted to their own condition.[14] A new star appearing

To remember all the coin which passes through my hands, I note down a few coppers of foreign coins, Swedish coin, shield, three bars, lion, etc., 1763, measures one inch and 3-10; another 1747, similar; Russian, a warrior on horseback with a spear piercing a dragon, on the reverse a wreath infolding a cypher.

This was part of the entry for September 16, 1787:

> In removing a stone wall in Mystic or Medford, in 1783, there were found under it a large collection of brass pieces nearly square, mixed with the smallest brass coins of Europe, the whole half a peck. A few round ones have a fleur-de-lis stamped on each side of them. . . .

This on September 26, 1787:

> A coin circulated with the apparent authority of Vermont. A star with an eye in the centre and between the rays other stars in number thirteen. On the reverse a wreath in which is enclosed the cyphers U.S. Inscription Libertas et Justitia. 1785.[15]

The Columbia in the Pacific Northwest in what would later be the Oregon Territory. (*Ship Columbia in Oregon* sketch by George Davidson in the Bostonian Society, Boston)

His diary on October 3, 1787, included this, with no introductory comments:

> Silver and copper medals for Capt. Kendrick on a voyage to the Pacific Ocean. On one side a ship and sloop under full sail, with the words Columbia & Washington commanded by J. Kendrick. On the reverse the following, "Fitted at Boston, North America,

for the Pacific Ocean by" encircling the names of J. Barrell, S. Brown, C. Bulfinch, J. Derby, C. Hatch, J.M. Pintard, 1787. Kendrick sailed Sept. 20, 1787.

The cents and half cents are said to have the device on one side, the Spread Eagle of the Union, encircled with the word "COMMONWEALTH." On the reverse an Indian with his bow & arrow, surrounded with the word "MASSACHUSETTS." Coin of the Massa. Commonwealth.

The Columbia & Washington medal.
(Massachusetts Historical Society)

1776 Continental dollar struck in pewter.

Several years later on July 20, 1791, his entry included mention of another collector:

> Being Commencement at Cambridge [Harvard College], I set out for Cambridge from Deacon Ridgeway's and in a chaise went to Judge Winthrop's[16] with whom I spent the day. In the morning I entertained myself with his curious cabinet of Coins and Medals. It was large and not with any antiques, but it had a great variety of small pieces and may be deemed the best we have in this part of the country. It is improving its value by constant additions, but it requires too great an interest in this country, to have its full success.

The diary entry for September 15, 1791, verifies that Bentley had done some reading on numismatics and was a keen observer of current issues.

> Watson, in the fourth volume of his Chymestry, has the following: "It is reported of King James II, that he melted down and coined all the brass guns in Ireland and afterwards proceeded to coin the pewter with this inscription, Melioris Lessera Fati." The Congress in America had recoursed the same expedient; they coined several pieces of about an inch and a half in diameter, and of 240 grains in weight on one side of which was a circular ring near the edge, Continental Currency, 1776, and within the ring a rising sun with Fugio at the side of it, shining upon a dial under which was Mind Your Business. On the reverse were 13 small circles joined together like the rings of a chain, on each of which was inscribed the name of some one of the 13 states. . . .
>
> I have been particular in the mention of this piece of money because, like the leaden money which was struck at Vienna when that city was besieged in 1529, it will soon become a great curiosity. I have estimated the weight of a cubic foot of this Continental Currency. It weighs 7,440 ounces. This exceeds the weight of a cubic foot of our best sort of pewter, and falls short of that of our worst. I conjecture that the metal of this Continental Currency consisted of 12 parts of tin and one of lead.[17]

Bentley's diary entry on October 23, 1795, describes his work with an important cabinet (of which little is known today):

> Busied myself to provide catalogue of coins for Mr. [Samuel] Curwin's collection for Mr. Winthrop. Such collections are rare in this country and in some parts utterly unknown. This is the largest that I have ever seen. The real antiques in silver, are an Athenian City, a Greek City, a Consul, Scipio, Juba, Julius Caesar, Augustus, Tiberius, Claudius, Hadrian, Marcus Antoninus. There are also a considerable number of copper and Mantuans, which the connoisseurs must distinguish. Among the modern is to be found a MARYLAND coin, Cecilius C Lord Baltimore. A Specimen is to be seen of all the modern coinage in this collection.

This notation of April 10, 1802, tells more about Curwin:

> Last night departed this life Samuel Curwin, Esq., at 87. . . . He was a merchant of Salem. . . . The times of the American Revolution were no times for him. . . . He left America and went to England. . . . The remains of a valuable Library were sold just before his return by his nephew Richard Ward, Esq., and it was sacrificed. A rich collection of coins was robbed of its best pieces. . . . He was an excellent antiquarian and I profited much from the few things he had saved from the destruction which befell his library, cabinet and private papers.

In the same era several other museums and libraries added coins to their collections. The Philadelphia Museum (aka Peale's Museum and the American Museum), established by artist and naturalist Charles Willson Peale in 1784, had a cabinet of coins and medals which was sold to P.T. Barnum in the mid-1840s.

In March 1861 the rebellious Southern states needed paper currency for their newly formed Confederate States of America. They turned to an unlikely source: New York City.

The CSA "Montgomery Notes"

March 1861

The $1,000 "Montgomery Note," one of four denominations printed for the Confederacy by the National Bank Note Co. in the spring of 1861, before the Civil War commenced. The portrait of Senator John C. Calhoun of South Carolina is at the lower left, and that of Andrew Jackson is at the lower right. Both images were used widely elsewhere, including Jackson on a United States 2¢ "Black Jack" postage stamp. The overlapped petals surrounding the Roman number M in the denomination are of the "cycloidal configurations" patent held by National. Signed by Alex. B. Clitherall, register, and E.C. Elmore, treasurer of the CSA.

In March 1861 officials of the newly formed Confederate States of America desired to have paper money for their new country, never mind that the government of the United States of America, or Union, did not recognize the existence of the Confederacy. In March 1861 they made arrangements with the National Bank Note Co., located in *New York City*, to print new currency. This was done, and beautifully. The bills were imprinted with the location of Montgomery, Alabama. Today collectors call them Montgomery Notes.

The Act of March 9, 1861, authorized such notes. These instructions were given: "Notes are to be at one year at the rate of one cent per day for every hundred dollars. Put the calculation on the back. None to be below fifty dollars."[1]

The bills, today numismatically considered as *treasury notes*, were printed in March, the same month they were ordered, in sheets of four notes arranged $50-$100-$500-$1,000. The interest-bearing information was printed on the face of each note in the final version, with the back left blank. By April 2, a shipment of 607 sheets was in the hands of Secretary of the Treasury C.G. Memminger in Montgomery. They had barely escaped capture; officers of the ship carrying the CSA notes refused to comply with an order by federal authorities to stop and be boarded in the harbor of New York City. The bills were sent (likely in uncut sheets) on April 8 to Treasurer E.C. Elmore. Today, these are known as "Montgomery Notes" by numismatists. Later bills by other printers have the address given as Richmond, where the capital moved.

The Confederacy felt that more money could be raised by selling smaller denominations.[2] Accordingly, 999 half-sheets were printed with the $50 and $100 values. These denominations did circulate as currency.

$500 "Montgomery Note."

$100 and $50 "Montgomery Notes."

After war was declared on April 15, 1861, the National Bank Note Co. surrendered the Confederate plates to agents of the Treasury Department, and the American Bank Note Co. did likewise for plates it had made to produce CSA bonds.

Considering the animosity of the North toward the Confederacy, how did this unlikely scenario happen? Here is the story.

The Confederacy

There had been great friction between the North and the South for many years, resulting from slavery throughout Dixie, while in the North slavery was not permitted and the abolition movement was strong. Slave labor was necessary to raise and harvest the crops, especially of cotton, where unceasing toil under the hot sun was required. President James Buchanan, elected in 1856, spent the four years of his administra-

tion trying to appease both sides, but satisfied neither.

By early 1860 the presidential election of November 6 was in the offing, and hopefuls in the North and South were well underway in their planning. After much posturing the nominating conventions were held. On May 18 Abraham Lincoln was chosen by the Republican Party. The Democratic Party met in Charleston to pick a nominee, but confusion and dissention reigned and many delegates bolted. The result was that the Southern Democratic Party split off and chose John C. Breckinridge by default, and the Northern Democratic Party proposed Stephen A. Douglas, whose earlier debates with Lincoln had made national figures of both debaters . The recently formed Constitutional Union Party, which hoped to hold the North and South together, fielded John Bell of Tennessee. The campaign ensued. Key in Lincoln's platform was the abolition of slavery.

In November, Lincoln won by a landslide. This was unacceptable to many leaders in the South. They felt the abolition of slavery, if it happened, would destroy the economy. On December 20, South Carolina seceded from the Union, followed in short order by other states. In early 1861 the Confederate States of America was formed with its capital in Montgomery, Alabama (moved later that year to Richmond, Virginia). The new Confederacy desired to go about its business in a normal way, trading with other countries including the United States, referred to as the Union. Congress no longer had jurisdiction, and slavery could continue as before, with traditions dating back to before the Revolution. Presidents from the

South had been slave owners, starting with George Washington. In 1861, residents of the South knew of no other social system.

Southern militia began arming and training for the protection of their new nation. The Confederate government formed a committee to explore future relations with that *other* country, the United States of America, while much commerce continued in the meantime. In contrast, Northerners, probably the majority, were not interested in such a scenario. By then the Confederates were viewed with contempt by many as secessionists or rebels who needed to be brought back into the Union, and soon. In sharp contrast, many hoped for

$20 note of the Bank of Commerce, Savannah, Georgia, signed by G.B. Lamar as president. From a plate by Danforth, Wright & Co., Philadelphia and New York. Ink-dated May 4, 1857. The Bank of Commerce was one of the most important financial institutions in the South. It operated into the Civil War, and then closed.

George H. Lovett's "Gallery of Traitors" token of 1861 listed individuals formerly important in the United States who decamped to the Confederacy in 1861. This is no. 1 in the series, but no later tokens are known to have been issued. John Bell had been a candidate for the United States presidency in the election of 1860. Howell Cobb had been secretary of the United States Treasury.

peaceful coexistence and saw no reason to continue arguments about slavery and other matters. By that time there was great uncertainty in the economy. On January 15, 1861, the *London Post* told this:

> The monetary intelligence from America is of the most important kind. National

bankruptcy is not an agreeable prospect, but it is the only one presented by the existing state of American finance. What a strange tale does not the history of the United States for the past twelve months unfold? What a striking moral does it not point? Never before was the world dazzled by a career of more reckless extravagance. Never before did a flourishing and prosperous state make such gigantic strides affecting its own ruin.

At the time the federal government was indeed at an impasse. President James Buchanan in the last months of his presidency remained helpless. Cash reserves in the Treasury were low—the result of confusion caused by the succession, lack of revenue, and poor planning. Meanwhile, many congressmen, government appointees, and other officials left Washington and headed to the South to their homes and families. Secretary of the Treasury Howell Cobb was among them. This caused wide resentment, and many charges of disloyalty and traitorism were printed in the Northern papers.

Lamar, the Entrepreneur

To facilitate commerce with the Union and also to obtain needed items, the Confederacy made secret arrangements with Gazaway Bugg Lamar, a banker and businessman who was president of the Bank of the Republic, headquartered in its own impressive building at the corner of Broadway and Wall Street. The National Bank Note Co. was at the same address. Lamar was a man of considerable wealth, with investments in several different businesses, mainly in the South. In the 1850s an ocean-going steamship and a Nashville & Chattanooga Railroad locomotive had each been named after him. He was also involved in the Great Western Marine Insurance Company, based in New York but controlled by Southerners. Simultaneously, Lamar was president of the Bank of Commerce in Savannah, Georgia, one of the largest financial institutions in the South.

In the 1850s, as a supporter of James Buchanan during the presidential election of 1856, he established close ties with appointed officials in the federal government, including the head of the Custom House in New York City, who was empowered to examine, or else choose to overlook, certain maritime activities, including of Lamar's shipping interests. After Abraham Lincoln's election in 1860 and before the Confederate States of America was formed, rebellious South Carolina needed munitions. Through John B. Floyd, Buchanan's secretary of war, Lamar arranged for South Carolina to purchase 10,000 muskets from the federal arsenal at Watervliet, New York.

Georgia seceded from the Union in January 1861. Three days later, on the 21st of the month, New York City police superintendent John Alexander Kennedy confiscated 38 crates of weapons purchased for Georgia by Lamar, and awaiting shipment to the South. In retaliation, the governor of Georgia ordered the seizure of New York ships in the Savannah harbor. Finally, through action of Secretary of War Floyd and New York City mayor Fernando Wood, Lamar was able to resume filling various orders for arms placed by his friends in the South.

In March he placed the order for paper money with the National Bank Note Co., and in a separate transaction the American Bank Note Company was enlisted to make bonds for the new nation. No publicity was given to this or Lamar's other dealings, although they were legal at the time. At the time, the Confederacy officials and commercial interests of the Confederacy viewed New York City as a normal place to conduct to sell $1 million in Confederate bonds through Lamar's bank in New York City.[3]

The National Bank Note Co.

The National Bank Note Co. was organized in November 1859 by men who had been with Danforth, Perkins & Co. earlier. By that time the American Bank Note Company, formed in March 1858 by the consolidation of eight printing and engraving firms, had most of the business of printing paper money, bonds, stock certificates, and other security items. After the Panic of 1857, relatively few new banks were formed. Still, there was business in replacing older notes. Although the field of opportunity was narrow, several dozen banks switched from American to National, and National secured contracts with some newly formed banks.

The National notes were usually more ornate than those of its main competitor. Most were embellished with "cycloidal configurations," this being the process whereby repeated engraving, often including the denomination of the bill, was arranged in lobes or overlapping petals as well as in latticework overlays containing inscriptions. This technique was patented in 1860 and was trumpeted as highly important in preventing counterfeiting.

In 1860 contracts for security printing were made by National with the Treasury Department and the Post Office. (Postage stamps had always been printed by private firms, who often used bank-note vignettes to illustrate them.) Later, on August 15, 1861, National landed a contract to make all stamps for the next six years, a major coup. Later still, it printed certain federal currency.

When the National Bank Note Co. was formed in 1859, James T. Soutter, then president of the Republic Bank and the Great Western Marine Insurance Company (and married to G.B. Lamar's daughter), was named vice president and trustee. Souter's name was also on the side of a Nashville & Chattanooga Railroad engine. Connections were certainly complex! By arrangement between both of Lamar's banks, Bank of Commerce notes from Savannah could be redeemed at the Republic Bank in New York for a charge of three-tenths of one percent.

Fort Sumter

In the meantime in the North the government made plans to reinforce federal facilities in the South. Early in April a naval fleet with about 2,000 men and a large amount of supplies headed southward to reprovision Fort Sumter, in Charleston Harbor, and Fort Pickens, off Pensacola, Florida. Word of this reached General Pierre G.T. Beauregard, commander of the Confederate forces at Charleston. After communicating with his superiors, on April 11 he held a meeting with Major Robert W. Anderson, who was in charge of the fort and about 100 men, and commanded him to evacuate. This Anderson refused to do. Early the next morning fire from Fort Moultrie on the shore was opened. For the next 34 hours bombardment reduced most of the fort to rubble. Miraculously, no lives were lost. On April 15, President Lincoln and Congress declared war. In the North this became known by some as the War of the Rebellion or the War of 1861. "Civil War" as a general term did not come until later. In Dixie many called it the War of Northern Aggression.

On April 26, 1861, the *New York World* gave details of what happened with the bank-note companies. The day before, United States deputy marshals Bersch and Horton "made an important seizure" at the offices of the American Bank Note Company, of 18 printing plates made for the Confederacy. More from the account:

The officers of the company state that they ceased printing from them as soon as the president's proclamation was issued. The informer against them asserts that they were being printed as late as four days ago. An hour after the above seizure the United States deputy marshals entered the office of the National Bank Note Company and took into their keeping two plates of cancelled Treasury Notes of the Southern Confederacy, of the denominations of $50, $100, $500, and $1000.

The engraving of the plates is of the best quality, and not unlike the United States Treasury Notes now in circulation. The presidents of both companies are held to await investigation in the matter."

It was not until July 13, however, that Congress formally authorized Lincoln to suspend commerce between the North and the South (and it was not until August 16 that the ban was fully implemented).

Postscript

In May 1861 Gazaway Bugg Lamar left New York City and took up with the Confederate cause. Later investigations revealed that he had been in the slave trade in the late 1850s and that in late 1860 and early 1861, before the onset of hostilities, he had engaged in covert operations in New York City on behalf of the Confederacy, these beyond his facilitating the shipment of arms to South Carolina and Georgia.

Lamar was never called to account for any of his illegal or treasonous deeds. He continued to live well and enjoy his prosperity.

In January 1861 Congress conducted investigation into certain questionable activities of Secretary of War John B. Floyd. It was learned that the shipping partnership of Russell, Majors & Waddell and several other express companies were in deep financial troubles in the late 1850s. Certain of these virtually bankrupt firms had close connections to Secretary Floyd, who started a letter-writing campaign to persuade bankers and other moneyed interests to loan large amounts of money against expected revenues from freighting contracts to be placed by the War Department. From March 1858 until just before the election of 1860, the incredible sum of $5,036,127 was placed through what became known as "Floyd acceptances," as Floyd endorsed the loan papers with his own signature. It was a sure-fire investment.

With fresh money on hand Russell, Majors, & Waddell set about reorganizing their businesses, renaming one the Central Overland, California & Pike's Peak Express Company (an appealing title, as Colorado was in the midst of the "Pikes Peak or Bust" gold rush). The company circulated information that it was going to get a contract for overland mail valued at up to $900,000 per year. However, the contract did not materialize, and other operations experienced great problems as well. When the first Floyd acceptances came due, there was no money to pay. In September 1860 a meeting of acceptance holders was held in St. Louis, where it was stated than an infusion of an additional $200,000 would carry the company through the temporary crisis, which was also alleviated with

money embezzled from the federal Indian Trust Fund. The situation came out in the open in December 1860 when it was realized that the Floyd acceptances were completely worthless.

With such information on hand, on January 29, 1861, three perpetrators, including Floyd, were indicted by the government for conspiring to "combine, confederate and agree together by wrongful means to cheat, defraud, and impoverish the United States." This included stealing or falsifying records of federal bonds and trust funds, arranging for large shipments of munitions to be shipped to the South, and other actions.

Floyd resigned his Cabinet post and decamped to the South, where he became an important official in the Confederacy. George H. Lovett, New York die sinker, soon memorialized him on his "Gallery of American Traitors" medal of 1861.

CHAPTER 42

An Extraordinary Gem

The record-breaking 1794 silver dollar, the first coin to sell for more than $10 million.

What does it take for a coin to break the $10 million ceiling?

A $10 Million 1794 Silver Dollar

The silver dollar of 1794, the first year of issue, has always been one of my favorite coins. It is estimated that about 140 survive from an original mintage of 1,758 pieces. Most of these show wear, often extensive. A very "nice" example in a major collection over the years was, and is, apt to grade Fine to Very Fine.

In 2012 Martin Logies, a specialist in dollars and the author of a book on early issues, consigned to Stack's Bowers Galleries his Cardinal Collection. The highlight among more than 100 scarcities and rarities was the finest-known 1794 dollar. The story was told in this news release.

> IRVINE, Calif. (January 24, 2013) — Leading rare coin auctioneer Stack's Bowers Galleries conducted one of the most highly-anticipated events in numismatic history on January 24, 2013 with the sale of the record-setting Cardinal Collection. The highlight of the evening was the $10,016,875 sale of the coveted 1794 Flowing Hair silver dollar, a superb Gem Specimen example, the finest known to exist. This set a new world-record price for any coin. Attended by hundreds of enthusiasts, collectors, investors and dealers, and resulting in nearly $27 million in rare coins crossing the block, the auction of The Cardinal Collection and other important consignments took place as part of the Stack's Bowers Galleries New York Americana Sale. . . .
>
> One of the greatest American numismatic landmarks, the 1794 Flowing Hair silver dollar is the finest known example of its kind, graded Specimen-66 by the Professional Coin Grading Service (PCGS) and the Certified Acceptance Corporation (CAC), leading certifiers of a coin's condition. A close study of its characteristics suggests that it may well be the first specimen struck of the first year of the silver dollar, and was carefully preserved for posterity.

This caused a lot of excitement—the first coin ever to cross the $10 million mark. Records are made to be broken, and in 1996 I had been auctioneer at the podium when the Louis E. Eliasberg Collection specimen of the 1913 Liberty Head nickel was sold for $1,485,000, the first coin ever to cross the $1 million threshold. I remarked to the audience at the 1794 dollar sale, perhaps not entirely in jest, that I hope to be around when the first $100 million coin is sold!

Minting the 1794 Dollars

The background of the first United States silver dollar may be of interest.

The Mint Act of April 2, 1792, authorized the production of silver dollars of 416 grains weight, with silver content of 371.25 grains, equivalent to .89243 fineness. The remaining metal was to be copper, added for strength. Mintage of precious metals was not allowed to commence, however, until certain Mint officers posted surety bonds of $10,000 each (even though in 1792 silver half dismes were struck in small numbers). Accordingly, regular production did not commence until 1794.

The Flowing Hair design used on the silver dollars of 1794 (and also 1795) and on the half dimes and half dollars with those dates was the work of Robert Scot, an engraver of metal printing plates (including for bank notes) and a die sinker. On November 23, 1793, Secretary of State Thomas Jefferson, who was in charge of the affairs of the Mint, wrote to Scot and sent him a commission to be engraver at the Mint. To Scot fell the task of cutting the dies for coinage, including those of the 1794 Flowing Hair dollar. In November 1794 John Smith Gardner was hired as his assistant, but by this time the initial delivery of silver dollars had been accomplished. Probably, Gardner worked on some of the 1795 and later dies. Mint records are silent on who engraved what, and today certain aspects of the pattern coins of 1792 remain a mystery—including the biography of "Birch," who signed a die.

A curious fact, apparently not mentioned in the literature prior to my publishing it in the early 1990s, is that while the eight stars on the left of the 1794 silver dollar are each oriented with a point toward the dentils (as standard), the seven stars on the right are each positioned differently, unique to 1794 in the early dollar series, with two points toward the dentils.

At the time the Mint did not have elaborate quality-control procedures in place, and it was difficult to produce planchets precisely of the required weight. Accordingly, the typical planchet was made slightly heavier than needed, and the weight was adjusted by hand filing to the correct level. Underweight planchets would have been useless, as their weight could not have been increased, and they would have had to have been discarded, to go through the entire process of melting, conversion to ingots, rolling the strip, and punching planchets again. Following a practice established earlier at other mints, lightweight planchets could be made useful by drilling a hole at their centers and inserting a silver plug of additional weight (more than the drilled-out metal) that extended slightly above each side. Such a planchet would become slightly overweight and could be adjusted to the proper standard.

A screw press suitable for striking coins up to the size of a half dollar was put into service. Production commenced, and about 2,000 1794-dated dollars were made. A couple hundred or so of these were found to be unsatisfactory. On October 15, 1794, a delivery of 1,758 pieces was made by the coiner. The die faces were not precisely parallel, resulting in weakness at the lower-left obverse and the corresponding area on the reverse, as is characteristic of all known examples in numismatic hands.[1]

After the initial effort at coining dollars, the project was abandoned, and a supply of silver-dollar planchets was put into chests for storage until a larger, satisfactory press could be installed, which happened in the spring of 1795. Thus, the mintage of 1794 dollars was much smaller than had been intended.

Numismatic Considerations

The Cabinet Collection of the Mint of the United States, by Mint Director James Ross Snowden, 1860, p. 107, told of the first coinage of dollars:

> The first deposit of silver bullion for coinage took place on the 18th day of July 1794. The deposit was made by the Bank of Maryland, and consisted of 'coins of France,' amounting to eighty thousand seven hundred and

fifteen dollars seventy-three cents and five-tenths ($80,715.735.)

The first return of silver coins from the Chief Coiner to the Treasurer was made on the fifteenth day of October, and comprised 1,758 dollars. The second delivery was on the first day of December, and consisted of 5,300 half dollars. This embraced the entire silver coinage of the year. There was a small coinage of half dimes, but they were only struck as pattern pieces, for the purpose of trying the dies, and were not regularly issued.

The types were as follows: Obv. A head of Liberty, facing to the right, with flowing hair. Above was the word 'Liberty,' and beneath the date '1794.' To the left of the effigy were eight stars, and to the right seven, fifteen in all. On the reverse was an eagle with raised wings, encircled by branches of laurel, crossed. . . .

The 1792 "half dimes," called *half dismes* in 1792, are the subject of chapter 1 in this book. Although the deposits of silver described above were important, it is thought that silver for the 1794 dollars was deposited by Mint Director David Rittenhouse and Charles Gilchrist, and the coins were delivered to Rittenhouse.

By early December 1794 a few of the new dollars had traveled north to the Granite State, where the *New Hampshire Gazette* reported the following on the 2nd of that month:

> Some of the dollars now coining at the Mint of the United States have found their way to this town. A correspondent put one into the editor's hands yesterday. Its weight is equal to that of a Spanish dollar, encircled by *Fifteen Stars*, and has the word "LIBERTY" at the top, and the date, 1794, at the bottom. On the reverse, is the *Bald Eagle*, enclosed in an *Olive Branch*, round which are the words "One Dollar, or Unit, Hundred Cents." The *tout ensemble* has a pleasing effect to a connoisseur; but the touches of the graver are too delicate, and there is a want of that boldness of execution which is necessary to durability and currency.

Recognition

Today, the 1794 dollar is recognized as a great classic, not only because it is rare, but because it stands as the first silver dollar produced by the fledgling Philadelphia Mint. From the inception of coin-auction sales on a large scale in the 1860s, to the present day, the appearance of a 1794 silver dollar in an auction usually has provided the opportunity for the cataloger to provide an extended comment. Similarly, 1794 dollars have occupied the spotlight in numerous dealers' fixed-price lists over the years.

Charles Steigerwalt, in *The Coin Journal*, September 1880, commented as follows concerning the 1794 dollar:

> The number of pieces coined in this year was not large and they have become very rare. Good specimens bringing about 50 dollars. The dies of the dollars and half dollars of this year were not sharp and the impressions are generally weak; good specimens being difficult to obtain.

When Ebenezer Locke Mason wrote *Rare American Coins: Their Description, and Past and Present Fictitious Values*, in 1887 he focused upon this coin and noted the following:

The 1794 United States silver dollar, which occupies the centre of the group in our illustration [a collage of coins at the top of the page], was authorized by an act of Congress, April 2, 1792, and was struck at the old Mint, opposite Filbert Street, in Seventh Street, Philadelphia, and is still standing. This dollar, which is considered very rare, commanded a premium of about $25 in 1860, and has steadily advanced in fictitious value from year to year, and commanded, in every condition, in 1885, the sum of three hundred dollars.

It is said that but few of the 1794 dollars were struck, and the earliest from the dies equaled Proof pieces in their glistening splendor. The British Museum contains the best known specimen of the 1794 dollar, and probably received it as a gift from our government the year it was coined.[2]

Over the years several different specimens of the 1794 dollar have been designated as Uncirculated by various catalogers. Today, fewer than 10 coins are believed to be MS-60 or finer by current grading interpretations. Nearly all 1794 dollars are in lower grades ranging from Good to Fine. Not many make the Very Fine grade, and perhaps fewer than 15 totally are Extremely Fine or better. Population report data from third-party grading firms are not particularly useful in determining the number of Extremely Fine 1794 dollars known, as a number marked "EF" (or the curious "XF") are, in my opinion, only VF. There seems to have been a grade escalation in regard to this particular date.

I look forward to cataloging other examples of the 1794 dollar over the years.

CHAPTER 43

One of the most curious chapters in the history of the Civil War—in some ways even humorous when reviewed today—had a numismatic connection.

The Great St. Albans Raid

It is October 19, 1864

Detail of a Vermont map showing St. Albans. The border with Canada is near the top margin. The town of Sheldon, also mentioned in the account, is seen up and to the right. (Thompson, *History of Vermont, 1842*)

The date is Wednesday, October 19, 1864. The place is St. Albans, Vermont, a quiet community of about 2,800 citizens on the shore of Lake Champlain at the northwest corner of the state, just below the border of Canada. The Civil War is in progress—distantly, in the South. Vermont is largely unaffected in a direct sense, although more than 34,000 of its young men are in the service (of whom more than 5,000 will never return). The economy of St. Albans, largely agrarian, is further enhanced by railroad machine shops and facilities that employ several hundred men. Three banks—two under state charter and one a National Bank—are busy with local and regional customers. A staffed recruiting station for the Union Army is also in the village.

It is an especially quiet day on the main street of St. Albans. Light rain in the morning has kept most people indoors. Main Street is muddy, and few people are to be seen. On this particular Wednesday, about 40 leading citizens are out of town, attending the session of the Legislature in Montpelier and the State Supreme Court in Burlington. Meanwhile, around the town, citizens are involved in everyday affairs, clerking in stores, conversing, catching up with office work—a very ordinary scene, nothing unusual. In contrast, yesterday was crowded with activity, as Tuesday was market day each week. The population about doubled as farmers, merchants, traders, tourists,

St. Albans, Vt. Main Street.

Main Street in St. Albans as it appeared in a postcard view early in the 20th century.

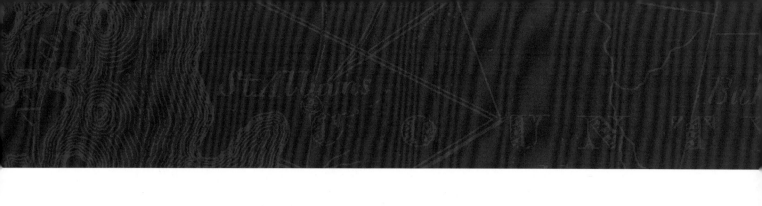

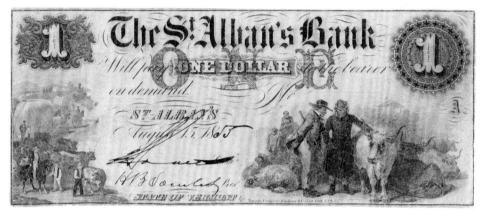

$1 note of the St. Albans Bank, 1863. Chartered by the state in 1853, it opened its doors for business on September 1, 1854. In October 1864 its capital was $150,000. On this note the bank title has an irrelevant apostrophe.

and others arrived to buy, sell, and exchange information. The village is easily accessible by road and by rail and is a popular regional destination.

Nine days earlier, on October 10, Bennett H. Young, age 21, and two companions had come to town on the Montreal Express train from Canada. They secured accommodations at the Tremont House on Main Street, which took in boarders. Three of their friends arrived the next day and checked in at the American House Hotel. The young men were a friendly bunch, typical tourists, and arrived from several different directions, including some from Chicago. Young read the Bible aloud in room 6, suggesting to guests who could hear him from the narrow hall that he was a theology student. He and his roommate, William Hutchinson, attracted the attention of two other boarders, Margaret Smith and Sarah Clark.

On the third day, Bennett had breakfast with the two girls. He invited Sarah to be his guest the next day for dinner at the American House, the finest dining spot in town. She was thrilled. During their repast they enjoyed each other's company, talked about the attractiveness of St. Albans, and discussed biblical prophecies. Afterward they walked around town and Sarah pointed out and discussed buildings and other points of interest, including Governor J. Gregory Smith's mansion on Bank Street, a highlight of the village. Sarah knew the governor's family well, and soon arranged a tour of the grounds for the next Saturday morning. In the meantime she was falling in love with Bennett, despite her roommate Margaret's advice that she learn more about him and go slowly. In due course Bennett and Sarah were guests at the mansion, where Bennett paid particular attention to the stable and its fine horses.

Bennett H. Young and his friends were sociable and of an inquiring turn of mind. Around town they asked many questions of local folk in a casual manner, such as which livery stables had good horses for rent. They visited the three local banks and tarried to watch business being transacted, making mental notes of where their safes were located and judging the temperament of the clerks and cashiers. As they hoped to go hunting, so they said, they checked on the possibility of borrowing or renting guns. On October 18, six more travelers from Canada arrived, with four of them checking into the Tremont House.

Today, the morning of the 19th, six more young men came to town and registered at the St. Albans House, while five others took accommodations in the American House Hotel.

Hmmm.

And Then. . . .

As to the sequence of memorable events in Saint Albans, this account is from the October 20, 1864, issue of the *Daily Spy*, a widely read paper published in Worcester, Massachusetts:

A Tragedy at St. Albans, Vermont

THREE BANKS ROBBED AND CITIZENS SHOT

ST. ALBANS, VT., Oct. 19.—An invasion of this town took place today. Some twenty or twenty-five armed desperadoes supposed to be in rebel employ, from Canada, made an assault on the several banks about 4 o'clock this afternoon. The National Bank was robbed of about $50,000, mostly in bills; the St. Albans Bank was robbed of between $70,000 and $80,000, and the Franklin County Bank of a considerable amount.

Some twenty horses were also seized by the desperadoes and carried off. Several citizens who resisted were deliberately shot, two were wounded seriously, and it is feared fatally, E.J. Morrison, a contractor, and C. Huntington, a jeweler. Several others are reported slightly injured. The raiders threatened to burn the town and left in the direction of Canada. A large part of armed citizens have gone in pursuit.

St. Albans is about eight miles from the Canada line, and three from Lake Champlain. It is the residence of Gov. Smith.

The attack began about 4 o'clock P.M. The cashier of one of the banks was locked up in his safe, where he remained a considerable time. The raiders came in the guise of travelers and may have been roving about town sometime before the attack.

The newspapers were abuzz with stories, often varying widely as to what happened. In its December 1864 issue, *Banker's Magazine* included this in its coverage:

Daring Robbery

One of the most daring bank robberies of the past fifty years was that of the banks at St. Albans, Vt., on the 19th of October, by a party of freebooters, since representing themselves as officers and men of the Confederate service.

They attacked and robbed the Franklin County Bank, the St. Albans Bank, and the First National Bank, all of that place. About half-past three two or three young men, very well dressed, and evidently men of intelligence, came into the St. Albans Bank. All were fair in appearance save one, who is described by our former townsman, M.A. Seymour, who was in the directors' room of the bank at the time, as of most malicious visage.

These fellows approached Mr. C.N. Bishop, teller of the bank, and, presenting a pair of pistols, proceeded to rob the institution. Mr. Bishop ran into the room where Mr. Seymour was, and attempted to bolt the door, but they were too quick for them, and, forcing the door, Bishop was dragged out by the throat, and Mr. Seymour presented with a rebel argument in the shape of a pistol at his head. They were then obliged to swear an oath of allegiance to the Southern Confederacy, and not to divulge any of these proceedings for two hours.

The leader of the party said: "We are here under the order of General Early. You have been down in the Shenandoah Valley, burned our houses, and wasted our property; and now we propose to pay you back in the same coin." Mr. Seymour, being an extremely good Union man, hesitated about taking the oath prescribed; but a threatened application of "cold lead" soon brought him to the rebel terms.

The First National Bank is comparatively a new institution, having been started last spring. The party who robbed this bank had a scrimmage before they went in with a young man

$5 note of the Franklin County Bank of St. Albans. This bank was chartered in 1849 with a capital of $100,000. After the 1864 raid the bank was distressed and went into liquidation. All provable debts were paid, after which it closed its doors forever.

named Blaisdell, clerk in an adjoining clothing store. He saw these armed men coming towards the bank, and started to notify the cashier that there was set of "blacklegs" proposing to visit him. Before he entered the bank, however, he was stopped by the raiders, who, presenting a pistol, after a brief scuffle marched him and other prisoners to the Green, where a guard was set over them.

Upon entering the bank Mr. Sowles, the

cashier, was urbanely invited to hand over what money he had and the keys of the safe. The request was complied with, the funds abstracted, and Mr. Sowles marched off to the Green. The losses of this bank amounted to $52,650, as follows: $29,650 in 7 3-10 Treasury bonds, in denominations of 50's, 100's, 500's and 1,000's; $15,000 in five percent legal tender interest bearing notes[1]; $8,000 in currency on New England banks and greenbacks.

A reward of one thousand dollars will be given for the necessary information which will lead to the conviction of any of the robbers, and all persons are cautioned against purchasing any of the above lost bonds, as payment has been stopped. After the raiders had procured their horses they congregated in front of the Amer-

$100 note of the Missisquoi Bank of Sheldon, Vermont, named for the Missisquoi River that flows nearby. Plate by the New England Bank Note Co.

ican, and near the store of George H. Farrar, when they strolled up and down Main Street, firing at random. Nearly all the parties implicated are now under arrest, and undergoing an examination at Montreal.

The Escape

On that fatal afternoon the citizens of St. Albans were frightened and confused. Some ran for shelter, and others took matters into their own hands. The workers at the railroad shops did not learn of the incident in time to help. The raiders, mounted on horses stolen from citizens and, as applicable, detached from their buggies and carts, plus seven taken from Fuller's livery, started on their way out of town, throwing "Greek fire," an inflammable concoction of phosphorus, on several buildings in an attempt to burn the village. At Atwood's and Brainerd's stores the fires were inconsequential. The American House Hotel was set on fire, but just a small part suffered damage. Shots were exchanged during these hectic moments, and Elinus J. Morrison, a contractor from New Hampshire who was doing the bricklaying during the construction the Welden House, was mortally wounded. Ironically, Morrison was later remembered as a Northerner who was sympathetic to the Confederate cause.

The raiders headed north toward the Canadian border. On the way they stopped at the Missisquoi Bank in Sheldon, but found the door locked. From there it was across the border to safety, setting small fires at two wooden bridges along the way. In ensuing days consternation and fear reigned along the towns in the United States that were close to Canada. A rumor arose that Burlington would be attacked next, with an even greater force, and that smaller towns would fall victim to depredations. Local guards and sentinels assisted by military personnel were on alert in many villages for the rest of the autumn and into the next year. Fear was widespread and facts were scarce.

The Rest of the Story

What was first thought to be a daring daylight robbery of several banks developed into an international incident. The raiders were, indeed, Confederate soldiers. Most were from Kentucky and all but one was from 20 to 26 years of age. Most of the men soon were arrested in Canada and sought protection under international law. Canadian authorities were indecisive and resisted the request to prosecute those in captivity and to issue arrest warrants for others at large. The raiders asserted that they were on a wartime exercise, for the glory of the Confederacy, and, seeking refuge in neutral Canada, they were immune from the laws of the United States.

In Washington, Secretary of War Edwin Stanton received word that St. Albans had been pillaged and set on fire by Southern raiders, after which the telegraph service to the District of Columbia failed. The next morning he learned the details of the robberies and escape. American troops were commanded to

Secretary of War Edwin Stanton with his son.

charge into Canada and capture the raiders by force. However, President Abraham Lincoln revoked the order, realizing that it would violate neutrality, and that an invasion of Canada could be construed as a warlike act. Such publicity would benefit only the

President Abraham Lincoln.

rebels and likely make Canada an ally of the Confederate States of America. For several years Canada had been a refuge for Northerners who sympathized with the Confederate cause. Later investigation revealed that the raid had been authorized by the Southern authorities and had been carefully planned.

On October 21, Secretary of State William H. Seward demanded that Canada turn the men and money over to American authorities. However, Lord Charles Monck, the governor general of British North America, directed that they be tried in court in Canada. The prisoners were taken to Montreal, where

crowds cheered them as they arrived. Soon they were taken to prison, but assigned to apartments that were pleasantly furnished in the manner of a fine hotel and given special food service. Bennett H. Young penned a nice letter to Sarah Clark, his former boarding-house friend in St. Albans, sending her $3 with a request for copies of the *Vermont Daily Messenger*, so he could read the accounts.

Secretary of State William Seward.

In Court

The court hearing of evidence began on November 7. The United States had observers on hand, but could not bring any attorneys to the court as none were licensed to practice in Montreal. Young, leader of the raiders, stated that the action was a military attack under the authority of the Confederate States of America, and nothing more. His statement included this:

The course I intended to pursue in Vermont, and which I was able to carry out but partially, was to retaliate in some measure for the barbarous atrocities of Grant, Butler, Sherman, Hunter, Milroy, Sheridan, Grierson and other Yankee officers, except that I would scorn to harm women and children under any provocation, or unarmed, defenseless and unresisting citizens, even Yankees, or to plunder for my own benefit.

After reviewing the testimony, Judge Charles-Joseph Coursol stated that in actuality he had no jurisdiction in the case as the raiders had not been arrested under legal warrants, and dismissed the prisoners to the cheers of onlookers. A waiting sleigh took Mr. Porterfield, a Confederate agent who had attended the proceedings, to a nearby bank where what remained of the stolen money had been stored. This was given to the agent, who distributed it to the prisoners. The value was calculated to be about $88,000 in terms of paper money, equivalent to about $50,000 in gold coins.

All of this was a curious and unexpected turn of events for President Lincoln and his advisors.

The released men then scattered in several directions. The United States raised sharp protests, including through Charles Francis Adams, United States minister to Great Britain, as Canada was a possession of that country. Call was made for a further investigation. Judge Coursol was commanded to appear before the Police Committee of Montreal after inquiries revealed that he had made certain arrangements with Confederate agents before and while the trial was in progress, suggesting what the verdict would be. He admitted that he had associated with Confederates, but declined to answer further questions. Coursol was suspended from his office, and the statement was made that he was indictable for malfeasance. Later, the attorney general restored him to the bench, and still later he was elected to several terms as mayor of Montreal.

The improprieties were considered, and Justice James Smith of the Superior Court issued a warrant for the re-arrest of the raiders, but only five could be found, one being Bennett H. Young. In the meantime, the freed men had turned over most of the St. Albans money to Clement C. Clay, the Confederate commissioner in Canada. A new trial was scheduled for December 27, then continued into the next year.

The trial took place early in 1865, and testimony was again heard, and again the raiders were victorious. Rousing cheers in the courtroom and outside were raised as the prisoners were given their freedom. Another arrest warrant was soon issued, and the men were taken to Toronto for yet another trial. Throughout these court scenes, United States representatives persisted that the actions of Young and his raiders were not those of soldiers, but of common criminals.

To counter this, and easily, the prosecution had a field day parading the similar and even worse depredations committed by Union soldiers on innocent people in the South, including in the Shenandoah Valley, where houses were pillaged. For good measure the defense attorney brought forth a volume of *The Rebellion Record*, published by Putnam in New York, and read this account of the invasion by Union troops of the quiet town of Darien, Georgia:

On June 11, 1863, an old ferry boat converted to a gunboat came up the Altahoma River to Darien. On board was a federal officer, Montgomery, commanding a party of Negro soldiers. Their purpose was to "present their compliments to the rebels of Georgia."

As they approached, they threw shells into the village scattering the terror-stricken inhabitants. Not a single armed person appeared at the wharf to dispute their landing or to offer resistance. Pickets were sent to the outskirts of the town; orders were given to take everything of value to the boat and then to burn Darien. Officers with squads started off in every direction. Soon they began to return to the boat loaded with all types of furniture, even pianos. Tools, mirrors, jewelry and money were taken. One private returned with a pair of chickens in one hand and leading a cow by the other. Papers, letters and books weren't neglected.

Darien contained between 70 and 100 houses on a street running along the river shaded on both sides by large oaks and mulberry trees. A town of age and respectability, it never looked so grand and beautiful as it did in its destruction. As soon as a house was ransacked the torch was applied, and by 6 o'clock the whole town was in a sheet of flame.

Montgomery's reason for the raid was, "The South must be conquered inch by inch and what we can't put a force in to hold ought to be destroyed." Later he described how the plunder was divided at camp and that "some of the quarters look really princely with their sofas and pianos."

The trial was still in progress when the war ended in April. The raiders were set free. Soon afterward the Canadian government made restitution to the Franklin County Bank of $31,000 of the paper money bearing the imprint of that bank, to the First National Bank $19,000 in paper money, and to the St. Albans Bank $20,000 in gold coins.

CHAPTER 44

A teenager too young to join the American Numismatic Association was allowed to have a bourse table at the annual convention. A reminiscence.

A Reminiscence of 1955

The Omaha Convention

Author's advertisement in the *Numismatic Scrapbook Magazine,* August 1955.

As I was a teenager not yet of the legal age of 18 in 1955, I was not eligible to become a member of the American Numismatic Association. So, I asked my father, Quentin H. Bowers, to join, which he did. Then I could read *The Numismatist,* the monthly journal, first-hand. At the time the ANA felt that youngsters could not be trusted. Reasons included that they were not old enough to make contracts, they lacked mature judgment, and, by gosh, they might return a coin a month or two later and demand a refund. Countless thousands of eager young people in the hobby were shut out. This was the era in which teenagers all across America had Whitman "penny folders" and dearly hoped to find a precious 1909-S V.D.B. cent. I started this way myself in the summer of 1952 at the age of 13.

In April 1955 this announcement was in *The Numismatist*:

Some additional bourse space is available for the annual convention of the ANA in Omaha, Neb., Aug. 24-27, 1955. Bourse space will be limited to not more than 40 so that adequate facilities, light, and aisle space will be available. All bourse space is in one room, around the wall in the room containing the membership exhibits, and fully air conditioned. Cost is $50, which includes full registration, badge and one banquet ticket.

Reservation with remittance should be sent to General Secretary Lewis M. Reagan, Box 577, Wichita, Kans. The Association reserves the right to decline any reservation, and those received after available space has been reserved will have to be declined.

I wrote to Reagan and asked if I could have a table. The secretary carried his office in his briefcase, figuratively, and took care of nearly all Association business, including awarding printing contracts, processing membership applications, and tending to convention details. He wrote back stating there were, indeed, a few spaces left and that I could have one if my father guaranteed my business there and if I could have another letter of recommendation. My dad did this, and Lee F. Hewitt, editor of the *Numismatic Scrapbook Magazine,* sent a warm comment that he had found me as an advertiser in the short time I had been with his magazine and by reputation to be very reliable and with a good amount of numismatic knowledge. I became one of 45 bourse-table holders, a few more than the ANA had planned, it seems.

My dad went with me to the convention and watched me as I bought, sold, and traded coins. He signed the convention register. Youngsters were not allowed to do so. Rumor had it that he was very wealthy and the backer of my business. In practice, he was a highly accomplished civil engineer and had a small business in this specialty. He did not collect coins.

By 1955 I had many clients and was, perhaps, America's leading dealer in the esoteric field of pattern coins (having bought and sold many that others, especially Abe Kosoff and Sol Kaplan, had bought at the King Farouk auction in Cairo in 1954), I was viewed as having almost unlimited funds at my disposal. I never said otherwise, but the truth was that our family was still of relatively modest means, and that every penny I had in the coin business I had earned myself—backed, for which I'm grateful, by a $6,000 loan from my father, and for which I insisted to pay interest at the bank rate, as I did.

One of my favorite pattern coins, the 1879 "School-girl" silver dollar by George T. Morgan.

By this time I had attended a number of coin shows and had been an active buyer in auctions, including from Stack's, New Netherlands, and the Hollinbeck Coin Co. At the first New York Metropolitan Numismatic Convention from May 6 to 8, 1955, I had my first bourse table—and spent three days in non-stop activity buying and selling. Apart from

attending club meetings and shows, my sales were conducted by sending letters to clients. It was a general rule, I was happy to learn, that most customers became steady buyers after their first order.

I had yet to publish my first printed catalog; that would happen with an issue dated September–October 1955. The reason is that once I had coins in stock they usually sold so quickly that there was no need to advertise them! The contents of this and other catalogs gave a glimpse of only a tiny fraction of what I bought and sold.

Medal forming part of the 1955 ANA convention badge.

At the Show

In terms of coin prices, my capital, perhaps $10,000 to $15,000 at the time of the ANA convention, including the loan, was equal to what it might take well over a million dollars to do today. As an example of this, at the convention Aubrey Bebee, who conducted the auction sale, showed me a gem 1796 quarter for which he had paid $200. "That was too much," he said apologetically, "but it is so-o-o-o nice!" Today the same coin would probably command several hundred thousand dollars![1]

B.A. Brown, a trader from Fallon, Nevada, who called himself a "butter-and-egg man," for that was his business back home, had a bourse table with piles of Uncirculated double eagles at $35 to $38 each, which

A beautiful Uncirculated 1796 quarter similar to the one I saw in 1955.

was not much more than the melt value. Gem Proof Barber half dollars worth $10 then became worth $5,000 or so in the early 21st century. A few dollars went a long way in buying coins in 1955!

An 1879 Flowing Hair $4 gold pattern Stella, one of a set of four patterns of this denomination made in 1879 and 1880.

The bourse was in the Grand Ballroom of the Sheraton-Fontenelle Hotel, a large space with an ornately decorated ceiling—dating back to the age of elegance earlier in the century. Dealer tables were placed all around the walls, and in the center were tables for educational displays. A kindly old gentleman, O.L. Harvey, from Seminole, Oklahoma, had a complete set of four 1879 and 1880 $4 gold Stellas on view. I had never seen such before, so he let me examine the plastic holder in which they were housed and see both sides of the coins.

Amon Carter Jr., William A. Philpott, and Bob Schermerhorn displayed cases of incredibly rare paper money, and John Rowe III, a member of the younger set who was to become a fine friend (we traveled by automobile across the American West in his new Thunderbird in 1961), had a currency exhibit as well. All hailed from Texas.

Bill Donlon of Utica, New York, exhibited his collection of Proof sets from 1858 onward, with all denominations from the cent to the dollar. Not long afterward his prize-winning collection was auctioned by Abe Kosoff. Dr. J. Hewitt Judd, here in his home town in Omaha, showed many of his spectacular pattern coins.

Among the coins I had for sale at the show was an 1849-O half dime, a worn example of this rare date and mint. A man came over to look at it, while I was talking to someone else. When I returned my attention, he had departed, as had the half dime. The dealer having the bourse table next to me, Charlie, a railroader who dealt in coins part time (and who wore the same tie, with a stain on it, each day at the show), told me that he knew the culprit, a well-known shoplifter, but there wasn't much that I could do about it as he needed to be caught in the act. I learned that others around the bourse were quite aware of him.

One of the more important dealers at that time was James, Inc., of Louisville, Kentucky, run by the Karp brothers. Among their specialties were Proof sets and groups of modern coins. In 1955 the demand for Proofs was so intense that the Mint placed restrictions on the number that any single person could order. Various dealers and investors got around this by having uncles, cousins, neighbors, and others, possibly even their pet cats, place requests for them. At the show David Karp had in his bourse table a neatly typed letter from the Mint, dated 1951, thanking him for his nice order for Proof sets. This was rather funny in 1955, as collectors then felt the Mint was against their interests, not for them.

Proof sets were indeed all the rage in 1955, and at the convention Sol Kaplan posted a list of bid and ask prices for modern sets of 1936 to date, changing certain values during the show. This created quite a stir, and at later conventions he set up a large chalkboard with this information. Kaplan's background was in the securities business (in addition to being a dealer in coins and stamps), and such "action" came to him naturally. At the convention I saw three complete 1915-S Panama-Pacific commemorative sets for sale, which was amazing. That reminds me to say that at a later show I needed such a set for a customer, and Kaplan, who had none in inventory, true to his stockbroker background, offered to sell me one "short." I demurred as I wanted to see it first. Although I always tried to cherrypick high-quality Uncirculated and Proof coins for my customers, most collectors and dealers in 1955 did not care whether a coin was average in quality or something better.

Page 2 offered gold coins. My gosh, how the prices have changed since then!

Q. David Bowers
- NUMISMATIST -

203 Second National Bank Building   Wilkes-Barre, Penna.

Tel. VAlley 3-8478

Sept. - Oct., 1955   No. 1

TERMS OF SALE

Remittance must accompany order unless you have established credit with me. Cash orders receive priority.

All items subject to prior sale. Remittances returned promptly on unfilled orders.

All material is sold subject to your satisfaction. Any returns must be made within three days of receipt.

This Bulletin lists a few of the choice items now in stock. May I suggest that you send your orders in early in order to avoid disappointment. Please include second choices wherever possible. All items are sent postpaid.

During the past year I have furnished many beautiful and rare items to collectors from all parts of the country. Your orders and correspondence have been a constant inspiration to me.

My display at the recent ANA convention in Omaha attracted considerable attention and I sincerely appreciate the many compliments received. During this trip I was fortunate in acquiring many beautiful coins, including

several collections. These coins are being catalogued for listing in future bulletins.

If you wish to sell any part or all of your collection, please note that I buy at prices which reflect the true quality and value of your material and will pay you immediate cash. My coin purchases amount to thousands of dollars each month. Write me today.

CHOICE UNITED STATES COINS
ARE MY SPECIALTY

The cover of my first printed catalog.

Interests and Specialties

In addition to patterns, I made a specialty of 19th- and early-20th-century Proof coins. By that time I had studied them very extensively, inspired by Walter Breen's *Proof Coins Struck by the United States Mint*, published in 1953 by Wayte Raymond. I had met Breen in New York City, where he worked for New Netherlands Coin Company, and plied him with technical questions. I was particularly intrigued with his listings of early Proof half cents by First Restrike and Second Restrike varieties. I had bought some such Proofs, but the only customer I could find who had an interest in them was Emery May (Mrs. Henry) Norweb. Others simply grouped them under the category of "restrikes with small berries."

I was always on the lookout for interesting and rare Proofs of various denominations, particularly for those dated before 1858, for most such early issues were not listed in the *Guide Book of United States Coins*, except for half cents and Liberty Seated dollars, and some dealers could not find customers for them. This may seem unusual when considered today, but most collectors in 1955 sought only items they could find prices and information for in what was (and still is) popularly nicknamed the "Red Book."

A 1786 Vermont copper struck in Rupert, the Republic of Vermont (which did not become a state until 1791), in 1786. Such coins were minted under rustic circumstances and show many surface irregularities.

CHARLES H. GOODWIN,
DRUGGIST & MANUFACTURING CHEMIST,
DEALER IN
Drugs, Medicines, Dye Stuffs, Perfumery and Fancy Goods.

A cent counterstamped USE G.G.G. & G.G.G.G. and an 1856 advertisement for the product.

Colonial and early American coins were another specialty, in particular the state copper coinages of 1785 to 1788 issued by Vermont (my favorite), Connecticut (another interest), Massachusetts (the most stereotyped and therefore the least interesting), and New Jersey. I was also intrigued by the secret Machin's Mills mint near Newburgh, New York, which I had read about in Sylvester S. Crosby's *Early Coins of America*, published in 1875 and still the standard reference in the 1950s—as it is, indeed, today!

In 1955 I became fascinated with counterstamped large copper cents and commenced building a collection. These were viewed as oddities of little value by other dealers, who often saved them for me and gave them to me as gifts! That changed in later years, of course, and today many such pieces have very strong values and appeal to a wide base of buyers. I still add occasional examples to my collection today.

In studying the catalog for the upcoming auction by Bebee's I concluded that the Proof 1867 With Rays Shield nickel was a bit scarcer than generally thought. At the auction I captured a gem for $610. This caused a great sensation at the time—a little kid paying $610 for a nickel! This augmented my reputation (which I enjoyed) that I would pay ridiculously high prices. As a result I was continually offered things by other dealers.

A gem Proof 1867 With Rays Shield nickel.

The secret was that I tried to buy very carefully, with knowledge of what I was doing. This did not always work out, but usually I made a profit. Besides, the coin market was in an upward trend, and a high price of 1955 might turn out to be a bargain a year later. As to the famous nickel, along came O.L. Harvey, who asked if I would take a profit, and I did. It was gone within a few hours after I bought it!

Reflective of market values at the time, a 1793 Liberty Cap cent, the Crosby 13-L variety, in Fine grade, sold for $310, and a rare 1799 in the same grade fetched $150. A Proof example of the ever-popular 1856 Flying Eagle cent reached $392.50, and an Uncirculated key-date 1877 cent found a buyer for $82.50, followed in due course by a like grade 1914-D at $85. A complete set of commemorative gold dollars and quarter eagles, 1903 to 1926, realized $461. Proof sets of 1950 and 1951, hot tickets in the marketplace, fetched $30 and $19 respectively.

B. Max Mehl

A highlight of the convention was a dinner one evening at the invitation of Abe Kosoff and his wife Molly. B. Max Mehl and I were their guests. I had read everything in print about Mehl—his advertisements and most of his auction catalogs—and rightfully considered him to be *the* great numismatic figure of the first half of the 20th century. I asked him all the questions I could think of, and suggested that he write his autobiography. "You know so much about me, why don't *you* write it," was his reply. I was much honored.

We were not strangers, as we had talked on the telephone. A few months earlier I had received a small printed catalog from him, apparently somewhat outdated, and saw an Uncirculated 1909-S Indian Head cent listed for $10. I called his office, announced my name, and asked for the Order Department. Instead, Mr. Mehl came on the telephone himself, and we chatted for a bit. I was in awe! It seems that he had heard of my little business and likened my activity to his own beginnings a half century earlier (he first advertised in *The Numismatist* in 1903).

"You know these cents are selling for about $30 now," he said. "However, you can buy some. How many do you want?" I took ten of them! They were *so*

nice that when I later offered them for $40 each they sold immediately.

At the show the Professional Numismatists Guild, which had been incubating since 1953, had its first official meeting at a breakfast event. Sol Kaplan was elected president, and James F. Kelly, of Dayton, Ohio, was chosen as vice president. C.C. Shroyer, of Fremont, Ohio, who had been helping with the formation of the Guild and had been its secretary-treasurer during its formation, was re-elected to that post. Abe Kosoff told me that when I reached the age of 21 he would sponsor me more membership. This happened in due course.

The attendance at the Omaha convention was excellent, and by show's end a record of 528 convention-goers was announced! A report of the event was given in *The Numismatist* in October.

Author's advertisement in *The Numismatist*, October 1955, the same issue that carried a report on the convention.

CHAPTER 45

In 2000 I covered the launch of the New Hampshire Statehood quarter for Coin World. *In 2013 it was an honor to do the same for the New Hampshire America the Beautiful quarter. This chapter's information from artist-sculptor-engraver Phebe Hemphill had never appeared in a numismatic publication before it was featured, in abbreviated form, in* Coin World.

The Statehood Quarters

1999 Delaware Statehood quarter dollar. The Washington obverse die was stock for the entire series.

The New Hampshire "America the Beautiful" Quarter

This is the story of the debut of the 2013 New Hampshire "America the Beautiful" quarter dollar, part of a program launched in 2010.[1] The inspiration for the "National Park quarter" program, as it is popularly called, came from the Statehood quarter series that honored each of the states plus the District of Columbia and five U.S. territories. The earlier program began in 1999 with the Delaware quarter, that state being the first in 1787 to ratify the new national Constitution.

2000 New Hampshire Statehood quarter dollar. Depicted is the Old Man in the Mountain in Franconia Notch in the White Mountains, an icon until it crumbled in 2003.

Progression continued in ratification order. In 2000 it was New Hampshire's turn. At 10 in the morning on Monday, August 7, that year, the launch ceremony was held at the New Hampshire Historical Society building across the street from the State House (state capitol building). Mint Director Jay Johnson arranged for me to conduct interviews with the Mint staff people on hand and gather information. United States Treasurer Mary Ellen Withrow and other dignitaries, federal and state, were in attendance. Subsequently, I reported the ceremony in a feature article for *Coin World*. In due course, 1,169,016,000 New Hampshire Statehood quarters were struck. That equaled more than three for every man, woman, and child in the United States. At the time, and still true today, the quarter was the highest-denomination coin of the realm, in practicality. Although Kennedy-design half dollars and presidential-design dollars continue to be produced I haven't seen a half dollar in change for years and I have never been handed one of the modern Sacagawea or Presidential coins.

As the years passed, Statehood quarters continued to be released at the rate of five designs per year, until finally the series was completed in 2009.

The 2000 New Hampshire quarter launch ceremony. U.S. Senator John Sununu is at the podium.

The author with U.S. Treasurer Mary Ellen Withrow at the ceremony.

The "America the Beautiful" Quarters

The good times came to an end. What to do next? Already, the Treasury Department and Mint had contemplated this question: could another series achieve popularity as well? At its September 21, 2004, meeting in Washington, the Citizens Coinage Advisory Committee (CCAC) discussed several possibilities including honoring national parks in each state. In other forums, ideas were shared as well. Finally, a measure for a series of national park quarters went through Congress, and on December 12, 2008, President George W. Bush made H.R. 2764, the District of Columbia and U.S. Territories Circulating Quarter Dollar Program Act, official.

The impending program was not without its flaws in logic. Certain national parks had already been depicted on the Statehood quarters, such as Yosemite in California. Other states, New Hampshire being an example, had no national parks at all. For these it was decided that a national forest or national historic site would suffice. In time the Mint decided to call the new coins "America the Beautiful" quarters. An added fea-

In the meantime the Treasury Department, the numismatic community, and many others realized that the Statehood quarter series was a dynamic influence in popularizing coins. Equipped with a folder or album, millions of people found it to be a pleasurable pursuit to track down as many different designs as possible in pocket change. Including Philadelphia and Denver mint varieties, this totaled more than 110 different possibilities from the various states and territories. In addition, special Proof strikes were priced at a premium and were struck at the San Francisco Mint. What fun!

The Gräbener press at the Philadelphia Mint, as photographed in March 2013.

ture was the separate minting of three-inch-diameter silver "coins" of the same designs, each containing five ounces of .9999 pure silver. These are strictly numismatic issues, sold at a premium by the U.S. Mint and not intended for circulation or monetary purposes. They are made one at a time on a huge Gräbener press in Philadelphia.

Public Reception

While the Statehood quarters played to a wide but steadily decreasing audience from 1999 to 2009, the National Park quarters did not attract widespread attention even at the starting gate or even among citizens of the various states featured. While collectors had found it easy enough to collect Statehood quarters as the names of each state were easily recognized, the America the Beautiful coins seemed to some to be obscure. The very first in the 56-coin series was launched in 2010 and featured Hot Springs National Park in Arkansas, the first established. Few people knew anything about that particular attraction. In the mid-1970s I went there to visit numismatist Robert Marks and to pick up his magnificent collection as an auction consignment. There were many rarities including an 1884 trade dollar (of which only 10 are known). The "park" is actually a city with shops, lots of old bath houses (once popular as spas), and the like. Very interesting to see. Perhaps if ARKANSAS had been lettered prominently at the top of the obverse of the quarters they would have been easier to identify and collect by state, rather than by design. Who knows?

Complicating matters, by 2010 America was in an economic recession, many banks and financial institutions were having problems, and there was not much interest in featuring and offering for sale the new quarters to bank customers. The combined mintage of Philadelphia and Denver quarters for Hot Springs National Park was 69,600,000 pieces In contrast, 72,200,000 were made for the last of the Statehood series, the Northern Mariana Territories, itself an even more unfamiliar location, it might seem.

It was not until autumn 2011 that the hundred-million mark was crossed, with 143,200 for the Chickasaw National Recreation Area in Oklahoma. The famous Yellowstone, Yosemite, and Grand Canyon issues of 2011 limped along with mintages of only 68,400,000, 70,000,000, and 72,000,000 respectively. I guess New Hampshire was lucky in 2013 with 176,400,000, which was more than double the quantity for the more famous (I think) Gettysburg!

I hasten to say that these mintages have nothing to do with the popularity or name recognition of the various parks. The production is based on the call placed by the Federal Reserve for distribution of quarters nationwide, not in the state commemorated. If there is a large demand for coins to use in commerce, whatever current issue is being produced is made in larger quantities. There was a great call for quarters when the New Hampshire issues were available, but not from banks in that state.

Accordingly, the New Hampshire quarter was impossible to find at regional banks. It turns out that many were released in Maryland and Virginia and none within the borders of the Granite State. At least, I was not able to learn of any. I purchased $1,000 face value of them from Littleton Rare Coin Co., who always buys quantities, paying a nominal premium for handling (the owner, Dave Sundman, and I are close friends). I gave several thousand of them to the Wolfeboro Area Chamber of Commerce, which passed them out at face value, one per person, to all who wanted one.

The economy and the reluctance of banks to accommodate their clients by ordering quantities combine to dictate mintages; the design of a given quarter has nothing to do with it. In a related vein the four different reverse designs of the 2009 Lincoln cent would have created great excitement if produced a few years earlier. With the country in recession, new coins for circulation were not needed, and public distribution of the cents was erratic. In New Hampshire I was not able to order any after applying to several banks.

The New Hampshire "America the Beautiful" Quarter

What a great chance was missed to have people of all ages buy and add to "penny" boards and albums.

With this prelude, now to the New Hampshire "America the Beautiful" quarter and how it was produced and distributed.

Phebe Hemphill, Artist and Sculptor

As an unexpected prelude, the time was August 1, 2012. The U.S. Mint had issued invitations to coin journalists, various national newspapers, television

Phebe Hemphill holds a historic galvano by sculptor A.A. Weinman, a design for a medal for the 1904 Louisiana Purchase Exposition.

The clay model for the New Hampshire quarter as it neared completion. The "White Mountain" inscription refers to the White Mountain National Forest. There is no peak with that name. Depicted is Mount Chocorua, instantly recognizable by residents of the Granite State, but not mentioned on the coin.

networks, and the like, to attend a preview of the new Visitors Center at the Philadelphia Mint.

As it turned out, Mary Counts (who married in 2013 and is now Mary Burleson), president of Whitman Publishing, and I were the only numismatic people on hand! There were more than a dozen others

from networks and newspapers, none of whom seemed to have any particular knowledge of coin manufacture and distribution—not unusual as such media people have so many different subjects to cover. Following remarks by Tom Jurkowsky, director of public affairs, the visitors broke into two groups to tour the various departments from beginning to end. These included seeing the designing of coins by sculptor-artists, the making of models and dies, and more, culminating in a tour of the production floor in which presses were busy stamping out different denominations.

Realizing that the coming year, 2013, would include the New Hampshire coin as part of the "America the Beautiful" program, during my stop in the Engraving Department I sought out the artist scheduled to work on the quarter. This turned out to be Phebe Hemphill, an accomplished sculptor and artist who, surprising to me, had already created two sketches, of which one had been selected from proposals submitted by several other talented Mint artists. She had in her office a clay model that more or less

Phebe Hemphill's adopted but not completed design showing Lake Chocorua in the foreground and the distinctive peak in the distance. Mount Chocorua, here in a lower profile than on the final motif, has been a favorite subject for artists and photographers for many years, this perspective being especially popular. The numeral at the lower right is the Mint's code for the design in the competition. The names of the artists were not given to the judges.

Detail of the area with the designer's PH initials (center of image).

The final design as used on the quarter. Certain details were changed, including making the distant peak more prominent.

One of several semi-final designs by other artists. This shows two deer with Lake Chocorua and Mount Chocorua in the distance.

Pattern or trial striking in clad metal of the reverse die of the New Hampshire National Parks quarter. Trial strikes are not saved. This is the first and only illustration of this coin! (Courtesy of Michael White of the U.S. Mint)

This motif is dominated by a songbird and trees with a mountain slope in the distance.

The New Hampshire "America the Beautiful" Quarter

Mount Chocorua is again the subject for this design which depicts a moose, an animal plentiful in the White Mountains.

The venue was Hanaway Hall. As is Mint policy, the National Forest people were called upon to make arrangements with local and regional people to attend, including schoolchildren. It was more of a White Mountain National Forest event than a U.S. Mint event. It, like other launches, was truly "down home." Mint staffers conducted a Coin Forum in Campton the previous evening, with general discussions, but with no coins exchanged. Eighteen people were on hand. I was not able to attend.

represented what the final product would be. Delighted and intrigued, I interviewed Phebe in some depth, and took notes and pictures. The quarter was to be released in early 2013.

As the launch time approached, I interfaced with Tom Jurkowsky and Acting Mint Director Dick Peterson and arranged telephone conversations and discussions with Phebe, who consented to an interview. The result was a unique view of the creation of a quarter design, the 16th in the series, from the first concept down to completion, a procedure, which I believe, had never been outlined in print before. Phebe's interview is included here in later paragraphs, together with my comments.

Phebe's list of accomplishments is quite lengthy. She certainly has turned out an amazing list of medals and coins for the Mint. Who knows? No doubt she might be the subject for a book some time in the future. In fact a great book subject would be the entire Engraving Department and the work they do now and have done in the past.

The New Hampshire Quarter Launch

The launch ceremony was scheduled to be held at Plymouth State University in Plymouth, New Hampshire, in the heart of the White Mountains, eight miles from Campton, a small town in which the White Mountain National Forest headquarters is located.

The stage in readiness for the New Hampshire quarter launch, Plymouth State University, February 21, 2013, in the heart of the White Mountains. The backdrop depicts scenes relating to the five America the Beautiful to be launched this year, beginning with New Hampshire at the far left.

I left Wolfeboro, New Hampshire, at 8:45 on Thursday morning, February 21, taking David Owen, our town manager, along for the ride. In about an hour we arrived at the university and went to Hanaway Hall, where most of the seats were already filled—with hundreds of eager elementary-school children from the area.

The Mint had reserved seats for us in the front row, and we sat with David Sundman who was on hand to represent Littleton Coin Company. Dave Owen was glad to meet Dave Sundman (lots of Daves

Hundreds of elementary-school children from the Plymouth and Campton district were on hand with their teachers to watch the ceremony and to each receive a sparkling new quarter.

here!) as he had been a Littleton client for many years. Members of the Nashua (New Hampshire) Coin Club were also in attendance—the "numismatic delegation," so to speak.

Everyone was set to witness an historic event. Children are, of course, the building blocks of the future and Mint ceremonies typically include them. However, unlike the 2000 Statehood quarter launch in New Hampshire, in which the number of children was rather modest, now an entire auditorium was nearly filled. On the stage at the left was the Plymouth Elementary School Band, which began the program with a selection of music. On the right of the stage were the fourth graders from the Campton Elementary School, who led the audience in the Pledge of Allegiance, followed by the National Anthem.

The Ceremony Begins

Shortly after 10:30 a.m., Bill Dauer of the National Forest Service went to the podium and introduced guests and gave opening remarks. It was evident from the outset that the White Mountain National Forest is more than just a tourist attraction to be visited on occasion; it is a part of New Hampshire life. I know that, of course, having lived in the Granite State for many years. The White Mountain Range, dominated by Mount Washington at 6,288 feet, which has an observatory at the top and prides itself as having the worst weather on earth, includes several dozen peaks of various heights. In and among the valleys are many

different towns. Accordingly, the White Mountains are just about everywhere in the North Country. When used as an adjective, *White Mountain* is singular, such as White Mountain National Forest. When standing alone, *White Mountains* is plural. There is no "White Mountain" entity, although that wording appears at the top of the obverse. It is the name of the chain of peaks.

Selected for depiction by Phebe Hemphill was Mount Chocorua, located in the town of Tamworth, rising above Lake Chocorua in a picturesque setting. With its rocky outcrop on top and distinct appearance, this has been a favorite for artists, photographers, and hikers for a long time. It is well memorialized in White Mountain art—a genre somewhat related to the Hudson River School—with nice depictions of landscapes with luminescent aspects. In the early-20th century the two-story Peak House hotel was prominently located on the slopes of Mount Chocorua, but it blew down in a terrific windstorm in 1917 and was never replaced.

Phebe Hemphill and the other artists were not given directions, but were shown many examples of White Mountain scenes from which they could select favorites. Everyone later agreed that Mount Chocorua was a great choice.

The first speaker after the introductory remarks was Congresswoman Ann McLane Kuster, one of New Hampshire's two lady representatives to Congress. Interestingly, the other two members of New Hampshire's delegation to Washington, Senator Jeanne Shaheen and Senator Kelly Ayotte, are also women, as is Governor Maggie Hassan. New Hampshire is the first state in the Union to be managed, in effect, by five ladies, a nice distinction.

Representative Kuster told of her own experiences in the White Mountains and her love of New Hampshire, and set the scene for a series of talks in which everyone paid tribute to the White Mountains, not from notes or from tourist guides, but from personal experience.

Acting Mint Director Richard Peterson at the podium. He gave a wide-ranging appreciation of the new quarter, enhanced by relating personal experiences of when he and his family lived in and enjoyed New Hampshire.

Then came remarks from representatives of senators Shaheen and Ayotte, after which Tom Wagner, White Mountain National Forest supervisor, acquainted the audience with various aspects of the scope, policies, and history of the National Forest.

Director Peterson at the Podium

Acting Mint Director Richard Peterson came to the podium next. In each of the Statehood quarter launches as well as the "America the Beautiful" quarter launches, a top official of the Mint is the keynote speaker. Typically he or she works from a sheet of notes in order to give informative remarks about a particular state (in the old Statehood series) or, in recent times, a national park, or a national something or other, in a ceremony usually held at a place unfamiliar to Mint leaders. "Canned" remarks result.

Not so here. The New Hampshire quarter was a remarkable exception. It turns out that Dick Peterson, retired Navy officer, used to be with the Portsmouth, New Hampshire Naval Base, a headquarters for submarines. He and his family lived in the Granite State, enjoyed the surroundings from the seacoast to the White Mountains, and still reminisce about their experiences. Dick's remarks were more than just general—he even named his favorite restaurants.

He then shifted to numismatics, telling of President Theodore Roosevelt's desire in 1904 to enlist America's most accomplished sculptor and engraver to redesign the entire spectrum of American coinage from the cent to the $20 double eagle. The sculptor accepted the challenge and set about work in his studio in Cornish, New Hampshire.

"Who was that sculptor?" Peterson asked the audience. "Coin collectors are not allowed to answer!"

Director Peterson with the author. The fast-paced program lasted slightly more than an hour.

Someone in the distance shouted, "Saint-Gaudens!" Right choice. Dick continued with his reminiscences.

Over the years I have been to quite a few launch ceremonies dating back to commemoratives of the early 1980s, but this was the finest keynote speech by a Mint official I have ever heard.

Free Quarters for the Younger Set

Next in the program was Maggie Hassan, newly installed governor of New Hampshire, a fine lady with

Governor Maggie Hassan welcomed a full auditorium dominated by children, but with many adults in attendance, including members of the Nashua Coin Club and other numismatists.

a ready smile, who told of her love of New Hampshire and delineated some of the policies she hoped to implement during her governorship. These involved educational, financial, physical, and other aspects of the Granite State. This part could have been a "political" speech given anywhere. Then she transitioned to the subject at hand, the White Mountains, and told of her experiences among the peaks and her love for them.

The ceremony then concluded, after which Representative Kuster, Governor Hassan, and Acting Mint

Director Peterson went into the audience, each carrying a sack of quarters to hand out to hundreds of outstretched hands. A happier scene could not be imagined!

Each coin had a P mintmark. Each one that I saw could be called a gem in condition—hardly any bagmarks at all. The coins were as brilliant and beautiful as the day they were struck.

As noon approached, David Owen and I headed toward the exit, stopping at tables by the Meredith Village Savings Bank in the lobby, arranged in cooperation with the Treasury Department, in which $10 bank-wrapped rolls of the new quarters were available—a minimum of one roll and a maximum of 10 rolls per person. Individual coins were not offered, as everyone who attended already had one free. I bought five rolls of quarters, and gave most of them to Town Manager Owen and asked him to give them out to the Wolfeboro Town employees (of which there are 82).

Nearby, Littleton Coin Company, whose headquarters is less than an hour's drive to the north, set up a display and gave away to all the children who wanted them specially packaged quarters plus album-boards to collect the "America the Beautiful" quarters. The exhibit was thronged.

Dave Owen and I then left the building, stopped for a nice lunch at the Common Man restaurant in Ashland, and returned to Wolfeboro early in the afternoon. Then came the writing and finessing of an article for *Coin World*, checking with Phebe Hemphill on details, and then going to press—a memorable experience recounted.

An Exclusive Interview with Phebe Hemphill

On February 20, 2013, I conducted an exclusive and far-ranging interview with artist-sculptor Phebe Hemphill (PH), touching upon aspects, most never chronicled in print before, of interest to numismatists.

QDB: Let's talk about the New Hampshire quarter. How were you selected to do the work on it?

The New Hampshire "America the Beautiful" Quarter

PH: It was an open competition. The sculptor-engravers here at the Mint were involved in it and also the Artistic Infusion Program artists who are an outside group of artists that the Mint uses as freelance designers. My design was chosen, and I got to sculpt it as well.

QDB: I have five images of proposals by various artists. I believe these are the semi-finalists. How many entries were there totally?

PH: Let me try to remember.

QDB: Approximately.

PH: There were some designs that were culled out and that didn't make it to the final round. So I believe that the ones that you are looking at would have been the final round.

QDB: Do all the sculptor-engravers at the Mint participate?

PH: Yes.

QDB: And who makes the final selection?

PH: There are two committees in Washington that recommend the winning design to the Mint; they are the CCAC (Citizens Coinage Advisory Committee) and the CFA (Commission of Fine Arts). They make recommendations, but it really is the Mint's decision.

Of the two proposals made by Phebe Hemphill, this is the one not adopted.

QDB: Is the decision at the Mint is made by Dick Peterson, the acting director? Or by the secretary of the Treasury? I believe that in years past it has been one or the other.

PH: It is usually on the secretary of the Treasury's desk and that's who signs off on these things, I think.

QDB: I'll look at the other designs, but Mount Chocorua was your pick? For example, there is Mount Washington, which is the largest mountain, so other people picked whatever they wanted?

PH: Yes.

QDB: Tell me a little bit about your career and I'll just listen.

PH: I was lucky. My grandfather was an amateur sculptor and I have a deep family connection to bas-relief sculpture. My grandfather's aunt studied with Augustus Saint-Gaudens at the Art Students' League back in the 1890s. My grandfather researched his aunt's work and uncovered a lot of her sculpture and information on her life. When I was young I would go into my grandfather's studio where he was practicing bas-relief sculpture. I was able to hang out with him while he was working. I then decided to go to art school at the Pennsylvania Academy of Fine Arts and was able to study traditional figure and portrait sculpture with EvAngelos Frudakis at his small academy in Philadelphia. It is this study, with a master sculptor, that enabled me to have a career in sculpture. After many years of freelancing for various collectible companies and working for toy companies I was hired at the Mint.

QDB: How long have you been at the Mint?

PH: I've been here since 2006. A thrilling moment was when I got here I was able to participate in the Tuskegee Airmen Congressional gold medal competition. My obverse was chosen so I got to sculpt that fairly soon after I got here.

QDB: Is the Tuskegee Airmen medal still available from the Mint?

PH: Yes.

QDB: Who did the reverse?

PH: Don Everhart did the reverse.

QDB: Don is certainly a creative person. I have a set of his Society of Medalists medals showing dinosaurs.

PH: He is the lead sculptor here.

QDB: So you did the Tuskegee Airmen? That was your first completed work?

PH: It wasn't my first, but it was the first big one that I was able to get involved in.

QDB: Now with the Tuskegee Airmen, how did you create the design? Or of any medal for that matter. Are you told what to do, or how do you go about creating a motif?

PH: That one was pretty wide open. They didn't want specific people depicted so I really had to make it all up, using references but not copying anything. That's the case with a lot of these design projects. There are problems with using disputed copyright images, so we try to come up with a lot of the designs on our own.

QDB: The back of the $10 bill until recently showed the Treasury Building with a little automobile in the corner. That was a Ford automobile done in 1928. This car soon became obsolete. The Treasury contemplated redesigning it for years afterward, but officials said "We can't do that, we can't depict a particular model. We could do it in 1928 but we can't do it now." So for years they talked about putting a new car in but they never did.

PH: I'm glad they didn't; I like the old one.

QDB: Tell me about some of the other things you've done. Have you done any of the Statehood quarters or any other National Park quarters?

PH: Oh yes. I was at the Mint when the National Parks program started and I got to do several. I did the Arizona Grand Canyon.

QDB: You need to redesign George on the obverse, by the way. He is far different in appearance than the motif's designer John Flanagan intended. Okay, tell me about the other quarters.

PH: Some parks really give a lot of specific reference material, and in the Arizona design they really wanted a specific photograph and angle. That park gave us the photographs, so we felt confident about reproducing the image. That one was from a very specific vantage point. I also did Mount Hood (Oregon), and they gave us almost no references, so we had to come up with some images on our own. The one I used was a geological survey image that was copyright free, of Mount Hood. I also got to sculpt the Yosemite quarter, although I did not do the design; my colleague Joe Menna did that.

QDB: So he designed it in sketch form and gave the sketch to you?

PH: That's correct. I sculpted the Gettysburg (Pennsylvania) quarter, which I really enjoyed. There has been some criticism about having a landscape on such a tiny coin from various people. I think one of the criticisms is that these landscapes become like a painting on a little coin and you really can't see it too well. But for the Gettysburg I tried to get as much dynamic sculpture into that little quarter to make that landscape pop off the surface as much as I could. I have an interest, an affinity, for these landscapes, so I am glad I got to do that one. I did not design Gettysburg; that was done by AIP artist Joel Iskowitz. The next one I sculpted was Chaco Culture (New Mexico), designed by Donna Weaver. She is no longer at the Mint, but she is an AIP artist designer who is very successful.

DB: Any more quarters in your list of accomplishments?

PH: For the previous quarter program, the 50 State quarters, I was able to sculpt one of the last in the series, the Oklahoma quarter, the scissortail flycatcher bird, which was designed by AIP artist Susan Gamble. I also sculpted the Northern Mariana Islands quarter that was designed by AIP artist Richard Masters.

QDB: You realize that you and other sculptor engravers are part of posterity. This means forever. Unlike a medal a coin gets listed in permanent reference books. Medals are great but they can be forgotten, but these coins will last forever so you are forever enshrined in the pantheon of American engravers. If I were an engraver that would

Phebe Hemphill's 2012 Chaco Culture
America the Beautiful quarter.

be a great distinction. I would rather design one coin than 27 medals. There are several medalists like Mr. MacMonnies, who did many, many medals years ago but never did a legal-tender coin, so few numismatists have ever heard of him and he is not memorialized in *A Guide Book of United States Coins*, the reference book everyone uses. Chester Beach, on the other hand, did coins and medals, and of course, Saint-Gaudens. Have you ever been to the Saint-Gaudens site in New Hampshire?

PH: It's funny. This is very coincidental. I have not been there in the summer but last weekend I attended a funeral for my uncle who lived in New Hampshire, very close to the Saint-Gaudens Site. So I was up in New Hampshire this past weekend and I drove by the site but of course it's not open in the wintertime.

QDB: The curator is Henry Duffy. He's a heck of a nice guy. He and the staff love Saint-Gaudens sculpture, so some time you should give him a call and go up and go through it.

PH: It's something I have always wanted to do.

QDB: Going back to Chocorua. Tell me about the computer versus pen-and-ink sketches. How do you create a design these days?

PH: We use Photoshop, which is typically thought of as photo-editing software, but you can also draw in Photoshop and this gives you a lot of design flexibility. So we design in Photoshop.

QDB: Do you have a stylus, or how do you do that?

PH: What we have is a Wacom Cintiq monitor, which is an interactive screen you can draw directly onto with the Wacom pen. The brush stroke gets immediately recorded in Photoshop.

QDB: So you have a pen, and if you want to do a tree branch you sketch it in on a screen by pushing on it with a pen.

PH: Yes, you draw it like a normal drawing, except that you are drawing on a screen and using Photoshop as your input program.

QDB: Do you save any of your earlier ideas or do they get erased as you go along?

PH: Oh no, that's the great thing about it. You can save infinite variations on these designs, and you will never lose anything as long as it's saved to your computer.

QDB: You created the sketch of Mount Chocorua and then you were told, okay, you won. What happened, step by step, after that?

PH: When I met you here at the Mint last August I showed you a clay. That's what I do first. I print out a transparency of my drawing, a piece of film that I can see through. This is used as a guide for creating the low-relief sculpture in clay. For the "America the Beautiful" quarters, I use an eight-inch-diameter coin basin blank which has been machined out of a high-density foam called REN. This is an exact upscale of the coin basin. I sculpt the image in a hard wax-like clay on this surface.

QDB: How long did it take for you to do that?

PH: The clay stage takes maybe a week and a half. And then when I get to a point where I can't go any further in the clay, I cast plaster over the top of that and I refine

Finessing the final design with computer technology.

QDB: Does anyone critique your work or tell you what to do or not to do?

PH: We have an internal review that all of us go through for each design, and then the final plaster model is scanned and converted to a digital sculpture file. At this stage I can make additional changes and further refine the sculpture using 3D software. Rendered images from the 3D digital sculpture are sent down to headquarters [the U.S. Mint office in Washington] and they review the image. So when everything gets the final okay there, that digital sculpture file is converted to tool paths to CNC-cut the master tooling for the quarters. The first reduction is a positive hub, and that is used to create master dies.

the surface in the negative plaster. Then that gets cast into a positive plaster, and that gets refined further, and I do that about two times. I cast one negative, one positive, a second negative, and the second positive is usually the final. The process of casting back and forth in plaster facilitates the drafting of the sculpture that is so critical for a successful coin.

QDB: Do you review the master tooling and the dies? Do they bring this to you and say "Hey Phebe, here it is. What do you think?" Or is it out of your hands by then?

PH: It's a little out of my hands. If there are any changes that need to be made at that point we go back to the digital file, make any changes in software, and then re-cut the steel. Our scanning and micro-milling technology is so exacting, the fidelity is so fantastic, that there is almost never a problem with regard to the fidelity of the cut steel to the original sculpture. Changes we do make are usually related to coining problems like relief height and draft angles.

QDB: Are there any trial strikings or anything? Does anyone hand you an early impression?

PH: Yes. There are trial strikes.

QDB: What happens to those? All the readers of this interview are going to want to know that.

PH: That's a really good question, what happens to them. I am not sure whether they get put into an archive or whether they get destroyed.

Working with the plaster model.

QDB: Could you find out for me and email me? The Smithsonian would probably like to have some.

PH: I'll try to get an answer for you.

[This was done through Tom Jurkowsky and Michael White of the Mint's Public Affairs Office, with Michael sending an image of such a strike. At present the policy is to destroy them, so as not to create numismatic rarities.]

QDB: Now the plaster you have. What happens to that?

PH: The final plaster is called the master, and that gets archived.

QDB: What about the [clay model] you showed me that was sort of green—what happened to that? It was sort of neat.

PH: I happen to have the very clay that I started on for that quarter. I don't know why I kept it. The original clay models are usually not kept because the sculpture gets greatly improved in the plaster stages.

QDB: Can you take it home and sell it?

PH: No, I can't do that.

QDB: If you create something can you take a sketch or anything and profit from it?

PH: No, not at all. That's strictly forbidden.

QDB: As far as one of the plasters go, maybe the New Hampshire State Historical Society might like that if it is just going to be filed in a room somewhere. I know Chief Engraver Elizabeth Jones pretty well and used to know her predecessor, the late Chief Engraver Frank Gasparro. They were both good acquaintances of mine and helped me a lot with research for certain of my books. Both of them had in their offices a lot of plaster sculptures looking like oversize Necco wafers against each other on the shelf. There was no particular attention paid to them and I hope they didn't get destroyed.

PH: No, the master plasters are kept. Now that we have the digital CNC system, though, it's not as important

because what is used to cut the coin is the digital file, and that is securely backed up and will always be available if there is any issue. So, I don't know how important these plasters are anymore, but we do keep the final ones.

QDB: When did you see your first struck New Hampshire coin?

PH: A couple of weeks ago when they were available in the gift shop here.

QDB: Did they give you one?

PH: I bought one. They don't give you free coins.

QDB: I guess the Mint doesn't give samples. This has been a very productive interview.

PH: I do have a funny story, if you have the time, regarding this quarter. My mother went to camp in the 1940s up there, on Lake Ossipee some miles to the east of Lake and Mount Chocorua, and she was playing around at camp up there on the lakes.

QDB: What was the name of the camp?

PH: Camp Winnemont.

QDB: Winnemont was owned by the Bentley family. Is your mother still living?

PH: Yes.

QDB: This camp was owned by the Bentley family. That was a girls' camp and then the boys' camp was Camp Wyanoke here in Wolfeboro. They had two camps. I will send you some pictures of Camp Winnemont from my collection of New Hampshire historical images.

PH: It's funny. I just found my mother in pictures on a web site of this camp and she's a 17-year-old.

QDB: It's a small world and, I hear tell, there are only 200 people in the world and they all meet each other! I will email you tomorrow when I get back after the ceremony just to send you some pictures for the heck of it. Where can [readers] learn more about your professional accomplishments?

PH: That's all online at the U.S. Mint web site.

QDB: This has been a great interview.

PH: Thank you very much.

The National Forest and Mount Chocorua

The White Mountain National Forest was established in 1918, the result of federal land purchase that began in 1914. At the turn of the 20th century much of the northern third of New Hampshire had been extensively logged, leaving bare landscapes. Many other areas, including the picturesque Franconia Notch (with the Old Man on the Mountains rock formation depicted on the 2000 New Hampshire Statehood quarter), was in private hands and, fortunately for posterity, untouched. Over the years, due to additional purchases plus assistance from private groups and associations, the White Mountain National Forest grew to encompass 750,852 acres, mostly in New Hampshire, but with nearly 6 percent in Maine to the east.

Today the National Forest includes areas for hiking, camping, skiing, and other nature-related activities. More than 100 miles of the famous Appalachian Trail winds through the terrain. The scenic Kancamagus Highway was constructed from the towns of Lincoln to Conway, going through landscapes not easily accessible otherwise, except on foot.

The National Forest comprises three discontinuous areas in which are six specially designated Federal Wilderness Areas. The expanse is so large and the natural landmarks so numerous that it is literally many parks in one. Franconia Notch is a prime attraction. In the Sandwich Range the Sandwich Notch Road, dating back to colonial times, was once the route for freight wagons going from Montreal to Portsmouth on the seacoast. Mount Washington and its observatory are a magnet for visitors, some of whom drive on the Auto Road to the top (also the scene of arranged races) or take the Cog Railway. In his New Hampshire launch ceremony, Acting Director Peterson said that his family had gone up the road in their car and had a bumper sticker to prove it. The White Mountain National Forest is likely the most visited such federal facility east of the Mississippi River.

Mount Chocorua is the easternmost peak in the Sandwich Range. The *Appalachian Mountain Club Guide* states that it, with a rocky picturesque cone as its summit, is one of the most photographed mountains in the entire world. Its height of slightly less than 3,500 feet makes it a popular climb and also a challenge for hikers who have a choice of several trails ranging in difficulty. The top offers panoramic views in all directions.

A legend has it that Chocorua was the name of a Native American who about the year 1720 was on friendly terms with settlers in the area, particularly the Cornelius Campbell family. Called away on a mission, Chocorua left his young son, Tuamba, in the care of the Campbells. The boy found and drank a poison fluid that was kept on hand to eliminate foxes that were depredating chickens. Chocorua returned and was told his son had died. Not long afterward, Mr. Campbell came home one evening to find that his family had been killed. He suspected Chocorua and chased him up the mountain that would later bear his name. Wounded by a bullet, Chocorua leaped from the rocky summit to his death, shouting a curse on the white settlers.

There are several versions of the story and the words uttered. "Chocorua's Curse," by Lydia Maria Child, published in The Token, 1830, gives these words:

> A curse upon ye, white men! May the Great Spirit curse ye when he speaks in the clouds, and his words are fire! Chocorua had a son—and ye killed him while the sky looked bright! Lightning, blast your crops! Wind and fire destroy your dwellings! The Evil Spirit breathe death upon your cattle! Your graves lie in the war path of the Indian! Panthers howl, and

A 1911 postcard showing Lake and Mount Chocorua, one of New Hampshire's most popular scenic views.

Detail of a 1906 postcard showing the Peak House, near the rocky top of Mount Chocorua. This accommodated overnight guests until it was blown down in a windstorm in 1917.

wolves fatten over your bones! Chocorua goes to the Great Spirit—his curse stays with the white men.

Cornelius Campbell was the first victim of the curse, the story goes. His body was found on the mountain two years later, partially eaten by wolves. Not a word of these stories has ever been confirmed by fact, but the legend endures in folk history and is memorialized on a roadside marker near the peak.

Phebe Hemphill

Phebe Hemphill is a graduate of the Pennsylvania Academy of the Fine Arts. She studied for three years with sculptor EvAngelos Frudakis in Philadelphia. In 1987, she joined the sculpture department at the Franklin Mint and for the next 15 years worked on many projects for the porcelain and medallic departments.

As a freelance sculptor, Hemphill has displayed her creative talents while working with various companies that produce figurines, medallions, dolls, toys, and garden ornaments. Prior to joining the United States Mint's team of sculptor-engravers in 2006, she was a staff sculptor for three years with McFarlane Toys in Bloomingdale, New Jersey. Hemphill's extraordinary sculptures have been exhibited with the National Sculpture Society, American Medallic Sculpture Association, West Chester University, and the F.A.N. Gallery in Philadelphia.

In 2000, Hemphill received the Alex J. Ettel Grant from the National

Mt. Chocorua from Chocorua Lake, oil on canvas, by American artist William Paskell circa 1900.

- 2009 American Platinum Eagle reverse (sculpting)
- 2009 District of Columbia and U.S. Territories Quarters Program—Northern Mariana Islands reverse (sculpting)
- 2009 First Spouse gold coin—Letitia Tyler obverse (design and sculpting)
- 2009 First Spouse gold coin—Margaret Taylor obverse (design)
- 2009 First Spouse gold coin—Sarah Polk obverse (design and sculpting)
- 2009 First Spouse gold coin—Sarah Polk reverse (design and sculpting)
- 2009 Louis Braille Bicentennial commemorative coin obverse (sculpting)
- 2009 Presidential $1 coin—John Tyler obverse (design and sculpting)

Sculpture Society, and in 2001, she received the Renaissance Sculpture Award from the Franklin Mint.

Coin Sculpting and Design Credits

- 2007 American Platinum Eagle reverse (sculpting)
- 2007 First Spouse gold coin—Abigail Adams reverse (sculpting)
- 2007 First Spouse gold coin—Thomas Jefferson's Liberty obverse (sculpting)
- 2008 50 State Quarters® Program—Oklahoma reverse (sculpting)
- 2008 Bald Eagle commemorative coin—gold obverse (sculpting)
- 2008 First Spouse gold coin—Louisa Adams obverse (sculpting)
- 2008 Presidential $1 coin—Martin Van Buren obverse (sculpting)
- 2009 Abraham Lincoln commemorative silver dollar reverse (design and sculpting)

- 2010 America the Beautiful Quarters Program—Grand Canyon National Park reverse (design and sculpting)
- 2010 America the Beautiful Quarters Program—Mount Hood National Forest reverse (design and sculpting)

- 2010 America the Beautiful Quarters Program—Yosemite National Park reverse (sculpting)
- 2010 American Platinum Eagle reverse (sculpting)
- 2010 First Spouse gold coin—Abigail Fillmore obverse (design and sculpting)
- 2010 First Spouse gold coin—Mary Todd Lincoln obverse (design and sculpting)

- 2010 First Spouse gold coin—Mary Todd Lincoln reverse (sculpting)
- 2010 Presidential $1 coin—James Buchanan obverse (design and sculpting)
- 2011 America the Beautiful Quarters Program—Gettysburg National Military Park reverse (sculpting)
- 2011 American Platinum Eagle reverse (sculpting)

The finished three-inch-diameter bronze Code Talkers medal. During World War II various members of Native American tribes were paired with each other at the ends of radio communications. They related secret military instructions in their tribal languages that were impossible for enemies to translate. The program was very effective. (U.S. Mint)

Presentation of Congressional gold medals to 25 tribes at the ceremony on November 20, 2013. These were the tribes to be honored on the series of Code Talkers medals, ongoing at the time. (U.S. Mint)

Phebe Hemphill at work on the clay model for the Meskwaki Nation Code Talkers medal, 2013.

- 2011 First Spouse gold coin—Eliza Johnson reverse (sculpting)
- 2011 First Spouse gold coin—Lucretia Garfield obverse (sculpting)
- 2011 Medal of Honor commemorative coin silver reverse (sculpting)
- 2011 Presidential $1 coin—James Garfield obverse (design and sculpting)
- 2011 United States Army commemorative coin—gold obverse (sculpting)
- 2012 America the Beautiful Quarters Program—Chaco Culture National Historical Park reverse (sculpting)
- 2012 First Spouse gold coin—Alice Paul obverse (sculpting)
- 2012 First Spouse gold coin—Frances Cleveland (variety 2) obverse (sculpting)
- 2012 First Spouse gold coin—Frances Cleveland (variety 2) reverse (sculpting)
- 2012 First Spouse gold coin—Suffrage Movement reverse (design and sculpting)
- 2012 Native American $1 coin—reverse (sculpting)
- 2012 Presidential $1 coin—Benjamin Harrison obverse (design and sculpting)
- 2012 Star-Spangled Banner commemorative silver coin obverse (sculpting)
- 2013 Five-Star Generals commemorative coin—clad obverse and reverse (design and sculpting)
- 2013 America the Beautiful Quarters Program—White Mountain National Forest reverse (design and sculpting)
- 2013 Girl Scouts of the USA Centennial silver dollar obverse (sculpting)
- 2013 Native American $1 coin reverse (sculpting)
- 2013 Presidential $1 coin—William McKinley obverse (design and sculpting)

Medal Sculpting Credits

- 2006 Norman E. Borlaug Congressional gold medal obverse (design and sculpting)
- 2006 Tuskegee Airmen Congressional gold medal obverse (design and sculpting)
- 2008 Senator Edward William Brooke Congressional gold medal reverse (design and sculpting)
- 2009 New Frontier Congressional gold medal obverse (sculpting)
- 2009 Women Air Force Service Pilots Congressional gold medal obverse (sculpting)
- 2011 September 11 National medal obverse (sculpting)
- Chocktaw Nation obverse, Code Talkers (sculpting)
- Crow Creek Sioux Tribe obverse, Code Talkers (sculpting)
- Meskwaki Nation obverse, Code Talkers (sculpting)
- Muscogee Creek Nation obverse, Code Talkers (sculpting)
- Osage Nation obverse, Code Talkers (sculpting)
- Ponca Tribe obverse, Code Talkers (sculpting)
- Santee Sioux Nation obverse, Code Talkers (sculpting)
- Seminole Nation obverse, Code Talkers (sculpting)
- Sisseton Wahpeton Sioux obverse, Code Talkers (sculpting)

The September 11 medal.

The Tuskegee Airmen medal.

CHAPTER 46

Completing a series is the goal of many collectors. In this chapter you will see two choices to consider.

Collecting by Coinage Years

Wide-Ranging Possibilities

A complete collection of United States coinage of the year 1816.

Every now and again a numismatist endeavors to focus on the coinage of a single year and obtain one each of the different denominations and mint-mark varieties minted, not including commemoratives, patterns, and others not intended for circulation.

The prize for the fewest goes to 1816, when the only denomination struck was the copper cent. In 1793 there were just two: the half cent and cent. In 1815 only the quarter, half dollar, and $5 half eagle were made. In 1799 the cent, dollar, $5, and $10 were the only denominations minted. Into the 20th century there are no record-breakers, but several years have relatively few denominations. In 1922 coinage included the cent; 1922-D, and 1922-S Peace silver dollars; and 1922 and 1922-S double eagles. In 1965 and 1966 Mint Director Eva Adams blamed coin collectors for a nationwide coin shortage, although the hoarding was done by the general public, not by numismatists. As punishment she ordered that mintmarks be eliminated for the coinage done at branch mints. Accordingly, the record shows that for these two years we only have mintmarkless (in any other era indicating "Philadelphia") coins from the cent to the half dollar, five denominations in all.

The Sweeping Panorama of 1873

The most famous specialist in forming a collection of a single date was Harry X Boosel, a Chicago collector active starting in the 1930s, who focused on the year 1873. It was Boosel (whose middle "name" was simply X, without a period) who publicized in the 1960s that for certain denominations of 1873 there were Open 3 and Close 3 variations in the date numerals. This difference in style came about early in 1873 when it was noticed at the Mint that the four-digit date logotype appeared at quick glance to be 1878. The last digit was modified in February and the knobs or balls on the 3 were spaced wider apart, creating the Open 3 style. In addition, and creating more

An 1873 trade dollar of the Philadelphia Mint, a tiny part of a set of 1873 coinage.

varieties, for the silver coins from dimes to silver dollars, those made after early in the year were of slightly higher weight; these were distinguished by having arrowheads placed at the date.

The 1873 year takes the cake for the number of different with 53 in all, quite a contrast with 1816! The coins include:

- 1873 Indian Head cent, Close 3
- 1873 Indian Head cent, Open 3
- 1873 nickel three-cent piece, Open 3
- 1873 silver three-cent piece, or trime, Close 3
- 1873 half dime, Close 3
- 1873-S half dime
- 1873 dime, Close 3
- 1873 dime, Open 3
- 1873-CC dime, Close 3 (unique today)
- 1873-CC dime, Open 3
- 1873 dime, Arrows at Date, Open 3
- 1873-CC dime, Arrows at Date, Open 3
- 1873-S dime, Arrows at Date, Open 3
- 1873 quarter, Close 3
- 1873 quarter, Arrows at Date, Open 3
- 1873-CC quarter, Close 3 (unique today)
- 1873-CC quarter, Arrows at Date, Open 3
- 1873-S quarter, Arrows at Date, Open 3
- 1873 half dollar, Close 3
- 1873 half dollar, Open 3
- 1873 half dollar, Arrows at Date, Open 3
- 1873-CC half dollar, Close 3
- 1873-CC half dollar, Arrows at Date, Open 3

- 1873-S half dollar, Close 3 (5,000 struck; none known today)
- 1873-S half dollar, Arrows at Date, Open 3
- 1873 Liberty Seated silver dollar, Close 3
- 1873-CC Liberty Seated silver dollar, Close 3
- 1873-S Liberty Seated silver dollar, Close3 (700 struck; none known today)
- 1873 trade dollar, Open 3
- 1873-CC trade dollar, Open 3
- 1873-S trade dollar, Open 3
- 1873 gold dollar, Close 3
- 1873 gold dollar, Open 3
- 1873 $2.50 gold, Close 3
- 1873 $2.50 gold, Open 3
- 1873-S $2.50 gold, Close 3
- 1873 $3 gold, Close 3
- 1873 $3 gold, Open 3
- 1873 $5 gold, Close 3
- 1873 $5 gold, Open 3
- 1873-CC $5 gold, Close 3
- 1873-S $5 gold, Close 3
- 1873 $10 gold, Close 3
- 1873-CC $10 gold, Close 3
- 1873-S $10 gold, Close 3
- 1873 $20 gold, Close 3
- 1873 $20 gold, Open 3
- 1873-CC $20 gold, Close 3
- 1873-S $20 gold, Close 3
- 1873-S $20 gold, Open 3

Into the Panic of 1837, coins of all denominations were hoarded, including copper cents. Chapter 33 tells of the situation. Many privately issued Hard Times tokens served as substitutes. The nickel-alloy small-diameter cents of Dr. Lewis Feuchtwanger were particularly popular at the time. They came close to setting the ongoing Mint standard for cents, until the director of that institution objected.

Dr. Lewis Feuchtwanger

Feuchtwanger Cents of 1837

Dr. Lewis Feuchtwanger was an entrepreneur and scientist who simultaneously ranks as one of the most important figures in mid-19th-century American numismatic history and in the study of mineralogical gems.[1] Born in Fürth, Bavaria, Germany, January 11, 1805, the son of a mineralogist,[2] he developed an interest in science at an early age. In 1827 he graduated as a medical doctor from the University of Jena, Thuringia, Germany, an institution with which he kept in contact for years thereafter. Seeking expanded opportunities, Feuchtwanger emigrated to America in 1829 and settled in New York City, where in time he opened the first German pharmacy. From this time onward he imported medicines, apparatus, chemicals, and other items from his native land.

By 1831 he set up a drugstore, curiosity shop, and museum at 377 Broadway, near the corner of White Street,[3] where he would remain until 1837. In 1831 also he publicized an alloy he had compounded before coming to this country. This was called Feuchtwanger's Composition, also occasionally referred to as American silver, a version of German silver, intended to imitate silver through an alloy of other metals, typically nickel, copper, and tin, sometimes with a trace of actual silver. This alloy was recommended as an ideal substitute for silver in many uses, including table and household goods, and for copper in coinage. It was more durable than pewter or, as sometimes branded, Britannia metal, whose composition is about 92 percent tin, 6 percent antimony, and 2 percent copper. In the early years he imported his alloy from Germany. Later he compounded it in New York City.

In addition to his business as a druggist and chemist,

> He also sold natural curiosities, such as rare minerals, gems, preserved reptiles, etc., a large collection of which he placed on exhibition at Peale's Museum and Gallery of Fine Arts at 252 Broadway,[4] and at a later time (in the 1850s) at the New York Lyceum of Natural History. At his Broadway store, "one door below White Street," he advertised "Nuremburgh Salve" and "Kreosote . . . a recent German discovery for preventing toothache." These nostrums seem to have been highly esteemed in their time.[5]

Dr. Feuchtwanger was a prolific advertiser in New York City newspapers.

To further the advance of agriculture, manufacture, and commerce the American Institute was founded in New York City in January 1828 and incorporated on May 2, 1829. Each year its Annual Fair (first held in October 1828[6]) would showcase various exhibits, which would in many instances be awarded a gold medal (highest honor), silver medal, or diploma (lowest recognition). In addition, if a medal had been given previously for a product, a suitably inscribed diploma would be awarded if it was deemed worthy of a later silver- or gold-medal honor. In 1834 Feuchtwanger was awarded a silver medal for the display of his Feuchtwanger's Composition and products made from it. Another silver medal was given to Feuchtwanger by the American Institute in 1835, and a third in 1836. Apparently, his displays were different each time.[7] Feuchtwanger also issued advertising tokens about the size of a quarter, one stating that the "American Silver

Composition" was ideal for instruments, beer pumps, pillars, grates, spoons, forks, and dinner sets. At the time he was at 377 Broadway.

By April 1837 Feuchtwanger moved his business a short distance to 2 Cortlandt (also spelled Courtlandt) Street, setting the scene for his popular "silver penny" and other issues, including quarter-size three-cent pieces made in two main styles: with the New York State arms and with an eagle similar to that used on his cents.

A Petition to Congress

In late summer and autumn 1837 Feuchtwanger spent much time and effort in trying to interest Congress in adapting his alloy to make coins. The new metal was said to have been "clean, while a durable material, of specific value, from which coins and all articles can be advantageously manufactured as are now wrought out of silver."[8] His ideas were outlined in a petition dated September 13, bearing the heading, 25th Congress, Document No. 7, House of Representatives, 1st Session, titled "Substitute for Copper. Memorial Lewis Feuchtwanger." The text noted:

Three-cent token made of Feuchtwanger's Composition. The obverse shows the state arms of New York. The stars and rosettes on the reverse are similar to those used on the R.E. Russell token illustrated later in this chapter. (HT-262, Low 117 variety)

> That your memorialist after repeated labors, has succeeded in making and perfecting a metallic composition, known as German silver, of clean, white, and durable material, of specific value, from which coins and all articles can be advantageously manufactured, as are now wrought out of pure silver.
>
> Your memorialist proposes to your honorable body to substitute this composition for the copper currency of the country, by striking off pieces of the size of a dime, and of the value of one cent, specimens of which he has prepared for inspection.
>
> Your memorialist proposes to furnish this substitute for copper as cheaply as copper is now furnished to

Eagle-design three-cent token made of Feuchtwanger's Composition. (HT-263, Low 118 variety)

the Mint, and is confident that the "silver cent" thus proposed as a substitute for the cent pieces will be more acceptable, more portable, and would be more generally used in making up the fractional parts of a dollar.

Your memorialist prays your honorable body to take the subject under your consideration, and, as in duty bound, will ever pray.

In Congress on September 13, Senator Thomas Hart Benton, of Missouri, presented Feuchtwanger's proposal "accompanied by specimens" for distribution to fellow legislators.[9]

To advance his proposal, the inventor prepared a "Circular," as it was titled, enclosing an example of a "silver penny" made of his American Silver, and with this text:[10]

I submit for your consideration a specimen of a one-cent piece made of American Composition, known by the name of German Silver, equivalent in value to One Cent in Copper, which I propose with the authority of Congress, to substitute for the existing unclean and unhealthy Copper Currency by which a handsome current coin may be obtained answerable for the fractional parts of a Dollar, and acceptable in the operations of trade and local purchases.

If this "Silver Penny" as I wish to have it designated shall be approved by Congress as a substitute for the one Cent pieces, I shall in that case, propose to remunerate the Mint for any loss sustained by the United States by the withdrawal of the Copper Coin. I am ready to contract for the delivery at the Mint of any amount of the Com-

position which Congress may authorize to be coined.

Dr. Lewis Feuchtwanger,
New-York City

It seems likely that the foregoing "Circular" as well as the proposal to Congress generated these two notices in the *U.S. Gazette*, Philadelphia, September 11 and 12, 1837:[11]

One Cent Pieces

Dr. Lewis Feuchtwanger, of New York, has issued a German silver penny, milled at the edge, on one side a fine bold eagle, and the reverse a wreath, with the words, 'one cent,' with his name on the circle. It is of the intrinsic value of one cent, and about the size of a dime. They are a first rate substitute for small change. One hundred makes a dollar.

The Cent

A friend called on us yesterday, with a sample of M. Feuchtwanger's coin of "one cent" to which we referred to in our morning's paper. It was a beautiful piece of money, if it may be allowed such a title, much more convenient in every way than the copper coin; and should silver and gold ever come again in fashion, we think this kind of "cent" would be a very excellent attendant.

The New York City *Evening Post* published this advertisement on October 19, 1837:

Hard Currency

Specie—One Cent Pieces.[12] The subscriber is furnishing the trade with his pennies of German silver, acknowledged by all persons who have had an opportunity of receiving them in exchange to be far superior to the dirty and unhealthy copper cents.

The tokens are neat, beautiful, portable, and of white metal; and he believes that when a sufficient quantity get into circulation the present flood of shinplasters, rags, &c. will immediately disappear, the more so as the intrinsic value of the one cent pieces bears a much greater resemblance to the real currency of the country, than the present flood of shinplasters with which the public are now so much imposed upon. Orders from the country are solicited and promptly executed.

Dr. Lewis Feuchtwanger
2 Courtlandt St.

And this in the *Baltimore Sun*, October 24, 1837:[13]

Metallic Currency

The country is flooded with copper medals of nearly the size and weight of cents, most of them bearing devices and inscriptions defamatory of the general government; but many are mere advertisements of goods and wares in copper. There are two manufacturers of them in Boston, and a hundred are made for thirty-five cents, affording a very fair profit to the maker. Perhaps an emission of German silver cents might suppress them.

The idea continued to command the attention of Senator Thomas Hart Benton, who on October 14, 1837, wrote to Mint Director Robert M. Patterson to endorse the idea. On January 4, 1838, Patterson replied with a long letter giving multiple objections, concluding with this:

On the whole, it is my decided opinion that it would not be proper to abandon our copper coinage in favor of the proposed substitute, and you will observe that, in presenting this opinion, I have not thought it necessary to bring to your view the many advantages belonging to the copper coinage; its profit to the Government, (the only pecuniary offset to the expense of the Mint), the hold which it has on the habits of the people, and the loss which would be sustained by its suppression, or the confusion which would arise from a double circulation of the same class.

At the time the Mint struck silver and gold coins at the request of depositors of those metals, charging only a nominal fee for doing so. In contrast, the profit between the face value and the significantly lower metal cost for copper used in half cents and cents went directly to the Mint's bottom line. Had Feuchtwanger's proposal been accepted, this advantage would have been lost.

His proposal rejected, perhaps at least in part because his asking price for the patent was said to have been $100,000 (although this was not specifically noted in the proposal), Feuchtwanger seems to have continued issuing his one-cent and three-cent pieces on a commercial basis, from dies dated 1837. Judging for the availability today of certain varieties, likely the cents were circulated to the extent of several million examples.

Feuchtwanger Cent Varieties of 1837

Hard Times tokens issued by Lewis Feuchtwanger, ONE CENT denomination, struck in Feuchtwanger's metal, reeded edge (except 7-J, silver, plain edge), are very interesting to contemplate and study.[14] It seems likely that the dies were made and the tokens were struck by Bale & Smith, 68 Nassau Street, New York City, from finished planchets supplied by Feuchtwanger, who is believed to have had complete facilities for rolling strips from ingots and for punching planchets from the strips. Bale & Smith did a wide-ranging business in tokens with customers on the East Coast.

The collecting of 1837 Feuchtwanger cents by die varieties has captured the interest and imagination of many numismatists over the years, including in recent times many readers of Russell Rulau's books on Hard Times and other tokens, which describe the die details. Rulau in the *Standard Catalog of U.S. Tokens* lists these as HT-268 and under that heading describes the varieties. Lyman H. Low in *Hard Times Tokens* lists the class as Low-120, without descriptions of the varieties.

Starting in 1997, by 2011 token collector, researcher, and dealer Stephen L. Tanenbaum had acquired all of the regular varieties except 3-C and 4-F. I embarked on a similar pursuit a few years later and was able to find all except the same two rarities. The awareness and popularity of Feuchtwanger cents has been enhanced by their listing as a general type in *A Guide Book of United States Coins* (the hobby's popular "Red Book").

Die Combinations of 1837 Feuchtwanger Cents

Feuchtwanger 1-A • Rarity-4 • *obverse 1*: Coarse dentils. Large date close to ground above, the 3 exceptionally large, the 7 very high. Snake's tongue slightly to the right of vertical. Seven tail feathers, four of them touching the ground. Known combinations: 1-A. • *Reverse A*: ONE very widely spaced. Small O's in COMPOSITION. A and P recut. Known combinations: 1-A, 2-A.

Feuchtwanger 2-A • R-5 • *obverse 2*: Similar treatment of the eagle to obverse 1. In date 18 low, small, closely spaced; 37 much larger, higher, also closely spaced. Eight tail feathers, five touching ground. *Grass is wavy or billowy and generally slants upward to the right. On the eagle's neck there are two raised bars, slanting down to the left and extending slightly into the field.* Of the tail feathers, four large feathers are delineated with their tips touching the ground, after which the fifth feather is not as well formed and may consist of two smaller feathers touching ground. In back below the wing, four feathers, the lowest being somewhat indistinct. Back loop of snake: More or less circular in shape; above 8. Known combinations: 2-A.

used with obverse 3 for which this is true). *Stems of the two upper inside berries of the right branch arise from innermost leaves almost at tips.* Known combination: 3-C. This and the 4-F are the Holy Grail varieties among circulation strikes of Feuchtwanger cents.

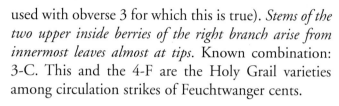

Feuchtwanger 3-D • R-7 • *Reverse D*: O in ONE slightly low. Right bow plainly overlaps left one. Right ribbon very close to both S and I. Known combinations: 3-D.

Feuchtwanger 3-B • R-3 • *obverse 3*: Date closely spaced, from smaller punches as on all to follow, and in a straight line on top. The 7 frequently shows crumbling between horizontal and upright; rim breaks down at lower right. Seven tail feathers, first two and fourth (latter recut) touching ground. Ground resembles pine branches. Known combinations: 3-B, 3-C, 3-D, 3-E, 3-G. • *Reverse B: Stems end in marked claws. 1st left inside berry has two stems. S in COMPOSITION very defective at top. Upright of F recut. N in COMPOSITION recut.* Known combination: 3-B.

Feuchtwanger 3-E • R-3 • *Reverse E*: IT about touch. E in ONE, T in CENT (left top) and P in COMPOSITION clearly recut. NT joined at top. Known combinations: 3-E (struck first), 4-E (struck last).

Feuchtwanger 3-C • R-8 • *Reverse C: Star close to final S in FEUCHTWANGER'S* (the only reverse die

Feuchtwanger 3-G • R-6 • *Reverse G*: 13 berries, the extra one just right of the bow. Berry near base of T in CENT attached to a leaf. Star too close to final N in COMPOSITION. Stems end in claws though not too distinctly. M P O spaced apart. Develops a crack through HTWANG, and another from wreath through final N to edge. N in ONE crumbles at base. Known combinations: 3-G, 5-G, 6-G.

Feuchtwanger 4-F • R-8 • *Reverse F: E (ONE) repunched at bottom.* Left stem with line at the end, giving it an appearance like a pen point. Ribbon end above O is solidly connected to bow and ends above the right side of P. Known combination: 4-F. This and the 3-C are the Holy Grail varieties among circulation strikes of Feuchtwanger cents.

Feuchtwanger 4-E • R-3 • *obverse 4*: In date 3 low, rather distant from 7 and often joined to it at top by a line. *Loop in snake's tail above and left of 1 in date*; in all other dies loop is above 18. Snake's tongue very long, very deeply forked. Back loop of snake: somewhat flattened; *centered to the left of 1*; a very distinctive diagnostic feature. Eagle's head droops. Eight tail feathers, three touching ground. • *Reverse E: NT solidly joined at top with a bar.* NE joined at top. Base of T (CENT) recut. Ribbon end above O is lightly connected to bow and ends slightly left of the center of the O. 13 Known combinations: 4-E, 4-F.

Feuchtwanger 5-G • R-2 • *obverse 5*: Date widely and evenly spaced; *slightly curved bar in ground directly above 83*. Seven tail feathers, only the second barely touching ground; fourth recut at tip. Ground resembles pine branches, but not as closely as obverse 3. First feather very close to ground above coil of snake; no vegetation in this area. In back below wing, six feathers with more or less rectangular ends; some slight vane details on feathers 2, 3, and 4. *Small curved line extends below bottom of leading edge of eagle's wing on right.* Back loop of snake: more or less circular, prominent beadlike segments evident; Centered over space between 1 and 8, and closer to 1. Reverse Die

State I: Perfect die. Reverse Die State II: Crack from wreath through left upright of N (COMPOSITION) to edge; this on about half of the extant pieces seen. On this die state a raised curved line develops at lower right of O (ONE), resembling a repunching. Reverse Die State III: Latest state seen. Lowest inside-left and second-lowest inside-right berries repunched to make them larger; lowest inside-left now has a hook or thorn projecting from it. Die crack from stem above 1st O (COMPOSITION) through tops of POSI. Rare. Known combinations: 5-G, 5-H.

Feuchtwanger 6-I • R-1 • *Reverse I*: 13 berries, extra one just left of bow, *and looking more like an extra stem*. E in CENT heavily recut. E in ONE high at base but in line with N at top. EU widely spaced; base of W significantly lower than left foot of A; R weak at top. Known combination: 6-I. • The most plentiful variety, probably at several times as populous as the next contender.

Feuchtwanger 5-H • R-1 • *Reverse H*: 13 berries, extra one just left of bow. E in ONE: top high at top and base. Crude recutting NE CEN; crumbling develops on these letters. Known combination: 5-H.

Feuchtwanger 6-RER • Rulau HT-309, Low-128; **• R-5 •** *Reverse RER*: R.E. RUSSELL at top border. At top center, three rosettes (center one larger; two smaller ones punched over stars) below which is I • O • U. In the fraction the denominator 2 is over an erroneous 1. Near bottom border, 12½ c, with three stars below (the center one being larger). From the left-center border continuing to the bottom border and ending at the center-right border are nine stars with stars 2, 5, and 8 being considerably larger than the others. Known combination: 6-RER.

Feuchtwanger 6-G • R-2 • *obverse 6*: Closely spaced date, bottoms in a straight line; 83 a little apart. Dash to left from upper serif of 1. *Base of eagle's neck smooth.* Seven tail feathers, four of them touching ground. Known combinations: 6-G, 6-I, 6-RER (Russell).

Aaron Packard, who has done extensive research in the field of tokens, has tentatively ascribed the token to Russell in Charleston, South Carolina, a dealer in botanical goods in the late 1830s and a bath house in connection with his Botany Garden.[15] The 12-1/2–cent denomination was popular at the time and was equal to one Spanish real or "bit."

The R.E. Russell token has been a well-known rarity for a long time. At the Thomas Birch & Sons sale of the S.W. Chubbuck Collection on February 27 and 2, 1868, one brought $10.25, twice the price of a 1796 quarter in Good grade that sold for $5 at the same event. When the collection of Matthew A. Stickney was auctioned by Henry Chapman in New York City, June 26 to 29, 1907, a Russell token brought $105, or about 10 times the typical price for an 1856 Flying Eagle cent in the marketplace! This was in an era of great passion for Hard Times and related tokens, when such pieces were widely publicized in *The Numismatist*, in dealers' catalogs, and elsewhere.

space between 1 and 8, closer to 8; somewhat similar to obverse 3, but with important differences. A very distinctive die. Known combinations: 7-J. • *Reverse J*: A carefully made die; wide spacing of border letters, good alignment, and with delicate features. Berry positions: Left outside berries opposite: Center of C / right side of upright of F / left of C. • Right outside berries opposite: Left upright of N / center of S / space between GE and slightly closer to E. Known combination: 7-J.

From 1862 to 1864 one-cent pieces were scarce in circulation and silver denominations were never seen, due to public hoarding. Among the currency substitutes was a "Feuchtwanger 9-cent strip," as illustrated. Nothing has been found concerning its issuer. These appear in the marketplace occasionally and are often collected in connection with encased postage stamps, an invention of the Civil War era.

Feuchtwanger 7-J Pattern • R-8, believed unique. Unknown to Russ Rulau. Could be designated as "HT-268-A." Pattern struck in silver, *plain edge*. Perfect dies. • *obverse 7*: 18 (1837) low, 3 high, 7 highest. Snake's tongue very short. Tail feather 1 embedded in top of coil of snake, feathers 2 and 3 touch ground, 3 close but with small plain space intervening. In back below wing, three feathers with vane details (superficially resembling these details in obverse 3, but with differences). Details of back wing (above top edge of front wing) incomplete. Eagle with very long tongue. Back loop of snake: more or less circular, prominent beadlike segments evident, centered over

"Feuchtwanger" 9-cent strip of three overlapping postage stamps in a copper frame with a Feuchtwanger-style eagle on the reverse. All seem to have been made by hand. Several dozen or so exist today.

CHAPTER 48

In his day Sherlock Holmes looked at the obvious, studied the information given to him, usually by Dr. Watson, then saw things that others overlooked. Generations later Yogi Berra said, "You can see a lot of things by just looking."

Acres of Diamonds

Perhaps like Edwin Parmele, proprietor of the Bowling Saloon in New York City in 1837, you will be "Quite Comfortable" by the time you reach this chapter! (Rulau HT-302, Low 268, by far the finest of three or four known; a Fine example with a cracked planchet was plated in the American Art Association catalog way back in 1886)

In the Footsteps of Sherlock Holmes: Numismatic Forensics

Years ago a motivational speaker told his audience that there were acres of diamonds at their feet free for the taking, but they needed to be recognized and picked up. Similarly, Holmes and Berra, mentioned above, found success by studying the obvious.

In numismatics there is endless opportunity to find interesting things, most of which have already been discovered, but many awaiting recognition. The 1938-D, D Over S, overmintmark mentioned in chapter 28 is a poster example. Not until 1962 had anyone among millions of coin collectors studied the common 1938-D Buffalo nickel carefully. Then two men working together found that on one curious, indeed inexplicable, coin there was an S mintmark clearly visible beneath the regular D. Excited about their discovery, they sent the information to the weekly newspaper *Coin World*. Editor Margo Russell contacted me about this seemingly unbelievable coin, I confirmed it, and the rest is history. Today the 1938-D/S nickel is a common variety!

In the series of federal coins most varieties have been carefully studied. And yet there are still opportunities. Similarly to the Buffalo nickel find, numismatist Harry W. Bass Jr. was the first to observe that on an often-seen variety of 1803 $10 gold coin there was a stray star on the reverse, in addi-

The newspaper *Alta California* noted on May 31, 1849, the existence of: "a five-dollar gold coin struck at Benicia City, though the imprint is San Francisco. In general appearance it resembles the United States coin of the same value, but it bears the private stamp of Norris, Gregg & Norris and is in other particulars widely different." Thus was announced the first coins to be struck in the California Territory using Gold Rush metal. The firm was in the plumbing and hardware-supply business in New York City, where the dies were probably made. The California coinage represented a short-lived venture that expired in 1850 after some $5 coins with that date were minted by the firm in Stockton.

tion to the normal 13. As mentioned in chapter 19, this spurred him onward to become one of the greatest researchers in the specialty of early American gold coins.

While I do not suggest that you will make any such startling discovery, the opportunity does exist, and hundreds of other collectors have scored home runs. More realistically, with the aid of a magnifying glass and a good measure of curiosity, you can examine coins in your possession and enjoy noting their unusual features. This pursuit is especially rewarding with early coins, tokens, medals, and bank notes from hand-made dies or individually made printing plates. If anything, numismatics is a very diverse pursuit. In looking through miscellany you will certainly whet your curiosity.

This chapter shares some such varieties I have found to be interesting—from rustic tokens to perfection in modern die making—a tiny tip of a very large numismatic iceberg.

In the spring of 1862 the city of New Orleans was occupied by troops of the Confederate States of America. Most coins had already disappeared from circulation. To fill the public need John B. Schiller, proprietor of the Sazerac (Coffee) House, obtained some 1860 (the year he became sole owner of the coffee house) Indian Head cents and stamped his name on the obverse and an X, for 10 cents, on the reverse. He paid these out and redeemed them at the enhanced value. He also issued paper scrip notes. Schiller died in 1867, leaving a fortune of $250,000. Today the cent is collected as part of the Civil War token series as Fuld variety LA-670-A-do. It is estimated that fewer than a dozen are known.

"To err is human, to forgive is divine," it is said. When an engraver errs in die making that is divine to numismatists. In 1787 an engraver was preparing the reverse of a Connecticut copper and instead of punching IN, the start of INDE, he punched FU, the start of Fugio—he thought he was working on a die for a Fugio copper. He realized his mistake and punched IN over the FU letters, traces of which can be seen. (Connecticut variety Miller 32.5-aa; Syd Martin Collection; Fugio variety Newman 13-JJ)

In the Footsteps of Sherlock Holmes: Numismatic Forensics

One of the simplest of all United States coins is this pattern silver three-cent piece of 1849, Judd-114, with the denomination given in two forms. It was made simply to test the striking of a silver coin of this new diameter. Regular-issue silver three-cent pieces, called trimes by the Treasury Department, were not made for circulation until 1851, at which time the design was much different, as also shown. Regular-issue trimes were made from 1851 to 1873.

This rare Series of 1875 $1 note of the First National Bank of Birmingham was, obviously, issued in Birmingham, Pennsylvania. Or was it? The bank was situated in Pittsburgh, which because of its steel industry was an American equivalent of Birmingham, England. The location should have read "Pittsburgh, Pa.," but an engraver at the American Bank Note Co., maker of the printing plate, did not know that! Hence the error in location.

Each of the National Bank notes in this series had a state seal at the left of the back, here the seal for Pennsylvania (see chapter 30 for the Colorado seal).

A matter of publicity. In 1858 several hundred pattern cents were made with an Indian Head obverse and laurel-wreath reverse, the same design as adopted for circulation the next year, in 1859. You can find the variety listed in *U.S. Pattern Coins* (by Dr. J. Hewitt Judd) as J-208. A high-quality Proof is worth several thousand dollars. In 1856 nearly a thousand pattern cents were made, and even more were restruck later. You can find the variety listed among regular issues in *A Guide Book of United States Coins*. A high-quality Proof 1856 costs in the tens of thousands of dollars (see chapter 6). What a difference publicity can make!

"The Smoker" has always been a favorite token. The die was made by F.C. Key & Sons and was combined with several different reverses, including this one for Joseph N.T. Levick, one of the leading numismatists of the day and an avid collector of tokens. In *100 Greatest American Medals and Tokens* this was voted as no. 63. Listed in the *Standard Catalog of U.S. Tokens 1700–1900* as Rulau NY-438.

If at first you don't succeed. . . . In his first full year of employment at the Philadelphia Mint George T. Morgan created his concept for a silver dollar, this at the request of Director Henry R. Linderman, who felt that better artwork could be obtained than that provided by Chief Engraver William Barber and his engraver son, Charles. The obverse of the illustrated 1877 half dollar was used as the motif for the standard silver dollar introduced in 1878.

The reverse with an eagle perched on a Roman standard was not used. Morgan liked it, and on the reverse of an 1879 pattern silver dollar used it again, but it did not find its way as a design used for a regular coin. Finally, years later, Morgan used it as the reverse for the commemorative quarter eagle made for the 1915 Panama-Pacific International Exposition, where it finally saw the light of day and thousands were sold.

In the Footsteps of Sherlock Holmes: Numismatic Forensics

The illustrated token was issued by Carpenter & Mosher, dry-goods merchants of Troy, New York. Both dies were cut in an amateurish manner by Benjamin True of that city. Édouard Frossard, writing in *The Coin Collector's Journal,* January 1886, gave this description: "Obv. A most disreputable head of Liberty, left. Upon the coronet, 'Troy.' Fourteen stars . . . *Rare.*" This particular example is either the finest or second-finest of only four known. One sold for $40,250 in 2008.

The desirability of rusticity: In American numismatics it is often the case that the more rustic or irregular a die is, the more interest it creates among numismatists. This is a concept that is appreciated once a collector is into the field for a year or two. In the meantime, to newcomers the idea seems strange. Copper cents of 1794 from hand-cut dies are more interesting to specialists than are copper cents of 1854, from dies made with improved systems so that all look more or less alike.

Rusticity to the extreme: This "blacksmith's token" combines a die for a Hard Times token of N. Starbuck & Son of Troy, New York, with a hand-made die said to have been created by a Montreal blacksmith. R.W. McLachlan, Howland Wood, Warren Baker, John J. Ford Jr., and other numismatists have studied these over a long period of time.

McLachlan wrote in the *American Journal of Numismatics,* volume XIX, 1884: "Previous to 1837 when the lack of specie caused copper change to be accepted in bulk, there lived in Montreal a blacksmith of dissipated habits. He prepared dies for himself, and when he wished to have a 'good time' he struck two or three dollars in these coppers and thereby supplied himself with sufficient change with which to gratify his habits." McLachlan heard the story from his mother, who grew up in Montreal, knew the blacksmith, and visited his shop in the 1830s. Interesting, but how did a Hard Times token die find its way to him? (HT-369)

The N. Starbuck & Son die used to make the blacksmith's token. (HT-368)

Now the forensics part. This illustration of HT-369 shows a crudely struck token. One might imagine that if the blacksmith struck a couple dollars' worth of these, the striking would have varied from one token to another. This illustration is of the same variety, a different example, sold from the John J. Ford, Jr. Collection by Stack's Bowers Galleries in August 2013, lot 21147, which realized $2,820. The features are identical on the Starbuck side, revealing that the die was mostly effaced by grinding before the blacksmith obtained it.

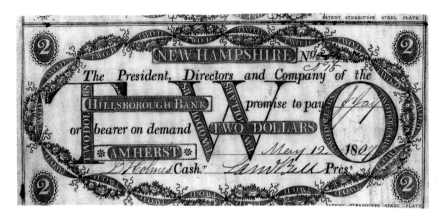

This $2 note was printed by Jacob Perkins of Newburyport, Massachusetts, an engraver and printer who supplied currency to many banks in the early-19th century. It was issued by the Hillsborough Bank of Amherst, New Hampshire, chartered by the state. There was a problem, however: the bank was operated fraudulently, with hardly anything in the way of assets. Large quantities of bills were made and distributed widely, including some shipped to distant Marietta, Ohio, to be passed out in commerce. Each note was signed by Samuel Bell, president. The venture collapsed in 1809, and its tens of thousands of dollars of currency became absolutely worthless, but the officers were never prosecuted. Bell went on to be elected governor of New Hampshire! Banking frauds were common, and there was little or nothing in the way of legislative oversight. Today such bills are enthusiastically collected.

In contrast to rustic early tokens, perfection in die making and striking is achieved with modern U.S. Mint commemoratives and other numismatic products, including this highly acclaimed 1988 Olympic Games $5 gold issue by Chief Engraver Elizabeth Jones.

Another example of perfection in die making is this $5 coin for the 1994 World's Cup. As to whether it is beautiful to behold is in the eye of the viewer. From rustic to sophisticated, dies of numismatic interest cover a wide range of possibilities, as illustrated in this chapter.

In 1916 the Standing Liberty quarter was introduced. Designed by sculptor Hermon A. Mac-Neil, the obverse featured the partially undraped figure of Miss Liberty and the reverse a flying eagle. Illustrated is a 1917 quarter from the Philadelphia Mint.

In the Footsteps of Sherlock Holmes: Numismatic Forensics

Partway through 1917 the design was modified to what is designated as Variety 2 today. Miss Liberty was reconfigured to appear in a coat of armor and the reverse was modified as well. For many years conventional numismatic wisdom was that the earlier semi-nude version of Miss Liberty was too "naughty," and a change was made accordingly. In actuality, MacNeil changed her to reflected armed preparedness in the World War then raging in Europe (America joined the Allies in 1918).

The diecutter for a Hard Times token of J.S. Pease & Co., St. Louis importers of hardware and cutlery, added the sentiment, HE WHO LIVES BY THE SWEAT OF HIS BROW SELDOM LIVES IN RUIN (Rulau HT-282, Low-257). There are many "sweat of his brow" quotations in history and literature.

Apparently, VAIN was found to be more appropriate than RUIN, perhaps drawing upon the works of Thomas Paine or another writer, so the RU in the last word was overpunched with VA, creating Rulau HT-282A, Low-258.

The partners in the firm were J.S. Pease and L.G. Irving (mentioned on the obverse). In St. Louis the firm was at 20 Main Street. In Albany, New York, the company was one of two agents for the Merchants and Millers Line of boats on the Erie Canal, the gateway for the importation of the items sold in St. Louis.

A coin without a country: an 1860 half dime with no mention of the United States of America. Mint Director James Ross Snowden had 100 of these struck as numismatic delicacies. You can find the variety listed in *A Guide Book of United States Coins*.

Just wondering. . . . How many recipients of this Civil War store card issued by a Cincinnati merchant, the variety known to collectors as Fuld OH-165-BJ-9a, realized that the German word for rabbit is Haas?

What might have been: In 1862, when the Treasury Department proposed issuing Legal Tender Notes, it was thought that the lowest denominations would be $1, $2, and $3, as these values were popular in the currency issued by state-chartered banks. The face design at the lower center had 1, 2, and 3 printed, with the denomination of a given note to be highlighted by giving it a white background, as on the $1 shown here (including a detail). Similar $2 notes were issued, but $3 bills were never made. The green reverses of these and other notes of the era gave rise to the term *greenback* for paper bills and also green being "the color of money."

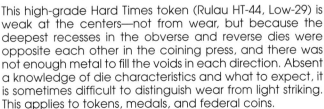

This high-grade Hard Times token (Rulau HT-44, Low-29) is weak at the centers—not from wear, but because the deepest recesses in the obverse and reverse dies were opposite each other in the coining press, and there was not enough metal to fill the voids in each direction. Absent a knowledge of die characteristics and what to expect, it is sometimes difficult to distinguish wear from light striking. This applies to tokens, medals, and federal coins.

One of my favorite coins, the MCMVII (1907) pattern $20 gold eagle, Judd-1905, using the Saint-Gaudens Indian Head obverse regularly seen on $10 coins, is unique. Its pedigree includes F.C.C. Boyd, King Farouk of Egypt, Dr. J. Hewitt Judd, the Wilkison family, and coin dealer Julian Leidman.

Minted from 1850 to 1933, the $20 double eagle was America's most popular gold coin for commercial and banking interests. Although certain varieties are rare and expensive, a six-piece set of the different types is affordable to many numismatists today.

Double Eagles and History

1849 gold dollar. (National Numismatic Collection, Smithsonian Institution)

A Beautiful Display of Double Eagles

Federal gold coins were first struck at the Philadelphia Mint in 1795. From then to the 1820s, sources of the metal were varied and often consisted of foreign coins that were melted. In the 1820s and 1830s Georgia and North Carolina were important producers of the metal, while the melting of foreign gold continued. The coinage denominations included $2.50, $5, and $10. The California Gold Rush changed everything. Beginning in 1848, vast quantities of that precious metal came on the market. By 1849, deposits of gold arriving in the East were unprecedented.

In 1849 Congress authorized two new denominations of gold coins—the dollar and the double eagle, the latter so named as it was twice the value of America's largest gold coin at the time, the $10 eagle. Gold dollars reached circulation in 1849. Pattern double eagles were made in that year, but production for circulation did not happen until 1850, when the Philadelphia and New Orleans mints struck large quantities.

The double eagle was the instantly favorite denomination for those engaging in large transactions in commerce. It took twice as much effort to coin two $10 coins as it did for a single $20, and eight times as much effort to coin an equal amount in quarter eagles. Production of double eagles was continuous from 1850 to 1916, then a lapse, then continuous again from 1921 to 1933. In the last year President Franklin D. Roosevelt decreed that citizens, numismatists excepted, must turn in their gold coins. This ended gold as a medium of exchange in American commerce.

Most people who had gold coins turned them in. This did not affect the typical citizen, as the country was in the depth of the Great Depression, and few had much money in *any* form, much less in gold.

Beginning in a large way in the mid-1870s many foreign nations and banks kept American double eagles as a reserve and store of value. Millions of coins remained on hand in overseas vaults when Roosevelt's order was given. Foreigners held on to their long-stored double eagles more tightly than ever, having no interest whatsoever in shipping them to the United States to be exchanged for paper money! Years later, ramping up in the 1940s, with dealer James F. Kelly leading the way, overseas hoards were tapped, in one country after another, bringing back to the United States millions of double eagles. Such pieces account for most of the coins in numismatic collections today.

Forming a Type Set of Double Eagles

From 1850 to 1933 there were only six different types or designs made in the double eagle series. Obtaining one of each motif is a fascinating pursuit today. All are relatively inexpensive in relation to premiums over the price of an ounce of gold bullion, except for the MCMVII, which was struck in limited quantities in December 1907 and, from the same dies, early in 1908.

In contrast, a complete collection of the more than 200 dates and mintmarks in various grades, not the highest for the rarities, would far exceed a million dollars in cost, not including the 1933, which is non-collectible. Rarities costing in the tens of thousands of dollars each include 1854-O, 1856-O, 1861 Paquet Reverse, 1870-CC, 1883, 1884, 1885, 1886, 1887, 1921, 1927-D, and all coined after 1928.

The standard composition of the $20 is 90 percent gold with 10 percent copper alloyed to add strength. The diameter is 34 mm and the weight is 516 grains. Liberty Head types from 1850 to 1907 have reeded edges, and the Saint-Gaudens types have lettered edges.

Proofs of the mirror type were made of most years of the Liberty Head types from the 1850s through 1907. Whether Proofs were made of the MCMVII is debatable. Of the two major third-party coin-grading firms, the Professional Coin Grading Service does not certify any as Proof, while the Numismatic Guaranty Corporation does. I have found no Treasury Department or numismatic references to Proofs in print before the mid-20th century.[1] Sand Blast Proofs were made of the 1908 and 1910 to 1915 Saint-Gaudens double eagles and Satin Finish Proofs were made for 1909 and 1910. Proofs, eminently desirable, are beyond the purview of the present chapter.

Following, I discuss each of the six types.

1850–1866 Liberty Head

Type 1
TWENTY D.
Reverse without Motto

Circulation-strike mintage: 23,538,945 (including 19,250 1861-S Paquet). Designed by James B. Longacre. His initials J.B.L. are on the neck truncation.

1852 $20.

Double eagles of the first type, made for circulation beginning in 1850 and continuing through 1866, are readily available in just about every grade desired.[2] Mintages were large for most issues, with New Orleans coins from 1854 to 1859 being exceptions. That mint had deteriorated since its opening in 1838 and was undergoing repairs. Double eagles of the 1860-O and 1861-O varieties were made in larger numbers. Many of the last were struck in early 1861 when New Orleans fell under the control of the State of Louisiana, which had seceded from the Union, and later under the Confederate States of America.

In 1861 a variety or sub-type was created by engraver Anthony C. Paquet, using tall letters on the reverse. This can be collected as a separate type, if desired, although over the years most numismatists have opted not to do so.

From late December 1861 until December 17, 1878, no double eagles were seen in circulation in the East or Midwest. They were plentiful in the vaults of banks and in the inventory of exchange brokers but could be obtained only by paying a premium in terms of paper money. In contrast, on the West Coast and areas eastward into the deserts and mountains, gold coins circulated at face value, but paper money was received only at a deep discount in comparison.

Until the turn of the 21st century, Choice Mint State double eagles of this type were rare, the only notable exception being 1861 Philadelphia coins. This changed with the discovery of several treasure-laden ships and recoveries of gold coins from them. The SS *Brother Jonathan*, lost at sea in 1865, was recovered and yielded hundreds of Mint State 1865-S double eagles, and some dated 1864 and a few earlier. I have fond memories of going out to sea off Crescent City, California, when the recovery was going on and also with my staff cataloging and offering the coins for sale at auction.

This find paled in comparison to the more than 7,500 coins, nearly all double eagles, including 5,402 of 1857-S, recovered by the Columbus-America Discovery Group in the 1980s and marketed by the California Gold Marketing Group (led by Dwight N. Manley) beginning in 1999. This is described in chapter 26. The wreck of the SS *Republic*, lost in 1865 while on a voyage from New York City to New Orleans, was recovered by Odyssey Marine Exploration and yielded hundreds of very attractive Mint State double eagles of this first type, some in high grades. The marketing was done by Odyssey, but I assisted with narrative for a book they published on the find.

I do not want to overlook the SS *Yankee Blade*, a passenger steamship lost in 1854 off the coast of Santa Barbara, California. Sometime after the 1960s a number of Mint State 1854-S double eagles appeared on the market, with no information being given as to who found them. There seem to have been several hundred in all, each with a lightly etched surface from sand washing over them underwater for more than a century.

In today's world of instant information and the desire for instant gratification, examples of the above treasure coins can be found easily enough. Although most buyers will glance at them briefly and then go on to other purchases, I suggest that you buy the books I and others have written about these—and spend several interesting evenings absorbed in the excitement and, if this word is appropriate, romance of the ships, how they were lost, and how their treasures were found.

1866–1876 Liberty Head

Type 2
TWENTY D.
Reverse with IN GOD WE TRUST

Circulation-strike mintage: 16,160,758. Longacre designs.

1868 $20.

This relatively short-lived double eagle type, with the same general obverse as the preceding but now with IN GOD WE TRUST on the reverse, is the scarcest of the six major styles of double eagles. Coins in grades from Very Fine to About Uncirculated are found easily enough, and the same is true for Mint State pieces in lower grades of MS-60 to 63. Problem-free MS-63 coins are somewhat scarce, and conservatively graded coins at the MS-64 and MS-65 levels are rare. Anything higher is seldom seen.

This era saw the opening of the Carson City Mint in 1870. Double eagles of 1870-CC are rarities, and those of 1871-CC and 1872-CC are scarce. Each of these three issues is usually in Very Fine or so grade when encountered. They seem to have circulated extensively on a regional basis.

Striking can be a problem with these issues, more so than in the types before and after. Check the hair detail of Miss Liberty, often unsatisfactory, and the centers of the stars, similarly less than sharp in many instances. The reverses tend to be struck up better, but, again, check all details including the eagle. The commercial certification services make no mention of weak striking, so cherrypicking is called for and can produce good results. If you want to learn more, check my *Guide Book of Double Eagle Gold Coins*, published by Whitman, or with a specialist of your choice, and you will find that certain dates and mints are sometimes found only lightly struck and never sharp, the famous 1870-CC being an example.

As noted above, no double eagles circulated in commerce in the East and Midwest. Business was conducted with paper money in the form of Legal Tender Notes and National Bank Notes. It was thought that after the Civil War ended, gold and silver coins would reappear in circulation. Instead, the public kept hoarding them, as the integrity of paper money was questioned, as was the status of the government's finances.

1877–1907 Liberty Head

Type 3
TWENTY DOLLARS
Reverse with IN GOD WE TRUST

Circulation-strike mintage: 64,137,477. Basic Longacre designs continued, with the denomination spelling changed by someone else (Longacre died on January 1, 1869).

era of this coinage. Mintages sometimes ran into the millions in the 1890s and early 1900s, with the result that many date-and-mintmark varieties are very common today.

I recommend that you select MS-63 as a minimum grade for a type set and suggest that even higher levels are available without paying a large premium. This is in dynamic contrast to the Type 2 double eagles, which are rarities at the gem level (MS-65 and above).

The striking is usually much better on this type than on the one before, although the hair details, stars, and reverse features should all be checked. A cherry picked sharp strike, easy enough to find, will cost no more than a weaker strike in the same MS numerical grade. Luster varies widely depending on the date and mint, a topic beyond discussion here, except that certain varieties such as 1901-S tend to be satiny while, for example, 1906-D tends to be "creamy."

MCMVII (1907) Saint-Gaudens High Relief

Type 4
Circulation-strike mintage: 12,867 (some of which were struck in January 1908). Designs by sculptor Augustus Saint-Gaudens.

1880-S $20.

MCMVII (1907) High Relief $20.

With massive finds in the Cripple Creek Gold District of Colorado and the Klondike in the Yukon, large quantities of gold came to the mints during the

This is the double eagle that everybody loves! The design showcases the artistry of Augustus Saint-Gaudens to its finest advantage, with the details in sculptured-like high relief, and obverse and reverse both being splendid in their layout. Fortunately, of the 12,867 pieces minted, about half exist today, providing ample opportunities for purchase. However, the demand is such that the pieces are hardly inexpensive.

The story of the creation of this coin is well known, and in 2002 in my *More Adventures With Rare Coins* book I devoted a chapter to it. Perhaps with Nathaniel Hawthorne's *Twice-Told Tales* people do enjoy rereading the familiar. However, I will be brief here.

In 1904 President Theodore Roosevelt was visiting the Smithsonian Institution's "Castle" building only a short walk from the White House. On display he saw coins of ancient Greece and marveled at their sculptured appearance, quite unlike the gold and silver coins being made in America. He contacted Augustus Saint-Gaudens, America's best-known sculptor, at his residence, Aspet, in Cornish, New Hampshire (now a National Historic Site well worth visiting). His *Shaw Memorial* in the Boston Common and his *Sherman Victory Monument* group on view at Central Park South were among his famous and highly admired productions. Roosevelt commissioned the artist to redesign the entire American coinage from the cent to the double eagle. Chief Engraver Charles E. Barber, viewed by many artists as having modest talent at best, protested. Traditionally the design of coinage was the challenge of the Mint staff. Outsiders were not welcome.

Work got underway, and a new double eagle motif began to be created. For the obverse *Victory* (also known as *Fame*, from the *Sherman Victory Monument*) was used, now slightly modified to show the United States Capitol and a radiant sun in the distance. For the reverse Saint-Gaudens created a version of a flying eagle, having stated to the president that his favorite motif on an American coin was that on the Flying Eagle cent of 1857. Both sides were in exquisite high relief. The sculptor died of cancer on August 3, 1907, his work nearly complete. The finishing touches were added by his assistant, Henry Hering.

Barber protested that the high relief was imprac-

tical and would not work on high-speed coining presses. Roosevelt called the project his "pet crime" and stated that if only one coin *per day* could be struck, that is how it would be. It did require three strikes of a medal press to make each coin. Accordingly, relatively few were made—just slightly more than 12,000, a record low by far for any of the double eagle types.

The MCMVII High Relief was a sensation and was widely admired in newspaper and other accounts. There was a great rush to acquire them. Bank tellers sold them at a profit. By the time the supply ran out the coins were bringing $28 to $30 each. In time the novelty passed, and many citizens spent them or in 1933 surrendered their coins when President Franklin D. Roosevelt called in all gold coins held by the public. Enough survived that today it is likely that at least 5,000 to 6,000 exist, representing about half of the mintage. Most of these are in varying degrees of Mint State, say MS-60 to MS-63, but with quite a few listed as MS-64 and MS-65. Lower grades such as Very Fine and Extremely Fine exist, but such coins were often used for jewelry or polished, or have other problems.

The striking is usually good, but check the central parts of the figure of *Victory*. Also check her left knee (which is a key point for abrasions, etc.) and the details of the Capitol building. Under magnification the die fields show myriad tiny raised curlicues and other die-finish marks, imparting a matte-like character to the luster. Varieties exist with a flat rim or a wire rim. I do not consider the difference significant at all, as the same dies were used to mint them, but because the popular *Guide Book of United States Coins* lists the distinction there is a demand for both.

1907–1908 Saint-Gaudens

Type 5
Arabic Numerals
No Motto
Circulation-strike mintage: 5,294,968. Saint-Gaudens design, extensively modified by Charles E. Barber.

Detail, 1908 No Motto $20, from the Wells Fargo Hoard.

1908–1933 Saint-Gaudens

Type 6
Arabic Numerals
With IN GOD WE TRUST

Circulation-strike mintage: 64,981,428. Modified Saint-Gaudens design, now with motto added.

1913-D $20.

During December 1907, in the time frame that MCMVII High Relief double eagles were being struck, dies in shallow relief, modified by Chief Engraver Charles E. Barber, were employed to strike quantities of this denomination for general circulation. The sculptured effect of the design was gone, and the Roman numerals were replaced by so-called Arabic numerals (1907, rather than MCMVII). This continued the next year with 1908.

Coins of this type lacked the IN GOD WE TRUST motto, as President Theodore Roosevelt personally objected to the use of the name of the Deity on coinage. However, in 1908 Congress restored the motto (which had been used on the $20 Liberty Head coinage of 1866 to 1907). Accordingly, the Type 5 was minted only for a short time—from December 1907 into the early summer of 1908.

Due to the repatriation of overseas holdings and to other sources, double eagles of the Without Motto (also called No Motto) design are plentiful in the numismatic marketplace today. I recommend that you opt for a coin in at least MS-63 grade, although 64 and 65 coins are plentiful, including gems from the famous Wells Fargo hoard discovered by Ron Gillio and his associates in the 1990s, consisting of 19,990 pieces. Most of these are quite attractive. Beyond that, watch out for wide differences of opinion, as the usual light striking of this issue plus other aspects combine so that what one expert can call MS-64, another might call About Uncirculated. This is a very tricky area, and perhaps to simply go with one holder certified as "Wells Fargo Hoard" will be the easiest route. (By the way, I have no connection of any kind with this particular find.) Otherwise, buy very carefully, and check for friction on the higher parts, most visible on the bosom of *Victory*.

Congress overruled President Theodore Roosevelt's objection to the motto on the double eagle, and beginning in August 1908 IN GOD WE TRUST was added to the reverse, above the sun. This basic motif was continued through 1933. In 1912 a slight modification was made by adding two tiny stars to the 46 already around the rim, reflecting the admission of Arizona and New Mexico to the Union, making a count of 48 states.

As a type, coins of this motif are common, and millions exist in Mint State, to which a lesser number of lightly worn coins can be added. Eye appeal can vary, especially among those of the earlier dates, 1907 to 1916, which tend to be less attractive than issues of the 1920s. The striking usually is good, but there are exceptions. Check the features of Miss Liberty, the details of the tiny Capitol building at the lower left, and other aspects. Some pieces have arc-like ridges around the periphery, a slight distance in from the edge, seemingly an artifact of extensive die use.

Next chapter: A special Type 6 double eagle, the end of the line.

CHAPTER 50

The 1933 double eagle was rare. Until 1944 none had been offered at auction. And then. . . .

On the Trail of the 1933 Double Eagle

Philadelphia, 1933: The Scene is Set

The Philadelphia Mint, where the 1933 double eagles were minted and stored. In 1937 most were melted into ingots.

In early 1933 the Philadelphia Mint routinely struck 445,500 double eagles.[1] America was deep in the Great Depression, and the coins were struck not because there was a demand in commerce for them, but to use gold bullion on hand. In the previous year, 1,101,750 $20 gold coins had been made. There was no call for the 1932 twenties either, and nearly all remained in vaults at the Mint. As to numismatic demand, there were probably fewer than 10 people assembling sets of twenties by date and mint. It was not at all unusual for the Mint to strike coins and not release them. This had happened recently with several issues of Peace silver dollars, which did have a good numismatic following, resulting in inquiries to the Mint.

On March 4, 1933, Franklin Delano Roosevelt was inaugurated as president of the United States. Although I was born a Republican, so to speak, as I write these words the Grand Old Party has not been so grand in recent years and has done a lot of self-destruction. The Democrats have had their share of problems as well. Although the setup is far from perfect, as Winston Churchill once observed, there is nothing better than the multi-party system, anywhere in the world. That said, it is my opinion that in the early 1930s Republican president Herbert Hoover was ineffective.

In the 1932 election Hoover sought reelection while Democrat Franklin Roosevelt sought to unseat him. Today it is my opinion that after George Washington, Roosevelt was probably the greatest president America ever had. If there is a competitor for the runner up, that would be Abraham Lincoln. Some time ago *The Economist*, my favorite magazine, rated Roosevelt as one of the greatest ever, stating simply, "He saved the world." However, from a *numismatic* viewpoint, he earned low marks—this also being my opinion. And, when 1933 double eagles are discussed, everyone has opinions.

The nation was in the midst of the worst economic depression in its history, and there was no sign that the situa-

President Franklin D. Roosevelt. (Bureau of Engraving and Printing)

tion was improving. In his inaugural address Roosevelt paraphrased the Bible and stated that as an early order of business he was going to drive the money-changers from the temple. As it turned out, his administration would also drive double eagles from the temple and just about everywhere else, and would harass at least one species among money changers (if numismatists can be called that). It should be noted that Roosevelt was a man of wealth and had enjoyed a life of luxury.

Although Roosevelt is said to have collected coins, I have not been able to learn much about his numismatic proclivities. His collection must have been modest at best. Not so with stamps, as he was an ardent philatelist. He even had James Farley, his postmaster general, make up all sorts of "private rarities" for himself and his friends—which caused such a ruckus among stamp collectors and dealers that he was forced to have the Bureau of Engraving and Printing make more of them, so everyone had a chance.

No doubt, if Roosevelt had been a serious numismatist, he would have created some fancy patterns or other delicacies—who knows? This does show that he didn't mind exercising his power to create rare collectors' items—and, presumably, if one or a few of his friends wanted some of those 1933 double eagles, they could have had them for face value. Or, perhaps Roosevelt could sin in philately, but be saintly at all times in numismatics. Again, who knows?

William H. Woodin

On March 5, 1933, Roosevelt tapped as his secretary of the Treasury none other than William H. Woodin, longtime numismatist whose two prime specialties for study were patterns and *gold coins*. This was the first time in American history that a dedicated and highly skilled numismatist and numismatic scholar and author had served in the post. Woodin was a very successful businessman who maintained residences in Berwick, Pennsylvania, and New York City.

In popular terminology Woodin might be called a Renaissance Man—with many talents in many fields: writer, musician, aesthete, an observer of and

American Numismatic Society

New York

BROADWAY BETWEEN 155TH & 156TH STS.

Organized 1858.   Incorporated 1865.

PRESENT EXHIBITIONS:

Medals, Coins & Decorations

of the Present War.

Medals of Lafayette & Naval Victories.

All collectors and students are cordially invited to make use of the extensive Library of the Society, and every facility will be offered to numismatists in examining and studying the large collection of coins and medals that may not be on exhibition.
Open to the Public daily, 10 A. M. to 5 P. M.   Sundays, 1 to 5 P. M.

COUNCIL

EDWARD D. ADAMS	ROBERT JAMES EIDLITZ	JOHN REILLY, JR.
W. GEDNEY BEATTY	ARCHER M. HUNTINGTON	ELLIOTT SMITH
BAUMAN L. BELDEN	EDWARD T. NEWELL	JOHN I. WATERBURY
F. C. C. BOYD	STEPHEN H. P. PELL	WILLIAM H. WOODIN
HENRY RUSSELL DROWNE	WILLIAM POILLON	

From the early 1900s onward William H. Woodin was deeply involved in numismatics, with a particular interest in gold coins. This August 1917 roster of the American Numismatic Society lists him as a Council member, as he was for many years. He was also a founder of the New York Numismatic Club and coauthor in 1913 of the standard reference on U.S. pattern coins.

participant in the world around him—whose contributions are still important today. He enjoyed what he did, relaxing in such diverse activities as playing the guitar in bed and whiling away the hours by looking at die details of 1795-dated gold half eagles to study their characteristics and differences.

He composed music, and his *Oriental Suite* was performed by the Berlin Philharmonic Orchestra. Another of his compositions, *Franklin D. Roosevelt March*, was obviously of a political slant. He collected rare and interesting books. In numismatics he wrote the text for *United States Pattern, Trial and Experimental Pieces* (published by the American Numismatic Society in 1913), formed a great collection specializing in gold, and intended to write a book on half eagles, including the aforementioned issues of 1795, but never did. He was also interested in *current* coinage, so much so that at a meeting of the New York Coin Club on the evening of December 11, 1914, Thomas L. Elder told the members that he had written to the government regarding the great need to improve the tired silver designs by Charles E. Barber, in use since 1892 and liked by hardly anyone. Elder suggested that a committee be appointed to address the subject, and that Woodin would be first choice as its chairman. Somehow, Woodin always found time from his duties in managing the highly successful American Car and Foundry Company to attend to numismatic matters.

Hmm. . . . For the first time and only time in American history the secretary of the Treasury is a longtime numismatist with a specialty in gold coins, and who knows most of the leading collectors and dealers. Interesting situation, this!

William H. Woodin.

New Regulations

On March 6, 1933, just two days after his inauguration, President Roosevelt issued Proclamation 2039, an order which closed all banks on this day, a Monday, beginning the so-called Bank Holiday. Banks that met certain financial tests were allowed to open for business by week's end, but many others remained closed until they could increase their capital. Many institutions went into receivership, or were forced to merge with stronger banks, or were acquired at bargain sales by their competitors.

Roosevelt also proclaimed that all gold bullion and all gold coins should be returned to the Federal Reserve System banks, exceptions being rare and unusual coins for collectors (including a provision that up to four specimens of a given variety of $2.50 could be retained, as these had been scarce for a long time). Numismatists were allowed to buy, sell, and trade gold coins, but anyone else had to get a special license. Failure to comply meant the potential of jail. At the time Prohibition was also in effect, and someone buying and selling ardent spirits could land in jail as well—as many had been by this time. Prohibition was repealed on December 5, 1933.

I cannot fail but to paraphrase a comment that Louis E. Eliasberg made:

> "If in 1932 a man walked down a street in Baltimore with a bottle of whisky in one hand and a double eagle in the other hand, he was committing a criminal act: by having the bottle.
>
> "If in 1934 the same man walked down a street in Baltimore with a bottle of whisky in one hand and a double eagle in the other hand, he was committing a criminal act: by having the double eagle."

By any interpretation, *any* coin of the current year would have been of numismatic significance and worth to a collector keeping up to date with coinage. Woodin was familiar with this, as for generations the building of sets of various denominations had been the main way to collect. There is *no way* that Woodin would have suggested otherwise. Moreover, the Treasury price list of 1932 (the latest-dated I have seen from this era) offered current double eagles for this very purpose—knowing that numismatists would want one of the latest date. In this instance the 1932 was offered for sale at face value.

Minting the 1933 Double Eagles

The mintage of 1933-dated double eagles commenced by March 15, and on this day bags totaling 25,000 1933 $20 pieces were delivered to Mint cashier Harry Powell. Under Mint practice dating back for generations, coins in the hands of the Mint cashier could be paid out without any further special instructions. While at the time the Treasury might not have been actively paying out $20 pieces or other coins for paper money, it seems quite certain (at least to me!) that someone trading like for like could have obtained such pieces.

By March 24 some 100,000 1933 double eagles had been minted, and by the 27th of April, a further 200,000 double eagles had been struck. It would seem that it was the intent of Secretary Woodin to use these in commerce sometime in the future, or else they would not have been made. If it had not been so, then per current Treasury Department practice, such as at regional government assay offices, gold not intended for circulation would have been cast into ingots—a far simpler procedure. By May 19 the total was increased by a further 145,500 1933 double eagles struck. By all indications, this was to be a *common-date* double eagle. Certainly, at the Mint in early 1933, no one would have considered it a rarity. As Roosevelt had called for double eagles to be surrendered by the public, there was no intention of paying them out in commerce. It would seem logical, however, that if someone had asked Secretary of the Treasury Woodin to arrange to obtain a few pieces in exchange for coins of other dates, the answer could not have been other than "Yes."

Here is what numismatic historian R.W. Julian found:

> The first delivery—on March 15—was for 25,000 pieces plus an additional 25 reserved for the annual Assay Commission. . . .

On the same day that double eagle coinage began, the Bureau of the Mint wrote Lewis Froman of Buffalo, New York, indicating that gold bullion could be deposited and that it would be paid for by the mint in gold. The letter, which was signed by Acting Director Mary M. O'Reilly in the absence of Director Robert J. Grant, noted that in this way "such a transaction neither increases nor depletes the stock of gold in the Treasury."

The letter is critical to understanding how the mints were operating in March 1933 and in particular the Philadelphia Mint, the closest one to Froman. When O'Reilly spoke of not depleting gold in the Treasury she clearly did not mean the Federal Reserve as is shown by another letter found in the archives. . . . This second letter, written to the Herff-Jones Company of Indianapolis on March 14 is also signed by O'Reilly and stated that Secretary Woodin had issued an order the previous day releasing Federal Reserve gold; when one releases gold—without a corresponding input of Treasury stocks—full Federal Reserve levels could not be maintained.[2]

Again, it seems to me that neither Secretary Woodin nor anyone else would have objected if someone had brought an earlier-dated double eagle to the Mint, and requested a 1933 coin in exchange.

Edgar H. Adams, a friend for decades and coauthor of the 1913 pattern book, told the American Numismatic Association convention in August 1933: "Secretary of the Treasury Woodin is a coin collector of the first rank and the possessor of the finest and most complete collection of pattern and trial coins ever brought together."

To reiterate, the secretary of the Treasury had a very large coin collection at the time, had served for years with the American Numismatic Society, and in 1933 knew most if not all of the leading coin collectors and dealers.

All was well on the coinage front in 1933, also with the printing of paper money, and other areas of interest to numismatists (who were not particularly concerned with Roosevelt's sly shenanigans in the making of new rarities among postage stamps). But, as the months went on, all was not well with Secretary Woodin. In declining health, on November 16 he advised Roosevelt of his situation, and on this day Henry Morgenthau Jr. was named as acting secretary of the Treasury. On December 31, Woodin resigned as secretary (effective January 1, 1934). He lingered in critical condition and died on May 3, 1934, of a throat infection. During his lifetime he is not known to have said or written anything unfavorable to a numismatist acquiring or holding a 1933 double eagle.

Henry Morgenthau Jr., acting secretary of the Treasury in 1933.

Meanwhile, on December 28, 1933, Acting Secretary Morgenthau issued an order for banks and individuals to surrender all gold coins and Gold Certificates in their possession, excepting numismatic coins and quarter eagles. For these surrenders they would be paid $20.67 per ounce, in contrast to the $34 per ounce being paid by the government for newly mined gold.[3] Regarding the $20 coins of 1933, it seems to me (again, opinion) that the Treasury would have recognized *current* double eagles to be of exceptional numismatic value, for, as noted, the Treasury itself had issued lists of modern double eagles for sale to collectors.

The Assay Commission

At the Philadelphia Mint on February 14 and 15, 1934, the U.S. Assay Commission met to review the prior year's coinage. Throughout 1933, samples had been taken from coins struck in precious metals (silver and gold) and set aside. The supply of such pieces was not large for that year, as dimes, quarters, and silver dollars were not made, and the only issues in silver were the 1933-S half dollar and some 1933-D Oregon Trail commemorative half dollars. Among gold coins there were $10 and $20 pieces bearing the 1933 date.

Among those on hand to check samples of these coins (to assure they were of correct weight and fineness) were at least two people with numismatic leanings. The U.S. Mint's chief engraver, John Ray Sinnock, was there, *ex officio*. Sinnock was quite aware that certain coins could have interest and value; a couple years later, he would have an example of the 1936 Elgin commemorative half dollar specially prepared (by treating its surface) to his order, and sent to the coin's designer, Trygve Rovelstad.[4] Later still would come the "special" cents of 1943 (at least one in copper) and 1944 (on overly thick planchets) that Sinnock made for himself.[5] If anything, many chief engravers over the years helped themselves to items of interest—witness the sale of numismatic rarities in the estate auction of Chief Engraver James B. Longacre (who served from 1844 to 1869) and the making to order of numismatic rarities by assistant engraver, later chief engraver, George T. Morgan (Sinnock's predecessor in the post). In more recent years, chief engraver John Mercanti purposefully declined to collect any of his own Mint creations, and those of his contemporaries, in order to avoid any appearance of such shenanigans.[6]

Another member of the Assay Commission in 1934 was the Honorable William A. Ashbrook, congressman from Ohio, whose deep interest in numismatics was longstanding. Years earlier, in 1908, as a new Democrat in Congress and as a member of the American Numismatic Association, he was named to serve on the Assay Commission. Presumably, Ashbrook must have liked the yearly routine immensely, for the records show that he was also on hand for meetings in 1910, 1915, 1917, 1918, 1919, 1920, 1922, 1924, 1927, 1928, 1929, and 1931. His attendance record is legendary in the annals of the Assay Commission, and has few challengers. (The most important exception was *numismatist* John Jay Knox, who served on 18 separate occasions from 1868 to 1890. Knox also happened to be deputy comptroller of the currency, an important Treasury Department post.)

Representative Ashbrook was not just a casual coin collector; he was among the most active of his era. Among other things, on October 1, 1908, he was elected to the board of governors of the American Numismatic Association, and in 1912 he was instrumental in assisting the ANA to get its congressional charter. In 1921 he joined Indiana congressman Albert Vestal in promoting the concept of the new Peace silver dollar. And Ashbrook was "an enthusiastic collector of U.S. gold and silver coins, which he kept in the vault of a bank in his hometown. Shortly afterward the bank was burglarized and practically his entire collection was stolen. This misfortune caused him to lose the greater part of his interest in collecting."[7]

On hand at the Assay Commission meeting in 1934 were 446 double eagles of 1933 (some 500 had been set aside, but earlier, on February 2, a quantity of 34 was returned to the Mint cashier or to a vault and also at an earlier time melted in an assay test). The commissioners selected 9 coins from the sample of 446; these were assayed and the results were found to be satisfactory. At the risk of belaboring the obvious, it seems to me that there was every indication that these coins would sometime be used in circulation (despite a growing set of rules), or else the time and expense of assaying was being deliberately wasted. Throughout the entire thread of the 1933 double eagle

The Honorable William A. Ashbrook.

story, logic must be relied upon, as well as knowledge of Mint procedures and traditions.

In summary, we have the incontrovertible fact that in 1933 the double eagles of that year were minted under the direction of Secretary of the Treasury William H. Woodin, recognized as one of America's greatest collectors and scholars in the field of *gold coins*. We also have the fact that at the 1934 Assay Commission many 1933 double eagles were on hand, and the senior member of the Commission personally specialized in collecting *gold* and silver coins.

Hmm. . . . Interesting, I would say again!

The Continuing Scenario

On October 9, 1934, a letter from the acting superintendent of the Philadelphia Mint to the director of the Mint in Washington *routinely* transmitted two 1933 Philadelphia double eagles to the United States National Museum without any mention that these had any "special" characteristics of any kind, nor were there any restrictions against trading one as a duplicate (in earlier times the Mint Collection curator had occasionally disposed of coins for one reason or another). The coins were supplied by Mint cashier George McCann (who had been in the post since March 20, 1934, and thus was a newcomer to the 1933 scenario). Although no records have been located, he probably had no information as to whether his predecessor had exchanged 1933-dated double eagles for other dates on a like-for-like basis from inventory on hand.

In the meantime, the stash of 445,500 1933 double eagles, minus various pieces that had strayed hither and yon, remained in storage in vaults at the Philadelphia Mint. At the Mint not much care was paid to such things, and on occasion loose double eagles of unknown dates were seen strewn around the vault floors, and, sometimes, no one knew where particular coins were being kept.[8]

In the meantime, all around the United States, well-meaning citizens dutifully turned their double eagles and other gold coins in to banks and to the Treasury Department. Not much track was kept of exactly what was turned in, this being part of traditional operations. (Amazingly, Treasury records do not reveal that even a *single* copper half cent was actually turned in after that denomination was terminated in 1857! Similarly, the Mint kept no records of the Proof Indian Head cents, nickel three-cent pieces, or Shield nickels minted before 1878! And no records at all were kept of 90 percent or more of the thousands of pattern coins made in the 19th century.)

Indeed, the Mint had always had difficulty keeping track of what it did with regard to paying out coins to collectors and dealers. For years, Philadelphia dealers had been buying coins from Mint employees.

Although many examples could be given, a short list includes John W. Haseltine selling coins for Mint officers, Henry Chapman buying rare gold issues of 1907, and Chief Engraver George T. Morgan selling Proof Morgan and Peace silver dollars in 1921. Although certain of these situations have been documented in numismatic circles, it was longstanding Mint practice to keep few records, not even on obvious items sold to collectors, such as patterns and certain Proof coins. In *United States Pattern Coins* as editor I commented:

> The scenario of producing over 1,500 varieties of patterns from 1859 to 1885, in total tens of thousands of individual coins, necessarily involved many people. It seems that *no records were kept by the Mint or the Treasury Department*, and in 1887 when a new director of the Mint endeavored to look into the matter, all he could find was that in 1868 some aluminum strikings of Proof coins had been made. Since then, research in other Mint records, in the committee reports of Congress, and in other places has furnished documentation on a few additional varieties, but for well over a thousand varieties there is no historical record.

Actually, this lack of attention to details had great numismatic benefits, for the late Abe Kosoff told me that one of the main sources for New York City coin dealers during the 1930s and early 1940s consisted of bank and Treasury Department employees who captured rare gold coins turned in by the public, exchanged common varieties for them, and sold the rarities into the numismatic market. These included double eagles dated 1932 and 1933.

Fortunately, Mint employees, officially or *unofficially*, continued to be helpful to numismatists for a long time afterward. In an interview published in my *Silver Dollars and Trade Dollars of the United States: A*

Complete Encyclopedia, John J. Ford Jr. told of the days circa 1963 when he was dealing in bulk silver dollars:

> [We were selling] Federal Reserve Bank sealed bags of silver dollars, all which were Uncirculated, and all of which had a little hole in the bag burned with a cigarette. A supplier with access to the Federal Reserve bank vault would get permission to take a cigarette in there, and he'd burn a whole in the bag and then he put his eye up to the hole and put a flashlight on the other side of the bag to illuminate through the canvas the other side of the bag, enough so he could see the front of one coin and the back of another to find out the date and the mint and to see if they were all Brilliant Uncirculated.

Perhaps a purist would fault bank and government employees for rescuing gold coins in the 1930s, but, collectively, numismatists can be grateful—perhaps it was done in the patriotic spirit of defying government regulations (remember the Boston Tea Party?), for Roosevelt had repudiated all contracts payable in gold coins, had stated that citizens who owned Gold Certificates promising to pay in gold could now go fly a kite, etc., etc.

Collecting 1933 Double Eagles

Various 1933 double eagles found their way out of the Mint and ended up in the possession of several collectors and dealers, including, over a period of time, F.C.C. Boyd (who displayed his at the New York ANA convention in 1939, the same year that the World's Fair was staged there), Jake Shapiro (known as "J.F. Bell," the famous Chicago numismatist), T. James Clarke (distinguished numismatist and one-time ANA president, from Jamestown, New York), Colonel James W. Flanagan (of Palm Beach, Florida, whose systematic collection of double eagles was consigned to

Stack's for auction sale), Charles M. Williams (Cincinnati insurance executive who owned many other rarities and who sold many of his coins through Numismatic Gallery in 1950 under the title of the "Adolphe Menjou Collection"), L.G. Barnard (of Memphis, a man who collected quietly), James Stack (who kept a suite in the Hotel Roosevelt, New York City; no kin to the professional numismatists of the same surname, although Stack's handled his collection years later), and dealers Ira S. Reed (well-liked Philadelphia dealer who in 1941 conducted the ANA convention sale), Israel SwITT (dealer in gold coins, jewelry, etc., who, like other dealers, often bought coins from bank and government employees, in an era when scarce-date gold coins were being turned in by the public), B. Max Mehl, James G. Macallister (who with Wayte Raymond cataloged the J.C. Morgenthau & Co. coin auctions), Abe Kosoff (one of the most enthusiastic dealers in New York City), Max Berenstein (of Bern's Antiques in New York City, whose family helped him in the business of Bern's Antiques), Smith & Son (in Chicago), and others. Abe Kosoff bought a small supply of them and sold four to R.E. ("Ted") Naftzger Jr. Israel SwITT, a Philadelphia dealer, had at least 10 that were found among his estate effects and were seized by the government in the early 21st century.[9]

To the above lengthy list can be added King Farouk of Egypt, who in 1944 obtained a 1933 double eagle from Mehl, and from the Treasury Department obtained a license for its export.

A Change of Circumstances

During the decade of the 1930s no one knew how rare the 1933 twenties were. In 1939 at the ANA Convention, F.C.C. Boyd opined that just four were known, that being conventional wisdom of the time. In the late 1930s there was scant information available in numismatic circles as to which of the later Saint-Gaudens double eagles were rare and which were common. As late as 1949, B. Max Mehl stated in the Green Collection catalog that he thought that only *three* examples existed of the 1924-S double eagle, and

The 1933 double eagle reputed to have been purchased by King Farouk of Egypt (seen here in a 1939 portrait).

Word reaches us at the time of going to press of the death on December 20 of Hugo Landecker, of San Francisco, California, a member of the ANA. It is reported that officers said his death was caused by poison. He was found in his office by friends, who called an ambulance, and he was taken to a police emergency hospital, where he lived only a few hours. Mr. Landecker was a jeweler and had been a collector of and dealer in coins in San Francisco for many years and was one of the best liked and most respected members of the Pacific Coast Numismatic Society of San Francisco.

He was convicted a week previously of the illegal possession of gold and had been sentenced to prison for two years, but was released on $10,000 bail pending an appeal. He had been denied probation. He was 58 years old and is survived by his wife and five children.

Landecker had been a numismatist and rare-coin dealer of high esteem and repute. Just about any jeweler or rare-coin dealer could be a "criminal" if certain aspects of the draconian federal rules were enforced—it was illegal to own a Gold Certificate, for example! No, this was not Nazi Germany, it was the United States, sadly to say. Related scenarios about the deaths of moonshiners and other Prohibition violators of the 1920s and up to December 5, 1933, could be told.

In February 1944, Stack's announced in *The Numismatist* that they would be auctioning the gold-coin collection of Colonel James W. Flanagan, including a 1933 double eagle as lot 1681. Excitement prevailed, as no specimen of this date had been auctioned before. In the words of R.W. Julian, here is what happened next:[10]

that the 1926-D was in the same category. That would make them, again per conventional wisdom, even rarer than the 1933.

The stringent regulations formulated in 1933 and 1934 against the holding of gold coins were rigidly enforced by federal officials, and over a long span of years after that numerous collectors and dealers were arrested and prosecuted for various "crimes" related to such. No case was more unfortunate than that of a San Francisco dealer, whose untimely end was reported thus:

While the Farouk specimen was on its appointed way [to its new owner in Egypt], the coin and stamp columnist at the *New York Herald-Tribune*, Ernest Kehr, was wondering why the 1933 double eagle in the Flanagan collection was so rare that it rated special mention in the Stack's advertisements. He wrote the Mint Bureau asking how many had been actually issued. The letter wound up on the desk of Dr. Leland Howard, who could find no official distribution of the coins in question.

Dr. Howard, who seems to have had a general dislike of collectors, then notified the Secret Service of the Great Crime that had been perpetrated. This was clearly So Important that critical war-time investigations might have to be delayed while Special Agents investigated this Terrible Event. And so they did. . . .

The Secret Service agents who investigated sometimes made little effort to spell names correctly and some of the facts were out in left field. . . . Some of the people and groups named, for example, included "Maxx" [Max] Mehl, Abe "Kasoff" [Kosoff], John "Sennett" [Sinnock], and the "Numismatic Association of America" [the American Numismatic Association].

Hopefully, better attention to accuracy was paid to other things the Secret Service was doing! A reading of once-confidential documents relating to the above suggests that it would not take much alteration to change it into a scenario for a modern version of a Keystone Kops comedy (Mack Sennett, where are you now that we need you)!

If such a comedy is ever done, the "Woodin wink" should not be omitted. Again, from R.W. Julian:

> In their investigations agents interviewed long-time Philadelphia coin dealer Stephen Nagy, whose numismatic contacts were legendary even then. In the early April 1944 discussion Nagy claimed never to have owned or sold a 1933 double eagle. Oddly enough, however, Nagy did mention that he had seen five of the coins in the possession of Treasury Secretary Woodin and that the latter had indicated, with a wink, that he had several more.
>
> Nagy had visited Woodin in the latter's Treasury office, thus indicating that the visit was planned and that the two men were good friends.

Indeed, the two had known each other for decades, and for both of them one of the highlights of their numismatic careers is when Woodin bought from Nagy and his associate J.W. Haseltine the two varieties, each unique, of the 1877 $50 gold patterns, featured in an article, "The World's Highest-Priced Coins," in *The Numismatist*, July 1909. Although I had several discussions with Nagy in the 1950s, I never thought to ask him about 1933 double eagles. Perhaps I should have.

Exposing F. Leland Howard

F. Leland Howard was a curmudgeon and probably a grafter, in 1944 the acting director of the Mint, but by the time I became acquainted with him in the 1960s he was director of the Office of Domestic Gold and Silver Operations. He played the simultaneous roles of poobah, stuffed shirt, high muckety-muck, and dictator to anyone who wanted to import gold coins.[11]

I recall an instance in which I and an associate

had some double eagles imported from Switzerland, with permission from Howard's office. The coins arrived, I was told, but I could not have them until the paperwork was finalized, which I hoped would be within a day or two. A week passed, then more time. I telephoned Howard, and he told me that his desk was awash with all sorts of requests, documents, etc., and that it would be quite a while before he could find mine and approve of the shipment. He was simply too busy, etc. However, there was a solution: he gave me the name of, apparently, a "pet" customs broker in New York (where the coins had arrived), who took care of it immediately, working with Howard! I found this to be obscene, if not illegal, and complained to a friend who held office in Washington, who told me to forget about it, pay my fees to the broker, and move on, as this was all part of the game. I would never win if I pursued Howard, I was told—his office had more tenacity, could call the Secret Service at its command, and could outlast and out-finance anything I, a young coin dealer, could ever do.

Moreover, Howard had life-or-death (so to speak) powers over which coins could be imported and which could not. For example, a super gem Mint State set of 1937 (coronation year of King George VI) British gold coins was illegal to import or own (jail and fines were the penalty!), while Proofs could be.

Back to 1944: At the behest of self-appointed czar F. Leland Howard, the Secret Service swooped down on collectors and dealers, seized all the 1933 double eagles they could find, including the one scheduled to be auctioned by Stack's, and interviewed dealers and others, and filed lengthy reports and correspondence amounting to hundreds of pages. Perhaps the nation's interest would have been better served if these agents had worked against German espionage, for in this year Hitler was killing millions in concentration camps and elsewhere, and America was fighting the greatest war in its history. However, *logic* and *common sense* have no place at all in the story of the 1933 double eagle, as you probably have figured out by now!

Frank Leland Howard in 1939, around the time he began serving as assistant director of the U.S. Mint.

On April 6, 1944, the chief of the Secret Service received a memorandum from the Treasury Department to the effect that records "do not show that any payments of 1933 double eagles were authorized to be made by the United States Mint, Philadelphia, to any Federal Reserve Bank or branch." Of course, this was true, but not at all relevant to the legality of the coins—indeed it is *farcical*, for the cashier at the Philadelphia Mint for years sold coins at face value to visitors at the Mint without the coins leaving the premises beforehand! The naïve writer of this "research report" apparently supposed that the Mint shipped coins to the Federal Reserve, after which someone at the Federal Reserve trotted back to the cashier at the Mint and returned some of the coins so they could be sold or exchanged as souvenirs. In modern parlance, "give me a break!"

By the way, I love the Treasury Department dearly, and in my career (which began some years after the 1944 capers), I have authenticated many coins for the department. At its request I gave an address (in the auditorium of the Federal Reserve Bank) for the Bureau of the Mint at the 200th anniversary on April 2, 1992, of the 1792 Mint Act. I have testified on the Mint's behalf in Congress, and I have enjoyed knowing the fine Mint directors and key personnel of recent years. On referral of the Smithsonian Institution I assisted an economist for the Federal Reserve System in the preparation of a paper on American monetary history. However, I feel that Leland Howard was a scoundrel of the worst type (with reference to numismatics), and that it is not too late for the Treasury, or even the president of the United States, to repudiate his actions. More about this below.

King Farouk

As related above, in 1944, before Leland Howard interjected himself into the scene, the government routinely gave an export license to permit King Farouk to buy a 1933 twenty from B. Max Mehl. Up to that time the 1933 was not viewed by anyone as anything other than a rare late-date double eagle. This coin was kept in the monarch's collection, until he was tossed off the throne by a military junta in 1952. He fled into exile, leaving behind his collections of coins, stamps, pornography, jewelry, etc. In early 1954 his coins were auctioned by Sotheby's of London.

Farouk decamped to Rome, where he grew increasingly corpulent, meanwhile living in a modest apartment in the company of two bodyguards, a cook, a maid, a male secretary, and a lady named Irma, this according to a recollection of his longtime numismatic dealer and friend Hans M.F. Schulman, who kept in touch.

Farouk hoped that General Gamal Abdel Nasser and his military contingent would be the victims of another coup, and that his young son, Fuad (also spelled Fouad), would become the next Farouk on the throne of Egypt. Meanwhile, rumors circulated that the former king had squirreled away a lot of money in Switzerland. If this was the case, he did not seem to be enjoying its benefits, for while he lived comfortably in

King Farouk of Egypt.

exile, there was no evidence of ostentation, again according to Schulman. Farouk, who had grown to become so fat that he could hardly move, died on March 18, 1965.

Auction Record Set

At the auction in Cairo in early 1954, the 1933 double eagle was withdrawn from the sale, went into hiding for a long time, and then is said to have reappeared in London in the 1990s (or perhaps even earlier). There were various stories of how it got there—"a camel driver had it," "a Cairo jeweler was the owner." Facts were scarce.

In the mid-1990s the so-called Farouk double eagle was purchased by London dealer Steve Fenton. As coin dealers are apt to do (in order to make a living, pay expenses, etc.), Fenton arranged for the sale of the coin, enlisting the aid of Jay Parrino, well-known

American dealer. In the Waldorf Astoria Hotel, New York City, under a veil of secrecy (actually, most big coin deals, with or without 1933 double eagles, are usually done in secret, for security reasons), the effort was made to sell the coin for $1.5 million. The buyer was a Secret Service "plant," in the best tradition of a James Bond novel. The date was February 8, 1996. The battle plan devised in 1944 by F. Leland Howard was dusted off, Parrino was accused of illegal actions, and the coin was seized.

To defend the 1933 double eagle, their investment in it, and their personal honor, Messrs. Parrino and Fenton engaged the legal services of Barry H. Berke, a highly competent and very intelligent New York attorney, who in turn enlisted me as a lead expert witness, used the talents of R.W. Julian as a researcher, and delved into a huge archive of previously unseen Secret Service and Treasury Department records (copies of which were numbered for ease of evaluation and then sent to me). Meanwhile, the coin was in the custody of the U.S. Attorney in New York. Not long after Berke engaged my services, I received a call from a government agent asking me if I would help *them* with research, but I said I was already spoken for! Sort of amusing, perhaps ironic, I thought at the time. However, if the Treasury had enlisted me first, my comments would have been the same: F. Leland Howard did not know what he was doing, the entire 1944 double eagle seizure was a farce and had no basis in Mint practice or tradition, and, my gosh, let the new owner enjoy the coin.

Barry Berke won his case, sort of. A compromise was effected whereby the coin, now with a Farouk pedigree inferring legality of ownership, was consigned to Stack's and Sotheby's as partners, with the proceeds to be divided between Fenton and the Treasury Department.

In July 2002, it crossed the auction block in New York City and set the world's record price for a coin at that time: $7,590,020. Stack's and, later, Stack's Bowers Galleries, featured this in advertising for a long time afterward and still does. (Records are made to be broken, and Stack's Bowers Galleries did this with the $10,016,875 sale of the gem 1794 dollar discussed in chapter 42.)

As to other 1933 double eagles now in hiding or seized by the government, I broached the suggestion to a Treasury official that these coins might be "pardoned." Off the record I was told that the matter was so complicated at this point that it might be impossible to undo the perceived wrongs, as reparations could be claimed by heirs of the owners of the pieces seized in the 1940s, and, more recently, the government was a partner in a commercial numismatic transaction in which a government decree confirming the legality of the Fenton-Farouk coin may have resulted in the coin bringing more money than might have been the case otherwise.

As to the "rest of the story": As 1933 double eagles are not readily collectible today, and as there are so many more interesting facts and sidelights to their story, perhaps the best thing to do is to buy or borrow a copy of David E. Tripp's *Illegal Tender*, a book that attracted a lot of attention when it come out in 2004. Also acquire a copy of my *Guide Book of Double Eagle Gold Coins*, published by Whitman in 2004. For an opposing viewpoint on the government's reasoning, read Edmund Moy's commentary (from the perspective of a retired director of the U.S. Mint) in *American Gold and Platinum Eagles*.

As I write these words it seems that within the borders of the United States, all by itself the coin auctioned in 2002 will stand as unique as a legal collectible. As such its fame will endure. However, should other 1933 twenties come out of hiding and be legalized, they will remain first-class rarities, perhaps comparison-wise on a par with the famous 1804 silver dollar, of which 15 are known.

CHAPTER 51

The wife of Ambassador R. Henry Norweb, Emery May Holden Norweb became interested in numismatics as a child and pursued coins, tokens, and medals for the rest of her long life. She was a fine friend to me, and it was an honor to present her estate collection at auction and to write a book about her.

Emery May Holden Norweb

The *Grande Dame* of Numismatics

Emery May Holden Norweb on the cover of the February 22, 1966, issue of the *Sunday Plain Dealer Magazine.*

Among my favorite memories are those of Mrs. R. Henry Norweb (who sometimes gave her name as Emery May Holden Norweb) and of her family. The Cleveland *Plain Dealer* called her "an art expert and collector, civic worker, Grande Dame of Cleveland society and the only woman to become president of the Cleveland Museum of Art." I think the title *Grande Dame of Numismatics* would fit equally well. Wonderfully, my memories also extend to her descendants—not often the case with numismatic personalities who have played major roles in my life.

I first met her at a coin convention in the mid-1950s. By that time she was known as the owner of one of the finest coin collections ever formed in America. I liked her immediately and was honored that she took a liking to me, a teenager who had a lot of enthusiasm and a growing business. Remarkably, within two or three years she and her husband, Ambassador R. Henry Norweb, began asking me for advice! In turn, I delighted hearing "coin stories" from them. Later, when I wrote a book about collector Virgil M. Brand, who had died in 1926, leaving behind the greatest private coin collection ever formed—about 350,000 items—she was the only person I could find to interview who actually knew Virgil.

Emery May was born in 1896, the daughter of Albert Fairchild Holden, a highly successful owner of mining properties who enjoyed collecting coins as a pastime and who was a second-generation

Liberty Holden, who started the family coin collection.

Albert Fairchild Holden.

numismatist. Albert's father, Liberty Holden, began the family collection years earlier.

When she was a child in elementary school her father had Emery May take Sylvester S. Crosby's 1875 *Early Coins of America* book and attribute coins. She did this, assigning Crosby numbers to Massachusetts silver coins and other colonial pieces. Imagine that! As the years went by, father and daughter continued to enjoy the family collection. When an auction catalog arrived in the mail, he would pick out items of interest, then discuss them with Emery May. "Should *we* bid on this?" Or, "Look through this catalog, and put a pencil mark on any item you think we should add to *our* collection." This was done with the famous Wilson Collection in 1907, for example. At the time she was still a couple of years away from being a teenager.

Emery May Holden as a teenager.

After her father's passing in 1913, it was natural that Emery May should continue in numismatics. And she did, with a passion. She was strong-willed from the start, a family characteristic. In April 1914 readers of *The Numismatist* saw a listing for Emery May Holden as new member No. 1,176 of the Amer-

ican Numismatic Association. Her address was Station H in Cleveland, wherever that was. She remained a member until her passing in 1984, or 70 years—a record of longevity not equaled by anyone else.

Sketches of Her Life

When the World War was raging in Europe but before the United States was involved she ran off to France and joined the Ambulance Corps. While there she met and fell in love with R(aymond) Henry Norweb, who

The staff at the American Embassy in Paris. Ambassador William G. Sharp is at the center. R. Henry Norweb is standing, third from the left.

was born to a wealthy family in Nottingham, England. The Norwebs moved to America in 1907 to settle in Elyria, Ohio. After graduating from Harvard in 1916 he went to Paris in 1917 as secretary to Ambassador William G. Sharp. Although Emery May's family members liked R. Henry, they thought she should slow down the romance—too much too soon—this per her recollections to me years later. However, she would not be deterred. The couple married in 1917.

In 1918 they had a son, Harry Jr., and two other children, and they lived happily ever after. R. Henry became a career diplomat and was posted at various places around the world.

Wherever he was posted, Ambassador Norweb held a reception every day in the embassy at 4:00 p.m. So if somebody came in and said, "Look, I'm a very important person from Portland, Oregon, you know," or something similar, the receptionist would reply, "Come by at 4 o'clock this afternoon and the ambassador will be delighted to see you." At the appointed hour visitors would be entertained with tea and cookies, pleasantries would be exchanged, and then everyone would go their separate ways. One family photograph shows such a reception with four uniformed color guards—lending dignity and formality.

Mrs. R. Henry Norweb in her twenties.

All the while, Mrs. Norweb pursued numismatics, specializing in American coins from the colonial era down to the current time, using her father's collection as a base. In time she acquired one of nearly everything, usually in the finest possible condition. At regular intervals they would return from whatever embassy they were serving to their main home at Bratenahl, a suburb of Cleveland with its own Lake Erie shorefront (and a short drive from Euclid Beach Park, now closed, but famous in its own day).

This reminds me that sometime in the 1950s a great contretemps arose when the government wanted to put a Nike anti-missile base on the shore too close to the Norweb mansion for the ambassador to be comfortable. I have forgotten how that played out.

The Norweb coin collection was stored in the safe-deposit area in the lower level of the Huntington Bank in nearby Cleveland. The bank had several large rooms nearby. Often, Ambassador and Mrs. Norweb would prepare a picnic lunch, complete with a bottle of wine, and pack it into a nondescript case. Upon entering the safe-deposit area they would request use of a room. Then the lunch would be opened, coins would be studied by Mrs., while the ambassador read a book. Two or three hours later, the remnants of lunch would be packed away—no bank attendants the wiser—and the coins returned to safe deposit. All of these details are from things related to me at the time and later.

When I was a teenager in the coin business nearly all of the old-timers were nice to me—B. Max Mehl and Abe Kosoff being just two of many. When selling a coin I described it as accurately as I could, trying to place myself in the position of the buyer. I would never say anything I did not believe to be true. I wouldn't say that a coin was a gem if it was not. I might say that "This rare 1916 quarter is scratched on the obverse, but on the other hand it's only $75 so it's a good filler. If you want a filler, buy it." I found that people responded very well to my letters and other offers, as at the time there was a lot of promotion and hype in the marketplace. Mrs. Norweb, a consummate connoisseur, took a liking to me early on, as I mentioned. She also liked Ken Rendell, who was a young collector-dealer friend of mine at the same time. I treated her with respect and as a friend.

Apparently, this was in contrast to the usual reception whereby dealers viewed her as a walking checkbook. At conventions they would fall over themselves trying to get her to stop by their tables so they could give a sales pitch. This she did not like at all, for she knew what she wanted, was able to judge quality and price, and did not want to be "sold" anything. Years later she discussed a lot of this with me, and it helped clarify some of the things I had observed when I knew her as a youngster.

In 1957 I paid a record $4,750 for an 1894-S dime. In 1958 Ambassador and Mrs. Norweb bought it from me for $6,000. The Norwebs had a summer place in Boothbay Harbor, Maine, and a residence occupying an entire floor of River House in New York City (where Henry Luce, founder of the Time-Life business, lived), these in addition to their embassy residence (which changed from time to time). Occasionally Ambassador Norweb, who was also interested in coins but not a passionate collector, took me as his guest for dinner at Keen's Chop House in New York City, then to a meeting of the New York Numismatic Club. The subject one night was Hard Times tokens, and each member was to bring examples if he or she owned them, or, if not, to participate in the discussion. This program feature was always fun.

Mrs. Norweb was gracious and generous to people she liked. However, if someone tried to pull a fast deal or deceive her, as John J. Ford Jr., once did, then they were forever cut off as a coin supplier. I have forgotten the details, but they went something like this: John had bought a rare colonial coin for, say, $2,000 and offered it to Mrs. Norweb with "I just paid $4,500 for this, and you can have it for $5,000." Not long afterward Mrs. Norweb was talking to a dealer who said, "I had a colonial I was going to offer to you, but then John Ford came along and bought it." She learned the price and told John, "I don't care what you paid for it, but to lie to me is not acceptable. Please do not contact me again." For many years she had been one of his most important clients.

I always called her "Mrs. Norweb." I was never invited to call her Emery May or anything other than Mrs. Norweb, and I never heard anyone other than *Coin World* editor Margo Russell call her anything else.[1]

Group photograph taken at the 1964 ANA convention, left to right: Ambassador R. Henry Norweb, *Coin World* editor Margo Russell, Director of the Mint Eva Adams, Mrs. Norweb, and convention chairman Robert McNamara. (*Coin World*)

Mrs. Norweb knew what she wanted. And she was always direct and to the point, in a nice way. I'd say, for example, "Mrs. Norweb, I have a coin that's on your list," and offer her a Proof half cent variety (she collected originals as well as both varieties of Small Berries restrikes for the various dates), or a rare colonial coin. "The price is $300." Once, she passed such an offer, and I said, "If it makes a difference, perhaps I can do a bit better than $300." To this she said, "Dave (she always called me Dave), you know if I wanted to buy it I'd pay $300 for it. I don't want to buy it."

Occasionally Mrs. Norweb had run-ins with people who tried to be too clever. John Ford wasn't the only dealer who tried this and lost. She told me what happened when she was in the American contingent to the King Farouk Collection auction held in Cairo, Egypt, in February and March, 1954. Farouk had been deposed and the military junta in charge of the country was selling what they called the Palace Collection. Many coins, including great rarities, were lumped helter-skelter in miscellaneous lots. One particular lot was described something like, "Collection of United States nickels from 1866 to 1950." It included the rare 1913 Liberty Head, but I don't think this was even mentioned in the catalog!

Mrs. Norweb was able, through diplomatic connections or something, to have that coin removed from the lot and sold separately as an addendum to the main lot. She didn't want to bid on it personally, for fear that someone would simply run her up on the price, thinking he could charge her more later, at retail. At the sale Abe Kosoff and Sol Kaplan were partners in bidding, and both knew Mrs. Norweb as a client. She said to Kaplan, "Buy this coin for me. Okay?"

Kaplan nodded his assent. Soon the coin was his, for slightly less than $4,000, a price that he realized was a great bargain. After the sale session, Mrs. Norweb thanked Kaplan, who then came back with a comment to this effect: "There is a complication. First of all, you know, you got it for much less than you said. But that's not the complication. The complication is that I got a wire from another client in the United States since I talked to you—I haven't talked to you since this morning, and he said to buy it at any price. So I can't really sell it to you at the price I paid."

Needless to say, this scenario did not play well with Mrs. Norweb. She did get her coin and at the bid price. She never spoke to Kaplan again for the rest of her life.

(Some years later I assisted her with an appraisal of the 1913 Liberty Head nickel, and its transfer as a gift to the National Numismatic Collection at the Smithsonian Institution in Washington.)

I almost landed an 1804 dollar for Mrs. Norweb. I was attending the Stack's sale of the Fairbanks Collection (formed by Ben Koenig) to buy for inventory. Ambassador Norweb enlisted me to secretly bid on his behalf on lot 576, an example of what B. Max Mehl used to call "the King of American Coins." He sat in the room in a position that enabled me to watch his signals. The coin opened in the five-figure range, but when it crossed the $20,000 mark I and another bidder were the only ones remaining in competition. My final bid was $27,000, after which the ambassador dropped out. The coin was sold to a representative (as I learned later) of Samuel Wolfson, a Florida theater magnate.

Mrs. Norweb addressing participants at the 1973 International Numismatic Congress held at the American Numismatic Society. (Margo Russell, *Coin World*)

(One of Harvey Stack's favorite stories told of a man who in the 1950s came with his young son into the Stack's store on West 57th Street in New York City. The boy was trying to fill Whitman folders for Lincoln cents. Harvey and the father talked, and soon the father was deep into coins, including rarities. That was Samuel Wolfson.)

Ambassador and Mrs. Norweb were deeply involved in the American Numismatic Society until they resigned their positions, after which each was named a life councilor, a rare distinction. Their benefactions to the ANS included gifts of a 1787 Brasher doubloon and many rare colonial coins. At the time the Society was housed in its museum and headquarters on Audubon Terrace at 155th Street and Broadway in New York City. This had been opened in 1908, paid for by donations from the Huntington family, and by the 1970s was one of the most delightful numismatic haunts imaginable—what with its huge library, helpful staff, and collections that could always be examined. I joined in 1958 and was later made a fellow.

Mr. Norweb was a person who liked to be in control, which I probably am too. So it was with her children. When she was, say, in her seventies and her children were perhaps in their thirties and forties she wanted a report from each of them every day on their activities. And everybody had a time. I'm not making this up. Like maybe Albert was to call at 7:18 in the morning, and R. Henry Jr. at 7:23—they all had their times.

At the family place in Boothbay Harbor there was a big living-room rug. In later years her grandchildren would visit in the summer. So true to Mrs. Norweb's character, the room was divided off with invisible lines—you can be in this corner, and you can be in this corner, you can do this, you can do that. All the kids had specific procedures to follow.

Postscript

Emery May Holden Norweb was blind in her later years but remained in good spirits and with her memory as sharp as a tack. She was always a positive-thinking person. She kept in touch by telephone with Margo Russell, me, and some other friends from her numismatic days. Over a period of time I asked her a lot of questions about things she did and people she knew. In the process I learned much that might not have been otherwise recorded. She passed away in comfort at the Cleveland University Hospital on March 27, 1988, and was widely mourned.

In due course the Norweb numismatic estate became available. When this happened, her son, R. Henry Jr., and his wife Libby simply said to me, "Come and get the collection." We didn't even negotiate. Whatever we did would be fine. And it was. In a

series of sales the Norweb Collection created attention worldwide, record prices were attained, and even today it is mentioned when great collections are discussed. When we had the honor of cataloging and presenting the collection for sale we used such terms as *choice*, *gem*, *superb*, etc., in the adjectival grading system, plus numbers for copper coins (this was before the ANA adopted standard numbers for grading). Her code was in just three steps: 1. Circulated. 2. Uncirculated. 3. Proof. With Mike Hodder I researched and wrote a book, *The Norweb Collection: An American Legacy*. Mike, one of the most knowledgeable professionals ever to be on our staff, also did much of the cataloging of subsequent sales.

The Norweb family gave a picnic for our staff afterwards. Several dozen of us—spouses and children too—went to Boothbay Harbor and were treated with a cruise followed by a lobster-fest. As we were all seated I stood up to thank Henry Norweb (R. Henry Jr.) and his family. I had hardly started, when he stood up and said, "Stop that. First of all I learned, from having my parents in the ambassador service, you don't say thank you's for thank you's. I'm thanking you and your staff, you're not thanking me!"

However, I did persist and was able to express my appreciation.

Some years later we were given the Norweb Collection of Canadian coins to sell, an Ultra High Relief MCMVII (1907) Proof double eagle, and one of the greatest collections of George Washington coins and medals ever formed.

R. Henry Norweb Jr.

It is appropriate for me to tell more about R. Henry Jr. and his family, also a wonderful part of my memories. The younger Henry, who was nicknamed Harry, was a numismatist who specialized in coins of Brazil. As he said, he did not want to take on the "ready-made" collection of his mother, but desired to have his own challenges.

Harry was born on August 19, 1918, in, of all places, a bomb shelter in Paris where his mother had

R. Henry Norweb Jr.

been taken in anticipation of a German air raid. As a child and as a young adult he was mainly educated in foreign schools by private tutors as he traveled to various embassy postings where his father served as a counselor or ambassador, including in Japan, the Netherlands, Chile, Bolivia, the Dominican Republic, Peru, and Portugal. In 1940 he followed in the footsteps of his grandfather and father and earned a degree from Harvard University, his in American history. Following family tradition, his mother assigned him and his sister Mary to attributing Connecticut coppers—one of the most technical of American specialties—by the system devised by Henry C. Miller years earlier. He was not yet a teenager.

As an adult he also became closely connected with the American Numismatic Society, joining in 1956 and in 1978 being elected to the ANS Council, where he succeeded his father, who had been a councilor since 1960. He was elected first vice president in 1984 and remained there until 1990, when he succeeded Harry Fowler as president. In 1994 he stepped down, but continued to serve on committees and help in other ways. Beyond numismatics he was executive director of the Holden Arboretum in Cleveland and

was on the board of various civic and other organizations including the Cleveland Orchestra and the Western Reserve Historical Society.

While Harry's mother Emery May was a "coin person" of outstanding knowledge and discrimination and was an ardent pursuer of anything numismatic upon which she set her sights, it is probably correct to say that her son, R. Henry Jr., was a "people person" first and a "coin person" second.

In 1984 in New York City a special dinner and reception was held by the ANS to honor R. Henry Norweb Jr. Numismatists, family members, and admirers from many points of the compass gathered for an evening of conviviality and appreciation held in a marble mansion a few steps off Fifth Avenue. All too soon the event ended, and people went their separate ways.

Harry Norweb died on June 6, 1995, following a coma sustained when he was walking on the shore at his summer home in Maine and slipped on a moss-covered rock. If there is any consolation in his passing it is that he is believed to have suffered no pain. However, no one had a chance to say good-bye. His obituary in the Cleveland *News Herald* included this:

> Any list of the kindest and most decent people who have ever graced this portion of the earth would have to include R. Henry Norweb, Jr., somewhere near the very top. Norweb embodied all the finest qualities that cause some human beings to rise above the crowd and cause others to exclaim, "Why can't everybody be like that?"
>
> He was well-mannered, gentle, generous, and an inspiring role model to be the kind of citizen he was. There are many ways in which Norweb will be remembered for his contributions to make our world a better place to live. . . .
>
> In 1944 he married Elizabeth

Gardner, of Maine, who was his constant companion for the next fifty years, during which they raised three wonderful children and enjoyed many things together. . . .

On June 20 a special memorial service was held for him at the Trinity Cathedral in Cleveland. An overflow crowd gathered to pay respects to their dear friend and to hear a eulogy delivered by retired newspaper publisher (Cleveland *Plain Dealer*) Thomas V.H. Vail, a relative and childhood chum. Among Vail's comments were these:

> Henry Norweb was the perfect gentleman. I never heard him say a bad word about anyone. Much as I will miss Henry I cannot feel sorry for him. He lived a long and wonderful life. He had a marriage made in heaven. He enjoyed the delightful family he and his wife created. He had a splendid professional career.
>
> We all know our beginning, but we do not know our end. Whatever our time frame turns out to be, from start to finish we should do what one prominent American challenged us to do: "Do what you can where you are and with what you have."
>
> This was Henry Norweb from beginning to end. He did the job in his diplomatic way, with the highest integrity of purpose, and with a sense of humor. I shall, like all of his family and friends, remember Henry Norweb in that way. . . . He set an example for all of us to follow. I could say no more about anyone!

He was survived by his wife Elizabeth (Libby), sister Jeanne Catherine, son Harry, daughter Emery May, and daughter Connie Abbey, and their families and children.

To know the Norwebs was to like them. As noted in the introduction to this chapter, they were among the most important people in my life in numismatics.

What a nice way to end this book.

NOTES

Chapter 1

1. Dye, of shady reputation, was earlier a leading publisher of counterfeit-detecting newsletters that rated the value of bank notes and the banks that issued them. His opinion could be bought, as reflected in his dishonest reporting of bills of the Litchfield Bank in Connecticut in the late 1850s and other illegal actions reported in the press at the time. His 1883 *Encyclopedia* was impressive in size but was scarcely noticed or quoted by numismatic writers and catalogers of the time.

2. The first person in modern times to revisit the possibility of two striking events was Carl W.A. Carlson, in his 1982 article in *The Numismatist,* "Birch and the Coinage of 1792." Pete Smith independently came to the same conclusion in 2013 after studying the half disme's die-state progression. See Leonard Augsburger, Joel Orosz, and Pete Smith, "1792: Birth of a Nation's Coinage," Money Talks presentation, ANA World's Fair of Money, Chicago, August 15, 2013.

3. Modern research is reflected in the work by Joel Orosz and Len Augsburger, *The Secret History of the First U.S. Mint.* Certain details were also given in "The 1792 Half Disme: America's Most Distinctive Coin," a special essay by Augsburger, Orosz, and Pete Smith, published in the January 2013 Cardinal Collection catalog by Stack's Bowers Galleries.

4. From a discussion between Joel Orosz and the author, August 30, 2013.

5. Joel Orosz, communication to the author, August 21, 2013.

6. *Ibid.*

Chapter 4

1. Letters from Jared Sparks, *Franklin's Works,* as quoted by William Sumner Appleton, *American Journal of Numismatics,* November 1867, pp. 63–64.

Chapter 5

1. Certain of this text is adapted from an article the author wrote for *COINage* magazine, submitted June 1, 2005.

Chapter 6

1. Walter Breen, *Encyclopedia of Proof Coins,* p. 245.

2. The Washington Cabinet suggestion is incorrect, as James Ross Snowden did not begin his campaign to add to this display until early 1859. However, the Mint did supply rare coins to collectors at the time, and had been doing so for many years.

Chapter 7

1. Communication to the author, May 24, 2013.

Chapter 8

1. This chapter is from my "Coins and Collectors" column in *The Numismatist,* July 2011, here slightly adapted. Certain information appeared earlier in my "Joys of Collecting" column in *Coin World.* Thanks to David Sundman, Wendy Beattie, Bill Maryott, *Coin World,* and David Schenkman for providing information. For additional information see my 1996 book, *American Coin Hoards and Treasures.*

Chapter 9

1. In the 1850s showman Yankee Robinson counterstamped half dollars with FREE TICKET TO YANKEE ROBINSON'S QUADRUPLE SHOW. Of course, the "free ticket" had to be surrendered at the door!

2. T. Allston Brown, *A History of the New York Stage,* volume I, 1903, pp. 361, 362.

3. *New York Herald,* September 1, 1856.

4. *New York Tribune,* July 9, 1857.

5. Boston *Herald Traveler,* January 29, 1858.

6. *New York Tribune,* February 20, 1858.

Chapter 10

1. The New York City exhibition with the Crystal Palace was a privately funded project and is not considered to be an official world's fair.

Chapter 11

1. Gene Hessler, *U.S. Essay, Proof and Specimen Notes,* pp. 98–102.
2. Thomas F. Morris (Jr.) was an avid numismatist and historian. In particular, he contributed much to the pages of the *Essay-Proof Journal.* His 1934 article in *The Numismatist* stated that the first notes had a word in the Constitution spelled as TRANQUILLITY, instead of TRANQUILITY, as it is on the original document; "while none of these notes were recalled, the plate was re-engraved to the correct spelling and the later notes indicate that the error does not occur." This is fiction as plate 1, still in existence, does not have the variant spelling.
3. Frank DeWitt in *The Numismatist,* July 1940.
4. Expanded information can be found in the *Comprehensive Catalog of U.S. Paper Money,* sixth edition, Gene Hessler, pp. 108–118 (also the source for the newspapers cited here).
5. "Testimony taken [in 1897] by the Committee appointed to Investigate the Bureau of Engraving and Printing," 55th Congress, 3rd Session, Senate, Document 109, Part II, March 3, 1899.
6. Much of this chapter has been adapted from my text in two books issued by Whitman Publishing: the *Whitman Encyclopedia of U.S. Paper Money* and, with David M. Sundman, *100 Greatest American Currency Notes.*

Chapter 12

1. For the first part of this chapter I give a nod posthumously (and by a long time) to John Allan, in essence my co-author.
2. The other two Americans were Mr. Paine, of New York City, and Thomas Lyman, listed as "United States," but with no specific location. Little is known today of these two men. The set of Mudie's National Medals comprised 40 pieces dated from 1799 to 1817, mostly commemorating British military victories.
3. Canal project champion Colonel W.L. Stone, editor of the *Commercial Advertiser,* wrote the "Official Narrative of the Grand Erie Canal Celebration," and received a silver medal in recognition of his efforts. His account is cited in William L. Stone, *The Centennial History of New York City, from the Discovery to the Present Day,* 1876, p. 195.
4. *American Journal of Numismatics,* January 1883.
5. Many Wright family papers, engravings, and other items are preserved by the New-York Historical Society. Katherine Jaeger De Silva did research there on my behalf and furnished certain of the information used here.

Chapter 13

1. The illustrated Georgivs Triumpho copper is from the Roger Siboni Collection.
2. Notre Dame University web site, www.coins.nd.edu, conducted by Louis Jordan. The described coin is from the Robert H. Gore, Jr. Numismatic Collection.
3. *Ibid.*
4. The book included a steel engraving of a United States silver dollar dated 1804, a date that had been hitherto unknown to collectors.
5. The GEORGIVS spelling, with a V in place of the correct U, is as given in the book, but some sentences later Dickeson spelled it as GEORGIUS.
6. *Sic* is in the original text, pointing out the spelling is a variant. The popular "voice of the people" term is usually given as VOX POPULI or VOCE POPULI, not POPOLI.
7. Mike Ringo, "The Georgius Triumpho," *Colonial Newsletter* 35 (serial 100), July 1995, showed the punch identity with Crosby 1-A and also the 1 and 7 punches with counterfeit British halfpence of

1775 and 1776 and a counterfeit Irish halfpenny of 1776.

8. From the author's *Coin World* column, November 28, 2011.

9. The first such flight in America took place on January 10, 1793, when Jean-Pierre Blanchard went aloft in Philadelphia as thousands, including President George Washington, watched. Blanchard reached a height of about 5,800 feet and landed safely in Gloucester County, New Jersey.

10. Eric P. Newman, "New Thoughts on the Nova Constellatio Private Copper Coinage," *Coinage of the Confederation Period*, Coinage of the Americas Conference, Proceedings No. 11, held at the American Numismatic Society, October 28, 1995.

11. From Louis Jordan, Notre Dame University web site (www.coins.nd.edu): The one verified example of a TRIUMPHO reused as a planchet for a New Jersey copper is an example of a Maris 73-aa acquired by Dennis Wierzba from the Bowers and Merena sale of September 14, 1998. The TRIUM-PHO undertype was noticed after the purchase and has been verified by Michael Hodder and Mike Ringo. This discovery will be discussed in the upcoming summer 1999 issue of the C4 Newsletter. Breen (1987, p. 133) related several Maris 73-aa examples had been overstruck using the TRIUMPHO copper as the planchet, however these coins have not been verified. Mossman (1992, p. 271) was not able to confirm the use of the TRIUMPHO as an undertype for Maris 73-aa from auction catalog descriptions but he did list the TRIUMPHO as an undertype on the very rare Maris 35-W and possibly on a Maris 56-n Camel Head. Anton and Kesse (p. 45) have examined the Maris 56-n (which was formerly in the Spiro sale, lot 1571 and then in Bareford sale, lot 186) and determined it did not have a TRIUMPHO undertype. The Maris 35-W remains unverified.

Chapter 14

1. *Alexandria Gazette,* October 13, 1842, exchange item from Baltimore. This anecdote was republished many times, into the 1850s.

2. *Hartford Courant,* September 11, 1847. This anecdote was widely published during the next two years.

3. *New London* (Connecticut) *Democrat,* September 28, 1849.

4. *Louisville Journal,* September 15, 1858.

5. Milbourne Christopher, *Panorama of Magic,* 1962, p. 114.

Chapter 15

1. Dickeson suggests that the "milling of the edges"—the rim on the coins—is not sufficiently raised to protect the surfaces from contact marks and undue wear.

2. Significant contemporary accounts mentioned that they were in just one keg, and it was small. The hoard "grew" as later stories of it reach print, these being by people not involved in the original find or distribution.

3. Rarity information is from Walter Breen, *United States Minor Coinages 1793–1916*, p. 11.

4. Breen, *Encyclopedia,* 1988, p. 202.

Chapter 16

1. Rick Crandall, "Literature Discovery from America's First Coin-Op Museum," *Musical Box Society Bulletin* Spring-Summer 1981.

2. From a card preserved in the Warshaw Collection of Business Americana, Smithsonian Institution, Washington, D.C. The text has some historical errors—not surprising as it was printed in the 1930s, before any reference books on disc music boxes were available.

3. "Boyer Donates $100 Cook Book to Fred Mills," *Spinning Reels,* November 1941. "In his imposing

museum at 1700 South Wabash Avenue he has gathered the largest and most intriguing collection of machines ever assembled under one roof—hundreds of them—many of them more than half a century old—and every one in perfect operating condition."

Chapter 17

1. Sold by Stack's Bowers Galleries, August 2013, at the American Numismatic Association World's Fair of Money convention in Chicago.

Chapter 18

1. Lyon's Magnetic Powder was widely advertised on tokens.
2. *Journal of Commerce,* December 21, 1854.
3. *Frank Leslie's Illustrated Newspaper,* March 8, 1856.
4. This token was listed as No. 92 by Charles I. Bushnell in *An Arrangement of Tradesmen's Cards, Political Tokens, etc.,* issued in 1858.

Chapter 19

1. Today this coin is preserved by the Harry W. Bass, Jr. Foundation as No. HBCC-7001. In Bass's own inventory system it was no. 10,001.
2. *The Numismatist,* November 1966.
3. *Harry W. Bass, Jr.: Memories of His Life.*
4. *Councillor* is the spelling style used by the Society.
5. Photographs of the Bass Gallery are courtesy of the American Numismatic Association via Robert Kelley.
6. Texas Bank's "Know Your Directors" series, March 1962.

Chapter 20

1. *American Education Society Quarterly Register,* August 1840.
2. The State House was located on the village green behind the Central Church and was demolished in 1889 when it was in a state of disrepair.
3. *Art and Artists in Connecticut,* Harry Willard French, 1878.

Chapter 21

1. Exchange item in the *Times-Picayune,* New Orleans, June 16, 1876.
2. *Daily Graphic,* New York City, July 6, 1876.
3. *Commercial Advertiser,* New York City, August 22, 1876.
4. *New York Herald,* December 16, 1876.
5. *New York Herald,* October 7, 1877.

Chapter 23

1. *American Journal of Numismatics,* March 1868. Cogan had no first-hand knowledge of the activities of the Mint in the 1820s and 1830s, for he was living in England at the time and did not become involved in numismatics until the late 1850s, but probably heard this from W.E. Dubois. J.D. Dannreuther, who examined the set in 1997, observed that the cabinet includes a complete 1821 Proof set (cent, dime, quarter dollar, half dollar, $2.50 gold, and $5 gold), indicating that Eckfeldt and/or the Mint or a friend of the Mint was reserving interesting coins by this time; later, the silver coins were heavily polished by curators and staff, but the cent and gold coins remain pristine.
2. In his April 14, 1841, letter to Joel Poinsett, Gilmor mentioned he had suggested the general idea to Eckfeldt; by implication, the suggestion would have been made prior to the establishment of the Mint Cabinet (which was instituted in 1838).
3. "On the Utility of a Cabinet of Historic Coins," T. Louis Comparette, *The Numismatist,* March 1906.
4. Bowers, *Louis E. Eliasberg, Sr.: King of Coins,* 1996, Appendix II.
5. In 1869, Vattemare sold certain of his collections, including autographs, to the Imperial Library in St. Petersburg, Russia. Anecdotes concerning Vattemare are adapted in part from "The Vattemare Collection," *American Antiquarian,* January 1872, pp. 126–127.
6. In 1892 John Bigelow, former American consul,

donated many of Vattemare's papers, but not numismatic items, to the New York Public Library.

7. It is to be remembered that continuing supplies of precious metals were essential to the Mint's operation. Mint facilities were employed often in the assay of native metal and ore. As branch mints were established, more often than not they were sited near sources of gold or silver.

8. Term used for what would later be called Proof coins.

9. *American Journal of Numismatics,* October 1868.

10. An anecdote at best; Eckfeldt and Dubois at the Mint were well acquainted with rare-coin values.

11. *American Journal of Numismatics,* October 1887.

12. In actuality the 1876 Centennial Exhibition, held in Philadelphia, also produced a flood of cheap medals in white metal, aluminum, copper, and brass. However, the Mint's entry, a fine dollar-sized medal made in silver and other metals, was more artistic than anything the Mint produced for the Columbian Exposition. In 1876 a large coining press was brought from the nearby Mint to the Exhibition in Fairmount Park, and the silver impressions were struck *in situ* and retailed for $3 each (in contrast, bronze and gilt pieces were struck within the Mint and were sold for $1).

13. *American Journal of Numismatics,* July 1894.

14. Vladimir Clain-Stefanelli, "History of the National Numismatic Collections," p. 10.

15. *Ibid.* p. 3.

16. William Jones Rhees, *The Smithsonian Institution: Documents Relative to Its Origin and History,* volume 1, Washington, D.C., 1901, pp. 7 ff.

17. Vladimir Clain-Stefanelli, "History of the National Numismatic Collections," p. 4.

18. Belote (1881–1953) seems to have come to the Smithsonian in 1908, was assistant curator in 1909, then full curator of the Division of History at the Smithsonian; he remained in the post until 1950.

19. Vladimir Clain-Stefanelli, "History of the National Numismatic Collections," p. 28.

20. *Ibid.* p. 12.

21. *Ibid.* p. 28.

22. At the time the American Numismatic Association had no headquarters or museum facility of its own, and coins were lent to the Smithsonian to be kept with the Mint Collection. Years later they were retrieved, and today the ANA Collection is exhibited at ANA Headquarters, Colorado Springs, Colorado.

23. *The Numismatist,* October 1937.

24. Edgar H. Adams and William H. Woodin, *United States Pattern, Trial, and Experimental Pieces. Being a List of the Pattern. Trial, and Experimental Pieces Which Have Been Issued by the United States Mint from 1792 Up to the Present Time.* Woodin was the primary author; Adams (who was well known as a writer and researcher) took the photographs. The book, which endured as the standard reference until the publication of Dr. J. Hewitt Judd's volume in 1959, was published by the American Numismatic Society.

25. This was later given to the Library of Congress, which later routinely deaccessioned it as being redundant; fortunately, it was retrieved by a numismatist, and its significance was appreciated.

26. Elvira Eliza Clain-Stefanelli, "Old Friends–Common Goals: The Evolution of Numismatics in the United States," *American Numismatic Association Centennial Anthology,* 1991. Also comment by George Fuld to Q. David Bowers, January 1997: Fuld recalled with disapproval that potassium cyanide was used for many of the silver coins. Similarly, Vladimir Clain-Stefanelli, "History of the National Numismatic Collections," pp. 28, 29: Dr. William Blum of the Electrodeposition Section of the National Bureau of Standards was called in to prepare the cyanide formula; after which, per Stefanelli, 1970, the "entire collection" was sprayed with Krylon; "unfortunately, however, unskilled technical assistants often used the lacquer to excess with detrimental results to the appearance of some of the specimens").

27. Letter, May 11, 1999.

28. J. Saltus Sanford Jr., died on July 24, 1922, at the Hotel Metropole, London. At the time he was engaged to marry Mrs. Estelle Campbell of New York City, a widow. An account (Howard L. Adelson, *The American Numismatic Society 1858–1958,* pp. 214–215 and pp. 341–342, contains another, similar description of the event) later noted: "The coroner's inquest disclosed the fact that the day before his death he had purchased a small quantity of potassium cyanide for the purpose of cleaning some recent purchases of silver coins. Once in his room, Saltus ordered a bottle of ginger ale, and after his death, two glasses were found on the dressing table, the first contained the cyanide and the second the ginger ale. Mrs. Campbell told of having often seen Saltus clean coins with cyanide and of having begged him to give up using it, telling him that 'it was only a question of time when something awful would happen.' While Saltus was cleaning his new coins for presentation to the British Society he must have picked up the wrong glass." Today the American Numismatic Society gives an award in his name each year, as it has for decades—not an award for cleaning coins (perish the thought or, perhaps, perish yourself!)—but for medallic sculpture designs.

29. Vladimir Clain-Stefanelli, "History of the National Numismatic Collections," p. 30.

30. *Ibid.* p. 30.

31. *Ibid.,* chapter 71 (February 5, 1969).

32. *Abe Kosoff Remembers,* chapter 68 (November 20, 1968).

33. Conversation with the author, April 21, 1999. Also, *Coin World,* April 26, 1999.

Chapter 24

1. Decades later the ANA board of governors sought a designation for the Association's highest honor and wanted to use George F. Heath's name, but the Heath Literary Award was already in place. Someone clueless suggested the recently deceased Zerbe,

unaware that he was the greatest charlatan in ANA history. The Farran Zerbe Award was created. As today few other than scholars know that Zerbe was at the center of the first major scandal in Association history, all is well. Recipients of the award (of which I am one) are honored.

2. *The Numismatist,* February 1909.

3. Howard L. Adelson, *The American Numismatic Society 1858–1958,* plate opposite p. 157, identifies a dozen individuals among those attending.

4. From the Bowers and Ruddy catalog of the John W. Adams cents, 1982. In 1916 Gilbert's book, *The United States Half Cents,* was published, to remain the standard work in the series for decades thereafter. Of the work on 1796 half cents, Charles Davis (*American Numismatic Literature,* p. 90) commented: "A hurried attempt to classify this date. . . ."

5. In June and July 1980 in *The Numismatist,* Thomas K. DeLorey's study was published, "Thomas L. Elder, A Catalogue of His Tokens and Medals," which today remains the standard reference on Elder's extensive output.

6. Apparently a pun, "after a fashion" possibly pertaining to the "collecting" of money, although Hetty Green could have been a numismatist as well (her son, Colonel E.H.R. Green, was, if not a student a coins, an aggressive buyer of them; biographical notes concerning him are easily found on the Internet and elsewhere).

Chapter 25

1. A leading Japanese industrialist who collected these instruments paid two people to spend a year translating it into Japanese so he could read every word!

Chapter 27

1. Portrait by Alan Dietz, provided by John W. Adams.

2. From Mason, "The Numismatic Chums" installment of "Personal Numismatic Reminiscences,"

Mason's Coin Collectors' Herald, September 1882.

3. *Mason's Coin and Stamp Collectors' Magazine,* June 1867.

4. Mason, "Reminiscences of a Coin Collector," *Mason's Coin & Stamp Collector's Magazine,* November 1867.

5. Emmanuel Attinelli, *Numisgraphics,* 1876, pp. 92, 94. Attinelli was very skeptical of this claim.

6. *Mason's Coin and Stamp Collectors' Magazine,* July and August 1868.

7. *Mason's Coin and Stamp Collectors' Magazine,* May 1870.

8. For details on his auction career see John W. Adams, *American Numismatic Literature,* volume I, 1982.

Chapter 29

1. *American Journal of Numismatics,* May 1867, p. 9.

2. George B. Lincoln, no kin to the president, was a dry-goods wholesaler in Brooklyn who had met Abraham in a visit to Springfield a few years earlier and who supported his campaign. He was with Lincoln in early 1860, before the nomination, when he spoke at the Cooper Institute in New York City.

3. Located at 234 and 235 Broadway, the firm advertised widely in the city papers.

4. In 1860 Eli M. Robbins was a merchant at 112 Duane Street, not far from merchant George W. Bramhall at 108 Duane; George E. Royce and Gershom E. Hard were importers at 70 Reade Street. The 1860 census lists Bramhall as a clerk at an unspecified location.

5. This is significant as it shows that Scovill used Lovett dies. Conventional wisdom has had it that Lovett struck his own tokens. If so, at least some others were made by Scovill.

6. It seems that Lincoln scholars of the present era are not aware of this photograph, per Fred L. Reed, who has studied Lincoln images and portraits (see his *Abraham Lincoln: The Image of His Greatness* and *Abraham Lincoln: Beyond the American Icon*).

7. Dr. Montroville W. Dickeson, *The American Numismatical Manual,* 1859. Dickeson was mentioned several times in the Bramhall catalog, and certain Connecticut coppers were attributed to Dickeson types.

8. The main source of Bramhall's biographical information other than in numismatics was *History of the Ninety-Third Regiment, New York Volunteer Infantry, 1861–1865,* compiled by David H. King, Judson Gibbs, and Jay H. Northup, published by the Association of the 93rd Regiment in 1895.

Chapter 30

1. Caroline Bancroft, *Gulch of Gold, A History of Central City, Colorado,* 1959, is an excellent modern history of the city. There are extensive biographical notes and a portrait of Frank Young.

2. Bayard Taylor, *Colorado: A Summer Trip,* pp. 56–70.

3. H. William Axford, *Gilpin County Gold,* 1976, p. 13.

4. As republished in *New Life in New Lands: Notes of Travel,* 1872, pp. 77–79. Grace Greenwood was the nom de plume of Sarah J. Clarke, who in 1853 became Mrs. Leander Lippincott. From the 1840s onward she contributed articles to many magazines and newspapers.

5. The *New York Times,* June 18, 1859, and July 27, 1859, carried multiple dispatches from the West telling of Gregory's find and others involved in the rush for gold.

6. Later this became part of Wells, Fargo & Company, and still later was known as the Kansas Pacific Railroad Express Company, and still later the Pacific Express Company.

7. Frank C. Young, *Echoes from Arcadia,* 1903, p. 87.

8. As quoted by H. William Axford, *Gilpin County Gold,* p. 20.

9. Communication with the author, April 17, 2009.

10. Frank Fossett, *Colorado,* 1879, p. 71.

11. *Rocky Mountain Directory and Gazetteer for 1871,* S.S. Wallihan & Company, Denver, 1870, is the

source of much of the contemporary information given here.

2. Frank Hall, *The History of Colorado,* Volume II, p. 210.

3. Caroline Bancroft, *Gulch of Gold,* 1959, pp. 206–207.

4. Frank R. Hollenback, *Central City and Black Hawk, Colorado, Then and Now,* 1961, p. 27.

5. Peter Huntoon, *National Bank Notes.*

Chapter 31
1. Information captured September 17, 2013.

Chapter 32
1. Information from interviews conducted with Mint personnel in the late 1950s.

Chapter 33
1. Ronald E. Shaw, *Andrew Jackson 1767–1845,* 1969, pp. 23–28, text of message. Although earlier the Supreme Court in the case of McCulloch vs. Maryland had held that the charter of the Bank of the United States was indeed acceptable under the Constitution. There was much monetary turmoil during the second Bank's existence, and one needs but read a file of *Niles' Weekly Register* to learn about many problems within the bank itself and its branches.

2. Ibid., pp. 74–79, text of message read to the Cabinet, September 18, 1833, outlining the procedure. James Parton, *Life of Andrew Jackson,* volume III, 1861, p. 528.

3. *Niles' Weekly Register,* January 7, 1833, p. 297, showed a report from Secretary of the Treasury Levi Woodbury, January 1, indicating the amounts to be transferred to each of the states during the coming year. A detailed discussion of pet banks is beyond the scope of the present study. John M. McFaul, *The Politics of Jacksonian Finance,* 1972, devotes a chapter to "Domesticated Pets." Sample entry (p. 146): "The Treasury had carried a nominal deposit with the Albany [New York] Regency

Bank of $25 through 1833 and 1834, but in 1835 it was appointed a full-time pet, and the government balance swelled to over $100,000 by the end of the year. At the same time $5,500,000 in federal funds was on deposit in the three Wall Street pets."

4. Certain commentary is adapted from the writer's 1993 text, *Silver Dollars and Trade Dollars of the United States: A Complete Encyclopedia,* which contained much year-by-year economic news.

5. By this time in scattered other locations, several important banks had suspended, including the Planters and Agricultural banks in Natchez, Mississippi, on May 4, and the State Bank at Montgomery, Alabama, a few days later.

Chapter 34
1. John Pack, who wrote the John J. Ford Jr. sale descriptions quoted, suggested Chormann as an avenue for research. The prime source for this information and for the citations was *The Executive Documents of the First Session of the 36th Congress.*

Chapter 35
1. "Joseph H. Merriam, Die Sinker," by David E. Schenkman, *The Numismatist,* April 1980, is the first important modern study of Merriam's issues and is the standard source for a listing of varieties. *The Numismatist,* February 1905, continued A.R. Frey's article, "Tokens and Medals Relating to Numismatists and Coin Dealers," and discussed Merriam.

2. *Scout* as used here means to reject or ignore with derision or contempt; a lesser-known meaning of the word.

3. *Mason's Coin and Stamp Collectors' Magazine,* May 1869.

4. *Mason's Coin and Stamp Collectors' Magazine,* April 1870.

5. *Mason's Coin and Stamp Collectors' Magazine,* March 1871.

6. *Journal of the Civil War Token Society,* Fall 1976 issue.

7. The contest lasted 37 rounds and ended in a melee with Sayers weakened and with Heenan unable to see clearly. It was a draw, more or less. Each man was awarded $1,000 and a championship belt. Heenan did not accept his prize and challenged Sayers to a rematch, but this never took place.

Chapter 36

1. *Hazard's Register of Pennsylvania,* March 1833, pp. 154–158 (includes lists with marchers, text of orations, etc.); J. Thomas Scharf and Thomas Westcott, *History of Philadelphia 1609–1884,* published 1846.
2. As an exchange item in the *Newark Daily Advertiser,* October 21, 1836.
3. Caroline Tichnor, *Hawthorne and His Publisher,* 1913, pp. 214, 214.
4. Mrs. E.F. Ellet, *Women Artists in All Ages and Countries,* London, 1859, pp. 300–306, and other sources.

Chapter 37

1. Certain information is adapted from *Silver Dollars and Trade Dollars of the United States: A Complete Encyclopedia,* 1993.
2. Thresher had no way of knowing that dollars with eight tail feathers were made only in Philadelphia.
3. In my *More Adventures with Rare Coins* book, 2002, I devoted a chapter to the 1903-O dollar.
4. It will be remembered that Alexander Hamilton was at that time secretary of the Treasury.
5. According to the 1886 *Annual Report of the Director of the Mint,* quoted in the text describing the 1885-CC dollar.
6. This information was new to me until I encountered it in the *Comprehensive Catalog and Encyclopedia of Morgan and Peace Dollars,* Van Allen and Mallis, third edition, pp. 63 and 199.
7. Reference: His advertisement in *The Numismatist,* January 1964.
8. *Ibid.*
9. *Walter Breen's Complete Encyclopedia of Colonial and U.S. Coins,* 1988. This is not a reliable source in certain aspects. The problem today is that probably 10 percent of Breen's work is imaginative or unreliable—but which entries fall in that 10 percent is a matter of question.

Chapter 39

1. Certain commentaries have been excerpted or lightly edited.
2. Mayr was 15 years old.
3. In the 1950s Robert Botsford, who lived in Nescopeck, Pennsylvania, was a frequent correspondent with me and a fine supplier of coins. He had been a friend of the late William H. Woodin's and had on hand many items from the Woodin estate, including a large quantity of pattern cents and nickels of 1896, which he sold me.

Chapter 40

1. His biography is detailed in *The Eagle That Is Forgotten: Pierre Eugène Du Simitière, Founding Father of American Numismatics,* Joel J. Orosz, 1988.
2. Illustrated in Orosz, p. 40; the sketch is now owned by the Library Company of Philadelphia.
3. A similar motif and motto (expressed as SI COLLIDIMUS FRANGIMUR) was used on Georgia $2 notes of 1776 and $2 and $11 notes of 1777. The vases represented England and America, and the sentiment can be translated: "If we collide, we both shatter [and sink]." The newspaper notice of the 1776 Du Simitière medal is also cited in C. Wyllys Betts, *American Colonial History Illustrated by Contemporary Medals,* p. 248, as Betts-550, the sole entry under the heading "Continental Army," with this footnoted comment, probably by W.T.R. Marvin (who with Lyman H. Low co-edited the work of the late Betts): "The device of the floating jars, with its accompanying motto, is quite an old one (several medals bearing it being given by Van Loon); it was used on the Continental paper money. That of the serpent divided into thirteen pieces, each part lettered with the initial of one of

the Colonies, and the motto 'Join or die' was also a favorite Continental emblem." The Betts editors commented, "No impression of this medal is known to us." Apparently, none have come to light since that time. The discovery of such today would represent a sensational numismatic find. The Betts footnote reference is to Gerard Van Loon, *Historie Metallique des XVII Provinces des Pays-Bas*, LaHaye, 1732.

4. Newspaper name and location not given. Quoted in the *American Journal of Numismatics*, Volume 20–21, July 1886, page 22. The same *Journal* account noted that *The Journals of Congress*, November 29, 1776, page 485, recorded the $32 payment. Further, "P.E. Du Simitière was a painter from Geneva. He practiced taking portraits, but not until he had been in Philadelphia over twenty years. He made a collection in natural history for an institution in that city, and was living there in 1782."

5. Quoted in *The American Antiquarian*, September 1871.

6. Orosz, p. 31, quotes the letter.

7. Orosz, pp. 26–27, gives details.

8. Ibid., pp. 32, 67. Hour-long tours of Du Simitière's American Museum, which offered various artifacts, curiosities, etc., in addition to coins, were given for fifty cents; the proprietor conducted groups of up to eight people at a time through the facility. The New-York Historical Society, which today maintains the use of the hyphen in New-York, was organized on December 10, 1804, and incorporated February 10, 1809. By Augustus B. Sage's era of the late 1850s the Society had more than 25,000 books in its library and was located (since 1857) in a building at the corner of Second Avenue and 11th Street.

9. Clarkson sale advertisement reproduced by Orosz, p. 54.

10. Orosz, pp. 64–65, adapted from correspondence between Orosz and Eric P. Newman, and mention of Eliot in Newman's *The Secret of the Good Samaritan Shilling*, American Numismatic Society, 1959.

11. *American Journal of Numismatics*, August 1866, quoting the Proceedings of the Massachusetts Historical Society, 321, 332; similarly, AJN, January 1885, "Mr. John Andrews, of Boston, had a collection of coins as early as 1782."

12. Bentley's diary entries, incomplete in some instances, were also quoted in *The Numismatist*, January 1907 and June 1945.

13. Other related terms used in the early days to describe spurious copper coins include brummagem and bungtowns.

14. Transcribed as "have not before me" in the book, but possibly the handwritten manuscript said *now* instead of *not*.

15. Although certain 1785 and 1786 Vermont coppers had a somewhat similar stars-and-rays reverse, the reference is to the Nova Constellatio copper of 1785, a different issue believed by some authorities to have been struck in England.

16. Judge James Winthrop (1752–1821).

17. *Walter Breen's Complete Encyclopedia of U.S. and Colonial Coins*, 1988, p. 110, notes that nondestructive analyses performed on several Continental Currency pieces in 1963 and 1964 revealed that the metallic composition is 95 percent tin and 5 percent other metals (natural alloys), but with no lead evident.

Chapter 41

1. Letter, Memminger to Lamar, March 13, 1861.

2. On April 2, Elmore wrote to Lamar about the new currency: "There will arise one difficulty about the Treasury notes. There are too many of the $1,000 and too few of the $50 and $100. Our calls will be for the smaller issues. Is there any way by which impressions could be taken of part of the plate?"

3. Letter from Memminger to Lamar, March 23, 1861, citation from Thian's *Register*, 1880 (as are the other letters quoted).

Chapter 42

1. Certain information in this study is from R.W. Julian, letter to the author, December 7, 1992, and from contributions by Julian to *United States Silver Dollars and Trade Dollars: A Complete Encyclopedia*, published in two volumes in 1993.

2. In a conversation with the author, August 6, 1992, Jack Collins stated that in the course of his research involving 1794 dollars he had learned that the specimen in the British Museum had been cleaned to the extent that it showed extensive hairlines. Perhaps Collins's assessment was overly harsh, or natural re-toning over the intervening years lessened the appearance of the cleaning, as John Dannreuther noted in his August 2006 article, "U.S. Coin Highlights in the British Museum," that during a recent visit to the Museum he examined the 1794 dollar and found it to be "an original, well-struck Almost Uncirculated example," and commented that "in the past, this coin has been reported as harshly cleaned, but if there is cleaning under the toning, it is minor."

Chapter 43

1. No notes of this specific type were ever issued; there were Legal Tender Notes and, separately, Interest Bearing Notes. Accounts in *Banker's Magazine* and other publications often contained numismatic inaccuracies.

Chapter 44

1. I later realized that in Abe Kosoff's May 24, 1955, sale of the Edgar Levy Collection of quarter dollars an Uncirculated 1796 fetched $425. Thus, Bebee's $200 price was not so far-fetched after all. In the same Kosoff auction a Proof 1827 quarter brought $1,250, and an Uncirculated 1916 Standing Liberty went to a buyer for $240. Also, Walter Breen, *The Complete Encyclopedia of U.S. and Colonial Coins*, 1988, p. 299: "When Col. Green inherited his mother's millions, he became a collector of (among other things) railroad cars, pornographic films; and among his immense numismatic holdings was a hoard of over 200 Uncirculated 1796 quarter dollars, of which at least 100 were more or less prooflike—their fields more mirrorlike than on the others. Abe Kosoff and André DeCoppet dispersed many of these to date and type collectors during the 1940s." It is believed that Kosoff acquired the Green coins through Philadelphia dealer James G. Macallister; accounts vary. Separately, John J. Ford Jr., in a conversation with me on June 27, 1996, stated that in the 1940s he had inspected the quarters when they were part of the Green estate, but that James G. Macallister had bought them.

Chapter 45

1. This is based on coverage I did for *Coin World* in 2012 and 2013. Thanks to these people for help in various ways: Roger Belson, Tim Grant, Phebe Hemphill, Tom Jurkowsky, Jill Kimball, Evelyn Mishkin, Dave Owen, Acting Mint Director Richard Peterson, Steve Roach, David M. Sundman, Stephanie Westover, and Michael White.

Chapter 47

1. Adapted from a study of Feuchtwanger in *More Adventures With Rare Coins*, 2002.

2. Certain information is from *Appleton's Cyclopaedia of American Biography*, volume II, 1888, pp. 444–445.

3. *Longworth's American Almanac, New-York Register, and City Directory*, New York, Thomas Longworth, 1831, p. 272; "druggist." This is the earliest directory entry located for Feuchtwanger. For other information: *Longworth's American Almanac, New-York Register*, and City Directory, New York, Thomas Longworth, 1832 and later editions. In New York City at the time it was the practice for household renters to sign one-year leases, with May 1 being "moving day" for those going from one location to another—a coordination with minimized vacancies. Renters were apt to relocate

frequently—several times within a decade—as even a casual inspection of directory listings of the era will reveal.

4. A well-known token relating to this attraction bears the inscriptions: PARTHENON / NEW-YORK 1825 on the obverse; ADMIT THE BEARER/ PEALE'S MUSEUM & GALLERY OF THE FINE ARTS. The museum opened in a building known as the Parthenon, in late October of that year; earlier, Montaigne's Garden was on the site, and the Sons of Liberty held meetings there in the days prior to the American Revolution. Late in 1840 the name was officially changed to the New York Museum, by an act of the State Legislature, although it had been called that earlier. Also in 1825 the Castle Garden underwent extensive renovations, completed in late February (announcement in the *New-York Evening Post*, April 2, 1825). The lessees, Rathbone & Fitch, issued an oval pass or identification badge, from dies by Richard Trested, depicting the facility on one side, and engraved with the name of the holder of the badge. In time these became highly sought numismatic items, especially after Wayte Raymond gave special notice to an example in his extensive catalog of the W.W.C. Wilson Collection, November 1925. The New York facility, managed by Rembrandt Peale, later by Rubens Peale, was a later branch of Peale's Philadelphia Museum, founded by Charles Willson Peale (who named most his children after famous artists: Raphael, Rembrandt, Vandyke, Titian, and Rubens; plus Franklin, named after the statesman), which opened in his home in 1784, then in the facilities of the American Philosophical Society in January 1794, in which latter year-long admission passes were sold for a dollar. Raphael and Rembrandt Peale together, then Rembrandt alone, managed a branch in Baltimore (which was later closed; however, the same building is still used today as a city museum; it is the oldest building in the Western Hemisphere specifically designed as a museum and is still used as such [note from Joel J. Orosz]). In 1831 Peale's New York City museum changed $10 for a family membership for one year; $5 for a gentleman's membership (at any time he had the privilege of bringing a lady with him); general admission 25 cents; children, 12-1/2 cents. In 1831 the Siamese twins, Chang and Eng, were featured for a time.

5. Quoted, slightly revised, from *Hard Times Tokens*, Lyman H. Low, 1900, p. 49.

6. At the Masonic Hall, New York City. Registered attendance was 1,359, and receipts totaled $339. From this modest beginning, in 1829 the Fair attracted about a thousand exhibitors and was viewed by 5,884, with receipts adding up to $1,571.82.

7. In 1837 the Institute's library included more than 5,000 books. Premises were upstairs at 187 Broadway. Later, the Institute was in a four-story building at 351 Broadway.

8. 25th Congress, Document No. 7, House of Representatives, 1st Session, titled "Substitute for Copper. Memorial Lewis Feuchtwanger, September 13, 1837."

9. *Niles' National Register*, September 16, 1837, p. 41.

10. Copy furnished by Kenneth E. Bressett.

11. As cited by Eric P. Newman in "The Promotion and Suppression of Hard Times Tokens, proceedings of the Coinage of the Americas Conference, American Numismatic Society, held October 29, 1994"; published 1995, p. 124.

12. Specie properly refers to gold and silver coins, not to one-cent pieces or any other coins or tokens not in these precious metals.

13. *Ibid.*, p. 125.

14. Certain information from Lyman H. Low, *Hard Times Tokens*, 1900. Russell Rulau, *Standard Catalog of U.S. Tokens 1700–1900* (certain descriptive text for the dies). "Varieties of the Feuchtwanger Cent," *Numismatic Scrapbook Magazine*, November 1957, adapted from *Numisma*, published by

the New Netherlands Coin Co., August 1956. James Theodore Koutsoures, "The Identification of Feuchtwanger Cents, Low 120," undated.

15. Correspondence with the author, November 29, 2013. Also see the Nova Numismatics web site.

Chapter 49

1. The late Walter Breen made up or at least did not disclose documentation for the "guidelines" he published for "Proofs" in certain of his writings.

2. Certain information is from the author's *Guide Book of United States Type Coins*, published by Whitman.

Chapter 50

1. Much of this chapter has been adapted from my section on the 1933 $20 in my 2004 *Guide Book of Double Eagle Gold Coins*. My sources include information from R.W. Julian, communications and his 5,833-word manuscript "The 1933 Double Eagle," sent to me October 1, 2002; examination of huge files of Secret Service, Mint, and Treasury documents in cooperation with attorney Barry H. Berke; the auction catalog of Sotheby's / Stack's prepared mainly by David E. Tripp in 2002; Ed Reiter, "Canonizing the 1933 Saint," *COINage*, May 2002; Reiter, "Rendering Unto Seizer," *COINage*, September 2002; and conversations with Hans M.F. Schulman, R.E. ("Ted") Naftzger Jr., Michael Brownlee, Harry W. Bass Jr., Louis E. Eliasberg, and others. I have a very large file on this coin—perhaps material for a future book on the subject, although I have no plans in this direction.

2. Excerpt from "The 1933 Double Eagle," manu-

script copy to the author, October 1, 2002. It is not the intent of the writer to strengthen Julian's reputation in connection with his 1933 double eagle research, as such strengthening is hardly needed; his contributions to Mint history date back decades to his contributions to the *Numismatic Scrapbook* magazine, and today his word remains highly respected.

3. *The Numismatist*, February 1934.

4. Owned at one time by the writer, obtained from his widow, Gloria Rovelstad, and now in a collection in England.

5. Also handled by the writer.

6. Related in conversations with Whitman publisher Dennis Tucker.

7. *The Numismatist*, October 1938, in connection with a talk he gave at the ANA convention that year.

8. Treasury Department internal correspondence reviewed by the author in 2001.

9. Details of the case of Langbord v. the U.S. Treasury Department were played out *in extremis* in the pages of *Coin World* and *Numismatic News* beginning in 2008.

0. Excerpt from "The 1933 Double Eagle," manuscript copy to the author, October, 1, 2002.

1. Also see related comment by Walter Breen in his 1988 *Encyclopedia*, p. 376.

Chapter 51

1. If I were to name a Grand Dame of Numismatics No. 2 she would be Margo Russell.

Chapter 1

The 1792 Silver Half Disme

Most of the 200 to 300 surviving 1792 half dismes show extensive wear, so collectors seeking a pristine specimen are in for a long hunt. The coin is listed in the 2015 edition of the *Guide Book of United States Coins* (the "Red Book") at $8,500 in About Good condition—this grade indicating an example that is very heavily worn, with portions of the lettering and legends worn smooth, and the date perhaps barely readable. A few dozen About Uncirculated and Uncirculated examples exist, several of them in choice and gem Mint State—possibly from among the four coins said to have been set aside by Mint director David Rittenhouse. An AU example is worth about $175,000, while an Uncirculated half disme will fetch $325,000 or more. Superb gems have crossed the $1 million mark. In April 2006 a unique *copper* striking of the coin, in Specimen-67 condition, was sold by Heritage Auction Galleries for $1,322,500.

Chapter 2

Frank Gasparro and the Eisenhower Dollar

Eisenhower dollars are easy to find in the rare-coin marketplace, in grades ranging from high-end circulated to lower-end Uncirculated. Some of the early dates and varieties are elusive in MS-65 and higher grades. Collectors typically do not look for (or pay premiums for) lower-grade "Ikes," and in fact the coins can still sometimes be found in bank drawers or cash registers for $1 apiece. Coin dealers often have quantities for $1.25 or $1.50 or so in circulated grades—this price reflecting a markup for handling, storing, and other overhead costs. Numismatic author, researcher, and educator Bill Fivaz often carries Eisenhower dollars around to give as tips at face value and to spread knowledge of the hobby. "They always get attention," he notes.

When grading a Mint State Eisenhower dollar, look for abrasion and contact marks on the president's cheek, jaw, and temple. High-grade examples (MS-66 and better) can be worth significant premiums ($60 to $125 or more, depending on date and condition). Passionate collectors of the series eagerly seek the elusive highest grades; in April 2012, for example, a collector paid $1,725 for a silver-clad Variety 1 Bicentennial dollar in MS-68 condition—a coin worth perhaps $20 in MS-65. The market for ultra-high-grade examples of modern coins in all series that are common in MS-65 is somewhat speculative, and caution is urged.

Chapter 3

The 1950-D Jefferson Nickel Excitement

The 1950-D Jefferson nickel reached dizzying heights not long after its minting. The peak of the frenzy was $30 or a little more for a Mint State coin, in 1964. As mentioned in the chapter text, several rolls were sold in November 2011 for $340 apiece, which works out to $8.50 per coin. Today the *Guide Book* lists the retail value at $14 in MS-60, $16 in MS-63, and $20 in MS-65. Collectors who specialize in Jefferson nickels will pay premiums for high-grade examples with strong, full strikes. The fifth Professional Edition of the *Guide Book of United States Coins* (an expanded version of the *Red Book* for intermediate and advanced collectors, dealers, and investors) lists an MS-65 Full Steps coin at $60, MS-66 at $70, MS-66 with Full Steps at $150, MS-67 at $275, and MS-67 with Full Steps at an impressive $3,000.

Chapter 4

Revisiting the Libertas Americana Medal

With only 100 to 125 original copper strikings of the Libertas Americana medal known to exist, collectors can expect to pay $8,000 to $10,000 for an impaired Proof (grading less than Proof-60). At PF-60 the medal is listed in the 2015 *Guide Book of United States Coins* at $12,500; in PF-63, $18,000; and in PF-65, $45,000.

The silver strikings are even rarer, with only a couple dozen believed to exist today. These are worth $40,000 even in impaired Proof, up to $120,000 or more in higher grades. In March 2014 at the Whitman Coin & Collectibles Expo in Baltimore, a silver Libertas Americana in MS-62 condition was auctioned by Stack's Bowers Galleries for $111,625.

For an authentic example of the *gold* Libertas Americana medal, the sky would be the limit. Only two gold medals were made, for presentation to the king and queen of France by Benjamin Franklin, and today their whereabouts are unknown.

Chapter 5

Louis E. Eliasberg, "King of Coins"

As mentioned in this chapter, no matter how deep your pockets, a coin collection the likes of that assembled by Louis E. Eliasberg cannot be had for *any* price! Eliasberg collected one federal U.S. coin of every date-mintmark-and-denomination combination. Today certain of his old coins are held in museums and other inaccessible collections. It's a case of "close, but no cigar" for anyone seeking to recreate Eliasberg's famous feat.

Chapter 6

The Famous 1856 Flying Eagle Cent

Collectors and their checkbooks battle it out for the 1,500 or so 1856 Flying Eagle cents that still fly around the hobby community—a textbook example of supply and demand keeping prices on the rise. The 2015 edition of the *Guide Book of United States Coins* lists this series key at $7,000 in Good-4 condition (with all details worn but visible), $12,000 in Very Fine (with considerable detail visible in the eagle's right wing feathers and tail), up to $22,000 in MS-63 (with only light contact marks or blemishes in the prime focal areas). An MS-64 example was auctioned in April 2013 for $32,900, and the fifth edition of the Professional Edition *Red Book* lists the coin in MS-66 for $150,000. Most of this issue are Proof restrikes; the *Red Book* catalogs the coin in PF-63 at $17,500.

Chapter 7

The Rare 1876-CC Twenty-Cent Piece

If any American coin deserves a glowing description in an auction catalog, it's the 1876-CC twenty-cent piece. Stack's Bowers Galleries devoted some 3,000 words to the coin sold in January 2013 in the Battle Born Collection. Eager collectors showed their enthusiasm by bidding the MS-65 coin up to a final price of $564,000. This was no fluke; several years earlier, in June 2009, an AU-58 example was auctioned for $207,000. The 2015 *Guide Book of United States Coins* catalogs the 1876-CC at $175,000 in AU-50, $250,000 in MS-60, and $360,000 in MS-63. Definitely a coin for deep-pocketed connoisseurs!

Chapter 8

A Treasure Hidden in the Woods

The aluminum tokens of Miss M.J. Drury were offered for $95 apiece after they came to light in 1996. No other hoards have been discovered since then; the tokens, already scarce at the time, haven't become any more common. Inclusion in Russ Rulau's *Standard Catalog* and similar publicity can only increase their interest within the hobby community. That said, scarce exonumia (tokens and medals) can often be purchased for a fraction of the value of a federal coin of similar rarity, because of lower demand. Today an Extremely Fine or About Uncirculated example of the Drury token might sell for $100 to $150, assuming one of the handful of owners could be convinced to part ways with his little piece of New England.

Chapter 9

Don't Miss the Model Artistes

Counterstamps on old foreign coins are a numismatic delicacy, sought by only a small number of aficionados. To many modern collectors, "bright" and "pristine" are the order of the day, and a well-worn coin with its surface marred by an old stamp doesn't hold much appeal. However, those who do collect counterstamped coins are passionate in their pursuit. A Spanish-American two-reales coin marked to admit the bearer to a Model Artist's show could sell for $250 to $400 or so in today's marketplace, depending upon the boldness of the stamp and the elements still visible from the undertype.

Chapter 10

Numismatics and the Columbian Exposition

World's Columbian Exposition half dollars are among the most common of the "classic" (pre-1982) U.S. commemorative coins. It's not unusual to find a worn example in Grandpa's cigar box or in old coin collections; they circulated at face value as pocket change for many years after the Exposition closed down in 1893. The 1892 date is slightly less common than the 1893, and only

worth a few dollars more in higher grades. Coin dealers often have both dates in stock for $20 or so in About Uncirculated condition; an Uncirculated example will run from $30 to $90 in lower Mint State grades. The 2015 *Guide Book of United States Coins* lists the 1892 coin at $475 in MS-65 or $1,100 in MS-66.

The 1893 Isabella quarter, on the other hand, is considerably scarcer, with its original distribution of only 24,414 coins. Today's collector can expect to pay about $450 for an AU-50 example, $600 for an MS-63, or $5,500 for an MS-66.

Medals, tokens, and elongated coins from the Exposition are in strong demand, appealing not only to numismatists but also to collectors of World's Fair and exposition memorabilia. Elongated cents and nickels with the undertype dates visible generally sell for $35 to $50 for dates in the 1880s through 1893, and much more for a special coin such as a rare 1885 Liberty Head nickel. Foreign coins, silver denominations, and rarer types often sell for $100 to $200.

Chapter 11

The Ornate "Educational Notes" of 1896

The Series of 1896 $1 Silver Certificate is collectible in all grades, with prices ranging from a few hundred dollars into the thousands. The fourth edition of the *Guide Book of United States Paper Money* lists the note at $215 in Very Good, $300 in Fine, and $485 in Very Fine. Values jump dramatically in higher grades: $1,000 for Extremely Fine and $2,750 in Uncirculated. Prices are generally the same whether the note has the signatures of Tillman (register of the Treasury) and Morgan (treasurer of the United States) or Bruce and Roberts.

The $2 note in the Educational series is more costly, with prices for the type ranging from $575 in Very Good up to $6,000 in Uncirculated. As with the $1 note, there is a jump between VF and EF, from $1,350 to $3,750. Seasoned collectors definitely pay extra for quality in this series, for all three denominations. Again, the signature combination is not a major factor in market values, as collectors care more about type and grade for the $2 note.

The $5 Silver Certificate is the priciest of the three Educational Note denominations. The first two signature combinations (Tillman/Morgan and Bruce/Roberts) are worth about the same in grades up through Extremely Fine, while in Uncirculated the Bruce/Roberts note is worth slightly more. Values as reported in the *Guide Book of United States Paper Money* range from $825 in VG to $10,000 (or $10,500) in Unc. The third signature combination, Lyons/Roberts, is worth a premium in every grade—$850 in VG, $1,500 in Fine, $2,750 in VF, $6,000 in EF, and $11,500 in Uncirculated.

Chapter 12

The Erie Canal Medal

A classic example of American numismatic art, the Erie Canal medal ranges from affordable to expensive, depending on metallic composition and grade. A collector satisfied with a white-metal striking in impaired Proof (PF-50 to PF-58, indicating light wear or blemishes from poor storage and handling) might pay $500 to $600, while a silver striking in the same condition would cost $3,500 to $4,500. In higher grades (choice to gem, PF-63 to 65), a white-metal example is worth $900 to $1,300, and a silver medal from $6,500 to $8,000. From time to time the Erie Canal medal is found with the small round wooden box they were distributed in (as pictured in the chapter); this extra bit of historical memorabilia will add $200 to $300 or more of value.

Chapter 13
The Enigmatic Georgivs Triumpho Token
For the cost of dinner and an evening out for two, you can add an attractively circulated example of the historic Georgivs Triumpho copper token to your collection. The *Guide Book of United States Coins* (68th edition) lists the token at $110 in Very Good condition, $225 in Fine, $500 in Very Fine, $800 in Extremely Fine, $1,400 in About Uncirculated, and $6,000 in Uncirculated. As with all early copper coins and tokens, eye appeal comes into the equation, grading can be subjective, and authentication is important, especially for expensive high-grade pieces.

Chapter 14
Wyman the Wizard
As with the Model Artistes counterstamped coins in chapter 9, the value of a "Wyman the Wizard and Ventriloquist" piece depends on the boldness of the stamping and the visibility of the host coin's design elements. A collector can expect to pay $300 to $450 for a nice example of a counterstamped two-reales coin.

Chapter 15
Revisiting the Randall Hoard
Uncirculated large cents of the Liberty Head type are surprisingly affordable today, thanks in part to the Randall Hoard. An attractive brown MS-63 example will cost around $600 (dated 1817, 1818, 1819, or 1820) or $700 (1816)—not a bad price for a 200-year-old piece of American history. As noted in the chapter text, many of the coins pedigreed to the hoard are found with splashes of original mint-red color flecked and toned with darker brown and even black areas.

Chapter 16
The Many Interests of Alden Scott Boyer
Boyer, best remembered as a president of the American Numismatic Association, is representative of many famous numismatists in that he had multiple collecting interests. He was also a facile writer with the ability to write about almost anything and make it interesting. Beyond numismatics, today enthusiasts in the field of automatic musical instruments recognize him as a pioneer in collecting these items.

One of the famous coins connected to Boyer is the 1913 Liberty Head nickel, of which five are known. In 1920 Samuel Brown offered Boyer one of the coins, estimating its value at $750. Boyer wasn't interested. Today a collector would have to pay in the millions to acquire one. Three of the top 10 U.S. coin prices realized at auction are held by 1913 Liberty Head nickels. In January 2014 an example graded Proof-64 sold for $3,290,000.

Chapter 17
Take a Ride on the New York & Harlem Railroad
The New York & Harlem Railroad token has been famous for a long time. With fewer than 100 believed to exist, the appearance of an example at auction is always a special occasion. You can imagine how surprising it was in 2013 when long-hidden treasures from the John J. Ford, Jr. Collection were offered at auction by Stack's Bowers Galleries and 14 of these tokens were presented in the same sale, at the request of the estate. This afforded numismatists the opportunity to study the characteristics of multiple specimens side by side. Only two were fully struck. The market price was necessarily adjusted for a while. By now, most are widely dispersed. Depending on the strike and condition examples are worth in the range of $1,000 to $3,000 each.

Chapter 18
Show This Coin, See the Minstrel Show
Well-worn Spanish-American silver two-reales coins, common in circulation in the mid-1800s, were the ideal matrix for counterstamping with advertising—creating little billboards, so to speak, promoting things from patent medicines to, as seen in this chapter, minstrel shows. Liberty Seated half dollars were likewise useful. Geo. Christy and Woods Minstrels, Broadway Varieties, Sprague & Blodgett's Georgia Minstrels, and Sprague's Georgia Minstrels were among such advertisers. Today, examples with most or all of the lettering readable and with nice eye appeal generally sell for $250 to $500. The challenge is not in *paying for them*—rather, it's in finding them for sale. As a class such counterstamps are quite rare.

Chapter 19
Harry W. Bass Jr., Numismatist and Scholar
Harry Bass was a Renaissance Man, combining talents of management, research, and keen interest to accomplish many things in his life. In numismatics he was the very definition of a connoisseur. Every coin he owned he carefully studied under high magnification and carefully researched as to its die characteristics, rarity, and place in numismatic history. In parallel to collecting coins he built one of the finest private libraries, including auction catalogs of the 19th century onward. Today, selected coins from his collection are on loan exhibit at the American Numismatic Association headquarters in Colorado Springs. As *Guide Michelin* might say, it is worth a *detour* to visit. The "market value" of the

Bass collection is a matter of theory, as the coins are not for sale but are now kept for study and enjoyment.

Chapter 20
The 1838 New Haven Medal, a Numismatic Icon

The New Haven medal, available in two varieties, was famous to numismatists active in the 19th century. This was an era in which medals of historical importance outshone federal coin rarities when offered at auction. Since then, emphasis in the marketplace has changed, and today the New Haven medal is little known. Perhaps this book will change that. Auction prices are hardly standardized and have ranged from the low hundreds of dollars to close to $1,000. The Ford Collection copper medal crossed the block at $575 in 2004 and his silver medal sold for $1,380. It would probably bring several multiples of that price today.

Chapter 21
Take a Peek at the Parisian Varieties

To own one of these counterstamped half dollars is to own a coin with a fascinating story—as you have read in this chapter. Examples are fairly scarce, so the opportunity to buy is more important than the price paid. The offering of the John J. Ford Jr. estate coins in 2010 included pieces ranging in price from $188 to $1,528, the latter for an 1873-CC half dollar with Arrows at Date, Very Fine grade. An 1875-CC in Very Good sold for $1,200.

As is often true for tokens and medals, prices in the Ford sale were not standardized. Also, if these pieces had been offered singly over a period of time they probably would have brought higher sale prices. The group offering was the request of the executors. Today, several hundred dollars would seem to be a likely valuation for a Philadelphia Mint half dollar in Fine or Very Fine grade.

Chapter 22
Half Dimes for a Mint Cornerstone Ceremony

Examples of the 1829 half dime have always been in strong demand as the first year of the Capped Bust type. The 2015 edition of *A Guide Book of United States Coins* prices them in eight grades, from G-4 at $55 to MS-63 at $925. Gem MS-65 coins sell for several thousand dollars and a choice Proof with good eye appeal will cross the $10,000 line.

Chapter 23
The Coin Collection at the Smithsonian

The next time you are in Washington make the Smithsonian Institution a must-see. You will be delighted and amazed. Leave your checkbook at home, of course—none of the coins in the National Numismatic Collection are for sale. They belong to the American people.

Chapter 24
Thomas L. Elder, Outspoken and Dynamic

Elder created many medals, often satirical, in the early 20th century. Today these are highly collectible and typically sell for several hundred dollars each. His auction catalogs are also collectible. Most of them have coins, tokens, medals, and paper money arranged in miscellaneous order. Today, they are a rich mine for research.

Chapter 25
The Mentality of Collecting

It seems to be a true statement that those who are avid collectors enjoy life more, are never bored, and often live longer than the average citizen. Perhaps reading this chapter will give you some further inspiration. As for a "market value" for such things: who can put a price tag on happiness?

Chapter 26
The SS *Central America* Treasure

Coins and ingots from this fabulous treasure appear on the market frequently. The "poster coin" to own is the 1857-S double eagle, of which more than 5,000 Mint State coins were found in the shipwreck. The 2015 *Guide Book of United States Coins* prices generic 1857-S twenties in MS-60 grade for $5,750 and MS-63 for $9,000. MS-64 and 65 coins sell for significantly more. Ideally, you would purchase one in a certified holder marked with the *Central America* pedigree.

Chapter 27
Trying to Understand "Ned" Mason

Mason collectibles include his auction catalogs and magazines. The catalogs are not particularly memorable. In contrast his magazines, reprinted in a set by numismatic bookseller Charles Davis, are guaranteed to furnish many evenings of interesting reading. There are book dealers who specialize in numismatic literature; collectors can search their inventories or query them for Mason-related material. There is even a non-profit hobby organization dedicated to the study and collecting of numismatic literature: learn more about the Numismatic Bibliomania Society at www.coinbooks.org.

Chapter 28
A Curious Misplaced Mintmark

The 1975-D nickel with misplaced mintmark made its debut in *Coin World* in 2013 and in the *Guide Book of United States Coins* in 2014 (the 2015 edition, page 137). I only know of three examples, all in Very Fine or so grade, one of which I purchased for $25. We all have to wait and see if this variety catches on and if any Mint State coins can be found. Numismatics is a vibrant and active field, with new discoveries, new research, and changing interests; stay tuned. In the meantime, if you're offered one of these coins it would probably be wise to buy it!

Chapter 29
The Tokens of William L. Bramhall
The Bramhall tokens, formerly known mostly to specialists, will now via this book be introduced to thousands of others. Likely, to read about them will create a desire to own them. Prices vary in the hobby marketplace, but most examples in brass sell for several hundred dollars each. Silver rarities can challenge the $1,000 level.

Chapter 30
Rare Territorial Notes from Central City
The combination of a territorial imprint and a black charter number has created a note widely desired in the hobby community. Examples in Very Fine and Extremely Fine grades sell for several tens of thousands of dollars each and make headlines when offered at auction.

Chapter 31
Let the "Egle" Fly
Estimates of value for this mysterious token have ranged from $500 or so to $4,000. If someone can unlock the secret of this token and pinpoint the engraver and time and place of issue, and if a firm Mormon connection is established, all bets will be off.

Chapter 32
Memories of the 1955 Doubled Die Cent
This and the 1909-S V.D.B. are the two most popular Lincoln cents. The 2015 *Guide Book of United States Coins* charts these prices for the 1955 Doubled Die: VF-20 $1,800, EF-40 $2,000, AU-50 $2,200, MS-60 $2,700, MS-63 $3,750, and MS-65 with original color $15,000.

Chapter 33
Jackson: "I Take the Responsibility"
There are several hundred varieties of Hard Times tokens, of which a few dozen are related to President Andrew Jackson. Common varieties are very affordable in circulated grades such as Very Fine and Extremely Fine, from about $25 to $75. Choice Mint State tokens of common varieties have prices in the low hundreds of dollars.

Chapter 34
Chormann's Special Pattern Coins of 1860
Current market values tend to be in the range of $1,000 to $2,000 each. Now that these coins have been publicized it is likely that they will become mainstream for pattern specialists.

Chapter 35
"Good For a Scent"
These particular Civil War tokens are not rarities, but the punning motif and the dog head are compelling to many buyers, making them popular collectibles. In 2014 several sales for Very Fine and Extremely pieces took place, bringing prices from the high hundreds of dollars to slightly over $1,000.

Chapter 36
Meet William J. Mullen and His Medal
The typical copper Mullen medal in About Uncirculated grade (most examples show evidence of handling) sells for several hundred dollars.

Chapter 37
Those Carson City Morgan Dollars!
Carson City Morgan dollars are mostly from the U.S. Treasury hoard and are in Mint State. The 2015 *Guide Book of United States Coins* includes these values:

1878-CC — MS-63 $425 • MS-64 $600 • MS-65 $1,700

1879-CC, Large CC — MS-63 $7,200 • MS-64 $10,500 • MS-65 $30,000

1879-CC, Large CC Over Small CC — MS-63 $6,300 • MS-64 $9,900 • MS-65 $40,000

1880-CC, Parallel Arrow Feather (PAF) — MS-63 $700 • MS-64 $1,150 • MS-65 $2,700

1880-CC, Slanted Arrow Feather (SAF) — MS-63 $650 • MS-64 $700 • MS-65 $1,250

1881-CC — MS-63 $575 • MS-64 $600 • MS-65 $900

1882-CC — MS-63 $260 • MS-64 $285 • MS-65 $550

1883-CC — MS-63 $230 • MS-64 $250 • MS-65 $525

1884-CC — MS-63 $230 • MS-64 $250 • MS-65 $525

1885-CC — MS-63 $800 • MS-64 $850 • MS-65 $1,100

1889-CC — MS-63 $45,000 • MS-64 $70,000 • MS-65 $325,000

1890-CC — MS-63 $825 • MS-64 $1,500 • MS-65 $5,000

1891-CC — MS-63 $750 • MS-64 $1,250 • MS-65 $5,000

1892-CC — MS-63 $2,400 • MS-64 $3,250 • MS-65 $9,000

1893-CC — MS-63 $8,500 • MS-64 $16,000 • MS-65 $70,000

Chapter 38
Following the Oregon Trail
The market for all classic-era (1892 to 1954) silver commemorative coins has been very quiet in recent years. To buyers this means that many low-mintage varieties, including those in the Oregon Trail series, are very affordable. The 2015 *Guide Book of United States Coins* includes these values:

1926 (47,955 distributed) — MS-63 $180 • MS-64 $320 • MS-65 $450

1926-S (83,055 distributed) — MS-63 $180 • MS-64 $320 • MS-65 $435

1928 (6,028 distributed) — MS-63 $300 • MS-64 $380 • MS-65 $500

1933-D (5,008 distributed) — MS-63 $400 • MS-64 $500 • MS-65 $575

1934-D (7,006 distributed) — MS-63 $235 • MS-64 $350 • MS-65 $625

1936 (10,006 distributed) — MS-63 $220 • MS-64 $330 • MS-65 $435

1936-S (5,006 distributed) — MS-63 $230 • MS-64 $375 • MS-65 $500

1937-D (12,008 distributed) — MS-63 $250 • MS-64 $375 • MS-65 $435

1938, 1938-D, and 1938-S (6,006, 6,005, and 6,006 distributed, respectively) — Set of *three* varieties: MS-63 $600 • MS-64 $900 • MS-65 $1,350 (on a per-coin basis illogically the least expensive coins in the series)

1939, 1939-D, and 1939-S (3,004, 3,004, and 3,005 distributed, respectively) — Set of *three* varieties: MS-63 $1,700 • MS-64 $2,000 • MS-65 $2,850

Chapter 39
"What They Say" About the World's Greatest Hobby

Enjoying the "king of hobbies"—priceless. (To this chapter you can add *your* comments!)

Chapter 40
The Beginning of Numismatics in America

Let's look at the 1652-dated Massachusetts Pine Tree shilling—it was a classic coin when numismatics first became popular in America, and remains a classic today. The 2015 *Guide Book of United States Coins* includes these values: Good $700 • VG $1,100 • Fine $2,400 • VF $5,000 • EF $8,750 • AU $14,000 • Unc. $26,000.

Chapter 41
The CSA "Montgomery Notes"

The four Montgomery notes are everlastingly popular with collectors. The $500 and $1,000 are classic rarities and the $50 and $100 are famous as well. Prices vary in the marketplace. The populations listed here are courtesy of Pierre Fricke, 2014.

$1,000 "Montgomery Note" (137 known) — VF $45,000
$500 "Montgomery Note" (137 known) — VF $42,000

$100 "Montgomery Note" (190 known) — VF $21,000
$50 "Montgomery Note" (187 known) — VF $19,000

Chapter 42
A $10 Million 1794 Silver Dollar

The price for *the* coin was $10,016,875. As to other grades, the 2015 *Guide Book of United States Coins* suggests these values: About Good-3 $37,500 • G-4 $65,000 • VG-8 $95,000 • F-12 $115,000 • VF-20 $150,000 • EF-40 $200,000 • AU-50 $325,000 • MS-60 $650,000

Chapter 43
The Great St. Albans Raid

Signed and issued notes from the banks involved in this story appear occasionally in the marketplace. A typical Very Fine note is valued at $100 to $200 or more, depending on the denomination and eye appeal.

Chapter 44
A Reminiscence of 1955

Of the coins mentioned in this chapter, here are some modern-day values. The gem 1796 quarter at $200,000 would probably cross the auction block now for $1 million more or less. A set of Choice Proof 1879 and 1880 Stellas would go higher than $3 million. A complete set of Panama-Pacific commemoratives, five pieces in a copper frame, today would be worth $250,000 to $300,000 or more. Sadly, many sets have been broken up so the individual coins can be put in certified holders. The $610 Proof 1867 With Rays nickel would now sell for $50,000 to $75,000. Proof sets of 1950 and 1951, then worth $30 and $19 are worth $600 and $675 now, according to the 2105 *Guide Book of United States Coins*. A gem 1909-S Indian Head cent that cost $10 is now worth several thousand dollars.

Chapter 45
The New Hampshire "America the Beautiful" Quarter

You can easily find an About Uncirculated example of this coin in pocket change. A gem Mint State example might cost $1 at a coin shop and a gem Proof $3.

Chapter 46
Collecting by Coinage Years

Regarding a complete coinage set of the year 1816, this being a solitary one-cent piece, the 2015 *Guide Book of United States Coins* gives these values: G-4 $20 • VG-8 $27 • F-12 $45 • VF-20 $90 • EF-40 $190 • AU-50 $300 • MS-60 $500 • MS-63 Brown $700. As to other years, perhaps including your birth year, hasten to the Whitman.com Web site or your favorite bookstore or other seller and get a copy of the latest edition of the *Guide Book of United States Coins*.

Chapter 47

Feuchtwanger Cents of 1837

The most readily available variety, the combination of dies 6-I, sells for about $200 or so in Extremely Fine grade. A Mint State example will be considerably more expensive: in MS-63, $600 to $800, and in MS-65 perhaps $1,500, if you can find one. Rare varieties can sell for much more.

Chapter 48

In the Footsteps of Sherlock Holmes: Numismatic Forensics

In the *Guide Book of United States Coins* there are many curious and interesting coinage varieties. If research and history are your cup of tea, buy some books on tokens, medals, patterns, and other coins. Coin dealers and coin shows at the local, state, regional, and national levels present you with collectibles at every budget level, from shoestring to millionaire. You can even find valuable die varieties in pocket change for the cost of their face value. A world of enjoyment awaits you.

Chapter 49

A Beautiful Display of Double Eagles

Due to their gold content, their status as the highest regular-issue gold denomination, and the affordability of many varieties at just a modest premium over intrinsic value, double eagles are America's most popular gold series. The price of common issues in lower grades will fluctuate with gold bullion prices. Coins of types 3, 4, and 5 are usually not collected in grades below MS-60. For these types most collectors opt for MS-63 or better. The 2015 *Guide Book of United States Coins* gives these values for the most readily available varieties within the major types (based on a gold bullion price of $1,300 per ounce):

Type 1 (1850–1866 Liberty Head) — VF-20 $1,900 • EF-40 $2,250 • AU-50 $2,750 • AU-55 $3,250 • MS-60 $5,750 • MS-63 $9,000 (for 1857-S; all others are more)

Type 2 (1866–1876 Liberty Head) — VF-20 $1,950 • EF-40 $2,100 • AU-50 $2,850 • AU-55 $3,250 • MS-60 $5,500 • MS-63 $11,500 (for 1865-S; all others are more)

Type 3 (1877–1907 Liberty Head) — VF-20 $1,625 • EF-40 $1,675 • AU-50 $1,700 • AU-55 $1,725 • MS-60 $1,775 • MS-63 $1,950

Type 4 (MCMVII [1907] Saint-Gaudens) — VF-20 $9,750 • EF-40 $11,000 • AU-50 $12,000 • AU-55 $13,000 • MS-60 $16,000 • MS-63 $25,000

Type 5 (1907–1908 Saint-Gaudens) — VF-20 $1,575 • EF-40 $1,600 • AU-50 $1,625 • AU-55 $1,650 • MS-60 $1,700 • MS-63 $1,850

Type 8 (1908–1933 Saint-Gaudens) — VF-20 $1,575 • EF-40 $1,800 • AU-50 $1,625 • AU-55 $1,650 • MS-60 $1,700 • MS-63 $1,850

Chapter 50

On the Trail of the 1933 Double Eagle

The only 1933 double eagle deemed by the federal government to be legal for private ownership is the example said to have belonged to King Farouk of Egypt. In July 2002 it sold for $7,590,020 in a Sotheby's / Stack's auction. The other surviving 1933 double eagles—a mere handful—are owned publicly, by the American people, and therefore have no price tag.

Chapter 51

Emery May Holden Norweb

Among the books I have written are several numismatic biographies, including of Ambassador and Mrs. R. Henry Norweb, Virgil Brand, Augustus B. Sage, Louis E. Eliasberg, and Harry W. Bass Jr. I encourage you to track these down in the marketplace for used books. I further encourage you to build a nice numismatic library. The Whitman Web site offers many of my books as well as those of other authors in the hobby community.

Style Notes

Some quoted material has been lightly edited, but in all instances the original meaning has been preserved. Common misspellings have been corrected. Footnotes, including in quoted material, are those of the present author (Q. David Bowers) unless specifically noted otherwise.

Credits and Acknowledgments

Also see the notes section.

The **American Numismatic Society** provided a portrait of William L. Bramhall. **Richard August** made coins available for photography including a 1652 Pine Tree shilling. **Roger Belson** provided an image of a William Paskell painting. **Anne Bentley** and the **Massachusetts Historical Society** provided items for photography (including the Columbia & Washington medal), and research. **Wynn Bowers** reviewed certain chapters. **Karen Bridges** of **Stack's Bowers Galleries** provided many photographs. **Tom Denly** assisted with paper-money research, and shared images. **Bob Evans**, curator of the SS *Central America* treasure, helped with information. **Pierre Fricke** shared information about Confederate currency. **Rusty Goe**, leading light in the Carson City Coin Collectors of America group, provided certain information about the Carson City Mint and descriptions used in the 2012 sale of the Battle Born Collection. **C. John Ferreri** furnished a bank note. **Steve Hayden** supplied images of tokens. Illustrations of several double eagles from the **Robert J. Galiette** Collection were used. **Larry Goldberg** and **Ira Goldberg** provided two illustrations of large cents. **Tim Grant** of the U.S. Mint assisted during a Mint visit. **Ron Guth** supplied images. **David Hall** supplied images. Certain images are courtesy of the **Harry W. Bass Jr. Foundation**. **Phebe Hemphill** of the U.S. Mint was interviewed and supplied illustrations. **R.W. Julian** provided the author with certain research in the early 1990s that is used herein. **Tom Jurkowsky** facilitated arrangements with the U.S. Mint and the Treasury Department. **Christine Karstedt** of **Stack's Bowers Galleries** helped in many ways. **Rob Kelley** and the **American Numismatic Association** provided images of the Harry W. Bass Jr. Gallery. **John Kleeberg** made suggestions. The **Library of Congress** provided certain images. **Fred Michaelson** sent information relating to minstrelsy, counterstamps, and related items. **Evelyn Mishkin** assisted with inquiries. **Shaina Mishkin** took certain photographs. **Eric P. Newman** provided pictures of colonial coins. **Joel J. Orosz** wrote the foreword and also provided historical information. **John Pack** provided research information. **Andrew W. Pollock III** helped with archival research. Acting Mint Director **Richard Peterson** provided information and assisted with research. **Steve Roach**, editor of *Coin World*, helped in several ways. **Robert A. Schuman** furnished illustrations of rare Feuchtwanger cents. **Hugh Shull** provided a banknote image. **Roger Siboni** provided illustrations of early coinage. Photographs from the **Robert Simpson** collection of patterns were used. **Gene Smirnov** provided a portrait of Phebe Hemphill. **Stack's Bowers Galleries** provided access to their photographic archives. **David Sundman** and **Littleton Coin Co.** provided illustrations including of the Miller hoard in Vermont and helped in other ways. **Stephanie Westover** of Littleton Coin Co. furnished photographs. **Michael White** of the **U.S. Mint** helped in several ways. **Whitman Publishing** furnished certain photographs including a 1955 Doubled Die cent and other images, some by **Tom Mulvaney**. **Wendell Wilson** supplied a photograph of the "Ship of Gold" exhibit.

Q. David Bowers

has been in the rare-coin business since 1953. He is chairman emeritus of Stack's Bowers Galleries and is numismatic director of Whitman Publishing. He is a recipient of the Pennsylvania State University College of Business Administration's Alumni Achievement Award (1976); he has served as president of the American Numismatic Association (1983–1985) and president of the Professional Numismatists Guild (1977–1979); he is a recipient of the highest honor bestowed by the ANA (the Farran Zerbe Award); he was the first ANA member to be named Numismatist of the Year (1995); and he has been inducted into the ANA Numismatic Hall of Fame. He has also won the highest honors given by the Professional Numismatists Guild.

In July 1999, in a poll published in *COINage*, "Numismatists of the Century," Dave was recognized in this list of just 18 names. He is the author of more than 50 books, hundreds of auction and other catalogs, and several thousand articles including columns in *Coin World* (now the longest-running by any author in numismatic history), *The Numismatist*, and other publications. His books have earned more "Book of the Year" honors bestowed by the Numismatic Literary Guild than have those of any other author.

Of the most valuable collections ever sold at auction—the Ambassador and Mrs. R. Henry Norweb Collection ($24 million), the Garrett Collection for The Johns Hopkins University ($25 million), the John J. Pittman Collection ($31 million), the Harry W. Bass Jr. Collection ($45 million), the Eliasberg Collection ($55+ million), and the John J. Ford Jr. Collection (nearly $60 million), he has been important in all but one (the Pittman Collection, sold by the late David Akers). When the all-time-high record for any rare coin ever sold at auction was achieved, that of a gem Uncirculated 1794 dollar in 2013, Dave cataloged it and his firm sold it. No other auction house past or present has come even remotely close to this record of success.

Dave is a trustee of the New Hampshire Historical Society and a fellow of the American Antiquarian Society, the American Numismatic Society, and the Massachusetts Historical Society. He has been a consultant for the Smithsonian Institution, the Treasury Department, and the U.S. Mint, and is research editor of the *Guide Book of United States Coins* (the annual best-selling book in numismatics, the standard guide to prices, popularly known as the "Red Book"). In Wolfeboro, New Hampshire, he is on the board of selectmen and is the town historian.